TWENTY-THIRD ANNUAL REPORT

OF THE

BUREAU OF AMERICAN ETHNOLOGY

LITHO BY WALSWORTH PUB. CO., INC., MARCELINE, MO.

TWENTY-THIRD ANNUAL REPORT

OF THE

BUREAU OF AMERICAN ETHNOLOGY

TO THE

SECRETARY OF THE SMITHSONIAN INSTITUTION

1901–1902

J. W. POWELL
DIRECTOR

The Rio Grande Press, Inc.

GLORIETA, NEW MEXICO · 87535

Copy of First Edition from which this edition
was reproduced was supplied by
MacRae's Indian Book
Distributors
P. O. Box 2632
Santa Rosa, Calif. 95405.
With certain exceptions, exclusive distributor to
the book and museum shop trade

A RIO GRANDE CLASSIC
First published in 1904 as
Bureau of American Ethnology Report No. 23
for the years 1901-1902

LIBRARY OF CONGRESS CARD CATALOG NO. 74-124509
I.S.B.N. 87380-068-0

First Printing 1970

The Rio Grande Press, Inc.
GLORIETA, NEW MEXICO · 87535

Publisher's Preface

This lovely book (the 60th title in our continuing series of beautiful Rio Grande Classics) is a somewhat rearranged edition of the 23rd Annual Report (1901-1902) of the Bureau of American Ethnology of the Smithsonian Institution, published in 1904. It is a massive work by any measurement. The first edition contained 44 color plates (on 88 pages) and 180 black and white plates (on 360 pages), with some front matter not germane to the Zuñi study. As originally printed, the book weighs seven and three-quarter pounds. Any copy is considered a rare book, and a fine or superb copy will command a price well over $100.00 if it comes onto the rare book market these days (1970).

Since all of the full page art plates were originally printed on one side of the page only (both color and black and white), we found it technically desirable to reposition these plates to enable us to print them back to back. Thus our edition now weighs a little less than five pounds. Since the position of the art plates was not written into the text, the reader of either the first or our edition would in any event need to refer to the "List of Illustrations" at the front of the book. We have re-set the "List of Illustrations" to show the new page position number. The original folio pagination has not been changed.

We might mention a word or two about these black and white plates, as well as the color plates. For reasons now obscure, most of the black and white plates are halftone engravings of paintings of photographs. Apparently Mrs. Stevenson, or someone with her, took ordinary photographs perhaps not good enough for direct reproduction. Or, perhaps, the good Bureau of American Ethnology (in 1904) preferred paintings of Indian men not so unclothed as the photographs might have shown. Whatever the reason, the original black and white plates were not well printed in this book. We have been technically able to improve most of them, but the critical reader should bear in mind that the originals were not very good to start with.

The marvelous color plates in the first edition were printed by engravings on flat stones. This beautiful old technique is gone forever, replaced by what is called four-color process printing. There is some verisimilitude in color reproduction, with process printing, but all the miracle of modern technology cannot (in our opinion) match the surpassingly lovely craftsmanship of the old stone-plate printers.

We would like to say something about the fine artists who rendered paintings from photographs, but there is nothing in the book about them. About all we can do is point out their fine work as portrayed in the paintings.

In the first edition, the editor inserted a brief precis about the author, which we recite below verbatim:

Few of the great groups of American aborigines have proved of equal interest with the tribes of the arid region. The Pueblo towns were first visited by white men in 1540, when the Coronado expedition penetrated the vast plateaus of the Colorado and the Rio Grande, but the world knew little of the people until New Mexico passed into possession of the United States. During the middle of the last century, members of military exploring expeditions under Sitgreaves, Ives, Emory, Simpson, Whipple, and others prepared short accounts of their observations among the Pueblos, and later the Powell Survey in 1874, the Hayden Survey in 1874, and the Wheeler Expedition in 1879 brought several of the villages to public notice. More recently the Bureau of American Ethnology, as well as a number of other institutions, have conducted scientific investigations of importance among the Pueblo tribes.

The pueblo of Zuñi has attracted more attention than the other towns. In 1879 Mr. Frank Hamilton Cushing was selected by Major Powell to take up his residence in this pueblo with the view of mastering the language and of making a thorough study of the manners and customs of the people. Although the results of his researches have never appeared in full, a number of valuable papers have been published. *My Adventures in Zuñi* appeared in The Century Magazine for February to May, 1883. A series of articles on *Zuñi Breadstuffs* was published in The Millstone during 1884-1886. A memoir on *Zuñi Fetiches* appeared in the Second Annual Report of the Bureau; *Pueblo Pottery as Illustrative of Zuñi Culture Growth,* in the Fourth Annual Report, and *Zuñi Creation Myths* in the Thirteenth Annual Report. A work on *Zuñi Folk Tales* appeared after Mr. Cushing's death, and the great store of information obtained by him during his residence at Zuñi was utilized in a number of minor papers.

The Eighth Annual Report of the Bureau contains a *Study of Pueblo Architecture: Tusavan and Cibola,* by Victor Mindeleff. During the decade beginning with 1879 Mr. James Stevenson made extensive collections in Zuñi and other pueblos, illustrated catalogues of which were published in the Second and Third Annual Reports. Mrs. M. C. Stevenson accompanied her husband to the Pueblo country in 1879, and soon became interested in the study of this most fascinating people. Her visits have been repeated at frequent intervals down to the present year, and her observations are now brought together in the accompanying paper, *The Zuñi Indians Their Mythology, Esoteric Societies and Ceremonies.* Mrs. Stevenson has published a number of papers dealing with the particular phases of Zuñi life. *Zuñi and the Zuñians* was printed privately; *Religious Life of the Zuñi Child* appeared in the Fifth Annual Report of the Bureau; *From the Zuñi Scalp Ceremonial* in the Congress of Women, vol. 2, Chicago, 1894; *Zuñi Ancestral Gods and Masks* in the American Anthropologist for 1893; *Zuñi Mythology* in the memoirs of the International Congress of Anthropology, Chicago, 1894, and *Zuñi Games* in The American Anthropologist for 1893.

In the accompanying paper Mrs. Stevenson does not attempt a monographic study of the Zuñis, the subject being too extensive for presentation in a single volume. Brief sketches describing the everyday life, arts, and customs of the people are given, but chief attention is devoted to the mythology, the esoteric fraternities, and the ceremonies of the people. These subjects are here presented in the detail which their importance demands. Mrs. Stevenson's prolonged visits to Zuñi and her intimate acquaintance with its people, especially with their inner life, give ample assurance that the true nature of the beliefs and practices of this tribe is here revealed.

Like the first edition of our recently-published *Aboriginal Indian (American) Basketry*, the first edition for the *The Zuñi Indians* from which we reproduced this edition came from Ken MacRae, MacRae's Indian Book Distributors, of Santa Rosa, Calif. Mr. MacRae will distribute this title exclusively to the book shop and museum shop trade, with certain exceptions, as he does also with *Basketry*. Mr. MacRae and his wife Diana are prominent in the Indian artifact business, and what we have seen of what they sell and trade has been of superior quality.

While we have always wanted to reprint this book ourselves, the project has been urged upon us by many interested (and interesting) people. Chief among these, to our pleasure, is Miss Octavia Fellin, librarian of the Gallup Public Library. Miss Fellin is one of the most knowledgeable people we know of on the subject of the Zuñi Indians (The Zuñi Pueblo is only 40 miles south of Gallup), as well as a good friend of The Rio Grande Press.

In any event, it is our pride and delight to bring this wonderful book back to life again. It is, in a sense, a genuine salute to the people of Zuñi Pueblo. We have visited the good Zuñi many times, and always we have been received with a courteous and friendly welcome. We remember once, visiting during a katcina ceremony . . . ah, but then, that is another story!

Robert B. McCoy

La Casa Escuela
Glorieta, N. M. 87535
September 1970

TWENTY-THIRD ANNUAL REPORT

OF THE

BUREAU OF AMERICAN ETHNOLOGY

TO THE

SECRETARY OF THE SMITHSONIAN INSTITUTION

1901–1902

J. W. POWELL
DIRECTOR

WASHINGTON
GOVERNMENT PRINTING OFFICE
1904

ACCOMPANYING PAPER

THE ZUÑI INDIANS

THEIR MYTHOLOGY, ESOTERIC FRATERNITIES, AND CEREMONIES

BY

MATILDA COXE STEVENSON

3

CONTENTS

CONTENTS 7

ILLUSTRATIONS

8

GENERAL VIEW OF ZUÑI

MUMMY CAVE IN CANYON DEL MUERTO

KO'THLUWALA'WA, JUNCTION OF LITTLE COLORADO AND ZUÑI RIVERS

THE ZUÑI INDIANS: THEIR MYTHOLOGY, ESOTERIC FRATERNITIES, AND CEREMONIES

By Matilda Coxe Stevenson

INTRODUCTION

During the last twenty-five years the investigations of archeologists and ethnologists in the United States have been largely directed to the southwestern region, especially to Arizona and New Mexico. This region appears to have been once quite densely populated, then desolated· by wars, and afterward held in precarious tenure by remnants of a dwindling race. The older ruins are found in the valleys, along the water courses, where the prehistoric people probably dwelt in peace and prosperity until, driven by a powerful foe from the homes of their fathers, they were forced to take refuge in recesses and caves in the canyon walls. These resorts are filled with the homes of the cliff dwellers. Many of the houses are well preserved, but most of the ruins of the valley are hardly more than crumbling heaps of stones, while among these everywhere are scattered the lares and penates of the ancients.

It can not be determined how many generations of cliff dwellers lived in these strange fastnesses; but that many of the stone structures of the cliffs are hundreds of years old may not be questioned. Some of these places have become inaccessible, owing to the wearing away of the approaches by the elements that fashioned the recesses of the canyon walls When the clouds of war grew less threatening, the people ventured to leave their fortresses, the scenes of long trials and many privations, and settled upon the mesas, or table-lands, which are so prominent a feature in the scenery of New Mexico and Arizona. The elevation of these sites enabled them to detect the approaching enemy; while in the valley below, along the streams that washed the bases of the cliffs, they sowed and gathered their crops. But the mesa top was far from the harvest field, and the women must have grown weary carrying the water vases and canteens up the steep acclivities of the rocky walls. In the course of time the mesa dwellers

13

ventured to descend to the valleys and to erect their dwellings upon the ruins of the towns where their forefathers had lived; there they at length regained their inheritance and reestablished their pueblos, which still endure, although within the past few years they have been rapidly changing under the influence of civilization. Thus was completed the cycle of vicissitudes in the history of these people—from valley to cliff, from cliff to mesa, and from mesa to valley again. The Hopi villages of Arizona and Acoma of New Mexico are still on mesas, but the people are gradually moving down into the valleys.

Much has been done, but more remains to be accomplished, before there can be hope of writing the history of the generations of men

FIG. 1—Morning prayer to rising sun.

whose records are found here and there on the canyon walls of the Southwest and whose traditions speak to us, however imperfectly, through the people now living in the pueblos of that region. Among the remnants of ancient tribes, the Zuñis, whose extreme exclusiveness has preserved to them their strong individuality, may claim perhaps the highest position, whether we regard simply their agricultural and pastoral pursuits or consider their whole social and political organization.

The quest for happiness is universal, and in their endeavor to attain this the Zuñis have developed a philosophy that has been profoundly influenced by their environment. Upon this philosophy is built a system of religion which, among its many interesting features, inculcates

truthfulness.   A Zuñi must speak with one tongue in order to have
his prayers received by the gods, and unless the prayers are accepted
no rains will come, which means starvation.   His voice must be gentle
and he must speak and act with kindness to all, for the gods care not
for those whose lips speak with harshness.   The morning prayer (figure 1) he must utter out of doors, looking toward the rising sun.   All
must observe continence four days previous to and four days following
the sending of breath prayers through the spiritual essence of plume
offerings, and thus their passions are brought under control.   They
look to their gods for nourishment and for all things pertaining to
their welfare in this world, and while the woof of their religion is colored with poetic conceptions, when the fabric is separated thread by
thread we find the web composed of a few simple, practical concepts.
Their highest conception of happiness is physical nourishment and
enjoyment, and the worship of their pantheon of gods is designed to
attain this end.

It has been said that the Pueblo Indians are attached to the Roman
Catholic faith; but such is not the case, at least with the Zuñis.   For
a time their ancestors were compelled to worship in that church, but
their pagan belief was not seriously affected thereby.   The ritual
pleased them, and they were allowed to decorate their walls with symbols of their own belief, and so the church became more or less an
object of interest to them, and to some extent the ritual of Catholicism
modified their own.   The Rio Grande pueblos, however, have been
brought more under the influence of the church, and superficial
observers have supposed them to be permanently Christianized.

In July, 1879, the birth year of the Bureau of Ethnology, an expedition was sent to make researches among the pueblos and the more
important ruins of New Mexico and Arizona, and at the same time to
make a special study of some particular pueblo.   Zuñi, in western
New Mexico, was selected as the place for the more detailed work.
Mr James Stevenson was placed in charge of the expedition, and with
a small party, including Mr Frank H. Cushing, Mr J. K. Hillers,
and the writer, started for Zuñi.

The first point of interest visited after leaving Las Vegas, N. Mex.,
then the terminus of the Atchison, Topeka and Santa Fe railroad, was
the ruin of the pueblo of Pecos, situated on a knoll about 100 feet
above the Rio Pecos, 25 miles south of east of Santa Fe.   At that time
the walls of the old church erected under the command of the Spanish
fathers were standing, and some of the interior wood carvings were
silent witnesses to the former presence of the conquerors.   With no
other implements than knives and stilettos the party worked during
the night, by the light of the brilliant moon, opening one chamber.   An
impression of a hand and arm in color, probably of a maiden, was found

on the wall.   Such evidences of maidenly vanity are still to be seen in pueblo houses of the present time.

Near one end of the town were the remains of two circular walls, which have been described by some writers as estufas, or fire houses, and are supposed to have been used for religious purposes by the former inhabitants of the pueblo.   Careful observation indicated that these particular inclosures were probably designed as reservoirs and were used for the storage of snow, to be consumed during the long droughts of that arid country.   Subsequently in the same year it was found that the Laguna Indians used similar stores of snow.   The Laguna women, in carrying water from distant springs when the reservoirs were exhausted, have worn a path 6 or 8 inches deep in the sandstone.   How pathetic is the story graven in the winding footway; what pages might be filled with this "testimony of the rocks."

The journey from the terminus of the railroad at Las Vegas to Zuñi was long and tedious, and the party felt deeply grateful to General Edward Hatch, then in command of the district of New Mexico, and to General J. J. Dane, district quartermaster, for their cordial compliance with the request of General Sherman to afford every facility in the way of transportation and otherwise.   Had it not been for the enthusiastic interest in ethnologic research of the General of the Army, the limited allotment for the expedition would necessarily have been largely expended for transportation and labor, and the scientific work greatly hampered.

Ten days were consumed in the journey from Santa Fe to Fort Wingate over the old Fort Wingate road, a thing of the past since the introduction of the railroad.   Every foot of the way bore evidence of former settlement.   When not visible on the surface, walls, stone implements, or fragments of pottery were readily revealed by a little work with the pick and shovel.

The warm welcome extended by General George P. Buell, then in command of Fort Wingate, was appreciated by the travelers, who had been constantly exposed to the burning sun of New Mexico for ten days.   After a short time spent in outfitting, the party proceeded to Zuñi, 45 miles distant.   Here they were made welcome by the native priests and other officials of the pueblo; and later, when a council was held and Mr Stevenson told them the object of his visit, they promised him every possible aid, a promise which they have sacredly kept.

Six months were spent in studying the religion and sociology of the Zuñis, in making a survey of the town and immediate vicinity, in securing photographs of the pueblo and the people showing various phases of their daily life, and in making a collection of ceremonial objects including a large number of fetishes, and of stone implements, fabrics, foodstuffs, and pottery.   Two images of saints and portions of the altar of the old Catholic church were obtained, the enamel finish on the face and limbs of the figures showing much artistic skill. The church objects were in the custody of one Mauritio, and in order to determine whether they might be removed a council of religious and civil officers was held. It was finally decided that it would be well to have these objects go with the other Zuñi material to the "great house" (National Museum) in Washington, where they would be preserved.

While the priests and other high officials favored photographing the ceremonials—in fact, seemed eager to serve the expedition in every way—the populace were so opposed to having their masks and rituals "carried away on paper," that it was deemed prudent to make but few ceremonial pictures with the camera, and the altars and masks were sketched in color by the writer without the knowledge of the people. The largest and most valuable collection, especially of fetishes and sacred vessels, ever secured from any of the pueblos was made at this time.

Before the collection was packed, General Buell left Fort Wingate for Colorado with his command and most of his transportation facilities to participate in the Ute war. After securing all the available teams in the country, Mr Stevenson found the number inadequate to convey the collections from Zuñi to the railroad. To ask for the few teams remaining at Wingate seemed presumptuous, yet it was necessary that something be done to get this material out of the Territory immediately. No one could tell what a day might bring forth in this frontier post, far from the railway and without telegraphic communication with the outer world. The Apaches were within striking distance and the Navahos were threatening an outbreak, while nearly the entire command of the military post was absent in Colorado. It was decided to communicate at once with General Buell and solicit aid. The result was that all the wagons except those in daily use at the garrison were assigned to Mr Stevenson, with a request that the transportation of the collection be hastened and the teams returned at the earliest possible moment. This generous act was profoundly appreciated. Had aid been withheld at this time much of the collection might never have reached the railroad.

The whole of the six months devoted to field work in 1879 was spent at Zuñi; and though the writer accompanied Mr Stevenson to the meetings of the various secret organizations, and though her relations with the Indians were of the most cordial nature, she obtained at this time but the merest suggestion of their inner life.

During 1880 all of the Rio Grande pueblos were visited. Photographs were made at each pueblo, and collections of stone implements, objects associated with the ritual, and pottery were secured. In 1881

Mr Stevenson returned to Zuñi, where six months were spent in ethnologic study and collecting. The Hopi villages and a number of ruins in the vicinity were visited in the winter of the same year.

In subsequent years further researches were made among the Rio Grande pueblos and the ruins of central and northern Arizona, and many objects of value were obtained. The pottery from the ruins was especially fine, many of the pieces rivaling in form and color the old Greek and Egyptian wares. One of the most interesting ruins was found in an arm of the canyon de Chelly. Although the main canyon had been previously visited, this arm, named the canyon del Muerto, from the exhumation of a number of mummies,[a] was unknown to the white man before the old Navaho chief, Ganado Mucho, who was Mr Stevenson's guide, led him, as a mark of special favor, into this hitherto unexplored field. Models of the ruins in the canyon del Muerto, constructed principally by Mr Victor Mindeleff, artist to the expedition, from the surveys, photographs, and sketches made at this time, are among the most interesting to be seen in the National Museum (see plate II).

The rich results from superficial excavations in New Mexico and Arizona, especially in the Hopi country, convinced Mr Stevenson that archeologic treasures lay hidden within the earth; but these he thought would remain undisturbed while he gathered objects of interest, both ancient and modern, from the many pueblos. For tourists and curiosity-seekers, fired with the desire for collecting, were effecting trades with the Indians, and many choice specimens were already crossing the seas; hence came the necessity for immediate action on the part of the Government collectors. It was hoped by Mr Stevenson that, when the materials to be found on the surface were safely deposited in the National Museum, a well-organized system of excavation throughout the Southwest could be begun. But exposure and overwork shortened the days of this earnest worker, and after his untimely death in 1888 it remained for Dr J. W. Fewkes, Dr Walter Hough, Dr George H. Pepper, and others to verify his opinions. The valuable archeologic collections made in recent years are evidence of the correctness of Mr Stevenson's convictions.

The writer has made several prolonged visits to Zuñi, and after many years of investigation and intimate acquaintance with the priests, theurgists, and the people generally, feels sufficiently acquainted with them, their life, and their thoughts, to venture a presentation of their esoteric beliefs, their rituals, habits, and customs. The limitations of this volume, however, make it necessary to give only a restricted account of many subjects that are deserving of more extensive treatment, and much material has been reserved for future publication.

---

[a] Mr J. Stanley-Brown was the first of the party to discover human remains in this canyon.

While the writer has gone deeply into the subject of the religion of the Zuñis, and is able to record the more important details of their philosophy, there are yet many fields to be worked, and an attempt at drawing final conclusions will not be made until more extensive studies of allied tribes have been undertaken. If that which is here presented serves as a basis for future investigation, and aids the Government to a better understanding of the North American Indians, the author will have succeeded in her purpose.

Whatever has been accomplished by the writer at Zuñi and elsewhere is largely due to the training and instruction received from her lamented husband and companion, James Stevenson. Much of the present volume is based on his notes and records. His plans for ethnologic research were far-reaching, and he expected to give many years to their completion. His life was devoted to the establishment and development of scientific institutions, and it is largely to his efforts, in support of those of Major J. W. Powell, that the Bureau of Ethnology owes its origin and success. His reputation for careful investigation, and a high sense of integrity, is too well known to require further comment in these pages.

To Mr W. H. Holmes, Chief of the Bureau of American Ethnology, the writer is indebted for uniform courtesy and for opportunities afforded in the prosecution of her recent studies in Zuñi. Acknowledgments are due for courtesies extended during the long period of the writer's investigations in the Southwest, among others, by Colonel G. G. Huntt, Captain Herbert H. Sargent, Captain Curtis B. Hoppin, Captain Guy Carlton, Dr Washington Matthews, Major Francis H. Hardie, Lieutenant Clarence R. Day, and Lieutenant H. B. Jordan, of the United States Army; Honorable Henry M. Teller, United States Senate; Honorable Robert Adams, jr., House of Representatives; Dr Reginald H. Sayre; Dr George Tully Vaughan, Assistant Surgeon-General Marine-Hospital Service; Mr J. D. McChesney, of the United States Geological Survey; Mr F. V. Coville, Botanist, Department of Agriculture; Mr J. N. Rose, United States National Museum; Mr P. C. Warman, editor, United States Geological Survey; Mr William Barnum of the Carnegie Institution; and Mr Douglas D. Graham, at present United States agent to the Zuñis. Mr Graham's interest in the success of the representatives of the Bureau of American Ethnology has been exhibited in the most effective manner for twenty years or more, and his generous aid, not only to the writer but to others in the employ of the Government who have visited Zuñi pueblo, has in many ways been invaluable.

The writer is under obligations also to her Zuñi friends, among whom are numbered not only the priests and theurgists, but also the women and children, who ever manifested a pleasing readiness to serve her.

She is especially grateful to the high priest of Zuñi; the sun priest; Nai'uchi,[a] elder brother Bow priest; Mesha, younger brother Bow priest; Kenoti, member of the Bow priesthood; the Ko'mosona, director of the fraternity devoted to anthropic worship; Sinahe (Dick), associate rain priest; Roman Luna, a theurgist; Hälian, son of Nai'uchi, and Nina, his daughter, who freely gave such aid and information as was sought. Among those, since deceased, who faithfully served the writer, and for whom she will ever retain the fondest remembrances, are Nai'uchi's wife; Lai'wa'silu'si, a former high priest; Pedro Pino,[b] a former governor; Jose Palle, a rain priest; and Wewha, the strongest character and the most intelligent of the Zuñi tribe within the knowledge of the writer.

MYTHOLOGY

GENERAL CONCEPTIONS OF THE UNIVERSE

Civilized man's conceptions of the universe are altogether different from those of primitive man. The former understands natural phenomena through analysis and correlation; the latter accounts for them by analogy. Civilized man lives in a world of reality; primitive man in a world of mysticism and symbolism; he is deeply impressed by his natural environment; every object for him possesses a spiritual life, so that celestial bodies, mountains, rocks, the flora of the earth, and the earth itself are to him quite different from what they are to civilized man. The sturdy pine, the delicate sapling, the fragrant blossom, the giant rock, and the tiny pebble play alike their part in the mystic world of the aboriginal man. Many things which tend to nourish life are symbolized by the Zuñis as mother. When a Zuñi speaks of the Earth Mother the earth is symbolized as the source, not only of all vegetal matter which nourishes man, but also of the game which gives him animal food. The earth is mother, the great one to whom all are indebted for sustenance.

The Zuñis believe that the earth is supplied with water by their dead of both sexes and all ages above infancy, and infants soon reach maturity after going to the undermost world whence the Zuñis came. The deceased always go first to Ko'thluwala'wa (Dance village), abiding place of the Council of the Gods, and they often return thither to dance in the great dance house. The deceased A'pi''läshiwanni (Bow priesthood) are an exception; they join the Ku'pïshtaya,[c] becoming lightning-makers.

The u'wannami (rain-makers) are controlled and directed by the

---

a Nai'uchi died in June, 1904.
b Pedro Pino and one other spoke Spanish fluently, the latter being able to read and write in this language. They had been taught by Spanish priests, who compelled them to give all their time to the language until they became proficient as interpreters. Two other men spoke a little Mexican.
c See p. 21.

Council of the Gods.   These shadow people collect water in vases and gourd jugs from the six great waters of the world.[a]   They are carried by the steam which rises from these springs to the upper plane, provided they are supplied with breath plumes, each u'wannami holding a group of these plumes in order to ascend.   Every individual in Zuñi makes these offerings each month at the time of full moon.   The u'wannami pass to and fro over the upper plane, protected from the view of the people below by cloud masks.   It is not the clouds which fall in rain; the u'wannami pour the water through the cloud masks. The clouds are produced by the breath of the gods and smoke, and, when it is understood that the greater the smoke offering the greater the inducement for the rain-makers to work, it is not surprising that smoking is one of the conspicuous features of the Zuñi ritual.   There is a time at the summer solstice when the torchbearer sets fire to everything in his way, from Ko'thluwala'wa to Zuñi.   The greater the smoke offering the heavier the cloud masks will be.

The Ku'pĭshtaya (lightning-makers) are mighty warriors who control the lightning arrows.   Each Ku'pĭshtaya has his ʻKĭä'ʻlawanni (deputy), and his ʻSi'kĭahaya (courier).   ʻKĭanil'ona, the greatest of the Zuñi ancestral gods (plate III), sits in state in Ko'thluwala'wa (plate IV), where the Council of the Gods appeals to him for water with which the u'wannami may water the earth, the male gods sprinkling with plume sticks dipped in gourd jugs of water and the female gods from vases.   The heavy rains are produced by the pouring of the water directly from the vases.   The u'wannami are sent to designated points by the Council of the Gods to water the earth according to the supplications of the Zuñis.

The varying forms of the clouds are significant to the Zuñi mind. Cirrus clouds tell that the u'wannami are passing about for pleasure. Cumulus and nimbus clouds indicate that the u'wannami will water the earth.   The smoke offerings which produce the clouds may have been sufficient to bring the rain; but this is not all.   The daily life, especially of the A'shiwanni (rain priests), must be such as not to offend the Council of the Gods, which controls and directs the rain-makers. Should this not be the case the Council of the Gods withholds its power, and the Su'ni-a'shiwanni, who send the cold winds from the northeast and northwest, would drive away the cloud masks.   Thus the Zuñis account for wind clouds.   The summer winds of the southwest and southeast are the breath of the u'wannami, who do not breathe from the mouth but directly from the heart.

These people rarely cast their eyes upward without invoking the rain-makers, for in their arid land rain is the prime object of prayer. Their water vases are covered with cloud and rain emblems, and the water in the vase symbolizes the life, or soul, of the vase.

---

[a] Referring to the springs of the six regions owned by ʻKĭanil'ona (owner of springs).

When the Ku'pĭshtaya communicate with one another, the ruler of the North dispatches his courier to the Ku'pĭshtaya of the West and the courier returns to his place in the North, the ruler of the West transferring the message to the South by his courier; in this way communication is held between the Ku'pĭshtaya of the six regions. The Zuñis have no fear of lightning, as the Ku'pĭshtaya never destroy the good in heart. One who is struck by lightning, no matter what his previous standing, must have possessed a bad heart. Thunder is produced by the rain-makers gaming with stones while the Ku'pĭshtaya are shooting their missiles. The rain-maker of the North rolls a stone to a fellow at some other point, and the one receiving the stone returns it; any number of rain-makers may join in the game. According to Zuñi philosophy thunder is produced in no other way.

The seeds distributed to the people by the personators of ancestral gods are recognized by the intelligent as only symbolizing the blessings which they desire and anticipate, yet each person receives the gift with the same solemnity and plants it with the same reverence as if it actually came from the god of seeds in the undermost world.

The sun is referred to as father, the ancient one. The moon is his sister; the Sun Father has no wife. All peoples are the children of the sun. Whatever the Zuñis fail to account for by incidents in the early stages of their existence is attributed to the agency of the Sun Father. Though the Zuñi philosophy, like that of other aboriginal peoples, is built on analogic reasoning, these savage philosophers certainly place entire faith in the first great cause, all-powerful, without beginning, without end.

CLASSIFICATION OF THE HIGHER POWERS

The higher powers of the Zuñis may be classed under seven heads, as follows:

1. *Universal.* A'wonawil'ona, the supreme life-giving bisexual power, who is referred to as He-She, the symbol and initiator of life, and life itself, pervading all space.

2. *Celestial, anthropic* (represented by persons wearing masks). The Sun Father, who is directly associated with the supreme power; he always was and always will be; he is the great god above all other anthropic and zoic gods; he is the giver of light and warmth, and through the supreme power the giver of life. The Moon Mother, giver of light at night, the divider of the year into months, and, through A'wonawil'ona, the delineator of the span of life—the supreme power gradually draws the mystic veil from the Moon Mother's shield, indicating birth, infancy, youth, and maturity; she draws the veil over the shield again, symbolizing man's passing on to the infancy of old age,

when he sleeps to awake in the abiding place of the gods;—and the Morning and Evening Stars.

3. *Celestial, anthropic* (represented in carvings and paintings). The Polar Star, all the fixed stars, the Morning and Evening Stars, the Galaxy, Orion, Pleiades, Ursa Major, Ursa Minor, and Ächiyälä′topa (the being with wings and tail of knives).

4. *Terrestrial.* Earth Mother, giver of vegetation.

5. *Subterranean, anthropic* (not personated). The Gods of War (represented by images of wood), children of the Sun Father, who have their successors but not impersonators on the earth; Po′shai-yänkĭ, the culture hero; and Corn Mother.

6. *Subterranean, anthropic* (represented by persons wearing masks and in one instance by an ophiomorphous image). Salt Mother, giver of herself; Corn Father, giver of himself; White Shell Woman, giver of herself; Red Shell Woman, giver of herself; Turquois Man, giver of himself; patronal and ancestral gods; the Plumed Serpent; and a number of foreign deities to be propitiated.

7. *Terrestrial and subterranean.* Zoic gods who play their part through the esoteric fraternities, eradicating the ill effects of witchcraft on individuals and interceding between the members of the fraternities and the Sun Father and Moon Mother, and between them and the anthropic gods.

BEGINNINGS OF THE UNIVERSE

The Zuñi ceremonies cluster about a cosmogony which serves to keep the beliefs alive and to guide both actors and spectators through the observances.

In the beginning A′wonawil′ona with the Sun Father and Moon Mother existed above, and Shi′wanni and Shi′wano′‘kĭa, his wife, below. Shi′wanni and Shi′wano′‘kĭa were superhuman beings who labored not with hands but with hearts and minds. The rain priests of Zuñi are called A′shiwanni and the Priestess of Fecundity is called Shi′wano′‘kĭa, to indicate that they do no secular work; they give their minds and hearts to higher thoughts in order that their bodies be so purified they may enter into communion with the gods.

All was shi′pololo (fog), rising like steam. With the breath from his heart A′wonawil′ona created clouds and the great waters of the world. He-She is the blue vault of the firmament. The breath clouds of the gods are tinted with the yellow of the north, the blue-green of the west, the red of the south, and the silver of the east of A′wonawil′ona. The smoke clouds of white and black become a part of A′wonawil′ona; they are himself, as he is the air itself; and when the air takes on the form of a bird it is but a part of himself—is himself. Through the light, clouds, and air he becomes the essence and creator of vegetation. The Zuñi conception of A'wonawil'ona is similar to that of the Greeks of Athena.

It is not strange, therefore, that the A'shiwi[a] cover their altars with symbols of cumulus and nimbus clouds, with "the flame of the cloud crest," and "the blue of the deep wells of the sky," and use all these, woven into plumes, to waft their prayers to the gods, and have as their symbol of life, embracing all the mysterious life-securing properties, including mystery medicine, an ear of corn clothed in beautiful plumage; for the spirit of A'wonawil'ona is "put into and upon this created form." The name of this symbol, mi'li, is but another word for corn, and the ĕt'tonĕ, the most sacred fetish of the A'shiwanni, is another symbol of life, including rain and vegetation.

While every Zuñi is taught that in inhaling the sacred breath from his fetishes or in breathing upon the plumes he offers to the gods he is receiving from A'wonawil'ona the breath of life or is wafting his own breath prayers to his gods, only the few have any conception of all that is implied in their observances or fully appreciate the poetic nature of their myths.

After A'wonawil'ona created the clouds and the great waters of the world, Shi'wanni said to Shi'wano''kĭa: "I, too, will make something beautiful, which will give light at night when the Moon Mother sleeps." Spitting in the palm of his left hand, he patted the spittle with the fingers of his right hand, and the spittle foamed like yucca suds and then formed into bubbles of many colors, which he blew upward; and thus he created the fixed stars and constellations. And Shi'wanni was well pleased with his creation. Then Shi'wano''kĭa said "See what I can do," and she expectorated into the palm of her left hand and slapped the saliva with the fingers of her right, and the spittle foamed like yucca suds, running over her hand and flowing everywhere; and thus she created A'witelin 'Si'ta (Earth Mother).

CREATION OF THE A'SHIWI AND THEIR COMING TO THE OUTER WORLD

Shi'wanni and Shi'wano''kĭa were the parents of the A'shiwi, who were created in the undermost world, being born as infants; not, however, at long intervals, but in rapid succession, until many were born.

Yätokĭa (Sun Father)[b] created two sons, Kŏw'wituma and Wats'usi, by impregnating two bits of foam with his rays. These Divine Ones

---

[a] A'shiwi, the people, the reference being to the Zuñis only. Shi'wi is the singular form.

[b] Yätokĭa means the holder or bearer of light. The sun itself is conceived as a shield of burning crystal, which the Sun Father, who is anthropomorphic, carries as he makes his daily journey from east to west. Prayers are addressed to the invisible and esoteric bearer of (the power behind) the shield, who travels over the road of day seated on a colossal turquois, wearing beautiful buckskin clothing and many necklaces of precious beads.

a　A HARD CLIMB

b　PICTOGRAPHS ON CANYON WALL AT HÄN'ʟ̣IPÍNKĬA

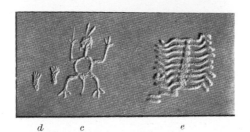

PICTOGRAPHS ON WALL OF INNER CHAMBER AT HÄN'ʼLIPÏNKÏA

MASK OF ᵀKĬÁNĬLONA (OWNER OF SPRINGS): FRONT AND REAR VIEWS

a MASK OF KÓYEMSHI; b, c MASK OF KÓMOKÁʺTSI; FRONT AND REAR VIEWS

ascended to their Sun Father over a road of meal, which they made by throwing the meal upward.

The Sun Father, wishing to bring his children from the undermost world to his presence, provided each of the Divine Ones with an a'mitolan pi'ᵗlännĕ (rainbow), wil'lolonannĕ sho'liwe (lightning arrows), and a ᵗkĭa'alännĕ (cloud shield), and directed them to go to the undermost world and bring his children to his presence. They rent the earth with their lightning arrows and descended into A'witĕn te'hula (fourth world).[a]

When the A'shiwi inquired of the Divine Ones "Who are you? Whence did you come?" they replied "A'chi ana pi'akoa" ("The two come down").

The undermost world was so dark that the people could not see one another, and they trod upon one another's toes. Their houses were but holes in the earth, and their food was seed grass. In order to see the people Kŏw'wituma laid dry grass upon the ground and placed his bow on the grass, and by rubbing his arrow, with a rotary motion, upon the bow he produced fire, and lighted the grass, using it as a torch to carry about among the people. Many could not look on the fire, for their eyes were not good for light, while others fell back crazed with fear. Kŏw'wituma said: "You have but few people." The elder ones replied "We have many," and they called those who were absent.

The Divine Ones, throwing out a line of meal, produced light, which guided them to the north, where they cut an ä'shekĭa (pine tree of the north, Pinus ponderosa var. scapulorum) with stone knives, and returning, planted it for the people to ascend to the third world, A'wisho te'hula (water-moss world). Here the Divine Ones threw out meal to the west, which produced light to guide them thither; and there they cut a kĭa'läᵗsilo (spruce of the west, Pseudotsuga douglassii), and returning, they planted it for the people to ascend to the second world, Pä'nanula te'hula (mud world). Here the Divine Ones, led by the line of meal which they threw out, went to the south and cut a ᵗhlan'ilkoha (aspen of the south, the quaking aspen, Populus tremuloides) and returning, they planted it for the people to ascend to the first world, La'tŏwᵗte'hula (wing world; from yä'tokĭa la'tŏwwe, sun's wings, the rays of the sun being referred to as wings). It was in this world that the A'shiwi first saw the faintest light of day; hence the name. Throwing out a line of meal to the east, the Divine Ones visited this direction, where they cut a lo'kwimo (spruce of the east, silver spruce, Picea pungens), and returning, they planted it for the people to ascend

---

[a] Te'hula refers only to underworlds. Uhl'onannĕ is the term for the outer world, or this world. The undermost world bears several other names: An'nociyan te'hula (world of utter darkness, blackness-of-soot world); Lu'hote kĭa'pīnna; lu'hote (fine earth or dust); kĭä'pīnna (uncooked, not hardened by fire).

thereby to the outer world,[a] Te′kohaiakwi u′kwa′ikĭa (light-of-day place). The Zuñis, in speaking of Te′kohaiakwi u′kwai′ikĭa, add yäm Yä′tokĭa Tä′ʻchu (my Sun Father), yäm A′witelin ʻSi′ta (my Earth Mother), u′natikĭanapkĭa (I inhale the sacred breath). The place of coming through to this world is called Ji′miᵗkĭanapkĭatea, a word full of occult meaning, having reference to an opening in the earth filled with water which mysteriously disappeared, leaving a clear passage for the A′shiwi to ascend to the outer world.

The Divine Ones and the A′shiwi spent some time in each world as they ascended, and many of the A′shiwi who were left behind struggled on after the others. The A′shiwi had constant rainfall during their ascent to the outer world, which was reached just as the Evening Star, who is second warrior to the Sun Father and follows after him, rose above the horizon.

Songs of the Divine Ones over the Ĕt′towe

In the lower world the A′shiwi had rain priests (A′shiwanni; singular, shi′wanni), of whom six were assigned to the six regions. Each shi′wanni possessed an ĕt′tonĕ,[b] most sacred of their fetishes, which he brought to this world wrapped in a mat of straw in a crude basket, pressed to his breast. Kŏw′wituma and Wats′usi, the Divine Ones, having knowledge that the A′shiwanni possessed ĕt′towe, made a meal painting of a′wehlwia′we (cumulus clouds) on the ground and on the road, and the A′shiwanni placed their ĕt′towe on the painting. The Kĭa′kwemosi, Shi′wanni of the North, sat next to the road, on the south side, the road being the dividing line; the Shi′wanni of the West and Shi′wano′ʻkĭa sat on his right. The Shi′wanni of the South sat next, the Shi′wanni of the East being on his right. The A′shiwanni of the Zenith and Nadir sat next, and after them four other A′shiwanni, Kŏw′wituma sitting at the end of the line. Four A′shiwanni sat on the other side of the road, with Wats′usi north of them. Yä′nŏwwuluha, a man of great heart and wisdom, sat before the meal painting to the north of the line, and the A′shiwi gathered around on the north, west, and south of the painting. They sang the songs of the Divine Ones for rain, that the earth should abound in kĭa′ᵗsanna (grass seed), the only food then known to the A′shiwi. They sat singing in low tones until midnight. Then, leaving their ĕt′towe in place on the painting, the Divine Ones and the A′shiwanni retired a short distance and ate. After eating they slept awhile,

---

[a] In an earlier publication it was stated that the A′shiwi ascended to the outer world through a huge hollow reed. The student of mythology labors under many difficulties, none of which are more perplexing than that of distinguishing between the tribal cosmogony and the winter tales of special narrators. The intimate acquaintance with the Indians of the Southwest acquired by the writer through later investigations has served to mark quite definitely the differences between their mythology and their winter tales.

[b] Plural ĕt′towe. The etymology of this word is not known, but it implies invariable bringer of good.

and then returned to the painting and, taking their seats, resumed their prayers. At this time Mo'yächun'hlan'na (Great Star, the morning star), the first warrior to the Sun Father, could be seen, but faintly at first through the delicate showers. When the people saw the star they exclaimed "Our Father comes," but the Divine Ones declared "He is not your Sun Father, but his warrior who comes before." Later, when the sun appeared, the people fell on their faces in fear; but the Divine Ones cried: "Be not afraid; it is your Sun Father."

At this time the Kïa'kwemosi went over the eastern road and, planting te'likinawe (prayer plumes) which the Sun Father had sent him by the Divine Ones, prayed, saying: "My Sun Father, my Moon Mother, I give to you te'likinawe."

KŎW'WITUMA APPOINTS YÄ'NŎWWULUHA DEPUTY TO THE SUN FATHER

When the Kïa'kwemosi returned to his place by the meal painting, Kŏw'wituma, pointing to the ĕt'towe, which were concealed with the mat covering, asked Yä'nŏwwuluha "What are these?" and he replied "'Kïa'ĕt'tonĕ chuĕt'tonĕ."[a] Then Kŏw'wituma said: "You are able to tell me of these precious things; your heart is good; your head is good; I will make you pe'kwĭn (deputy) to my Sun Father." Yä'nŏwwuluha remained standing on the meal line and near the painting, while the birds of the six regions came in succession and sang.

Kŏw'wituma called first O'noʰhlikïa (bird of the North, Icteria longicauda, long-tailed chat). On arriving he perched on the eastern end of the meal line and sang for rains and lightning. The bird kept his place after he ceased singing. Then Kŏw'wituma called Mai'ya (bird of the West, Cyanocitta macrolopha, long-crested jay). This bird perched next to O'noʰhlikïa on the meal line, and repeated the songs for rains and lightning. He, too, remained in his place after singing. Kŏw'wituma next called Mu'la (bird of the South, macaw). Mu'la stood on the meal line next to Mai'ya and sang songs for rains and lightning. After these songs Kŏw'wituma called Kïä'tetäsha (bird of the East, Pipilo megalonyx, spurred towhee). This bird repeated the songs for rains and lightning, having his place on the meal line next to Mu'la. Kïa'wuloʰki (bird of the Zenith, Progne subis, purple martin) was called next. His place was on the meal line after Kïä'tetäsha. He, too, sang songs for rains and lightning. The last bird called by Kŏw'wituma was He'alonsĕt'to (bird of the Nadir, Passerina ciris, painted bunting). This bird stood on the meal line beside Kïa'wuloʰki and sang for rains and lightning.

The birds remained in place on the line while Kŏw'wituma said to

---

[a] A full explanation of the ĕt'towe will be found in the chapter on the A'shiwanni (Rain priesthood).

Yä′nŏwwuluha: "These birds shall be your ĕt′towe." The birds then flew away to their homes.

Yä′nŏwwuluha, passing around by the north side back of the meal painting, took his seat on the line to the left of the Kĭa′kwemosi, by order of Kŏw′wituma. Then Kŏw′wituma had the Shi′wanni of the Zenith move with his ĕt′tonĕ to the end of the line of A′shiwanni on the south side, and had Yä′nŏwwuluha take his place in the line as Shi′wanni of the Zenith and pe′kwĭn[a] (deputy) to the Sun Father. Kŏw′wituma again had the two A′shiwanni on the immediate right of Yä′nŏwwuluha move with their ĕt′towe to the end of the line on the south side; he then took his place by the side of the pe′kwĭn, with Wats′usi sitting to the right of him. The prayers and songs over the ĕt′towe were continued eight days and nights, the A′shiwanni retiring each evening for refreshment. There were no houses yet, and each shi′wanni made a place for his ĕt′tonĕ by using four stone slabs. On the ninth day the A′shiwanni, by direction of the Divine Ones, began building houses of large reeds and earth.

The A′shiwi were queer beings when they came to this world. They had short depilous tails, long ears (at night they lay on one ear and covered themselves with the other), and webbed feet and hands, and their bodies and heads were covered with a′wisho (moss), a lengthy tuft being on the fore part of the head, projecting like a horn. The Zuñis do not believe that they ever existed in other than human form. After the A′shiwi moved to a spring not far distant from their place of nativity, which they named A′wisho, the Divine Ones amputated the tails and ears and cut the webbed feet and hands with their stone knives. The people then bathed, for they were very unclean.

Coming of the Hopis, Pimas, and Navahos

The Mu′′kwe (Hopis) followed the A′shiwi to this world four years (time periods) after all the A′shiwi arrived. The Coconino Pimas came four years after the Mu′′kwe, and the Ä′pächu (Navahos) followed four years after the Coconino Pimas. All these peoples came from the undermost world, passing, like the A′shiwi, through three worlds before reaching this world. The Zuñis do not pretend to account for the origin of the other pueblo peoples.

The villages of the A′shiwi and Mu′′kwe were not far apart in the undermost world, and the two peoples, though not related and speaking different languages, communicated with one another and were friendly. After the Divine Ones had arranged for the A′shiwi to go to the outer world, they visited the Mu′′kwe, delivered the message from the Sun Father, that he wished them to come into his presence, and gave them

---

[a] Pe′kwĭn, when used without explanation, will refer to the Shi′wanni of the Zenith, earthly deputy to the Sun Father.

te′likinawe which they had prepared for them; and the Divine Ones instructed the Mu′‘kwe how they should proceed to the outer world. The Mu′‘kwe themselves cut the trees by which they ascended to this world. The Divine Ones worked only for the A′shiwi, and, as has been stated, they traveled with the A′shiwi from the undermost to this world and remained with them until they had found the Middle place. When the Mu′‘kwe reached this world they did not make a cloud symbol upon the ground and they did not sing, for they did not have the Divine Ones to teach them. The Mu′‘kwe came through Ii′mikĭanakate′a, a short distance north of the point of egress of the A′shiwi. After the A′shiwi had been four years at A′wisho, the Mu′‘kwe moved southeast of Ii′mikĭanakate′a and not far from A′wisho. Here the Divine Ones cut the webbed fingers and toes and amputated the tails of the Mu′‘kwe.

ZUÑI EXPLANATION OF THE PRESENCE OF MEXICANS

Two Mexicans, man and wife, who appeared in this world at the time the A′shiwi arrived remained with them for some time. The Coconino Pimas remained with the A′shiwi long enough to teach them some of their songs, which have descended to the Shu′maakwe fraternity. The Navahos separated from the others. The Coconino Pimas were the last to leave the vicinity of Ii′mikĭanakate′a. They were very thirsty during their journey and could find no water; finally they discovered fox tracks and followed them, for they knew that the tracks would lead to water. After proceeding some distance they were led into a deep canyon (Coconino), where they remained, building permanent homes for themselves. Some few of the A′shiwi went with the Coconino Pimas[a] to the canyon and thus became permanently separated from their people. The Coconinos met a shi′wanni (rain priest) of a strange people upon reaching the depth of the canyon.

A Mu′‘kwe when walking about one day discovered a village and visited it, inquiring of the people, who were A′shiwi, whence they came and whither they were going. "We are in quest of the Middle place," they replied. After a time all the Mu′‘kwe but the Corn clan (the Zuñis do not know where or when the Mu′‘kwe received their clan names), moved west, then east. After many struggles with enemies in the valleys and in canyons the Mu′‘kwe built their homes on mesas.

COMING OF THE WITCHES AND THE INTRODUCTION OF CORN

While the A′shiwi were at A′wisho the Divine Ones organized four esoteric fraternities (see Esoteric fraternities). The A′shiwi were happy here. Day after day they were followed by those who had failed to come to this world with them, for many, becoming tired had fallen back. Every time the A′shiwi heard a rumbling of the earth (earth-

---

[a] The Zuñis declare that some few of the Coconino words are the same as their own.

quake) they knew that others were coming out. They would say
"My younger brother comes;" or, "Some of my people come." The
exodus from the underworlds continued four years.[a] The last observed
to come forth were two witches, a man and a wife, who were all-powerful for good or evil. Kŏw'wituma and Wats'usi, hearing a rumbling
of the earth, looked to see who had arrived, and met the two witches,
whose heads were covered with loose hoods of coarse fiber blowing in
the breeze. Kŏw'wituma inquired of the witches: "Whither are you
going?" They replied: "We wish to go with your people to the Middle place of the world." Kŏw'wituma said: "We do not want you
with us." The witches, holding seeds in their closed hands under
their arms, said: "If we do not go we will destroy the land. We have
all seeds here." When the Divine Ones again told the witches they
were not wanted, they declared that it would not be well if they were
not allowed to go, saying: "We have all things precious for your people." The man, extending his closed hand over the seeds, said: "See,
I wish to give this to the Kĭa'kwemosi; and I wish him to give us two
of his children, a son and a daughter. When we have the children the
corn shall be his." "Why do you wish the children?" asked Kŏw'-
wituma. "We wish to kill the children that the rains may come."

The Divine Ones hastened to repeat what they had seen and heard
to the Kĭa'kwemosi, who replied: "It is well." When the witches
appeared before the Kĭa'kwemosi and claimed two of his children, he
said: "I have no infant children; I have a youth and a maiden; what
do you wish to do with them?" "We wish to destroy them." "Why
do you wish to destroy my children?" "We wish to destroy them
that there may be much rain. We have things of great value to you,
but we must first have much rain." "It is well," said the Kĭa'kwemosi; and when the youth and maiden slept the two witches shot their
medicine into their hearts by touching the children with their hands,
causing their deaths. Their remains were buried in the earth, and the
rains fell four days. On the fifth morning a rumbling noise was heard,
and Kŏw'wituma saw the youth appearing from his grave. Again
there were four days of heavy rains, and on the fifth morning after
the resurrection of the youth a rumbling was heard, and Kŏw'wituma
saw the girl coming from the earth. The same night the two witches
planted all the seeds in the wet earth, and the following morning the
corn was a foot high and the other things were of good size. By
evening all was matured and the A'shiwi ate of the new food, but
they were not pleased; everything was hot, like pepper. Then Kŏw'-
wituma and Wats'usi called the raven, who came and ate much of the
corn and other things. Again the Divine Ones called the owl, who ate

---

[a] "Of old two days were as four years, and four days as eight years," reference being to time
periods. Years throughout this paper will refer to indefinite time periods, unless it is otherwise
explained.

the heart of the grain, leaving the remainder on the cob, so that the corn became soft. The Divine Ones then called the coyote to come and eat the corn; he ate of everything in the field. The raven, owl, and coyote, by eating of the food, softened and sweetened it so that it became palatable to the A'shiwi. Since that time the fields have had to be watched, for the raven takes the corn in the day and the coyote robs the fields at night. At this time the Divine Ones instructed the A'shiwi in fire making and cooking.

A'shiwi Continue their Journeying

While the earth was not muddy, it was so soft that the A'shiwi found difficulty in proceeding. Long years were consumed, and many villages were built, and then abandoned, as they pushed on in their quest for the Middle of the world. Even when they tarried at the towns which they built they were driven therefrom by the corruption of their dead, and they desired even to escape from the effluvium of their own bodies, which was unbearable. "It was like burning sulphur; it was an odor that killed." Repeated divisions of the people occurred during the years consumed in their migrations, some going to the north, others to the south; thus the Zuñis account for many of the ruins north and south of their line of march.

Witches Give Seeds to the Corn Maidens

Unseen and unknown, the Corn maidens came with the A'shiwi from the undermost world and remained with them until they had been four years at Shi'pololo kwi (Fog place), when they were discovered by the two witches sitting under a häm'pone (out-of-door covered place), a pavilion of pine boughs. The witches inquired: "Who are you?" The maidens replied: "We are the a'towa e'washtokïi (Corn maidens)." "Where is your corn?" asked the witches. "We have none." "This is not right. If you are Corn maidens you should have corn;" and, handing a yellow ear of corn to one of the maidens, the witches said: "You are the Yellow Corn maiden and a'wankïo'wu (great or elder sister)." To another they handed a blue ear of corn, saying: "You are the younger sister, the Blue Corn maiden; you two will be the directors or leaders of the others." Handing a red ear of corn to the third one, they said: "You are a younger sister, the Red Corn maiden." And to the fourth they handed an ear of white corn, saying: "You are a younger sister, the White Corn maiden." And to the fifth they said, as they handed her an ear of multicolored corn: "You are the Every-colored Corn maiden and a younger sister." And to the sixth they handed a black ear of corn, saying: "You are the younger sister, the Black Corn maiden." And to the seventh they handed an ear of sweet corn, saying: "You are the younger sister, the Sweet Corn maiden." And to the eighth they said, as they handed her squash seeds: "You are the younger sister, the Squash maiden." And to the ninth they handed watermelon seeds, saying: "You are the younger sister, the Watermelon maiden." And to the tenth they handed muskmelon seeds, saying: "You are the younger sister, the Muskmelon maiden."[a]

After receiving the corn the elder sister said "I will dance with my corn, and so will my sisters;" and she formed her sisters into two lines, facing the east that they might see the coming forth of the Sun Father. They danced all night under a bower walled with ho'mawe (cedar), whose roof was a'wehlwia'we (cumulus clouds) fringed with kĭä'lä'silo (spruce of the west). The witches observed the dance through the night, and in the morning continued their migrations with the A'shiwi, but said not a word to them of the Corn maidens, who remained at Shi'pololo kwi, where "they bathed in the dew (or mist), but did not drink of it."

ORIGIN OF THE ANCESTRAL GODS

After the A'shiwi had journeyed for many years from the far northwest in a southward and then in an eastward direction, the Kĭa'kwemosi decided to send two of his children, a youth named Si'wulu'si'wa and a maiden named Si'wulu'si'sa, to look for a good place to build a village. The two finally ascended a mountain, where the sister was left to rest while the brother proceeded to look over the country. Returning to the mountain top at midday he found his sister sleeping and was so enamored of her beauty that he embraced her. This act made her wildly angry. The result of his embrace was the birth of ten children that same night. This unnatural union caused an immediate change of tongue; but, though their language was changed, they understood each other perfectly. There was no change of appearance. The firstborn[b] was normal in all respects, but the other nine children did not possess the seeds of generation. The brother said to the sister: "It is not well for us to be alone; we will prepare a place for the others of ours." He descended the mountain and drew his foot through the sands and created two rivers (the Zuñi and the Little Colorado) and a lake, and in the depths of the lake a village. Si'wulu'si'wa and his sister also created two mountains, one of them to be his perpetual home. The village is Ko'thluwala'wa, having the great ceremonial house of the gods in its center. This house is provided with four windows, through which those not privileged to enter may view the dance. Only deceased members of the Ko'tikili (mythologic fraternity) go within

---

[a] The A'shiwi say that the Mexicans brought beans, but that they always had watermelons and muskmelons. Although the Zuñis make this statement, it is declared by the representatives of the Department of Agriculture that neither the watermelon nor the muskmelon are indigeneous to this country.

[b] Attention is called to an error regarding "the firstborn" in a paper published in the Fifth Annual Report of the Bureau of Ethnology, the notes for which were gathered during the writer's first visit to Zuñi.

STEVENSON] ORIGIN OF ANCESTRAL GODS 33

the walls. The name of the lake is Hätin ᵗkĭaiakwi (Listening spring), the reference being to hearing voices in the depths of the waters, but it usually bears the name of the village, Ko'thluwala'wa. We'nima, the archaic name, is commonly used in ceremonials.

The first group of A'shiwi to cross the river was the ᵗHle'wekwe ti'kili (Wood fraternity); and the children on their mothers' backs pinched and bit the mothers until they became alarmed and dropped their little ones into the water, when the children were at once transformed into ĕt'towa (tortoises), mi'ᵗkĭaᵗli (water snakes), tä'kĭa (frogs), and mu'tuli'ᵗkĭa (tadpoles). These transformed children descended from the river into the depths of the lake, where they were immediately restored to their normal condition; and they attained to the age of maturity at once, becoming the Council of the Gods, the prototypes of the Ko'mosona, first body of A'shiwanni, and Gods of War.

The following table gives the members of the Council of the Gods, and shows their relative positions and the corresponding positions of certain Zuñi priests:

Council of the Gods and their Warriors	*Zuñi Priests*
Pau'tiwa — Director-General of the Kok'ko	Ko'mosona—Director-General of the Ko'tikili
ᵗKĭäklo—Pe'kwĭn (deputy) to the Director-General of the Kok'ko	Ko'pekwĭn (deputy) to the Director-General of the Ko'tikili
Shu'laawiᵗsi—Pe'kwĭn to the Sun Father	Pe'kwĭn (deputy) to the Sun Father (Shi'wanni of the Zenith)
Sa'yatäsha	Kĭa'kwemosi
First Yä'muhakto	Shi'wanni of the West
Hu'tutu	Shi'wanni of the South
Second Yä'muhakto	Shi'wanni of the East
Säl'imobiya, warriors and seed-gatherers of Ko'thluwala'wa	Elder and younger brother Bow priests— Earthly representatives of the Gods of War

Si'wuluᵗsiwa and the nine last-born became Ko'yemshi (old dance men) (plate v), the father being the A'wan täᵗchu (Great Father), of the newly created gods, while Si'wuluᵗsiᵗsa became Ko'mokätsi (old dance woman) (plate v) and mother of the Kok'ko. All anthropic gods bear the name of Kok'ko.[a] The firstborn became Kor'kokshi (dancer for good). A'wan täᵗchu decided that he and his nine last-born should remain in the mountain of his creation[b] (peak to the left on plate III), on the opposite side of Ko'thluwala'wa from Mount Kor'kokshi, on which he embraced his sister, while Ko'mokätsi and the firstborn should live in Ko'thluwala'wa.

---

[a] Kă'kă, the term given by some writers instead of kok'ko, is the name for raven, and bears no relation whatever to the gods.

[b] Ko'yemshi mountain bears evidence of having once been a great center for making arrow points. The Zuñis, however, do not admit that genuine arrows were ever made by them. "Arrows were cast upon the earth by lightning-makers."

To those who followed the 'Hle'wekwe across the mystic waters the Divine Ones called "Wait until we speak;" and they charged the women not to be afraid of their children if they should pinch and bite, if they would bring them safely across the river. These children were subjected to no change except that their toes and fingers became webbed. The Divine Ones cut the webs with their stone knives, restoring the feet and hands to the normal form. After the remainder of the people had crossed the river, the Kĭa'kwemosi requested the Divine Ones to descend into the lake and look after the lost children. After the creation of the gods, which, according to Zuñi belief, was the beginning of the worship of the ancients, the A'wan tä'ᵗchu Ko'yem-shi deemed it best that these gods should not appear outside the dance house unmasked. He therefore created masks by placing his finger to his mouth and rubbing the spittle in a small spot on the floor of the dance house, a mask appearing almost immediately each time the finger touched the floor. Masks were made in this way for each god.

On entering Ko'thluwala'wa the Divine Ones found all the newly created gods wearing masks; but these were soon removed and placed by their sides, and the Divine Ones addressed them as "my children;" and the gods said "Sit down and tell us of our mothers." On learning that their mothers refused to be comforted they said: "Tell our mothers not to grieve for us; we are not dead; we live and sing and dance in this beautiful place. When they fall asleep they will wake here and return to the undermost world whence they came. Here we work for our mothers and all our people, and we are very happy." They also said to the Divine Ones "Look well at our masks and examine them;" and the Divine Ones looked until they knew the masks with their hearts; and said "El'lakwa cha'we (thanks, children)." On ascending from Ko'thluwala'wa the Divine Ones related to the Kĭa'kwe-mosi what they had seen.

After remaining for a time near Ko'thluwala'wa—which time might be called the mythologic period, for, according to Zuñi legend, they were in personal communication with their gods—the A'shiwi continued their travels, building villages from time to time, then deserting them to push on to the Middle of the world.

ORIGIN OF THE DIMINUTIVE GODS OF WAR

The A'shiwi had proceeded less than a day's journey from Ko'thlu-wala'wa, coming to the place that they afterward called Hanᵗlipĭnkĭa, when smoke was discovered in the distance. "Ha!" exclaimed the Kĭa'kwemosi, "there is a village. I wonder who these people are?" "We will see" said the Divine Ones; and two members of the Ne'wekwe ti'kili (Galaxy fraternity) were told to go ahead and hunt a trail. They refused, saying: "We are fighting men and we may meet some one and kill him, and thus get you into trouble." But the Divine Ones dispatched the two men, who had not gone far when they observed two women on the bank of a stream washing buckskin. They killed the women, who belonged to the village whence the smoke came; and as soon as the strange people learned of the murder they were enraged and at once attacked the A'shiwi, who fought two days, but without success. Then Kŏw'wituma and Wats'usi, having grown weary with fighting, for they had had many conflicts during their journey from the far northwest, requested their Sun Father to send two others to take their place as warriors.

In compliance with this wish the Sun Father caused a heavy rain to fall until the cascade of the mountain side no longer glided placidly over the rocks to the basin below, but danced along; and in her[a] joy she was caught in the sun's embrace, and bore twin children, who issued from the foam.

When Kŏw'wituma and Wats'usi looked toward the cascade they discovered two little fellows upon the water in the basin, whom they at once recognized to be of divine origin. Kŏw'wituma inquired of the tiny ones: "Who is your father?" U'yuyewi, the firstborn, replied: "The Sun is our father." "Who is your mother?" "Laughing water is our mother." "It is well; thanks; it is good," said Wats'usi; "I am weary with fighting, and I wish you two to work for me." "I am very small," said the firstborn (while the Divine Ones were somewhat below medium height, the newborn gods were diminutive in stature), "and do not know how to fight." "Yes," said Wats'usi, "you understand all about fighting." "Wait, wait," said the firstborn; but Wats'usi and Kŏw'wituma insisted, saying: "Your heart is good and we know you understand how to fight." "Is it so? do I understand how to fight? I guess my younger brother knows more than I." Ma't'sai'lema interrupted, saying: "My elder brother knows more than I." "All right," said the elder, "we will fight for you." Wats'usi said: "We have fought two days, but we can do nothing with the enemy. Many arrows have pierced the heart of the 'Cha'kwena who leads the opposing forces, yet she continues to pass to and fro before her army, shaking her rattle; and until these people can be conquered or destroyed we can not proceed in our quest of the Middle place of the world." The newborn gods of Laughing water replied: "We will join you. We may destroy the enemy; we may not." In times of peace both these gods bear the name of A'hayuta. When associated with war the elder is always referred to as U'yuyewi, and the younger as Ma't'sai'lema.

---

[a] The Zuñis attribute gender to all natural objects.

DESTRUCTION OF THE KĬA′NAKWE, AND SONGS OF THANKSGIVING

The day was still young when these gods requested Kŏw′wituma, Wats′usi, a man of the Coyote clan, and To′na O′ᵗsi (Turkey man[a]) to muster about a pottery drum and dance. The man of the Coyote clan was provided with a drumstick, such as is used at the present time for these drums. U′yuyewi, Maᵗsai′lema, all those who had participated in fighting, and the A′shiwanni joined in the broken circle around the group, each man in the circle having a woman of his paternal clan by his side.

By command of Kŏw′wituma the man of the Coyote clan gave four loud and distinct strokes upon the drum, and then beat it rapidly, which called forth seven beings from the depths of the earth, who took their places in the group. The circle moved slowly, with even, measured step. Those in the circle sang, Kŏw′wituma, keeper of the songs, leading the song. After four songs, or stanzas, the To′na O′ᵗsi struck the drum with his great claws four times, each time clearly and with great force. Each stroke caused the hearts of the enemy to tremble and jump with fear. He then beat rapidly upon the drum while those forming the circle sang four songs, after which the A′shiwi, accompanied by the Divine Ones, U′yuyewi and Maᵗsai′lema, advanced to meet the enemy, who were discovered to be the Kĭa′nakwe, though the A′shiwi called them the white people, because they all wore mi′has[b] (white cotton embroidered blankets).

The fighting continued four days. The Kĭa′nakwe were compelled to close their nostrils with raw cotton to avoid the sulphurous odors emitted from the bodies of the A′shiwi. At night each party fell back; the Kĭa′nakwe to their village, and the A′shiwi to Hän′ᵗlipĭnkĭa, where they danced and prayed throughout the night for rain.

The second night the Kĭa′kwemosi sent the Divine Ones to Ko′thluwala′wa to inquire if A′wan tä′ᵗchu Ko′yemshi could tell anything about the enemy, and to implore the Council of the Gods to cause rainfall, that the A′shiwi bowstrings, which were made of yucca fiber, might be made strong, and the bowstrings of the enemy, made of deer sinew, might be weakened. The A′shiwi secured their arrows for the engagement with the Kĭa′nakwe on Ko′yemshi mountain.[c] Mountain is to be seen at left of plate (see plate IV).

The prayers of the A′shiwi brought heavy rains on the third morning, and again they met the enemy. This time their forces were strength-

---

[a] This personage was a turkey of enormous size.

[b] The Zuñis say they never saw the mi′ha until they met the Kĭa′nakwe, but they afterward wove it of their native cotton. The modern mi′ha is made by the Hopi priests, and consists of commercial cotton in the body of the blanket and wools for embroidery. They are exclusively ceremonial and are the most valued of all fabrics known to these people. The principal designs in the embroidery are conventional butterflies and cloud and lightning symbols.

[c] As already stated, Ko′yemshi mountain, in the immediate vicinity of Ko′thluwala′wa, was found to have been a central place for arrow making.

ened by the Kok′ko, present at the request of U′yuyewi and Ma⁺sai′-
lema, who were now the recognized Gods of War.   Again Ku′yapäli⁺sa,
the ⁺Cha′kwena, walked in front of her army, shaking her rattle.   She
succeeded in capturing four of the gods from Ko′thluwala′wa—Kor′-
kokshi, the first born of Si′wulu⁺siwa and Si′wulu⁺si⁺sa; It′⁺sepäsha
(game-maker), one of the nine last-born; a Sa′ya⁺hlia (blue horn, a warrior god); and a Sha′läko (one of the couriers to the u′wannami
(rain-makers).   These gods succeeded in making their escape, but all
were captured except the Sha′läko, who ran so like a hare that he could
not be caught.

The Kĭa′nakwe had a dance in which the prisoner gods appeared in
celebration of their capture.   Kor′kokshi, the firstborn, was so angry
and unmanageable that Ku′yapäli⁺sa had him dressed in female attire
previous to the dance, saying to him: "You will now perhaps be less
angry."[a]

In the Zuñi dramatization of the Kĭa′nakwe dance of thanksgiving for the capture
of the gods the one personating the Kor′kokshi wears woman's dress and is referred
to as the ko′thlama, meaning a man who has permanently adopted female attire.
The custom of youths donning female attire at puberty, which exists to some extent
among the pueblos of New Mexico and Arizona, has given rise to conflicting statements.   An assertion made, not only by the writer after her first visit to Zuñi, but also
by others, was that these persons were hermaphrodites.   One is led into this error
by the Indians, who, when referring to men dressed as women, say "She is a man;"
which is certainly misleading to one not familiar with Indian thought.   Others claim
that men who are thus attired, who are regarded in a religious light, subject the
maidens of their tribe to their desires before their husbands are privileged to take
them unto themselves.   After more intimate acquaintance with the pueblos the
writer is able to give the facts as they are.   Men who adopt female attire do so of
their own volition, having from childhood hung about the house and usually preferring to do the work of women.   On reaching puberty their decision is final.   If they
are to continue woman's work they must adopt woman's dress; and though the women
of the family joke the fellow, they are inclined to look upon him with favòr, since
it means that he will remain a member of the household and do almost double the
work of a woman, who necessarily ceases at times from her labors at the mill and
other duties to bear children and to look after the little ones; but the ko′thlama is ever
ready for service, and is expected to perform the hardest labors of the female department.   The men of the family, however, not only discourage men from unsexing
themselves in this way, but ridicule them.   There have been but five such persons
in Zuñi since the writer's acquaintance with these people; and until about ten years
ago there had been but two, these being the finest potters and weavers in the tribe.
One was the most intelligent person in the pueblo, especially versed in their ancient
lore.   He was conspicuous in ceremonials, always taking the part of the captive
Kor′kokshi in the dramatization of the Kĭa′nakwe.   His strong character made his
word law among both the men and the women with whom he associated.   Though
his wrath was dreaded by men as well as by women, he was beloved by all the children, to whom he was ever kind.   Losing his parents in infancy, he was adopted by
an aunt on his father's side, and the loving gratitude he exhibited for his aunt and
her grief at his death afforded a lesson that might well be learned by the more

[a] The Zuñis assert this to be the first instance of a god or man appearing in woman's dress.

enlightened. Such was his better side. He was said to be the father of several children, but the writer knew of but one child of whom he was regarded as certainly being the father. The other ko'thlama, who was one of the richest men of the village, allied himself to a man during one of the visits of the writer to Zuñi, and to the time of her departure from Zuñi in 1897 this couple were living together, and they were two of the hardest workers in the pueblo and among the most prosperous. The third and fourth assumed woman's attire during the absence of the writer. The fifth, a grandson on the maternal side of Nai'uchi, elder brother Bow priest, donned the dress during the visit of the writer to Zuñi in 1896. The mother and grandmother were quite willing that the boy should continue in the work in which he seemed interested, but the grandfather, who was much disgusted, endeavored to shame him out of his determination to follow woman's work. He did not, however, attempt any authority in the matter, and on the boy's reaching manhood the trousers were replaced by woman's attire. There is a side to the lives of these men which must remain untold. They never marry women, and it is understood that they seldom have any relations with them.

At night, after the third day's battle, both parties fell back, as usual, and the A'shiwi danced and prayed. The rain continued to fall, and on the fourth morning moisture so affected the bowstrings of the enemy that they failed in most of their shots.

After many prayers and songs addressed by Kŏw'wituma to the Sun Father, the knowledge came to him that Ku'yapäli⁺sa carried her heart in her rattle. He aimed his arrow and, piercing the rattle, Ku'yapäli⁺sa fell dead. Her death caused a panic among her people, who retreated to their village, closely pursued by the A'shiwi; these captured the village and released the three gods, who returned to Ko'thluwala'wa. Another version says that U'yuyewi sent his younger brother to the Sun Father to solicit aid, and to learn how the heart of Ku'yapäli⁺sa might be reached; whereupon the Sun Father provided Ma⁺sai'lema, the younger God of War, with two turquois rabbit sticks, telling him to give one to his younger brother. On returning to battle, the elder brother threw his stick, but missed the rattle. Then Ma⁺sai'lema threw his stick, which struck the rattle, and Ku'yapäli⁺sa fell dead. The Kĭa'nakwe in desperate fear jumped into the waters of the black rocks, which Kŏw'wituma at once covered with stone slabs that the enemy might not return to the earth. Their ghost selves went to Ko'thluwala'wa. But two escaped this tragic death, a youth and a maiden, brother and sister, who hid in a cave in the rocks below the village.

After the A'shiwi captured the village they opened the gates of the corral in which all game was kept by the ⁺Cha'kwena (keeper of game) and said to the game: "We have opened for you the doors of the world; now you may roam where you will, about the good grass and springs, and find good places to bear your young; you will no longer be imprisoned within the walls, but have the whole world before you." Since that time game has roamed over the face of the earth.

VIEW OF OJO CALIENTE IN 1879

RAINBOW SPRING AT OJO CALIENTE

KÓLOOWISI (PLUMED SERPENT)

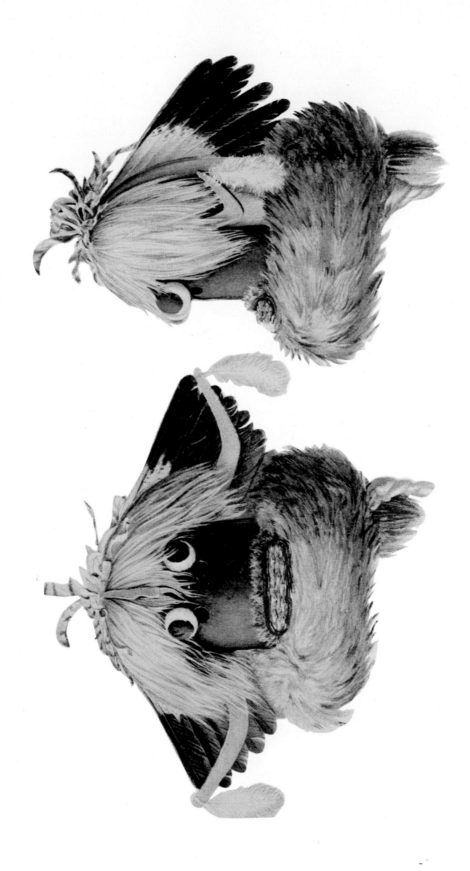

MASK OF A SAYAᵀHLIA (WARRIOR GOD)
front and side views

Kǐa′makǐa[a] is an extensive ruin about 50 miles south of Zuñi and a little off the trail to the Zuñi salt lake, standing upon the brink of the canyon wall of black rock, over which flow many springs of clear water as cold as ice. The village had been surrounded by a wall 5 feet thick. When the ruin was visited in 1884 the walls were standing to the height of 5 feet, and it was found that the masonry was superior to that of any ruin in the surrounding country. There were remains of several underground ki′wi'siwe (chambers dedicated to anthrophic worship). There was an additional inclosure whose eastern side was formed by the main wall of the village, which the Zuñis claim was a corral in which 'Cha′kwena kept all game. She allowed the game to go out to graze during the day, the young awaiting the return of their mothers in certain niches in the walls of the corral.

Hundreds of te′likinawe, offered by the Zuñis to the departed Kǐa′nakwe, dotted the canyon walls about the springs. The Zuñis never visit this ruin except by special permission of the Ko′mosona (director of the ki′wi'siwe) or Mo′sona (director of the personators of the Kǐa′nakwe).

After the conquest the A′shiwi again formed about the drum at Hän'lipǐnkǐa. The seven beings were again called from the earth; Ku′yapäli'sa's scalp was divided and held by a son of the man of the Coyote clan who beat the drum, and the ceremony held before going to battle was repeated. The songs were not for the destruction of the enemy, but were a thanksgiving for the scalps which bring good fellowship between the deceased enemy (ghost self) and the A′shiwi, and therefore much rain. After the close of the songs U′yuyewi and Ma'sai′lema declared that this ceremony must always occur after the scalping of an enemy.

The instruction by the beings who came from the earth at this time was that, when this ceremony should be repeated, the tepehan (pottery drum) must be struck the first time with such force that they could not fail to hear and be present, though invisible, to insure the correct singing of the songs.

Disaster again threatened the A′shiwi while they were still at Hän''lipǐnkǐa. The second danger arose from the wrath of their gods, instead of from a strange foe. Though continued supplications were made by the A′shiwi to the Council of the Gods for rain, their prayers remained unanswered, and drought was threatening starvation. The A′shiwi were beginning to fear that their A′shiwanni were not pure of heart, when it was discovered that the te′likinawe which had been deposited by the Kǐa′kwemosi and others had been stolen by a witch before the Sun Father had received the prayers which had been breathed into the plumes. The Divine Ones, however, recovered the stolen te′likinawe, which were again planted, and so the calamity was averted.[b]

---

[a] Kǐa′makǐa is from kǐam′amanĕ: plural kǐam′amawĕ, easy to break; pule kǐam-amanĕ, a shell easy to break, pu′we kǐam′amawe, shells easy to break, from the black rock of which the village was built, containing shells which broke from the slightest pressure after being removed from the rock.

[b] Hän'lipǐnkǐa (place of stealing) received its name from the occurrence described. Though Hän'lipǐnkǐa is well known to the present Zuñis, many of whom have visited the place, comparatively few understand why or how this place received its name. The A′shiwanni are superstitiously averse to any reference to the stealing of the te′likinawe

ORIGIN OF THE CLANS

It was at Hän'ᵗlipĭnkĭa that the A'shiwi received their clan names, which originated in this way: During their migrations the A'shiwi traveled in groups, so when the Divine Ones decided that the people should be gathered into clans they addressed each group, saying: "You will take unto yourselves a name." Of one group he inquired "What will you choose?" and they answered: "We are the Pi'chikwe (Dogwood people).ᵃ Another group having been questioned, they replied: "We are the To'wakwe (Corn people). Others chose to be the ᵗKoᵗloktakwe (Sand-hill Crane people), selecting this bird because it happened at the time to be flying by. Each name was chosen from some object seen at the time, and the totem of each clan was cut on the rocky walls; many of them are to be seen at the present time.

It has been mentioned that four fraternities were organized by the Divine Ones soon after coming to this world. These were the Shi'-wannakwe people, who do not fast from animal food, Ne'wekwe (Galaxy people), ᵗSän'iaᵗkakwe (Hunters), and ᵗHle'wekwe (Wood people). The mo'sona (director) of the Shi'wannakwe chose to belong to the To'nakwe (Turkey clan). The mo'sona of Ne'wekwe chose the ᵗKoᵗlotakwe (Sand-hill Crane clan); the mo'sona of ᵗSän'iakĭakwe also chose the ᵗTo'wakwe clan, and the mo'sona of ᵗHle'wekwe chose the ᵗKoᵗloktakwe, while his pe'kwĭn (deputy) chose to belong to To'wakwe (Corn clan). Since that time the a'mosi (directors) of these organizations have been chosen from the original clans, and the deputy to the mo'sona of the ᵗHle'wekwe must be of the Corn clan. It is not permissible in these cases, as it is with many others, for a child of the clan to fill the place.ᵇ

The first clan to prepare te'likinawe (prayer plumes) was the Pi'chikwe (Dogwood clan). These plumes are attached to slender sticks, themselves called pichiᵗhlame, the last syllable coming from ᵗhla'wa-psushle'a (making prayer plumes).

The Pi'chikwe clan was divided in the following manner: Yänŏwwu-luha, pe'kwĭn to the Sun Father, placed two eggs in a sacred basket of meal and deposited it on the floor before the ĕt'toweᶜ of the A'shi-wanni and requested all the people of the clan to choose an egg. All chose the beautiful blue egg; none would have the more homely one. But, alas! when the eggs were hatched the raven came from the blue egg and the macaw from the other. Yä'nŏwwuluha then said to some of the Pi'chikwe, "Henceforth you will be the Mu'la (macaw) Pi'chikwe." Others of this clan he called Kă'kă (raven) Pi'chikwe. Yä'nŏwwuluha sent the Mu'la to Mexico and with it a number of the Mu'la Pi'chikwe

ᵃ Pi'chi, from pi'chiko, dogwood (Cornus stolonifera); kwe (pl.) suffix, signifying people.

ᵇ A Shi'wi belongs to the mother's clan, and is regarded as the child of the clan to which his paternal parent belongs   The reader will bear in mind that whenever the child of a clan is mentioned in this paper. reference is to the clan of the paternal parent. See List of clans.

ᶜ See A'shiwanni (Rain priesthood).

to look for the Middle place, saying: "If you find it we will go there. The others will go eastward to look for the Middle place."

The Zuñis keep the location of Hän'ʼlipĭnkĭa from the knowledge of the white man. They declare that the writer was the first American to visit the sacred spot. It was out of the course of the Spanish invaders, and it is certain that no student has before seen the place. While a stage road from the railroad to St. Johns, Ariz., passes nearby, there is nothing in evidence to induce the traveler to alight. To avoid the high mesas the writer, with the younger brother Bow priest, a shĭ'wanni and theurgist, followed the old California wagon road over a desert country devoid of every vestige of animal life. Kwa'kina, an extensive ruin, was found 6 miles northwest of Zuñi. On reaching a miniature forest of scrub cedars, about 35 miles from Zuñi, a dry but otherwise attractive camp was made. At sunrise the following morning, after proceeding a mile or two, the road was left and an untraveled country followed 5 miles to the southwest, the Indians constantly asserting that water would be found nearby; finally the three Zuñis separated, each running many miles, but they returned without success. Determined to reach the destined point, they urged the writer to continue the journey, saying they would again hunt for water. On her refusal to comply with their wish, a dispute resulted which was soon quelled, however, and, after sharing water from the keg and canteens with the thirsty animals, all heads were turned toward Zuñi.

After a few days a new start was made by a more southern route. Pi'nanai, an extensive ruin on a knoll a mile west of Zuñi, on the St. Johns road, was passed. The St. Johns road was left to the south before reaching Ojo Caliente to avoid any questions as to the destination of the travelers which might be asked by the people of this village. The second morning out brought the party to a difficult road. After an unsuccessful attempt by the driver of the escort wagon to ascend, the wagon was practically unpacked and the material transported by the patient, faithful Indians. Finally, after strenuous efforts, the mules and wagons reached the summit (plate VI a). After a short distance had been traveled on the mesa, it became necessary to build a road in order to descend. One of the Indians, knowing the writer's objection to their driving her team, hurried to the top after the road had been improved, and, without warning, jumped into the wagon and started down the hill. His apology was: "I knew you would not let me drive if I asked you, and I was afraid if you drove you might be killed. It was better for me to die." After much trouble the party began traveling over the lowlands. After proceeding several miles ʼKia'napälto, the last of a series of springs, which figures in the ʼKiäklo myth (see page 85) was reached.

About 30 miles from St. Johns the travelers turned northward to traverse a country unknown to all, though two of the three Indians of the party had visited Hän'ʼlipĭnkĭa some years before by a trail which took them over an altogether different route, and had a vague idea of the proper course to take. An obscure wagon road was discovered by the Indian guide, leading up and down mesas, many being difficult of ascent. Finally the guide declared that the road must be left and the party go more toward the north. After traveling some miles in this direction the writer was obliged to stop her Indian companions and compel them to make camp. One of the Indians descended to the valley below to make a reconnaissance for water. He returned after dark with a specimen of a ceremonial stone knife, a red pottery bowl, and a quantity of fragments of pottery, telling the writer of extensive ruins where the specimens were found, and also brought the good news that the animals could be watered in the morning. By sunrise one of the Indians was off with the thirsty beasts to refresh them; the others packed the wagon and ere long the march to Hän'lipĭnkĭa was renewed. Five miles to the northeast the party came to the fissure in which Hän'lipĭnkĭa is to be found, and camp was made near a group of water pockets, the only drinkable water within miles. From this point the party proceeded on foot to where a sandstone bench is crossed to the north of the fissure, then turning southward a quarter of a mile was traversed, when a descent of 150 feet was made to a canyon 100 feet across at the point of descent. Turning toward the direction of the camp the party worked their way through a labyrinth of tall grass, rank weeds, and willows, which earlier in the season must have been impassable. The canyon narrowed toward the end, and at this point it is not over 15 feet wide. The walls were completely covered with pictographs (see plate VI b). An interesting feature of this canyon are the potholes, many of them large and deep, some forming a perfectly arched niche. It was in one of the latter that the Gods of War, U'yuyewi and Ma'sai'lema, are supposed to have been created.[a] This

FIG. 2—Ancient sun shrine

arch is near the point of the canyon, and it is sufficiently large to admit a person 5 feet 3 inches tall. An etching of the sun decorates this niche about 2 feet above the base. The younger brother Bow priest exhibited the keenest interest in imparting all that was to be learned about Hän'"lipĭnkĭa. Retracing their steps, the party found on the right a small natural chamber, about 10 by 10 feet, the walls and roof of which are sandstone. From this point the party with difficulty squeezed through a small opening at the base of the wall by lying flat on the ground; another and larger apartment was entered, roofed only by the firmament. Access to four other chambers is by narrow passageways. The walls in these places are also elaborate with pictographs, including clan totems.[b]

---

[a] See Origin of the Diminutive Gods of War.
[b] Pl. VII shows a number of symbols secured by the camera: a, Zuñi seal; b, sun; c, primitive Zuñi before the amputation of tail; d, feet after removal of web; e, unknown; f, altar; g, curious composite figure including deer.

The rain priest of the party, who is a member of the Shi′wannakwe fraternity, exclaimed upon seeing one of the altar etchings: "There is the altar of my fraternity." The discovery of these etchings settles the question that the pueblos, at least the Zuñi people, had tablet altars before the invasion of the Spaniards, and that they were not suggested to the Zuñis by the Roman Catholic altars.[a]

Curious water markings on an irregular broken surface are believed by the Zuñis to be the footprints of those who danced at Hän′ᶜlipĭnkĭa on the level above the canyon.[b]

The following morning a sun shrine, which no doubt had been covered and uncovered with sand many times, was discovered not many rods from camp. This shrine with its many fetishes was photographed and sketched and afterward removed, to be deposited in the National Museum at Washington.

A′SHIWI RESUME THEIR JOURNEYING

All obstacles having been removed, the main body of the A′shiwi continued eastward in their quest for the Middle of the world. In addition to the Divine Ones they now had with them the Gods of War— the gods born of Laughing water.

After the A′shiwi had been some time at ᶜKiap′kwena,[c] the director of the Ne′wekwe fraternity disappeared through Lu′kĭana ᶜkĭai′a and became the musician and jester to the Sun Father, accompanying him in his daily travels over this world; but he first instructed his people that he was to be personated annually by a member of the fraternity, when he would be present in spirit. This personage, as he appears in one of the Zuñi dramas, presents one of the most stately, picturesque, and dramatic characters to be imagined.

ADOPTION OF THE TWO SURVIVING KĬA′NAKWE BY THE A′SHIWI

The two Kĭa′nakwe, brother and sister, who escaped death at the hands of the A′shiwi conquerors by secreting themselves in a cave, subsisted for a long time on meal and rats, the meal being ground from the corn left by their people. The rats were caught in a trap set every night by the boy, who would go in the morning and fetch what he had secured. At night the girl roasted the rats, and in the morning made a stew of them.

Growing weary of this life, the brother decided they would start out into the world and see if they could not find some kind people among

---

[a] Although extensive studies of the rock writings of the Southwest have been made, the writer had never before found anything which would indicate the altar.

[b] See Destruction of the Kĭa′nakwe and Songs of Thanksgiving.

[c] Ojo Caliente, one of the three farming districts of the Zuñis, 15 miles south of west of the pueblo of Zuñi (see pl. VIII). The town takes its name from a number of springs at the place, three of which are sacred, each to a god. To′seluna ᶜkĭai′a, named from the tall grass which grows in the spring is dedicated to Ko′loowisi (Plumed Serpent), and three years out of every four the pilgrims of the summer solstice gather there. They go quadrennially to Ko′thluwala′wa. This spring also supplies the water for irrigating the farms of Ojo Caliente. A′mitolan ᶜkĭai′a (Rainbow spring), which is about 2 feet in diameter and quite deep, is sacred to the Sha′läko gods. The water of this spring is clear and cold, and is excellent to drink. Lu′ᶜkĭana ᶜkĭaia (ashes spring) is the spring of Bi′ᶜᵗsĭᵗsi, the original director of the Ne′wekwe fraternity. While numbers of te′likinawe are to be found at all these springs, Lu′ᶜkĭana ᶜkĭaia is the only one where a shrine appears to have been erected. The Zuñis claim that all the sacred springs are used for the gods to look through. A view of rainbow spring is shown in pl. IX.

whom they could live. Drawing near to the village of ʻKĭapʻkwena the youth said: "I see not far off a village; to-morrow I will go there." The sister begged him not to venture, fearing he would be killed. But he said: "It is better that we both die than live longer in the world alone." While they were yet talking, a youth from ʻKĭapʻkwena saw the boy and girl, and greeting them, inquired "Who are you?" "We are the last of our people, the Kĭaʻnakwe,"[a] said the boy, as he held two ĕtʻtowe to his breast. The girl having provided herself with two ears of white corn before leaving Kĭaʻmakĭa took them from her dress and, extending them toward the youth, said: "See, we are the Miʻkĭanakwe (Corn people)." "Will you go to our village?" said the youth. The boy replied: "To-morrow we will go, though I fear your people will destroy us, as they destroyed all my people."

The youth hurried to the village and told of his meeting with the boy and girl, and the Kĭaʻkwemosi, feeling compassion, sent for them to come to him. On their arrival the Kĭaʻkwemosi, addressing the two, inquired "Who are you?" And the girl again took from her dress the two ears of white corn, saying "See, we are the Miʻkĭa-nakwe;" and the boy displayed his two ĕtʻtowe. The Kĭaʻkwemosi was well pleased, and said: "You are the same as our people, the Toʻwakwe; you must live with us and be our children. You," addressing the boy, "are now old enough to have a wife; and you," turning to the girl, "a husband. You will have children, and they will be our children." He selected a woman of the Corn clan to adopt the brother and sister.

Another version of the story is that the boy, wandering off, ran upon the village of Ojo Caliente and, returning at night, said to his sister: "I have seen a town where people live; we will go to it." She replied: "They will kill us if we go." He said: "It is better that we should die like our people than live alone." The next morning they hurried through their breakfast and started for the village. Upon their arrival the boy called on the Kĭaʻkwemosi and was received kindly.

A'SHIWI FIND THE MIDDLE PLACE

Leaving ʻKĭapʻkwena, the Aʻshiwi migrated to Heʻshotaʻyälla, a small village, to find all the inhabitants but four either fled or dead from the effluvium of the Aʻshiwi. The houses here were built of reeds and earth, and the Aʻshiwi declared, "Our people built this village."[b] On entering one of the houses an aged man and woman, with two

[a] The Zuñis say the Kĭaʻnakwe were strangely marked. One half of the face was red, the other white, the dividing line running diagonally across the face. It has been so long since the boy and girl came to live with the Aʻshiwi that all traces of the mark have gone from their descendants, although an aged priest claims that he remembers seeing a very old woman so marked when he was a young child. The wife of the deceased Koʻmosona (director of the Koʻtikili), who preceded the present incumbent, is supposed to be a direct descendant of the Kĭaʻnakwe, and she is the Aʻwan ʻSiʻta (Great Mother) of the personators of the Kĭaʻnakwe. She bathes the head of each participant in the dance of the Kĭaʻnakwe and draws an ear of corn four times over the top of the head, saying: "I am of the Corn people; I do this that you may follow the straight road of the Sun Father."
[b] The Zuñis assert that their early ancestors had such dwellings before they built stone houses.

grandchildren, boy and girl, were discovered sitting by a meal symbol of clouds upon the floor. Their ears and nostrils were closed with raw cotton, and they were bending over a he'pik̆ia tehl'i (urinal) in which the old man had deposited sunflower and other medicine, the fumes of which they were inhaling to save them from the killing odors of the A'shiwi. Some of the A'shiwi exclaimed: "These people are dead." The old man replied: "We are not dead; we were the Yellow Corn people; you have destroyed or driven off all but ourselves; we are saved by inhaling my medicine, but it has made our corn, which we hold in our belts, black, and we are now the Black Corn people." Since that time they and their descendants have been called the Black Corn people.

Some of the A'shiwi wished to kill these people, but the Kĭa'kwemosi said: "No, they may have an ĕt'tonĕ." The Kĭa'kwemosi, endeavoring to learn more from the aged man, said: "We will cause your death if you remain here." "No, you can not do that; I possess great things," replied the old shi'wanni, pointing to his ĕt'tonĕ, which was immediately before him and over which he leaned to inhale the medicine from the bowl.

The Kĭa'kwemosi was pleased to find that the old man possessed an ĕt'tonĕ, and said to him, "You must remain with us; you will remain in your house four days and sing your songs for rain, and we will see what you can do with your ĕt'tonĕ (there were many houses in He'sho-tayalla, but all the others had been deserted, for the people fled from their houses before they died); then I will bring out my ĕt'tonĕ and sing my songs for rain." "No," said the old man, "you shall sing your songs first; you are perhaps greater than I." "No," replied the Kĭa'kwemosi, "you were here first, and you shall sing first." After much talking, the Black Corn shi'wanni went into retreat for four days and sang his songs for rain, and much fell; after the fourth day the Kĭa'kwemosi placed his ĕt'tonĕ in a room and sat four days and sang, and his songs brought much rain. The two became fast friends, and the old priest and his family were adopted into the A'shiwi tribe. Since his death his ĕt'tonĕ has been in the possession of the old priest's descendants, the Kwĭn'nakwe (Black Corn people).[a]

Through the friendship of the shi'wanni having this fetish in his keeping the writer was enabled to photograph by flashlight the chamber in which this ĕt'tonĕ is kept. (The ĕt'tonĕ is not in view in the picture.) This old priest was the keeper of the fetish Ko'loowi'si (Plumed Serpent), and had the privilege of painting an elaborate serpent on the wall of the chamber. Other ĕt'towe rooms do not have this decoration (see plate XXXVI).

---

[a] The ĕt'tonĕ, said to have come from the Shi'wanni of He'shotiyäl'la, was the fetish of an aged shi'wanni, the last of the Black Corn clan, supposed to be the direct descendant of the people of this village. Since his death in 1902 the ĕt'tonĕ (invariable bringer of good) has remained permanently in its resting place, as no other priest is privileged to bring it out.

Another village of the A'shiwi was Ma'ᵗsakĭa,ᵃ standing on a knoll less than 2 miles east of the present Zuñi. After a time the A'shiwi concluded that they were a little too far east for the center of the world. They abandoned their villages about Ma'ᵗsakĭa and built the town of Häl'ona (Ant place). Finally the ᵗKĭan'astepĭ (Hydrotrechus remigis), who came from the south, relieved the Zuñis of all anxiety by spreading his legs and declaring the Middle of the world to be directly beneath his heart. So the town of I'tiwanna (middle) was built, as indicated by ᵗKĭan'astepi, where the present pueblo of Zuñi stands, on the opposite bank of the river from Häl'ona. I'tiwanna and Häl'ona are frequently referred to as one and the same place.

The ĕt'tonĕ of the Kĭa'kwemosi rests in the room which is directly west of and below the ceremonial chamber of the Kĭakwe amosi (Directors of the house of houses), and is supposed to be the spot over which ᵗKĭan'astepi's heart rested, and therefore the Middle of the world.

He'patina, a shrine a short distance southwest of the village, symbolizes the Middle of the world. The Middle place, where the ĕt'tonĕ of Kĭa'kwemosi rests, is regarded as too sacred to be referred to, except by the Kĭakwe amosi themselves.

ORIGIN OF THE KO'TIKILI

A time came when Pau'tiwa, director-general of the Kok'ko, desired that the A'shiwi should be made personally acquainted with their gods, and that they learn in detail of their coming to this world and their migrations after reaching here. Pau'tiwa therefore chose ᵗKiäklo, his deputy, as narrator; and, in obedience to him, ᵗKiäklo passed from Ko'thluwala'wa to I'tiwanna on the backs of the Ko'yemshi.ᵇ He related to the A'shiwi the history of their coming to this world and their quest for the Middle place, and declared to the A'shiwi, before he departed, that in eight days all of the others (referring to the ancestral gods) would come from Ko'thluwala'wa, when they must be prepared to receive them, adding: "You must build six chambers, one for each of the six regions, which shall be dedicated to the Kok'ko."

After the departure of ᵗKiäklo the A'shiwi hastened to work, and the six chambers, which were called ki'wiᵗsiwe, one for each region, were in readiness when he reappeared to them. ᵗKiäklo visited each of the six ki'wiᵗsiwĕ remaining a short time in each, to announce the coming of the gods, and again departed over the western road to Ko'thluwala'wa; not, however, before a man of the Dogwood clan had examined ᵗKiäklo's mask, afterward making one like it.

The first body of A'shiwanni and others were gathered in He'iwa

---

ᵃ The first syllable, ma, from mawe (salt), so named from a Shi'wi, who, looking about the country soon after the people had settled at this point, discovered the Salt Mother near by.

ᵇ See p. 33.

(north) ki′wi^tsinĕ to greet the gods, who wore their masks to Iti′wanna, but removed them on entering the ki′wi^tsinĕ. A′wan tä′^tchu (Great Father) Ko′yemshi, addressing the A′shiwi, said, "Now you will look well at these masks." Pau′tiwa's mask was the first examined. Kia′-kwemosi, who belonged to the Dogwood clan, receiving it from the hands of Pau′tiwa, and inspecting it closely, said "Thanks, my child."[a] Afterward he made a counterpart of the mask worn by Pau′tĭwa.

The mo′sona (director) of the Ne′wekwe fraternity examined the mask of A′wan tä′^tchu Ko′yemshi and copied it; others of this fraternity copied the remaining nine masks of the Ko′yemshi. Then A′wan tä′^tchu Ko′yemshi, desiring to organize a fraternity by whom the gods should be personated, said: "I wish a Ko′mosona,[b] a Ko′pek-wĭn (deputy to the Ko′mosona), and two Ko′pi^tläshiwanni (warriors to the Ko′mosna and Ko′pekwĭn)." The Kĭa′kwemosi first chose a man of Deer clan, saying: "My child of Deer clan, I wish you to be the Ko′mosona of the Ko′tikili." And to another of the same clan he said: "My child, I wish you to be Ko′pi^tläshiwanni to the Ko′mosona." And selecting a man of Badger clan, he said: "My child, I choose you to be Ko′pekwĭn to the Ko′mosona." And he chose another of the same clan to be Ko′pi^ttläshiwanni to the Ko′pekwĭn.

The first body of the A′shiwanni then left the ki′wi^tsinĕ, and the newly appointed Ko′mosona divided the A′shiwi, regardless of clan, among the six ki′wi^tsiwe, to which they were to remain permanently allied. A′wan tä′^tchu Ko′yemshi then directed the gods whose masks had not been examined to separate and go to the other five ki′wi^tsiwe, where their masks should be copied. There were six Sha′läko (giant couriers to the rain-makers), and one was designated for each ki′wi^tsinĕ. The Council of the Gods, a Sha′läko, some of the Kor′kokshi, a body of ^tCha′kwena, and the Säl′imobiya (warrior and seed-gatherer) of the North remained in He′iwa (north) ki′wi^tsinĕ. A Sha′läko, Säl′imo-biya of the West, and a number of Kor′kokshi went to Mu′he‘wa (west) kiwi^tsinĕ. A Sha′läko, a number of Kor′kokshi, Säl′imobiya of the South, Mu′luktäkĭa, and the Kĭan′akwe went to Chu′pawa (south) ki′wi^tsinĕ (A, plate x). A Sha′läko, other Kor′kokshi, a body of Wa′tĕm^tla, and Säl′imobiya of the East went to O′he‘wa (east) ki′wi^tsinĕ. A Sha′läko, a body of ^tCha′kwena, other Kor′kokshi, and Säl′imobiya of the Zenith went to Up′^tsännawa (zenith) ki′wi^tsinĕ. A Sha′läko, a body of Wa′tĕm^tla, others of the Kor′kokshi, and Säl′imobiya of the Nadir went to He′kĭapawa (nadir) kĭ′wi^tsinĕ.[c]

---

[a] It must be borne in mind that these gods were the children of the A′shiwi.

[b] Ko, from Kok′ko; mo′sona, director.

[c] Since the organization of the Ko′tikili every male child must become a member of this fraternity in order to enter the sacred dance house in Ko′thluwala′wa. A dramatization of the coming of the gods to I′tiwanni occurs quadrennially, when the children receive involuntary initiation into the Ko′tikili.

DISCOVERY OF THE CORN MAIDENS

The witches who were with the A'shiwi never mentioned their meeting with the Corn maidens, and after the A'shiwi had settled at I'tiwanna, Kŏw'wituma and Wats'usi went on a deer hunt. On drawing near Shi'pololo they discovered, dancing under a häm'pone (pavilion of spruce boughs or, as some say, of cat-tails), these beautiful maidens, who had remained in the same place since the departure of the A'shiwi. Each maiden held a ʻhla'we in either hand brought from the under world consisting of a number of stalks of a white plant, each stalk abundant with delicate white plume-like leaves.

On their return to I'tiwanna the Divine Ones related to the A'shiwanni what they had seen, and these at once became eager to have the Corn maidens come to them. The pe'kwĭn to the Sun Father was delegated to bring them, that they might dance for the rains and the growth of corn. The Corn maidens accompanied the pe'kwĭn to I'tiwanna. Leaving them at Ku'shilowa (red earth), which place is a few rods east of the present village of Zuñi, he hastened to notify the A'shiwanni and Divine Ones, who were assembled in the O'he‘wa ki'wiᵗsinĕ. Kŏw'wituma and Wats'usi then went for the Corn maidens. The Yellow Corn maiden and four sisters accompanied Kŏw'wituma and the Blue Corn maiden and four sisters accompanied Wats'usi to the O'he‘wa ki'wiᵗsinĕ, where they sang and danced for a short while. No rattles, drums, or singers accompanied the Corn maidens at this time.

At midnight they were led by the pe'kwĭn, who was preceded by the other A'shiwanni and the Divine Ones, to a häm'pone of waving corn, in si'aa'ᵃ te'wita (the sacred dance court). A meal painting of cloud symbols had been made on the ground in the häm'pone where the Corn maidens danced.

During the dancing the A'shiwanni and Divine Ones fell asleep, and while they slept Pa'yatämu,ᵇ god of music, butterflies, and flowers, who was walking about the country, discovered the Corn maidens, and approaching the häm'pone, he took a seat at the northeast corner. Pa'yatämu thought the maidens were all very beautiful, but the Yellow Corn maiden was the most beautiful of all, and he said to himself "Ho'oh il äl'lanna (I wish to embrace her)." The Corn maidens, understanding Pa'yatämu's thoughts, were much afraid, and they ceased dancing and drew close to one another. The elder sister whispered to the others: "I think he will soon sleep, and then we will run away."

ᵃ The word means to break or tear apart. The te'wita was so named because the court often became so crowded as to endanger the breaking away of the walls.

ᵇ Pa'yatämu is diminutive and wears a crown of flowers, and with the sho'kona (his flute) he causes flowers to bloom and draws the butterflies of the world to him. His home is in A'mitolan te'poula (rainbow covering entrance) at the base of Shun'tekaiya, a mesa near To'wa yäl'lännĕ.

And when Pa'yatämu slept the Corn maidens ran off by the first light of the morning star to Ke'yatiwa shipololo' a'wehlwia'kǐai'a.[a]

The god of music soon awoke, and to his dismay found the maidens gone; and his heart was sorely troubled. The A'shiwanni and Divine Ones on waking were also astonished to see the Corn maidens gone, and looked everywhere, but could not find them. The A'shiwanni and Divine Ones having slept while Pa'yatämu was at the häm'pone, they did not suspect the cause of the flight of the Corn maidens. On reaching Ke'yatiwa, the Yellow Corn maiden, the elder sister, sent the Black Corn maiden to Ko'thluwala'wa to tell the gods of their fears. On delivering her message she was accompanied back to Ke'yatiwa by A'wan tä'tchu Ko'yemshi and Pau'tiwa,[b] both gods assuming the form of ducks; and the Corn maidens, who were in the spring, were now protected from view by the gods spreading their wings over the waters.

CREATION OF THE BEAST GODS

The Divine Ones, wishing that the world should be well guarded by those keen of sight and scent, visited Shi'papolima, home of Po'shaiyänkǐ, Zuñi culture hero, and his followers, and converted the medicine men who came to this world with Po'shaiyänkǐ into Beast Gods. They converted one into the Cougar, giving him the north region to preside over. Another was converted into the Bear to guard the west. A third was transformed into the Badger to guard the south. Another was converted into the White Wolf to preside over the east. A fifth was converted into the Eagle to guard the zenith, and another was transformed into the Shrew to guard the nadir or earth. Others were converted into rattlesnakes and ants to preside with wisdom over the earth.

ORIGIN OF THE BOW PRIESTHOOD

At another time U'yuyewi and Ma'sai'lema started on a journey, and discovering a beautiful woman in the distance, U'yuyewi exclaimed: "Who is that woman?" Ma'sai'lema replied: "I do not know." On reaching her, U'yuyewi asked: "Where do you live?" Pointing, she replied: "There is my house." "Where is your father? where is your mother?" "There in my house," replied the woman; and she then inquired of U'yuyewi "Where is your house?" He replied, pointing to the southeast: "There is my house; come with me to my house." The woman consenting, the three started in the direction indicated by

---

[a] Ke'yatiwa, cat-tails; shi'pololo, fog coming up like steam; A'wehlwia, cumulus clouds, 'Kǐai'a, spring.

[b] See p. 46.

U'yuyewi, the woman walking between them.   On their way U'yuyewi told her that his house was very beautiful; but he was lying to her. On reaching a cave in the rocks the woman asked: "Where are we?" U'yuyewi replied: " Here is my house."   At night the woman inquired: "Where shall I sleep?"   U'yuyewi said: "You will sleep between my younger brother and me."   U'yuyewi lay at the right of the woman and Maᵗsai'lema lay at her left.   Each placed an arm across the woman. Early in the morning U'yuyewi said: "Let us go now and look about the country."   "Whither are you going?" inquired the woman.   "Oh, to walk about," said U'yuyewi, who at the same time closed his left eye and winked at his brother with his right as a signal to be ready; and as U'yuyewi and the woman left the cave, Maᵗsai'lema struck her on one side of the head with his club.   Then U'yuyewi struck her with his club on the other side of the head, and the woman fell dead.   Taking her scalp, they went to the house of the Cougar of the North, who was very angry on learning what the two had done.   They then visited the house of the Bear of the West, where they were also denounced for the murder.   Then going to the house of the Badger of the South, they related their story, only to anger the Badger.   Again they told their story to the Wolf of the East, who also became very angry.   On reaching Shi'papolima they were kindly received by the ants, who, after listening to their story, asked them to sit down in the ceremonial chamber, where an altar stood in the west end of the room.

Presently a voice was heard calling: "Where are my husbands? I want my husbands."   And the Gods of War recognized the voice as that of the woman they had killed, and they told the mo'sona (director) of the Ant fraternity that the ghost woman had come.   He called to the woman to come in, and as soon as she entered the Gods of War again struck her with their clubs, and, carrying her out, threw her some distance.

Returning to the chamber of the ants, the Gods of War discovered the tracks of a chaparral cock, made during their absence.   The mo'sona, examining the footprints of the bird, inquired "What is this?" The Gods of War asked "Which way did the bird go?"   U'yuyewi said "It went out," but Maᵗsai'lema declared that the bird had passed in. "Then where is it gone?" they both cried; and after much hunting Maᵗsai'lema found it back of the altar.   U'yuyewi joined his younger brother behind the altar, and, holding the bird carefully, examined it and counted the tail feathers; and, passing to the front of the altar, he sat before it and said: "Listen! This bird has ten tail feathers; hereafter when a man takes a scalp he must observe continency and fast from animal food, grease, and salt for the period of ten days."   This fast is observed at the present time.   The closest relations were at that time established between the Gods of War and the ants.   U'yuyewi and Maᵗsai′lema left Shi′papolima at sunset to return to Häl′ona, carrying the Navaho woman's scalp with them.

Announcement was made in Häl′ona that the Gods of War were returning with a scalp; Kŏw′wituma and Wats′usi, the Divine Ones, and others went out to meet them and accompany them to the village. On reaching Häl′ona (the site of the present Zuñi) they encircled the village four times, each time drawing nearer to the center, and entered te′wita ᵗhlanna (large plaza), where the divided scalp was hoisted on a po!e, and thirteen days were spent in rejoicing.

On the evening of the last day a group was formed about a pottery drum in the te′wita, and a circle, composed of the A′shiwanni and others, surrounded the drum. The seven beings previously referred to were again called forth by the loud strokes on the drum, and the same songs were sung as at Hän′ᵗlipĭnkĭa.[a] After the songs, Kŏw′-wituma and Wats′usi, without rising from their seats, disappeared forever into the earth, making their perpetual home in the depths of the crater at the Zuñi salt lake.

The priesthood of the Bow was thus organized, with U′yuyewi and Maᵗsai′lema as the first directors, and the scene supposed to have been enacted at this time is dramatized upon the initiation of a victor into the priesthood of the Bow.

REDISCOVERY OF THE CORN MAIDENS AND THEIR RE-CREATION OF CORN

After flourishing four years (time periods) at I′tiwanna, the site of present Zuñi, the A′shiwi came to grief because of the witches destroying their corn and other food; and in their distress they called upon the Gods of War to aid them. The Gods of War instructed the kăkă (raven) to fly about and look for the Corn maidens. The raven returned to say that he could not find them. The Gods of War then called upon the owl to search at night for the Corn maidens, but he brought back word of failure. They then sent the hawk, who returned with no better news. Then the Gods of War and the A′shiwanni talked together and it was decided to ask aid of Biᶜ′ᵗsi′si, musician and jester to the Sun Father. For this purpose the Gods of War visited Lu′kĭana ᵗkĭai′a, the spring, into which Biᶜ′ᵗsi′si disappeared during the migrations of the A′shiwi, and said to him "We want you." "Why do you want me?" asked Biᶜ′ᵗsi′si. The Gods of War replied: "A′towa e′washtokĭi kwa′chua ho′nawa a′tä ᵗchu to′no te′shuna (The Corn maidens are gone; our fathers wish you to find them)." "Hai′i ho′o te′shuna (All right, I will find them)," replied Biᶜ′ᵗsi′si. He accompanied the Gods of War to I′tiwanna

---

[a] See Destruction of the Kia′nakwe and Songs of Thanksgiving, p. 36.

and went into the He'iwa ki'wi^tsinĕ, where the A'shiwanni were assembled. The Kĭa'kwemosi told Bi^{·″t}si^tsi of his wish, and he said "Ho'o a'wa a'wili i'änna (I will look for them all);" and the Kĭa'kwemosi replied "El'lakwa (Thanks)." The words between the Kĭa'kwemosi and Bi^{·″t}si^tsi were not spoken by the lips, but from the heart.

The A'shiwanni sat all night and all day in the ki'wi^tsinĕ, where there was no fire. They spoke not a word with their lips, and they did not eat, drink, or smoke. All their thoughts were given to the Corn maidens and to rain.

After leaving I'tiwanna, Bi^{·″t}si^tsi ascended a tall cottonwood tree[a] and looked all over the world. Finally he espied one of the maidens in the far south through the separated plumes of one of the duck's wings.[b] Descending from the tree, he hastened to tell the A'shiwanni and the Gods of War of his discovery. Again he spoke not with his lips, but with his heart. He was then carried by Yu'pia^thlan'na (Galaxy), who bowed to the earth to receive him, to Ke'yatiwa, and descending to the earth, he walked with great dignity, his arms crossed, to meet Pau'tiwa, to whom he spoke: "The A'shiwanni wish the A'towa e'washtokĭi' to come to them." The Corn maidens, hearing the words of Bi^{·″t}si^tsi, refused to go, saying "We are afraid." But Pau'tiwa said: "Your A'wan a'tä^tchu (Great Fathers, meaning the A'shiwanni) want you; you must go." All spoke with their hearts; hearts spoke to hearts, and lips did not move.

Bi^{·″t}si^tsi returned to I'tiwanna, followed by the A'wan tä^tchu Ko'-yemshi, Pau'tiwa, and the Corn maidens; the gods and Corn maidens remaining at Ku'shilowa, a few rods east of I'tiwanna, while Bi^{·″t}si^tsi went direct to the ki'wi^tsinĕ, where the A'shiwanni, who were still assembled, sat in line at the west end of the room and back of the cloud symbol of meal made by the pe'kwĭn. Their miwachi[c] were on the meal painting, and a line of meal extended from the cloud symbol to the ladder leading from the hatchway to the floor of the ki'wi^tsinĕ. A basket containing six te'likinawe stood by the meal painting—one yellow, for the Yellow Corn maiden of the North; one blue, for the Blue Corn maiden of the West; one red, for the Red Corn maiden of the South; one white, for the White Corn maiden of the East; another white dotted in all colors, for the Every-color Corn maiden of the Zenith, and a black one, for the Black Corn maiden of the Nadir.

[a] One or two A'shiwanni claim that Bi^{·″t}si^tsi did not ascend the cottonwood tree, but traveled by Yu'pia^thlan'na (Galaxy) south until he was over Ke'yatiwa; when, looking down, he discovered one of the maidens through the separated feathers in the duck's wing. The first version, however, is held by all the other A'shiwanni.

[b] It will be borne in mind that A'wan tä^tchu Ko'yemshi and Pau'tiwa had assumed the form of ducks.

[c] Singular mi'li, sacred fetish composed of an ear of corn surrounded by feathers.

VIEW OF OLDER PORTION OF ZUÑI SHOWING CHUʻPAWA KIʻWIʻSINĚ, CHAMBER DEDICATED TO ANTHROPIC WORSHIP, SHOWN AT A

TO'WA YÄL'LÄNNĚ (CORN MOUNTAIN)

IDOL OF ÁHAYUTA (ELDER GOD OF WAR)

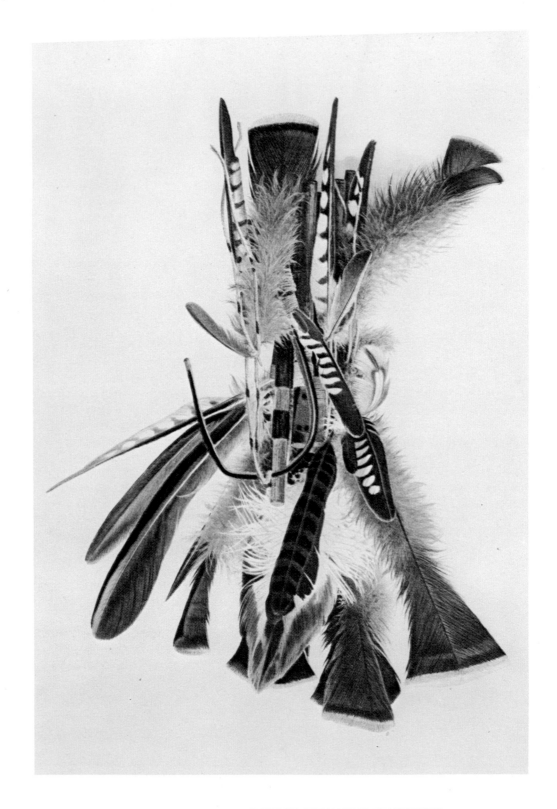

PRAYER PLUMES OF MEMBERS OF GREAT FIRE FRATERNITY
AT WINTER SOLSTICE

After announcing the arrival of the Corn maidens, Bi‴si‵si left the ki′wi‵sinĕ with the yellow te′likinanĕ (singular of te′likinawe) and, planting it, he returned to the kiwi‵sinĕ for the blue te′likinanĕ, which he planted a short distance beyond the yellow one. Returning to the ki′wi‵sinĕ, he took the red te′likinanĕ, which he deposited a short distance beyond the blue. Again returning to the kiwi‵sinĕ, he took the white te′likinanĕ and placed it a short distance beyond the red one. He then secured the every-colored te′likinanĕ and stood it in place, and went for the black te′likinanĕ and placed it a short distance beyond the every-colored one, near Pau′tiwa. The gods, being now in human form, were sitting south of the Corn maidens, who stood in line east and west. After depositing the last one, Bi‴si‵si passed from left to right around Pau′tiwa and the Corn maidens.

A′wan tä‵chu Ko′yemshi then went to I′tiwanna and returned to Ku′shilowa, preceded by the pe′kwĭn (deputy to the Sun Father). He circled round the Corn maidens and Pau′tiwa from left to right and took his position back of Pau′tiwa, who was now standing in line with the Corn maidens. Bi‴si‵si stood before Pau′tiwa and the pe′kwĭn was before Bi‴si‵si. In this order the four proceeded to I′tiwanna, followed by the Corn maidens.

The pe′kwĭn entered the ki′wi‵sinĕ and took his seat north of the meal painting. Pau′tiwa, following, passed up the meal line to the cloud symbol, then around by the north side of the painting and sat in line with the A′shiwanni, immediately back of the meal painting. He remained in the ki′wi‵sinĕ but a short time, not removing his mask while there. The pe′kwĭn smoked a cigarette, taking a whiff or two at a time, and waved it with an upward motion over Pau′tiwa. Each shi′wanni afterward sprinkled Pau′tiwa's mask with meal, and Pau′-tiwa passed down the south side of the room, throwing meal before him as he proceeded, and then ascended the ladder from the west side.[a] On leaving the ki′wi‵sinĕ Pau′tiwa returned directly to Ko′th-luwala′wa. When a short distance west of I′tiwanna he again assumed the form of a duck.[b]

The Corn maidens ascended, one by one, to the roof of the ki′wi‵sinĕ, where Bi‴si‵si awaited them. Each maiden first went to the northeast corner of the roof and faced north, while Bi‴si‵si waved his two eagle plumes about her, turning her completely around by his manipulation of them, that the rains of the north and of all the world might fall upon I′tiwanna. The maiden then passed to the northwest corner

---

[a] In descending the ladder of a ki′wi‵sinĕ one always steps from it on the right side, but it is ascended from the opposite side.

[b] The gods assume forms other than their own when they come up from Ko′thulwala′wa. Nothing would induce a Zuñi to shoot at game anywhere near Ko′thluwala′wa because of his fear that the animal might be an assumed form of a god.

and looked westward, and again the feathers were waved about her,
and she was turned that the rains of the west and of all the world
might fall upon I'tiwanna.   At the southwest corner the maiden looked
southward and was turned that the rains of the south and of all the
world might fall upon I'tiwanna; and again she stood at the southeast
corner and looked eastward and was turned that the rains of the east and
of all the world might fall upon I'tiwanna.   The maiden then descended
into the ki'wi͗sinĕ, Bi͈͗͗si͗si waving his feathers over her back as she
passed through the hatchway.   The same ceremony was repeated over
each Corn maiden on the roof before she descended into the ki'wi͗sinĕ.
The Corn maidens on entering the ki'wi͗sinĕ passed up the meal line
and sat on the ledge north of the line, each maiden sitting to the left of
the one who preceded her.   After all were seated in the ki'wi͗sinĕ, the
pe'kwĭn dipped two eagle-wing feathers six times for the six regions
into a bowl of medicine water which stood before the meal painting,
and sprinkled first the a'wan kĭow'u (elder sister) Yellow Corn maiden,
by striking the plume held in the left hand with the one held in the
right.

As soon as all the maidens had entered, Bi͈͗͗si͗si with arms folded
appeared in the ki'wi͗sinĕ and, standing near the hatchway, spoke
with his lips, addressing the A'shiwanni: "Hom a'täͨchu ko'naton sun'-
hakĭanap'kĭa (My great fathers, I greet you)."   The A'shiwanni replied,
also with their lips: "Kets'anishi (All good come to you)."   Bi͈͗͗si͗si
then left the ki'wi͗sinĕ, returning to Lu'kĭanaͨkĭaia'.   Then the Yellow
Corn maiden accompanied the Kĭa'kwemosi to his home; the Blue Corn
maiden to the home of the Shi'wanni of the West; the Red Corn
maiden to the home of the Shi'wanni of the South; the White Corn
maiden to the home of the Shi'wanni of the East; the Multicolored
Corn maiden to the home of the Shi'wanni of the Zenith, and the Black
Corn maiden to the home of the Shi'wanni of the Nadir.   Each maiden
bathed and rubbed her body hard from head to foot, and what of her
being she rubbed off she left with the shi'wanni whom she accompanied.   Thus the Kĭa'kwemosi became the possessor of yellow corn,
the Shi'wanni of the West of blue corn, the Shi'wanni of the South
of red corn, the Shi'wanni of the East of white corn, the Shi'wanni of
the Zenith of multicolored corn, and the Shi'wanni of the Nadir of
black corn.

The Corn maidens returned to their home at Ke'yatiwa, and the
pe'kwĭn brushed the meal of the cloud symbol together with his eagle
plumes and, lifting it with his hand and plumes, deposited the meal in a
sacred meal basket, afterward throwing it into the river, to go to
Ko'thluwala'wa as an offering to the Council of the Gods.

When that which the Corn maidens had left of themselves had been
planted, and the corn had grown a foot high, they were requested by the
A'shiwanni to come again to I'tiwanna and dance, that the corn might

grow. The pe'kwĭn, who was sent to bring the Corn maidens,[a] returned with them at sunset, going at once into the O'he'wa ki'wĭ'sĭnĕ, where the A'shiwanni and Divine Ones had assembled. The A'shiwanni sat in line back of a cloud symbol of meal that had been made by the pe'kwĭn previous to his going for the Corn maidens. He now drew a line of meal from the cloud symbol eastward, which he embellished with mi'wachi (ears of corn surrounded by plumes) and other sacred objects.

Passing north of the meal painting, the pe'kwĭn took his seat immediately back of it. The Corn maidens proceeded up the meal line, and five of them took seats north of it, the elder sister being at the east end, while five sat south of the meal line, the Blue Corn maiden being at the east end of that line. U'yuyewi passed before the Corn maidens north of the meal line and gave to each a te'li-kinanĕ, the color of the stick being appropriate to the region to which the maiden belonged. He placed the te'likinanĕ between the clasped hands of the maiden, and, clasping her hands with his own, waved them to the six regions, with prayers for rains to come from the six quarters of the world. Maᵗsai'lema passed down the line on the south side and gave, with the same ceremony and prayers, a te'likinanĕ to each maiden on that side. After the distribution of the te'likinawe the a'wan kĭow'u, accompanied by U'yuyewi and a Pi'ᵗläshiwanni (member of the Bow priesthood), and the younger sister Corn maiden, accompanied by Maᵗsai'lema and a Pi'ᵗläshiwanni, visited He'patina (a shrine symbolic of the Middle of the world), for the water vases left there before they fled from Pa'yatämu. The vases secured, the Yellow Corn maiden with U'yuyewi and the Pi'ᵗläshiwanni went to Kiä'ᵗsi 'kĭaia', a small spring a few miles north of I'tiwanna, and collected water; and the Blue Corn maiden, accompanied by Maᵗsai'lema and his accompanying Pi'ᵗläshiwanni, visited 'Kĭa'nayalto (a spring in a high place), in the foothills of To'wa yäl'lännĕ (Corn mountain).

When the Yellow Corn maiden with her attendant returned to the ki'wĭ'sĭnĕ, she passed up the meal line and took her seat at the west end of the north line of maidens. The Blue Corn maiden passed up the meal line and took her seat at the west end of the south line of maidens. The water vase of the Yellow Corn maiden was placed on the north and that of the Blue Corn maiden on the south side of the painting. Taking the vase of the Yellow Corn maiden in his hand, the pe'kwĭn sprinkled her and her line of sisters with plumes dipped in the water. He then received the vase of the Blue Corn maiden and sprinkled her and her line of sisters. The first body of A'shiwanni sat in silence, and the maidens also spoke not a word.

The maidens afterward danced in the ki'wĭ'sĭnĕ to the music of two

---

[a] Nai'uchi, elder brother Bow priest, and also Shi'wanni of the Nadir, until his death in June, 1904, alone claimed that the Gods of War and not the pe'kwĭn went for the Corn maidens.

choirs. One choir sat in the southeast corner of the ki′wiᵗsinĕ; the other was grouped in the northeast corner. These choirs had been taught appropriate songs for the occasion by Kŏw′wituma and Wats′usi. The maidens on the south side, holding their beautiful ᵗhla′we (a number of white stalks covered with white plume-like leaves), danced first to the accompaniment of the choir in the southeast corner of the ki′wiᵗsinĕ. Then the maidens on the north side danced to the music of the choir grouped in the northeast corner.

At midnight the A′shiwanni, Gods of War, the maidens, and the members of the choirs left the ki′wiᵗsinĕ for si′aa′ te′wita, where they sat under a häm′pone of kiä′läᵗsi′lo constructed by the A′wan tä′ᵗchu, pe′kwĭn, and Piᵗᵗläshiwanni Ko′yemshi. Near the west side in the middle of the häm′pone a meal painting of clouds had been made by the pe′kwĭn. The A′shiwanni, carrying their mi′wachi from the O′heᵗwa ki′wiᵗsinĕ, deposited them in line on the cloud symbol. U′yuyewi laid upon the meal painting a folded white cotton embroidered kilt having a broad band of blue-green painted on it, symbolic of the vegetation of the world, and painted at each end of the band was the game of sho′liwe, the game itself being tied to one corner of the kilt and a game of ti′kwanĕ being tied to another corner. The pe′kwĭn sat immediately back of the painting. The other A′shiwanni sat in line on the west side of the häm′pone. The Corn maidens took seats in the häm′pone corresponding to those occupied in the ki′wiᵗsinĕ, the a′wan kĭow′u sitting at the east end of the north line, and the Blue Corn maiden at the east end of the south line, these two being the directors of the other maidens. Their te′likinawe were placed by their sides next to the meal line.

A fire made by a man of the Badger clan burned in the plaza before the häm′pone that all present might be seen. No youths could enter the häm′pone where the beautiful maidens were, and every protection was thrown around them that they might not again be frightened away. The Corn maidens slept till dawn, the A′shiwanni, Divine Ones, and warriors remaining awake to protect them.

At daylight the Gods of War, knowing that Pa′yatämu lived in the midst of fog and cloud, thought it would be well to seek his aid, and visited his house under the rainbow.[a] Pa′yatämu returned with the Gods of War to I′tiwanna, going at once to the house of the Maᵗᵗke ᵗsan′nakwe (Little Fire fraternity), where he was joined by the eight members of the order he had originated some time before.[b] They went together to the plaza at the northeast corner of the häm′pone, from which point Pa′yatämu had previously observed the Corn maidens. The flutes given them by Pa′yatämu were laid across a large and beau-

---

tiful medicine bowl and covered with a white embroidered cotton kilt.

The Corn maidens danced from daylight until night. Those on the north side, passing around by the west, joined their sisters on the south side, and, leaving the häm'pone, danced in the plaza to the music of the choir at the southeast corner of the häm'pone. After they had all returned to their places the maidens on the south side, passing by the west, joined their sisters on the north and danced in the plaza to the music, not only of the choir on that side, but also of the group of trumpeters led by Pa'yatämu. The maidens were led each time to the plaza by either their elder sister Yellow Corn maiden, or the Blue Corn maiden, and they held their beautiful 'hla'we in either hand. The Corn maidens never appeared again to the A'shiwi, for soon after the dance described they were destroyed by the great fire which swept over the earth.[a]

ORIGIN OF ANIMAL FETISHES

After the A'shiwi settled at I'tiwanna, U'yuyewi and Maᵗsai'lema lived with their grandmother at Shop'ᵗhlua yälläkwi, not far from I'tiwanna. While these diminutive Gods of War were great in heroic deeds they were also very mischievous. On one occasion when they appeared in I'tiwanna U'yuyewi took his position on the east and Maᵗsai'lema stood on the west, opposite his brother. The elder held his game of ho'kĭamonně close to his breast and, calling to his younger brother, requested him to catch the ball of the game, which he would roll to him. After Maᵗsai'lema received the ball he returned it to his elder brother in the same manner. Maᵗsai'lema had the games of ti'kwaně and sho'liwe, which he held to his breast. Each one had a turquoise rabbit stick, which the boys of the village observed with envy. U'yuyewi threw his rabbit stick cutting his younger brother open from throat to abdomen, and Maᵗsai'lema fell. U'yuyewi patted his hand over his mouth, giving the war whoop, but not loud, and pressed his hands upon his brother, and Maᵗsai'lema rose unharmed. Then Maᵗsai'lema threw his stick at his elder brother, cutting him across the waist, and U'yuyewi fell as one dead. Maᵗsai'lema hastened to him, repeated the war whoop, and pressed his hands to his elder brother, and he arose unharmed. The A'shiwi youths looked on amazed, and begged that they might use the rabbit sticks, but U'yuyewi and Maᵗsai'lema replied: "They are for us alone; these are our games."[b]

---

[a] The 'Hla'hewe drama, which in the past was played quadrennially in August when the corn was a foot high, is similar to the myth here described, with the exception of a few changes made, the Zuñis say, by the pe'kwin at the first production of the drama. This drama has not occurred since 1891, when the writer observed it in all its details. It is held specially sacred by the Zuñis, and they prefer not to enact it in the presence of strangers; hence, as most of the ceremonies must be held outdoors, it is not likely to occur again.

[b] See Games.

The Gods of War continued throwing the rabbit sticks at each other, first one and then the other jumping up unharmed. Finally, after much persuasion on the part of the A'shiwi youths, the gods threw their rabbit sticks at them, striking one at a time until many lay upon the ground. All who were struck were immediately killed. The mothers of these youths, wondering at the absence of their children, went in search of them, to find only their dead bodies; and the women were greatly enraged.

The gods returned to their home as though nothing unusual had happened, and their grandmother was unaware of the trouble they had caused until informed by the parents of the deceased children, whereupon she whipped the gods. They afterward told her that she had better hurry away, for they intended to burn I'tiwanna. Very early in the morning the grandmother ran to Ma'kĭaiakwi, a low mountain not far south of the present Zuñi, leaving the Gods of War alone at the house. After talking together U'yuyewi and Ma'sai'lema decided that their grandmother was too near, for they were very angry with the A'shiwi and intended to destroy everything in the world about them; so they called to their grandmother to go farther, and she hastened to the place now occupied by Ma'we'sita (Salt Mother).

The gods shot lightning arrows with their rainbow bows into the heart of the shield of burning crystal carried by the Sun Father, and immediately the world was ablaze. The A'shiwi were not destroyed by the fire because their bodies still retained the hardness of iron, the condition in which they were when they came from the underworlds to this world; but the Corn maidens were destroyed and many animals were burned and converted into stone, some of them becoming diminutive. Thus the A'shiwi account for the size of many of their animal fetishes, which they believe to have originally been living creatures. Many of the birds were also burned. 'Ko''loktakĭa (sand-hill crane) ran to Ko'tina yäl'lännĕ, near Ojo Caliente, but was burned before he could reach the summit of the mountain. He is now to be seen on the spot where he was overtaken by the catastrophe, converted into stone.

ORIGIN OF THE ZUÑI SALT LAKE

Four years after U'yuyewi and Ma'sai'lema set fire to the world they went to 'Kĭa'nanaknana, a spring at the black rocks, about 5 miles east of present Zuñi, then the home of Ma'we'sita. They had lived there four years when 'Hli'akwa[a] (Turquoise) came to the black rocks. Ma'we inquired of him: "Who are you?" He replied: "I am 'Hli'akwa, from Wehl''hluwalla (Santo Domingo).[b] I was of no

---

[a] The perfect blue is the male; the off-colored is the female.

[b] The turquoise mines best known in New Mexico are about 15 miles by trail from the pueblo of Santo Domingo. Previous to their being possessed by white men they were the resort of Indians in quest of turquoise.

value there. The elder and younger brother Bow priests gave me to women to pay them for granting their evil desires, so I came away. After I left, A′ne ′hlawi (a certain bird) 'shot' small stones from his mouth upon the elder and younger brother Bow priests and the women as they entered my home, and another bird caused a rock to fall and cover the entrance, leaving but a crevice through which thin sheets of he′we (a wafer-like bread) and a tiny jug of water were passed to them. In four days they all died. When the rock was removed from the entrance of the house it was discovered that they had become large rattlesnakes. These snakes were short, and their bodies were thick." Ma′we declared: "I also am too near my people to be of value; I will go far away." The Gods of War, hearing the remarks of Ma′we, said: "Mother, if you go far away you will be of much greater value, and we will go with you." Together with ′Hli′akwa, the Gods of War and Ma′we left ′Kĭa′nanaknana.

Before leaving the black rocks Ma′we saw a youth, who in answer to an inquiry said he was of the Tä′kĭakwe (Frog clan). " Well," said she, "in four years I wish your people to come here and put my house in good order." Since that time the people of the Frog clan have taken great care of this spring.

′Kĭa′nanaknana is sacred to the A′shiwanni. The basin formed by the spring is about 15 by 20 feet. Terraced ledges extend around it beneath the surface of the water. It could not be learned whether these ledges were produced by deposits from the spring or were artificial.

This spring is cleaned after the installation of a new pe′kwĭn, and at such other times as may be deemed necessary, by members of the Frog clan and their immediate families, by order of the pe′kwĭn. He commands: "In eight days the water shall be removed from ′Kĭa′nanaknana and the spring shall be well cleaned. Bowls must be made for dipping the water."[a] On the eighth day after this announcement the pe′kwĭn awaits a short distance from the village the coming of those designated to clean the spring. The men are dressed in cotton trousers and shirts. European dress, so much in vogue at the present time, even in ceremonials, must not be worn on this occasion. The women wear their ordinary dress, their best moccasins, many necklaces, and white cotton blanket wraps bordered in blue and red. Each person carries a bowl with four la′showawe (one or more plumes attached to cotton cord) and four te′likinawe wrapped in·corn husks. The la′showawe are carried in the bowls. All these plumes were prepared by the fathers or brothers of the women who are present. The la′showawe are offered to the deceased A′shiwanni, and the te′likinawe to the u′wannami, of the four regions.

---

[a] Female members of the Frog clan and women closely related in consanguinity make the bowls, which have four small openings equidistant, near the rim.

The pe'kwĭn precedes the party to the spring, and, when all are gathered on the bank, he offers a prayer for rain and crops, and then directs the men to enter the water. They remove their trousers and begin at once to fill the vases, which they hand to the women, who pass other vases to the men and empty the water contained in those received by them. In this way the spring is cleaned, the men descending from terrace to terrace.

When the work is completed each person attaches la'showawe to the four openings in the bowl, and the pe'kwĭn, receiving one bowl at a time, deposits it on one of the terraces. These ledges are literally covered with bowls, which have been deposited from time immemorial.[a]

When the pe'kwĭn comes from the basin of the spring he receives the four te'likinawe from each person and bunches them in a kĭa'ĕt-chinĕ (a number of prayer plumes wrapped together) and, attaching a stone sufficiently heavy to carry this to the bottom of the spring, casts it into the center of the water, which is now only a few inches in depth, with the following prayer: "We pray that the u'wannami will work for us, that our crops and the crops of all the world may be watered and be plentiful, that our people and all people may be happy, that our people may not die but sleep to awake in Ko'thluwala'wa."

On leaving Kĭa'nanaknana, Ma'we and 'Hli'akwa assumed the form of birds, and in their flight Ma'we, striking a certain projecting point of rock, passed through the rock, leaving an opening. Here she dropped the eagle plume that was tied to her hair; it petrified as it stood perpendicularly in the ground and became a monument many feet high. This monument and the opening in the rock are to be seen at the present time.

On reaching a beautiful lake, about 45 miles south of the present Zuñi, the Gods of War decided that they had gone far enough, and Ma'we agreed to stop with them, but 'Hli'akwa declared that he must go farther. Though 'Hli'akwa endeavored to persuade Ma'we to journey on, she refused, and finally he said: "You may stop here because you are not of so great value as myself; this is too near home for me." So he journeyed on to the southwest and made his home in a high mountain protected by many angry white and black bears.[b] Ma'we made her home in the lake, and the Gods of War selected a mountain rising from the lake for their home.

---

[a] These sacred objects will soon be scattered, as the secret of burying the vases beneath the water has become known to the men now employed in constructing the Government dam for these Indians. This spring will be in the bed of the great reservoir.

[b] The writer was bound to secrecy regarding the home of 'Hli'akwa. The Zuñis make pilgrimages thither for the purpose of collecting turquoise. On these expeditions they are always provided with te'likinawe and sacred meal. The plumes are offered to the angry bears who guard 'Hli'akwa, and the meal is sprinkled upon the beasts, when, the Zuñis say, they become friendly and allow them to approach.

FLIGHT OF THE A′SHIWI TO TO′WA YÄL′LÄNNĔ AND THEIR RETURN
TO THE VALLEY

The A′shiwi were not destined to remain undisturbed. They were compelled by a great flood to seek refuge on a mesa near by, which they named To′wa yäl′lännĕ (plate XI) from the quantity of corn they carried from the lowlands to the mesa, the corn occupying much room in their houses. During the stay of the A′shiwi on the mesa a cave in the southwest wall of To′wa yäl′lännĕ took the place of He′patina in symbolizing the Middle of the world. The Zuñis claim that many sacred objects were secreted in this cave during the Spanish conquest (see A plate L).

Though this table-land stands hundreds of feet above the valley the waters rose nearly to the summit and caused consternation among the A′shiwi, who feared that the flood would sweep them from the face of the earth. It was finally decided that human sacrifice was necessary to appease the angry waters. Consequently a son and a daughter of the Kĭa′kwemosi[a] were dressed in their most beautiful clothes, adorned with many precious beads, and then cast into the great sea. The waters immediately began to recede, and the youth and maiden were converted into stone. This columnar rock, known as the "Mother rock," stands for all time as a monument of the peril from which the A′shiwi were happily delivered (plate XII).

The A′shiwi were glad to descend to the valley, for their trials were great when living on the mesa and the maidens had grown weary carrying water up the steep acclivity. They rebuilt Ma′ᵗsakĭa, Häl′ona, or I′tiwanna, and a number of other villages. The most easterly was Kĭa′kĭima, and Ha′wiku was the most westerly, Ma′ᵗsakĭa being the center of priestly power. But now their peace was disturbed by the Navahos and Apaches, who made repeated attacks, plundering and killing many of their people. Thrilling stories are told by the present Zuñis of attacks of the Navahos upon their ancestors, and how the women and children were brutally murdered during the absence of the men from their homes. But the Navahos did not always get the better of the community dwellers. The Zuñis relate one instance when their people let it be known that they were to have a great dance in the si′aa′ te′wita, and so induced many of the enemy, who were ever ready to observe the ceremonials of the A′shiwi, to be present. The plaza was crowded with the Navahos, when, at a signal from one of the A′shiwi, war clubs did lively work, almost every Navaho present being clubbed to death.

---

[a] See A′shiwanni (Rain priesthood).

ANTHROPIC WORSHIP AND RITUAL

Kiʻwiʻsiwe and their Functions

The Zuñi kiʻwiʻsiwe (chambers dedicated to anthropic worship) are above ground, rectangular, and constructed of stone. The exterior walls are roughly plastered, but the interior walls are smoothly finished like those of dwellings. They are entered through a hatchway quite different from that found in the roofs of other buildings. Each kiʻwiʻsinĕ has a couple of openings in the front wall for the admission of light; in early days these were never closed, as those not privileged to do so would never look in the direction of the kiʻwiʻsinĕ while a ceremonial was proceeding within. At present these openings are filled with wads of cloth to prevent the intrusive eyes of strangers. There is an interior door leading to the adjoining dwelling. The fire altar (see plate xx), which is constructed of stone slabs, is immediately beneath the hatchway, so that the smoke can readily escape.

As has been stated, the A'wan tä'ᵗchu Ko'yemshi appointed a man of the Deer clan as Ko'mosona[a] director of the Ko'tiliki (mythologic fraternity) and director-general of the kiʻwiʻsiwe, and a man of the same clan as his warrior, and he selected a man of the Badger clan as Ko'pekwĭn (deputy) to the Ko'mosona, and a man of the Badger clan as warrior to the Ko'pekwĭn.

There is a great variety of anthropic gods in the Zuñi pantheon, many of them ancestral. Certain gods are allied to particular kiʻwiʻsiwe, their dances being under the special direction of the o'taikĭa mo'sona (dance director) of the kiʻwiʻsinĕ, to which the personators of these gods belong.

There are six kiʻwiʻsiwe, dedicated to the six regions. The one for the north is He'iwa (building up wall, so named because the people were constantly tearing down and rebuilding the kiʻwiʻsinĕ), and it stands on the north side of si'aa' te'wita[b] (sacred dance court), though not on the north side of the village. The one for the west, Mu'he'wa (manure house; this kiʻwiʻsinĕ was originally built of blocks of manure), is not on the west side of the village, but stands rather to the center of the group of kiʻwiʻsiwe. Chu'pawa (corn house; this name was derived from the people in the olden times popping corn in the kiʻwiʻsinĕ) is dedicated to the south, and is in the southern portion of the village, but not on the south side. As it is south of the main group of houses it

---

[a] The fact that the Deer clan is almost extinct causes much anxiety to the Zuñis. The present warrior to the Ko'mosona belongs to the Bear clan, owing to their inability to find a man of the Deer clan among the A'pi'ᵗläshiwanni (Bow priesthood) to fill the place.

[b] Si'aa', to break or tear apart. This te'wita received its name because of the danger of the surrounding walls falling because of the large crowds of spectators who gathered on the roofs to observe the ceremonies in the court.

may originally have been on this side of the village. The one for the east is O′he‘wa (brains; this ki′wiᵗsinĕ received its name from a certain god who requested the people of his ki′wiᵗsinĕ to make snowbird traps and catch birds. Upon the god's return the birds were given to him, and he requested the people of the ki′wiᵗsinĕ to boil the birds and to crush the kernels of squash seeds with water on a stone and throw them into the pot with the birds. When the seeds boiled they resembled brains, and the people named the ki′wiᵗsinĕ after the squash seed, calling it brains. Another version gives the name "brains of game"). Up′ᵗsannawa (few people; derived its name from its members being reduced), which is dedicated to the Zenith, and O′he‘wa are east of the others, but they are hardly east of the center of the present village. He′kĭapa (back wall, referring to the opposite from the east, which is always "the before" with the Zuñis) is dedicated to the Nadir, and is on the west side of the village. When possible, all ceremonial chambers extend east and west, symbolic of the daily course of the Sun Father.

Each ki′wiᵗsinĕ has its dance director, who is the superior of his ki′wiᵗsinĕ, and he leads the songs and dances, his position being always midway the line of dancers, and a corps of wor′we (managers) who are appointed for life, though they may be impeached for proper cause. The o′taikĭa mo′sona decides when the dances of his ki′wiᵗsinĕ shall occur, excepting at the time of the semiannual ceremonies of the Kor′kokshi,[a] which are controlled by the Ko′mosona (director-general) of the ki′wiᵗsiwe after consulting with the first body of A′shiwanni (rain priests). In a sense the o′taikĭa mo′sona controls these also, for though the Ko′mosona notifies him that the dances must occur, the specific time is decided upon when he communicates his wish to one of the first body of A′shiwanni that his people will dance for him—that is, the Kor′kokshi of his ki′wiᵗsinĕ will dance in connection with the retreat of the shi′wanni for rain. Each ki′wiᵗsinĕ has dances in association with one of the first body of A′shiwanni. The dual system so complete with the Zuñis is expressed in the coupling of the ki′wiᵗsiwe.

While the ki′wiᵗsiwe are ordinarily referred to in the following order—He′iwa as elder brother to Mu′he‘wa, Chu′pawa as elder brother to O′he‘wa, and Up′ᵗsannawa as elder brother to He′kĭapawa—they are differently classified for the Kor′kokshi dances. He′iwa is elder brother to O′he‘wa, Mu′he‘wa is elder brother to He′kĭapawa, and Chu′pawa is elder brother to Up′ᵗsannawa when the dances are produced in the He′iwa, Mu′he‘wa, and Chu′pawa, the younger brothers, according to the above relation, supply the goddesses for the Kor′kokshi This order is reversed when the O′he‘wa,

---

[a] Kor′kokshi (dancers for good) are the u′wannami (rain-makers).

He'kĭapawa, and Up'ᵗsannawa take up the dances. Then they become the elder brothers, the younger brothers, as before, supplying the goddesses.

The ki'wiᵗsinĕ which is to furnish the Kor'kokshi upon the return of the party from Ko'thluwala'wa or Kĭap'kwena at the summer solstice (see page 158) begins the Kor'kokshi dances of winter. If a request is made at this season by the Ko'mosona, Ko'pekwĭn (deputy to Ko'mosona), or A'shiwanni, including the elder and younger brother Bow priests, for the gods to repeat these dances the second day in the plazas, they must remain during the night in the ki'wiᵗsinĕ, and may dance if they choose, but they do not visit the other ki'wiᵗsiwe after the first night. The same rule is adhered to if they dance the third and fourth days in the te'witas. Under no conditions can the Kor'-kokshi dance more than four days in the winter. They must never dance but one night and day in the summer, for so the gods have commanded.[a] The first dances of the Kor'kokshi in summer occur when the Ko'mosona and his party return from their pilgrimage to Ko'thluwala'wa or Kĭap'kwena. Each ki'wiᵗsinĕ, including the one to which the Ko'mosona belongs, takes its turn sexennially in furnishing dances for this occasion. They always gather in the ki'wiᵗsinĕ to which the Ko'mosona is allied and dance here and in the house of the Ko'pekwĭn during the night, and in the plazas the following day.

Those who are to personate the Council of the Gods[b] and the Ko'yemshi gather in the Ko'pekwĭn's house, and the personators of the Sha'läko, with their fellows and wor'we, assemble in the ki'wiᵗsinĕ of the Ko'mosona, except when the Chu'pawa takes its turn in furnishing the Kor'kokshi; then the Sha'läko of this ki'wiᵗsinĕ, with his younger brother or alternate, is present in the Ko'pekwĭn's house, and their wor'we go to the ki'wiᵗsinĕ.

The Great Fire fraternity always assembles in the Ko'pekwĭn's house for the summer solstice ceremonies, but the Ko'mosona may select the fraternity he wishes to have perform in the ki'wiᵗsinĕ.

No other dances are allowed during the summer dances of the Kor'kokshi. The Kor'kokshi remove their masks in summer when in the ki'wiᵗsinĕ. In winter they go over the western road to remove their masks and disrobe. Dances may occur at any time from the winter solstice to the summer solstice by the wish of the dance director of a ki'wiᵗsinĕ.

Dances for rain sometimes occur at the farming districts. After dancing one or more days the dancers usually walk to Zuñi, retire to the ki'wiᵗsinĕ of the o'taikĭa mo'sona who has charge of the dance, and dance during the night. The dances are repeated in the plazas the

[a] Nai'uchi had the dance repeated in summer, but this was stopped, as it is against the old custom of the Kor'kokshi to appear more than one day in the te'witas.

[b] See p. 33.

following day. Each ki'wi^tsinĕ has a dance of thanksgiving and also for rain at the gathering of the crops, the dancers departing over the western road.

All male children must be received into the Ko'tikili, in order to enter the sacred dance house of Ko'thluwala'wa after death, and at the time of involuntary initiation the child becomes allied to one of the ki'wi^tsiwe.

Women may join a ki'wi^tsinĕ under certain conditions, but their initiation into the Ko'tikili is rare. Occasionally when a woman is ill and the treatment of one or more theurgists fails, her family may think she has been frightened by one of the personators of the gods, and they try to decide who caused the trouble. When the person has finally been decided upon he is requested to appear before the girl. He visits the house dressed in the full regalia of the god he personated at the time he was supposed to have frightened the girl, and proceeds to instruct her in the importance of the religious duties which must be performed by her should she become a member of the Ko'tikili. At the next involuntary initiation ceremonies of the Ko'tikili the girl passes through the rites with the infant boys. She walks back of the one who is supposed to have frightened her, he becoming her ceremonial father, while the young boys are carried on the backs of their ceremonial fathers. The voluntary initiation of the girl is no less severe than that of the boys.

In 1902 there were four female members of the Ko'tikili. Two of these were in Mu'he'wa ki'wi^tsinĕ, both young married women. One has three children, the other none. Chu'pawa has one girl who joined the Ko'tikili at the time of the last involuntary initiation previous to the writer's visit to Zuñi in 1902; she is not married. The O'he'wa has one female member; she is the eldest of the female members, is married, but is childless. These women take part in the masked dances, personating the goddesses.

The ki'wi^tsinĕ to which the child shall belong is decided upon at his birth. He must join the ki'wi^tsinĕ of the husband of the doctoress who receives him at his nativity. If several female physicians be present, which is usually the case, each is desirous to secure the child as it comes into the world. The husband of the fortunate physician serves as godfather in both the involuntary and voluntary initiation. If the doctoress has no husband, her eldest son takes his place; if there is no son, her eldest brother acts.

The initiatory ceremonies are supposed to be performed by direct command of Pau'tiwa (director-general of Ko'thluwala'wa), who sent ^tKiäklo[a] from Ko'thluwala'wa to I'tiwanna to notify the A'shiwi that the gods would come in eight days to give to the children the sacred

---

[a] ^tKiäklo is an ancestral god and deputy to Pau'tiwa.

breath of life, so that after death they might enter the dance house at Ko'thluwala'wa before proceeding to the undermost world whence they came.

Pau'tiwa decided that one of the gods must go to I'tiwanna (site of the present Zuñi) to relate to the people their history after leaving the undermost world and to prepare them for the coming of the gods to bless the male children with the sacred breath of life that they might enter into the everlasting happiness of the sacred dance house. 'Kiäklo was chosen as a sagacious god to perform this service. Before he started on his mission, Pau'tiwa gave him a duck skin filled with seeds, with shells about its neck, to be used as a rattle. He was carried to I'tiwanna by the ten Ko'yemshi, who sang to him as they proceeded, each Ko'yemshi taking his turn at bearing 'Kiäklo on his back.

A body of four men have this history myth in their keeping. Two of them must be of the Dogwood clan and the two others must be children of the same clan—that is, their paternal parents must belong to this clan.[a] The men of the Dogwood clan may belong to either the Parrot or the Raven division of the clan.[b] Upon the death of a member of this organization a successor is chosen by the first body of A'shiwanni and the director of the organization. Death is the punishment for betrayal of the trust reposed in these men. This organization meets four consecutive nights until midnight in the months of February and March to rehearse the iliad of their race. They meet one month in the house of a member of the Dogwood clan, and the next month in the house of a child of the Dogwood clan. The first body of A'shiwanni holds meetings simultaneous with those of this organization. Plume offerings to the Council of the Gods and ĕt'towe (see page 163) are prepared at these meetings.

The drama occurs quadrennially, beginning in April, by direction, as is supposed, of the Council of the Gods, when a member of the organization takes his turn in personating 'Kiäklo, the performance being an exact representation of the visit of 'Kiäklo and the other gods of I'tiwanna.

The ceremonial begins with the ten Ko'yemshi and the personator of 'Kiäklo visiting their shrines, located at the base of the knoll upon which the shrines dedicated to the Council of the Gods stand. At the rising of the morning star the personators of the Ko'yemshi, well laden with food collected from the people of the village, go to their shrine, where they deposit te'likinawe. After making a fire they group themselves about it and enjoy their feast. The personator of 'Kiäklo, following a little later, deposits plumes at his shrine,

b At the time the writer secured this myth the director of the body, a man about 30 years of age, was a member of the Parrot division of the Dogwood clan. The other keeper from this clan, who is much older, belonged to the Raven division of the clan. The two remaining were respectively members of the Corn and Frog clans.

a

b

VIEWS OF MOTHER ROCK, WEST SIDE OF TO'WA YÄL'LÄNNĚ (CORN MOUNTAIN)

KO'LOOWISI (PLUMED SERPENT) WITH HEAD THRUST THROUGH TABLET

MASK OF SHITSÚʻKIǍ (GAME EATER): FRONT, SIDE, AND REAR VIEWS

MASK OF KWEʹLELE (FIRE MAKER TO SHITSUʹKʹIÄ): FRONT AND SIDE VIEWS

which is but a short distance from the other, and joins the Ko'yemshi in the feast.   Here the ordinary dress is replaced by religious paraphernalia.

The personator of 'Kiäklo has his body painted with the pinkish clay found near Ko'thluwala'wa.   He wears buckskin trousers fringed on the outside and reaching to the feet, a white cotton shirt, and a white embroidered Hopi kilt, across which a band of blue-green is painted, with a conventional design of the game sho'liwe at each end of the band.   The blue-green of the band symbolizes the vegetation of the world.   The kilt is held on by an embroidered sash and a red belt, and a fox skin is pendent at the back.   A folded mi'ha (sacred embroidered blanket) is worn over the shoulders.   Dance moccasins complete the costume.   The mask, which is of hide, covers the head; it is painted white, the back being decorated with a frog or toad and several tadpoles in black.   A rainbow extends over the upper portion of the front of the mask, which has circular eye and mouth holes.   Three lines, symbolic of rain, radiate from the lower portion of each eyehole. A fox skin finishes the base of the mask.   The personator carries a duck skin filled with seeds, with a string of shells around the neck, which he uses as a rattle.   The Ko'yemshi also have their bodies painted with the pinkish clay universally used by the personators of the anthropic gods; their masks are freshly colored with the same pigment; they wear the black kilt and pieces of the same material tied around the base of the mask.

The drama begins with the Ko'yemshi carrying 'Kiäklo on their backs to the village, just as the god is supposed to have traveled from Ko'thluwala'wa to I'tiwanna, and the song of the personators of the Ko'yemshi is supposed to be the same as that sung by the gods at that time.   The song is begun as soon as they start for the village and continued until 'Kiäklo has taken his seat in the ki'wi^tsinĕ.

Free Translation of Ko'yemshi Song

I

We come out from the fourth world; we carry our grandchild on our backs.   We come out.

A ----ha' ---- i ---hi' ----a ----ha' ---- i ---hi'.

He remains on our backs and looks to the six regions, my poor grandchild.

Hurry and call for rains, my poor grandchild, you whom I carry on my back.

II

We come out from the fourth world; we carry our grandchild on our backs.   We come out.

A ---ha' ---- i ----hi' ----a ----ha' ---- i ---hi'.

He remains on our backs and looks to the six regions, my poor grandchild.

Hurry and call for seeds, my poor grandchild, you whom I carry on my back.

Song of the Ko'yemshi

I

A'witĕn	te'hula	hon[a]	u'kwai'i;	yäm	nana	se'topa;	hon	u'kwai'i.
Fourth	world	we	come out;	our	grand-child	carry on backs.	We	come out.

A ----ha' ---- i ----hi' ----a ----ha' ---- i ---hi'.

Lĕs'si	te'kwĭn	tu'nawa	lu'chupächi,	i'yo	ho'ma	nana.
To the	six regions	look;	remains on our backs,	poor	my	grand-child.

Hä'nate	ʻkĭa'shima	we'atina,	i'yo	ho'ma	nana,	to'o	ho'o	se'toye.
Hurry,	rains	call for,	poor	my	grand-child,	you	I	carry on my back.

II

A'witĕn	te'hula	hon	u'kwai'i;	yäm	nana	se'topa;	hon	u'kwai'i.
Fourth	world	we	come out;	our	grand-child	carry on backs;	we	come out.

A ----ha' ---- i ----hi'. --a ----ha' ---- i ---hi'.

Lĕs'si	te'kwĭn	tu'nawa	lu'chupächi,	i'yo	ho'ma	nana.
To the	six regions	look;	remains on our backs,	poor	my	grand-child.

Hä'nate	to'shona	we'atina,	i'yo	ho'ma	nana,	to'o	ho'o	se'toye.
Hurry,	seeds	called for,	poor	my	grand-child,	you	I	carry on my back.

---

[a] Hon is a contraction of hono, we (two or more).

III

We reach the last spring on the road carrying our grandchild on our backs.

A____ha'____i____hi'____a____ha'____i____hi'.

We reach the middle spring on the road with our grandchild on our backs.

A____ha'____i____hi'____a____ha'____i____hi'.

IV

We see the prairie-dog girls and the prairie-dog women enter their place below.

A____ha'____i____hi'____a____ha'____i____hi'.

V

Ha'aiyu, ha'aiyu; we will reach there in one, two, three, four steps.
Call for rains, our poor great-grandchild, continue to call for rains. It is beautiful, beautiful here.[a]

A____ha̦'____i____hi'____a____ha'____i____hi'.

III

ᵗKĭa'na	päl'to	o'nakona	yäm	nana	se'topa,	hon	a'wiya;
Spring	last	road	our	grand-child	carry on backs	we	come to;

A____ha'____i____hi'____a____ha'____i____hi'.

ᵗKĭa'na	i'tiwa	o'nakona	yäm	nana	se'topa	hon	a'wiya.
Spring	middle	road	our	grand-child	carry on backs	we	come to.

A____ha'____i____hi'____a____ha'____i____hi'.

IV

ᵗKu'shi	e'washtokĭi	ᵗku'shi	a'makĭi	i'ami	a'hakwi	te'maiän
Prairie-dog	girls,	prairie-dog	women	their	stone place	see

pia'   kwa'to.
below   enter.

A___ ha'____i____hi'____a____ha'____i ___hi'.

V

Ha'aiyu,	ha'aiyu;	to'pa,	kwĭl'li,	hai'i,	a'witĕn	i'techuna
		one,	two,	three,	four	steps

ye'liyuᵗhlau'
reach there.

I'yo	ho'nawa	a'wan	nana	ᵗkĭa'shima;	we'atiua,	te'hatou.
Poor	our	great-	grand-child	rains	call for,	continue to call for.

E'lu   e'lu   li'ᵗla.
Beau-tiful,   beau-tiful   here.

A____ha'____i____hi'____a____ha'____i____hi'.

---

[a] I'tiwanna (the old Zuñi).

VI

Ha′aiyu, ha′aiyu; we reach there in one, two, three, four steps.
Call for seeds, our poor great-grandchild, continue to call for seeds.
    Beautiful, beautiful here.[a]
        A_ _ _ _ha′_ _ _ _i_ _ _ _hi′_ _ _ _a_ _ _ _ha′_ _ _ _i_ _ _ _hi′.

VII

Our poor great-grandchild, our poor great-grandchild, carried on our
    backs.
You wish to go about carried on our backs.
      A_ _ _ _ha′_ _ _ _i_ _ _ _hi′_ _ _ _a_ _ _ _ha′_ _ _ _i_ _ _ _hi′.

VIII

Our great-grandfather duck came out a short time since from the old
    dance village[b] by the mountains.[c]

VI

Ha′aiyu,   ha′aiyu;   to′pa,   kwĭl′li,   hai′i,   a′witĕn   i′techuna
                       one,   two,   three,   four   steps
ye′liyuᵗhlau′.
   reach there.

I′yo   ho′nawa   a′wan   nana   to′shona   we′atina,   te′hatou.
Poor   our   great-   grand-   seeds   call for,   continue to
                         child   call for.
E′lu,   e′lu   li′ᵗla.
Beau-   beau-   here.
tiful,   tiful
       A_ _ _ _ha′_ _ _ _i_ _ _ _hi′_ _ _ _a_ _ _ _ha′_ _ _ _i_ _ _ _hi′.

VII

I′yo   ho′nawa   a′wan   nana,   i′yo   ho′nawa   a′wan   nana,
Poor   our   great-   grand-   poor   our   great-   grand-
                        child,   child,
Se′towi hon′te.   To′o a′luᵗsema,   se′towi ho′ma, se′towi ho′ma.
Carried on my back.   You wish to go about,   carried on my back,   carried on my back.
       A_ _ _ _ha′_ _ _ _i_ _ _ _hi′_ _ _ _a _ _ ha′ _ _ i_ _ _ _hi′.

VIII

I′ᶜwayusha′,[d] i′ᶜwayusha′, i′ᶜwayusha′, huna′, i′ᶜwayu huna′.
      A_ _ _ _ha′_ _ _ _i_ _ _ _hi′_ _ _ _a_ _ ha′_ _ _ _i_ _ _ _hi′.

La′lekhoᵗli i′yokwi we′nima yäl′läa′ ho′nawa a′wan   nana[e]
There   [referring to Ko′thluwala′wa and the   our   great-   grand-
          two mountains near by]   father
iwayusha′ kwai′i ko′wa.[f]
duck   come out short time.

---

[a] I′tiwanna.
[b] Ko′thluwala′wa.
[c] Referring to the two mountains near Ko′thluwala′wa, sacred to the ancestral gods.
[d] Referring to the duck rattle given to ᵗKiäklo by Pau′tiwa (director-general of Ko′thluwala′wa).
[e] Nana is used both for grandfather and grandchild.
[f] The first eight stanzas are sung on the way to the ki′wiᵗsinĕ, see pl. XA.

IX

You have reached the ki'wi^tsinĕ; ascend the ladder.
You will enter the ki'wi^tsinĕ, and here you will sit down.   Hasten and
  enter; hasten and stand.
Inside you will see your fathers[a] all seated calling for rains.
   A....ha'....i....hi'...a....ha'....i....hi'.

X

Our great-grandfather duck came out a short time since
From the old dance village by the mountains.

XI

You have reached the ki'wi^tsinĕ; ascend the ladder.
You will enter the ki'wi^tsinĕ, and here you will sit down.
Hasten and enter; hasten and stand.
Inside you will see your fathers all seated calling for seeds.
   A....ha'....i....hi'...a....ha'....i...hi'.

IX

Li'^tla to'o i'ya; li'^tla to'o ye'maku.
Here you come; here you go up.

Li'^tla to'o kwa'to; li'^tla to'o i'mu.
Here you enter; here you sit down.

A'uthluwa^tla kwa'to; a'uthluwa^tla ye'li.
Hasten enter; hasten stand.

Te'^tlaku i'yäm to'o a'tä^tchu a'wunatikĭa;
Inside your you fathers will see;

Ti'nanuliye yäm to'o ^tkĭa'shima we'atina.
All sitting down your you rains calling for.

  A....ha'.. .i....hi'....a....ha'....i...hi'.

X

La'lekho^tli i'yokwi we'nima yäl'läa' ho'nawa a'wan nana
There [referring to Ko'thluwala'wa and the our great grand-
  two mountains near by]   father

iwayusha' kwai'i ko'wa.
duck came out short time.

XI

Li'^tla to'o i'ya; li'^tla to'o ye'maku.
Here you come; here you go up.

Li'^tla to'o kwa'to; li'^tla to'o i'mu.
Here you enter; here you sit down.

A'u^thluwa^tla kwa'to; a'u^thluwa^tla ye'li,
Hasten enter hasten stand,

Te'^tlaku yäm to'o a'tä^tchu a'wunatikĭa;
Inside your you fathers will see;

Ti'nanuliye yäm to'o to'shona we'atina.
All sitting down your you seeds calling for.

  A...ha'....i...hi'....a....ha'....i... hi'.[b]

---

[a] A'shiwanni (rain priests). [b] Stanzas IX, X, and XI are sung on the roof of the ki'wi^tsinĕ.

XII

Hasten, hasten, a'haya, hasten, hasten, a'haya.

> A____ha'____i____hi'____a____ha'____i____hi'.

A'haya, hasten, hasten, hasten, hasten, hasten, hasten, hasten.

XII

Iku',   iku',   a'haya;   iku',   iku',   a'haya.
Hasten,   hasten,   a'haya;   hasten,   hasten,   a'haya.

> A___ ha'____i____hi'____a____ha'____i____hi'.

A'haya,   iku',   iku',   iku',   iku',   iku',   iku',   iku'.
A'haya,   hasten,   hasten,   hasten,   hasten,   hasten,   hasten,   hasten.

Ascending to the roof of the Chu'pawa ki'wi'sinĕ, the Ko'yemshi, who is carrying 'Kiäklo, seats him upon a blanket. Before 'Kiäklo enters the ki'wi'sinĕ the following dialogue takes place between him and the Ko'yemshi:

'Kiäklo. 'Kiäklo, 'Kiäklo, 'Kiäklo, Ho'o kwa'to (I enter).

Ko'yemshi. Klu'u (Good-by).

'Kiäklo. Ton o'tiptu (You will dance).

Ko'yemshi. Eh Si, hon o'tipshe (Yes, we will dance).

'Kiäklo. Ho'o sham'li kwai'i (In the morning I will come out).

The first body of A'shiwanni, the Ko'mosona, the Ko'pekwin, and the people of the Chu'pawa ki'wi'sinĕ are assembled to receive 'Kiäklo. The pe'kwĭn (sun priest) and the three members of the organization to which the personator of 'Kiäklo belongs sit in line on the north ledge. A line of meal extends from the base of the ladder to the ledge on the north side of the ki'wi'sinĕ and is crossed by four equidistant lines of meal. When 'Kiäklo descends into the ki'wi'sinĕ he stands at the base of the ladder while the Ko'yemshi, who remain on the roof, repeat the twelfth stanza of the song four times. He now steps upon the first cross line and remains while the same stanza is again repeated four times, and this repetition occurs as 'Kiäklo stands on each cross line. On reaching the end of the line 'Kiäklo takes his seat and repeats the history myth, which is begun at sunrise.[a]

---

[a] This most sacred of myths was secured first from the director of the body of men who have it in their keeping and afterward from a second man of the body, neither one knowing that the other had recited the myth. The only difference in these two recitations was the addition of two words by the second man. This is the only instance where the writer has not had all oral information verified by three or more priests or theurgists.

HISTORY MYTH OF THE COMING OF THE A'SHIWI AS NARRATED BY ᵗKĬÄKLO

The following are the principal characters and objects which appear in this history.

Pi'ᵗläshiwanni te'yona, elder and younger brother Bow priests of the place.
Pi'ᵗläshiwanni te'yona,

Pau'tiwa, director-general of Ko'thluwala'wa.

ᵗKĭäklo, deputy to director-general.

A'wan tä'chu Ko'yemshi, great father of the ancestral gods.

KĬa'kwemosi, director of the house of houses.

Pe'kwĭn, deputy to the Sun Father.

Ét'towe,[a] fetishes for rains and fructification.

[Free translation]

Narrator. Now we (the Zuñis) come through the hole which is emptied of water for our passage and afterward fills with water, and we inhale the sacred breath of A'wonawil'ona.[b] While we are in the fourth world, the blackness-of-soot world, our great fathers, Bow priests of the place, work for us. The elder brother does not care to perform the mysteries alone, but wishes his younger brother to join him in his wonderful work.

Elder brother. This light (pointing above) is what we are looking for. I have thought it all over. I want my younger brother of the place very much.

[Text and interlinear translation.]

Narrator.

No'mihlte hon ji'miᵗkĭanapkĭatea.[c]
Now   we   Ji'miᵗkĭanapkĭatea.

A'witĕn te'hula, an'nociyän te'hula. Ho'no li'ᵗla a'teyaye'.
Fourth   world,   blackness-of-soot   world.   We   here   remain.

Ho'nawa   a'wan   a'täᵗchu   a'piᵗläshiwanni   te'yona,
Our   great   fathers,   Bow priests   of the place,

I'mätiĕlᵗla,[d]   yäm yu'yanamonakĭa.[e]
Do not wish,   possessing all knowledge, fearing nothing to gain the end.

Elder brother.

Lu'kĭa   te'kohannan   teshuna'kĭa.   Zem'akwiwe   ya'kĭakĭa.
This   light of day   looking for.   Mind   finished.[f]
[pointing above]

Yäm   suwe   te'yona   än'teshema   ti'kĭa.
My   younger brother   of the place   want   very much.

---

a See p. 163.

b See p. 22.

c Referring to water disappearing for the time being from the opening in the earth through which the A'shiwi came to this world (see p. 26).

d Referring to the Divine Ones not wishing the A'shiwi to remain in the undermost world.

e The term is applied to one possessing all power and using the power only for good. It is in this reference the term is applied to the Pi'ᵗläshiwanni te'yona. The elder brother did not wish to perform the mysteries alone, but desired that his younger brother should join him in his wonderful work.

f Referring to having thought a matter over.

Narrator. The younger brother hastens.

Younger brother. Now, do you want me very much? What do you wish? What do you wish to say? Do you wish a great talk? All right; let me know what you wish to talk about.

Elder brother. I am thinking all the time of one thing; for many days I have concentrated my thoughts on the one thing; I am thinking seriously that I will remain here for a time to aid my people.

Narrator. The elder and younger brothers of the place talk to one another.

The two cut down the pine tree of the North (Pinus ponderosa); the two cut down the spruce (Pseudotsuga douglassii) of the West; the two cut down the aspen (Populus tremuloides) of the South; the two cut down the silver spruce (Picea pungens) of the East.[a]

Elder brother. Over there in the fourth (undermost) world, we sit down to talk together on serious subjects.

Narrator.

A'nanamei'kĭashetikĭäkĭa.
He hastened.

Younger brother.

E'mala kĭäma,	ho'mo	to'o	an'teshema	ti'kĭa;	ma'imati?
Now	me	you	want	very much;	what do you wish?

Chaup hincho'li	pe'nane te'yu'hlanna	te'akĭana?
What do you wish to say	talk big	have?

Te'wunau'sona,	ho'mo	to'o	yu'yakĭäkĭa.
All right,	me	you	let know.

Elder brother.

Ho'o	u'sona i'semaku'na.	Ho'o	te'wananĕ te'yakĭana.
I	thinking always of one thing.	I	many days one place think on one thing done.

Narrator.

An su'we	te'yona	le'achi iyäntikwa'kĭa.
His younger brother of the place		they [b] talk to one another.

Ä'shekĭa	a'chi	kĭa'wulkwikĭa;
Pine tree of north	the two	cut down;

Kĭa'lä'silo	a'chi	kĭa'wulkwikĭa;
Spruce tree of the west	the two	cut down;

'Hlän'ilkoha	a'chi	kĭa'wulkwikĭa;
Aspen of south	the two	cut down;

Lo'kwimo	a'chi	kĭa'wulkwikĭa.
Silver spruce of the east	the two	cut down.

Elder brother.

Thlo'kwa	a'witĕn	te'hula	ho'no	ti'nan	'la'kiye.
Over there	fourth	world	we	sat down together to talk on serious subjects.	

---

[a] It is understood by the narrator and others that the trees of the four regions were used as a means of ascent from the lower worlds.

[b] Referring to the elder and younger brothers.

Over there in water-moss (third) world, we sat down to talk together on serious subjects.

Over there in mud (second) world, we sat down to talk together on serious subjects.

Over there in wing (first) world,[a] we sat down to talk together on serious subjects. Over there our fathers[b] are near by. We see all of our children; they are not happy there. It is dark inside; we can not see one another.

We step on one another's toes. We are looking for the light; all must look for it; this light (pointing above) we are looking for. I have thought it over; this is what you want very much; all wish our rain-priest father of the North.

Narrator. They[c] talked to one another. The two wished the rain priest of the North very much.

Thlo′kwa a′wisho te′hula ho′no ti′nan ′la′kiye.
Over there water-moss world we sat down together to talk on serious subjects.

Thlo′kwa pä′nula te′hula ho′no ti′nan ′la′kiye.
Over there mud world we sat down together to talk on serious subjects.

Thlo′kwa la′tow[a] te′hula ho′no ti′nan ′la′kiye.
Over there sunbeam world we sat down together to talk on serious subjects.

Thlo′kwa le′witea yäm a′tä*chu.[b]
Over there near by our fathers.

A′wa ho′nawa te′apkunan u′natikĭakĭa.
All our children see.

Elth′kwa e′lutea te′ämmĕ.
Not happy there.

Ko′wi te′kwĭn u′lia; elth′kwa ho′no i′yunawamĕ.
Little dark inside; can not we see one another.

Ho′no i′yachu′shle nan′nule.
We step on one another.

Lukĭa te′kohannan te′shunakĭa; zem′akwiwe yakĭakĭa.
This light [pointing above] looking for; mind finished.

Le′nakĭa to′o thlo än′teshema ti′kĭa.
That is what you all want very much.

Tĕmta′i pĭsh′le shi′wanni ho′nawa tä*chu i′likĭana.
All want north rain priest our father have.

Narrator.

Le′achi[c] i′yantikwakĭa. A′chi pĭshle shi′wanni än′teshema tikĭa;
They talked together. The two, north rain priest want very much:

---

[a] Wing; in this world was seen the first glimpse of sunlight, the beams penetrating through the opening in the earth. Sunbeams are called the sun's la′tŏwwe (wings). All this is distinctly understood by those versed in the ′Kiäklo myth.

[b] A′shiwanni (rain priests).

[c] Elder and younger brother (Divine Ones).

He hastened, carrying his precious things[a] clasped to his breast.

Elder brother. All wish our rain-priest father of the West.

Narrator. They talked together. The two wished the rain priest of the West very much. He hastened, carrying his precious things clasped to his breast.

Elder brother. All wish our rain-priest father of the South.

Narrator. They talk together. The two wish the rain priest of the South very much. He hastens, carrying his precious things clasped to his breast.

Elder brother. All wish our rain-priest father of the East.

An'anamei'kĭashetikĭäkĭa,   yäm   ĕl'leteliwe   yäm   ʻkĭaĕttowe,[a]
He hastens,   his   precious things, his   rain and crop
                                                              fetishes,

yäm chu'ĕttowe, yäm mu'ĕttowe, yäm ʻhle'ĕttowe ʻhle'iyan
his rain and crop his rain and crop his rain and crop carries
    fetishes,   fetishes,   fetishes

te'chikĭanapkĭa.
at his breast.

Elder brother.

Tĕmta'i käl'ishi shi'wanni ho'nawa tä ᵗchu i'likĭana.
All want west rain priest   our   father   have.

Narrator.

Le'achi i'yantikwakĭa. A'chi kälishi shi'wanni an'teshema tikĭa.
They   talked together. The two, west rain priest   want   very
                                                               much.

An'anameikĭashetikĭäkĭa,   yäm   ĕl'leteliwe,   yäm   chu'ĕttowe,
He hastened,   his   precious things, his   rain and crop
                                                        fetishes,

yäm mu'ĕttowe,   yäm ʻthle'ĕttowe   ʻhle'iyan te'chikĭa'napkĭa.
his rain and crop his rain and crop   carries at his breast.
     fetishes,   fetishes

Elder brother.

Tem'ta'ʻi äla'ho shi'wanni ho'nawa tä ᵗchu i'likĭana.
All want   south rain priest our   father   have.

Narrator.

Le'achi i'yantikwakĭa. A'chi älaho shi'wanni än'teshema ti'kĭa.
They   talked together. The two, south rain priest want   very
                                                              much.

A'nanamei'kĭashetikĭäkĭa,   yäm   ĕl'leteliwe,   yäm   ʻkĭa'ĕttowe,
He hastens,   his   precious things, his   rain and crop
                                                        fetishes,

yäm chu'ĕttowe,   yäm mu'ĕttowe,   yäm ʻhle'ĕttowe
his rain and crop his rain and crop his rain and crop
     fetishes,   fetishes,   fetishes

ʻhle'iyan te'chi kĭa'napkĭa.
carries   at his breast.

Elder brother.

Tĕmta'i te'makoha shi'wanni ho'nawa tä ᵗchu i'likĭana.
All want east   rain priest our   father   have.

---

[a] Fetishes to bring rains and crops.

Narrator. They talk together. The two wish the rain priest of the East very much. He hastens, carrying his precious things clasped to his breast. They stoop over and come out through the place [a] which was filled with water, the water disappearing for the time being to permit the A'shiwi to pass. The two meet.

Elder brother. All wish the Middle place; we must look for the Middle of the world; we are on the road. Our great fathers and our people stop here together.

Narrator. Our great fathers talked together. Here they arose and moved on. They stooped over and came out from the fourth world, carrying their precious things [b] clasped to their breasts.

Narrator.

Le'achi	i'yantikwakĭa.	A'chi	te'makoha shi'wanni	än'teshema
They	talk together.	The two,	east rain priest	want

ti'kĭa.
very much.

A'nanamei'kĭashetikĭakĭa,	yäm	ĕl'leteliwe,	yäm	ᵗkĭa'ĕttowe,
He hastens,		his	precious things,	his	rain and crop fetishes,

yäm	chu'ĕttowe,	yäm	mu'ĕttowe,	yäm	ᵗhle'ĕttowe
his	rain and crop fetishes,	his	rain and crop fetishes,	his	rain and crop fetishes

ᵗhle'iyan	te'chi	kĭa'napkĭa.
carries		at his breast.

Yäm	ᵗkĭashima	te'litokwi [a]	i'tinakna,	kwai'ikĭa.
Our water		inside place	stoop,	come out.

A'chi	i'onaĕllatekĭa.
The two	meet. [c]

Elder brother.

Tĕm'ta'i	i'tiwannan	te'shuna	ho'no	a'wona	i'likĭana.
All want	middle	looking for	we	road	have.

Ho'nawa	a'wan	a'täᵗchu	yu'ᵗlakĭtina.
Our	great	fathers	stop together.

Tĕmĭs'kon?	ho'nawa	yu'ᵗlakĭtina.
All here?	we	stop together.

Narrator.

Ho'nawa	a'wan	a'täᵗchu	le'achi	i'yantikwakĭa.
Our	great	fathers	they	talked together.

Ĭs'ko	thlu'walemaku;	a'witĕn	te'hula [d]	i'tinakna,	kwai'ikĭa.
Here	they arose;	fourth	world	stoop,	come out.

Yäm	ĕl'leteliwe,	yäm	ᵗkĭaĕttowe,	yäm	chu'ĕttowe,	yäm
Their	precious things,	their	rain and crop fetishes,	their	rain and crop fetishes,	their

mu'ĕttowe,	yäm	ᵗhle'ĕttowe	ᵗhle'iyan	te'chi	kĭa'napkĭa.
rain and crop fetishes,	their	rain and crop fetishes	carry		at their breasts.

---

[a] Referring to the A'shiwi (Zuñis) coming through Ji'mĭᵗkĭanapkĭatea to this world (see p. 26).

[b] Ĕt'towe, fetishes to bring rains and crops.

[c] The elder brother precedes the younger to this world, and they are followed by many people. The younger one, following later, joins his brother, and the others come after him; hence the expression.

[d] The narrator, after mentioning the arrival of the A'shiwi in the outer world, goes back and relates their coming through the inner worlds.

They stooped over and came out from moss world, carrying their precious things clasped to their breasts.

They stooped over and came out from mud world, carrying their precious things clasped to their breasts.

They stooped over and came out from wing or sun rays world, carrying their precious things clasped to their breasts.

They stooped over and came out and saw their Sun Father and inhaled the sacred breath of the light of day.

Second-world place, third-world place, fourth-world place.[a]

Following their road of exit, they stooped over and came out.

They walked this way.

They came to the gaming-stick spring.

They came to the gaming-ring spring.

They came to the Ne'wekwe[b] baton spring.

They came to the spring with prayer plume standing.

They came to the cat-tail place.

They came to the moss spring.

They came to the muddy spring.

They came to the sun-ray spring.

They came to the spring by many aspens.

They came to shell place.

I'tinakna,   kwai'ikĭa.   A'wisho   te'hula   i'tinakna,   kwai'ikĭa.
Stoop,   come out.   Moss   world   stoop,   come out.

Pä'nanula   te'hula   i'tinakna,   kwai'ikĭa.
Mud   world   stoop,   come out.

Latôw   te'hula   i'tinakna,   kwai'ikĭa.
Wing   world   stoop,   come out.

Yäm   yä'tokĭa   tä'chu   än'tekohannanĕ   u'natikĭanapkĭa.
Their   sun   father   light of day,   inhale the sacred breath.

Kwĭl'li   kĭana'na   hai'i   kĭana'na   a'witĕn   kĭana'na.
Second-world place,   third-world place,   fourth-world place.

Yäm   o'neya'hlan   kwai'ina   i'tinakna,   kwai'ikĭa.   Kĭa''la   a'wakĭa.
Their   great road   exit   stoop,   come out.   This way   come.

Yä'munĕ   'kĭai'akwi   a'wikĭa.   'Si'kon   'kĭai'akwi   a'wikĭa.
Gaming-stick   spring   come to.   Gaming-ring   spring   come to.

Tä'nin   'kĭai'akwi   a'wikĭa.   Ta'melän   'kĭai'akwi   a'wikĭa
Ne'wekwe   spring   come to.   Prayer plume   spring   come to.
baton   standing.

Ke'yatiwa   kwi   a'wikĭa.   A'wisho   'kĭai'akwi   a'wikĭa.
Cat-tail   place   come to.   Moss   spring   come to.

Pä'nanulin   'kĭai'akwi   a'wikĭa.   La'tŏw   'kĭai'akwi   a'wikĭa.
Muddy   spring   come to.   Sunbeam   spring   come to.

'Hlän'ihlkoha   'kĭai'akwi   a'wikĭa.   U'pu'lema   kwi   a'wikĭa.
Aspen   spring   come to.   Shell   place   come to.

---

[a] Referring to passing through the interior worlds.

[b] Galaxy fraternity.

They came to dragon-fly place.

They came to flower place.

They came to the place of trees with drooping limbs.

They came to fish spring.

They came to young-squash spring.

They came to listening spring.[a]

Our great father old dance man; our great mother old dance woman.[b]

They possess much knowledge; they finished the rivers.[c]

They possess much knowledge; they made Ko'thluwala'wa mountain.

Elder brother. All wish our great fathers, the ᵗKĭa'ĕttowe, Chu'ĕttowe, Mu'ĕttowe, ᵗHle'ĕttowe (rain and crop fetishes.)

Narrator. They passed between the mountains.[d] It is far to the Middle of the world.

Pä̆ᵗsi[e]　shi'na　kwi　a'wikĭa.　U'teyan　ĭn'kwi　a'wikĭa.
Dragon fly　name　place　come to.　Flower　place　come to.

Ta'piliyänku　kwi　a'wikĭa.　Käsh'ita　ᵗkĭai'akwi　a'wikĭa.
Trees with drooping limbs　place　come to.　Fish　spring place　come to.

Mo'län[f]　ᵗkĭai'akwi　a'wikĭa.　Hä'tin[a]　ᵗkĭai'akwi　a'wikĭa.
Young squash　spring　come to.　Listen　spring　come to.

Ho'nawa　a'wan　tä̆ᵗchu　hona'wa　a'wan　ᵗsi'ta.
Our　great　father,　our　great　mother.

Yäm　änikwa　nan'nakkĭa.
They　know　many things.

A'chi　ᵗkĭap'yaᵗhlannĕ　ya'kĭakĭa;　yäm änikwa　nan'nakkĭa.
The two,　rivers　made;　they know　many things.

Ä'chi　Ko'thluwala　yäl'lännĕ　an'nimukĭa.
The two　Ko'thluwala'wa　mountain　made.

Elder brother:

Tĕm'ta'i　hona'wa　a'wan　a'tä̆ᵗchu　i'likĭana　ᵗkĭa'ĕttowe,
All want　our　great　fathers　have　rain and crop fetishes,

chu'ĕttowe,　mu'ĕttowe,　ᵗhle'ttowe.
rain and crop fetishes,　rain and crop fetishes,　rain and crop fetishes.

Narrator:

Kĭăᵗla　a'wimpikwaiikĭa　kwai'ikĭa.　La'lekhoᵗli　i'tiwanna.
Come　passed between,　come out.　There where　middle.

---

[a] Hä'tin means to listen, to hear, and is the name for the waters of Ko'thluwala'wa. The expression has reference to the hearing of voices in the depths of the water.

[b] The two original ancestral gods (see p. 33).

[c] The brother makes the beds of the rivers (Zuñi and Little Colorado) by drawing his foot through the sands, and the sister follows in the path (see p. 32).

[d] References to the ĕt'towe being carried by the A'shiwanni between Kor'kokshi and Ko'yemshi mountains, which are near Ko'thluwala'wa, as the A'shiwi proceed in their quest for the Middle place.

[e] Pä̆ᵗsi is archaic for shu'makolowa (plural shu'makolowe), dragon fly, one of the rain symbols of the A'shiwi.

[f] This spring is associated with the Ko'yemshi gods (see p. 33).

Our great fathers![a] our great mothers![b]

Here we will sit perfectly still for days, which will be precious, and our hearts will speak with the gods of the inside water place;[c] all wish to meet together.

Sun priest (deputy to Sun Father). Here we will sit perfectly still, not moving body or limb; where can we talk together?

Kĭa'kwemosi (Director-general of the House of Houses). Sun priest of the Dogwood clan knows.

Sun priest. Much thought has been given to finding a place; one has been found; give no further thought to it.

Narrator. Our great fathers[d] sit perfectly still. There we can talk with them. Now all my children are happy together.

Hona′wa   a′wan   a′täᵗchu[e]   hona′wa   a′wan   a′ᵗsita,

Our   great   fathers,   our   great   mothers,

Liᵗla   ho′no   yuᵗlakĭt′ikĭa,   a′wante′wananně   a′kĭa.[f]

Here   we   sit perfectly still,   precious days   continue.

Yäm   ᵗkĭa′shima   te′litokwi.   Těmᵗla   än′teshema   ti′na   i′wokwikĭa.

Our   water   inside place.   All   wish   meet   together.

Pĕ′kwĭn:

Liᵗla ho′no yuᵗlakĭtikĭa. Ho′ᵗli ko′na te′kwiyashuwan te′yakĭa′na?

Here   we   sit perfectly still.   Where   can   talk to one another   together?

Kĭa′kwemosi:

Pi′chikwe   a′nota   pe′kwĭn[g]   shi′wanni   lu′kon   a′nawakĭa.

Dogwood   clan   sun   priest,   he   knows.

Pĕ′kwĭn:

An′ᵗseman a′ninena; kĭa′me ton an′ᵗseman a′ninenawe.[h]

A place has been found; give no further thought to it.

Narrator:

Hona′wa   a′wan   a′täᵗchu[d]   yuᵗlakĭtikĭa.

Our   great   fathers   sit perfectly still.

Ma′leko[c]   yä′shuwan   te′yakĭana.

There   we can talk   together.

La′ki   ho′ma   a′wan   te′apkunan   kets′anishi   a′teyakĭa′na.

Now   my   all   children   happy   together.

---

[a] ᵗKĭa′ĕttowe (see p. 163).

[b] Chu′ĕttowe (see p. 163).

[c] Ko′thluwala′wa.

[d] The gods of Ko′thuluwala′wa.

[e] The ᵗkĭačttoně (ᵗkĭa from ᵗkĭa′we, water) is referred to as father, the chu′ĕttoně (chu from chuwe, seeds) as mother.

[f] The unexpressed idea is that one will remain perfectly quiet, not moving the body or limbs, during the days of retirement. The expression is used for the retreat of the A′shiwanni (see Rain priesthood). After a period of fasting and continence, perfect repose of body, and concentration of thought, the physical and grosser nature becomes separated from the spiritual nature, leaving it free to commune with A′wonawil′ona (see p. 22) and the gods.

[g] The literal translation of the word pe′kwĭn is deputy, and in the above case the reference is to the deputy of the Sun Father. This priest, however, is referred to simply as the sun priest or priest of the Zenith.

[h] This expression is not translated literally. The meaning is that much thought has been given to finding a place for the retreat of the rain priests.

M. W. Wright Gill.

GROUP OF NE'WEKWE (GALAXY FRATERNITY). HE'IWA (NORTH) KI'WI'SINĔ, CHAMBER DEDICATED TO ANTHROPIC WORSHIP, IN REAR

BAUBLE OF NE'WEKWE (GALAXY FRATERNITY)

MASK OF PAU'TIWA front and side views

CLOUD SYMBOL AND FETISHES OF THE SHÍWANNI (RAIN PRIEST) OF THE NADIR

Here we finish our prayer plumes.

There [a] our fathers the Council of the Gods will receive them.

Pau'tiwa. Our great fathers, ᵗKĭa'ĕttowe, Chu'ĕttowe, Mu'ĕttowe, ᵗHle'ĕttowe, passed between the mountains to find the Middle of the world, where they sit perfectly still.

Who is a good man? Who possesses much wisdom?

A member of the Council of the Gods. Over there, in the room above, sitting in the hatchway. Everybody knows ᵗKĭäklo of the place; this man knows much.

Pau'tiwa. Now, I wish some one to tell him to come.

Narrator. He hastens, comes in, and sits down.

Li''la   ho'nawe   te'likinawe   a'yakĭanap'kĭa.
Here   our   prayer plumes   finished.

La'lek   la'ki   ho'nawe   a'täᵗchu   i'likĭana.
There   now   our   fathers   have.

Yäm   ᵗkĭa'shima   te'litonan'kwi   i'änteshema.
Our   water   inside place   wish.

Te'likinawe   a'yakĭanap'ᵗkĭa,   la'lekhoᵗli   ho'nawa   Kok'ko A'wan.
Prayer plumes   finished,   there   our   Council of the Gods.

Te'likinawe   i'tiuhlᵗla,   kĭanapkĭa. [b]
Prayer plumes   placed together,   finished.

Pau'tiwa:

Ho'nawe   a'wan   a'täᵗchu   ᵗkĭa'ĕttowe,   chu'ĕttowe,   mu'ĕttowe,
Our   great   fathers

   ᵗhle'ĕttowe,   a'wimpikwekĭa,   kwai'ikĭa; [c]
                   passed between,   come out;

La'lekhoᵗli   i'tiwanna   le'anakĭa'nankwi   yu'ᵗlakitikĭa.
There   middle   name place   sit perfectly still.

Li''la   ko'lehoᵗli   ᵗse'manapkĭa.   Chaup   ᵗse'mak   änikwa   kian'na.
Here   how   think.   What   man   knows   much.

A member of the Council of the Gods:

ᵗHlo'kwa   te'koskwa   im'koskwi.
Over there   room above   sitting in hatchway.

E'ᵗsakĭanna   ᵗKĭäklo   te'yona;   lu'kon   ᵗse'mak   änikwa   kian'na.
Everybody knows   ᵗKĭäklo   of the place;   this   man   knows   much.

Pau'tiwa:

Te'wuna   än'teshema   ti'nawe.
Now   wish   tell him to come.

Narrator:

A'nanamei'kĭashetikĭakĭa, [d]   ikia,   imiteᵗla'kukĭa.
He hastened,   came,   sat down.

---

[a] Referring to Ko'thluwala'wa.

[b] Referring to planting prayer plumes, which are afterward received by the gods of Ko'thluwala'wa.

[c] Referring to the ĕt'towe passing between the mountains near Ko'thluwala'wa

[d] Referring to ᵗKĭäk'lo.

ᵗKïäklo. I am here.   What do you wish of me?   You wished me to
  come.   What do you wish to say?   Do you wish to talk much
  together?

Pau'tiwa. There in I'tiwanna (Middle name place) our great fathers
  sit perfectly still.

  You will tell the great ones to count the days one by one, and in
  eight days the gods will go over the road and meet all our fathers.
  We will go over the road and meet them; we will meet all our fathers.

  Now, think of some.   Perhaps all are gathered.   Good!   No, I
  have not my North father of the place, the god with the scapula
  of the yellow deer of the North; the god with the scapula of the

---

ᵗKiäklo:

  Li'ᵗla,   kon   iyanteku'nakĭa?
  Here,   what do you wish of me?

  E'malakĭama   ho'o   to'o   än'teshema   ti'napkĭa.
  Now   I   you   wish   come here?

  Ma'imati   chaup   hĭn'choᵗli   pe'nane   teyu   ᵗhlanna?
  Now   what wish   talk   big?

  ᵗHlan'na   pe'nän   te'yakĭäna?
  Big   talk   together?

Pau'tiwa:

  La'lekho'ᵗli   i'tiwanna   le'anakĭa'nankwi
  There   middle   name place

  Ho'nawa   a'wan   a'täᵗchu ᵃ   yu'ᵗlakĭtikĭa. ᵇ   A'wona   ĕllatekia'na. ᶜ
  Our   great   fathers   sit perfectly still.   Road   meet.

  A'wa   yal'lenan   pi'lakĭana.
  All   count   days one by one,

  La'lekho'ᵗli   yäm   a'täᵗchu   to'no   a'wona   ĕl'latekĭa'na.
  There   your fathers   you   road   will meet.

  A'wati   tela'ma   to'no   i'techuna   i'ku   kia'tekwi. ᵈ
  Four   steps   you   will take   hasten   reach place.

  Lĕs'si   te'wanna,   hĭn'choli   hai'elikkĭa   te'wakia.
  So many days,   wish   eight   days.

  Te'aan'na   tĕmᵗlamo   yäm   a'täᵗchu   a'wona   ĕl'latekĭa'na.
  After   all   our   fathers   road   meet.

  Yäm   a'täᵗchu ᵉ   tĕmᵗlamo   ho'no   a'wona   ĕl'letekĭa'na.
  Our   fathers   all of them   we   road   meet.

  E'malákĭama,   i'yantesemanawe. ᶠ   Ho'lon   tĕmᵗla   ha'pona   kok'shiye.
  Now,   think of some.   Perhaps   all   gathered,   good.

  Elth'ᵗla,   kwali'wan   ĕm'pishlan kwinta'na ho'o   tä'ᵗchu   i'li   te'yona.
  No,   not this way   north   my   father   have of the place.

  Kok'ko   ᵗhlup'ᵗsina   kĭai sälimon   ᵗhlupᵗsina   il'ona;
  God   yellow   deer scapula   yellow   got;

  ᵃ A'shiwanni (rain priests).
  ᵇ A'shiwi (the Zuñis) have found the Middle place and ceased their journeying.
  ᶜ Referring to the A'shiwi meeting the gods from Ko'thluwala'wa.
  ᵈ Present site of Zuñi.
  ᵉ The A'shiwi (Zuñis).
  ᶠ Reference to thinking of men who will serve the purpose.

blue deer of the West; the god with the scapula of the red deer of the South; the god with the scapula of the white deer of the East; the god with the scapula of the every-colored deer of the Zenith; the god with the scapula of the black deer of the Nadir.

I wish the god with wood ears on his mask very much.

I wish the god with the wool cap very much.

I wish the god possessing many deer very much.

I wish the god A'nahoho[a] very much.

I wish the god Shu'laawiᵗsi very much.

I wish the gods who carry reed staffs ornamented with twigs of the spruce tree of the west[b] very much.

I wish the shaker, the great director, who goes about, very much.

I wish all of the gods with blue-horned masks very much.

Kok′ko	ᵗhli′anna	kĭai sälimon	ᵗhli′anna	il′ona;
God	blue	deer scapula	blue	got;
Kok′ko	a′hona	kĭai′ sälimon	a′hona	il′ona;
God	red	deer scapula	red	got;
Kok′ko	ko′hanna	kĭai′ sälimon	ko′hanna	il′ona;
God	white	deer scapula	white	got;
Kok′ko	ᵗsi′lipäna	kĭai′ sälimon	ᵗsi′lipäna	il′ona;
God	every color	deer scapula	every color	got;
Kok′ko	shikĭan′na	kĭai′ sälimon	shikĭanna	il′ona;
God	black	deer scapula	black	got;

| Än′teshema | ti′nakĭa. | ᵗHle′lashoctipona | än′teshema | ti′nakĭa. |
| Want | very much. | Wood ear | want | very much. |

| U′poyona | än′teshema | ti′nakía. |
| Wool cap | want | very much. |

| Na′wisho[c] | än′teshema | ti′nakĭa. | A′nahoho | än′teshema | ti′nakĭa. |
| Deer | want | very much. | Anahoho | want | very much. |

| Shu′laawiᵗsi | | än′teshema | ti′nakĭa. |
| Deputy to the Sun Father in Ko′thluwala′wa | | want | very much. |

| ᵗSi′tonnĕ | ᵗhle′onna[d] | än′teshema | ti′nakĭa. |
| Spruce of the west | held in hand | want | very much. |

| Hä′shi[e] | ati′nakwe | a′wan | mo′sona | än′teshema | ti′nakĭa. |
| Shaker | goes about | great | director | want | very much. |

| Sa′yaᵗhlia | a′wa | än′teshema | ti′nakĭa. |
| Horn blue | all | want | very much. |

---

[a] This mask is white with a black hand over the face.

[b] Mu′luktäkĭa (tall thin gods).

[c] So named because this god possesses many deer.

[d] The name which is usually applied to the ᵗSi′tonne gods is Mu′luktäkĭa (tall thin god). A frog decorates the back of the mask. The personators of these gods carry long reed staffs with spruce twigs attached in the middle. These staffs have feather ornamentation of a variety of bird plumes.

[e] This name is applied to ᵗKiäklo, as he continually says "häshi" and shakes his body as he proceeds and sprinkles meal when he comes at sunrise following the appearance of the gods on the eighth day (see p. 96). He comes from Ku′shilowa, and after visiting the four te′witawe (plazas) departs while it is still early day over the western road.

I wish the Plumed Serpent very much.

I wish the god Suti'ᵗki[a] very much.

I wish the suckling very much.

I wish the old dance men[b] very much.

Great father of the Ko'yemshi. Now, do you want me very much?

Pau'tiwa (addressing great father Ko'yemshi). You will go over the road with ᵗKiäklo and meet our fathers at the Middle place. You will carry this[c] for your rattle when you go to meet your fathers.

Narrator. ᵗKiäklo comes out[d] and sits down. He looks to the six regions and calls: "ᵗKiäklo, ᵗKiäklo, ᵗKiäklo, ᵗKiäklo grandfathers;[e] where are you? Carry me on your backs."

Ko'loowisi[f] än'teshema ti'nakĭa. Su'tiᵗki än'teshema ti'nakĭa.
Plumed Serpent want very much. A small bird want very much.

ᵗSi'ᵗsikĭa[g] än'teshema ti'nakĭa. Ko'yemshi[h] än'teshema ti'nakĭa.
Suckling want very much. Old dance man want very much.

Great father of the Ko'yemshi:

E'malakĭama ho'ma to'o än'teshema ti'nakĭa?
Now me you want very much?

Pau'tiwa (addressing ᵗKĭäklo):

L'alekho'li i'tiwanna kwi yäm a'täᵗchu.
There Middle place our fathers.

To'no a'wona ĕl'latekĭa'na.
You road will meet.

Lu'kĭa to'o iᵗleyana[c] yäm a'täᵗchu to'o a'wona ĕllatekĭä'na.
This you hold your fathers you road will meet.

Narrator:

ᵗKĭäklo imuna kwai'ikĭa.[i] Lĕs'si te'kwi tu'natikĭa.
ᵗKĭäklo sits down, comes out. To the six regions looks, and calls.

ᵗKĭäklo, ᵗKĭäklo, ᵗKĭäklo, ᵗKĭäklo.

A'nana,[e] hop tona'wakia? Hom i'seto'nawe.[j]
Grandfathers, where are you? Me carry on backs.

---

[a] A small bird.

[b] Ko'yemshi (see p. 33.)

[c] Referring to a duck skin filled with seeds and having a string of beads about the neck to serve as a rattle.

[d] Referring to the coming of ᵗKiäklo from the depths of the lake to the shore.

[e] The Ko'yemshi.

[f] Ko'loowisi came from the waters of the west, appearing to the A'shiwi for the first time when they went to To'wa yällänĕ to escape the great flood which swept over the earth. The impression of his head is still to be seen on the mountain side where he stopped to rest. Ko'loowisi did not return to the western waters, but went to Ko'thluwala'wa, becoming the seed-bearer of the gods to the A'shiwi.

[g] ᵗSi'ᵗsikĭa names the infants at involuntary initiation; hence the appellation "suckling."

[h] The Ko'yemshi, who were in their mountain, heard as one hears from lightning, and the A'wan täᵗchu (great father Ko'yemshi) went at once to the lake by the inner road through the mountain.

[i] ᵗKĭäklo ascends the ladder to this world from the abiding place of the Council of the Gods and sits on the bank of the lake.

[j] The Ko'yemshi, hearing in their mountain home, come to the borders of the lake, and ᵗKĭäklo mounts the back of the pe'kwĭn (deputy to the great father Ko'yemshi).

The old dance men, hearing ꞌKiäklo call, come from their mountains to the lake. ꞌKiäklo mounts the back of the deputy to the great father of the old dance men, and looks to the six regions. ꞌKiäklo, looking to the east, sees four roads close together.

ᵗKïäklo. We will take the middle road. We will come this way. Grandfathers, you will sing.

Narrator. ꞌKiäklo now recounts the travels of the ancients to the Middle of the world.

ᵗKïäklo. We come this way. We come to a large lake; here we get up and move on. We come to a valley with watercress in the middle; here we get up and move on.

We come to the stealing place; here we get up and move on.

We come to houses built in mesa walls; here we get up and move on.

We come to the last of a row of springs; here we get up and move on.

We come to the middle of a row of springs; here we get up and move on.

Lĕssi　te′kwi　te′tuna　cho′kĭa. [a]
To the　　six　　regions　　looks.

ꞌKiäklo te′luwankwi ta′na a′witĕn a′na o′neya hlawe
ꞌKiäklo　east looks　this way　four　separate　roads　close

wo′kĭapa　u′natikĭa.
together　　sees.

ᵗKïäklo:

I′tiwa　o′neyaᵗla′kowa　kĭäthl　ho′no　a′wonakĭa.
Middle　road　　　　come　we　this road.

A′nana,　te′nanawe. [b]　Kĭäthl　ho′no　a′wonakĭa. [c]
Grandfathers　sing.　　Come　we　this road.

ᵗKĭatu　hlan′na　kwi　a′wikĭa;　ĭs′ko　ᵗhluwal′emaku.
Water　big place　come to;　here　get up; move on.

Te′wulᵗla　i′tiwa　piꞌᵗkĭaia　kwi　a′wikĭa;　ĭs′ko　ᵗhluwal′emaku.
Valley　middle　watercress place　come to;　here　get up; move on.

Hän′ᵗlipĭnkĭa　kwi [d]　a′wikĭa;　ĭs′ko　thluwal′emaku.
Stealing　place　come to;　here　get up; move on.

He′ipächi　kwi [e]　a′wikĭa;　ĭs′ko　thluwal′emaku.
Wall-built　place　come to;　here　get up; move on.

ᵗKĭaia′　pälto　kwi　a′wikĭa;　ĭs′ko　thluwal′emaku.
Last series of　place　come to;　here　get up; move on.
springs.

ᵗKĭaia′　i′tiwa　kwi　a′wikĭa;　ĭs′ko　thluwal′emaku.
Middle series of　place　come to;　here　get up; move on.
springs.

---

[a] Referring to ꞌKiäklo.

[b] The song of the Ko′yemshi is begun when the gods start for I′tiwanna. Whenever the Ko′yemshi cease singing, ꞌKiäklo strikes the one who carries him with his rattle and calls for more singing.

[c] ꞌKiäklo now recounts to the A′shiwi the travels of the ancients from Ko′thluwala′wa to I′tiwanna.

[d] So named from plume wands, deposited for rain, which were stolen by a witch, thus causing the rains to cease. The plume wands were afterward secured by a shi′wanni (rain priest), thus averting calamity.

[e] Cliff dwellings.

We come again to the middle of a row of springs; here we get up and move on.

We come to the house of Ko'loowisi; here we get up and move on.

We come to watercress place; here we get up and move on.

We come to a small spring; here we get up and move on.

We come to a spring in a hollow place in a mound, hidden by tall bending grasses; here we get up and move on.

We come to ashes spring; here we get up and move on.

We come to high-grass spring; here we get up and move on.

We come to rainbow spring; here we get up and move on.

We come to place of the Sha'läko; here we get up and move on.

We come to the place with many springs;[a] here we get up and move on.

We come to moss place; here we get up and move on.

I'tiwa ᵗkĭaia'[b] kwi a'wikĭa; ĭs'ko thluwal'emaku.
Middle series of place   come to;   here   get up; move on.
     springs

Ko'loowisi ᵗkĭakwe kwi a'wikĭa; ĭs'ko thluwal'emaku.
Plumed Serpent   house   place   come to;   here   get up; move on.

Piᵗkĭaia kwi a'wikĭa; ĭs'ko thluwal'emaku.
Watercress   place   come to;   here   get up; move on.

Kĭatsi ᵗkĭaia' kwi a'wikĭa; ĭs'ko thluwal'emaku.
Small   spring   place   come to;   here   get up; move on.

Po'showa[c] kwi a'wikĭa ĭs'ko thluwal'emaku.
Spring in cavity   place   come to;   here   get up; move on.
   in a mound

Lu'kĭana ᵗkĭaia'kwi a'wikĭa; ĭs'ko thluwal'emaku.
   Ashes   spring   come to;   here   get up; move on.

To'seluna[d] ᵗkĭaia' a'wikĭa; ĭs'ko thluwal'emaku.
High-grass   spring place   come to;   here   get up; move on.

A'mitolan ᵗkĭaia'kwi a'wikĭa; ĭs'ko thluwal'emaku.
Rainbow   spring   come to;   here   get up; move on.

Sha'läko ᵗkĭaia'kwi[e] a'wikĭa; ĭs'ko thluwal'emaku.
Sha'läko   spring   come to;   here   get up; move on.

ᵗKĭap'kwena kwi·[f] awiᵗkĭa; ĭs'ko thluwal'emaku.
Many-springs   place   come to;   here   get up, move on.

U'hana[g] kwi a'wikĭa; ĭs'ko thluwal'emaku.
Moss   place   come to;   here   get up, move on.

---

[a] Named by the Spaniards Ojo Caliente.

[b] The two springs are called the middle springs, as they are supposed to be centrally situated between the others mentioned.

[c] A spring so covered by bending grasses from all sides as to leave but a small opening, which can be seen only when one is very near. The spring referred to is sacred to the gods of Ko'thluwala'wa.

[d] The largest of the springs at Ojo Caliente.

[e] During the A'shiwi migrations the Sha'läko gods appeared to them through this spring; hence the name. The places here mentioned were named by the A'shiwi as they stopped from time to time in their quest of the Middle place. ᵗKiäklo relates to those of I'tiwanna the places named by their fathers.

[f] ᵗKiap'kwenakwi or ᵗKiapkwena is the Zuñi name for Ojo Caliente.

[g] U'hana is another name for a'wisho (moss); it is also the Zuñi name for wool.

We come to stone-lodged-in-a-cleft place; here we get up and move on.

We come to stone-picture place;[a] here we get up and move on.

We come to poison-oak place; here we get up and move on.

We come to a spring in a mesa wall; here we get up and move on.

We come to rush place; here we get up and move on.

We come to a place of bad-smelling water; here we get up and move on.

We come to the place of sack of meal hanging;[b] here we get up and move on.

We come to the blue-jay spring;[c] here we get up and move on.

We come to Corn mountain; here we get up and move on.

We come to the spring at the base of the mesa;[d] here we get up and move on.

We come to the ant-entering place; here we get up and move on.

We come to vulva[e] spring; here we get up and move on.

A'ᵗlapäᵗsi   kwi   a'wikĭa;   ĭs'ko   thluwal'emaku.
Stone held between place   come to;   here   get up; move on.
two other stones

A'ᵗsina'kwi   a'wikĭa;   ĭs'ko   thluwal'emaku.
Stone-picture place come to;   here   get up; move on.

Pi'shuᵗkĭaia'kwi   a'wikĭa;   ĭs'ko   thluwal'emaku.
Poison-oak spring   come to;   here   get up; move on.

ᵗKĭa'nuhlᵗhla'kwi   a'wikĭa;   ĭs'ko   thluwal'emaku.
Mesa wall spring place come to;   here   get up; move on.

To'loknäna   kwi   a'wikĭa;   ĭs'ko   thluwal'emaku.
Rushes   place   come to;   here   get up; move on.

ᵗKĭa'techi   kwi   a'wikĭa;   ĭs'ko   thluwal'emaku.
Bad-smelling   place   come to;   here   get up; move on.

O'pompia[b]   kwi   a'wikĭa;   ĭs'ko   thluwal'emaku.
Sack of meal   place   come to;   here   get up; move on.
hanging

A'yaya[c]   ᵗkĭaia'kwi   a'wikĭa;   ĭs'ko   thluwal'emaku.
Blue-jay   spring   come to;   here   get up; move on.

To'wa   yäl'la   kwi   a'wikĭa;   ĭs'ko   thluwal'emaku.
Corn   mountain   place   come to;   here   get up; move on.

I'teᵗla'kup   ᵗkĭaia   a'wikĭa;[d]   ĭs'ko   thluwal'emaku.
At the base of   spring   come to;   here   get up; move on.
mesa

Häl'on   kwa'ton   a'wikĭa;   ĭs'ko   thluwal'emaku.
Ants   entering   come to;   here   get up; move on.

Ä'sha[e]   ᵗkĭaia   a'wiᵗkĭa;   ĭs'ko   thluwal'emaku.
Vulva   spring   come to;   here   get up; move on.

---

a Rocks with pictographs.

b O from owe, flour (corn or wheat); pompia, hanging.

c So named from the blue jays gathering about the spring to drink.

d Corn mountain.

e So named because the rock from which the water flows resembles the vulva.

We come to a spring high in the mountain; here we get up and move on.

We come to Apache spring;[a] here we get up and move on.

We come to coyote spring; here we get up and move on.

We come to salt place; here we get up and move on.

We come to a place with fumes like burning sulphur; here we get up and move on.

We come to ant place; here we get up and move on.

We come to the Middle place.

'Kĭäklo (addressing the A'shiwi). In a short time my fathers, whom I have there,[b] will meet you on the road. You will meet together. They will come, and will give to all your children more of the great breath; the breath of A'wonawil'ona; the breath of the light of day.

'Kĭa'nayältokwi   a'wikĭa;   ĭs'ko   thluwal'emaku.
Spring in high place   come to;   here   get up; move on.

Wila'ᵗsu'kĭa[a]   'kĭaia   a'wikĭa;   ĭs'ko   thluwal'emaku.
Apache   spring   come to;   here   get up; move on.

Sum   'kĭaia   a'wikĭa;   ĭs'ko   thluwal'emaku.
Coyote   spring   come to;   here   get up; move on.

Ma'ᵗsakĭa[c]   kwi   a'wikĭa;   ĭs'ko   thluwal'emaku.
Salt   place   come to;   here   get up; move on.

Ko'lin   'kĭaia'kwi[d]   a'wikĭa;   ĭs'ko   thluwal'emaku.
Odor of burn-   spring   come to;   here   get up; move on.
ing sulphur

Häl'ona[e]   kwi   a'wikia;   ĭs'ko   thluwal'emaku.
Ant   place   come to;   here   get up; move on.

I'tiwanna[f]   kwi   a'wikĭa.
Middle   place   come to.

'Kĭäklo (addressing the A'shiwi).

We'ᵗsimte'nalapa   la'lek   ho'na   a'tä'chu   i'lona.
In a short time   here   my   fathers   have.

To'no   a'wona   ĕl'latena'wa.   To'no   a'wona   ĕl'latekĭa.
You   road   will join you.   You   road   meet together.

To'ma   a'wa   te'apkunawe   a'wan   pi'nan   te'liyana'wa.
Your   all   children   great   breath   we give more.

To'no   te'kohanna   yän'ichiyanap'tu.[g]
You   light of day   inhale.

---

[a] So named because it resembles certain springs of the Apache Indians. 'Kĭaki'ma is another name for this spring, which is near a ruin of the same name.

[b] Ko'thluwala'wa.

[c] Ma'ᵗsakĭa—ma—from mawe (salt), is so named from a man having visited the Salt Mother before she left her home a few miles east of I'tiwanna and returned with a small quantity of salt to this place.

[d] The shrine symbolizing the Middle of the world, the spot upon which He'patina stands. It is claimed that this place received the name of Ko'lin from a tuft of grass pulled up by the ancients exposing black water having the odor of burning sulphur. The shrine is a few hundred yards southwest of Zuñi.

[e] Halona is the village which was occupied by the A'shiwi previous to their settling at I'tiwanna. The two are separated by the Zuñi river.

[f] Supposed to occupy the middle of the world.

[g] The body of one wearing a mask becomes the abode of the god he impersonates; he blows from his heart the breath of A'wonawil'ona upon the plumes or the hand and carries these to the mouth of another, that the sacred breath may be inhaled. The breath of A'wonawil'ona is everywhere; it is life itself.

As the narrator does not remove his mask, and as he speaks very rapidly, much that is said is lost to the hearers. Though it is supposed that this iliad is recited for the express purpose of instilling the history into the minds of the people, it is really intended that the people shall be informed about it but vaguely. The statement that this narration is begun in one ki'wi^tsinĕ and continued through ᵗKiäklo's visit to the other five is erroneous. It is repeated in full in each ki'wi^tsinĕ.

When it becomes necessary to quench his thirst, ᵗKiäklo takes popcorn water (made by grinding popped corn and mixing it with cold water) through a reed which is passed through the mouth hole of the mask. This is his only nourishment during his visit to I'tiwanna.

The directors and laymen of each ki'wi^tsinĕ are assembled to receive ᵗKiäklo, who goes directly from one to the other in the following order, and in each repeats the sacred story from beginning to end. He goes from Chu'pawa to Mu'he'wa at noon, O'he'wa at sunset, Up'ᵗsannawa at midnight, He'iwa at rising of the morning star, and He'kĭapawa at dawn, each move being made on the back of a Ko'yemshi. He leaves the He'kĭapawa in the morning about 7 o'clock, and departs over the western road to return to Ko'thluwala'wa. He talks more rapidly in the He'iwa and He'kĭapawa ki'wi^tsiwe than in the others, because the time is limited.

RABBIT HUNT WITH THE GODS.

The rabbit hunt in which personators of the gods take part occurs quadrennially after the visit of ᵗKiäklo to the village, but may occur oftener in times of great drought.

The first body of A'shiwanni including the elder and younger brother Bow priests meet in the ceremonial chamber of the latter, where they spend the night, and at sunrise the warrior of the fraternity of Hunters who is either the elder or younger brother Bow priest, notifies the fraternity that a hunt by the Kok'ko (anthropic gods) will occur in four days. Those who are to personate the gods in the hunt prepare te'likinawe the day following this announcement. They meet the same night in their ki'wi^tsiwe, rehearse their songs, and smoke.

ᵗSi'ᵗsikĭa (the suckling) and the Ko'yemshi go about the village on the fourth day inquiring for the boys to be initiated into the Ko'tikili. The male children four or five years of age are brought forward by their mothers, who declare that their little ones have no name, and request that they be named by the Ko'yemshi and ᵗSi'ᵗsikĭa, who have the naming of the children. They name girls only when they are to join the Ko'tikili. Pregnant women visit the ᵗCha'kwena[a] (who is

---

[a] The ᵗCha'kwena is the deceased Ku'yapäli^tsa (female warrior) of the Kĭa'nakwe, who carried her heart in her rattle as she walked to and fro before her army during the engagement with the A'shiwi. She was also keeper of all game (see Destruction of the Kĭa'nakwe and songs of thanksgiving).

personated by a man) in the He'kǐapawa ki'wi^tsině the same day, and wash off the pinkish paint which covers her limbs. The dress of the 'Cha'kwena at this time hangs from both shoulders and fastens up the front. The Zuñis say: "In the olden time dresses were worn in this fashion." The 'Cha'kwena gives te'likinawe to the women, to be offered to the A'wan 'Sita (Great Mother) of the children of To'wa yäl'lǎnně (Corn mountain). These te'likinawe are deposited at the mother rock (see plate XII) below the summit of this mesa. The husbands of the women frequently accompany them on this pilgrimage, which means much to them.

Later in the day the 'Cha'kwena, wearing her mask, which covers the face only, passes through the village telling the people she will give to them the game of the world. At this time 'Cha'kwena and the other gods receive many donations of food. The Säl'imobiya (warriors and seed-gatherers) of the six regions announce that they will bring all seeds to the people. After sunset these gods go over the western road and deposit the collected corn in the river for the gods at Ko'thluwala'wa, but the remainder of the food is brought back to the village and eaten. The 'Cha'kwena on the following day plants the te'likinawe given her by the personators of the gods who are to take part in the hunt.

The 'Sän'iakǐakwe assemble in their fraternity chamber on the night previous to the hunt, and the personators of the gods, including the 'Cha'kwena, wearing the masks and other paraphernalia, go from the He'kǐapawa ki'wi^tsině to the fraternity chamber of the 'Sän'iakǐakwe and dance to the accompaniment of the rattle, drum, and song of the fraternity.

The first body of A'shiwanni meet the same night in their ceremonial chamber. At sunrise on the following morning the 'Sän'iakǐakwe join the A'shiwanni. 'Cha'kwena leaves the He'kǐapawa ki'wi^tsině and, passing by the north side of the village, enters Si'aa' plaza from the east side. Proceeding to the center of the plaza, she passes to the north, west, south, and east, starting each time from the center, and then makes a circle from left to right four times around the plaza, that the rain-makers of the four regions and those of the world, the circle symbolizing the world, may cause the rains to fall upon Zuñi. She then ascends a ladder and enters the ceremonial chamber of the A'shiwanni and sits on a sacred embroidered blanket spread upon a box and crossed with sacred meal, indicative of the four cardinal points. The priest of the Zenith (sun priest) places a hand on each shoulder and motions her to the six regions, the Zenith and Nadir being indicated by a sort of raising and lowering of the shoulders, and attaches a fluffy eagle plume, colored red, to the scalp lock. The elder and younger brother Bow priests make fire with the fire sticks in the chamber of the A'shiwanni, and torches of cedar fiber are ignited. The 'Cha'kwena, accompanied by two

Ko′yemshi carrying the lighted torches, and the younger brother Bow priest follow the ′Sän′iakïakwe, who leave the chamber for the western road, carrying bread made by the wives and daughters of the first body of A′shiwanni.   The Ko′yemshi set fire to the grass and other vegetation as they proceed.   The Säl′imobiya of the six regions, ′Hle′lashok-tĭpona (Wood-ears), U′poyona (Wool-cap), and Na′wisho (Owner of many deer), pass over the road, following the ′Cha′kwena, and, after reaching a certain point, the yellow Säl′imobiya of the North halts; the others proceed some distance, when the blue Säl′imobiya of the East stops; and so these gods take their positions in file at about equal distance apart.

A Sa′ya′hlia (blue horn), who deposits a reed cigarette in ′kĭawiyu l′aknakwi (a deep place in the river bed some distance west of the village), returns and joins his three associates, who go through the village with other gods, notifying the people that the hour for the hunt has arrived and calling on them to prepare for it.   They use their giant yucca on all who are not fortunate enough to get out of the way.   All hasten to have their hair done up, it having been washed in yucca suds.   No one can take part in a religious ceremonial without first having the hair washed.   Many are mounted and others are on foot.   Should a personator of a god wish to mount, he steps to one side with a member of his ki′wi′sinĕ, the equestrian dismounts and puts on the mask, and the other takes the saddle.   Maidens ride behind their fathers or brothers.   The Sa′ya′hlia follow separately, each with a party of pedestrians, and when they reach the Säl′imobiya of the North, this god chases the party to where the Säl′imobiya of the West stands, and returns to a point a few yards in advance of his former place.   The same party is then chased to the next god by the Säl′imobiya of the West, who returns to a point some yards in front of his former position.   In this way the party passes all the gods, and the gods at the same time advance some yards.   This plan is pursued with each Sa′ya′hlia and his party.   Finally all reach the ′Sän′iakïakwe, who are waiting in the timbered country.

A low tree is fired near the base with a burning torch, and the fraternity, gods, and others, with prayers, cast bread into the flames as food for the gods.   Those offered by the ′Sän′iakïakwe are invocations to the deceased members of the fraternity to aid them in the hunt.   The ′Cha′kwena prays to the goddess whom she personates, imploring her to send many of her children (rabbits) to the Zuñis. The others address the gods in general, praying that they will influence the mother of game to send her children to them and that the rain-makers will water the earth.   All excepting the gods pass their rabbit sticks through the flames for success in the hunt.   A large circle is formed around the preserve by starting in opposite directions.   The ′Cha′kwena and ′Säni′akïakwe remain within the circle and with the firebrands drive the rabbits out from their hiding places among the trees. The rabbits are killed by the gods and others with the rabbit stick. The gods never take up the rabbits they kill, but the women run from their places to collect them and return again to the circle. When a god fails to kill a rabbit which runs between himself and another man, and the man kills it, the latter strikes the god over each arm and leg; but should the god slay the rabbit he whips the man; if both fail, they whip one another. The women endeavor to catch the rabbits with their hands as they pass by, but are not often successful. The unsuccessful one receives four strokes across the back from the gods.

The first rabbit killed has its nose cut and is handed to the ꞌChaꞌ-kwena by a maiden, and the ꞌChaꞌkwena rubs the bleeding nose down her legs on the inner sides, that the Aꞌshiwi (Zuñi) girls may hasten to arrive at the age of puberty and that they may be prolific in child-bearing.

After the first hunt is finished the circle is broken, and the women who have charge of the slain rabbits carry them to the moꞌsona (director) and peꞌkwĭn (deputy) of the ꞌSänꞌiakĭakwe, who stand facing the east, each holding a firebrand. They pick off a bit of fur from the tip of the tail of each rabbit and place this fur in the firebrands, for future success in the hunt. The rabbits are laid on their sides on the ground, with their heads to the east and facing south, and all draw near, pray, and sprinkle them with meal.

All the rabbits that are secured in the hunt, except the one carried by ꞌSiꞌᵗsikĭa to Heꞌiwa kiꞌwiᵗsinĕ, are conveyed by the director of the ꞌSänꞌiakĭakwe to the ceremonial chamber of the first body of Aꞌshi-wanni and presented to them. The rabbits are laid on the floor, with their heads to the east, and an ear of corn is placed between the fore paws of each rabbit (see plate CVI b). All present, including the members of the household, gather around, offer up a prayer, and sprinkle meal. A feast is then enjoyed, and some of the food is car-ried from this chamber to Heꞌkĭapawa kiꞌwiᵗsinĕ by the women of the house. The rabbits presented to the first body of Aꞌshiwanni are stewed in vessels used exclusively for ceremonial cooking, and at sun-rise the meat is cast into the fire, with a prayer to the gods to eat: "My fathers, my mothers, my children, eat." ꞌSiꞌᵗsikĭa flays his rabbit and fills the skin with cedar bark. A pinch of meal is placed in the filling, symbolic of the heart, a hollow reed is run from the mouth through the filling, and gypsum is placed in the eye sockets.

After the return of the gods from the hunt they pass about the village before entering Heꞌkĭapawa kiꞌwiᵗsinĕ. There is dancing in the six kiꞌwiᵗsiwe throughout the night. During the evening the ꞌChaꞌkwena, led by the Koꞌmosona, encircles the village, and on reaching a point on the north side she leaves the Koꞌmosona, proceeds some distance north of the village, and deposits food offerings in an excavation made for the purpose, that the A'shiwi women may pass safely through parturition; that the children may live and grow to maturity, and that the women may be prolific. The ᵗCha'kwena repeats her prayer on the three following evenings at the three other cardinal points. The gods appear for three successive evenings for a time in the streets of the village, and dance during the night in He'kĭapawa ki'wiᵗsinĕ and in the ceremonial chamber of the ᵗSän'iakĭakwe. The ᵗCha'kwena spends the four days following the last deposition of food in the He'kĭapawa ki'wiᵗsinĕ lounging on her bed, suggestive of a woman after accouchement. Any woman having lost children may remain in the ki'wiᵗsinĕ at this time, the ᵗCha'kwena preparing a sand bed for her.[a]

The first morning the woman is in the ki'wiᵗsinĕ she bathes the goddess and dresses her in a new gown with embroidered sash and a woman's belt tied at the left side; a pair of moccasins of fine white deerskin and elaborate necklaces and bracelets of precious beads are put on, and blue yarn is attached to the right wrist and a bow wristlet to the left; the mask is then placed over the face. The goddess is supplied with a gourd rattle, which she carries in her right hand, and a bunch of te'likinawe is carried in the left hand. A fawn skin hangs below the breast. In this regalia the ᵗCha'kwena follows the Ko'mosona from the ki'wiᵗsinĕ, with the four Sa'yaᵗhlia behind her and after them the Ko'pekwĭn and two Ko'piᶜᵗläshiwanni. The last three stand off a distance while the others approach the house south of the ki'wiᵗsinĕ. The ᵗCha'kwena, standing in the doorway, extends the te'likinawe she carries into the room four times, and the four Sa'yaᵗhlia, who are close to her, extend their bows in the same manner. Afterward the matron of the house comes forward and hands various kinds of bread to the ᵗCha'kwena, who hands the larger pieces to the Ko'mosona or Ko'pekwĭn, to be deposited in a blanket that is spread on the ground, and places the small pats in the fawn skin she wears, to be afterward given to the gods. The family of the house now sprinkle the ᵗCha'kwena and Sa'yaᵗhlia with meal. Many houses are visited, and food is collected in the manner described.

Men who participate in the hunting of large game give te'likinawe to the ᵗCha'kwena, Ku'yapäliᵗsa having been the original owner of all game, for success in the hunt. The first body of A'shiwanni and such women as wish to become mothers make offerings of te'likinawe to Ku'yapäliᵗsa. Long prayers are repeated with each presentation. This goddess is soon laden with plume offerings, which she carries attached to a string. Every house on the ground floor is visited by ᵗCha'kwena and her party. Those living above descend to make their offerings of food. When a sufficient quantity has been gathered the blanket is removed by the Ko'piᶜᵗläshiwanni and carried to

---

[a] Zuñi women are confined on sand beds.

He'kǐapawa ki'wiᵗsinĕ. When the fawn skin can no longer hold the contributions its contents are emptied by a Ko'piᶜᵗläshiwanni into a sack which is carried for the purpose. After Cha'kwena has concluded her visits through the village, she passes, with her associates, over the western road, led by the Ko'mosona for a distance, and the food collected in the fawn skin is deposited with te'likinawe and prayer meal in an excavation in the river bank made by wor'we (managers) from the He'kǐapawa ki'wiᵗsinĕ. Long prayers are offered by all present. The opening is afterward covered, Cha'kwena removes her mask, and the ceremony in which she figures is concluded.

Coming of Ko'loowisi (Plumed Serpent) and Involuntary Initiation into the Ko'tikili

Those who are to personate the gods at the coming of Ko'loowisi spend the greater portion of their time in the He'kǐapawa ki'wiᵗsinĕ during the eight days preceding the appearance of the fetish. The first seven mornings they go to collect wood, which they bring on the backs of burros. On the sixth morning the Säl'imobiya from the other ki'wiᵗsiwe, each with his younger brother, or fellow, meet in He'kǐapawa to decide upon the fraternities that are to be invited to the ki'wiᵗsiwe to participate in the coming ceremonies, each Säl'imobiya except the one in He'kǐapawa being privileged to have a fraternity of his choice in his ki'wiᵗsinĕ. The Great Fire fraternity must always be in He'kǐapawa for this occasion.

Each personator of a god who is to accompany Ko'loowisi to the village selects a young man and provides him with a gourd jug with which to visit To'seluna, a sacred spring at Ojo Caliente, and get water and the tall grass which grows in the spring. The party of young men returns in the evening in time to join the personators of the gods, who have gathered at a certain point some distance west of the village, ready to accompany the Ko'loowisi, which has been taken to this point, entirely secreted by its priest, or keeper.

The figure of Ko'loowisi, which is constructed of deerskin, is about 5 feet long and 8 inches through the thickest part of the body. The under portion is painted white and the back is black, covered with duplicate curves in yellow and blue-green to designate the scales of the serpent. A rod of cottonwood extends through the fetish, symbolizing the spinal column. A miniature stick with plumes attached, representing the heart, is secured at the middle of the rod. Hoops of slender pieces of cottonwood, representing the ribs of the serpent, extend from the neck to the lower end. A deerskin tongue, colored red, hangs from the mouth, which is provided with teeth. Plumes stand from the top of the head, which is made of a gourd. The throat is wrapped with a fox skin[a] (see plate XIII). The procession as it

---

[a] An exact model, made for the writer by a priest associated with the fetish, is in the United States National Museum.

SUN PRIEST

AGED MAN OF DEER CLAN

ᵀHLELH PONNĔ (HEAD-DRESS) WITH TABLET ORNAMENTED WITH CLOUD,
SUN, CRESENT, AND STAR SYMBOLS

a *b* *c*

MASK OF A SHÍWANNI (RAIN PRIEST) OF THE KĬÁNAKWE: FRONT, SIDE, AND REAR VIEWS

enters the village is impressive. The head of the fetish passes through a tablet ornamented with cloud symbols (see plate xiv), which is supported on each side by a man of Chu′pawa ki′wiᵗsinĕ. Two other men carry on each side a spruce tree which so covers the Ko′loowisi that only the head is distinctly seen. The tail of the fetish, which is held by the left hand of the priest, or keeper, and the ᵗsu′ᵗhlan′na (great shell), on which he constantly blows, are hidden from view by the trees.

The Ko′loowisi is accompanied by Pau′tiwa (director-general in Ko′thluwala′wa), the Säl′imobiya (warriors and seed-gatherers) from the six regions, many other gods, and a number of men from Chu′pawa ki′wiᵗsinĕ. Su′tiᵗki, a bird fetish, follows after Ko′loowisi. The gods are grouped at the side and back of the fetishes. The Ko′loowisi is carried to each ki′wiᵗsinĕ in the order visited by ᵗKiäklo. On entering He′kĭapawa the Ko′loowisi is deposited north of the altar, with its head to the east, and the two trees are so placed as to quite cover the fetish except the head. The tablet through which the head was thrust is deposited back of the altar, the gourd jugs of water brought from To′seluna spring are placed before the fetish north of the meal line, which extends from the altar, and the grass from the spring is laid upon the jugs. The ki′wiᵗsinĕ is decorated with two pictures of Ko′loowisi, which extend along the north and south walls, the heads almost meeting at the altar. The priest of the Ko′loowisi and Pau′tiwa remain with the fetish. The former constantly blows the shell, making it appear that the serpent is keeping up a continuous roaring. The other personators of the gods go to their respective ki′wiᵗsiwe, where the members are assembled to receive them. The Ko′yemshi, who are supposed to be returning after carrying ᵗKiäklo back to Ko′thluwala′wa, come to the village after the others and proceed to their ceremonial chamber. The gods dance throughout the night, visiting one ki′wiᵗsinĕ after another, observing the order in which the regions are named—North, West, South, East, Zenith, and Nadir.

At the rising of the morning star the gods who accompanied the Ko′loowisi gather in the He′kĭapawa from their ki′wiᵗsiwe, and make offerings of grains of corn and other seeds, which are received by the director and deputy of the Great Fire fraternity. The yellow Säl′imobiya of the North has yellow corn, that of the West blue corn, that of the South red corn, that of the East white corn, that of the Zenith multicolored grains of corn, that of the Nadir black corn; the Ko′yemshi native squash seeds, An′nahoho gourd seeds, Shu′laawiᵗsi corn of all colors, and Na′wisho sweet corn. Each one presents a plume wand with his offering. These wands are afterward planted at the apexes of sand mounds in the Chu′pawa and O′heʻwa ki′wiᵗsiwe. The gods now leave the ki′wiᵗsinĕ and go over the eastern road, which leads to Pescado, one of the farming districts. After proceeding about a mile they remove their masks and take from their hair a la'showannĕ (plume attached to a cotton cord), consisting of a single feather of a woodpecker, and attach it to a sprig of coyote weed. "This feather is used because the woodpecker ascends and descends the trees headforemost and can peck into the hardest wood." The masks are replaced, and the gods return to their respective ki'wi⁺siwe and await the coming of ⁺Kiäklo at daylight.

⁺Kiäklo, who on the present occasion is called Hä'shi (shaker), accompanied by two Mu'luktäkĭa, two Kĭa'nakwe, director and warrior, two or three Säl'imobiya, two or three Sa'ya⁺hlia, and usually one or two ⁺Cha'kwena gods,ᵃ comes over the eastern road to Si'aa' te'wita. The two Mu'luktäkĭa dance in the center of the te'wita, while Hä'shi tramps about sprinkling a line of meal after him and calling to the others to follow.ᵇ When the gods reach He'kĭapa te'wita the Mu'luktäkĭa dance immediately before the opening in the wall of He'kĭapawa ki'wi⁺sinĕ through which the head of Ko'loowisi has been thrust, the tablet being attached to the opening of the outer wall. The head of the serpent protrudes at intervals, touching the Mu'luktäkĭa while they dance. Hä'shi now repeats the running about and sprinkling of meal behind him, calling to the others to follow. After a short time Hä'shi, with his followers, departs over the western road, while the Ko'yemshi and Säl'imobiya, and others of the six ki'wi⁺siwe who may have been spectators, return to their respective ki'wi⁺siwe.

Later in the morning the directors of the different ki'wi⁺siwe and some six or eight others go to the He'iwa ki'wi⁺sinĕ, where members of the Great Fire fraternity have already carried materials for a sand or dry painting. A disk is formed of sand, which may be gathered from any place, but usually from the creek. A deep, small-necked, archaic bowl, greatly prized by the Zuñis, decorated with toads, tadpoles, and dragon flies, is placed by the director of the Great Fire fraternity in the center of the disk of sand. This bowl is referred to as the spring. The water in it must have been brought from ⁺Kĭa'nanaknan'na (a spring sacred to the rain priests), and must contain mosses, such fishes as may be found, frogs, and also a water snake, if one can be secured in this particular spring. The water is dipped by a member of the Frog clan. A ground color of white covers the sand, and one of the artists of the fraternity, chosen by the director, delineates upon it pictures of the Säl'imobiya, ⁺Kiäklo, and other gods. There must be as many gods represented

---

ᵃ These ⁺Cha'kwena bear no relation to the ⁺Cha'kwena (Ku'yapäli⁺sa) before mentioned.

ᵇ The man who personates Hä'shi is not the same as he who represents ⁺Kiäklo when he recites the iliad, though he wears the same mask and regalia; nor are those who accompany him the men who are to personate the gods when the children are initiated into the Ko'tikili. These are now present as spectators only.

in this painting as there are children to be initiated. The director of the Great Fire fraternity remains constantly by this painting, leaving it only occasionally to observe the progress of the work done by members of his fraternity in Chu'pawa and O'he'wa ki'wi'siwe.

There are fifteen sand mounds made in each of these ki'wi'siwe for the fifteen gods who are personated.[a] The men who make the mounds remain to look after them. The gods for whom the mounds are made in the Chu'pawa are the six elder brothers Säl'imobiya, two elder brothers Na'wisho, elder brother 'Hle'lashoktĭpona, elder brother U'poyona, two elder brothers An'nahoho, Shu'laawi'si, 'Si'tsikĭa, and Awan tä'tchu (Great Father) Ko'yemshi. The younger brothers of the gods, except Shu'laawi'si, 'Si'tsikĭa, and A'wan tä'tchu Ko'yemshi, visit the O'he'wa ki'wi'sinĕ. Shu'laawi'si, 'Si'tsikĭa, and Awan tä'tchu Ko'yemshi go from one ki'wi'sinĕ to the other.

As soon as members of the Great Fire fraternity leave for the two ki'wi'siwe to make the sand mounds Shu'laawi'si, led by his ceremonial father, leaves the Up'tsannawa to visit the O'he'wa, where he is joined by the two An'nahoho, and the four proceed to He'iwa ki'wi'sinĕ, where the director of the Great Fire fraternity dips water from the "spring" with an ancient shell attached to a long stick of cottonwood and gives to each a drink. At this point the choir of the fraternity sing to the accompaniment of the rattle and drum. The water is drunk to make the gods angry, and the pe'kwĭn (sun priest) says: "Those of you who drink this water are privileged to strike all men and women you may meet, except those that you find lying down, standing close to the wall or by a ladder or under one, or carrying an ear of corn or a vase of water; or pregnant women, men wearing plumes in the hair or buckskin around them, officers of the fraternity who take part in the ceremonies, or those who have worked on the sand painting and mounds." The gods and others who had previously visited the ki'wi'sinĕ and partaken of the water also received instructions from the pe'kwĭn to whip the people. These gods break large quantities of pottery, and as each piece is thrown to the ground they cry: "Pa'chu a'shetu (Death to the Navaho)." Baskets are broken by the other gods and burned by the lighted brand of Shu'laawi'si, and they cry: "Le'na Pa'chu an ham'pone cha'pitu (In this way burn the Navaho camp.)" The populace and Säl'imobiya give the war whoop during the destruction of pottery and baskets.

The Ko'yemshi ascend to the roof of the He'iwa ki'wi'sinĕ and listen to 'Si'tsikĭa, who has not left the ki'wi'sinĕ and is now on the ladder which passes through the hatchway. He holds the stuffed rabbit skin with gypsum eyes, previously referred to, near his mouth, and the

---

[a] Illustrations of these sand paintings may be found in "The Religious Life of the Zuñi Child," Fifth Annual Report of the Bureau of Ethnology, p. 539–555.

rabbit is supposed to be saying: "Your little grandfather is hungry; he wishes something to eat; bring him some food." The Ko'yemshi, in obedience to the little grandfather's request, go to the homes of the children who are to be initiated and have been previously named by ᵗSi'ᵗsikĭa and the Ko'yemshi. The first boy visited gives an eating bowl full of cooked yellow beans, the next gives a bowl of blue beans, the next a bowl of red beans, the fourth a bowl of white beans, the fifth a bowl of beans of all colors, the sixth a bowl of black beans. The other children give dried peaches, stewed meat, etc. The bowls of food are carried to the He'iwa ki'wiᵗsinĕ by the Ko'yemshi, who hand them through the hatchway to persons inside. ᵗSi'ᵗsikĭa does not receive the bowls himself. Wor'we (managers) from the other ki'wiᵗsiwe go to He'iwa and carry off their share of the food, each party partaking of the feast in its own ki'wiᵗsinĕ after the gods have finished their tour of destruction. About this time each godfather carries a la'showannĕ to the He'iwa ki'wiᵗsinĕ, giving it to the director of the Great Fire fraternity, who places it on the head of one of the pictures of the sand painting.

The godfathers of the boys who donate beans have their la'showawe placed on the heads of the Säl'imobiya of the six regions, each la'showannĕ being placed on the head of the god associated with the region of the color of the beans, the color of the figures having nothing to do with the ki'wiᵗsinĕ the boy is to enter; but, apart from the feathers of the godfathers of the boys who have donated the beans of the colors of the six regions, the feathers are placed on the heads of the figures as the director may decide. As soon as each father is informed upon which figure his plume is placed he leaves the ki'wiᵗsinĕ to prepare for the involuntary initiation of his godchild.

The pe'kwin leads the gods from He'kĭapawa ki'wiᵗsinĕ, where they assembled after their feasts in their respective ki'wiᵗsiwe, to Si'aa' te'wita. Entering by the eastern covered way, he sprinkles a line of meal from the entrance of the plaza to the He'iwa ki'wiᵗsinĕ and forms a circle of meal at the base of the ladder which leads to the roof of the ki'wiᵗsinĕ. He crosses the main line of meal at equal intervals with lines of meal of the different colors associated with the six regions, beginning at the east entrance, to indicate the positions the gods are to take. He again returns to the east entrance and places the Ko'pekwĭn, deputy to the Ko'mosona, the Ko'mosona, and the gods in proper order, standing each one, with a hand on each shoulder, on a cross line of the meal; they all face north. The position of the gods is as follows: The Säl'imobiya of the North stands next to the Ko'mosona, then follow in order the Säl'imobiya of the West, Säl'imobiya of the South, Säl'imobiya of the East, Säl'imobiya of the Zenith, Säl'imobiya of the Nadir, ᵗHle'lashoktĭpona, U'poyona, An'nahoho, Shu'laawiᵗsi, ᵗSi'ᵗsikĭa, and Great Father Ko'yemshi. The other Ko'yemshi mark a place with the feet for each god to place his extended foot while striking the children.

The child, who is carried on the back of his godfather, wears a cotton shirt and two blankets, and is held on the back by two additional blankets and a piece of canvas which take the place of the bison robes used in olden times. As the godfathers pass before the gods the children are struck four times by each god with bunches of giant yucca. The Ko'mosona and Ko'pekwĭn take no part in the whipping. After the godfather passes the line of the gods, he steps into the meal circle and ascends the ladder to the roof of the ki'wiᵗsinĕ, where the child is stood at the hatchway if he is old enough to walk down the ladder, otherwise the godfather carries him into the ki'wiᵗsinĕ. He removes the la'showannĕ from the proper sand figure and ties it to the child's head, and the director of the Great Fire fraternity gives the child a drink from the "spring." The water is dipped with the old shell referred to. After all the children have the plumes tied to the hair they are told to step upon the sand painting, their breasts and other portions of their bodies being touched with the sand. The children are now carried on the backs of their godfathers to the plaza and seated on the ledges that extend around the square, the godfathers standing behind them. The wife and daughter of each godfather stand on each side of the child, who now has only three blankets over him, holding a piece of canvas which secretes the child. After the godfathers leave the ki'wiᵗsinĕ the director of the Great Fire fraternity ascends with the spring bowl and, dipping water with the shell, gives those who are assembled on the roof of the ki'wiᵗsinĕ drafts of the sacred water.

A square formed by four crosses of meal, symbolizing the four regions, each cross with its four points symbolizing the same, is made in the plaza by the Ko'mosona. Four Sa'yaᵗhlia, selected by the Ko'pi‘ᵗläshiwanni from some one ki'wiᵗsinĕ, stand each on a cross. The one on the northeast cross faces north, the one on the northwest faces west, the one on the southwest faces south, and the one on the southeast faces east. After a time the four gods turn, facing the points directly to their left, and in this way they make a circuit of the four regions, after which the Ko'mosona leads the Sa'yaᵗhlia from the northeast cross past the children, beginning with the child nearest the east entrance. The god endeavors to locate the child under the canvas by touching it with his foot. Each child is struck once; then the Sa'yaᵗhlia from the northwest cross passes by the children and strikes each one twice. Three strokes are given each child by the Sa'yaᵗhlia from the cross at the southwest point, and four strokes are given by the one from the southeast cross.

The four Sa'yaᵗhlia now form a line, facing north, and the child nearest the east entrance is carried on the back of the godfather;

the little one, now having but two blankets and the canvas over him, is struck four times by each Sa'ya͏ᵗhlia. Each child is carried in turn by these gods. After passing the gods, the godfather continues to his home, where he and the godchild join in a feast, after which they go to either the O'he‘wa or the Chu'pawa ki'wi͏ᵗsinĕ. When the gods leave the plaza they repair to the He'kĭapawa, where all the other gods are assembled; there they have a light repast, and then arrange the corn to be delivered by the Ko'loowisi in the ki'wi͏ᵗsiwe. When all who are privileged, including the first body of A'shiwanni, the Ko'mosona and others, are gathered in Chu'pawa and O'he‘wa ki'wi͏ᵗsiwe the gods in He'kĭapawa separate into two bodies, going to the two ki'wi͏ᵗsiwe in the order before described. All but one of the gods enter the hatchway headforemost; facing the north, and catching the rung of the ladder with one foot, then the rung below by the bended knee, they descend the ladder in this manner to the fire altar; and with head on the slab of the altar make a somersault into the room.

A sacred embroidered blanket is attached to the wall at the west end of the room, one is placed on the ledge immediately below, and many strings of precious beads and an old red, black, and green yarn belt hang on each side of the blanket on the wall. U'poyona, who is the first god to enter the ki'wi͏ᵗsinĕ, and who walks down the ladder instead of going headforemost, takes his seat before the blanket. As each god makes a somersault into the room he hops like a frog past the mounds on the south side, and then around on the north side. As ͏ᵗHle'lashoktĭpona (Wood-ears) passes U'poyona this god leaves his seat and hops on all fours after him. As each god reaches the appropriate mound he halts on all fours to the north of it, and when all are in position they simultaneously jump on their mounds, remove the plume wands, and, jumping off in the same fashion, pass to the children who are between the extended knees of their godfathers. Each godfather sits on the ledge between his wife and daughter.

Each god blows four times upon the plume wand he carries, each time passing it before the child's lips, giving to him the sacred breath of the god. After this ceremony all the gods except Shu'laawi͏ᵗsi, ͏ᵗSi'͏ᵗsikia, and Great Father Ko'yemshi depart by the western road. The three last named proceed to O'he‘wa ki'wi͏ᵗsinĕ and there join the younger brother gods in similar ceremonies. Later in the evening Su'ti͏ᵗki, the bird fetish which announces the coming of Ko'loowisi, is carried from the He'kĭapawa ki'wi͏ᵗsinĕ to the roof of Chu'pawa. The pole is projected through the hatchway, and by an ingenious arrangement of cord the bird is made to run back and forth, while a second man uses a whistle of most curious workmanship[a] that is hidden under his blanket. The bird is supposed to chirp and warble,

---

[a] This whistle was secured for the United States National Museum.

notifying those in the ki'wi'sinĕ of the coming of Ko'loowisi. Finally
the bird halts at the far end of the pole, and all, including the children
in the ki'wi'sine, draw their hands to their mouths, inhaling the breath
from the sacred fetish. While this is being done the man with the
whistle blows out his breath four times.

This ceremony with the bird is repeated at O'he'wa ki'wi'sinĕ, and
afterward the two men with the bird fetish pass out over the western
road.[a] Ko'loowisi is the next to visit the ki'wi'siwe, going first to
Chu'pawa. The serpent is carried now just as it was brought to the
village. The slab is held firmly while the head is projected through
the hatchway into the ki'wi'sinĕ. Water from the To'seluna spring is
secretly emptied from a gourd jug into the body of Ko'loowisi, and it
pours from his mouth into bowls held by the Ko'mosona, the Ko'pekwĭn, and two Ko'pi'läshiwanni. The grains of corn of different colors,
which are now mixed, are afterward put into the serpent and received
in baskets from its mouth by those who receive the water. The to'selu
(long grass) from the spring is thrown through the hatchway, while the
children's eyes are covered in order that they may not know that it
does not come from the mouth of the serpent.

Ko'loowisi is now carried to the hatchway of O'he'wa, where the
offering of seeds and water is repeated. Each child receives a bowl,
which is a present from the godfather made by a female member of
his family, containing sacred water from the Ko'loowisi. The Ko'pekwĭn gives a handful of the mixed corn to each boy and to each godfather, and a roll of the long grass is also handed to each child. Should
there be an oversupply of the grass it is given to the godfathers. As
soon as these distributions have been made to the children in Chu'pawa
ki'wi'sinĕ the Ko'mosona, Ko'pekwĭn, and two Ko'pi'läshiwanni proceed
to the O'he'wa ki'wi'sinĕ and take part in similar ceremonies. After
receiving the gifts of the gods the children are carried to their homes
by their godfathers. The water is drunk by the boy and his immediate family and is also used to sprinkle the stacked corn. The long
grass is deposited with the stacked corn, and the seeds are planted
separate from the others in the field in the coming spring.

After the ceremonies in the ki'wi'siwe the gods deposit the plume
wands from the mounds and food in a large excavation west of Zuñi,
which is afterward covered. They then return to the village, with their
masks secreted under blankets, each going to the house where his mask
is kept and returning it to the keeper with appropriate prayers. As a
a number of masks are often kept in one house, several personators
of the gods meet there and are served with an elaborate feast. Previous to the feast, however, each personator of a god removes all of his
clothing but the breechcloth and is bathed by the women of the family.

---

a The two men mentioned have entire charge of the bird fetish and the whistle, and their office is
for life.

At sunrise the morning after initiation the child goes to the house of his godfather, where the plume is removed from his hair and the head is bathed by the wife; then the godfather returns the plume to its place and gives the boy four ears of corn and te'likinawe, after which the child has his morning meal at the house of his godfather. After the meal the godfather carries the child to Ku'shilowa (red earth), a short distance east of the village, removes from his hair the plume, and plants it in the earth, and the child deposits his te'likinawe. He plants the corn the coming year in his fields.

Thus closes this curious involuntary ceremonial of initiation of the Zuñi boy into the Ko'tikili, an initiation for which the godfather is mainly responsible. The boy must take upon himself the vows as soon as he is old enough to fully understand the requirements resting upon a member of this fraternity.

VOLUNTARY INITIATION INTO THE KO'TIKILI

Voluntary initiation occurs when the boy is 12 or 13 years of age. He decides for himself, but the elders do not fail to have him understand the importance of the step.

The initiation described was witnessed in 1891. By 1 o'clock in the day the He'iwa k'iwi⁺sinĕ (see plate xv)[a] contains a large number of people, including several boys to be initiated. Each boy sits by the side of his godfather (the same godfather acting for involuntary and voluntary initiation) on the south or east ledge of the room. The first body of A'shiwanni (rain priests), the Ko'mosona, and the Ko'pekwĭn sit on the south ledge, to the west. Four Sa'ya⁺hlia stand on the north side of the ki'wi⁺sinĕ and west of the center of the floor, facing south. The long goat's wool used for hair on these masks is tied with yucca ribbons, so that the eyeholes of the mask may not be covered. The Ko'yemshi (see plate v a),[b] who have charge of the bunches of giant yucca, hand a bunch to each Sa'ya⁺hlia (see plate xvi).

One of the boys is a Sia youth, who is included in the number to be initiated in order that the Sia Indians may use the Ko'yemshi masks which they possess, all who formerly had this privilige being now dead. This boy is accompanied to Zuñi by one of the principal rain priests and two theurgists of his tribe. The director of the Shu'-maakwe fraternity was chosen as his godfather. As this youth has not received involuntary initiation in Zuñi, he must pass through a more extended ceremonial than the others. He is the first one brought forward.

---

[a] In the plate the He'iwa ki'wi⁺sinĕ occupies only the left-hand portion, reaching nearly to the window.

[b] Although the masks of the ten Ko'yemshi are similar, each one has its special knob and mouth forms.

The godfather folds four large blankets separately into squares and two women lay them over the Sia boy's back while he bends forward. A large piece of double canvas is now thrown over the boy, completely covering him. His back is bent until one could sit upon it. The godfather, who leads the novice, holds the canvas together under the chin so that the boy can scarcely see. The women who place the blankets walk on either side of the boy, who stops before the Saʻyaʻhlia at the east end of the line. This god strikes the boy four times with all his strength across the back with the yucca. The four strokes are repeated by each Saʻyaʻhlia in turn, the novice being led by his godfather from one to the other and then to the northwest corner of the room where he stands facing north. The Saʻyaʻhlia now stand in line north and south and face east. The boy is again led before the gods to be whipped with the yucca. The one at the north end of the line strikes him first. He passes four times before the Saʻyaʻhlia, and each time the gods give him one stroke each with the yucca. The blows are counted aloud by the Koʻyemshi, who stand by and furnish the gods with fresh bunches of yucca as needed. One of the women who accompany the boy is now led by the godfather before the gods. She bends forward and receives on her back one stroke of the yucca from each Saʻyaʻhlia, they having resumed their position on the north side of the room. Two blankets are removed from the boy's back and he is again led before the gods, each one striking him with force four times across the back. Judging from the smothered groans, the strokes are keenly felt by the boy. After the third whipping the boy and the godfather each take meal from a cornhusk held by the godfather and sprinkle the Saʻyaʻhlia, and after the blankets are removed the godfather attaches a fluffy eagle plume to the hair of the boy, who again appears in his calico shirt and trousers.

A blanket of ordinary thickness and a deerskin are used for voluntary initiation. The novices pass but once before the Saʻyaʻhlia, receiving from each of these four gods four strokes with giant yucca delivered with all their strength, and though every effort is made by the novices to keep silent, their smothered groans are pitiable to hear. When all of the novices have received their chastisement they return to their seats, each one going to the side of his godfather, who places his hands over the eyes of the boy while the four Saʻyaʻhlia gods remove their masks. The Koʻyemshi do not take off theirs. After the boys are whipped the two Koʻyemshi go to the roof of the kiʻwiʻsinĕ to see that no one intrudes while the masks are being removed. Every initiate has a rain-maker's mask given him by his godfather, which becomes his personal property, and is buried after his death. When the godfathers remove their hands from the eyes of the boys, the novices discover for the first time that the supposed gods are but men. Four of the boys stand before the four Sa′ya‘hlia, each god placing a mask on the boy before him and handing him his yucca. The novices now pass down the line of gods, the first boy striking the first god once over the right arm and then the left, the right ankle and then the left. He repeats the strokes with each god, the other boys doing the same. Passing on, they afterward form into line and again approach the gods, each boy being vis-a-vis to the god whose mask he wears. Each god removes his mask from the boy's head and the novices return to their seats, when four others pass through the same ceremony.

After all the boys have been initiated the gods replace the masks over their own heads and the godfathers are struck by each god over the limbs, as heretofore described. Afterward each shi′wanni is struck in the same manner. The Ko′mosona informs the boys that if they divulge the initiatory secrets, especially those associated with the masks, their heads will be cut off with a stone knife.

After the initiation a feast is served in the ki′wi‘sinĕ, the food being brought to the hatchway in the roof by the families of the Sa′ya‘hlia. After the feast the boys pass out one by one with their godfathers. The Sa′ya‘hlia go to the plaza while the Kor′kokshi are dancing and run up the ladder and over the housetops, using their yucca freely. Women are whipped to cure them of bad dreams.

As the writer was closeted in the ki′wi‘sinĕ, she could not observe the ceremonies in the plaza at this time; but on a similar occasion she remained in the plaza instead of going into the ki′wi‘sinĕ, and the scenes observed at that time, which are virtually the same each year, are here given.

There are thirty-one Kor′kokshi u′wannami (rain-makers) dancers in the plaza. Seven are goddesses. Those representing women wear the ordinary black woven dress and white blanket wraps, bordered top and bottom in blue and red, blue knit leggings, many necklaces, and turquoise earrings. Their hands and arms are colored pink and their feet yellow. The hair is parted over the top of the head and down the back, and done up on either side over forms made of wood and wrapped with native blue yarn. After one side is wrapped, the person whose hair is being dressed holds the yarn tightly until the hairdresser rolls the rest of the hair, when it also is wrapped with yarn. A bang of goat's wool 4 inches deep passes around the head. The woman's mask, which covers only the face, is white, with a black beard about 6 inches long. Each personator of a woman has a large white fluffy eagle plume tied to the forelock, except one who has two plumes, which are somewhat smaller than those worn by the others. They carry spruce twigs in both hands.

Those personating the male gods have their legs and arms painted yellow to the knees and elbows; yellow lines run from the elbow up the arm and down the back and breast on each side. They wear the conventional dance moccasins, with porcupine anklets, white cotton embroidered kilts fastened at the right side, a white fringed cotton sash, and a Zuñi woman's belt which is carried around the waist and looped at the right side. A fox skin is pendent at the back. Bunches of native blue yarn with sleigh bells are worn below the knee, the yarn hanging in tassels. A tortoise-shell rattle hangs at the calf of the right leg. Blue yarn is wound around the right wrist and a bow wristlet is worn on the left. In addition to the elaborate necklace, each dancer wears a hank of blue yarn around the neck. Spruce twigs stand out from the belts, and also from the leather armlets, which are cut in points colored blue-green, and a banded turkey feather is suspended from each point by a buckskin thong several inches long. The hair, which has been plaited to make it wavy, falls over the back, and three white, equidistant, fluffy eagle plumes are attached to a string hanging down the back. A bit of cylindrical wood about 1½ inches long and one-fourth inch in diameter is tied to the lower end of the string to keep it in place. A bunch of yellow parrot plumes stands on the fore part of the head at the line from which the bang falls. The masks, which are rectangular and shaped to fit the face, are blue-green, blocked at the base in black and white, symbolic of the house of the clouds, and have a black beard. The gods carry gourd rattles, colored pink, in the right hand and small spruce twigs in the left.

The dancers are led by a man of the ki'wiᵗsinĕ dressed in velveteen knee breeches with a line of silver buttons on the outer sides, buckskin leggings, red garters, moccasins, a black native wool shirt trimmed with red and green ribbons over a white shirt, and a yucca ribbon around the head. A white fluffy eagle plume and a small bird plume are attached to the forelock; a buckskin folded lengthwise hangs over the left shoulder. This man carries a mi'li (see page 416) and a meal basket in the left hand and sprinkles meal with the right.

The dancers enter the Si'aa' te'wita from the western way and leave it by the eastern covered way. One personating a goddess walks by the side of the foremost dancer. All personating the gods form in line, facing north. The leading goddess stands vis-a-vis to the dancer she accompanies, while the other six personators of goddesses face the dancers in the middle of the line. The leader of the song and dance always stands midway down the line. The god at the east end of the line and his vis-a-vis turn to face the man who precedes the dancers, and dance a moment or two, while the others, except those personating women, continue the dance, facing north. The six women face the men. In a short time the two at the end of the line resume their former position, and the leader, who is not a dancer, passes down

the line in front of the dancers to the group of Ko'yemshi standing
north and near the west end of the line of dancers. The leader prays
and sprinkles each Ko'yemshi with meal. The dancers continue the
song and dance to the accompaniment of the rattle. After a time they
turn, forming into single file facing the east, and so they reverse several times. The step in the dance is of dull uniformity, the balancing
being done with the left foot, while the right is raised slightly above
the ground and put down squarely with a stamp.

After the Kor'kokshi dance once they retire for a time to the
ki'wiᵗsinĕ whence they came. They are soon followed to the plaza by
four Sa'yaᵗhlia, who remain a short time, brandishing their huge
bunches of giant yucca, causing men, women, and children to get out
of their way. They retire to the He'iwa ki'wiᵗsinĕ, where they, with
two Ko'yemshi, pass the boys assembled there through voluntary
initiation into the Ko'tikili.

Eight of the Ko'yemshi remain in the plaza, where they are joined by
members of the Ne'wekwe (Galaxy) fraternity, who have their entire
bodies painted ash-color, with curves of black under each eye and over
the upper lip. Their heads and ears are covered with ash-colored
cotton skullcaps ornamented on the top and over the ears with ribboned corn-husk rosettes. Native black-wool breechcloths are worn.
A bunch of unspun black yarn hangs about the neck and a string of
it is tied around the left ankle. One man has his body and limbs
encircled by bands of white paint. Each is provided with a large
blanket, which is worn most of the time, for the day is extremely
cold, and each carries his baton (see plate xv, Group of Ne'wekwe),
the harlequin's bauble (see plate xvII). Throughout the afternoon
during the interval of the Kor'kokshi dancing the Ko'yemshi and
Ne'wekwe hold high carnival, delighting the hundreds of spectators
with their buffoonery.

Women of the higher rank gather inside the houses or on elevated
galleries to witness the ceremonials in Si'aa' te'wita. Others sit on
the house tops or on blankets spread on the south side of the plaza.
The return of the dancers is always the signal for the cessation of all
nonsense, and these clowns, with great seriousness, attend to the wants
of the Kor'kokshi, some portion of their regalia not infrequently
requiring attention. The warrior of the Ko'yemshi whirls the rhombus
during the dancing, calling upon the rain-makers to gather, the Kor'-
kokshi being their personators.

After the fifth dance a bowl of food is brought to the plaza, and
after the food is eaten by the Ne'wekwe one of them brings a bowl of
urine and drinks and gargles his throat with it, and places it in the
northwest corner of the plaza when the dancers are seen advancing.
It is drunk after the dancers leave the plaza.

After the sixth dance the Ko'yemshi and Ne'wekwe gather in the northeast portion of the plaza, the latter having laid aside their batons. One Ne'wekwe beats a drum, while the others burlesque the dancers who are now absent from the plaza. The scene becomes hilarious when a Ne'wekwe ascends a ladder and, entering a house, soon emerges with a urinal filled to the brim, which he brings to the plaza and passes to his three fellows, each one drinking from the bowl.[a] When the vessel is empty he places it, inverted, over his head, and a fellow hastens to lick the drops which fall from the bowl to the ground. The man with the urinal finally falls to the ground and smashes the bowl. The four Ne'wekwe play at being intoxicated from the draft, their antics exceeding anything before observed by the writer. They come nearer falling to the ground without so doing than could be imagined. One man, tumbling into the arms of another, exclaims: "Father, why am I crazy?" One of the four is a peerless harlequin. They hold a regular drunken dance, throwing their arms up, and with the Ko'yemshi sing to the accompaniment of the drum. A man falling from a ladder, a rung having slipped out, causes great merriment.

At 4.30 the Kor'kokshi come to the plaza for the seventh time, when the innovation occurs of forming into file facing west and dancing a moment before forming in line facing north. The leader of the dancers now stands west of them instead of east. After the dance, which does not close until the shadows of evening are falling, the Kor'kokshi leave the plaza by the western street.

Although a boy at voluntary initiation into the fraternity of the Ko'tikili joins the ki'wi*sině to which his godfather belongs (see page 65), it sometimes, though seldom, occurs that a man from choice leaves his ki'wi*sině to become associated with another. In such case he may return at any time to the one of his boyhood. Also, when improper conduct is observed between a man and the wife of one of his fellow-members, the offender is expelled, whereupon he seeks admittance into one of the other ki'wi*siwe. Sometimes, however, the efforts of members to expel an objectionable person are futile. For example, the director of a certain ki'wi*sině discovered that undue intimacy existed between one of his fellow-members and his wife, and, after denouncing the man, he left the wife's house never to return. A meeting of the members of the ki'wi*sině was held, and not only the director but the Ko'mosona (director-general of ki'wi*siwe), he being also a member of this ki'wi*sině, demanded the dismissal of the guilty man. But their demands were overruled, whereupon the Ko'mosona, the director of the ki'wi*sině, and three others left and became members of the Chu'pawa.

---

[a] The Ne'wekwe are the only Zuñis who eat and drink filth. It is the aim of each member of this fraternity to outdo the others in everything disgusting.

CALENDAR AND CALENDRIC CEREMONIALS

CALENDAR

The year (te'pikwaï'i) is divided into two seasons, each consisting of six months (te'lakwaï'i). The month is divided into three parts, each part being called topïnta as'tĕm'la (one ten).

According to Zuñi calculation, when the rising sun strikes a certain point at the southwest end of To'wa yäl'länně (Corn mountain) it is the winter solstice. Then the sun moves to the north, passes the moon at A'yonawa yäl'länně and continues round to a point northwest of Zuñi which is called Yäl'lä 'hlan'na (Great mountain), where it sets consecutively for four days at the same point. The last day is the summer solstice.

The names of the months are given below. It will be observed that those for the months December to June are indicative and that the same names are repeated for the other six months.

WINTER MONTHS. I'kopu (turning or looking back[a]), December; Taiyämchu (limbs of trees broken by snow), January; O'nänulakïakwamě (no snow in the road), February; 'Hli'tekwakïa 'sanna (little wind month), March; 'Hli'tekwakïa 'hlan'na (big wind month), April; Kwashi'ämme (no name), May.

SUMMER MONTHS. I'kopu (turning or looking back), June; Taiyämchu (limbs of trees broken by snow), July; O'nänulakïakwamě (no snow in the road), August; 'Hli'tekwakïa 'sanna (little wind month), September; 'Hli'tekwa'kïa 'thlan'na (big wind month), October; Kwashi'ämme (no name), November.

WINTER SOLSTICE CEREMONIES

Yä'tokïa (sun father) i'tiwannan (middle) kwǐ (place) te'chi (reaches there) is a reference to the shortest day in the year, the winter solstice.

Though the ceremonies of both seasons extend through some days, the first day on which the people en masse plant te'likinawe (prayer plumes) is designated as the solstice. The day chosen for the winter solstice celebration is the 21st or 22d of December. The pe'kwǐn (sun priest) is alone responsible for the calendar. He is usually correct in his calculations, but has been known to be in error. Such was the case in 1896, when the pe'kwǐn (see plate XVIII) had but recently replaced his predecessor. The former sun priest had been dismissed from his high office by the word of the Shi'wano''kïa (Priestess of fecundity), who enjoys such prerogative; she declared the failure in crops due to the bad heart of the pe'kwǐn. Many ventured to hint that he possessed the diabolical powers of witchcraft. After prolonged discussion by the first body of A'shiwanni (rain priests) and others over the time designated by the new pe'kwǐn, his decision was confirmed.

---

[a] The reference is to the Sun Father's turning back after reaching the point referred to at the southwest end of To'wa yäl'länně. He is supposed to pause here for a time before returning on his course.

NEW YEAR FIRE IN HE'IWA (NORTH) KI'WI:SINĔ CHAMBER DEDICATED TO ANTHRŌPIC WORSHIP

SHRINE OF YOUNGER GOD OF WAR ON TO'WA YÄL'LÄNNĚ (CORN MOUNTAIN)

a

b

a MASK OF KÓTHLAMA, FRONT VIEW; b HEAD OF PERSONATOR OF KÓTHLAMA, REAR VIEW

MASKS OF A'PI''LÄ̈SHIWANNI (WARRIORS) a OF THE NORTH, b OF THE WEST,
c OF THE SOUTH: FRONT AND SIDE VIEWS

The sun priest makes daily observations of the sunrise at a petrified stump which stands on the outskirts east of the village, and sprinkles it with meal when he offers his matins to the rising sun. When the sun rises over a certain point of To′wa yäl′länně he informs the elder brother Bow priest, who notifies the first body of A′shiwanni, and they meet the same night in the ceremonial chamber.[a]

The following morning the pe′kwĭn prepares four te′likinawe for the Sun Father and Moon Mother and, carrying them up the steep acclivity, deposits them at a shrine on To′wa yäl′länně. The four te′likinawe are tied into groups of twos, each group having a blue stick for the sun and a yellow one for the moon, which is referred to as sister of the sun. The lower end of each stick is tipped with black to indicate feet, and the top is beveled, with three black dots on the beveled surface indicating eyes and mouth. Under tail and breast feathers of the eagle and plumes of the birds of the six regions are attached to each stick.

The fourth morning following he deposits four te′likinawe in the field[b] to the deceased a′pekwĭn (sun priests). The sticks of these are black with turkey plumes attached. On the fourth morning after this he returns to the sun shrine on To′wa yäl′länně and deposits four te′likinawe. On the fourth morning next succeeding he plants four te′likinawe in the field to his predecessors. Again on the next fourth morning he deposits four te′likinawe at the sun shrine on To′wa yäl′länně. On the fourth morning following thereafter he plants four more te′likinawe in the field to his deceased predecessors. The pe′kwĭn must observe continency from four days previous to the first planting of the plumes to four days following the last deposition of these offerings, and he must fast from animal food four days following the offerings made to the sun, but this fast is not observed in planting te′likinawe to the deceased a′pekwĭn.

The morning following the final planting of the te′likinawe the pe′kwĭn announces from the house top that the winter solstice will occur in ten days. Then the rising sun will strike the point referred to as the Middle place, after which it returns over the road it has traveled. The pe′kwĭn continues his daily visits to the petrified stump to pray and sprinkle meal to the rising sun.

Studies of the winter solstice ceremonies were made in 1891 and 1896; and as each annual festival is substantially the same only the one for 1891 will be described. It must be borne in mind that the dates vary

---

[a] While this room is the ceremonial chamber of the first body of A′shiwanni, who are known as the Kĭa′kwe amosi (Directors of the house), the house referred to being the perpetual home of the ět′toně (see p. 163) of the Shi′wanni of the North, it is spoken of as the house of this shi′wanni in consequence of his being the possessor of the sacred fetish, which rests in the room immediately over the center of the world; and, as has been stated, the Shi′wanni of the North is always referred to as the Kĭa′kwemosi (Director of the house), while the others of the first body of A′shiwanni are spoken of as Shi′wanni of the West, South, etc.

[b] Fields throughout this paper refer to ground under cultivation.

somewhat in different years. While the actual ceremonial continued eleven days, beginning on the 22d of the month in 1891, for convenience of reference the four days prior to this date will be included in the enumeration of days. The references in the following account are therefore from the first day to the fifteenth inclusive, the fifth day being the actual beginning of the ceremonial.

The first four days are consumed by the first body of A'shiwanni, not including the Shi'wano''kĭa (Priestess of Fecundity), who assemble in the houses of the Kĭa'kwe amosi in the preparation of te'likinawe. Besides their individual prayer plumes to the sun and their ancestors, each shi'wanni makes a te'likinanĕ to the sun, one to the moon (the two being wrapped together with native cotton cord), and four to each of the six regions for the deceased A'shiwanni of these regions. The te'likinawe of the Priestess of Fecundity are made by the first body of A'shiwanni. She prepares a ha'kwani (a number of cotton-cord loops), symbolizing a sacred white blanket. The Kĭa'kwemosi and the Shi'-wanni of the Nadir each make a te'likinanĕ, the stick measuring from the inner side of the elbow to the tip of the middle finger. That of the Kĭa'kwemosi is to the u'wannami (rain-makers) of the six regions or the whole world, and that of the Shi'wanni of the Nadir, who is also elder brother Bow priest, is to the Ku'pĭshtaya (lightning-makers), with whom the deceased A'pi''läshiwanni (Bow priests) work. The elder and younger brother Bow priests prepare offerings to the Gods of War, and four to the lightning-makers (deceased A'pi''läshiwanni) of each of the six regions. All except the individual offerings of these priests are grouped together into a kĭa'ĕtchinĕ (a group of te'likinawe), the two longer te'likinawe made by the Kĭa'kwemosi and Shi'wanni of the Nadir being in the center. The Shi'wanni of the Nadir holds the te'likinawe in place while the younger brother Bow priest wraps the base with thread made of yucca. The kĭa'ĕtchinĕ is placed on the meal painting in the He'iwa (North) ki'wi'sinĕ[a] the fourth evening.

This group of te'likinawe is offered to the gods with prayers for the pure hearts of the people, the appearance of a'wehlwia'we (cumulus clouds), shi'pololowe (fog, clouds like the plains), wil'lolonannĕ (lightning), rains, and much water in the rivers and lakes. Should the hearts of the people be not pure, it could not be expected that the Sun Father would combine with the Council of the Gods in directing the u'wannami to favor Zuñi-land. The Ko'mosona and his associates prepare their prayer plumes in the room adjoining the Mu'hewa (west) ki'wi'sinĕ, to which he belongs. He also has one te'likinanĕ, as long as from the inner side of the bend of the elbow to the tip of the middle finger, which is offered to the Council of the Gods. Members of the fraternities, except those of the 'Hle'wekwe (Sword swallowers), also gather in their ceremonial chambers on the first day and prepare te'likinawe.

---

[a] See Ki'wi'siwe and their functions.

This is a busy season with the fraternities, and the floors are covered with groups of men with their medicine boxes beside them and plumes of all colors lying about. They prepare te'likinawe not only according to the custom of the fraternity in which they hold membership, but according to the orders to which they belong, the fraternities in most instances being composed of several orders. They go from one ceremonial chamber to another to prepare the appropriate offerings, for it is quite common for a Zuñian to hold membership in two or more fraternities. The A'pi‘‘läshiwanni as such prepare te'likinawe to the Gods of War and to their predecessors. The members of this organization also prepare the appropriate offerings for the other fraternities in which they hold membership.

Each member of a mystery medicine order, and many of the fraternities have the order of Mystery medicine, makes offerings to the sun and moon—four to the deceased members of the fraternity, one to Po'shaiyänkĭ,[a] and one to Po'shaiyänki's fellow. The ends of the offerings made to the two latter personages are cut square across, with a Greek cross on the top,[b] but the offerings of the A'shiwanni to Po'shaiyänki are serrated on the top, symbolic of cumulus clouds. A miniature crook and corn planter, each having a la'showannĕ (one or more plumes attached to a cotton cord) attached, are grouped with the offerings to Po'shaiyänki. The crook, which symbolizes longevity, is deposited with the prayer beginning "I walk with this cane," which signifies that the one who speaks prays to grow old; not to die, but to sleep and awake as a little child with the others, reference being made to the ancients.

The officers of the order of mystery medicine make te'likinawe to the Beast Gods of the six regions, to their deceased predecessors of the order, and four to deceased members at large. A member at large may only make an offering to the Beast God of one of the six regions. The A'pi‘‘läshiwanni prepare four to the deceased of their fraternity who preceded them as warrior guardians of the altars and medicine. Such orders of fraternities as have patron gods make additional offerings to them. The offerings of boys who have received only involuntary initiation into the Ko'tikili (mythologic fraternity) and those of the women and girls are made for them by their fraternity fathers. When the fraternity parent is a woman, her fraternity father prepares her te'likinawe and those for her fraternity child, should the child not be a member of the Ko'tikili.

Although it is considered out of order, a man sometimes makes his fraternity offerings at his mother's or wife's house. Each man pre-

---

[a] Po'shaiyänkĭ is the Zuñi culture hero who gave to them oxen, sheep, and raiment.

[b] Although the superstition regarding the Spaniards is still so great that no word of Mexican must be spoken in the presence of a te'likinanĕ, many of the aged theurgists declare that the cross in the marking on the offering to Po'shaiyänkĭ is symbolic of Catholicism, as their culture hero was a Catholic.

pares his individual offerings, one to the sun and four to his ancestors in his mother's house; at least such was the custom. The writer has observed these te'likinawe being made in the wife's house. The husband makes the individual offerings for the wife and children in the wife's house, including such boys as have not received voluntary initiation into the Ko'tikili. Should the father not be living the eldest son fills his place. Each female has one offering to make to the moon and three to her ancestors. Infants have two to their ancestors, none to the sun or moon. A very young infant sometimes has but one, to its ancestors. Procrastination is a common fault of the Zuñis, and consequently many must hurry to complete the individual plume making on the fifth day, the day on which the offerings are made.

On the evening of the second day all the fraternities except the ᵗHle'wekwe, ᵗKo'shiᵗkwe (Cactus), and A'piᵗⁱläshiwanni convene, each having its tablet altar erected. The members of the A'piᵗⁱläshiwanni go to their respective fraternities to fill their places as guardians of the altars and fetishes.

These synchronous meetings continue eight nights; they last until midnight on the first three nights. The women and children return to their homes to sleep, while the men sleep in the ceremonial chamber. The fourth night's ceremonies continue throughout the night, closing after sunrise. Again they convene, retiring the first three nights at midnight, and on the fourth night the ceremonies continue until after sunrise. The sick are healed at this season, but there is no initiation.

The visiting of one fraternity with another at this time is common. An invitation is extended by a mo'sona (director) of one fraternity to the corresponding officer of another. The former, calling upon the latter and presenting him with a small quantity of meal wrapped in a corn husk, invites him and his associates to come to his chamber and assist in healing the sick. These invitations are not confined to those who practise in a similar way.[a]

Images of the Gods of War (A'hayuta) are begun in the house of the aged man of the Deer clan (see plate XIX) on the third day. He fashions the idol of the elder God of War, while a man of the Bear clan makes that of the younger, both gods on this occasion bearing the name of A'hayuta. The games to accompany the idol of the elder god are made by a member of the Deer clan, and those for the younger

[a] The writer was present during a ceremonial of the Shu'maakwe (see Esoteric fraternities) when certain members of the Ma'ᵗke ᵗhlan'nakwe (Great Fire fraternity) by invitation practised their mystery medicine upon the sick of the Shu'maakwe, who do not possess the secret. On another occasion she was present when the patron gods of the Shu'maakwe danced at a meeting of the Ma'ᵗke ᵗhlan'nakwe, and members of this fraternity visited the chamber of the Shu'maakwe the same night and practised their mystery medicine. There was a special meeting of the Shu'maakwe fraternity previous to the solstice of 1896 to initiate the new Ko'mosona of the Ko'tikili into the fraternity, that he might be provided with a mi'li (see p. 416). The Kîa'kwemosi wished him to possess the sacred fetish for his visit to Ko'thluwala'wa (see pl. IV) upon the occasion of the summer solstice ceremonial. The Ko'mosona was not a member of any esoteric fraternity previous to his initiation into the Shu'maakwe.

are made by a member of the Bear clan. Two other men, belonging respectively to the Deer and Bear clans, make each four te'likinawe. The reason for confining the preparation of these idols and their games to the Deer and Bear clans is given in the words of the elder brother Bow priest:

When the two gods were once going about the country, the elder spoke, addressing the younger: "Who is your father? The deer is mine." The younger, who was just a little more venturesome and braver than the elder, replied: "The bear is my father."

At this season the images are carved from po'la (Populus fremontii). For the scalp ceremonial they must be made of ä'shekïa (Pinus ponderosa) that has been struck by lightning.

Seven members of the A'pi‘‘läshiwanni are designated by the elder brother Bow priest to make the paraphernalia for the elder God of War, and the same number are appointed by the younger brother Bow priest to prepare that for the idol of the younger God of War. One warrior makes a tablet, a second makes a staff, a third makes a shield. The hoop of the shield, large enough to encircle the bended knee, is first wrapped closely with cotton cord, and afterward the space is filled with netting. The idol stands on this shield. A fourth warrior makes the ko'lannanʰhla'kwikïa an te'likinawe (a serrated projection from the umbilicus to which plumes are attached, symbolic of clouds and lightning). All varieties of seeds are deposited in the cavity before the projection is inserted. The plumes attached waft specially valuable prayers to the gods for rain. A fifth makes a diminutive bow and arrow, shield, and war club, which are attached to the projection. A sixth warrior makes the war club. A seventh a tehl'nanĕ (a stick with plumes attached) of he'sho (piñon), measuring from the bended knee to the heel. After the idols are modeled they are decorated. The base of each idol is covered with a wad of yucca fiber,[a] held in place by a rope of the same.

Yucca cord also serves to support the plume offerings afterward made to the gods by members of the Bow priesthood. A belt of raw cotton is wound round the idol. A fine cotton cord hangs at the neck, from which an abalone shell is also pendent, but these are obscured by other adornments. When all is completed the idols are stood in state, facing east, near the north end of the room in which they have been fashioned. Two men, one of the Deer clan and the other of the Bear clan, serve as sentinels or special watchers over the idols until they are taken to the He'iwa (north) ki'wiʰsinĕ. Many come to offer prayers

[a] The yucca leaves are boiled, then run through the mouth, the fiber being partially separated by the teeth. They are afterward completely parted by the fingers. The mass is laid away until required, when it is sufficiently moistened with water to render it pliable. A cord is made by first arranging the yucca into a strand of the length required, then dividing it into two. The pieces are rolled separately with one hand at the same time on the knee, and afterward twisted into a cord without raising the material from the knee. The cord is rubbed with meal until it is quite white.

and sprinkle the gods with meal. Each member of the A'pi‘‘läshiwanni leaves a te'likinanĕ in the belt of each idol.

The maker of the sacred fire of the new year is chosen by the Kĭa'-
kwemosi and notified by the Ko'pekwĭn, who immediately after sunrise
carries a small quantity of prayer meal wrapped in corn husks to the
house of the selected party. Clasping the latter's hands with both of
his, and still holding the meal, the Ko'pekwĭn delivers his message and
prays. The office of fire-maker is filled alternately by a member of
the Badger clan and a child of that clan (see List of clans). He often
becomes the personator of the god Shu'laawi‘si in the Sha'läko ceremonial the following autumn, but this is not always the case.

The plucking of an eagle occurs in the house of a prominent shi'wanni
(not one of the first body of A'shiwanni) on the fourth day. The
process is as follows: The male members of the family are busy
arranging plumes for their te'likinawe, when the stepson of the shi'-
wanni is dispatched for an eagle (the eagles are kept in cages), which
is brought into the room under cover of a heavy blanket. Before
removing the blanket entirely, one man catches the feet and another
holds the head of the bird. The blanket is spread on the floor, and
the eagle is held on it. An ear of white corn is held to the east of the
eagle, the head of the bird being to the west. Then the plucking
begins, which requires some time, after which the feathers are deposited in an Apache basket. During the plucking a gourd of powdered
ke'chipa (kaolin) is brought in by the elder daughter of the house, who
washes several of the eagle plumes in water and holds them near the
fire. When dry, the feathers are rubbed with the kaolin to whiten
them. The younger daughter mixes a quantity of kaolin with water
in a small bowl and places it north of the eagle. After the plucking
is completed the stepson lifts the ear of white corn, and biting off several grains takes a mouthful of the kaolin mixture. The man at the
head of the eagle holds its mouth open while the other, standing with
his head some distance above the eagle's, ejects the mixture of kaolin
and chewed corn into the eagle's mouth; then, throwing the remainder
from his mouth over the eagle, he rubs that which remains in the
bowl over every spot where the white fluffy plumes should grow.
The corn is used that the plumes may soon grow, as corn comes up,
and the kaolin that the plumes may be white. While this is going
on in the center of the room the old shi'wanni sits with his back to the
fire, with piles of plumes before him and a basket on the ledge by
him, filled with plume sticks. When the plumes are all assorted into
groups he attaches them to the sticks. After each te'likinanĕ is completed he breathes upon it and offers a prayer. The eagle is carried
under cover of the blanket to his cage, where he remains in comparative peace until required for another plucking.

The preparation of wheat and corn bread for the feasts that follow is elaborate.   The light bread, which is made into fanciful shapes, is baked in the ovens which illuminate the town on the fourth night, this being the last opportunity for their use until the ten days devoted to the ceremonial expire.

At noon on the fourth day the new-year fire-maker starts on his tour through the village for wood.   He collects a fagot of cedar from each house, the person giving the wood offering a prayer that the crops may be bountiful in the coming year.   As the wood is collected it is tied together, and when the fire-maker has a load he carries it to the He′iwa ki′wiᵗsinĕ, entering through the hatchway in the roof.   As soon as the wood is deposited he starts for more, and he continues until every house in Zuñi has donated its share.

The ki′wiᵗsinĕ is entered each time through the hatchway, and the collector also leaves by the same entrance.   Upon leaving the ki′wiᵗ-sinĕ after having deposited the last load of wood, the fire-maker goes to the house directly east of it, where he collects coals from the fire-place with two pieces of wood, and returns through a communicating door between the house and the ki′wiᵗsinĕ.   After depositing the coals at the fire altar, he arranges a portion of the wood in a square, log-cabin fashion, to a height of about 18 inches.   The fire (see plate xx), which is lighted at sunset, is called ma′ᵗke tĕsh′kwi (fire not to be touched, sacred fire).[a]

At sunset the pe′kwĭn makes a meal painting on the floor at the west end of the ki′wiᵗsinĕ, he being the only shi′wanni present at the time.   Later on he places on the painting the kĭa′ĕtchinĕ, composed of the te′likinawe prepared by the first body of A′shiwanni.

The first body of A′shiwanni assemble at night in the ki′wiᵗsinĕ, and at midnight the idols of the Gods of War are brought to it from the house where they have stood in state.   The pe′kwĭn, who leads the party, carries a meal basket and sprinkles first the idol of the elder God of War and afterward that of the younger, while he stoops before and between the idols.   The elder brother Bow priest, after placing a te′likinanĕ in the belt of each of the idols and sprinkling both with meal, takes his position north of the pe′kwĭn who now stands a short distance from the idols.   The younger brother Bow priest makes his offerings to the gods in the same manner, and stands south of the sun priest.   Each whirls a rhombus.[b]

After prayers the procession leaves the house in the following order: The pe′kwĭn leads, sprinkling meal as he proceeds.   He is

---

a Tĕsh′kwi is applied to all sacred objects, such as altars, dry paintings, shrines; to the ashes and sweepings which are kept for ten days; also to fasts, such as shi′li (meat) tĕsh′kwi, machi′kwa (sugar) tĕsh′kwi.

b This instrument, which is composed of two slender slats of wood attached by a string, is extensively known among savage peoples.   It is sometimes called bull roarer, and is said to be used to work savages into frenzy.   Such is not the case with the Pueblo tribes, among whom the rhombus is whirled to create enthusiasm among the u′wannami (rain-makers).

followed by the priest of the pa'ĕttonĕ[a] carrying his fetish which bears his name; after him is a priest of the ᵗsuᵗhlan'na (great shell), carrying the shell; then the Kĭa'kwemosi bearing his ĕt'tonĕ; then the aged man of the Deer clan, carrying the idol of the elder God of War. The two men of the Deer clan follow with the paraphernalia of the god; then a man of the Bear clan with the idol of the younger God of War, and after him two other members of the Bear clan bearing the paraphernalia of this god. The elder brother Bow priest walks to the right of the pe'kwĭn and the younger brother Bow priest is on the right of the man at the end of the file, each whirling his rhombus as he proceeds. After entering the ki'wiᵗsinĕ the fetishes and idols are placed on the meal painting, the idols and paraphernalia being deposited by the pe'kwĭn. The A'piᶜᵗläshiwanni are present in a body, having left their various fraternities for this purpose, and at this time they sing the song which is sung after sunset in the closing scene of the scalp ceremony (see A'piᶜᵗläshiwanni, page 605).

The ceremonies in the ki'wiᵗsinĕ continue throughout the night. The Gods of War are thus honored that they may intercede with the rain-makers for rains to fructify the earth. At sunrise the idols are carried by the elder and younger brother Bow priests to their respective homes, each being accompanied by a warrior bearing the games and paraphernalia of the gods. Each idol is placed in the west end of the large chamber and the paraphernalia are arranged about it (see plate XXI).[b]

As soon as the idol and its belongings are placed in position by the elder brother Bow priest and his associates, they offer prayers and sprinkle meal. Then the family of the former gather about the idol to pray and make offerings of precious beads, etc., and they sprinkle sacred meal. Many from outside, of both sexes and all ages, come to the gods to pray and make offerings of one or more precious beads.[c]

After depositing a little food south of the idol, and then breakfasting with his family, the elder brother Bow priest ties a reddish, fluffy plume

[a] The pa'ĕttowĕ (singular pa'ĕttonĕ: pa from Pachu, Navaho) are sacred fetishes of the A'piᶜᵗläshiwanni (Bow priesthood) which protects them from the enemy.

[b] Plate XXI was made from a case in the National Museum, the objects being placed according to photographs and sketches made of the group in the house of the elder brother Bow priest in 1896. The idol is a very old one, secured through Nai'uchi for Mr Stevenson from the shrine on To'wa yäl'lännĕ (Corn mountain) in 1881. It has been redecorated after the sketch made of the one observed in the winter solstice of 1896. All the coloring used on it is native. The white top of the idol with black rectangles signifies a white cloud cap with black rain clouds—the house of the clouds. The tablets, staffs, war club, and the te'likinawe, except four, were made by the elder brother Bow priest, who also made the feather bow and arrow, which is to be seen immediately before the idol. The other te'likinawe were fashioned by the aged member of the Deer clan. The games (see Games, p. 317) were made by members of the same clan. All was done by direction of Nai'uchi, the elder brother Bow priest, that the writer might have a facsimile of the idol of the elder God of War as he appears in his (the elder brother Bow priest's) house at the winter solstice.

[c] During the time the idol is in the house, Nai'uchi, the most successful practitioner in Zuñi, treats several patients who come to him. In each case he relieves the sufferer by pretending to extract the cause of the disease from the body; wrapping the ejected material in a husk, he carries it from the house. Nai'uchi does not practice medicine through his association with the Bow priesthood, but through his membership in other esoteric fraternities.

to his forelock, removes a die (grain of corn) from one of the cups of the game i'yänkolo'we, and hands it to the associate warrior, who wraps it in a corn husk while the elder brother Bow priest ties the four cups together. The associate binds the two games of sho'liwe together and gathers all the games into his blanket over the left arm. The elder brother Bow priest removes the yucca rope with the te'likinawe attached, and, stooping before the idol, holds the plumes near its base while he prays. He now deposits the feather bow and arrow in a hu'chipone (deep basket), and the idol with all its adornments is stood in the basket. The rope containing the te'likinawe is placed next, and the food which was south of the idol is wrapped in the cloth and put into the basket. He now hangs his war pouch over his shoulder, rolls a quantity of prayer meal in a piece of cloth, and tucks it into his belt. Wrapping his blanket about him, he provides himself with a rhombus and, supporting his basket with his left arm, leaves the house, whirling the rhombus with his right hand. He is followed by his associate carrying the remaining paraphernalia of the god in the blanket over his left arm while he whirls a rhombus with the right hand. During their progress through the village the two are frequently stopped by those who wish to pray before the idol and sprinkle meal upon it. On reaching the shrine on U'hana yäl'länně the idol placed the previous year is removed and the new one substituted, with its paraphernalia about it, just as it is seen in the house of the elder brother Bow priest. The idol of the younger God of War is carried in the same manner to a shrine on To'wa yäl'länně (see plate XXII).[a] The only difference observed in the two images is that the one representing the younger god has a zigzag stick, symbolic of lightning, running up from the top of the cloud cap on the head.

The A'shiwanni and officers of the fraternities deposit their te'likinawe on the fifth day at the appropriate shrines, while all others plant theirs in the fields, the fraternity offerings being deposited in the excavations with the individual offerings.

The Kĭa'kwemosi carries the kĭa'ĕtchině, composed of the prayer plumes of the A'shiwanni, and the ha'kwani, made by the Shi'wano'-'kĭa, to the base of Ma'ʼsakĭa (a ruin on a knoll), where the kĭa'ĕtchině is deposited. Both the plumes and the ha'kwani are offerings to the u'wannami A'shiwanni (rain-maker priests). The pe'kwĭn alone visits the shrine on the summit of the knoll, but no plume offerings are deposited here. This shrine (see figure 3) consists of a stone wall, semicircular in form, about 3 feet high, the inner space being 3 feet wide and opening to the east. A sandstone slab, about 2 feet high and 14 inches wide, with a symbol of the sun 4 inches in diameter etched upon it stands against the apex of the wall. A smooth-surfaced stone on which are cut a number of lines is inserted in each side of the wall

---

[a] See p. 606.

about 8 inches above the base. Some of the priests declare that the lines on the south side of the wall indicate the number of years the previous sun priest held the office, and the one on the north side the number of years the present incumbent has served.[a] Nine concretions form a square on the ground before the etching of the sun, and there are three smaller ones in line in front of these. Concretion fetishes, valued as bringing fructification to the earth, are to be found in all the fields. A small flat stone rests on two of the larger concretions.

The same morning, about 9 o'clock, members of the order of Pa'yatämu of the Little Fire and Cimex fraternities, playing on their flutes, ascend To'wa yäl'länně to To'mapa, a shrine in the west side (see plate XXIII) halfway up the mesa, and deposit their offerings to the god,

FIG. 3—Sun shrine at Ma'⸤sakĭa.

while officers of other fraternities carry their offerings to various shrines. The ⸤Ko'shi⸤kwe deposit te'likinawe at this time, but they hold no ceremonial in their chamber.

There is no exception to the rule of members at large of fraternities planting their fraternity offerings at this season in the same excavation and at the same time as the family deposit theirs. It is usual for all the members of a household to go together; in fact, in all observations made by the writer, such has been the case. Husbands deposit their offerings in the fields of the families of their wives, and vice versa. A hole about 14 inches square and the same in depth is made by a man of the household, and the plumes, which are carried to the fields on the fifth day, wrapped together with corn husks, are sepa-

---

[a] The statement regarding the lines was made previous to the appointment of the present sun priest.

rated and deposited, the father standing his te'likinawe, including those of his ti'kili (fraternity), in one end of the excavation, the mother placing hers in the other end, and the children depositing theirs between. The infant is carried to the field on the mother's back, and with its tiny hand, guided by the mother, plants its plumes. These offerings may be planted any hour between sunrise and sunset (see plate XXIV). Those who are absent on long journeys or those too ill to leave the house have their offerings deposited for them by some member of the family. All must have the head bathed with yucca suds previous to depositing the plume. There may be exceptions to this rule, such as a young child suffering with a cold.

The sun rose in splendor on the morning of the fifth day, making brilliant the mantle of snow that covered the earth. The valley was sparkling white, and the mesa walls were white, with here and there a patch of dark blue, the pines veiled by the atmosphere. The snowy plain was a vast kaleidoscope from morning until evening, the devotees in their bright clothing going to and returning from their sacred mission.

One description of a family planting prayer plumes will answer for all, and the writer will describe the one in which she took part, having been expected to perform this sacred office with one of the families.

On the present occasion the male head of the house is an associate shi'wanni. Those who accompany him are his wife, mother-in-law, daughter about 10 years of age, a younger one of 4 years, a son 8 months old, the younger brother of his wife with his wife and infant, a girl of 12 years, daughter of the younger brother Bow priest, who is the elder brother of the associate shi'wanni's wife, and the writer. The associate shi'wanni hands the writer the te'likinawe he has made for her, saying: "Though you are a woman you have a head and a heart like a man, and you work like a man, and you must therefore make offerings such as men make."

The party proceeds to a melon patch of the associate shi'wanni, where he makes an excavation about 14 inches square and of the same depth, using an old saber for the purpose. The excavation completed, all except the two infants remove the corn husks which wrap the te'likinawe and, after sprinkling prayer meal in the excavation, proceed without formality to plant te'likinawe. Each man deposits as his individual offerings one te'likinanĕ with its stick colored blue to the Sun Father and four with sticks colored black to his ancestors. The younger brother of the wife plants, in addition to his individual te'likinawe, offerings as a member of the Great Fire fraternity (see plate XXV),[a] one to Po'shaiyänki (culture hero), one to the younger brother, or fellow, of Po'shaiyänki. The one to Po'shaiyänki has

---

[a] It should be noted that the te'likinawe on pl. XXV are inverted. To get a proper view of the prayer plumes the plate should be reversed. Through inadvertence in the color printing this mistake occurred.

attached a miniature crook, symbolic of longevity, the other a miniature corn planter bound to it, to bring much corn in the coming year. He also plants one to the Cougar of the North, to the Sun Father, and to the Moon Mother, the two latter being bound together. Some of the te'likinawe have pendent la'showawe (one or more plumes attached to cotton cord). Those having the la'showawe bear the prayers for rains, and those without are for clouds and other things.

Each female, including the child of 4 years, plants one te'likinanĕ with the stick colored yellow to the Moon Mother, and three with the sticks colored black to her ancestors. Each infant offers one or two te'likinawe with sticks colored black to its ancestors. The writer deposits one to the Sun Father and four to ancestors. In addition to the individual plumes, both the wife and elder daughter of the associate shi'wanni, as members of the Shu'maakwe fraternity, deposit two te'likinawe to Shumai'koli and two to Sai'apa (patron gods of the fraternity), one to the ettonĕ,[a] and four to the deceased members of the fraternity.

After the te'likinawe are all stood in the ground each person takes a pinch of meal brought by the mother-in-law in a cloth and, holding the meal near the lips, repeats a prayer for health, long life, many clouds, much rain, food, and raiment, and the meal is sprinkled thickly over the plumes. The little child seems to understand perfectly her duties and prayers. The tiny babies have their hands dipped into the meal and held over the plumes. These plumes remain uncovered until sunset the following day, that the Sun Father, in passing over the road of day, may receive the prayers breathed upon the meal and into the plumes, the spiritual essence of the plumes conveying the breath prayers to him. The excavations are afterward so covered that no one could discover that the earth had been disturbed.[b]

After the te'likinawe are deposited no animal food or grease càn be eaten or touched with the hands for four days, those excepted being members of the 'Sän'iakïakwe (Hunters) and Shi'wannakwe (those who do not fast from animal food) fraternities and children receiving nourishment from their mothers. As the latter take milk, they may eat grease. The first body of A'shiwanni must fast from animal food and grease and observe continence for ten days from this time.

There must be no trading of any description for four days, and to begin trading before ten days have expired is indicative of plebianism. No ashes or sweepings may be taken from the house during this period, and no artificial light must appear outside the house, not even a burning cigarette, nor the flash of firearms, no matter how great the

---

[a] See A'shiwanni (Rain-priesthood), p. 163.

[b] When the associate shi'wanni visited the excavation in the evening after the plume planting, the writer accompanied him and induced him to let her have the complete set of plumes which were planted the previous day. These te'likinawe are deposited in the United States National Museum in an excavation as they appeared in the field at Zuñi.

distance from the village. The words of a shi'wanni will give an idea of the dread these people have of failure in the custom concerning firelight: "Why did the woman [reference to the camp manager of the writer] go outside last night with a light? She was seen by one of my neighbors. Alas! alas! alas! I will have no crops for four years. I shall be poor. Rains will come and fall all around my fields, upon the fields of my brothers, but none will come to me." The writer endeavored to console him by saying that he could not possibly be responsible for the acts of one of her party. "It was done from my house and I must be the sufferer. Did she carry a lamp or candle?" When informed that a candle was carried, distress was again depicted on his face. "It might have been better had she carried a lantern, for then the light would have been at least partially housed."

On the morning of the fifth day the fire-tender covers with ashes the coals on the fire altar in the ki'wi'sinĕ and goes to his home for his breakfast. After his meal the fire-tender deposits his individual te'-likinawe and returns to the ki'wi'sinĕ where a fire burns throughout the day. At night he covers the coals with ashes before he sleeps. In the morning the fire is again kindled from the coals. After a time the fire-tender covers the coals with ashes and goes a distance from the village for cedar, to be consumed on the fire altar. On his return in the evening, after he has taken his meal in his own house, he again rekindles the fire, which burns until he is ready to sleep, when he covers the coals as before. He leaves the ki'wi'sinĕ only to eat and to go for wood each day until the closing of the festival. No food must be taken in the ki'wi'sinĕ for ten days. If this rule should be broken, the offender would not only have his crops destroyed by crows and mice, but would be in great danger of death.

There is no perpetual fire kept in the ki'wi'siwe of any pueblo, nor has there been one since the introduction of matches among the Indians and since they have found their way to the woods clear from enemies. In times past the scarcity of wood near home and the danger attending journeys for wood, which was brought upon their backs (as they had no beasts of burden until the invasion of the Spaniards), compelled the strictest economy in fuel and necessitated a central fire for each village. This not only gave warmth to a large number of priests while they performed their religious and other duties, but furnished coals with which to light small fires elsewhere when needed for domestic and other purposes. Fire furnishes warmth and light after the sun is gone to his home for the night, and it cooks the food and conveys the spiritual essence of food to the gods. Fire is therefore a goddess, second in importance only to the sun. Thus the elements attending the physical wants become features of the psychical.

From the fifth to the eighth day the pueblo is buzzing with the mills and the songs of the grinders, and on the eighth day every household is busy preparing varieties of food, for on the following morning the fraternities will adjourn, when meat may be eaten and the appetite generally sated.

On the eighth day there are still more extensive preparations of te'likinawe.   All are busy in chambers of the fraternities and elsewhere. While this day is especially set apart for making the offerings to be deposited on the ninth day, several days must be consumed by many who have not only their own te'likinawe to make but those of their fraternity children.   No one who has not received voluntary initiation into the Ko'tikili is privileged to fashion the sticks or attach the plumes, although women sometimes color the sticks.   There is, however, an exception to this rule.   When a woman has severed her connection with the U'huhukwe (Eagle down) fraternity,[a] she must then prepare the offerings for it, she having been instructed by her fraternity father.

The only persons exempt from offering te'likinawe on the ninth day are females who are not associated with a fraternity and young male children who have not received voluntary initiation into the Ko'tikili. Each member of the Ko'tikili deposits one te'likinanĕ to the sun, one to the moon, four to the Kok'ko A'wan (Council of the Gods), and others to the game animals, birds of the six regions, birds of summer, birds of winter, and to Po'shaiyänki for all domestic animals.

The old proverb, "When you are in Rome do as the Romans do," is sometimes observed in Zuñi.   For example, a Hopi Indian, married to a Zuñi woman and therefore a resident of Zuñi, is seen sitting in the midst of a group of his people (visitors to the village) in the southwest portion of the room of José Palle, a shi'wanni, and all are preparing te'likinawe that are quite different from those offered by the Zuñi.   The son of the shi'wanni by a former wife, one by his present wife, a stepson, and two adopted children, nephews of the wife, one of whom wears female attire, sit on the ledge in the northeast portion of the room, all busily engaged preparing their te'likinawe.   The shi'wanni himself sits some distance from the family in the east end of the room.   Medicine boxes and Apache baskets are before and beside him.   His wife busies herself making te'likinawe of the U'huhukwe fraternity, from which she has resigned.   Two children amuse themselves with plumes given them by their grandfather. One young mother, tying a plume to her infant's hair and providing him with a ceremonial rattle, teaches him to dance.   Thus the children begin at the tenderest age to prepare for their future duties, those features which delight their infantile minds becoming the ritual associated with their worship.

The Hopi resident makes for each person present, including the children and the writer, a la'showannĕ of two fluffy eagle plumes and two pine needles, which he presents with prayers for rain to fructify the earth, that the crops may be bountiful, and for the good health and long life of all.   The la'showannĕ is tied to a strand of hair at the left

----
[a] See Esoteric fraternities.

TO'MAPA, A SHRINE IN WEST WALL OF TO'WA YÄL'LÄNNĚ (CORN MOUNTAIN)

M. Wright Gill.

FAMILY STARTING FOR THE FIELD TO DEPOSIT PRAYER PLUMES AT WINTER SOLSTICE

MASKS OF A'PI'ᵗLAṢHIWANNI (WARRIORS): a OF THE ZENITH, b OF THE NADIR,
c OF THE MOSONA OF THE KĨA'NAKWE   FRONT AND SIDE VIEWS

MASK OF SHUĹAAWIᵗSI (DEPUTY TO THE SUN FATHER); FRONT AND SIDE VIEWS

side of the head near the crown. He sets the basket containing the other la'showawe made by himself and his people on the north ledge of the room, and he and his party leave the house.

When the others complete the preparation of their offerings, the baskets containing them are also deposited on the ledge. Such objects are never touched or in any way disturbed by the children. About 8 o'clock supper is served. The Hopi resident and the two sons-in-law of the house, being present, participate in the meal. No animal food appears. Considerable time is consumed over the meal, and it is after 9 o'clock when the mother and elder daughter begin their ablutions preparatory to attending their fraternity. Their hair has already been washed. The bath and toilet are made in the general living room. Each woman stands before a large bowl of water and, without removing her camis, bathes the entire body. No member of a fraternity would dare omit the daily bath during a ceremonial. Such neglect would cause great offense to the Beast Gods, who would visit their wrath upon the offender. After the daughter has bathed she washes her husband's head in yucca suds and proceeds to brush and do up his hair. The younger daughter performs the same service for her husband, who holds his infant on his lap, caressing him, except at times when the child is coaxed away by his grandparents or other relatives present, all seeming ready to suspend more weighty matters to fondle the tiny one.

Twelve members of the Chu'pawa ki'wit'sině, including the pe'kwĭn (deputy to the priest of the Kĭa'nakwe),[a] arrive from time to time. The pe'kwĭn arranges a number of te'likinawe, which he brings with him, into groups, wrapping them at the base with corn husks, and deposits them in a flat basket. In the meantime José Palle's two sons-in-law depart for the chamber of the Shi'wannakwe fraternity. The elder daughter has her hair dressed by the adopted son, who wears feminine dress. She then attires herself in her best gown and belt. The many necklaces of the father are divided by him between his wife and daughter. Each woman has her own silver necklaces, but is ready to add all the ko'hakwa (white shell beads), turquoise, and corals that can be secured. Great pride is felt over the display of such wealth at these ceremonials. The writer has seen children of four or five summers loaded with necklaces, marveling that the weight could be carried in the dance. The elder daughter assists her 8-year old child to bed in the west end of the room and starts for her fraternity. Her infant nephew begs to accompany her, his attachment for his aunt seeming to be as great as that for the mother, and he is caught up on her back with a blanket and carried off to the fraternity. Her younger sister, after filling a pottery basket with sacred meal and returning it to a niche in the south wall, lies beside the niece.

The members of the Chu'pawa ki'wi'sině who are present chat and

---

a See p. 36.

smoke and repeat te'lapnawe (tales) until midnight, when they hold an interesting ceremonial not directly connected with the winter-solstice festival, but relating to the calendar. The chairs are removed, the floor is swept, and the party take their seats on their wadded blankets or on the ledge, forming a broken circle near the fireplace, in which may be seen a large vessel, balanced on stones, containing a stew of meat and hominy, and two large pumpkins roasting before the fire. The men remove their moccasins. The shi'wanni of the Kĭa'nakwe (see page 36), who is the man of the house, forms the central figure and is raised above the others by his wadded blanket being placed on a low box. He faces east. A large Apache basket containing his te'likinawe, offerings to the Council of the Gods, two small vases of the roots and blossoms of te'na'säli (mythical medicine plant bearing blossoms of the colors of the six regions), and several buckskin medicine bags, are placed before him. Other baskets holding similar te'likinawe belonging to the others of the group are handed him. He removes the buckskin medicine bags from the larger basket, lays them on the floor between himself and the basket, and transfers the groups of te'likinawe from the smaller baskets to the larger one, arranging them artistically, so that the feather ends radiate and the la'showawe attached to the te'likinawe fringe the edge of the basket.

The shi'wanni makes a cross of meal south of the basket and one in the center of it, and deposits a stone cougar, 8 inches long, colored yellow, the mouth, tail, and feet black, on the cross south of the basket. Another basket is now handed to the shi'wanni, which he holds on his lap, and to which he transfers the two packages of te'na'säli. He then proceeds to empty the bags. Removing one fetish at a time, he examines each, and, if a prey animal, deposits it in the basket on his lap, with the head to the east. There are as many as forty of these stone fetishes, mostly prey animals, ranging from 1½ to 4 inches in length. A few are concretions, sacred to the fields. As an evidence of the extreme conventionality of these fetishes, the shi'wanni finds it necessary, when handling some of the more ancient ones, to consult several of his party as to what animals they might be. Each animal fetish carries an arrow point on its back, held on with strings of precious beads wrapped around the image.

The man to the left of the shi'wanni also has sacks of fetishes. Removing each fetish separately from the sack, he holds it until it is received by the shi'wanni, who places it with the others. When all the fetishes have been deposited, the shi'wanni again sprinkles a cross of meal in the larger basket, and handles each package of the tena'säli separately. Each fetish is deposited in the large basket with the same care as when it is placed in the smaller one. He sets the smaller basket between the larger one and the large fetish of the cougar, being careful to so place the basket that the la'showawe in the larger one fall over it. The second man to the left of the shi'wanni, his stepson, makes a cigarette of native tobacco and, after lighting and drawing on it an instant, hands it to the man at his right, who takes a whiff and passes it to the shi'wanni, who takes eight long whiffs, each time blowing the smoke over the basket of plumes and fetishes. The shi'wanni then returns the stump of the cigarette to the man at his left, the collector of the te'na'säli. The first associate to the shi'wanni, who sits on his right, after consuming all but a bit of the cigarette, deposits it by the large stone cougar. Each cigarette of native tobacco afterward smoked by the associate is deposited by this fetish after the better part has been consumed.

Cigarettes are smoked by all the party during the ceremonial, but not more than one or two smoke at the same time. After the shi'wanni's first smoke he takes a pinch of meal in his right hand and repeats a long litany, responded to by the others. At the close of this prayer he sprinkles the meal he holds over the cougar and basket of plumes and fetishes, and then all take a pinch of the meal from the basket and simultaneously offer a short prayer and sprinkle the plumes and fetishes, drawing from them the sacred breath. The song now begins, led by the shi'wanni. It opens low in a minor key, swelling until the notes are rich and full. This song, less monotonous than usual, is offered to various beings of the six regions, who are addressed in succession. The first prayer is to a group belonging to the Sia cosmogony, whom the writer has never before heard mentioned in Zuñi ritual. These beings are the Yellow Woman of the North, the Blue Woman of the West, the Red Woman of the South, the White Woman of the East, the Every-colored Woman of the Zenith, and the Black Woman of the Nadir. The Cougar of the North, the Bear of the West, the Badger of the South, the White Wolf of the East, the Eagle of the Zenith, and the Shrew of the Nadir play an important part in this ritual.[a]

The old shi'wanni, sitting in light or shadow according to the uncertain flickering of the fire light in the quaint fireplace, with silvery hair and a countenance impressed with the superstitions peculiar to his race and depicting the most intense earnestness, is a picture not to be forgotten. He is surrounded by his associates, who are also intent upon having their songs pass over the straight road of truth. The songs and prayers are to bring rains to fructify the mother earth, who gives to her children the fruits of her being if prayers are offered with a pure heart. The song closes at the rising of the morning star, which announces that the Sun Father is coming from his house, when all repeat a short prayer and inhale the sacred breath of A'wonawil'ona.[b]

---

[a] This prayer song was recognized as being in the Sia language, and on being questioned the shi'wanni, who was not a little chagrined at the discovery, said: "The song came to us long ago, so long that the fathers of the father's fathers could not tell when."

[b] See Classification of the higher powers, p. 22.

The stone fetishes are returned to the buckskin medicine bags by the owners, and the te′nasᵗsäli is restored to the vase by the man whose special care it is to guard the sacred mythical medicine plant. The participants in this ceremony now go to their homes or fraternities, and return after sunrise for their te′likinawe, which may be planted in the fields any time during the day.

An incident occurred on the eighth evening that is worthy of mention. A flayed bear was brought to the pueblo by some Navahos and presented to the mo′sona (director) of the Hä′lo‘kwe (ant) fraternity, who at once convened the fraternity. The altar was erected and the a′kwamosi (maker of medicine water) consecrated the water. The bear was butchered, and in an inner room, during the night, was cooked in immense caldrons in the broad fireplace with awning by female members of the fraternity. The other members spent the night in singing and dancing. In the early morning the cooked meat was brought in, with other food, in large bowls. The mo′sona placed the bear's skull in a flat basket in which he had made a cross of meal, symbolic of the four regions, and deposited the basket before the altar, the top of the head to the east. A woman prepared a bowl of yucca suds and each person present dipped his two ceremonial eagle plumes into the suds and brought them forward over the top of the skull. The woman who prepared the suds afterward washed the skull, and the mo′sona painted the lower portion of it black and the upper portion yellow. The top of the head was spotted over with micaceous hematite. A salmon-colored fluffy eagle plume was attached to the top of the skull and a similar one to the base. After the skull was decorated the a′kwamosi sprinkled it with meal, having first thrown medicine water over it, and all present sprinkled meal upon it. The skull was afterward carried in state to To′mapa, a shrine in the west wall of To′wa yäl′-länně (see pl. XXIII).ᵃ Each member of the fraternity having prepared a te′liki-naně, these were arranged in a flat basket, the plume ends radiating, and the skull was placed in the center. The woman who washed the skull carried it and was followed by four officers of the fraternity, who sang to the accompaniment of the rattle. Each man wore the deerskin hood of the personators of the Sha′läko, which may be worn by officers of fraternities on such occasions as described.

The first body of A′shiwanni gather on the eighth day in the He′iwa ki′wiᵗsině, where they remain during the night and prepare te′likinawe, some of which are deposited at sunset on the evening of the ninth day in a spring or water pocket, through which the Kok′ko (anthropic gods) are supposed to view this earth from the undermost world.

On the ninth day the first body of A′shiwanni, the Ko′mosona, the Ko′pekwǐn, and two Ko′pi‘ᵗläshiwanni meet in the dwelling of the Ko′mosona, his wife's house, and prepare te′likinawe. Each shi′wanni makes four offerings to Pau′tiwa. The others present make each two te′likinawe to be offered to that god. The Ko′mosona groups all the te′likinawe into a kǐa′ětchině. On the same day the people of the Corn clan and the children of the clan ᵇ assemble in the house of the father or head of the clan to choose a man to personate Pau′tiwa (see page 33), who is known at this time as the Kom′häᵗlikwi.ᶜ The head of the clan presents prayer meal wrapped in a corn husk to the party chosen to represent the Kom′häᵗlikwi, notifying him that he is to personate this god

ᵃ Skulls of the prey animals of the six regions are deposited at this shrine.
ᵇ See List of clans.
ᶜ Dance witch or witch of the Kok′ko.

in the coming ceremony. A prayer is offered for a good heart to the chosen party and for rains to fructify the earth. Each man present makes four te′likinawe to Pau′tiwa. When the prayer plumes are completed the head of the clan groups them into a kĭa′ĕtchinĕ, which is afterward given to the personator of Pau′tiwa.

Pau′tiwa appears three times annually in Zuñi. When he comes to announce the closing of the winter solstice ceremonial the personator must be of the Corn clan or a child of this clan, the corn being selected every other year. When Pau′tiwa comes on the evening of the closing ceremonies he must be of the Dogwood clan or a child of this clan, the Dogwood clan being represented every alternate year, and being chosen for this occasion by the mo′sona of Shu′maakwe fraternity, who selects him irrespective of the Parrot and Raven divisions of this clan (see page 40). When Pau′tiwa comes for the mo′lawe festival [a] the personator must be of the Ai′yahokwe (a certain plant) clan or a child of this clan, the Ai′yahokwe being represented every alternate year.

Five members of the Sun clan and five of the Corn clan, besides the personator of Pau′tiwa or Kom′hä′likwi, assemble in the house of the latter soon after his appointment, and each one present makes four te′likinawe to the Council of the Gods. After the offerings are completed the men carry them to the Ko′mosona, who puts them with the offerings made by his party, wrapping the group of te′likinawe at the base with cotton cord, and hands the kĭa′ĕtchinĕ to the Kom′-hä′likwi, who with his party is dispatched to plant these plumes.

The five men of the Sun clan precede the others in file, the fifth one carrying a ta′sakwĭnnĕ (ancient corn planter). He is followed by the Kom′hä′likwi bearing the kĭa′ĕtchinĕ. The five men of the Corn clan follow in file. All carry a mixture composed of ground abalone shell, ko′hakwa (white shell), and turquoise, which they sprinkle as they proceed. This mixture is prepared by a woman of the Sun clan, and is made especially for the occasion. When some distance west of the village the man who carries the corn planter makes an excavation on the bank of the river, using the corn planter to loosen the earth, which he throws out with his hands. The process is somewhat tedious, but continues until he has excavated to the depth of his waist and some 2 feet in diameter. He must reach considerable water. After the Kom′hä′likwi deposits the te′likinawe in the excavation, all sprinkle the plumes with meal and pray for rains, then the opening is filled by the man who made it.

On the tenth day the otaikĭa mo′sona (dance director) of each ki′wit-sinĕ, with several associates, awaits in his ki′wit-sinĕ the coming of the Kom′hä′likwi, who arrives at midnight. He dodges about and disappears in the dark corners to avoid the light and the view of the people, just as witches do; hence the name. Ascending the ladder to the roof, he throws a pinch of meal through the hatchway, and marks four lines with meal on the crossbar of it, which indicates that after

---

[a] See Annual festival of the Sha′läko, p. 277.

four days shall have passed ashes may be carried outside, or that the těsh'kwi (fast) closes. After visiting the ki'wi'siwe he disappears over the western road. Each day one line of the meal is rubbed off by the otaikĭa mo'sona.

During the fourteenth day the first body of A'shiwanni, the Ko'mosona, Ko'pekwĭn, the two Ko'pi'läshiwanni, and the fire-tender are engaged in the He'iwa ki'wi'sině preparing te'likinawe to the Council of the Gods, the six Sha'läko, four Sa'ya'hlia, and Bi'''si'si. Those to the latter are designated mo'lawe a'wan te'likinawe, they being associated with Bi'''si'si, the original mo'sona of the Galaxy fraternity, at the time of his appearance in the festival of the mo'lawe.[a] In addition to these offerings, others are made every four years to 'Kiäklo,[b] and to the Kĭa'nakwe,[c] who are personated quadrennially. At the same time the A'wan tä'tchu Ko'yemshi[b] is chosen from the designated fraternity by the elder brother Bow priest, who is also Shi'wanni of the Nadir, the several fraternities alternating annually; and while it is customary for the A'wan tä'tchu Ko'yemshi to select his nine associates from the fraternity to which he belongs, they are sometimes chosen at large from the people.

The Great Fire fraternity is also assembled in the ki'wi'sině at this time, with other members. The mo'sona of this fraternity directs two of its members to visit 'Kĭa'nanaknana, a spring at the black rocks east of Zuñi, and collect water. A gourd jug covered with a network of cotton cord, with four fluffy white eagle plumes attached, is handed to one of the men, who holds it in his left hand and receives four te'likinawe in his right. These plume offerings are to the Sun Father, deceased Kĭa'kwe amosi (rain priests) of the North (rain priests of the Zenith), and rain priests of the Nadir. The second man receives four te'likinawe to the Sun Father, deceased rain priests of the West, South, and East, which he carries in his left hand, while in his right he has a rhombus, which he whirls as he follows the other man to the spring. The leader carries meal in his belt, which he throws before him as he proceeds. Reaching the spring, the te'likinawe are deposited, and the jug is filled with water.

The same morning the Ko'mosona selects a man of the Deer clan and one of the Corn clan to visit a spring at 'Kiap'kwena (Ojo Caliente). The man of the Deer clan leads. He carries in his left hand a water jug similar to that borne by the member of the Great Fire fraternity, and five te'likinawe, which are to be offered to Council of the Gods. In his right hand he carries a rhombus. The man of the Corn clan carries in his left hand a similar jug and five te'likinawe, as offerings to Council of the Gods and the Sha'läko. He carries a rhombus

---

[a] See Annual festival of the Sha'läko, p. 277.
[b] See Origin of ancestral gods, p. 33.
[c] See Destruction of the Kĭa'nakwe and songs of thanksgiving, p. 36.

in his right. These te'likinawe are deposited in the spring, and the jugs are filled with water. This couple returns the same evening, though the spring is 15 miles from Zuñi. Should they become weary, they sprinkle meal before them, with a prayer to the Council of the Gods for strength of heart and limb. Upon their return from ᵗKĭa'-nanaknana the men pass to the right of the ladder, and after descending into the ki'wiᵗsinĕ turn to the left and advance to the director of the Great Fire fraternity, who stands by the meal painting. After receiving the jugs, the director stoops and empties the water into his medicine bowl with the prayer: "Ho'mo a'täᵗchu u'wannam-a'shiwanni yäm ᵗkĭa'shima yäm to'shonannĕ yäm ᵗhli'towe yäm wil'lolonannĕ yäm ku'lulunannĕ yämᵗhlash'shiakĭa (My fathers, rain priests, rainmakers, give to us water, seeds, rains, and lightning. Let us have thunder. Let us be white-haired with age)." The unexpressed thought is that they may be made happy with the fruits of the earth and live to old age, to sleep, not die, and awake in Ko'thluwala'wa (the abiding place of the Council of the Gods; see plate IV). The two members of the Great Fire fraternity take their seats with their fraternity. The Ko'mosona receives the jug brought by the others and pours the water into his medicine bowl with a prayer similar to that offered by the director of the Great Fire fraternity.

On the fourteenth day the first body of A'shiwanni, the Ko'mosona, and the Ko'pekwĭn consult together in the He'iwa ki'wiᵗsinĕ as to who shall personate certain gods and who shall entertain the Council of the Gods and Sha'läko in the coming autumn. This privilege is asked by such men of the village as desire to build new homes or renovate old ones, those having good hearts and being fitted to fill the positions receiving much consideration; the decision is made by the elder brother Bow priest. There are always eight new houses to be blessed by the gods.

A meal painting, quite different in character from the one symbolic of clouds seen on the fourth day, is made by the Ko'pekwĭn before sunset on the fourteenth day. The former painting is the property of the Gods of War, and must never appear except in connection with them. The latter is used in reference to the Kok'ko. The cloud symbols of the other fraternities are different from either of those mentioned. A large fire burns on the fire altar day and night during the fourteenth day.

The Sa'yaᵗhlia masks (see plate XVI) that were deposited by the meal painting are soon removed and worn by the personators of these gods, who appear as warriors for a short time in the streets of the village and then return to the ki'wiᵗsinĕ. They and the personators of Shits'ukĭa and Kwe'lele (two gods from Shi'papolima ᵃ) wear their

---

ᵃ See Esoteric fraternities.

masks throughout the night and move about continually without taking seats (see plates XXVI and XXVII).

The personator of Pau'tiwa appears in the ki'wi⁺sině after dark, and his mask (see plate XXVIII) is removed and placed by the meal painting, the man himself taking his seat immediately back of it between the lines of men of the Dogwood and Sun clans.

The ledge around the room is filled with spectators, all males who have passed their voluntary initiation being privileged to enter the ki'wi⁺sině. The Sa'ya⁺hlia, Shits'ukĭa, and Kwe'lele are tenacious in their prerogative of whipping those who are found dozing or who attempt to depart from the ki'wi⁺sině during the night. No one must sleep while in the ki'wi⁺sině, nor must one, after entering, leave before morning. The members of Great Fire fraternity and of the He'iwa ki'wi⁺sině alternate in singing to the accompaniment of the rattle and drum.

There is constant smoking, and a quantity of popcorn water is drunk. No article that has touched grease must be used in dipping this water.

Mr. George M. Landers, of Connecticut, a Representative in the Forty-fourth and Forty-fifth Congresses, desiring to aid in Christianizing and civilizing the Zuñis, gave to an Indian, who was spending the winter with the writer, a large box of cutlery and silverware, thinking that this Indian, having had the environment of civilization for six months, would carry back its influence to her people. When the writer visited Zuñi about two months after the return of the Indian to her home, she found that the steel knives had been distributed among the rain priests and others, for the purpose of fashioning te'likinawe, and that the large silver spoons were used with popcorn water, which is drunk in certain ceremonials. The forks were playthings among the children, the Indian to whom the things were given having returned to the use of her fingers in place of the knife and fork. Yet this Zuñian, during her six months' stay in Washington, came in contact only with the highest conditions of culture, dining and receiving with some of the most distinguished women of the national capital.

The songs and dancing of Shits'ukĭa and Kwe'lele continue until the rising of the Morning Star (warrior to the Sun Father), which is carefully watched for by men who ascend the ladder to the hatchway. When announcement is made of the appearance of the star, Kwe'lele and the director of the order of Kok'ko ⁺hlan'na (Great god) of the Great Fire fraternity[a] take their seats near the fire altar. Kwe'lele places his horizontal fire stick on the floor and proceeds to produce fire by friction. A quantity of crushed cedar fiber having been placed beside the horizontal stick, a second stick held in the hand is rubbed in a rotary manner upon the one on the floor. After Kwe'lele has worked a while, the director of the order of Kok'ko ⁺hlan'na takes the stick, and, after a time, produces sparks, which ignite the crushed fiber. Lifting the fiber in both hands, he waves it sidewise until there is sufficient fire to light the brand. (The breath must never be blown upon the fiber, for this would so offend the gods that no rains

---

[a] See p. 407.

would come.) Kwe'lele rises and touches his brand to the light, after which the director throws the crushed fiber into the flames of the fire altar. The fire tender lights a similar brand at the fire altar, and the party leaves the ki'wiᵗsinĕ in the following order: Shits'ukĭa, carrying a rhombus in his right hand and an ear of yellow corn in his left; the Ko'pekwĭn, with a basket of sacred meal and his mi'li in his left hand, while with his right he throws meal before him; the pe'kwin, who carries a basket of meal and an ear of blue corn in his left hand and sprinkles meal with his right; the fire-tender, carrying in his blanket over his left arm four ears of corn with te'likinawe in the center and a firebrand in his right hand; the Kŏ'mosona, carrying his mi'li and basket of meal in his left hand and sprinkling meal with his right; Pau'tiwa, wearing a white cotton shirt, embroidered sash, four mi'hawe (sacred embroidered blankets), white deerskin leggings fringed at the sides, and dance moccasins; his mask is elaborately decorated; on his left arm are many te'likinawe, including offerings from each member of the first body of A'shiwanni, while with his right hand he sprinkles meal, which he carries in his sash; four Sa'yaᵗhlia, who carry bows and arrows in their left hands, and bunches of yucca in the right; four men of the Sun clan; Kwe'lele, who follows a short distance from the others, carrying a firebrand and crushed cedar fiber in his right hand, and in his left fire sticks, from which the fire is made.

The party proceeds to Ku'shilowa (red earth), a short distance east of Zuñi, where the fire tender lays his burning brand on the ground and Kwe'lele places his brand south of it. The Ko'pekwĭn runs a line of meal between the two brands, which are a short distance apart. Shits'-ukĭa stands north of the brand of the fire tender and Kwe'lele stands south of his own brand. The fire tender stands just west of the meal line and Pau'tiwa stoops with bended knees behind the fire tender. The four Sa'yaᵗhlia stand a short distance back of Pau'tiwa, the remainder of the party forming in groups north and south and back of the others, all facing east. Those grouped at the back sprinkle meal on the gods and draw in the sacred breath. The te'likinawe are now deposited in a circular excavation, an arm's length in depth, made by the ceremonial father of Pau'tiwa, a member of the Sun clan, he having preceded the others from the ki'wiᵗsinĕ in time to have the excavation in readiness. The fire tender separates his corn from the te'likinawe and carries it home. The father of Pau'tiwa covers the offerings with earth, leaving no trace of the excavation.

The plume offerings are made to the Sun Father, Council of the Gods, Sa'yaᵗhlia, Shits'ukĭa, Kwe'lele, u'wannam A'shiwanni,[a] Ku'pĭsh-taya,[b] and Po'shaiyänki.[c] The prayers offered on this occasion are for rain, snow, and warmth from the Sun Father to fructify the mother earth, that she may give in abundance the fruits of her being, all seeds

---

[a] Rain priests (rain-makers).　　[b] Lightning-makers.　　[c] Culture hero.

being mentioned, and for raiment, each article being named.   For the latter Po'shaiyänki is appealed to.

The exit of the party from the ki'wiᵗsinĕ is the signal for all families to begin the cleaning of their houses.   Each female member of the family except the one making the bread, no matter how young, if she can walk and carry a small basket or bowl, goes to the nearest field of the family and deposits sweepings; ashes with live coals are deposited separately.   To the sweepings she says: "I now deposit you as sweepings, but in one year you will return to me as corn."   To the ashes she says: "I now deposit you as ashes, but in one year you will return to me as meal."   Both the ashes and sweepings are sprinkled with meal, and prayers are offered.   The one who is making the bread afterward goes to the heaps, repeating prayers and sprinkling meal. The te'likinawe, which are kept with the ashes and sweepings for ten days, are then deposited in the fields.

After the return of the party to the ki'wiᵗsinĕ, where the A'shiwanni, the Great Fire fraternity, and others have awaited them, the Great Fire fraternity sing to the accompaniment of the rattle and drum, and the four Sa'yaᵗhlia, Shits'ukĭa, and Kwe'lele dance until after sunrise. Having extinguished his firebrand at Ku'shilowa, Kwe'lele brings it with him to the ki'wiᵗsinĕ and after sunset deposits it on the road to Ko'thluwala'wa.   All go to their homes to eat except the four Sa'yaᵗhlia, Shits'ukĭa, and Kwe'lele, who must remain in the ki'wiᵗsinĕ.

An aunt on the paternal side, or some woman of the father's clan, calls through the hatchway in the roof of the ki'wiᵗsinĕ to the fire tender.   He ascends to the roof and accompanies her to her house, where she washes his head with yucca suds and bathes his body for purification and longevity, that he may not die, but sleep to awake in Ko'thluwala'wa.   After eating in the aunt's house, the meal including animal food, the fire tender returns to the ki'wiᵗsinĕ.   When the others who left for breakfast have returned, the pe'kwĭn selects separately from a basket tray a number of te'likinawe to be distributed to persons chosen to fill certain offices, which appointments were discussed on the previous day.

The pe'kwĭn hands each te'likinanĕ separately to the elder brother Bow priest, the following words being repeated with the presentation of each: "Täᵗchumo" (father), said by receiver; "täl'emo" (father's brother's son), said by the giver; "pa'pamo" (elder brother), said by the receiver; "su'emo" (younger brother), said by the giver; "kä'kiamo" (mother's elder brother), said by receiver; "kä'simo" (mother's younger brother), said by giver; "na'namo" (grandfather), said by receiver; "tosh'limo" (grandson), said by giver; "äl'limo" (great-grandfather), said by receiver; "u'waikiämi" (great-grandson), said by giver.   Each offering is to the god the chosen party is to personate; the offerings for those who have been appointed to entertain the Sha'läko remain in the ki'wi⁺sinĕ until they are taken in charge by Pau'-tiwa later in the day. The elder brother Bow priest distributes the others soon after he receives them. The presentation of the te'likinawe indicates that the parties are chosen for the office and must repair to the ki'wi⁺sinĕ. They are as follows: Those to personate Shu'laawi⁺si,ᵃ Sa'yatäsha, two Yä'muhakto, Hu'tutu, Pau'tiwa, A'wan tä'⁺chu Ko'-yemshi,ᵇ and Bi'"⁺si⁺si.ᶜ Every fourth year the personator of ⁺Kiäklo and the priest or the director of the Kĭa'nakwe are included, the ceremonies in which these gods figure occurring quadrennially.

The elder brother Bow priest returns to the ki'wi⁺sinĕ and is soon followed by those to whom he has given the te'likinawe. These offer-ings remain in the house of each man until he has filled the position for which he is chosen.

On entering the ki'wi⁺sinĕ these men take their seats on a plank extended from one box to another. The personator of Shu'laawi⁺si is the first addressed, the pe'kwin presenting to him the appropriate offer-ing from the basket containing the te'likinawe. The sticks of these offerings are as long as the space between the carpus and the tip of the middle finger. The stick for Shu'laawi⁺si is black, spotted with yellow, blue-green, red, and white, and feathers of the turkey, duck, and the birds of the six regions attached. The priest stoops before the chosen personator of Shu'laawi⁺si, and, placing the te'likinanĕ in his hands, clasps them with both of his and prays for rain, corn, much water over the earth, long life, and all good things. The te'liki-nanĕ is now passed downward several times before the face in order that the selected one may draw the sacred breath from the plumes. The same ceremony is repeated by the pe'kwĭn with Sa'yatäsha, Hu'tutu, the two Yä'muhakto, A'wan tä'⁺chu Ko'yemshi, and Bi'"⁺si⁺si. The sticks of all except the Ko'yemshi are colored yellow, while that of the Ko'yemshi is colored black, and all are decorated with feathers of the eagle, turkey, duck, and the birds of the six regions. After the presentation of the te'likinawe the chosen personators of the gods leave the ki'wi⁺sinĕ, the personator of Sa'yatäsha taking to his home all the te'likinawe excepting those of the Ko'yemshi and Bi'"⁺si⁺si.

Shits'ukĭa and Kwe'lele perform during the day on the roof of the ki'wi⁺sinĕ. All the exposed parts of Shits'ukĭa's body, including the upper legs, are painted white, with this symbol ✕ just above the knees, formed by scraping off the white paint. He wears a white cotton shirt, an embroidered Hopi kilt fastened at the right side, an embroidered Hopi sash, and a woman's belt around the waist looped on the right. A fox skin is pendent at the back of the waist. A sacred embroid-ered blanket is doubled and fastened over the right shoulder, passing

ᵃ Shu'laawi⁺si must belong to the ki'wi⁺sinĕ of the Zenith.   ᵇ See p. 33.   ᶜ See p. 408.

under the left arm, both arms being perfectly free. Several strings of archaic black and white beads, with an abalone shell attached, pass over the right shoulder and under the left arm; the deerskin leggings are fringed at the side, native black yarn is tied around the legs below the knees and hangs in tassels, with sleigh bells attached; dance moccasins are worn. On some occasions it has been observed that Shits'ukĭa wears white cotton leggings knit in fanciful designs. These are unquestionably of Spanish origin. A bow wristlet is on the left wrist and native blue yarn encircles the right. The mask (see plate XXVI) is white with designs of lightning in yellow and blue, and a cornstalk runs over the forehead. A deer tail hangs on each side of the mask above the colored wheels that symbolize corn and squash blossoms. White fluffy eagle plumes and yellow parrot feathers decorate the top of the mask and long parrot plumes and fluffy eagle feathers stand up at the back of the mask; an aigret of hawk plumes is below this group. A collarette of spruce is worn at the base of the mask. Shits'ukĭa carries a rhombus in his right hand, which he uses constantly, and yucca in his left.

Kwe'lele has his body colored black except the upper legs, which are painted white, the white beginning some inches above the knees. He wears an embroidered Hopi kilt fastened at the right side and held on by a Hopi woman's belt with a white cotton fringed sash; a fox skin is pendent at the back. He has green armlets just above the elbows, with spruce twigs standing from the upper sides. A bow wristlet is on the left wrist and native blue yarn on the right, the yarn hanging in tassels. Strings of archaic beads, similar to those worn by Shits'ukĭa, hang in the same way over the shoulder. He wears dance moccasins and anklets embroidered with porcupine quills, and carries bunches of yucca in the right hand and fire sticks in the left. The mask (see plate XXVII) is black, with plume decorations similar to that of Shits'ukĭa; bells of white paper hang on each side of the mask. Shits'ukĭa and Kwe'lele walk about over the roof for sometime; meanwhile crowds are gathering in the plaza and on the house tops.

The ladder leading into the ki'witᵗsinĕ has a horizontal bar (symbolic of the bow of the Sa'yaᵗhlia) attached to it several feet above the hatchway, which is fringed with black goat's wool about 5 inches deep. A squirrel skin is pendent at the middle of the bar, and each end is decorated with white fluffy eagle plumes. The songs of the Great Fire fraternity are to be heard within during the time the two gods are on the roof. As the afternoon draws to a close Shits'ukĭa and Kwe'lele descend into the ki'witᵗsinĕ, and soon reappear with ears of sweet corn strung together horizontally with strings of yucca, which they throw to the populace. The corn has been cooked in the husk, which is afterward removed. It has been mentioned that no meals are served in the ki'wi⁺sinĕ during the winter solstice ceremonial; no rains would come if food should be eaten there at this season. This custom and that of throwing food to the populace are associated with the legend here introduced.

Legend related by We'wha

The gods of Chi'pia[a] were hungry. They had no meat, and they were hungry for meat. There had been no rains for a long time, but there had been a little lightning. Shits'ukĭa said to Kwe'lele: "I think I will go to-morrow to look for deer." The ancestral gods of the A'shiwi were also hungry, but the gods of Chi'pia did not know this. Shits'ukĭa and Kwe'lele were so hungry that they ate their moccasins, and Shits'ukĭa ate his earrings of deer tails; and so in the morning he started after deer. There was no game in his country, and he considered: "Which route shall I take? I think I will go to the west, whence the lightning came; the deer, I guess, live there." He was barefoot and poorly clad, for he had eaten everything; he had only a little meal of sweet corn and a few seeds of the same. The afternoon of the fourth day he came to tall green grass, and sitting in the grass were two sisters washing a buckskin. When they discovered the stranger they turned a large pottery bowl over the buckskin. Shits'ukĭa, approaching them, inquired: "What are you doing?" "I have been washing." "What have you been washing?" "I have been washing myself." "No," said Shits'ukĭa, "I know what you have been washing; you have been washing buckskin." "Did you see?" "Yes; I saw you a long time. I have been watching you." The girls then removed the bowl and showed the buckskin, and then continued their washing. When it was done, one said, addressing her sister: "Now we will go home." The girl then invited Shits'ukĭa to accompany her home. These people were the Kwal'ashi kwin'na (Black raven). These raven people then lived in a high mountain. On reaching the house the father exclaimed: "Who is that boy who has come?" The mother also asked the question. The daughter replied: "I don't know; he has been traveling four days and nights." The father said to the elder girl: "Well, he will be good for your husband." The parents were eating and had much meat before them. They invited Shits'ukĭa to eat. The father had just returned from the cornfield. After he had finished his meal he said to the stranger: "I will take you for my son. You are poor. You will live with me. Look at both my children. You shall have one as your wife. Look at both and tell me the one you choose." Shits'ukĭa replied: "I wish the elder daughter for my wife." "It is well," said the father. At bedtime the father said: "I guess you are very tired. You will sleep alone with your wife in the upper room." On reaching his room Shits'ukĭa found his bed made of deerskins. He slept all night with his wife. When they arose in the morning the father said: "Now I will show you all our game—elk, deer, antelope, rabbits, and rats." Going a short distance away, he exclaimed: "Ah, ha, my children, I am glad to see you; good day." The game answered: "Kets'anishi (all good come to you)." Shits'ukĭa said to the game: "I am hungry and want meat. Which of you shall I kill?" An elk replied, "Kill me;" and Shits'ukĭa killed the elk, flayed him, and then returned to the house. For four days he killed deer and dried the meat. The fifth day he asked the father: "Where is a good place to plant my corn? I have a few seeds." "A little way off there is a good place." "Well, I have lots of meat. I will take it with me and stay two nights at the field." He went off and planted the corn; he did not intend to sleep in the field. That night he wrapped the meat up in a skin and went to Ko'thluwala'wa. Pau'tiwa was delighted to see the meat. He asked: "My child, where did you find the deer?" "I sat outside my house

---

[a] Chi'pia is the abiding place of certain gods who preceded the Zuñis to this world. It is located, according to Zuñi history, near Shi'papolima, the home of the Zuñi prey gods.

after sundown and saw a little lightning. I thought I would look for my children in the direction whence it came, and I found them." He told the story of meeting with the Kwal'ashi people. He remained all night at Ko'thluwala'wa. Shits'ukïa said: "Pretty soon I will steal all the game." He also told of his planting the corn. "Well," said Pau'tiwa, "your corn will be ripe in four days and I shall be contented to have you steal all the game; my people are very hungry for meat." All night they talked. Pau'tiwa went out and brought in a beautiful girl and said: "When you bring the deer, then this girl shall be your wife. I sent the eagle for game and he returned without having seen it. I also sent the hawk, and he returned without having seen any. But you are wiser than the others; you are my child." Shits'ukïa returned early in the morning to where he had planted the corn. The corn was already quite high—over a foot. He hoed the ground and sang till sunset, and then returned to the Kwal'ashi people and slept that night with his wife. He said to the father: "My corn is good; it is already quite high." He remained four nights with these people, going each day to his cornfield. He also killed many deer, and dried the meat. The fourth day he said to the Kwal'ashi man: "Now I am going to my cornfield. My corn I think is ripe. Now I will roast some corn."

Shits'ukïa went to the field, and made a great fire at night and threw the corn in, and all the gods came from Ko'thluwala'wa and ate the corn and meat. After all had gathered, Shits'ukïa said to the cougar: "Father, I wish you to come to me." And in a little while the cougar appeared. He then called the bear, then the lynx, and then the coyote. Shits'ukïa said to the cougar: "Father, what will you have to eat? Will you have the rabbit?" "No." "Will you have the antelope?" "No; I wish the deer." He then said to the bear: "My father, warrior, what will you have to eat?" "I will have the same as the cougar—the deer." He then said to the lynx: "My warrior, what will you have? Will you have the deer?" "No." "Will you have antelope?" "No; I want the rabbit. I do not run about much; I will eat the rabbit." Then he asked the coyote: "What will you have? Will you have the rabbit?" "No." "The antelope?" "No; I will have the deer." "Well, let us go." And they all went to the deer house. When they came close to the great stone fence which surrounded the game he said to all: "We must not speak loud." And on reaching the gate he spoke to the deer, saying: "Deer, my children, come hither; my father and warriors wish to eat; whom shall I kill?" A deer replied: "Kill me." "Come outside, my child," said Shits'ukïa. "Where shall I go? It is dark, I can not see." "Here; come out." The deer passed out the door. The cougar made a second attempt before he caught the deer. Then Shits'ukïa called the bear. The hair was so heavy over his small eyes that he could hardly see. "Stand here," said Shits'ukïa. A second deer was called. When the deer passed out of the gate the bear walked about, but could not see the deer; the deer went far away, and the bear failed to catch him.[a] Shits'ukïa said: "Now you have failed to catch the deer; no longer shall you eat deer. You will be my warrior still, but you shall eat only medicine."[b] Then Shits'ukïa called the lynx, who has eyes like the cougar, and he caught the rabbit and ate it. Then the coyote was called up, and the deer came, as for the cougar. "Pass out," said Shits'ukïa. The coyote had fallen asleep, and awoke after the deer had passed, exclaiming: "Where is the deer?" "He has gone," Shits'ukïa said, "go after him." But with all the coyote's running he could not catch the deer. When he returned Shits'ukïa asked him if he had caught the deer. The coyote replying in the negative, Shits'ukïa said: "Well, hereafter you shall not eat the meat of any animal. You shall eat only blood. In the past the

---

[a] "The cougar has eyes like fire and sees all things. The bear only walks about slowly, continually dropping chips."

[b] This medicine is found in the earth by the bear. Whenever the Zuñis see him, he is still walking around, dropping chips and hunting in the earth for his medicine. In the old time Shits'ukïa gave the bear the medicine, which he still eats.

KO'YEMSHI GODS ON HOUSE TOP

SHRINE TO ANTHROPIC GODS ON KOR'KOKSHI MOUNTAIN

MASKS OF HE'HEA̋ (BLUNDERER) OF THE SOUTH: FRONT, SIDE, AND REAR VIEWS

a

b

c

MASK OF HE′HEĂ (BLUNDERER) OF THE NADIR: FRONT, SIDE, AND REAR VIEWS

coyote ate only blood, and therefore the fetish sus'ki (coyote) is dipped into the blood of the deer. The cougar and bear fetishes also eat blood of the deer.

Then Pau'tiwa and Shits'ukĭa both said to the game: "My children, you shall no longer stay here. We will open the gates that you may pass over the earth and eat the grass of the earth." The game had but little to eat in their stone house. Pau'tiwa said: "You will find good places where you can have your young, and when we want food we will kill and eat you, and your otherselves will come and live in my house." And all the game passed out of the gates. One of the Kwal'ashi, hearing, ran to tell the others, and all left the house to see, and they cried: "Who has let out our game?" Shits'ukĭa at once spat out the medicine[a] Pau'tiwa had given him over the Kwal'ashi people, and they all turned into ravens and, croaking, flew away, to return no more to their homes.

The collecting of the corn and throwing it to the people, amid shouts and cheers of the latter, continue for some time. When throwing it Kwe'lele holds the yucca in his left hand. Previous to the distribution of the corn each time Shits'ukĭa and his associate walk about over the roof of the ki'wĭᵗsinĕ hooting in a peculiar way. Their dexterity in throwing the great bunches of corn, often as many as a dozen at once, is remarkable.

The water collected on the fourteenth day is drunk late in the afternoon of the following day, that of the Great Fire fraternity being administered by the director of the fraternity, and that from ᵗKiap'kwena by the Ko'mosona. The water is dipped with a shell, the one receiving the draft saying, "täᵗchumo" (father), and the giver replying, "pa'pamo" (brother). Pau'tiwa, Shits'ukĭa, Kwe'lele, and the four Sa'yaᵗhlia do not take this water. Should they drink of it the Council of the Gods would refuse to water the earth. The pe'kwĭn receives his two drafts before leaving the ki'wĭᵗsinĕ to accompany Pau'tiwa on his round of the ki'wĭᵗsiwe.

Late in the afternoon five men of the Sun clan are seen coming over the plain a considerable distance south of the village. When they left the ki'wĭᵗsinĕ they carried the mask and paraphernalia of Pau'tiwa, the personator of this god having also gone from the ki'wĭᵗsinĕ. Soon after the men of the Sun clan are seen Pau'tiwa is discovered coming from the south also, but he is nearly a quarter of a mile east of the group, and is alone. His dress is the same as previously described. He carries in each hand a number of plume wands strung together with yucca thread, with loops at the top of each group to serve as handles. The base of each wand is wrapped with a bit of corn husk. He has also a large bunch of te'likinawe in each hand. A diminutive game of ᵗsi'kon tikwanĕ, a slender stick with a hoop colored blue attached, is carried in the right hand, the whole elaborately dec-

a This medicine was given to Shits'ukĭa by Pau'tiwa when he first visited Ko'thluwala'wa after Pau'tiwa told him he wished him to steal all the game. Shits'ukĭa replied that perhaps the Kwal'-ashi people had good heads and would find out and kill him. Then Pau'tiwa gave him the medicine and said it would destroy the people. Shits'ukĭa returned to Ko'thluwala'wa with Pau'tiwa, and lived there a long time, and had the girl as his wife. He did not take his Kwal'ashi wife with him when he returned to his home. On his return he passed south of I'tiwanna (Zuñi). Shits'ukĭa and Kwe'lele still visit Ko'thluwala'wa.

orated with eagle plumes and feathers of the birds of the six regions. This game must be held until Pau'tiwa deposits it after leaving the pueblo at sunset.   Pau'tiwa also has in his left hand a kĭa'puli 'hla'si-tonnĕ (a twig, suggestive of the Navaho scalp,[a] having a crow's feather and owl plume attached, which must have dropped from the birds).

Pau'tiwa proceeds with a slow, even tread.   He circles round the village four times, coil fashion.   The first circle is a short distance from the village, the last through the streets of the town.   After the fourth circuit he stops beside a house on the east side of the village. A stone slab, 8 by 12 inches, concealing a recess in the wall is removed by the matron of the house and laid on the ground some minutes previous to the arrival of Pau'tiwa.   A man of the Sun clan and two of the Dogwood clan, one grandfather to the other, form a group by the house on this occasion.   The man of the Sun clan personates Pau'tiwa's father; the others, his elder and younger brothers.   The younger brother assists Pau'tiwa to detach the te'likinawe to be deposited in the recess which runs some 2½ feet along the wall and is 8 or 10 inches deep.   Much of this space is filled with these offerings previously deposited, many of them looking quite as fresh as the new ones.[b]

The te'likinawe deposited by Pau'tiwa are offered to the sun and moon, to the former the blue stick and to the latter the yellow.   The upper ends of both are beveled to represent the face; three black dots denote the eyes and mouth.   These offerings are for the increase and perpetuation of vegetable and animal life, especially that of the Zuñis.   The plumes are deposited with prayers, and then Pau'tiwa sprinkles them with meal which he carries in his belt and proceeds to a house on the north side of the village.

As soon as Pau'tiwa leaves, the matron of the house appears, carrying a small copper kettle of plaster.   The younger brother of Pau'-tiwa after replacing the slab in the wall hastens after the party, leaving the woman to secure it with the plaster; she leaves no trace of the excavation.   The ceremony of depositing te'likinawe is repeated at houses on the north, west, and south sides of the village, and at two houses in the inner streets for the zenith and nadir.   When these offerings to the sun and moon have all been deposited, Pau'tiwa goes to the He'iwa ki'wi'sinĕ as the sun is sinking behind the horizon.   He is received at the base of the outer ladder by Shits'ukĭa, Kwe'lele, and the pe'kwĭn, who carries a basket filled with te'likinawe.   The ladder is sprinkled with meal by Shits'ukĭa and the pe'kwĭn, and Pau'tiwa sprinkles it as he ascends by throwing the meal up before him.

---

[a] In times of hostility the Navahos pass about at night, like the owl, and inform the enemy of the Zuñis of their whereabouts.

[b] Mr Stevenson during his explorations among the ruins of the Southwest found many objects in the walls of cliff and mesa houses which had been deposited in the same way.

As soon as Pau'tiwa reaches the roof of the ki'wi'sinĕ, he throws the symbol of the Navaho scalp into the ki'wi'sinĕ, which indicates that the song must cease. Stooping, with bended knees, and facing east, he separates two plume wands from the others, one to be given to the man who is to personate a Sha'läko in the coming autumn, and one for the man who is to entertain the god. The sticks of these wands are the length of the bended elbow on the inner side to the tip of the middle finger. Pau'tiwa deposits them with four smaller te'likinawe while he prays, on the end log of the hatchway, this opening of the ki'wi'sinĕ being finished on the four sides with substantial logs, and draws four lines of meal with his index and second fingers on the inner side of the log upon which he places the plumes, meaning that the gods will come four times, the reference being to the Säl'imobiya bringing seeds from Ko'thluwala'wa (abiding place of the Council of the Gods).

Pau'tiwa now sprinkles meal through the hatchway. Rising, he kicks the twig, which has been thrown out upon the roof, four times with his left foot, symbolic of the treatment of the Navaho scalps. He then lifts the twig in his left hand and, descending the outer ladder, departs with those who await him at the base of the ladder to Chu'-pawa ki'wi'sinĕ.[a] Shits'ukĭa leads, whirling the rhombus, and is followed by the pe'kwĭn and Kwe'lele. Shits'ukĭa and the pe'kwĭn, on reaching the ki'wi'sinĕ, sprinkle the ladder with meal, and pass beyond to allow Pau'tiwa to approach. He sprinkles meal upon it as he ascends to the roof, and repeats the deposition of the te'likinawe as described. After all the ki'wi'siwe have been visited Pau'tiwa and his party proceed to the northwest corner of the village, where he turns to face the east, and receives from a woman of the Dogwood clan, she facing north, a ha'kwani (a number of cotton loops symbolizing the sacred embroidered blanket). The woman, in presenting the ha'kwani, repeats a long prayer for food and raiment.

The three gods leave the village by the western road, and are supposed to go to Ko'thluwala'wa, where Shits'ukĭa and Kwe'lele spend a night, after which they return to their home in the east, passing south of Zuñi in their journey. In reality they go to a bend in the river which serves as the greenroom. The pe'kwĭn accompanies them a short distance. Handing the plumes he carries to Pau'tiwa, to deposit on the road to Ko'thluwala'wa, he returns to the village. After depositing the te'likinawe, the gods disrobe, their masks and paraphernalia being brought to the village under the blankets of those dispatched for the purpose. After the departure of Pau'tiwa, those who are in the He'iwa ki'wi'sinĕ go to their homes to eat, with the exception of the four Sa'ya'hlia, who must remain in the ki'wi'sinĕ to receive the 'Cha'kwena,[b] who arrives soon after dark. Those in the other ki'wi'siwe

---

a The entrance to this ki'wi'sinĕ may be seen in the center of pl. x at a point marked A.

b See p. 89, note a.

also return to their homes for food. The chief wor'li [a] of each ki'wi^tsině carries the plume wands and te'likinawe left by Pau'tiwa to his home.

The personator of the ^tCha'kwena must be a man of the Badgeɪ clan. As the ^tCha'kwena proceeds to the He'iwa ki'wi^tsině, all pregnant women hasten to look upon her, that they may pass through the trials of parturition safely and without pain. The ^tCha'kwena descends into the He'iwa ki'wi^tsině, and the gods accompanying her tramp about over the roof. She sits by the Sa'ya^thlia, to whom she speaks for a few minutes. While here ^tCha'kwena is visited by personators of her people, the Kǐa'nakwe from Chu'pawa ki'wi^tsině. She does not stay long, soon leaving for Si'aa' te'wita (sacred dance plaza) by the eastern covered way, having entered it from the west, and passing to the east side; thence by the north way to the southwest corner, whence she departs from the village. As she proceeds, she prays for the good health of the people, their increase, more game, and bountiful crops.

After accompanying the ^tCha'kwena a short distance from the village the other gods return. The A'toshle, angry gods, remain in the town and announce that four times the gods will come: "For so my grandfather," referring to Pau'tiwa, "he who has been here, has said." The A'toshle go about the village scolding the men and women and frightening the children, who stand in abject fear of them. Many of the people of the Chu'pawa ki'wi^tsině remain in the He'iwa to see the whipping, by the Sa'ya^thlia, of those who wish to be cured of headaches and bad dreams. These gods show little mercy in the use of their great bunches of yucca.

About 11 o'clock great excitement prevails over the arrival of the ^tHle'lele. In the old time these beings wore, in addition to the breechcloth, a bison robe over their backs, the hair inside; at present, owing to the scarcity of these robes, a sheepskin or piece of canvas is usually substituted.

Large fires burn in every house and bonfires light up the village everywhere. This is a real gala time for the youngsters, who are permitted to keep the fires blazing. All hands pelt the ^tHle'lele with coals of fire as they pass through the streets, calling for fire: "More fire. Give us more beautiful flowers," referring to the coals of fire.

The dancing continues in all the ki'wi^tsiwe until long after midnight, when the gods depart over the western road. Previous to their departure the Säl'imobiya carry baskets of seeds into each ki'wi^tsině, giving a portion of the contents to each person present. The seeds, which are afterward planted, are sure to yield bountifully if those to whom they are given have good hearts.

---

[a] The wor'we (plural for wor'li) of the ki'wi^tsiwe are also the Sha'läko wor'we, the chief wor'li selecting such members of his ki'wi^tsině as he may choose to have serve with him in attending upon the Sha'läko. The wor'we are appointed for life. In case one should die the chief wor'li chooses a man to fill the vacancy. When a chief wor'li dies the next in rank takes the office.

The visits of the Säl'imobiya, with the dances and distribution of seeds, are repeated at each ki'wĭᵗsinĕ every fourth night until the four visits have been made. Each member of the Ko'tikili carries a bowl of food to the road leading to Ko'thluwala'wa, praying as he goes that the gods will bless the A'shiwi with rain to fructify the earth, that she may bear to them the fruits of her being. The food is emptied into the river as offerings to the Kok'ko A'wa (all the gods).

The Sa'yaᵗhlia leave the He'iwa ki'wĭᵗsinĕ after the whipping, but return at midnight and are sprinkled with meal by the Ko'pi⁽ᵗⁱläshi-wanni, after which they depart over the western road, accompanied by the ᵗHle'lele.

When the Sa'yaᵗhlia leave the ki'wĭᵗsinĕ the mi'wachi (plural of mi'li, see page 416) and other objects are removed from the meal painting, and the Ko'pekwĭn gathers the meal of the painting together and deposits it in the circular hole in the floor of the ki'wĭᵗsinĕ (symbolic of the entrance to the undermost, or fourth world), with a prayer for corn and all the fruits of the earth, and the winter solstice ceremonies are closed.

WINTER DANCES OF THE KOR'KOKSHI

On the day following the winter solstice ceremonies, about sunset, the chief Sha'läko wor'li of each ki'wĭᵗsinĕ calls upon some man to notify the older and more important members of his ki'wĭᵗsinĕ to meet in his (the wor'li's) house at night. When all are gathered some one present asks the wor'li: "What do you wish to say?" He replies: "What do you think? What man will take the te'likinanĕ (referring to the wand to be given to the entertainer of the Sha'läko)? What man will entertain the Sha'läko in his house?" Someone present replies: "I will receive the te'likinanĕ and have the Sha'läko in my house." The wor'li then stands and hands over the wand with the words: "I pray that all things will be well with you; I pray that you may have much rain, that you will have much corn and all things to eat, that your family may keep well, and that you may all live, not die, but sleep, and awake in Ko'thluwala'wa." The wor'li then selects a man to serve as elder brother Sha'läko and gives to him the other wand, composed of feathers of eagles' legs, of ducks, and of birds of the six regions.

The wor'li blows his breath upon the plume wand four times, each time drawing it before the mouth of the chosen man, and prays: "May you speak with one tongue; may you be gentle; may you be good to others, that we may have much rain, much corn, all things to eat, and all clothing. May your life be long, and may you pass over your road to the end and sleep, not die, to awake in Ko'thluwala'wa." The four smaller te'likinawe left at each ki'wĭᵗsinĕ by Pau'tiwa are also given to the chosen personator of the Sha'läko. The wor'li then selects a man to act as younger brother Sha'läko, and the chosen Sha'läko breathes four times upon the plume wand he has received, and each time passes it before the mouth of the chosen younger brother, repeating the prayer that was said by the wor'li to him.[a] The elder brother Sha'läko now passes the wand before the mouth of all the men present.

At sunrise on the following morning, accompanied by his younger brother, he visits the houses of all members of his ki'wiᵗsinĕ, including the youngest children, excepting those who were gathered at the wor'li's house on the previous night, and passes his plume wand, as before described, before the mouth of each. He selects four men to act as Mo'lawe (fruit and seed bearers) from such houses as he may choose while he is making his round of calls.

On the same morning the wife and daughters of the man who is to have the Sha'läko dance in his house go through the town and notify all persons connected with the family by consanguinity, and also the close neighbors and the people of the clan, to come to the house. No time is set for the visit; sometimes only one or two women with their children will meet there, at other times large numbers may chance to come together. The men and their wives and children go at different times. The man of the house stands before each guest and breathes four times upon his wand, passing it each time before the lips of the other, who inhales the sacred breath or better part of the man. On the fourth day after Pau'tiwa leaves the plumes at the hatchways of the ki'wiᵗsiwe the people of each ki'wiᵗsinĕ meet in the house of their chief Sha'läko wor'li to discuss what dances they shall have as soon as they can get the masks ready. It is usual to select gods whose masks are easy to prepare.

The people of companion ki'wiᵗsiwe often dance together, one ki'wiᵗsinĕ inviting the people of the other. This is done by the wor'li sending some of his people to the companion ki'wiᵗsinĕ, when those who wish to dance go to the wor'li's house on the same evening and say: "We will dance with you." It is usual for the guests to prepare their own masks to suit the dance in which they are expected to join, and they must not only prepare te'likinawe of the ki'wiᵗsinĕ to which they belong, but must make others for the one in which they are to dance. It is the privilege of guests to make a choice among the masks belonging to the ki'wiᵗsinĕ in which they are to dance, and they may appropriate any mask they wish. For instance, the wor'li may have decided that two of his men should personate the A'toshle, but, should a guest choose one of these masks, it is given to the latter. When Ko'yemshi masks are chosen they are secured from a man of Eagle clan who has charge of these particular masks. Only seven of

---

[a] Should one of these men be caught fighting or quarreling or intimate with any woman except his wife, he is expelled, and another is chosen to fill his place.

the Ko'yemshi masks, however, may be borrowed; those of the three officers—Great Father, deputy, and warrior—must not be borrowed on this occasion. The guest carries his two eagle-wing feathers, which are associated with the esoteric fraternities, and four te'likinawe to be offered to the deceased wor'we of the ki'wiᵗsiwe with the prayer: "Take all disease from our people." The head wor'li receives the te'likinawe.

The dances occur in the ki'wiᵗsiwe the fourth night and the gods appear in the plaza on the fifth morning after Pau'tiwa announces the coming of the gods. The A'toshle do not dance in the plazas, but go about the village, and are joined later in the day by some of the Ko'yemshi. As they approach a house blank cartridges are sometimes fired by a man of the house at the A'toshle, symbolizing that the Navaho will be frightened away or killed and not enter the Zuñi homes. When an A'toshle falls as if dead the door of the house is closed upon him, and he soon rises and walks away. At other times the A'toshle and Ko'yemshi are shot, symbolizing the killing of game. The one who fires the shot is sure to be successful in the hunt. The one supposed to be shot falls to the ground, the hunter places a hand each side of the mask and draws in the breath, and the game is carried into the house, laid upon a blanket on the floor with the head to the east, facing south, and an embroidered sacred blanket is spread over him. All present sprinkle meal upon him, and the children are told that the A'toshle who was shot is now a deer. All the personators of the gods return at dusk to the ki'wiᵗsinĕ, remove their masks, put on their ordinary dress, and return to their homes. Each chosen Sha'läko, with his younger brother, goes over the western road and plants the four te'likinawe in an excavation the depth of the lower arm. Prayer meal is sprinkled in and the excavation is covered; this is repeated for all the ki'wiᵗsiwe. A week or more is consumed with these particular dances and exhibitions. On the day following the last of these performances the Ko'pekwĭn makes four te'likinawe, and plants them in his cornfield to the Council of the Gods and the rain-makers.

The following is a description of the first of the Kor'kokshi ceremonies in the winter of 1891. The fourth afternoon following the planting of prayer plumes by the Ko'pekwĭn two Mu'luktäkĭa gods (see plate LXXIII) from the He'iwa ki'wiᵗsinĕ, this being the one which begins the Kor'kokshi dances,ᵃ visit the other ki'wiᵗsiwe, going first to the He'kĭapawa, where the two men who are to act as Sha'läko and his younger brother the following autumn and the chief officers of the ki'wiᵗsinĕ are gathered to receive them. They announce: " On the fourth night the gods will come [referring to the Kor'kokshi]."

―――――――――――

ᵃ The ki'wiᵗsinĕ that is to furnish the Kor'kokshi dancers for the summer solstice ceremonies begins the Kor'kokshi dances of the preceding winter.

The two gods sit facing east. The wor'li lights a reed cigarette of native tobacco and waves it to the six regions, each time taking a puff. He then hands it to one of the gods, who pushes back his mask and repeats the puffing of the cigarette, also motioning it to the six regions, and then returns the cigarette to the wor'li, who again extends it to the six regions, puffing each time. He next hands it to the second god, who repeats the performance and returns the cigarette to the wor'li, who now deposits it in a basket tray. The wor'li then inquires of the gods: "Why are you here?" The gods reply: "I come that you may raise much corn and all things to eat, that you may have many children, that you may be happy, and to tell you that the gods will be here on the fourth night; prepare for them." A long prayer is then repeated by these gods in the archaic tongue and in it a history is given of their coming to this world and of their migrations, the springs they passed, etc.

The Sha'läko wor'we and two men who are to act as the Sha'läko and his younger brother each give te'likinawe to the gods. The elder brother god, standing about the center of the room, now draws four parallel lines of meal extending east and west, and places a cigarette which he carries and a corn-husk package of meal on the south line. The gods now leave the ki'wiᵗsinĕ, the wor'li takes the package of meal and cigarette, and all present smoke the cigarette and wave it to the six regions for rain. The wor'li carries the package of meal home with him. The ceremony described is repeated in each ki'wiᵗsinĕ visited, except that no package of meal is left. Then they return to the He'iwa and disrobe.

There may be some dances in the plaza during the tour of these gods, but these have no direct connection with the gods or with what they have to say. The two who make the announcement of the coming of the gods deposit the te'likinawe given them on the banks of the river in an excavation the depth of an arm to the Council of the Gods and the rain-makers. The excavation is covered after meal has been sprinkled in it.

It is the business of two men in each ki'wiᵗsinĕ to collect the dancers. These men are called o'taikᵃ pe'yenakwe (dance talkers). They address the men they wish to have dance. The men often decline, but afterward yield to persuasion. The same men take part as often as the Kor'kokshi dance of a ki'wiᵗsinĕ is repeated, as others who have not rehearsed the songs would not be sufficiently familiar with them. On the fourth afternoon following the announcement by the two gods they repeat their tour of the ki'wiᵗsiwe, remaining but a short time in each one, to announce that the gods, referring to the Kor'kokshi, will come at night, and this night is referred to as Kok'ko A'wan i'tiwannan (great gods in the middle, meaning that the great gods come in the middle of the year).

While the two gods from the He′iwa ki′wiᵗsinĕ are notifying the people of the other ki′wiᵗsiwe that the gods will come at night, two men from He′iwa go through the village collecting corn and all varieties of cultivated seeds in their blankets. At the same time the wor′we and members of all the ki′wiᵗsiwe excepting He′iwa prepare te′likinawe for the Kok′ko A′wan (Council of the Gods), which are made into a kĭa′ĕtchinĕ by the head wor′li of each ki′wiᵗsinĕ.

On the return of the seed-gatherers they empty the contents of their blankets on one blanket. The corn is removed from the cob and the seeds are mixed together, equally measured into five parts with a basket tray, deposited in five sacks, and placed before the altar of the fraternity chosen by the chief wor′li of the ki′wiᵗsinĕ to receive the gods and furnish music. There are elaborate preparations throughout the day for the entertainment of the gods. Every member of the Ko′tikili, including the women, deposits food of every variety that has been made in the home into the river to na′nakwe (grandfathers) and ho′takwe (grandmothers).

After the two Mu′luktäkĭa have announced "The gods will come to-night," they return to the He′iwa ki′wiᵗsinĕ. The people of each ki′wiᵗsinĕ, including those who are to personate the Kor′kokshi (the female Kor′kokshi represent such women as belonged to the Ko′tikili when they were alive, and symbolize fecundity) proceed to their homes to eat, and afterward go to the house of the head wor′li of their ki′wiᵗsinĕ. Later on, the personators of the Kor′kokshi go to the river bank a short distance west of the village. They are covered with their blankets, which hide the masks. Each Kor′kokshi deposits his tortoise-shell rattle, which is worn on the calf of the right leg, on the ground and places his mask upon it,[a] and sprinkles the sacred objects with meal and prays, addressing the rain-makers: "Come, let us go to our people and dance and make rain for them." Then, addressing the Sun Father and Council of the Gods, they say: "I hope you will let me live. May I have a good heart. May I raise much corn and many sheep and have all things to wear. Let me be happy; let all people have much and be happy." The Kor′kokshi then come masked to the village, and after dancing in the four plazas they retire to the He′iwa ki′wiᵗsinĕ and dance. The fraternity stops singing as soon as the Kor′kokshi are heard without.[b]

---

[a] If the mask is not to be worn, then only the rattle is laid on the ground. When the Kor′kokshi dance in winter they may be masked or not, according to the dictates of the dance director, when they come over the western road. If they are masked, they dance in the four plazas before retiring to their ki′wiᵗsinĕ. If they are not masked, they go directly to the ki′wiᵗsinĕ.

[b] The Kor′kokshi can wear their masks in their own ki′wiᵗsinĕ and others as they choose, except those of the ki′wiᵗsinĕ of the Zenith. They must always wear the mask when dancing, not only in other ki′wiᵗsinĕ, but in their own.

After the Kor'kokshi have danced and sung songs that have been
made for the occasion by members of the ki'wiᵗsinĕ, five of the goddesses take each a sack of seeds from before the altar.   The person
who was chosen Sha'läko of this ki'wiᵗsinĕ and who is now personating a Kor'kokshi, receives a bunch of reed cigarettes wrapped in a
corn husk from the head wor'li of the ki'wiᵗsinĕ, and taking a pinch
of meal from the bowl before the altar places it in his sash and leads
the dancers to the other five ki'wiᵗsiwe, the same ceremonies being
repeated in each.   They usually go to the nearest one first, but the
director of the dance, who is always midway the line of dancers, has
the privilege of choosing.   There are gods, but no Kor'kokshi, in
the other ki'wiᵗsiwe, and these gods must complete their dances before
stopping, so that it sometimes happens that the Kor'kokshi must wait
outside, for the others must not dance when the Kor'kokshi are dancing.

On reaching the roof of each ki'wiᵗsinĕ the leader of the dancers
takes the meal from his belt, waves it to the four regions, and throws
it through the hatchway, trying to strike the small excavation before
the fire altar that is symbolic of the entrance to the undermost world,
at the same time exclaiming: "A'wisho, althtiha (Water moss, open
the door);" and all draw in the sacred breath.   The water-moss world
being next above the undermost, if the door be opened, the rain-
makers may come from there and be present in the ki'wiᵗsinĕ.   The
Kor'kokshi now descend the ladder, make the circuit of the room, form
in single file, facing east, and, turning to the north, begin the dancing.
The bearer of the cigarettes soon approaches the chief wor'li of the
ki'wiᵗsinĕ, puts a pinch of meal from his sash into his left hand, places
one of the cigarettes upon the meal, takes both hands of the wor'li in
his, and waves them to the six regions, saying: "May my Great
Fathers bring much rain; may my Great Fathers bring many seeds."
One of the goddesses then advances with a sack of seeds and deposits
it by the second wor'li.   The several wor'we and aged men of the
ki'wiᵗsinĕ sit in line on the south side of the room near the west end.
The two Kor'kokshi return to the line of dancers, and each wor'li and
aged man in turn holds the sack of seeds close to his face and prays.
After which the wor'li who received the cigarette lights it, and after
puffing it passes it down the line for each to smoke.

The women of the house adjoining the ki'wiᵗsinĕ and their immediate friends are present and give food to such dancers as appear when
the Kor'kokshi are not there.   The women also sprinkle the gods
with meal.   The dances may be repeated several times at the request
of the members of the ki'wiᵗsinĕ.   After the Kor'kokshi have danced
in a ki'wiᵗsinĕ the people of it, who dress in the house of the wor'li,
visit their ki'wiᵗsinĕ and receive from the Sha'läko wor'li of their
ki'wiᵗsinĕ the kĭa'ĕtchinĕ composed of te'likinawe made by members

of each of the other ki'wi^tsiwe. After prayers they go to the ki'wi^tsině
furnishing the Kor'kokshi, and, passing around in an ellipse, form in
single file, facing north, and dance. In a short time the one who is
to personate a Sha'läko, and who carries the kĭa'ĕtchině, advances to
the wor'we and elderly men and hands the kĭa'ĕtchině and a reed
cigarette to the chief wor'li. He holds both hands of the giver of the
cigarette, who stoops before him and prays. At the close of the
prayer the god returns to the line of dancers.

The kĭa'ĕtchiwe (plural of kĭa'ĕtchině) are kept in the homes of those
who receive them, the chief wor'li selecting men for this purpose,
until after the morning meal, when each man deposits his in a place
associated with the region of his ki'wi^tsině. They are deposited as follows: The one from the ki'wi^tsině furnishing the Kor'kokshi deposits
the kĭa'ĕtchině at a spring associated with the region of his ki'wi^tsině;
the next kĭa'ĕtchině is deposited in an arroyo or a small canyon; the
next, in a cornfield of the region with which the ki'wi^tsině is associated;
the next, on the road running west from the village; another, at a
still greater distance on the western road; the last, in the bed of the
river some miles west of the village.

These dancers, who may be masked or not according to the choice
of the director, the exception being the Ko'yemshi who must invariably wear their masks,[a] continue around to the other ki'wi^tsiwe, giving
one reed cigarette to each wor'li of a ki'wi^tsině.

After each body of dancers has made a tour of the ki'wi^tsiwe, they
spend the remainder of the night dancing in their own. As soon as
the visiting dancers leave a ki'wi^tsině, a wor'li passes around among
the people carrying the sack of seeds and gives a handful to those
present, including women and children. The seeds are carried home
and planted the coming season with those given by the Ko'loowisi,
apart from the other seeds. A draft of medicine water is administered by the director of the fraternity to all unmasked dancers and
others who may be in the ki'wi^tsině during the ceremonies. He
sprinkles the masks, dipping two eagle plumes into the water. All
dancers are sprinkled with meal at the close of each dance.

Each ki'wi^tsině is supposed to follow in regular succession in presenting the Kor'kokshi, but this does not always happen; for instance,
if a head wor'li of the ki'wi^tsině is engaged with his fraternity, the
dance of his ki'wi^tsině is delayed until he is free, and it not infrequently
happens that some other ki'wi^tsině takes the place of the one which
would come in regular order.

While the Kor'kokshi dances are classed among the most sacred
observances, for the rain-makers themselves are not only personated

---

[a] The masks of the Ko'yemshi are frequently worn by others than the real Ko'yemshi, and in such
cases they must be returned to the keeper of these masks at the close of the dances, no matter
what the hour may be.

but are spiritually present, they also furnish great entertainment to the people. The sacred dance court of the Zuñis is not only their temple where they invoke their god, but it is their theater where they gratify their love for the spectacular.

From the close of the Kor'kokshi dances to the latter part of March the ki'wiᵗsiwe hold a variety of dances, which furnish great interest and enjoyment to the people. When a wor'li or some prominent member of a ki'wiᵗsinĕ wishes to have a dance, he calls at some house where he will find a number of his people gathered, as it is customary for people of a ki'wiᵗsinĕ to meet almost nightly, when not otherwise engaged, in the different houses of the members. He says: "I wish to have a dance; let us arrange for it." They begin making songs at once—there are song-makers in Zuñi as well as elsewhere. The wor'li makes four te'likinawe on the following day and plants them during the same afternoon to the Kok'ko A'wa (all the gods), and the dance occurs on the fourth night. On the fourth afternoon the wor'li makes a reed cigarette, carries it to the house of the Great Father Ko'yemshi, or to the director of a fraternity, and presents it, with the request that the recipient furnish Ko'yemshi for the dance.

The wor'li and dancers assemble in the ki'wiᵗsinĕ and dance and sing during the night. The man who is selected by the wor'li to act as leader, or priest, of the dancers goes to the ki'wiᵗsinĕ, where he remains while the others visit the house of the Great Father Ko'yemshi, or the director of a fraternity, as the case may be, and dance. At dawn they go to the river bank, deposit their tortoise-shell rattles, and, putting on their masks, sprinkle meal and pray. They wear their ordinary dress, and on their return to the village dance in the four plazas. The Ko'yemshi do not appear at this hour with the dancers, who go later to their homes and eat, after which they bathe and wash their hair if only the sho'yannĕ (mask which covers only the face) is worn. After the bath they carry their dance paraphernalia to the ki'wiᵗsinĕ, the masks being already there. The leader, dressed in his regalia, returns to the ki'wiᵗsinĕ in the morning to lead the dancers.

SUMMER SOLSTICE CEREMONIES[a]

Though the visits of the pe'kwĭn (deputy to the Sun Father and Shi'wanni of the Zenith) to the petrified stump referred to in the winter solstice ceremonies are continued daily for the purpose of offering meal and prayers to the rising sun, no further observations are made from this point after those for the winter solstice. The pe'kwĭn observes Yäl'län ᵗhlan'na (Great mountain), a mesa northwest of Zuñi, from the shrine at Maᵗsakĭa (see figure 3) for a number of

---

[a] Yä'tokĭa teᵗchi (sun reaches there), the summer solstice, is indicated by the setting sun striking a certain point on a mesa northwest of Zuñi.

evenings prior to the summer solstice.   The sun strikes a certain point
of this mesa at sunset for five consecutive days.   The Zuñis say that
the Sun Father rests five times in succession over this mesa in his daily
journeys over the world.   At other times he does not halt twice in the
same place.   Upon the first observation of the sun at this point the
pe′kwĭn informs the elder brother Bow priest, who is also Shi′wanni
of the Nadir, and he notifies the first body of A′shiwanni.   They
gather the same evening in the ceremonial chamber of the Kĭa′kwemosi
(Shiwanni of the North).

The following morning the pe′kwĭn makes four te′likinawe and ties
them in pairs, to be offered to the Sun Father and Moon Mother.
Those for the sun have their sticks colored blue and those for the
moon yellow.   He plants them at a shrine on Yäl′län ᵗhlan′na.   The
fourth day following he prepares four te′likinawe to the deceased
a′pekwĭn (sun priests) and plants them in his field.   On the fourth
morning following the deposition of these plumes he plants two to the
sun and two to the moon on Yäl′län ᵗhlan′na; the fourth morning afterward he repeats the planting of four te′likinawe to the deceased
a′pekwĭn in the field; again on the fourth morning succeeding he
plants two to the sun and two to the moon on Yäl′län ᵗhlan′na, and
the fourth morning afterward he deposits four to the deceased a′pekwĭn
in the field.   The same fast is observed by the pe′kwĭn in connection
with the planting of these plumes as that practiced in depositing the
plumes previous to the winter solstice.

At early dawn of the last day of depositing the plumes he announces
from the roof of the ceremonial house of the Kĭa′kwemosi that yä′tokĭa
teᵗchĭ (summer solstice) will occur on the eighth day after the issuing
of this notice.   As he stands facing the rising sun while making the
announcement to the people, it is believed that he is repeating the
words given him at the time by the Sun Father.   At this season
the pe′kwĭn is supposed to have direct communication with the Sun
Father.   In addition to the notice, the pe′kwĭn says: "I wish my
children to make te′likinawe to my Sun Father, Moon Mother, and to
the u′wannami (rain-makers).   I wish the A′piᵗläshiwanni (Bow priesthood) to make te′likinawe to Ku′pĭshtaya and to the u′wannam A′piᵗlä-
shiwanni."[a]   Though he looks upward as he speaks, his words are
heard by the mass of people who have congregated for the purpose.
In 1891 the solstice occurred on June 21, and the ceremonies of that
year will be described.

Two days previous to the solstice the first body of A′shiwanni assemble in the ceremonial chamber of the Kĭa′kwemosi and prepare te′li-
kinawe, and the Ko′mosona and Ko′pekwĭn prepare te′likinawe in

---

[a] Deceased members of the Bow priesthood become lightning-makers and work with Ku′pĭshtaya,
the chief of lightning-makers.

their respective houses. All the fraternities except the 'Hle'wekwe and A'pi‘‘läshiwanni convene on the day previous to the solstice and remain in session throughout the day and night; the members of the latter fraternity meet with those to whom they are allied. Altars are erected in the ceremonial chamber and embellished with the mi'wachi and other fetishes. Medicine water is consecrated by the a'kwamosi (maker of medicine water), and suds from certain roots are made, symbolic of clouds. The day is consumed principally in the preparation of te'likinawe to Kok'ko A'wan (Council of the Gods). There are no fetishes of the Beast Gods present at this time, but at night prayer songs are offered to these gods to invoke their influence upon the u'wannami. The members of the A'pi‘‘läshiwanni offer special prayers to Ku'pĭshtaya and u'wannam A'pi‘‘läshiwanni. Prayers are also offered to Pa'yatämu (god of music). The songs are sung to the accompaniment of the rattle, no drum being used on this occasion. The closing song to the rising sun, when the flute is played, is exceedingly impressive. The te'likinawe prepared by members of the fraternities are deposited, with their individual offerings, on the day of the solstice in the manner described on page 119.

Pottery is made and decorated on the three following days. Though pottery may be made at any season, this is a special time for the working of this art, and women and girls are to be found busy molding clay or painting in every house in Zuñi. Pottery is fired on the fourth day, when the village at night is ablaze and has the appearance of a smelting town of civilization. A bit of wafer bread, the spiritual essence of which is believed to feed the spirit of this object, is deposited in each piece of pottery as it is balanced on stones to be baked (see plate LXXXVIII).

The first body of A'shiwanni prepare te'likinawe in the ceremonial chamber of the Kĭa'kwemosi on the fifth day following the solstice. The men prepare those for the Shi'wano'‘kĭa (Priestess of fecundity). Each shi'wanni makes two to the sun, two to the moon, four to the u'wannami of each of the six regions, and four to his deceased predecessors. The offerings are made into a kĭa'ĕtchĭnĕ, which is carried by the Kĭa'kwemosi and his first associate to ‘Kĭa'nanaknana, a spring in the lava beds some miles east of Zuñi, and is sunk in the waters of the spring. The Kĭa'kwemosi carries a gourd water jug covered with a network of cotton and with white fluffy eagle plumes attached, which he fills from the spring while his associate whirls a rhombus. On his return he goes into retreat with his ĕt'tonĕ for eight nights, accompanied by his associates and the Shi'wano'‘kĭa.[a]

On the last night of his retreat, which is the night of the return of the pilgrims from Ko'thluwalawa, he makes a cloud symbol of meal and

---

[a] Each member of the first body of A'shiwanni follows in order in going into retreat (see p. 180).

M. Wright Gill

KOR'KOKSHI GODS DANCING IN PLAZA ATTENDED BY KO'YEMSHI GODS AND NE'WEKWE (GALAXY FRATERNITY)

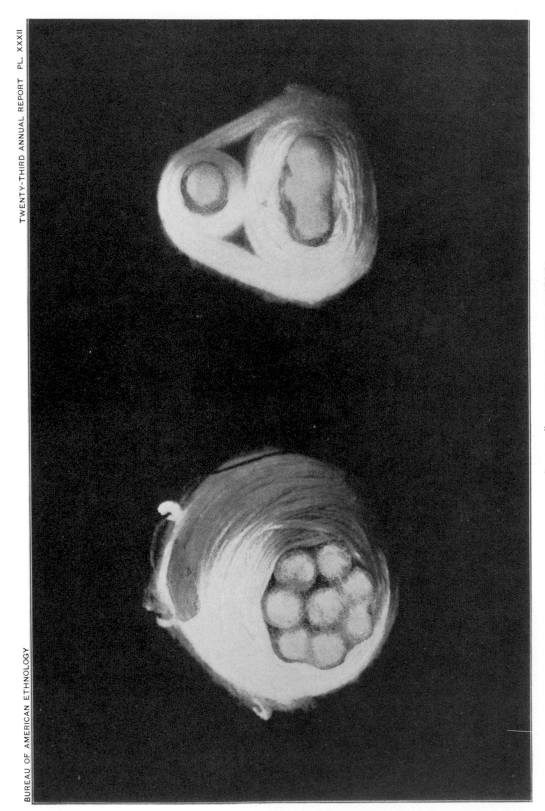

END VIEW OF ĔT'TONĔ, FETISH OF RAIN PRIESTS

MASK OF SAYATÄSHA (RAIN PRIEST OF THE NORTH): FRONT AND SIDE VIEWS

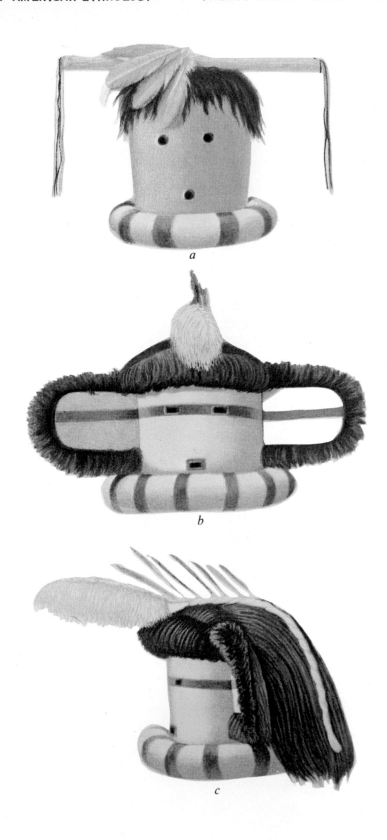

a MASK OF YÄ̈'MUHAKTO b, c MASK OF HU'TUTU
front and side views

corn pollen on the floor, which is embellished with his ĕt'tonĕ and other
fetishes, including the mi'wachi of himself and associates. The jug of
water, which is also placed by the painting, is afterward emptied into
a medicine bowl and drunk on the closing night of the ceremonies by
those present, it being the privilege of the families of the shi'wanni and
his associates, including the youngest children, to gather in the chamber
on that night. The party in retreat rarely speak, and they sing but
little until the last night, when they invoke the presence of the u'wannami. They sit most of the time perfectly quiet, giving their thoughts
to their desired object, that the u'wannami may water the earth.
Their prayers go from their hearts to the Sun Father and the u'wannami without spoken words. Should the Shi'wano'ʻkĭa be nourishing
an infant, the child is brought into the ceremonial chamber by a female
relative and handed to the mother in perfect silence, who, after feeding
the child, returns it in silence to the bearer, who leaves the chamber
without a word. The thoughts of the A'shiwanni at this time must not
be given to earthly things. The pe'kwĭn visits the Kĭa'kwemosi during his retreat, as he does all the others of the first body of A'shiwanni
during their retirement.

On the eighth day the A'shiwanni of the West, South, East, Zenith,
Nadir, and the elder and younger brother Bow priests, join the Kĭa'-
kwemosi and his associates who are in retreat, and prepare te'likinawe
in the ceremonial chamber of the Kĭa'kwemosi. The Ko'mosona and
Ko'pekwĭn with their Ko'piʻʻlāshiwanni, six men to act as Sha'läko [a]
and their alternates (each of the six men who are to personate the
Sha'läko and each of the alternates has two associates present, whose
duties are to prepare the masks and paraphernalia of the Sha'läko),
the personator of Shu'laawiʻsi, a man designated as his father
(whose duty it is to prepare the mask and attend to the general adornment of the person of the Shu'laawiʻsi), Sa'yatäsha, first Yä'muhakto,
Hu'tutu, second Yä'muhakto, and ten men who prepare the masks and
dress of the last four mentioned (see page 33) gather in the chamber
adjoining the Mu'heʻwa ki'wiʻsinĕ, the one to which the Ko'mosona is
allied, for the purpose of preparing te'likinawe. Each person present
makes four to the Council of the Gods, and each one who is to personate a god in the Sha'läko festival the coming autumn makes four
additional offerings to the god he is to represent. The te'likinawe
must be completed by noon and deposited in basket trays.

The personators of the ten Ko'yemshi (see page 33) are busy at the
same time in a house chosen by the A'wan tä'ʻchu (Great Father)
Ko'yemshi making their plume offerings; but one other besides the
Ko'yemshi is present, he being a man who labors for them. Each one
makes four te'likinawe to the Ko'yemshi and four to the Council of

---

[a] See Annual festival of the Sha'läko, p. 227.

the Gods. The offerings of the Ko'yemshi must also be completed and deposited in basket trays by noon. Immediately after noon the Ko'yemshi, who are now termed the Du'mĭchĭmchĭ, leave the house. They are nude, excepting a bit of old black cloth about their loins, their hair hanging loose before each shoulder. They proceed in file, each man grasping with both hands the string which holds the loin cloth of the man preceding him. As they pass through the streets women on the house tops pour over them water into which sacred meal has been sprinkled, with a prayer for rain. Though this scene causes merriment among the spectators, it is of a strictly religious character. After passing through the streets the Du'mĭchĭmchĭ retire to dry themselves, after which they put on their masks and visit the house tops (see plate XXIX) and, after making a tour of the village, return to their ceremonial chamber, resume their dress, and then retire to their homes, when the name of Du'mĭchĭmchĭ is renounced.

Near sunset the Ko'mosona makes a meal painting in Mu'he'wa ki'wĭᵗsinĕ, where a number of his associates are gathered, and deposits about it sacred objects, including a kĭa'ĕtchinĕ composed of the plume offerings in a basket tray, making a long prayer for rains to fructify the earth.

All now go to their homes to eat. They do not abstain from animal food, as at the winter solstice, as Shits'ukĭa[a] plays no part at the present time. After eating, all return to the ki'wĭᵗsinĕ, when the Ko'mosona and Ko'pekwĭn each make three po'newe (singular, po'ne), reeds filled with native tobacco, the tobacco being pressed in by the use of a slender stick or the quill end of a plume. After the reeds (which are as long as from the metacarpus to the tip of the middle finger) are filled they are colored black, each one wrapped in a corn husk, and deposited in an Apache basket, which is set by the meal painting. Those who are to personate the Sha'läko and their alternates are present.

Members of the Great Fire fraternity visit the ki'wĭᵗsinĕ, wearing ordinary dress and each carrying a rattle. They sit south of the meal painting and sing invocations to the Beast Gods of the six regions, to Ä'chiyälä'topa (a being of the zenith with wings and tail of knives), and to their original director. One song is addressed to each being, imploring his intercession with the u'wannami for rain. The song closes at midnight with the drawing of the sacred breath of A'wonawil'ona,[b] and the Ko'mosona, without rising from his seat, offers a prayer to the Council of the Gods for rain. The director of the Great Fire fraternity afterward prays to the Council of the Gods, and the sacred breath of A'wonawil'ona is inhaled by all present. The Ko'mosona hands one of the wrapped cigarettes to the Sha'läko wor'li of the He'iwa ki'wĭᵗsinĕ; returning to the basket, he takes a second cigarette

---

[a] See p. 135.   [b] See p. 22.

and hands it to the Sha'läko wor'li of the ki'wi^tsiné of the west. The remaining cigarettes are in turn distributed to the Sha'läko wor'we of the other ki'wi^tsiwe, and all but the Ko'mosona, the Ko'pekwĭn, and their A'pi^tläshiwanni leave the ki'wi^tsiné for their homes, each Sha'läko wor'li carrying home his cigarette in a corn husk.

Those who are to make the pilgrimage to Ko'thluwala'wa and those who are to aid them in getting off are astir betimes on the following morning. The Ko'yemshi gather in their ceremonial chamber and certain others join the Ko'mosona in the Mu'he'wa ki'wi^tsiné, others start directly from their homes. After the Ko'yemshi collect their te'likinawe from the basket trays they proceed to the Mu'he'wa ki'wi^tsiné when the Ko'mosona divides the kĭa'ĕtchiné which has stood on the meal painting in the ki'wi^tsiné, giving a portion of the te'likinawe to the Ko'pekwĭn and keeping the others for himself. He is also provided with te'likinawe made by men of his (the Deer) clan, and the Ko'pekwĭn has offerings made by a man of his (the Bear) clan. Each places his te'likinawe in a hu'chapone (deep basket), which is carried on the back and held in place by a strap crossing the chest or forehead. A long-necked ancient gourd jug is provided with a sprinkling stick, colored black, and freshly painted for each occasion. The bulb of the jug is partially covered with cotton netting, around the bottom of which four white fluffy eagle plumes are arranged at equal distances. The jug is carried in the right hand by means of a cotton cord, which forms a handle, and four te'likinawe to the Council of the Gods and a crooked stick, symbolic of longevity, are held in the left. Prayer meal, which is carried in the belt, is thrown out with the right hand in a line before them as they proceed. The two Ko'pi^tläshiwanni whirl rhombi, calling the clouds to gather. The director of the fraternity of Hunters carries on his back a hu'chapone filled with te'likinawe.

The Great Father Ko'yemshi carries a kĭa'ĕtchiné in a piece of white commercial cotton cloth, which passes over the right shoulder and across the back, and is tied in front. He and his nine fellows each carry four te'likinawe to the Council of the Gods. The ceremonial father of Shu'laawi^tsi carries four te'likinawe for the Council of the Gods and the personator of Shu'laawi^tsi the same number. Those who personate Sa'yatäsha, Hu'tutu, the two Yä'muhakto and the six Sha'läko, with their alternates, each carry four te'likinawe to the Council of the Gods.

The party leaves the village about 8 o'clock in the morning, barefoot and clad in ordinary dress, which is new for the occasion.[a] The Ko'mosona, with his Ko'pi'^tlashiwanni on his right, leads the party.

---

[a] In the past the party has always made these journeys on foot; but at the present, while the Ko'mosona, Ko'pekwĭn, the two Ko'pi^tläshiwanni, and Ko'yemshi adhere to the old custom, others proceed to the base of the mountains on burros.

The ceremonial father of Shu′laawiᵗsi, the personators of Shu′laawiᵗsi, Sa′yatäsha, Yä′muhakto, Hu′tutu, a second Yä′muhakto, and the Sha′läko, with their fellows, come next. The director of the Hunters fraternity follows some distance behind alone,[a] and after him a man of Deer clan and one of Badger clan go on burros. After these follow the Ko′pekwĭn with his Ko′pi′‴lashiwanni and then the ten Ko′yemshi.[b]

After sunset the canteens are filled at a spring, then the party ascends a mountain, where they camp for the night. After the evening meal the Ko′mosona requests the party to dance. Early in the morning they proceed on their journey, arriving at the forks of the road. A mile or so from Ko′thluwala′wa the Ko′yemshi take the right-hand trail, which leads northwest to their mountain. The Ko′mosona and others take the left-hand trail, which carries them southwest to Kor′kokshi mountain, which they ascend.[c]

The Ko′mosona and Ko′pekwĭn, each with his Pi′‴läshiwanni, the one to the Ko′mosona preceding and carrying a torch, enter a cave on the summit of the mountain. They are supposed to go by an inner passageway to the depths of Ko′thluwala′wa and return. Each carries a number of te′likinawe, which are deposited within the cave.

The Zuñi priests humbug their people by declaring that there is a direct passageway from this cave to the dwelling place of the Council of the Gods in the depth of the lake, and that, opening from this passageway, there are four chambers, equal distances apart, where those privileged to enter the underground road may rest on their journey to and from the lake. A stone which was carefully placed to conceal the entrance to this shallow cave was removed in 1881 by Mr Stevenson, and two of his party and himself, including the writer, succeeded in squeezing in to the depth of 16 feet. At the end of this passageway they found a space of not more than 3 feet. It was examined carefully by candlelight, and it was discovered that nothing of any size could pass beyond. Numbers of te′likinawe were found in the passageway.

The visit of Mr Stevenson and the writer to Ko′thluwala′wa was interesting. Spending one night in St. John, Ariz., they left there with a view to visiting the lake. Most cautiously they approached their Indian guide on the subject, but on learning their object he declared they must not go. Extreme persuasion was necessary to induce him to guide them to the sacred spot. As the day advanced and the party proceeded on their journey the old Indian, so fearless in battle, became greatly alarmed; he declared the marshy ground which the party crossed with difficulty was made so by the gods who did not wish them to approach the lake; his usually merry voice was reduced to a whisper; in fact before camp was made he was unable to speak. He said to the writer: "If you insist on going, I will show you the way, but I shall offend the gods and I shall surely die." Finally, after the party had traveled for several hours, he said in a low whisper: "We will camp here." As the writer could see no water, she thought the Indian had yielded to his superstitious

---

[a] The director of the Hunters and his deputy alternate in the quadrennial visits to Ko′thluwala′wa.

[b] In the intervening years the personators of the gods, including the Ko′yemshi, visit a spring south of Zuñi, while the others go to To′seluna spring at Ojo Caliente.

[c] These mountains are prominent landmarks. According to a Zuñi legend, Kor′kokshi mountain is the spot where their first ancestral god and goddess originated; and the other is the home of the Ko′yemshi. It was on Ko′yemshi mountain that the Gods of War prepared for the attack upon the Kĭa′nakwe. The vast amount of flint chips show it to have been a great center for arrow-making.

fear. Just then a Mexican youth appeared, and the writer inquired of him if a lake was near. He replying in the affirmative, the old Indian whispered: "And you have seen it?" "Yes." "And you have looked into it?" "Yes," replied the Mexican, looking up with surprise. "And you were not afraid?" "No; why should I be afraid?" The youth was still more puzzled when the old man said to the writer: "He has looked into the waters of the Kok'ko A'wan and he did not die." The superstitious notion is that anyone who looks on the waters of this lake, unless by special permission of the Ko'mosona, will die in four days.

In deference to the wishes of the old guide the party camped half a mile from Ko'thluwala'wa. When they remounted to visit the lake no amount of persuasion could induce the Indian to accompany them, but some time later, when they had completed the circuit of the lake, they discovered the old man as near the water as the marshy ground would permit, engaged in prayer. The headkerchief had been removed, a custom usually observed by these people when taking part in any religious ceremony. He stood erect, his hair blowing in the breeze. His right hand was extended toward the setting sun, and with it he was scattering prayer meal toward the lake. He gave no evidence of being aware of the approach of others until his prayer was completed, then turning with the old smile upon his face and his eyes again bright, he exclaimed: "I am very happy, and yet, I know I must die. I shall be contented to die, for I have looked upon the waters of the house of my departed fathers." He had approached the lake on foot, as this sacred ground must not be desecrated by the tread of beasts. The old Indian desired to remain behind after camp was broken, but the writer determined not to be separated from him. Several times he urged her to follow the party, but she insisted upon waiting for him. Finally he said: "Well, I suppose you must see all." Whereupon he took a large quantity of bread, which he had secreted behind a tree, and consigned it to the camp fire, with a prayer to the dead that they would intercede with the Sun Father and the Kok'ko A'wan for his people and all the world. The old man had observed a strict fast during his stay in this camp for the purpose of saving his food to offer to the departed.

In crossing a low mountain not far from the lake several pieces of pinkish clay were collected. This is greatly prized by the Zuñi, who believe that if the smallest portion should be parted with no rain would again fall upon the land. The priests claim that this clay comes directly from the house of the Council of the Gods in the depths of the lake. The Indian guide could not be persuaded to touch a piece, and when he found that he could not make the party desist from gathering it he begged that they would not let it be seen in Zuñi.

The main road had scarcely been reached when two Zuñi Indians appeared, returning from a visit to Camp Apache. They expressed surprise at the meeting, and the guide was not long in informing them that Mr Stevenson had been to St John to see a collection of ancient pottery which had been found in a cave by a Mexican, and he adroitly endeavored to have the Indian travelers continue their journey. His efforts to ward off any suspicion of the party having visited Ko'thluwala'wa was dramatic. He kept the attention of the visitors so riveted upon his fictitious narration of the visit to St John, describing the bowls of turquoise and other precious beads found with the pottery, that there was no time for inquiry on the part of the visitors. He recited many anecdotes of his trip, all originating within his brain. His hearty laughter became contagious, and so the night passed without his permitting the others to sleep or even to lie down; they must have no time for thought or dreams.

The punishment for visiting the lake without the permission of the Ko'mosona is not only death within four days by the anger of the gods, but severe corporal punishment and perhaps death by the order of the Ko'mosona.

While the Ko'mosona and party are in the cave the personators of the Council of the Gods and Sha'läko deposit te'likinawe at a shrine on the summit of the mountain to the west (see plate xxx). There are many precious beads and large numbers of te'likinawe in position at this shrine, and hundreds of the plume offerings lie scattered about, having been removed to make room for others.

The Ko'yemshi make offerings at a shrine on their mountain, and by the time the others are through with their ceremonies on Kor'kokshi mountain the Ko'yemshi are coming over the trail singing.

Song of the Ko'yemshi at Ko'thluwala'wa

Ha'liliko,   ha'liliko,   a'yaltonanĕ,   a'yaltonanĕ.
Mountain   mountain   walking on the   walking on the
  sheep,   sheep,   mountain edge.   mountain edge.
Lilth'note wa'ᵗsuᶦsukɪ̈a a'thlashi   a'lana ye'maku a'lana ye'maku.
  Here   gopher,   old,   many   go up,   many   go up.
Ha'liliko ha'liliko a'wuhlᶦhlananĕ   a'wuhlᶦhlananĕ
Mountain   mountain   walking below,   walking below.
  sheep,   sheep,
Lilth'note wa'ᵗsuᶦsukɪ̈a a'thlashi   a'lana pan'iyu alana pan'iyu.
  Here   gopher,   old,   many come down, many come down.

Both parties gather on a hill to the east of the lake. The Ko'mosona and Ko'pekwĭn remove their clothing preparatory to entering the lake. They tie up their hair and secure their many necklaces around their throats. Each one suspends a sack from his neck in which to place the tortoises they may secure. The Great Father Ko'yemshi gives the kĭa'ĕtchinĕ he carries to the Ko'pekwĭn and the director of the Hunters fraternity hands his to the Ko'mosona. The two, owing to the marshy condition of the ground, approach the lake on their hands and feet, somewhat in the fashion of frogs. They deposit the kĭa'ĕtchinĕ which they have brought from Zuñi and the others in the water, weights being attached for the purpose of sinking them. The kĭa'ĕtchiwe are offered to the Council of the Gods without being separated, with prayers for rain, and also that their otherselves, the tortoises, may come out through their doors, their homes being deep in the water. Four holes are supposed to exist in the walls of the lake, which are termed the home of the tortoises. The Ko'pekwĭn also deposits fire sticks, which are old and used only for this occasion, into the lake, after applying a coat of mud from the lake, he having previously made notches on the horizontal stick. These sticks are of giant yucca stalks and must be broken, not cut, from the plant. When depositing the fire sticks he offers a prayer for much rain.

Others of the party gather as near the lake as the marsh will permit, and each one plants four te'likinawe to his ancestors. All, including the Ko'mosona and Ko'pekwĭn, return to the hill and dress, after which they take their evening meal. After dancing for a time, they again undress and go as near as possible to the lake, where each one deposits food. Those who are to personate the Council of the Gods and Sha′-läko in the coming autumn offer the prayers while at the lake which they will repeat at the time of the Sha′läko festival. They now proceed to the south side of the lake and dance. At the close of the dance they return to the hill and retire for the night. In the early morning the Ko′mosona, Ko′pekwĭn, and the two Ko′pi′′läshiwanni return nude to the lake and gather cat-tails (Typha latifolia), which they distribute to the others. The pe′kwĭn also secures the fire sticks which he deposited in the water on the previous evening.

Before departing for the lake the Ko′mosona dispatches most of the party for tortoises with the words: "Go, look for our otherselves." Only members of the fraternity of Hunters may strike the tortoise with the rabbit stick; others pat them with their hands until the head is projected, when a string is tied around the neck.

A favorite place for the tortoise is said to be the house of the deer, a spring a short distance from Ko′thluwala′wa, above the general level of the country, and so named because deer congregate there to drink. An underground passage is supposed to extend from this spring to the lake; in fact, Ko′thluwala′wa is said to be connected with all sacred springs and lakes by underground roads.

After the return of the Ko′mosona and Ko′pekwĭn from the lake to the hill the sacred fire is made by wood friction. A small quantity of cedar fiber is crushed and deposited on the ground and the stick, to be used horizontally, with bits of mud attached to each point where the other stick is to be used, is laid upon it. The Ko′mosona,[a] Ko′pekwĭn, the two Ko′pi′′läshiwanni, the personator of Shu′laawi[t]si for the coming autumn, the ceremonial father of Shu′laawi[t]si, and other members of the Badger clan, form a broken circle. The process of fire making begins with the Ko′mosona, who, after using the drill, passes it to the Ko′pekwĭn who sits at his left. After the first handling of the drill these two do not touch it. The sticks being damp, a long time is required in making the fire. It would not do to work on a spot that had been touched with a drill. When combustion occurs and the crushed fiber is ignited, the one who produces the fire lifts the fiber, holding it in partly closed hands, moving them back and forth that the fiber may be fanned by the breeze. The breath must never be blown upon it, as this would so offend the Council of the Gods that there would be no rain. If rain is not the result of the fire making, the hearts of those who work with the drill are not good.

The cedar brand is ignited from the burning fiber, which is now thrown into the spring with a prayer for rain. The one who produces

[a] The Ko′mosona being a child of the Badger clan (see List of clans) is privileged to use the fire drill.

fire and lights the brand is termed Shu'laawi'si, but he must not be confounded with the one who is to personate Shu'laawi'si in the autumn festival of the Sha'läko. He lays the brand on the ground, the burning end to the east, this being the signal for the return to Zuñi. Extra brands are held in readiness, as the sacred fire must not die out on the way. As they proceed they sing, and the two Ko'pi·'läshiwanni whirl their rhombi, imploring the u'wannami (rainmakers) to water the earth. When they are a short distance from Ko'thluwala'wa, the pinkish clay used by the personators of the gods is collected by the Ko'mosona and others.

As they proceed, Shu'laawi'si runs about setting fire to grass, trees, or whatever comes in his way, that smoke may rise in clouds like the breath clouds from the gods of Ko'thluwala'wa.[a] When crossing from one side to the other of the procession, Shu'laawi'si must pass back of it, never before. The Council of the Gods hold te'likinawe between their hands, not the actual plumes offered by the Zuñi, but the ghost-selves of the plumes, and blow them to the heavens, they forming clouds as they ascend. "Breath comes from the mouths of the Kok'ko A'wan like steam."

The party returns to the mountain or ridge where they camped on their journey to Ko'thluwala'wa. Shu'laawi'si builds a fire at a distance from the others and lays his firebrand near by, the end pointing to the east. The Ko'mosona and Ko'pekwĭn each place beside the firebrand their gourd jugs, which they filled with water from the spring, the home of the deer, near Ko'thluwala'wa. After dancing until midnight, the party rest and sleep until early morning, when they start for Zuñi. They visit the springs of Ko'loowisi (Plumed Serpent) and Kok'ko 'hlan'na (great god) of the Ne'wekwe (Galaxy) fraternity as they pass through Ojo Caliente. Shu'laawi'si continues the destruction of whatever may come in his way.

The party is met by the Kor'kokshi, who on the present occasion are representatives of the Heiwa ki'wi'sinĕ, about 1½ miles southwest of Zuñi. A bonfire is lighted here, just as at the camping place, from the brand that is afterward laid on the ground, the burnt end to the east, and the jugs of water brought by the Ko'mosona and the Ko'pekwĭn are placed either side of it at the west end. The party from the lake, except the Ko'yemshi, are seated facing east, while the Kor'kokshi, who have donned their masks and paraphernalia, dance. The Ko'yem-shi, likewise, are attired in their scanty ceremonial dress, including their masks. On proceeding to Zuñi the brand is ignited at the bonfire and is now carried by the one who is to personate Shu'laawi'si in the Sha'läko ceremonial of the coming autumn.

---

[a] When the fence of a ranchman was burned some years ago, the Zuñi regarded this American, as they called him, as a most depraved character because he objected to the burning of his fence when the object was to bring rains.

The Ko'mosona leads the party, carrying his gourd jug of water; his Ko'pi‘‘läshiwanni is at the right, whirling the rhombus; the Kor'-kokshi follow, with those who are to personate the Sha'läko on either side. The Ko'pekwĭn, carrying his jug of water, follows next, with his Ko'pi‘‘läshiwanni whirling the rhombus; the personator of Shu'-laawi‘si with his firebrand held horizontally, the burning end to the front, is next to the Ko'pekwĭn. Those who personate the others of the Council of the Gods proceed on either side of the Kor'kokshi, carrying great bunches of cat-tails, and several have rhombi which are kept in constant motion. On reaching the village at dusk the party visits He'kĭapa (back wall) plaza, and after the Kor'kokshi dance here the procession passes up the west street to the north of the village and a short distance down the street and enter Ko'china (rat) plaza. After a dance here they pass to ‘Si'aa' te'wita, sacred dance plaza, and, after one dance, they visit te'wita ‘hlanna (great plaza), where they give one dance.

The Ko'mosona, followed by his Ko'pi‘‘läshiwanni, now leads the Kor'kokshi and those who are to personate Sha'läko, with their attendants, into the Mu'he‘wa ki'wi‘sinĕ. The Ko'pekwĭn with his Ko'pi‘‘-läshiwanni leads to his home, the wife's house, those who personate the Council of the Gods and the Ko'yemshi.

The Hä'lo‘kwe (Ant fraternity) has its altar erected in the Mu'he‘wa ki'wi‘sinĕ. The altar is embellished with mi'wachi and other fetishes, and a bowl of medicine water is in front of it. The fraternity is grouped south of the altar, which faces east. The tortoises are deposited in a large bowl of water which is set before the altar, and the cat-tails are stood either side and rest against it.

The altar of the Great Fire fraternity is placed in the home of the Ko'pekwĭn, with mi'wachi and many other fetishes about it, and a bowl of medicine water deposited before it. Tortoises and cat-tails are also placed by this altar. The members of this fraternity are grouped south of the altar with their rattles ready to furnish music for the dance. This fraternity is alone privileged to meet in the Ko'pekwĭn's house at the summer solstice.

Soon after entering the house, Shu'laawi‘si knocks off the burning end of his brand at the fireplace and lays it before the altar of the Great Fire fraternity. The Kor'kokshi remove their masks and change their ceremonial dress for ordinary clothing, and all except the Ko'mosona, his Ko'pi‘‘läshiwanni, and the officers of the fraternity go to their homes for refreshment. The wife of the Ko'mosona and the women of her family bring food to the ki'wi‘sinĕ for those who remain. After the evening meal nothing must pass the lips of the actors excepting the drafts administered by theurgists until afternoon of the day following. The Ko'pekwĭn, his Ko'pi‘‘läshiwanni, and the officers of the Great Fire fraternity remain in the house of the former, his wife and family and clan relations serving food to them, while the others go to their homes to eat. All gather later in the evening.

The Kor'kokshi prepare themselves in the ki'wi⁺sinĕ for the dance, the masks being discarded for the night dancing. The Ko'mosona leads the Kor'kokshi from the ki'wi⁺sinĕ to the Ko'pekwin's house. He carries his mi'li and meal basket in his left hand and sprinkles meal with his right from the time he enters the house until the dancers form in line. After one dance, they return to the ki'wi⁺sinĕ, accompanied by two Ko'yemshi wearing masks. In this way the Kor'kokshi dance alternately four times in the Ko'pekwĭn's house and the ki'wi⁺sinĕ. In the former place the Great Fire fraternity sing to the accompaniment of their rattles and in the ki'wi⁺sinĕ the Ant fraternity furnishes the music. When the Kor'kokshi are not present in the Ko'pekwĭn's house, Shu'laawi⁺si, the Ko'yemshi, and others dance.

The night is passed in dancing, and at daylight the Ko'mosona, holding a corn husk of mud from Ko'thluwala'wa, dips his index finger into the mud and anoints the breast, the palm of the right hand, and the sole of the right foot of each of the Kor'kokshi, who are now standing, saying: "Kok'ko A'wan hĕl'li⁺kwe kwa ho'o än'teshema to'o i'ton, kwa än'teshema to'o tu'tu (I anoint you with the mud of the Council of the Gods; I do not wish you to eat; I do not wish you to drink)." A fast is observed from this time until noon. After the anointing the Kor'kokshi prepare themselves to dance, after which the Ko'mosona, taking a large medicine bowl, prepares paint with the pinkish clay from Ko'thluwala'wa. Calling to him each man who personates a Kor'-kokshi god, he asks each in turn where he will have the paint applied, and, dipping his index finger into the bowl, daubs the paint on the spot indicated—foot, hand, shoulder, or elsewhere. Then handing the bowl of paint to the dance director, he tells him that the Kor'kokshi are to paint themselves. Each man covers his face, body, arms, hands, feet, and his legs nearly to the thighs, with the paint. The Ko'mosona now calls the eight men who personate the Kor'kokshi goddesses, and after asking them a similar question daubs them with yellow paint, mixed in a medicine bowl, brought also from the neighborhood of Ko'thluwala'wa. Addressing the chief goddess, who stands midway in the line of the goddesses in the dance, and, handing over the bowl of yellow paint, he directs that all shall decorate their persons. The hands and arms to the elbows and feet and legs to the knees are painted. The ceremonial dress is now put on and the tortoises are distributed as far as they will go; others carry gourd rattles only.

The bowl containing the tortoises is deposited near the middle of the floor before the dancers are supplied, where it remains throughout the day. The tortoises[a] are returned to the bowl each time the Kor'kokshi come to the ki'wi'sinĕ.

The Ko'yemshi are the first to visit 'Si'aa' te'wita in the early morning, this being the morning which closes the retreat of the Kĭa'kwemosi. They are led by the Ko'pekwĭn, carrying his mi'li and meal basket in his left hand and sprinkling meal with his right. Each Ko'yemshi has a bunch of cat-tails in his left hand and a rattle in his right. They present the cat-tails to the Shi'wano''kĭa (Priestess of fecundity), who descends from the ceremonial chamber of the Kĭa'-kwemosi to receive them. The ceremonial chamber of the Kĭa'kwemosi is in the second story of a house opening on the Si'aa' te'wita. Returning to the chamber, the Shi'wano''kĭa hands the cat-tails to the Kĭa'kwemosi, who lays them near the meal painting on the floor.

The Ko'yemshi are followed by the Kor'kokshi led by the Ko'mosona who wears a white shirt, white embroidered kilt held on by an embroidered sash tied at the right side, blue knit leggings, and red garters. The feet are bare. A line of pinkish clay extends across the nose and under the eyes. There are thirty gods, of whom twenty-eight are Kor'kokshi and two are younger brothers of Pau'tiwa, director-general at Ko'thluwala'wa. One of the brothers stands midway the line and leads the dances. There are eight goddesses. One walks beside the foremost dancer in the file, and faces him in the dance. The others are companions to the gods, who number from thirteen to nineteen, inclusive, in the line. The Kor'kokshi dance in He'kĭapa and Ko'china plazas before going to Si'aa'. The arrival of the Kor'kokshi in Si'aa' te'wita is the signal for the Kĭa'kwemosi to play his flute in the ceremonial chamber. After the first dance in the plaza, the Kĭa'kwemosi descends from the ceremonial chamber and passes from west to east down the line of gods, halts for a moment before the Ko'mosona, and then passes by the goddesses. He sprinkles each goddess and the cat-tails[b] she carries with meal and then receives the cat-tails and returning down the line of gods he sprinkles them and the cat-tails with meal, receiving from each god, except six, the cat-tails he carries. He then halts before the Ko'mosona and, sprinkling a line of meal down the mi'li, which the Ko'mosona holds in his right hand, offers a prayer.

The Kĭa'kwemosi returns to the ceremonial chamber and deposits the cat-tails by the cloud symbol on the floor (see page 150). Leaving the Si'aa' te'wita, the Kor'kokshi proceed to the te'wita 'hlanna, and, after

---

[a] After the ceremonial the tortoises are taken home by those who caught them and are hung by their necks to the rafters till morning, when they are thrown into pots of boiling water. The eggs are considered a great delicacy. The meat is seldom touched except as a medicine, which is a curative for cutaneous diseases. Part of the meat is deposited in the river, with ko'hakwa (white shell beads) and turquoise beads, as offerings to Council of the Gods.

[b] The stems of the cat-tails are afterward used by the A'shiwanni for te'likinawe.

dancing there, they return to the ki'wi'sině, lay aside their masks, indulge in a smoke, and rest a short time. The dancing in the four plazas is repeated four times before noon. The fourth time they dance in the Si'aa' te'wita the Ko'mosona, who leads the file of dancers, tells the Great Father Ko'yemshi that it is time to eat.

After this dance the Kor'kokshi are followed for the first time by the Ko'yemshi, who have previously awaited them in the Si'aa' te'wita. After dancing in the te'wita 'hlanna the Ko'mosona leads the Kor'kokshi to Mu'he'wa ki'wi'sině, and the Ko'yemshi follow the Ko'pekwĭn to his house. Great feasts are spread in both houses, those who have spent the night in the two places being still present.

There is no dancing in the house of the Ko'pekwĭn during the day, and no one but the Ko'pekwĭn and the Ko'yemshi leave the house. Those who are to personate the gods at the Sha'läko festival receive instructions in their duties in the He'iwa ki'wi'sině during the day. The Ko'mosona administers to each one in the Mu'he'wa ki'wi'sině from a shell' the water from the spring, which has been previously emptied from the gourd jug into a medicine bowl, saying "Drink." The one receiving the draft says: "Tä''chumo" (father). The Ko'mosona replies: "Täl'lemo" (younger one). After all have been helped, the Ko'mosona says: "I am well pleased, my children; you have danced four times; we will dance no more now, for neither did the people of old. You may drink all you wish." The water vases brought in by the women of the Deer clan are soon surrounded by the thirsty men who have neither eaten nor drunk since the previous evening. The same is repeated in the Ko'pekwĭn's house, water being carried thither by women of the Badger clan. They indulge in a great feast served by women of the Deer and Badger clans.

After smoking and resting for a time the dancing in the four plazas is repeated four times. The fourth time they dance in the Si'aa' tewita (see plate XXXI) the Ko'mosona again tells the Great Father Ko'yemshi that it is time to eat. After dancing in the te'wita 'hlanna, they return to the ki'wi'sině and to the house of the Ko'pekwĭn, where a second feast is enjoyed. Here they smoke and have their heads washed in yucca suds by women of the Deer and Badger clans. The summer solstice ceremonies, strictly speaking, are now over, yet it is but the beginning of the Kor'kokshi dances for rains to fructify the earth that the crops may grow, the Kor'kokshi being personated in turn from the five other ki'wi'siwe.

A'SHIWANNI (RAIN PRIESTHOOD)

The rain priesthood consists at the present time of fourteen A'shi-wanni (those who fast and pray for rain), the elder and younger Bow priests, and Shi'wano'ʻkĭa (Priestess of fecundity). Of the A'shiwanni, six are known as Kĭa'kwe a'mosi (directors of the house). The house referred to marks the middle of the world, and is the ceremonial house of the Kĭakwe amosi. A room in this house, in which the ĕt'tonĕ of the Shi'wanni of the North is kept, is supposed to be directly over the center of the world. While the term Kĭa'kwe a'mosi is applicable to the A'shiwanni of the six regions, the Shi'wanni of the North, being the head of the priesthood, is always referred to as the Kĭa'kwemosi; the others are termed the Shi'wanni of the West, the Shi'wanni of the South, etc. Throughout this paper the term Kĭa'kwemosi will refer to the Shi'wanni of the North. The six regions in order are North, West, South, East, Zenith, and Nadir, the center being always subsumed. The A'shiwanni are described by the Zuñi as those who do no secular work, and it is their special duty to fast and pray for rain.

Each shi'wanni, excepting the Shi'wanni of the Zenith, is the possessor of an ĕt'tonĕ, which is supposed to have descended directly from the shi'wanni who brought it in a basket[a] clasped to his breast from the undermost to the outer world. The ĕt'tonĕ is dual: ᵗkĭa'ĕttonĕ and chu'ĕttonĕ (see plates xxxii and xxxiii). The ᵗkĭa'ĕttonĕ (the first syllable, ᵗkĭa, is from ᵗkĭawe, water) consists of four hollow reeds, each of the length of the middle finger measured on the under side, one reed being thicker than the rest. All contain water.

FIG. 4—Toad kept in ĕt'tonĕ reed, actual size.

The larger one also contains in the water a diminutive toad (Bufo punctatus, figure 4), which seems to thrive in its restricted quarters. The ends of the reeds are closed with a blackish clay, said by the A'shiwanni to have been brought from the undermost world, and native cotton. The chu'ĕttonĕ (the first syllable, chu, is from chu'we, seeds) is composed of eight hollow reeds filled with all the edible seeds known to the A'shiwi (Zuñis) and closed at the ends with native cotton. Originally the reeds contained only kĭa'ᵗsanna, the only food then known to the A'shiwi. Each group of reeds is wrapped with cord of native cotton, the end of the cord on the ᵗkĭa'ĕttonĕ being left free, to symbolize the tail of a toad, which would indicate that the A'shiwi were aware of the evolution of the toad from the tadpole. A number of precious beads are attached to the cord wrapping of the ĕt'tonĕ, and a fine arrow point rests on the top.

[a] See p. 26. Since the A'shiwi learned the art of making pottery the ĕt'tonĕ has rested in a vase instead of a basket.

The sacredness of the ĕt′tonĕ is indicated, not only by its prominence in legend, but by the care with which it is guarded. The writer was fortunate in being able to handle and examine the ĕt′tonĕ of Nai′uchi, since deceased, Shi′wanni of the Nadir, who was also elder brother Bow priest. On removing the toad from the reed it was found to be in a lively condition. The writer is indebted to Nai′uchi for models of the sacred fetish, which are in the National Museum.

When the A′shiwi were divided into clans these sacred objects became associated with the clans chosen by their possessors, and while an ĕt′tonĕ may pass from a shi′wanni of the parent clan to one of the children of the clan,[a] it remains in the care of a woman of the parent clan, when not in the hands of the shi′wanni, this office passing from mother to daughter or from sister to sister.

When not in use each ĕt′tonĕ rests in a sealed vase in a special chamber in the dwelling house of its keeper. The chamber has no windows, and the door is kept sealed except when the sacred fetish is brought to a larger chamber in the same house for the winter and summer retreats or is taken from the house for the ′Hle′wekwe ceremonial.[b] Should there be a small opening in the roof of the chamber of the ĕt′tonĕ, it is covered with a slab set in plaster, and is opened only for the purpose of sprinkling meal into the chamber during a retreat of the shi′wanni and his associates. Two of the ĕt′towe are supposed to have come from the conquered Kĭa′nakwe, to have been brought by the boy who, with his sister, was adopted by the A′shiwi. The aged woman who has the care of these fetishes is said to be the direct descendant of the foster mother of the brother and sister.

Through the earnest persuasion of a nephew to the shi′wanni possessing these fetishes, the wife being also in sympathy with his wishes, the aged woman in charge of them (his mother-in-law) was induced to allow the door of the room to be opened. The entire family incurred danger in giving their assistance. The front chamber was carefully guarded, so that no one should enter an inner room into which the sacred apartment opens. It was necessary to be expeditious, there being no surety against intrusion, for, according to the custom of the A′shiwi, the people of the same clan are regarded as one family and have access to all parts of a house. While the old woman was opening the sealed door of the room containing the ĕt′towe the writer, with the assistance of the nephew, hurriedly prepared her flashlight and camera, and in a few moments a picture was taken. The illustration (figure 5) shows the room, which is about 7 by 5 feet, with two vases containing the sacred objects and other fetishes associated with the ĕt′tonĕ. The door was soon closed again and sealed with plaster. The family was in

[a] See List of clans.   [b] See ′Hle′wekwe fraternity.

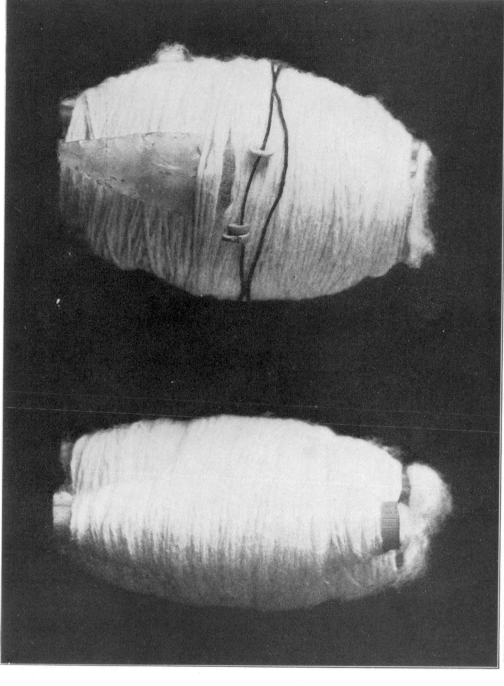

TOP VIEW OF ĔT′TONĔ, FETISH OF RAIN PRIESTS

CLOUD SYMBOL AND FETISHES OF SHIWANNI (RAIN PRIEST) OF THE NADIR PREVIOUS TO THE PLACING OF THE FRUIT AND GRAIN OFFERINGS

MASK OF SĀ́LIMOBIYA (WARRIOR) OF THE ZENITH
front and side views

MASK OF SÄ'LIMOBIYA (WARRIOR) OF THE NADIR: FRONT AND SIDE VIEWS

great distress, the young wife being prostrated with fear, for she knew that if her husband and mother were detected in this breach of trust their lives would be in great danger. When the writer expressed her thanks, the wife, after her condition had improved, said: "We are all very much afraid and very unhappy, but we were glad to serve you." Two ĕt'towe rest undisturbed in sealed vases in their chambers, the divisions of the A'shiwanni to whom they belong having ceased to exist because the families privileged to form these divisions have either expired or been considered unworthy to join the sacred priesthood.

Except the Shi'wanni of the Zenith, who is pe'kwĭn (deputy) to the Sun Father, each shi'wanni has a corps of associates, including a woman,

Fig. 5—Room of ĕt'towe of Corn clan.

except the shi'wanni possessing the Kĭa'nakwe ĕt'towe. He has no female associate, as none has ever been found possessing a sufficiently good heart for this position. One of the duties of the women associated with the A'shiwanni is the grinding of white corn into a coarse meal in the family mills. This kĭa'waiawe (prayer meal) is mixed with crushed turquoise, ko'hakwa (white shell), and abalone shell. The wife, daughter, or sister of the pe'kwĭn grinds that which he uses.

This priesthood is confined to families, the rule being that each member of a division of the priesthood must be of the clan or a child of the clan of the shi'wanni of the division. The son or brother of the shi'wanni fills a vacancy, preference being given to the eldest son. There are exceptions, however, to this rule, such as the Shi'wanni of the Zenith, who is appointed by the first body of A'shiwanni from the Pi'chikwe (Dogwood clan), and may belong to either division of the clan (see page 40), the directors of the 'Hle'wekwe and Shu'maakwe fraternities. The ĕt'tonĕ of the Shu'maakwe is distinctly different from the others. The songs over this ĕt'tonĕ are in the Pima tongue.[a]

The associate priests are in the line of promotion, but should the first body of A'shiwanni consider one unworthy of advancement,[b] it convenes, and a discussion occurs in regard to the proper party for the place. This meeting, however, appears to be a mere formality, it being the prerogative of the shi'wanni in whose division an appointment is to be made to select the man. Nevertheless, he addresses the priesthood, saying, referring to himself and his associates: "We do not know who is best. We leave the selection to you." At the same time he has already made known his choice. The Kĭa'kwemosi, who is the head of the priesthood, formally requests the elder brother Bow priest to notify the person of his appointment. The elder brother Bow priest enjoys great power in Zuñi, and nowhere is this superior personage (earthly representative of the elder God of War) more revered than in the first body of A'shiwanni. Though the female associate of the Kĭa'kwemosi, whose position is quite different and far superior in character to that of the other female associates, she being Shi'wano''kĭa (Priestess of fecundity), is present at these meetings, she holds her peace when one is to be appointed, but is free to express herself when there is any suggestion of impeachment. Any shi'wanni or associate may be impeached for proper cause.

Some years since, the Shi'wano''kĭa denounced the pe'kwĭn, Shi'wanni of the Zenith, declaring the droughts and failure of crops to be due to his impure heart. She even expressed her suspicion of his being a sorcerer. Some one must be held responsible for the absence of rains, and the poor pe'kwĭn, a most excellent man, was the victim. He was impeached and removed and, after much discussion, a young man of the Raven division of the Dogwood clan was selected to fill the place. The Kĭa'kwemosi dispatched the elder and younger brother Bow priests to make the announcement to the chosen party. The mother, who was present, wept bitterly and begged her son not to accept the position, saying to the elder brother Bow priest: "He is so young, and he might make some mistake, and then perhaps he would be condemned as a sorcerer." The mother's grief touched the heart of the son, and he declined the honor which he most earnestly desired to attain. Another meeting of the A'shiwanni was held, when a man of the Macaw division of the Dogwood clan was chosen, and in due time he was installed in his high office.

The A'shiwanni are becoming much concerned regarding the successors of the Kĭa'kwemosi and pe'kwĭn. They say it is hard to find good men who are eligible, either of the Dogwood clan or children of

---

[a] See Shu'maakwe fraternity.

[b] The vital requisite is that one shall be pure of heart, otherwise his prayers for rain would avail nothing, and in this arid land, where the greatest boon to man comes from the clouds, it means much to these people to have an infallible rain priesthood.

the clan. It was due to the impossibility of finding suitable persons that the present Kĭa′kwemosi had but one male associate for some time. He is the eldest son of the former Kĭa′kwemosi and nephew of the present one, and will in time attain that position. The present Kĭa′kwemosi and his predecessor were brothers.

The following is an enumeration of the A′shiwanni as it existed in November, 1896:

Kĭa′kwemosi (Shi′wanni of the North), Dogwood clan, younger brother of his predecessor; first associate, Turkey clan,[a] son of the former Kĭa′kwemosi and nephew on the paternal side of the present one; second associate, Dogwood clan; third associate, vacant, no eligible person being available; fourth associate, Shi′wano′′kĭa, Dogwood clan, elder sister of the former and the present Kĭa′kwemosi.

Shi′wanni of the West, Dogwood clan, deceased; first associate, Sun clan, son of the deceased shi′wanni;[b] second associate, Dogwood clan, younger brother of the deceased shi′wanni; third associate, Dogwood clan; fourth associate, a female, Dogwood clan.

Shi′wanni of the South, Badger clan; first associate, Badger clan; second associate, Badger clan; third associate, Badger clan; fourth associate, a female, Badger clan.

Shi′wanni of the East, Eagle clan; first associate, Eagle clan; second associate, Eagle clan; third associate, Eagle clan; fourth associate, a female, Eagle clan.

Shi′wanni of the Zenith, Dogwood clan.[c]

Shi′wanni of the Nadir, Eagle clan; first associate, Sand hill crane clan, son of the shi′wanni; second associate, Eagle clan, younger brother of the shi′wanni; third associate, Eagle clan; fourth associate, a female,[d] Eagle clan.

Seventh shi′wanni, Eagle clan; first associate, Eagle clan; second associate, Eagle clan; third associate, Eagle clan; fourth associate, a female, Eagle clan.

Eighth shi′wanni, Dogwood clan; first associate, Dogwood clan; second associate, Dogwood clan; third associate, Dogwood clan; fourth associate, a female, Dogwood clan.

Ninth shi′wanni,[e] Black Corn clan; first associate, Black Corn clan; second associate, Ai′yaho‘kwe (a plant); third associate, Corn clan; fourth associate, a female, Corn clan.

Tenth shi′wanni, Chaparral Cock clan, director of Shu′maakwe fraternity; first associate, Dogwood clan, deputy to director; second associate, Sand hill crane clan, maker of medicine water; third associate, Sun clan, warrior to the fraternity; fourth associate, a female, Ai′yaho‘kwe, great mother of the fraternity.

Eleventh shi′wanni, Sun clan; first associate, Sun clan; second associate, Sun clan; third associate, Sun clan; fourth associate, a female, Sun clan.

Twelfth shi′wanni, Corn clan; first associate, Corn clan; second associate, Corn clan; third associate, Corn clan; fourth associate, Corn clan.

---

[a] At the time of his father's death this man was too young to be associated with the A′shiwanni.

[b] The vacancy caused by the death of Lai′wa‘silun′kĭa, Shi′wanni of the West, was not filled immediately because the A′shiwanni were doubtful for a time whether the first associate possessed a sufficiently pure heart; but after considerable discussion it was decided that the son of the former shi′wanni should be advanced to his father's position. Lai′wa‘silun′kĭa's death was followed by the demise of the female associate, whose place was filled by her mother's sister's daughter. Nai′uchi, elder brother Bow priest, declared that, though this woman was pure of heart, no other of her immediate family should succeed her, as her brother was a sorcerer, and he had strong suspicions of the father. The father held the important position of scalp custodian in the A′pi‘ᵘläshiwanni (Bow priesthood).

[c] Pe′kwĭn (deputy) to the Sun Father; he has no associate.

[d] Nai′uchi, as Shi′wanni of the Nadir, is preparing his grandchild, the daughter of his first associate, to fill the place of female associate when the present incumbent shall have passed away.

[e] The ninth shi′wanni is the possessor of the ĕt′tonĕ secured, according to Zuñi legend, through the aged shi′wanni of the Black Corn clan, who was found with his wife and two grandchildren in the village He′shotiyälla, west of I′tiwanna, and who became allied with the A′shiwi (see p. 45).

Thirteenth shi′wanni, Corn clan; first associate, Corn clan; second associate, Corn clan; third associate, Corn clan; fourth associate, a female, Corn clan.

Fourteenth shi′wanni, Corn clan; first associate, Corn clan; second associate, Corn clan; third associate, Corn clan; fourth associate, a female, Corn clan.

Fifteenth shi′wanni,[a] Coyote clan.

Sixteenth shi′wanni,[a] Frog[b] clan.

INSTALLATION OF AN ASSOCIATE SHI′WANNI OF THE NORTH

An elaborate ceremonial of installation occurs when the appointee is received as an associate shi′wanni. He passes from this position to that of shi′wanni without further ceremonial of special importance.

The ceremonial described began about midday on December 13, 1896, in the ceremonial chamber of the Kĭa′kwemosi, where all such ceremonies associated with the first body of A′shiwanni take place. The man to be installed was a nephew of the Kĭa′kwemosi. He belonged to the Dogwood clan, was married, and did not appear to be over 20 years of age. Each shi′wanni was accompanied by his male associates; and each director of a fraternity, having been notified in the early morning by the elder brother Bow priest, was accompanied by his fellow-officers. The Shi′wano′′kĭa and the writer were the only women present. In most cases a fraternity has but one warrior, owing to the limited membership of the A′pi‘′läshiwanni. The only fraternity not represented as a body is the A′pi‘′läshiwanni, the members of this organization appearing separately with the other fraternities to which they are allied as warriors.

The first body of the A′shiwanni, including the first associate of the Kĭa′kwemosi, the elder brother Bow priest and the Shi′wano′′kĭa, have seats in the south end of the room and east of the doorway. As each division of A′shiwanni or group of a fraternity arrives it finds seats which are most agreeable on the ledge which extends around the room, and after the ledge is filled seats are taken on the floor, the room becoming crowded.

Great ceremony is observed on entering the chamber. As the groups come in each man of a group greets those present, who in return make response. The second party of the group entering does not extend this greeting until that of the first one has been responded to. Moccasins are removed after entering the room. The Kĭa′kwemosi acts as master of ceremonies until the arrival of the younger brother Bow priest, whose duty it is to look to the seating and to see that no one sleeps during the long ritual. The associate shi′wanni to the Kĭa′kwemosi spreads a large blanket on the floor near the first body of A′shiwanni and places on the blanket a large, fine white buck-

---

[a] These are extinct. The two ĕt′towe of these shi′wanni are the ones referred to as remaining permanently in sealed vases.

[b] The writer believes when a specimen is secured and examined it will be found to be a toad and not a frog. Until then she gives the common translation of the Indian word tä′kĭa (frog).

skin, furnished by the Kĭa'kwemosi, with the head to the east. He receives from the Kĭa'kwemosi a small buckskin sack containing corn pollen, and proceeds to sprinkle a line of pollen from one extremity of the deerskin to the other, great care being observed that the line of pollen shall be perfectly straight and end in the center of the mouth portion of the skin. Quantities of necklaces of coral, turquoise, and ko'hakwa beads, furnished by the Kĭa'kwemosi and other A'shiwanni, are laid over the line of pollen, forming a slight ridge, this line being symbolic of the road of life and truth, the road which must be followed in order to win the favor of A'wonawil'ona.[a]

The decoration is somewhat different when a pe'kwĭn (deputy to the Sun Father)[b] is installed. A sun symbol, composed of a disk colored blue-green, with three dots of black representing eyes and mouth, encircled by a block of black and white, symbolizing the house of the clouds, and four lines of pollen extending from four points of the periphery, is made in the center of the deerskin. The line of pollen and beads on the skin is broken by the disk. A line of meal extends from the deerskin to the entrance of the chamber, and the meal is crossed near the skin. The novice stands upon the deerskin, and the A'shiwanni and others in turn stand upon the cross line of meal. The novice is appealed to to do his duty as becomes the deputy of the Sun Father; to follow the straight road of the Sun Father, which will insure the good of his people. Should he find evil or discontent in his heart, to take it out and throw it behind him; and to keep straight in the path of truth and virtue. The sun priest prays that the blessings of A'wonawil'ona may continue, and that the Sun Father may not send his son (the rainbow) to call the rain-makers from above to send them elsewhere. He prays that all people of all lands may be bountifully supplied with food and clothing, and that his people and all other people may have no great sickness among them, and that they may be preserved from death. He also addresses prayers to Ko'hakwa (white shell) mother[c] of the sun, and Ma'we (salt) sister[c] to the sun.

The novice now takes a seat west of the deerskin and near it. Each person present removes the head-kerchief before taking part in the ceremony. Soon after noon the pe'kwĭn takes the hand of the novice, who rises and stands in the center of the skin facing east, with a foot on each side of the line of pollen and beads. The pe'kwĭn, still facing

---

[a] See Classification of the higher powers.

[b] The pe'kwĭn to the Sun Father is supposed to practice celibacy, and from the time of assuming his office to regard his wife, if he have one, as a sister, he remaining in the family and she performing all the domestic duties as before. Should celibacy not be strictly observed, the A'shiwi would soon die and I'tiwanna become depopulated. At least such is said to have been the ancient law, but at present the pe'kwĭn resumes conjugal relations when not occupied with his religious duties, from which he is seldom free. He must be so pure of heart that he can make no mistakes, otherwise he would not keep the calendar correctly, and the people would be overwhelmed with infinite troubles.

[c] Mother and sister are figurative.

the novice, places his arms about the shoulders of the novice, who
places his around the pe'kwĭn's waist, and prays. The pe'kwĭn then
places his hands behind him and clasps each hand of the novice by
placing his fingers across the palm and his thumb on top of the hand;
and, bringing the clasped hands around raises them nearly to the
novice's chin, and prays four times; the novice responds "Yes" each
time. During the prayers the pe'kwĭn draws the novice's hands to
his own mouth and breathes upon them; then he moves them downward four times before the mouth of the novice that the latter may
receive the sacred breath of A'wonawil'ona. When the pe'kwĭn
closes his prayers the first associate Shi'wanni of the West clasps
each hand of the novice, the pe'kwĭn being careful not to relinquish
his hold until his successor shall have taken the novice's hands. This
requirement is strictly observed throughout the ceremonial. The
second associate Shi'wanni of the West is the next to appear before
the novice and prays with him, and after him each shi'wanni with
his associate, the Shi'wano''kĭa excepted, in the same order in which
they go into retreat. Then follow the officers of the Shi'wannakwe,
the Ne'wekwe come next, then the 'Sän'iakĭa'kwe, followed by the
'Hle'wekwe, then the Ko'mosona (director of the Ko'tikili), the
Ko'pekwĭn (deputy to the Ko'mosona), two Ko'pi''läshi'wanni (warriors to the Ko'mosona and Ko'pekwĭn), and then the officers of
the Hä'lo'kwe. The last fraternity to take part is the 'Ko'shi'kwe.[a]
When the warrior of this fraternity has closed his ceremony the
pe'kwĭn takes the novice's hands from those of the Pi''läshiwanni
and conducts him to his place, not loosening his hold until the new
associate shi'wanni is seated. The associate to the Kĭa'kwemosi, who
arranged the deerskin, now removes the beads, returning them at
once to their owners. Beginning at the east end of the buckskin, he
raises it slightly so as to throw the pollen toward the center; he now
shakes the sides and other end of the skin for the same purpose, and
gathers the pollen into a corn husk, which he folds and hands to the
Kĭa'kwemosi, who ties the package with a ribbon of corn husk and
deposits it in his pouch. The associate also folds the deerskin and
hands it to the Kĭa'kwemosi, and afterward removes the blanket.

The Kĭa'kwemosi now removes his head-kerchief in preparation for
his part. He offers a long prayer, which is responded to occasionally
by those present. When this prayer is over all join in another prayer,
and at its close the younger brother Bow priest repeats one much
like that offered by the Kĭa'kwemosi, the difference being that the
younger brother Bow priest appeals to the Gods of War (who are
associated with the lightning-makers) in addition to other gods.

---

[a] The fraternities mentioned will be fully explained under the heading " Esoteric fraternities."

All the prayers, which are repeated in low and impressive tones, are much the same, the burden being that the incoming shi′wanni may be pure of heart, live the straight life indicated by the line of pollen and beads;[a] and so please A′wonawil′ona, who is life itself, that the people may be blessed with much rain so that all seeds may develop; and that they may have long life, without death, and grow to that old age when one sleeps to awake young again in Ko′thluwala′wa (abiding place of the Council of the Gods). It could not be discovered that any other special instruction was given to the novice. The symbolic lines over the deerskin seemed to be so full of meaning as to render spoken words unnecessary.

Many pleasantries and jokes are indulged in under the breath during the long ritual, and commercial tobacco is constantly smoked by those who are waiting their turn. The only service performed by the Shi′-wano′ʻkĭa is the supplying of corn husks from an adjoining room for the smokers.

At the close of the ceremony, which continues six hours, the new associate shi′wanni, who remains in position four hours, and showing no signs of exhaustion until the last moment, is escorted to his dwelling, the wife's house, by the elder and younger brother Bow priests. There is no further ceremony over him until he meets with the Kĭa′kwemosi and other associates in the winter retreat, when the dual fetish ʻkĭa′ĕt′-tonĕ and chu′ĕt′tonĕ is placed in his hands that he may draw from it the sacred breath.

Preparation and Planting of Te′likinawe

The preparation and planting of te′likinawe are among the principal features of Zuñi worship and ritual. Thousands of these plume offerings are made annually. Every god and goddess in the Zuñi pantheon receives his or her particular offerings, which are readily distinguished by them. Individual offerings are insignificant compared with those made by the various fraternities and organizations.

The first body of A′shiwanni make offerings each month at the appropriate points of the compass. At each place an excavation is made, in depth equal to the length of the arm of the man who removes the earth, and te′likinawe, with meal ground from toasted sweet corn and kĭa′waiawe (prayer meal) are deposited. The sweet corn is first sprinkled into the opening, then the prayer meal, after which te′likinawe are planted to the sun, moon, deceased predecessors, and others. The portion of the stick symbolizing the face always faces the east. The elder and younger brother Bow priests make additional offerings to the lightning-makers of the six regions, the A′piʻᵗläshiwanni becoming after death colaborers with Ku′pĭshtaya, the lightning-

---

[a] This straight road must be followed in order to receive the gifts of the gods.

makers. The first prayer is to the Earth Mother to invoke the Sun Father's embrace to warm her children (fruits of the earth) into being. Prayers are also offered to the deceased predecessors.

The plume stick indicates to whom the te'likinanĕ is offered, and the plumes attached convey the breath prayers to the gods. The breath of the prayer combines with the breath of the gods to whom it is offered to form clouds, behind which the rain-makers work. After the prayers the excavation is covered so that no trace of it remains.

The preparation of te'likinawe is as follows: The first stick is measured by the hand, the part of the hand used depending on the length of the stick required. Sometimes the under side of the middle finger is used; then again, the length of the stick is equal to the distance from the metacarpus to the tip of the middle finger. Others are measured from the carpus and still others from the inner side of the bend of the elbow to the tip of the middle finger. After the first stick is cut it is used as a measure for the others. As each stick is made it is laid carefully in a basket tray or on the floor beside the worker until all are completed. The plumes are then attached with cotton cord, the character of the plumes depending on the character of the person to whom the offering is to be made. The offerings are again laid side by side, but once more are removed for the coloring of the sticks. If a la'showannĕ (one or more plumes attached with cotton cord) is added, the string of the latter is dotted four times in black, symbolic of rain clouds.

The plumes used by the A'shiwanni are fluffy eagle plumes, from the under wing, and feathers of the birds of the six regions. To these are added butterflies, each shi'wanni using those of the color appropriate to the region he represents; darning needles (Enallagma exulans Hagen), and artificial flowers of the te'nas'säli (mythical medicine plant bearing flowers of the colors of the six regions). Each of the fourteen A'shiwanni has two paint pots of black and one of red earth. These earth paints are supposed to have come from the undermost world. The pots, when not in use, are covered with buckskin securely tied with cotton cord, to which bits of turquoise, ko'hakwa, and abalone shell are attached. The sticks of the te'likinawe offered for cold rains and snows are colored with paint from one of the black pots and those for the summer rains are colored with paint from the other, an exception being when neither paint is used, but instead paint used by laymen. Should the paint of the A'shiwanni be used in the month of May, cold winds would come and destroy the fruit. At this time the paint in common use for the te'likinawe is employed by the A'shiwanni.

Winter Retreat of the Shi'wanni of the Nadir[a]

One of the most pleasing ceremonies observed during the writer's studies among the Zuñis was the occasion of the winter retreat, in 1896, of Nai'uchi, Shi'wanni of the Nadir. Every opportunity was given to observe closely all the features of the ritual and to photograph, by flash light, the elaborate meal painting with its interesting embellishments.

The day is spent in silent prayers for rains and at night Nai'uchi and his associates, who have gathered in the large chamber of the house in which the ĕt'tonĕ is kept, are joined by their families, including the youngest infants. The vases containing the ĕt'tonĕ and other sacred objects are brought from the ĕt'tonĕ chamber, which adjoins this room. The shi'wanni begins a pollen and meal painting in the eastern end of the room, the painting extending from the north toward the south, by running a line of meal south; he afterward forms lines at right angles by sprinkling meal from the east. and again from the west, to the main line. He now outlines the cloud symbol, using his two eagle-wing plumes to efface any imperfections. Afterward he adds slightly to the length of the main line of meal, and an associate on the opposite side continues the line. The shi'wanni and his third associate sit on wadded blankets west of the meal line, and his first and second associates sit on the east side. After the meal line is completed, the shi'wanni fills in the outlines of the cloud symbol with white meal, while an associate on the other side outlines six scallops in meal, corn pollen, and charred corncob, which vary in size, the largest being next to the cloud design, east of the line of meal and connected with it. The associate west of the line forms circles by adding similar scallops on his side, and the circles are filled in with meal. The shi'wanni now proceeds to empty one of two vases.

A number of concretion fetishes are removed and deposited in a basket containing eight mi'wachi.[b] These are most sacred fetishes and emblems of mystery medicine. They are afterward handed one by one to an associate opposite, who places them along the meal line. Other stone objects from a medicine box and buckskin sacks are added until the line seems a solid mass of irregular stones, some of them very attractive. A reed flute is laid on one side.[c]

As soon as the shi'wanni has handed over many objects to the associate he proceeds to arrange the fetishes about the cloud symbol. A most beautiful obsidian knife, 8 inches in length, is deposited on the east side of the painting; then one, half the size, on the opposite side. The shi'wanni afterward distributes a number of arrow points of

---

[a] While each shi'wanni, with his associates, makes a retreat of one day and night in winter, when the ĕt'tonĕ and other fetishes are placed about a meal painting, the summer retreat is for a longer period.

[b] See p. 416.

[c] This flute was secured after Nai'uchi's death for the United States National Museum.

various sizes and forms over the cloud symbol, and an arrow point is placed at the end of each of the two lines radiating from the extreme end of the meal and pollen circles.

Nai'uchi and an associate each form a small cross of meal on opposite sides of the meal line by running four lines inward to the center, symbolic of the four regions. The cross is encircled with meal, symbolizing the whole world. The circle is afterward covered with strings of precious beads, which form a cincture pad, upon which the two men place medicine bowls. The eight mi'wachi[a] are placed in line across the back of the cloud symbol, and tortoise shells, the first objects taken from the second vase, are deposited at either end of the line of mi'wachi. The shi'wanni now bathes his hands in prayer meal and removes the dual et'tonĕ from the vase, the wrappings about each part forming a sort of square package. These are laid back of the line of mi'wachi for a short time, and then the shi'wanni opens each package in the most reverent and impressive manner, for they are almost too precious to be touched even by the hands of the shi'wanni himself. This dual fetish is placed midway on the cloud symbol, the ʰkia'ĕt'tonĕ being east of the chu'ĕt'tonĕ (see plate XXXIV). A more solemn occasion than that of the placing of the ĕt'tonĕ on the cloud symbol and the ceremonies attending its presence could not be imagined. All hearts and minds are filled with the adoration of the holiest of fetishes, with hopes for the dualistic influence upon the gods to water the earth. This is a supreme moment with the Zuñis, and can be compared only with the administering of the Holy Eucharist in the Roman Catholic church.

Nai'uchi now raises the third associate, who has recently been ordained, by taking both hands in his, and stands him next to the mi'wachi and cloud symbol. The shi'wanni again washes his hands in meal and, taking the kia'ĕt'tonĕ in his right hand and the chu'ĕttonĕ in his left, he holds them with the clasped hands of the newly ordained associate and makes a long prayer, that the man may walk in the straight road of day, be pure of heart, and so please the gods that they will make the earth rich with her being. This prayer is repeated over the new associate by the other two in turn, each washing his hands in meal before handling the ĕt'tonĕ. When the second associate closes his prayer Nai'uchi receives the ĕt'tonĕ, first having rubbed his hands with meal, and returns its two parts to the meal symbol. The new associate is now seated in his former place by Nai'uchi, who places his hands on the associate's shoulders, motioning to the six regions, and gives him a push into his seat, resuming his own.

---

[a] The beautiful mi'wachi displayed at the ceremony of the ĕt'tonĕ are the property of the A'shiwanni by virtue of their membership in the order of O'naya'nakia (mystery medicine) of an esoteric fraternity. The altars seen during the ceremonies associated with anthropic worship are also the property of these fraternities, who are present by invitation, to furnish music for the dances of the gods.

Nai'uchi calls for a vase of water, which is brought by the female associate, and, dipping six gourdfuls, empties it into the medicine bowl on the west side of him, and hands six gourdfuls to the associate opposite, who empties the water into the medicine bowl on his side of the line. The shi'wanni now sprinkles meal into his bowl and drops six concretion fetishes for fructification separately into the water; as he holds each one he prays to the u'wannami (rain-makers) of one of the six regions. The associate forms a cross of powdered root and encircles the cross with it, afterward sprinkling the root over the surface of the water.

After Nai'uchi, with long prayers, consecrates the water in his bowl, he stands and whirls the rhombus, while the associate whips the mixture in his bowl into frothy suds, symbolic of clouds. A single reed is used in making the suds, a more slender one being applied to keep them in place in the bowl.[a]

The other associate on the east side plays the flute. All this is an invocation to the gods for rain—the one great and perpetual prayer of the people of this arid land. The shi'wanni now lays aside the rhombus and, dipping his two eagle plumes into the consecrated water, sprinkles the offerings. This dipping of the plumes into the water and sprinkling is repeated six times, and quiet reigns for a short while. Again the shi'wanni stands and whirls the rhombus while an associate plays the flute, and the recently ordained member shakes the rattle of shells suspended from a crooked stick to which plumes are attached. This rattle is used only in ceremonials of the A'shiwanni. The other associate constantly sprinkles meal over the meal line, beginning always at the far end of the line, with prayers, which continue throughout the ceremony of invocation to the rain-makers,[b] to enter and pass up the line of pollen and meal. The shi'wanni and associates each in turn sprinkle meal up the line, though the shi'wanni is the principal actor. All night the appeal to the gods continues in low, weird, yet musical tones. The invocation is as follows:

Invocation to the U'wannami

I

Come you, ascend the ladder; all come in; all sit down.
We were poor, poor, poor, poor, poor, poor,
When we came to this world through the poor place,
Where the body of water dried for our passing.

---

[a] The Sia Indians are much more expert than the Zuñis in making suds and keeping the mass in place. It was not observed that the Sia used the extra reed, yet they bank the suds much higher than the Zuñis.

[b] It will be borne in mind that the rain-makers are the deceased A'shiwi.

Banked up clouds [cumuli] cover the earth.
All come four times with your showers,
Descend to the base of the ladder and stand still;
Bring your showers and great rains.
All, all come, all ascend, all come in, all sit down.[a]

[The above stanza is repeated four times.]

II

I throw out to you my sacred meal that you may all come.
Hold your gaming-stick; throw it forward; all come.
Hold your gaming-ring; throw it forward; all come.
All come out and give us your showers and great rains; all come,
That the seeds may be strong and come up, that all seed plants may come
    up and be strong.
Come you that all trees and seeds may come up and be strong.
Come you hither; all come.

III

Cover my earth mother four times with many flowers.
Let the heavens be covered with the banked up clouds.
Let the earth be covered with fog; cover the earth with rains.
Great waters, rains, cover the earth.   Lightning cover the earth.
Let thunder be heard over the earth; let thunder be heard;
Let thunder be heard over the six regions of the earth.

IV

Rain-makers, come out from all roads that great rivers may cover the earth;
That stones may be moved by the torrents;
That trees may be uprooted and moved by the torrents.
Great rain-makers, come out from all roads, carry the sands of our earth
    mother of the place.
Cover the earth with her heart,[b] that all seeds may develop,
That my children may have all things to eat and be happy;
That the people of the outlying villages may all laugh and be happy;
That the growing children may all have things to eat and be happy.
This way[c] our great father ˡkïa′ĕttonĕ wishes you to come.
This way[c] our great mother chu′ĕttonĕ wishes you to come;
That we may have all kinds of seeds and all things good;
That we may inhale the sacred breath of life;
That our fathers ˡkïa′ĕttowe and our mothers chu′ĕttowe may bring us happy
    days.
Let our children live and be happy.
Send us the good south winds.
Send us your breath over the lakes that our great world may be made beau-
    tiful and our people may live.

---

[a] At these words the A′shiwanni sprinkle meal up the line of fetishes, symbolic of the rain-makers passing over the meal line.

[b] Reference to rains. The unexpressed idea is, water is the heart and life of the earth.

[c] Reference to the spirits of the rain-makers passing over the meal line to the ĕt′tonĕ.

V

> There, far off, my Sun Father arises, ascends the ladder, comes forth from
>   his place.
> May all complete the road of life, may all grow old.
> May the children inhale more of the sacred breath of life.
> May all my children have corn that they may complete the road of life.
> Here sit down; here remain; we give you our best thoughts.
> Hasten over the meal road; we are jealous of you.
> We inhale the sacred breath through our prayer plumes.

In the summer retreat of the A'shiwanni thunder stones are brought out and during the invocation to the rain-makers are rolled down the line of meal and pollen to a disk formed by two concentric circles of corn pollen just beyond the arrow points at the far end of the meal and pollen line (see plate XXXV). The shi'wanni is the first to roll the stone, and his associate removes it from the disk, which is spoken of as the house of the thunder stone, and, returning to the meal painting, starts it down the line. In this way the shi'wanni and his associates take their turns in rolling the thunder stones. These stones vary from 1¼ to 4 or 5 inches in diameter and are among the most sacred objects to be found among the Zuñis, who believe that these stones were dropped to the earth by the rain-makers while playing their games.[a]

At the rising of the morning star a kĭa'ĕtchinĕ (group of te'likinawe wrapped together at the base) is carried by the first associate shi'wanni to a field of Nai'uchi's; he is accompanied by another whirling a rhombus. Each is provided with a long necked gourd jug, the bulb covered with cotton netting and having four white fluffy eagle plumes attached at equal distances around the lower edge of the netting. Meal ground from roasted sweet corn and prayer meal are sprinkled into an excavation[b] and the te'likinawe are placed with the eyes looking to the east, as the A'shiwanni express it, each te'likinanĕ having three black dots on the upper end of the stick, representing eyes and mouth. A prayer is repeated by the two associates after the te'likinawe are planted; meal is sprinkled during the prayer. The jugs are filled from a spring, and the two return to the ceremonial chamber. The first associate deposits the water into a medicine bowl on the floor on the northeast side of the cloud symbol; the other hands his jug to the shi'wanni, who empties the water into a bowl west of the painting.

The women join in the song for a short time, after which the offerings made by the women are distributed among the shi'wanni and his

---

[a] A fine specimen of a thunder stone of a highly silicified volcanic rock resembling chalcedony has been secured and deposited in the National Museum.

[b] Excavations used for the offerings of the A'shiwanni at the time of their winter and summer retreats are made with the ʦemĕ (ancient bean planter), the depth being the length of a man's arm.

associates. Plate XXXV shows the offerings, consisting of ears of corn, bowls containing grains of corn of various colors, bead necklaces and bangles made of meal in imitation of silver, and young shoots of peach trees with artificial fruit of dried he'palokïa[a] and sweet corn. Both are ground, the latter after it has been boiled, made into a stiff paste with cold water, and molded into balls and tinted.

All included in the ceremony move the objects up and down in time to the songs of thanksgiving to the gods for the gifts that have been received. The moving of the brilliant corn and highly decorated baskets by the men and women, the beautiful arms of the latter being exposed, is the rhythm of motion. The songs of thanksgiving, with the raising and lowering of the offerings, continue without cessation fifty minutes, after which a low prayer is made by Nai'uchi, and the offerings are removed to another part of the room.

The maker of the suds pushes his cloud bowl forward to a group of women, and each takes a handful of suds and rubs it first on her chest, then over her arms and legs. The bowl is afterward carried around the room, that all may bathe with the suds. The third associate carries the bowl of consecrated water, administering a draft from a shell to all present. He begins at the west end of the room, giving it to the shi'wanni and associates last.

After partaking of the consecrated water, the shi'wanni removes the mi'wachi one by one from the painting, carefully blowing off any meal that may have dropped on the feathers, and returns them to the basket. He next removes the chu'ĕttonĕ, while the associate by his side takes the ᵗkïa'ĕttonĕ. They blow off every particle of meal that may have remained on the fetishes. Each fetish is first wrapped in a piece of cotton cloth, then in deerskin, and then carefully tied. The shi'wanni now tenderly returns the chu'ĕttonĕ to the vase, and after receiving the ᵗkïa'ĕttonĕ from the associate deposits it by the side of the other. While the fetishes are being placed in the vase the two associates opposite the shi'wanni are engaged in returning the stone fetishes to the medicine box and sacks from which they were taken. After all objects are removed the second associate sweeps the meal and pollen into a heap, and, carrying it to the river, casts it into the waters, that it may go to Ko'thluwala'wa.

Without further ceremony the owners of four of the mi'wachi, who are related to the shi'wanni or associates, leave the chamber with their fetishes. The fetishes directly associated with the ĕt'tonĕ are returned with it to its room. Then the shi'wanni and associates have their heads bathed by the female associate, after which the usual feast is served, which Nai'uchi, his associates, and their families enjoy. First, however, a portion of the food is gathered by the shi'wanni and associates and cast into the fire, to be conveyed to the ancestral gods.

---

a See p. 365.

ROOM OF ĒT'TONĒ, FETISH, OF SHI'WANNI (RAIN PRIEST) OF BLACK CORN CLAN

HÄM'PONE (PAVILION) OF THE 'HLA'HEWE, PERSONATORS OF THE CORN MAIDENS

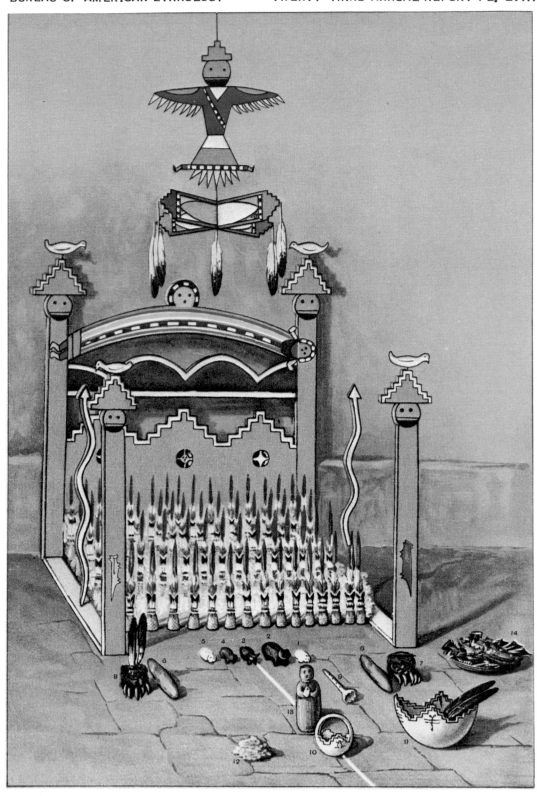

ALTAR OF ÚHUHUKWE (EAGLE DOWN FRATERNITY)

ALTAR OF ᵀSANÍAKIAKWE (HUNTER FRATERNITY)

SUMMER RETREAT OF A SHI′WANNI

An account of the summer retreat of the shi′wanni possessing the ĕt′tonĕ, which is supposed to have come from the Black Corn clan, was given the writer by the shi′wanni himself and verified by the third associate, one of the brightest Indians in Zuñi.

The house in which the ĕt′tonĕ of the Black Corn clan is kept is one of the oldest in the village. It is accessible on one side from a street and on the other from a plaza. The room of the sacred fetish is on the ground floor, but can be entered only by a ladder from an upper chamber. This room is not over 8 by 4 feet and has a low ceiling. Its walls are elaborately decorated with cloud symbols and two Ko′loowisi (plumed serpents). The sacred frog, wearing a cloud cap with lightning shooting forth, stands with each foot on the tongue of a Ko′loowisi. This decoration, which is not to be found in the other chambers of the ĕt′towe, is due to the fact that the shi′wanni at the time referred to also had charge of the Ko′loowisi fetish (see plate XXXVI).

The room where the retreat is made is directly above the chamber of the ĕt′tonĕ, and there is an opening 12 by 18 inches in the floor, through which meal is constantly sprinkled during the retreat. At other times this hatchway is closed by a stone slab set in plaster.

The shi′wanni and his associates gather in the chamber of the ĕt′tonĕ at sunrise on the fifth morning of the retreat. The shi′wanni makes a cloud symbol of corn pollen and white meal on the floor, and the ĕt′tonĕ separated into its two parts, with other fetishes and arrow points, are placed thereon, the ĕt′tonĕ being the most important object. The shi′-wanni and associates descend to this chamber on the three following days at sunrise, noon, and sunset to invoke the presence of the gods. On the eighth and last day of the retreat a similar painting to the one in the room below is made on the floor of the upper room, and an even more elaborate display is made, when the families consanguineous to the shi′-wanni and his associates gather for the night, presenting a most interesting picture, similar to that described in the ceremony of the Shi′-wanni of the Nadir. The te′likinawe are planted in the manner described in the winter retreat of the Shi′wanni of the Nadir.

On the morning that the retreat closes, an excavation is made, in the manner heretofore described, close to the one that was dug at the beginning of the retreat, and te′likinawe are deposited just as they were on the first day in the other excavation. Both openings are now covered, the first remaining open until the second one receives the te′likinawe.

At sunrise the heads of the shi′wanni and the three associates are washed by the female associate, after which a feast is enjoyed. Then the shi′wanni and associates each place food in a fine basket, and carrying it to the fireplace, where there are a few embers, consign it to the fire with prayers to the ancients of all regions, the dead Zuñis, to water the earth. The retreat of all the A′shiwanni are for the same object—rains to fructify the earth—and the ceremonials vary but slightly.

Order of Retreat of the A'shiwanni in 1891

The following is the order of retreat of the A'shiwanni as observed by the writer in the summer of 1891:

Kĭa′kwemosi retires June 26; leaves retreat July 4.
Shi′wanni of the West retires July 4; leaves retreat July 12.
Shi′wanni of the South retires July 12; leaves retreat July 20.
Shi′wanni of the East retires July 20; leaves retreat July 28.
Shi′wanni of the Zenith retires July 28; leaves retreat August 1.
Shi′wanni of the Nadir retires August 1; leaves retreat August 5.[a]
Shi′wanni of Eagle clan retires August 5; leaves retreat August 9.
Shi′wanni of Dogwood clan retires August 9; leaves retreat August 17.
Shi′wanni of Black Corn clan retires August 17; leaves retreat August 25.
Shi′wanni of Shu′maakwe fraternity (Chaparral Cock clan) retires August 25; leaves retreat August 29.
Shi′wanni of Sun clan retires August 29; leaves retreat September 2.
Shi′wanni of Corn clan (Kĭa′nakwe) retires September 2; leaves retreat September 6.
Shi′wanni of Corn clan retires September 6; leaves retreat September 10.
Shi′wanni of Corn clan retires September 10; leaves retreat September 14.

′HLA′HEWE CEREMONIAL FOR RAIN AND THE GROWTH OF CORN

The drama of the ′hla′hewe (singular ′hla′ha),[b] which is enacted quadrennially in August when the corn is a foot high, is supposed to be a reproduction of the ceremonies held at the time of the third appearance of the Corn maidens before the A′shiwi, and is regarded as one of their most sacred festivals. Great preparations were made by the A′shiwi for the third coming of the Corn maidens, who were to dance that rains would come and water the earth, that the new corn might be made beautiful to look upon, and that the earth would furnish all food for nourishment. While the drama must be played once in four years, it may occur more often by order of the first body of A′shiwanni.[c]

In 1890 there was a special play of the ′Hla′hewe, owing to the fact that the former pe′kwĭn (sun priest) had bèen impeached for having caused a drought, and it was necessary that the new incumbent should become acquainted with this drama, in which he plays an important part. The Zuñis declare this celebration of the festival brought so much rain that they danced all night in mud instead of on the hard ground. When the writer visited Zuñi in 1891, she expressed regret to the Kĭa′kwemosi (rain priest of the North) and the elder brother Bow priest that she had failed to be present at the drama of the ′Hla′hewe in the previous year, and asked if it were not possible to repeat the ceremony. Whereupon the Kĭa′kwemosi declared that this could not be done as

---

[a] The elder and younger Bow priests also make a retreat at this season.
[b] ′Hla′ha, rabbit skin blanket. The name signifies fecundity.
[c] The writer learned when at Zuñi in 1902 that the ′Hla′hewe drama had not been performed since 1891, owing, the Indians said, to their wish to keep the sacred ceremony from the eyes of Americans.

his people would at once suspect him of holding a festival in order that the writer might make notes and pictures. After much consulting between the Kĭa′kwemosi and elder brother Bow priest, they concluded that as certain prisoners at Fort Wingate, from Oraibi (a Hopi village), supposed by the Indians to be sorcerers, had stated that they would cause a drought throughout the Pueblo country if they were not liberated,[a] they might include the ᵗHla′hewe drama among the additional ceremonies, as it was of special value for rains.

While the drama is known as the ᵗHla′hewe, the dancers and the choirs form into two parties, one side being called ᵗHla′hewe, the other Sho′ko‘we (singular sho′kona, flute), having reference to Pa′yatämu (god of music, flowers, and butterflies).

The first body of A′shiwanni assemble in the house of the Shi′wano′‘kĭa (priestess of fecundity), to arrange for the drama which is to occur in eight days. They decide who shall perform the parts in the drama for which permanent actors are not provided. The Shi′wano′‘kĭa is present, but remains silent.

The following table gives the participants in the ᵗHla′hewe and the mode of selection:

TABLE OF PARTICIPANTS

First body of A′shiwanni, women who officiate with mi′wachi.[b]

ᵗHla′hewe	Sho′ko‘we
A′wan mo′sona (director-general).	A′wan mo′sona.
Vice a′wan mo′sona.	Vice a′wan mo′sona.
Two he′kupowanhak′tona (virgins who dance at sunset), impersonated by females.	Two ushän′ashutĕ (virgins who dance at sunset), impersonated by females.
One sho′lipsimonthle′ona (virgin who dances with the he′kupowanhak′tona), impersonated by a male.	
Two ᵗkĭa′punakwe, virgins (water-sprinklers), impersonated by a youth and a maiden.	Two ᵗkĭa′punakwe, impersonated by a youth and a maiden.
Man of Frog clan.[c] Position permanent.	
One a′shuwahänona (plume-waver), also called shuts′ina after the hawk whose plumes he carries.	
Ten mi′laiiläpo′na (personators of the Corn maidens), the two females personating the Yellow and Blue Corn maidens being designated as a′mosono′‘kĭa (directresses-general).	Ten mi′laiiläpo′na.

[a] "These men are not only sorcerers but thoroughly imbued with the lore of medicine." They spread consternation among the Pueblos, not only of Hopis and Zuñis, but of the Rio Grande Indians as well, and all were having extra prayers and dances.

[b] See p. 416.

[c] The present incumbent is warrior to the Snake fraternity.

Four ʻkĭa′potiikwe (dance at sunrise),
    impersonated by females.   Four ʻkĭa′potiikwe.
One ya′pota (symbolizer of corn), a male,
    who dances that the ears of corn may
    be perfect.
Four ʻhla′he o′tiikwe (female dancers)   Four Sho′ko o′tiikwe (female dancers).
Mo′sona (director) and vice mo′sona of   Mo′sona and vice mo′sona of choir.
    choir.
Ten singers and a drummer.   Ten singers and a drummer.
                                    Mo′sona of flutists and nine additional
                                        flutists.

The A′wan mo′sona and vice A′wan mo′sona of both sides, he′kupowanhak′tona, A′shuwahänona of the ʻHla′hewe, and ushän′ashutĕ of the Sho′koʻwe side are selected by the pe′kwĭn and notified by the elder brother Bow priest. The man of the Frog clan is notified by the elder brother Bow priest. The sho′lipsimonthle′ona is chosen and notified by the elder brother Bow priest. The ʻkĭa′punakwe, mi′laiiläpo′na, and ʻkĭa′potiikwe of both sides are chosen and notified by the pe′kwĭn. The ya′pota, ʻHla′he o′tiikwe, and choir of the ʻHla′hewe side are chosen and notified by the A′wan mo′sona of this side, and the Sho′ko o′tiikwe and choir of the Sho′koʻwe side are chosen and notified by its A′wan mo′sona. The mo′sona of the flutists is notified by the A′wan mo′sona of the Sho′koʻwe side, and he in turn notifies the other flutists.

A′wan mo′sona and vice A′wan mo′sona of both sides may belong to any clan. The he′kupowanhak′tona and ushän′ashutĕ are children or grandchildren of the first body of A′shiwanni. They must abstain eight days from animal food and salt. Should they not be virgins, the green corn would be destroyed by worms. The sho′lipsimonthle′ona must be a son or grandson of one of the first body of A′shiwanni, and he must abstain eight days from animal food and salt. In the ceremony described the sho′lipsimonthle′ona is personated by a grandson of Nai′uchi, Shi′wanni of the Nadir and elder brother Bow priest. This youth adopted female attire several years after the ceremony here described.

The ʻkĭa′punakwe of the ʻHla′hewe side must be of the Dogwood clan or children of the clan,[a] and the ʻkĭa′punakwe of the Sho′koʻwe side must belong to the Corn clan or be children of this clan. They must abstain from animal food and salt four days, which fast begins the morning they go to the häm′pone (pavilion).

The A′shiwanni, having enjoyed a feast, retire from the house of the Shi′wanoʻʻkĭa at midnight and sleep until dawn in their homes, when they again gather in her house and prepare la′showawe (singular la′showanĕ, one or more plumes attached to a cotton cord), each consisting of a tail and a wing feather of the ʻhlai′aluko, mountain bluebird (Sialia arctica). The two feathers are joined at the quill ends so as to form a V and wrapped with cotton cord. The feathers to be given to men are from the male bird, those for the women from the female bird. When the la′showawe are completed the elder brother Bow priest is first dispatched for the A′wan mo′sona and vice A′wan mo′sona of the ʻHla′hewe, who accompany him to the house of the Shi′wanoʻʻkĭa, and then for those who are to fill similar positions on the Sho′koʻwe side. Again the elder brother Bow priest leaves the house and returns with the he′kupowanhak′tona and sho′lipsimonthle′ona.

_____

[a] See List of clans.

Each party brought by the elder brother Bow priest is presented with a la'showannĕ by the pe'kwĭn, who says to each: "May your heart be good; may you have good thoughts; may you speak with one tongue, that the rains may come."

The pe'kwĭn gives additional la'showawe to the A'wan a'mosi to be distributed by them among the others. The la'showannĕ is attached to the left side of the head of each recipient by the cotton cord from which the feathers are suspended and by a strand of hair. These la'showawe are planted in the fields with te'likinawe on the morning after the close of the drama. All now return to their homes, the pe'kwĭn carrying the remaining la'showawe. After eating he visits the houses of the ᵗkĭa'punakwe, notifying them of their appointment and giving to each a la'showannĕ, which he attaches to the hair on the left side of the head.

The two choirs in separate houses begin practicing the night they are notified. The A'wan a'mosi and A'wan a'mosono'ᶜkĭa are present at the rehearsals. The A'wan a'mosi join in the songs, but the A'wan a'mosono'ᶜkĭa are silent. On the day following the notification the two choirs assemble at dawn in the Shi'wano'ᶜkĭa's house to accompany the dancers. The ᵗHla'hewe choir group in the southeast corner of the room and the Sho'ko'we choir[a] in the northeast corner.

The first body of A'shiwanni sit in line on the south ledge which extends around the walls of the room. Two large Apache baskets containing ears of yellow corn, symbolic of the Yellow Corn maiden, and two filled with blue corn, symbolizing the Blue Corn maiden,[b] stand in line, the baskets of yellow corn being north of the others in the west end of the room. The A'wan mosono'ᶜkĭa personating the Yellow Corn maiden sits back of the baskets of yellow corn, and the A'wan mosono'ᶜkĭa personating the Blue Corn maiden sits back of the baskets of blue corn. Each woman has a pottery meal basket in front of her.

The ᵗkĭa'potiikwe dance at sunrise, first on the Sho'ko'we side, when they carry yellow corn from the baskets, and afterward on the ᵗHla'hewe side, when blue corn is carried. In the former case the yellow corn is given to the dancers by the A'wan mo'sono'ᶜkĭa personating the Yellow Corn maiden, and they are led to the floor by the A'wan mo'sono'ᶜkĭa personating the Blue Corn maiden. She remains but a few moments on the floor, but afterward returns and continues dancing for a short time after the ᵗkĭa'potiikwe retire. Before the yellow corn is exchanged for the blue, the Shi'wano'ᶜkĭa takes the clasped hand of each dancer, the corn being held between the hands,

---

[a] The Zuñis claim that the songs of the Sho'ko'we are sung in their ancient tongue, and the Laguna Indians also claim that these songs are in their archaic tongue. The Zuñis in general resent the claim of the Lagunas, but a number of their priests have stated that the old tongue of the Zuñis is the same as the ancient language of the Lagunas.

[b] Yellow is the color for the north, the Yellow Corn maiden representing that region; and blue is the color for the west, the Blue Corn maiden being the representative.

and passes the corn three or four times before the lips of the girl, with a prayer that she may inhale the sacred breath of life. The dancers now pass to the A'wan mo'sono''kĭa of the Sho'ko'we side, who repeats the passing of the corn before the lips of the 'kĭa'potiikwe and returns it to the basket. The A'wan mosono''kĭa of the 'Hla'hewe side, who is now in her place by the baskets, gives blue corn to the 'kĭa'po-tiikwe, and they are led to the floor by the A'wan mosono''kĭa of the Sho'ko'we side. She, too, remains only a short time, but returns and stays on the floor dancing until the 'kĭa'potiikwe have returned the blue corn, when she returns to her place and the 'kĭa'potiikwe leave the chamber.

The girls who act as 'Hla'he and Sho'ko o'tiikwe gather in an adjoin-ing room and come forward as required, eight at a time, with the ya'pota in the middle of the line. They begin to dance as soon as the 'kĭa'potiikwe have retired. The dancers are attired in their ordinary dress, but are careful to wear their best moccasins and elaborate necklaces. They repeat the performance of the 'kĭa'potiikwe. They carry first the yellow corn, and afterward the blue corn, receiving the corn and returning it in the manner previously described. They are led to the floor first by the A'wan mo'sono''kĭa of the 'Hla'hewe side and afterward by the A'wan mo'sono''kĭa of the Sho'ko'we side, in the same manner as the 'kĭa'potiikwe. The corn is passed before their lips first by the Shi'wano''kĭa and afterward by the A'wan mo'sono''kĭa, as described above. After the first set of girls and the youth have danced with the yellow and blue corn, they retire, and another set take their places. The dance continues, except dur-ing the noonday feast, until the arrival of the he'kupowanhak'tona, sho'lipsimonthle'ona, and Ushäna'shutt an hour before sunset, when they take the floor. These dances occur on three alternate days in the house of the Shi'wano''kĭa.

On the seventh morning the two A'wan a'mosi, with their vicars and men selected by them, construct an extensive häm'pone in the Si'aa' te'wita, sacred dance court, immediately in front of the He'iwa ki'wi'sinĕ (ceremonial house of the Kĭa'kwe a'mosi), the lower door of the house opening into the west side, or back, of the häm'pone. Heavy poles support the beams and over them is canvas covered with spruce (Pseudotsuga douglassii) boughs, the edge of the roof being fringed with spruce and cedar boughs, and the south wall formed of spruce and a small quantity of cedar. The personators of the A'wan tä'ᵗchu (Great Father), the pe'kwĭn, and the Pi''ᵗläshiwanni (warrior) of the Ko'yemshi[a] gather the boughs and place them in position.

The first body of A'shiwanni, the A'wan a'mosi with their fel-lows, the mi'laiiläpo'na, and the two choirs assemble in the O'he'wa

---

[a] See p. 33.

ki'wiᵗsinĕ,[a] the pe'kwĭn having previously made a cloud symbol of
meal on the floor, extending a line of meal eastward from the symbol.
Later he forms four concentric circles of meal, on which he places
a medicine bowl, after which he arranges the mi'wachi of the A'shi-

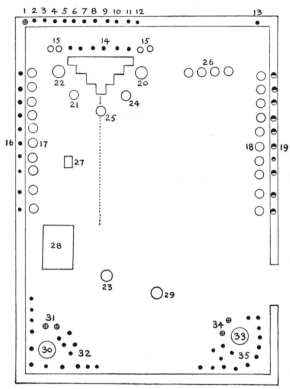

Fɪɢ. 6—Diagram of the ᵗHla'hewe ceremony in the ki'wiᵗsinĕ: 1, Shi'wano''kia; 2, younger brother
Bow priest; 3, Shi'wanni of the West; 4, Shi'wanni of the South; 5, Shi'wanni of the East; 6, 7, ᵗkĭa'-
punakwe (youth and maiden); 8, Kĭa'kwemosi; 9, associate Kĭa'kwemosi; 10 and 11, ᵗkĭa'punakwe
(youth and maiden); 12, pe'kwĭn (sun priest); 13, elder brother Bow priest; 14, mi'wachi; 15,
water jugs and vases of the ᵗkĭa'punakwe; 16, mi'laiilapona of ᵗHla'hewe side; 17, baskets of mi'laiilapona of ᵗHla'hewe side; 18, baskets of mi'laiilapona of Sho'ko'we side; 19, mi'laiilapona of Sho'-
ko'we side; 20, basket of corn and te'likinawe; 21, basket of corn of ᵗHla'hewe side; 22, medicine
bowl; 23, basket of corn of ᵗHla'hewe choir; 24, basket of corn of Sho'ko'we side; 25, prayer meal
basket; 26, baskets of corn; 27, blanket; 28, fire altar; 29, basket of corn of Sho'ko'we choir; 30,
drum of ᵗHla'hewe choir; 31, directors of ᵗHla'hewe side; 32, ᵗHla'hewe choir; 33, drum of Sho'ko'we
choir; 34, directors of Sho'ko'we side; 35, Sho'ko'we choir.

wanni in line on the west side of the cloud symbol (see figure 6). The
preparations and ceremony in O'he'wa ki'wiᵗsinĕ were as follows:

The men assemble in the ki'wiᵗsinĕ and prepare te'likinawe. After
eagle, turkey, and other plumes are attached to the upper ends of the
sticks, they are colored black. A diminutive crook (symbolic of longevity), with la'showawe attached, is bound with cotton cord to each

---

[a] Some years ago the ceremony here described occurred in the Mu'he'wa ki'wiᵗsinĕ owing to the
O'he'wa being unfit for occupancy.

te'likinanĕ, and the te'likinanĕ with its companion is wrapped in a corn husk which only partially covers the plumes, the wrapping being secured by a ribbon of husk. The te'likinawe thus wrapped are deposited in baskets of corn, the feathers fringing the edge of the baskets, which are in position by the cloud symbol. These offerings are made to the rain-makers to induce them to intercede with the Sun Father, that he may embrace the rains of the earth, that the corn may grow to be beautiful to look upon and good to eat. The 'Hla'hewe and Sho'ko'we choirs deposit their te'likinawe in separate baskets.

After the te'likinawe are completed the Kĭa'kwemosi takes his seat by the medicine bowl. A woman places a vase of water and a gourd by him, and he dips six gourdfuls of water from the vase, emptying it into the bowl. He now drops six a'thlashi (concretions; sacred to the mother of corn of the six regions) separately into the medicine bowl, raising high each stone and praying before depositing it into the bowl (22 of figure 6). After the consecration of the water a blanket (27 of figure 6) is spread upon the floor a short distance in front of the cloud symbol. The pe'kwĭn takes his seat to the west of the blanket; the elder brother Bow priest sits south and the younger brother Bow priest north of it. The ten mi'laiiläpo'na of the 'Hla'hewe side are seated in line south of the meal line extending from the meal symbol, and the ten mi'laiiläpo'na of the Sho'ko'we side are seated in line north of the meal painting. Some of these women are white-haired and aged. Each has a basket of corn before her. Those of the Sho'ko'we side have, in addition to the corn, 'hle'we (tablets) ornamented with sun, moon, star, and cloud symbols, with white fluffy eagle plumes surmounting the tablets. Those of the 'Hla'hewe side have 'hla'we (slender stems of a plant) about 18 inches long, painted white and adorned with delicate white duck feathers in groups of two, the space between being of the width of the first three fingers placed crosswise within a few inches of their ends. Each basket is covered with a white embroidered kilt. The choir of the 'Hla'hewe side is grouped in the southeast corner and that of the Sho'ko'we side in the northeast end of the room. The flutists prepare te'likinawe in the ceremonial chambers of the Ma'ᵗke 'Sän'nakwe (Little Fire fraternity) and Pe'shäᵗsilo'kwe (Cimex fraternity). The ears of corn, tied together in twos, are taken from the baskets in turn by the A'wan a'mosi of the choirs and the others, and deposited on the blanket to the right of the elder brother Bow priest, who at intervals holds a bunch of the corn between his hands and prays. He afterward makes a cavity in the end of each ear. After each ear is prepared by him he hands it to the pe'kwĭn, who deposits seeds in the cavity and passes it to the younger brother Bow priest, who seals the opening with a paste of yucca fruit softened in the mouth before it is applied. The younger brother Bow priest lays each ear as it is completed to his left on the blanket, and it is returned by the proper parties to the baskets. Afterward the corn is placed with that stacked in the house of each individual who receives it.

After the preparation of the corn the mo'sona of the ᵗHla'hewe choir passes to each mi'laiiläpo'na of his side and tells her in low tones to go to the Sho'ko'we choir and ask them to work for the ᵗHla'hewe. As each man is interrogated he replies "Yes," in a voice scarcely audible. The women return to their seats and the members of the Sho'ko'we choir sit on their wadded blankets before the basket of corn and, facing the mi'laiiläpo'na, prepare the ᵗhla'we. Each ear of corn to be carried by the dancers is surrounded and hidden by the ᵗhla'we, each one being separately bound to the corn with cotton cord. The cord is held between the teeth during the wrapping. When all the stems are attached, short dark eagle feathers, plumes from the birds of the six regions, and white sage blossoms are arranged upright around the ear of corn, and a piece of native white cotton cloth is placed over the base of the corn, extending several inches upward and heavily wrapped with the cotton cord. A diminutive crook, with la'showawe attached, is tied to each ᵗhla'we to be carried in the left hand of the dancer. The ᵗHla'hewe choir sings while the Sho'ko'we choir works on the ᵗhla'we. The song is addressed to A'wan ᵗSita (Great Mother) corn: "See, I dress your children [referring to the corn] in beautiful feathers and mi'hawe (sacred embroidered blankets). I pray that you will send to us many of your children another year." Upon the completion of the ᵗhla'we they are laid across the baskets of corn of the mi'laiiläpo'na of both sides, and the mo'sona of the Sho'ko'we tells the mi'laiiläpo'na of his side to request the choir of the ᵗHla'hewe to work for them. The requests and replies are made in undertones. Members of the ᵗHla'hewe choir sit before the baskets of corn of the mi'laiiläpo'na and prepare the ᵗhle'we. An ear of corn, surrounded with feathers and white sage blossoms, is attached to the inner side of the tablet.[a] The ᵗhle'we are also laid across the baskets of the mi'laiiläpo'na of both sides. The embroidered kilts are removed each time to allow the ᵗhla'we and ᵗhle'we to be placed in the baskets.

At sunset each of the first body of A'shiwanni deposits four te'liki-nawe, the sticks colored black, with feathers of the eagle, turkey, and birds of the six regions attached, and six grains of corn of the colors of the six regions, beneath the floor of the ki'wi'sinĕ through the circular opening (symbolic of the entrance to the undermost world). The offerings are made to the Council of the Gods and deceased A'shi-

---

[a] Some slight mistakes made in the arrangement of the feathers about one of the ears of corn was at once noticed by one of the women of the Sho'ko'we side. She immediately called the attention of a member of the choir of her side to the error, which he corrected.

wanni of the six regions for rains, and to Pau'tiwa[a] that the sun may embrace the earth that she may be fruitful.

The four ᵗkĭa'punakwe,[b] one couple accompanied by a man of the Dogwood clan and the other by a man of the Corn clan, come to the ki'wĭᵗsinĕ. They are met by the pe'kwĭn, who leads them down the room to seats at the west end.

The two youths wear white cotton shirts, embroidered kilts about their loins, and finely dressed white buckskins tied about the neck and falling over their shoulders far below the waists. Each carries a perfect ear of corn secreted in the front of the sash which holds the kilt; they wear dance moccasins. The maidens are dressed in mi'hawe worn as dresses and fringed white cotton sashes. A perfect ear of corn is secreted in the back of each sash. They wear ordinary moccasins, but of fine quality, and both the youths and the maidens wear turquoise earrings and elaborate necklaces.

The pe'kwĭn gives to each ᵗkĭapuno'na (singular of ᵗkĭa'punakwe) six te'likinawe, one for each of the six regions, with a la'showannĕ attached to each; a butterfly the color of the region represented is also attached to each te'likinanĕ. An awehlwia tehl'i (cloud vessel), which is a pottery vase with serrated rim, and decorated in clouds, rain, and tadpoles, and is suspended with cotton cord, and an ear of corn with which to sprinkle the water to be collected are given to each maiden. The youths have each a ᵗkĭa'pokĭatommĕ (long-necked gourd jug), the bulb covered with a netting of native cotton cord, to which fluffy eagle plumes are fastened. A reed in each jug, having a la'showannĕ tied to it, is to be used as a sprinkler. The two ᵗkĭa'punakwe of the ᵗHla'hewe side collect water from ᵗKĭanayälto (spring in high place), in the foothills of Corn mountain, where they deposit their te'likinawe to the deceased A'shiwanni, Pau'tiwa, and A'wan ᵗSita (Great Mother) corn, that the rains may come and the earth be embraced by the Sun Father, that she may give to the people the fruits of her being. The ᵗkĭa'punakwe of the Sho'koᶜwe side visit ᵗKĭä'ᵗsiᵗkĭai'a (small spring), a few miles north of Zuñi, and deposit their te'likinawe, with prayers similar to those offered by the others, and bring water. As soon as the ᵗkĭa'punakwe leave, the mi'laiiläpo'na of the ᵗHla'hewe side, led by the A'wan a'mosono'ᶜkĭa, form in line down the center of the room, holding a ᵗhla'we in each hand, and dance to the music of their choir, who sing to the accompaniment of the rattle and drum. The mi'laiiläpo'na of the Sho'koᶜwe side, who hold the ᵗhle'we, repeat the dancing to the music of their choir. The two sides dance alternately until midnight in the manner described.

---

[a] See p. 33.

[b] In the ceremonial described the youth of the ᵗHla'hewe side is a child of the Dogwood clan; he belongs to the Badger clan. The maiden belongs to the Dogwood clan and is the daughter of the Shi'wano'ᶜkĭa, who is of the Dogwood clan. The youth of the Sho'koᶜwe side belongs to the Corn clan and the maiden is a child of that clan. At the next festival the youth of the ᵗHla'hewe side must belong to the Dogwood clan and the maiden must be a child of the clan, and the youth of the Sho'koᶜwe side must belong to the Corn clan and the maiden must be a child of the clan.

The ᶜkĭa'punakwe return a short time before midnight with water from the springs visited, each party escorted by a member of the A'pi·ᶜläshiwanni (Bow priesthood). Each ᶜkĭapuno'na, in addition to the vases of water, brings young cornstalks with the roots.

The pe'kwĭn receives the cornstalks and stands them on each side of the cloud symbol in line with the mi'wachi and places the water vases and jugs on the circles of meal formed when he made the cloud symbol. The ᶜkĭa'punakwe resume their seats. The elder and younger brother Bow priests stand on each side of the cloud symbol, the elder brother being on the north side, and whirl the rhombi for the rain-makers, while the Kĭa'kwemosi, remaining in his seat, plays on the flute (not that of Pa'yatämu, but the smaller flute of the A'shiwanni). At the same time a man of the Frog clan smokes a cigarette of native tobacco, puffing the smoke into the medicine water and over the vases and jugs of water and green corn, and both choirs sing, that the earth may be abundantly watered.

After the cigarette is smoked the two male ᶜkĭa'punakwe sprinkle water from their gourd jugs over the cloud symbol and objects about it, including the green corn, all the baskets of corn, from which the kilts have been removed for the purpose, and each person present. The female ᶜkĭa'punakwe repeat this sprinkling. After a long prayer by the pe'kwĭn the procession forms to proceed to the häm'pone in the Si'aa' te'wita. The elder brother Bow priest leads. He carries his mi'li and a kilt, which has a broad band of blue-green (symbolic of the vegetation of the world) painted across it, with a conventional design of the game of sho'liwe[a] at each end of the band. The design is formed by the use of a number of yucca splints crossed at right angles to form squares. These are laid on the cloth, and yellow and black paint is applied in the squares, which denote the sho'liwe reeds grouped ready to throw. The yellow indicates the north country, whence the A'shiwi came, over which the Kĭa'kwemosi, Shi'wanni of the North, has care, whose breath must be pure so that this region may always be fruitful and beautiful to look upon. The black is symbolic of the earth over which the Shi'wanni of the Nadir has care, whose prayers must be pure that the earth may be made good for man to walk upon. The diagonal line through each square is symbolic of the straight road of the Sun Father. The kilt is shaped to form an equilateral triangle, a fluffy eagle plume being fastened to each point. A game of sho'liwe[a] (arrow reeds) with plumes attached is tied to one corner and a ti'kwanĕ[a] (gaming stick) with plumes attached is tied to another corner.

The pe'kwin follows the elder brother Bow priest, carrying a sacred meal basket in his left hand and throwing the meal in a line before him with his right. Not being a member of the order of O'naya'nakĭa (Mystery medicine), he does not possess a mi'li. The ᶜkĭa'punakwe

a See Games.

follow next in file, a youth before each maiden.   The mi′laiiläpo′na of
the ‘Hla′hewe and Sho′ko‘we, walking side by side, each party led by its
A′wan mosono′‘kĭa, come after the ‘kĭa′punakwe.   Each mi′laiiläpo′na
carries on her head a basket containing corn and other seeds, two ‘hla′we,
two ‘hle′we, and te′likinawe, covered with a white embroidered kilt.
Four A′shiwanni walk in file on one side of the mi′laiiläpo′na, and a
shi′wanni and the Shi′wano′‘kĭa, who carries a basket of all kinds of
seeds on her head, are on the other side.   The younger brother Bow
priest follows next.   A man of the Badger clan carrying a pottery bowl,
which is hidden from view by a red blanket, containing coals from the
fire altar in the ki′wi‘sině, walks to the right and back of the younger
brother Bow priest, and behind him the ‘Hla′hewe choir in a group,
the mo′sona and vice mo′sona leading side by side, this group being
in line with the others.   The drummer, who is a short distance to
the right, carries his vase-shaped pottery drum in his left arm and
the hooped drumstick in his right hand.   The Sho′ko‘we choir follow
in the same order, their drummer being slightly to the left.   The
flutists come next in a group, led by their mo′sona and his deputy
walking side by side.   They all have their flutes to their lips, but do
not play.   The procession passes under the eastern covered way to the
häm′pone in the Si′aa′ te′wita, and proceeds by the south side of the
häm′pone to their places (see plate XXXVII).   The elder brother Bow
priest deposits his mi′li at the northwest corner of the cloud symbol,
a painting of meal similar to the one in the ki′wi‘sině having been
previously made by the pe′kwĭn in the häm′pone.   He lays the folded
kilt on the symbol and takes his position by the west wall on the
north side.   The pe′kwĭn, following the elder brother Bow priest,
places his meal basket by the cloud symbol, and takes his place by
the west wall.   The ‘kĭa′punakwe of the ‘Hla′hewe side hand their
jug and rain vase to the pe′kwĭn, who steps forward to receive them;
he deposits them on the south side of the cloud symbol, and the youth
and maiden take their places.   The ‘kĭa′punakwe of the Sho′ko‘we
side pass by the west to the north where the pe′kwĭn receives their jug
and vase and deposits them on the north side of the cloud symbol,
and the ‘kĭa′punakwe pass to their positions by the west wall.   The
mi′laiiläpo′na of the ‘Hla′hewe side remain in file, facing east after
they enter the häm′pone.   Those of the Sho′ko‘we side pass around
by the west wall to the north side to their places; they also face
east.   The other A′shiwanni take their positions in line on the west
side of the häm′pone, and the choirs of the two sides are grouped
at the southeast and northeast corners.   (Figure 7 shows position of
participants in ‘Hla′hewe ceremonial in the plaza.)   The flutists stand
a short distance from the Sho′ko‘we choir, outside the häm′pone.

    The flutes are about 27 inches long.   The gourd cup at the end of each is decorated on the outer side with yellow, blue, red, black, and white cloud symbols. The concave or inner side has a ground

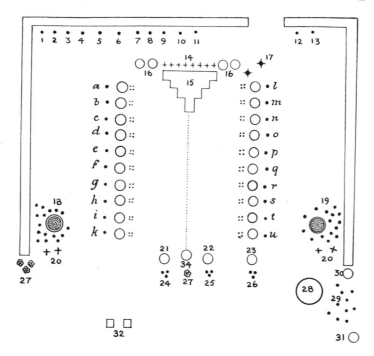

FIG. 7—Positions of participants in the ʻHlaʹhewe ceremonial: 1, younger brother Bow priest; 2, Shiʹwanni of the West; 3, Shiʹwanni of the South; 4, Shiʹwanni of the East; 5, ʻklaʹpunakwe (boy); 6, ʻklaʹpunakwe (girl); 7, Klaʹkwemosi; 8, associate Klaʹkwemosi; 9, ʻklaʹpunakwe (girl); 10, ʻklaʹpunakwe (boy); 11, peʹkwin (sun priest); 12, elder brother Bow priest; 13, Shiʹwanoʻʻkla (Priestess of fecundity); 14, eight miʹwachi; 15, meal painting symbolic of clouds; 16, water jugs and vases of the ʻklaʹpunakwe; 17, baskets of corn and teʹlikinawe of the Shiʹwanoʻʻkla; 18, choir and drum of ʻHlaʹhewe side; 19, choir and drum of Shoʹkoʻwe side; 20, aʹmosi of the two sides; 21, basket of corn belonging to the moʹsona of ʻHlaʹhewe; 22, basket of corn belonging to the moʹsona of Shoʹkoʻwe; 23, basket of corn belonging to the moʹsona of flutists; 24, teʹlikinawe of the ʻHlaʹhewe choir; 25, teʹlikinawe of the Shoʹkoʻwe choir; 26, teʹlikinawe of flutists; 27, trees; 28, pottery bowl supporting the flutes; 29, flutists; 30 and 31, baskets of corn of flutists; 32, excavations in which corn and teʹlikinawe are deposited; 33, pottery bowl over coals; 34, bunch of teʹlikinawe. a to k inclusive, miʹlaiilȧpoʹna of ʻHlaʹhewe side; each has her basket of corn and four teʹlikinawe by her side. l to u inclusive, miʹlaiilȧpoʹna of Shoʹkoʻwe side; each has her basket of corn and four teʹlikinawe by her side.

color of white or blue-green, upon which butterflies and dragon flies are painted. The edges of the cups are scalloped, each scallop being tipped with a fluffy white eagle plume. The flutes are laid across a bowl 18 inches in diameter, the edge of which is serrated, and the bowl is decorated with rain symbols on a white ground. This bowl contains medicine of Pa'yatämu, supposed to be composed of the flowers of the te'nasᵗsäli (mythical medicine plant having blossoms of the colors of the six regions), the hearts of butterflies, and dragon flies. The flutes are partly covered by a white cotton embroidered kilt having the same decoration as that carried by the elder brother Bow priest.

The A'shiwanni are dressed in white cotton shirts and trousers and red silk headbands. The elder and younger brother Bow priests have the war pouch added to their dress. The two choirs are attired, according to the taste of the individuals, in cotton or calico shirts and trousers, with fine silk scarfs wrapped like a turban around their heads. They wear all the beads they possess and as many more as they can borrow. The mo'sona of the ᵗHla'hewe choir has a line of micaceous hematite across his face just below the eyes, indicative of the prominence of his office. The mo'sona of the Sho'ko'we choir has a line of corn pollen under the right eye and a line of micaceous hematite under the left. The corn pollen signifies that he is to fast and pray and to practice continency one night.

The flutists wear white cotton shirts under the native wool shirts, which are elaborately trimmed with green and red ribbons that extend in festoons across the back. Velvet knee breeches, lined on the outer side with silver buttons, the ordinary moccasins, and buckskin leggings are worn. The hair is parted on top and the front locks are folded over on each side of the forehead and tied with bunches of red and green ribbons. The back hair is done up in the usual knot or bow. They make an elaborate display of beads and necklaces. Each flutist has a line of pollen, supposed to be from the te'nasᵗsäli, under the right eye and a line of micaceous hematite under the left. The line of pollen of the te'nasᵗsäli indicates that those so decorated sing the songs of Pa'yatämu. The A'wan a'mosi and their fellows are dressed similar to the flutists, but their hair is done up in the usual way and silk bandas are worn. Their faces are streaked across under the eyes with micaceous hematite after they return from their morning meal, which is taken in their homes. The A'wan a'mosono'ᶜkĭa personating the Yellow and Blue Corn maidens wear their ordinary dress with a white blanket bordered in blue and red, which is fastened sufficiently low to expose the necklaces. A white embroidered sash is so arranged about the waist that the upper corners meet in front and the lower ones fall apart. A plumule ear of corn, symbolic of A'wan ᶜSita (Great Mother corn), is carried in the back of the sash, but is hidden from view by the mi'ha. The breast is covered with precious beads. The hair is parted down the back, and each side is rolled and crossed so as to hang in a loop

M.Wright Gill

'HLA'HEWE, PERSONATORS OF THE CORN MAIDENS DANCING IN PLAZA

HE'PATINA, SHRINE SYMBOLIZING CENTER OF THE WORLD, WITH FRONT SLAB REMOVED

SHÁLÁKO (GIANT COURIER GODS OF THE RAIN MAKERS) PRECEDED BY HIS ALTERNATE

SHÚLAAWIˀSI (DEPUTY) PRECEDED BY KÓTHLUWALÁWA, HIS CEREMONIAL FATHER

across the back of the head, and this is wrapped with native blue yarn; bangs cover the face, and a white fluffy eagle plume is tied to the forelock. The other mi'laiiläpo'na wear their ordinary black embroidered dresses and blanket wraps, and their hair is done up in the usual manner. All wear white moccasins with finely finished black soles.

All but the two choirs and the flutists remain standing until the 'Hla'hewe and the Sho'ko'we choirs have each sung, the latter being accompanied by the flutists. After each song the choir repeats a prayer aloud. The others now take seats, the mi'laiiläpo'na keeping their places, sitting upon boxes or chairs covered with robes or blankets placed for them. The A'wan mosono''kïa of each side takes the front seat, with her deputy (younger sister) back of her.[a] The A'wan mosono''kïa of the 'Hla'hewe side must belong to the Dogwood clan, and the one back of her must be a child of this clan. The mi'laiiläpo'na at the west end of the line must also belong to the Dogwood clan. The A'wan mosono''kïa of the Sho'ko'we side must belong to the Corn clan, and the one back of her must be a child of this clan. The one at the west end of the line must belong to the Corn clan. As has been stated, the other mi'laiiläpo'na may belong to any clan. The mi'laiiläpo'na of the 'Hla'hewe side deposit their baskets by their left side, standing their te'likinawe to the left of the baskets. Those of the Sho'ko'we side place their baskets on the right and their te'likinawe to the right of the baskets. Other baskets and te'likinawe are deposited in front of the häm'pone and midway.

After the songs all remain quiet until morning, and they are closely watched by the elder and younger brother Bow priests lest they sleep. At sunrise the eight 'kïa'potiikwe, having slept two nights in the house of the Shi'wano''kïa, come to the häm'pone, where four are dressed by members of the 'Hla'hewe choir and four by the Sho'ko'we choir. The ordinary black dress is not removed, a mi'ha being placed over it and fastened, like the dress, on the right shoulder, the deep embroidery being at the top. A second mi'ha is used for a skirt only, and is fastened at the back, the deep embroidery being at the bottom. That the outer skirt may be sufficiently short, the blanket is turned over at the top, forming a sort of standing ruffle above the white cotton fringed sash. The moccasins are of finely dressed white buckskin with highly polished black soles. Each girl wears a profusion of fine necklaces, and the wrists are adorned with bunches of dark blue yarn hanging in tassels and tied with strings of red yarn. The hair hangs loosely down the back, and bangs cover the face. The

---

[a] The elder sister Yellow Corn maiden is represented by the foremost woman in the line on the north side, and the younger sister Blue Corn maiden is represented by the foremost woman on the south side; those next to these two are their ceremonial younger sisters.

dress complete, the ˈhlelhˈpone[a] (see plate XXXVIII) is placed on the
head.   When the ˈkĭaˈpotiikwe are ready for the dance those who
were dressed on the Shoˈkoˈwe side pass around by the west side of
the hämˈpone and join the others on the south.   Each dancer is supplied with two ˈhlaˈwe by the miˈlaiiläpoˈna, and they are led to the
plaza by the Aˈwan mosonoˈˈkĭa of the ˈHlaˈhewe side who throws meal
before her as she proceeds.   She joins in the dance for a short time
and returns to her seat.   The ˈkĭaˈpotiikwe face the east while dancing.
After one dance to the accompaniment of the ˈHlaˈhewe choir, the
dancers return to the ˈHlaˈhewe side, each handing her ˈhlaˈwe to a
miˈlaiiläpoˈna and receiving two ˈhleˈwe instead.   They now pass by
the west side around to the Shoˈkoˈwe side and out into the plaza, led by
the Aˈwan mosonoˈˈkĭa of the Shoˈkoˈwe side, who also sprinkles meal
as she advances.   She joins the ˈkĭaˈpotiikwe in the dance for a short
time, and then returns to the hämˈpone.   When dancing for the Shoˈ-
koˈwe side they have the additional music of the flutists.   After the
dance the ˈkĭaˈpotiikwe return to the hämˈpone by the Shoˈkoˈwe side,
those representing the ˈHlaˈhewe passing around to their own side.

The girls are now stripped of their regalia and return to their homes.
They are no sooner departed than eight Muˈluktäkĭa (certain anthropic
gods) arrive by the eastern covered way.   The Koˈmosona, director-
general of the Koˈtikili (mythologic fraternity), having been notified
by the elder brother Bow priest that he desired the services of eight
Muˈluktäkĭa, gave the order for them to appear.   As soon as the Muˈluktäkĭa reach the center of the plaza they begin dancing, turning first one
way then another, and dropping grains of corn of the colors of the six
regions, which are carried in a white embroidered sash worn by each
dancer.   After a short appearance in the plaza for the purpose of dropping the corn, the Muˈluktäkĭa disappear by the western covered way,
and the Aˈshiwanni gather up the corn.   Each shiˈwanni drops six
grains, every grain being of the color of one of the six regions, into each
of the two square excavations, the one on the north having been made
in the early morning by the Kĭaˈkwemosi and the one on the south by
the peˈkwĭn at the same hour.   They carry the rest of the corn with
them, passing down the Shoˈkoˈwe side and up the ˈHlaˈhewe side,
each shiˈwanni giving six grains of corn of the six colors to each

---

[a] The ˈhlelhˈpone is a ceremonial headdress. A circle is formed of a slender bit of wood, and four
additional pieces are attached to the band at equal distances, coming together at the other ends,
forming a sort of miter. A fringe of black goat's wool, in the present instance about 3½ inches deep,
extends around the band. A tablet similar to those carried in the hands stands out from the center
of the miter, and a thin fringe of goat's wool, 4 inches deep, dyed red, hangs at the base. Serrated
pieces of wood, symbolic of clouds, attached to the bands stand in the arches. Each cloud symbol
is tipped with a fluffy eagle plume. A bunch of yellow parrot plumes stands at the back of the
ˈhlelhˈponĕ, with an aigret of shorter parrot plumes and fluffy eagle feathers at its base. Long
streamers of red and green ribbon hang from the aigret. The ˈhlelhˈpone, like other ceremonial
objects of the Zuñis, are freshly decorated whenever they are to be used. The decorating is done in
the houses of eight men designated by the Aˈwan aˈmosi, and they are carried to the hämˈpone
when the morning star appears above the horizon.

mi'laiiläpo'na. They next distribute the corn to the members of the 'Hla'hewe choir, then to the 'kĭa'punakwe, the Shi'wano''kĭa, the Sho'-ko'we choir, and last the flutists. After the corn, which is supposed to have been blessed by the gods, is distributed, the Kĭa'kwemosi deposits four te'likinawe in the excavation on the north and the Shi'wanni of the Nadir deposits four in the one on the south to the deceased A'shi-wanni; they cover the plumes with earth and obliterate all traces of the excavations. The two choirs and flutists now go to their homes for refreshment. Upon their return all the others leave except the 'kĭa'punakwe, who must remain and eat he'we (wafer bread), made of corn meal mush. They may drink coffee when they have it.

All the participants in the drama return to the häm'pone before 9 o'clock, when the Mu'luktäkĭa reappear through the eastern covered way with four spruce trees, each tree borne by two of the gods, of whom the foremost has the trunk on his shoulder, while the other has his right arm around the top of the tree. They post one of the trees midway and in front of the häm'pone and three at the south end. The Mu'luktäkĭa dance about during the planting of the trees. When they have finished they leave the plaza by the west entrance and pass over the western road to Ko'thluwala'wa (abiding place of the Council of the Gods). In reality they go about half a mile to a bend in the river, where an embankment protects them from view, and remove the regalia of the gods they personate. They are followed by two men, who keep well to their left and are apparently unconscious of the presence of the Mu'luktäkĭa. Their mission is, however, to bring back the masks and other paraphernalia hidden under their blankets.

As soon as the Mu'luktäkĭa leave the plaza, the general dancing of the 'Hla'he o'tiikwe and Sho'ko o'tiikwe begins. The female dancers remain in the house of the Shi'wano''kĭa until their services are required, when four of them are led by the A'wan mo'sona of the 'Hla'hewe side and four by the A'wan mo'sona of the Sho'ko'we side through the eastern covered way to the häm'pone, those for the 'Hla'hewe entering on the south and those for the Sho'ko'we on the north. Four of the girls are dressed by members of the 'Hla'hewe choir and four by members of the Sho'ko'we choir on their respective sides, their regalia being identical with that worn by the 'kia'potiikwe, including the 'hlelh'ponně.

The men who personate the ya'pota[a] may remain in the plaza observing the drama until such time as they are wanted for the dance. The ya'pota, who personifies A'wan tä''chu (Great Father of corn), enters the häm'pone on the 'Hla'hewe side. He is dressed by a member of the choir of this side. He wears a white embroidered kilt fastened at the right side and held on by a sash tied on the same side. A fox

[a] Several men take their turn in representing ya'pota.

skin hangs pendent at the back, and a perfect ear of corn—not a grain must be missing—is worn in the back of the belt, though carefully concealed from view. Spruce twigs standing erect are fastened about the waist. The hair hangs down the back, with two white fluffy eagle plumes fastened one below the other. The front bangs cover the face, which is painted white, and there are daubs of the same paint on each breast, shoulder, scapula, upper arm, and leg above the knee. Dance moccasins are worn, with anklets blocked with black and white porcupine quills, and hanks of native blue yarn hanging in tassels, with sleigh bells attached, are worn below the knees. Four strings of olive shells and black stone beads hang over the right shoulder across the chest and back. These beads, which are claimed to be very old, are the property of the elder brother Bow priest and are greatly treasured by him.

Each dancer, including ya'pota, holds a 'hla'we in each hand received from the mi'laiiläpona. The dancers of the 'Hla'hewe side are joined by those of the Sho'ko'we side and pass in file, the ya'pota midway, to the plaza, led by the A'wan mosono''kïa of the 'Hla'hewe side, who throws meal in a line before her as she advances. A line is formed facing the east, and after dancing a while they turn and form into file facing south and dance again (see plate XXXIX). This movement is repeated throughout the dance, with an occasional change by turning all the way round.

The ya'pota uses his left foot principally to balance himself, violently moving the right foot up and down. The women keep their feet close together, slightly raising the heel, the motion being principally from the knee. All extend their arms before them and keep time with the songs of the 'Hla'hewe, entreating the Sun Father to embrace the Earth Mother that she may give to them the fruits of her being. Shortly after the dance begins, five women,[a] wearing their black dresses and blanket wraps, come from the ceremonial house of the Kïa'kwemosi and pass through the häm'pone on the 'Hla'hewe side to the plaza. Each woman passes her mi'li before the mouth of each dancer, who draws a breath from it, and they return to the house by the 'Hla'hewe side. The dance continues fifteen minutes, when the dancers return to the häm'pone, those of the Sho'ko'we side, who enter first, passing around to the north side.

The 'hla'we are received by the mi'laiiläpo'na. The A'wan mosono''kïa lingers in the plaza a moment or two after the others leave, dancing slowly back to the häm'pone as she faces east. On taking her seat she deposits her 'hla'we in the basket beside her.

The dancers now receive the 'hle'we, and those on the 'Hla'hewe

---

[a] These women, who approach the different dancers with their mi'wachi, are the Shi'wano''kïa and the wives of the first body of A'shiwanni.

side, including ya′pota, pass by the west wall to the Sho′ko‘we side
and, joining the others, proceed to the plaza, led by the A′wan
mo′sono′‘kĭa of the Sho′ko‘we side.   The Sho′ko‘we choir is joined
by the flutists.   The dance is nearly the same as before, the difference
being that the ᵗhle′we are moved downward, while the song implores
Great Mother of corn to give them many of her children during
the coming year.   After the dance they return to the Sho′ko‘we side,
the A′wan mosono′‘kĭa lingering, as before, a short time in the plàza;
those belonging to the ᵗHla′hewe pass around to the south side.

The same persons who dressed the male dancer and the girls now
disrobe them and prepare for another set of dancers, who appear as
soon as the others are gone, led by the A′wan a′mosi of the two sides.
The new set is dressed as before described.   The start this time is
made from the Sho′ko‘we side.   After four sets of girls have danced,
as described, a feast is served, seventy-five great bowls of food and
coffee being brought by women and placed in two rows on either side
in the häm′pone.   After all the participants in the drama have partaken of stewed mutton with chili and hominy, stewed peaches, wafer
bread, and coffee the remainder of the food is carried around and
distributed among the spectators.   While the more exclusive women
with their children observe the ceremonies from windows opening
into the plaza or seated on blankets and robes on the south side of the
court, the house tops are crowded with persons of both sexes and all
ages, wearing their best clothes and most elaborate blankets and exhibiting the most intense interest in all that is passing before them.

Dancing is resumed after the feast, each side having five dances
before the arrival of the sunset dancers.   The he′kupowanhak′tona
and sho′lipsimonthle′ona appear before the ushän′ashutĕ.   The two
girls are dressed behind a blanket held by the elder brother Bow
priest and another shi′wanni.   The Kĭa′kwemosi assists the girls for
a time, then the elder brother Bow priest takes his place and completes the dress.   Their attire is like that of the ᵗkĭa′potiikwe.
After the he′kupowanhak′tona are dressed they retire to a lower room
in the ceremonial house of the Kĭa′kwemosi which opens into the
häm′pone.   There their hair is parted over the head and down the
back, done up on both sides over wooden forms used exclusively for
ceremonial hair dressing, and then wrapped with native blue yarn.
Sho′lipsimonthle′ona's dress is like that of ya′pota, with long strings
of turquoise beads hanging from his ears.   He wears three white
fluffy eagle plumes down the back of the hair, instead of two, but
he does not have the ear of corn in his belt.   While the girls are
having their hair dressed the elder brother Bow priest spreads
two blankets, one upon the other, on the floor of the häm′pone
on the ᵗHla′hewe side toward the west end.   A low box is placed

on the west side of the blanket rug, upon which a shi'wanni takes
his seat, and one of the he'kupowanhak'tona partly reclines on
the rug with her head held between the hands of the shi'wanni, he
he being careful to keep her hair from the face. The elder brother
Bow priest spreads a white cotton cloth over the body of the girl,
and the pe'kwĭn colors her chin and lower jaw black with paint supposed to have been brought by the A'shiwanni from the undermost
world. A line is first drawn across the face near the upper lip, black
is laid on below this line, and then corn pollen is applied to the upper
portion of the face. The black is symbolic of rain clouds and the
pollen of the fruits of the earth. The girl now stands while the process is repeated with the other he'kupowanhak'tona and the sho'lipsimonthle'ona. When the face decorations are finished the blankets
are folded into smaller proportions. The pe'kwĭn sits on the box,
which remains in place, and two A'shiwanni hold a blanket protecting
him from view while he prepares a he'kupowannĕ, which consists of an
ear of corn and eight te'likinawe (offerings to the Sun Father, Moon
Mother, and Corn Mother) secured in a mi'ha, which is folded into
a strip about 8 inches wide and 36 or more inches long. The end
containing the corn and te'likinawe rests on the head. The embroidered portion forms the lower end of the scarf-like piece. On completing the he'kupowannĕ the pe'kwĭn resigns his seat to the elder
brother Bow priest, who makes a second he'kupowannĕ. On its completion the two are placed on the heads of the he'kupowanhak'tona,
and pounds of ko'hakwa (white shell beads), turquoise, and coral
necklaces are heaped upon each package. Each he'kupowanhak'tona
gives an additional touch to the hekupowannĕ to properly balance it
on the head before proceeding in file, with sho'lipsimonthle'ona
between them, to the plaza. The girls carry 'hla'we, and the youth
carries in his right hand te'likinawe, with a hoop (world symbol)
colored blue with la'showannĕ attached, and the folded kilt from the
meal painting in the häm'pone; and in the left hand the Kĭa'kwemosi's
mi'li. The three are led to the plaza by the A'wan mosono''kĭa
of the 'Hla'hewe side, who remains a few moments in the plaza and
then retires to the häm'pone, then the vice A'wan mosono''kĭa appears
and continues dancing after the others, who dance but fifteen minutes.
They must not turn their faces from the east until they enter the
häm'pone. The he'kupowanhak'tona do not venture to raise their
heads for fear of dropping the he'kupowannĕ.

The pe'kwĭn removes the he'kupowannĕ from the heads of the he'kupowanhak'tona and hands them to two men, who hold them in the left
arm, much as an infant in civilization is carried, and proceed with them
to the plaza. They face the east and pray, sprinkling meal from a meal
basket held in the left hand. Each has an attendant who stands north

of him. After the prayers the party return to the häm'pone, and the bearers of the he'kupowannĕ are relieved of the sacred objects by the elder brother Bow priest, who in turn hands them to the pe'kwĭn, who holds them gently in his arms while he stands in the center of the plaza and prays to the Sun Father to give health, happiness, and long life to his people. He prays that they may be blessed with the all-pervading life of A'wonawilo'na.[a] Moving the two he'kupowannĕ round in a circle, he draws from them the sacred breath, deposits them in a large bowl with serrated edge, and spreads an embroidered kilt over them.

The ushän'ashutĕ are dressed and painted like the he'kupowanhak'tona, and, carrying he'kupowannĕ specially prepared for them, repeat the ceremony of the he'kupowanhak'tona with every detail. The flutists accompany the Sho'ko'we choir when the ushän'ashutĕ dance, but they do not play for sho'lipsimonthle'ona. The Shĭwano'-'kĭa and other bearers of the mi'wachi, who bless the ushän'ashutĕ with their life-givers (see page 416) in the manner described, leave the plaza by the eastern covered way.

A'shuwahänona now appears for the first time. He is dressed by a member of the ʻHla'hewe choir like sho'lipsimonthle'ona, except that he wears two plumes on the back of his hair instead of three; his moccasins are painted white and there are daubs of paint on them from the pinkish clay found near Ko'thluwala'wa.[b] He has a bit of hawk medicine (a root) in his mouth and he carries a hawk plume in each hand, which he waves as he dances to the music of the choir of the ʻHla'hewe side. The choir sings the Shuts'ina yai'na (song of the hawk), which is an invocation to this bird that those who dance and sing may not be made tired. The A'wan mosono''kĭa of the Sho'ko'we side joins the A'wan mosono''kĭa of the ʻHla'hewe side, each wearing a ʻhlelh'ponnĕ on her head and carrying ʻhla'we. The A'wan mosono''kĭa of the ʻHla'hewe side precedes A'shuwahänona, and the one of the Sho'ko'we side follows after him to the plaza. After dancing about fifteen minutes they start for the ʻHla'hewe side of the häm'pone, and the leader, as she passes in, turns and pushes A'shuwahänona back, and he returns to the center of the plaza and dances a few minutes longer, keeping time with the ʻHla'hewe choir by the most violent motion of the arms and legs, while he strikes one plume with the other. On entering the häm'pone the A'wan a'mosono''kĭa are relieved of their ʻhlelh'ponnĕ and ʻhla'we and return to their seats.

A'shuwahänona now enters the häm'pone on the ʻHla'hewe side. Passing first by the ʻHla'hewe choir, he waves his plumes about their heads; and, extending his arms before him, he strikes the underside of the plume held in his left hand with the one held in his right, waves his plumes in a circle, and strikes them toward the earth in the manner

---

a See Classification of the higher powers. b See pl. IV.

described.   At this moment all expectorate, that they may have good hearts and much strength for the song and dance.   A'shuwahänona repeats the ceremony with the plumes over the A'shiwanni, Sho'ko'we choir, flutists, the mi'laiiläpo'na of the Sho'ko'we side, and those of the 'Hla'hewe side; he then removes his regalia, assisted by a member of the 'Hla'hewe choir, and leaves the plaza by the eastern covered way.

The elder brother Bow priest now ties a white fluffy eagle plume to each tree with a cotton cord, that the plume may convey the breath prayers to the u'wannami (rain-makers) to water the earth.   After the plumes are attached to the trees, there are ten dances by the 'Hla'he o'tiikwe and Sho'ko o'tiikwe, which continue the best part of the night.[a]

The pottery bowl, which has remained over the coals, is removed at dark and a large fire is lighted from the coals, wood having been placed near by.   The legend says that a light must be kept so that the Corn maidens may be carefully watched and protected.   All through the long night the dancers are ever ready to perform their part.   The pe'kwĭn leads the man of the Frog clan to the häm'pone at earliest dawn, and he sits on a wadded blanket immediately back of the cloud symbol, facing east.   He holds an ear of corn, a miniature crook with eagle and turkey plumes and feathers from the birds of the six regions attached, and two te'likinawe in his right hand.   He prays for rains, and just as the plaza is bathed in sunlight, the te'likinawe of the mi'laiiläpo'na and mi'wachi, obedient to his command, fall over.[b]

Following the all-night dancing, the four 'kĭa'potiikwe, led by the A'wan mosono'·kĭa of the 'Hla'hewe side and four by the A'wan mosono'·kĭa of the Sho'ko'we side come to the plaza before sunrise and enter the häm'pone from the south; the 'kĭa'potiikwe led by the A'wan mosono'·kĭa of the Sho'ko'we side pass around to the north, and are dressed as before described.   After the girls of the 'Hla'hewe side are robed in their regalia they join the others on the north, when all are led to the plaza by A'wan mosono'·kĭa of the Sho'ko'we side, who throws a line of meal before her as she proceeds.   Each girl carries the 'hle'we, which she constantly moves toward the earth during the dance.   They are accompanied by the Sho'ko'we choir and flutists, neither the musicians nor these particular dancers ceasing for a moment from sunrise until 9 o'clock, for the dancers must not return to the häm'pone until the cloud symbol is bathed in sunlight.   During

---

[a] When a woman wishes to leave the häm'pone for any purpose during the night she is attended by a member of the choir of her side.   Such attendants are called Pi'ʻläshiwanni.   The elder brother Bow priest acts in this capacity several times during the night, and the younger brother Bow priest watches carefully that no one associated with the drama sleeps.   To sleep at this time would give great offense to the gods whom they address.

[b] The ear of corn is afterward placed in the stacked corn in his house, the two te'likinawe are deposited south of the village on the road to the shrine of the Snake fraternity, and the crook is returned to the elder brother Bow priest.   As the man of the Frog clan does not possess a crook he must borrow one.   He is called by the pe'kwĭn to take part in the 'Hla'hewe ceremonial because he possesses such valuable songs for rains that mi'wachi and te'likinawe obey his commands.

the dancing several of the mi'laiiläpo'na of the Sho'ko'we side come
to the plaza and pass ᶜhle'we before the mouths of the dancers. The
miwachi bearers make frequent visits to the plaza to pass the mi'wachi
before the lips of the dancers, that they may inhale the breath of life,
the breath of A'wonawil'ona.

The ᶜkĭa'punakwe appear about half past 7 o'clock, already attired in
their ceremonial dress. They are led by the pe'kwĭn first down the
Sho'ko'we side, when they sprinkle each basket of corn, the youths with
the reeds dipped into their gourd jugs of water and the maidens each
with an ear of corn dipped into her cloud vessel. They continue round
to the south and down the ᶜHla'hewe side, sprinkling the baskets of
corn on that side; they then go out into the plaza, where they form
into line, facing east, back of the ᶜkĭa'potiikwe. At the same time
the elder brother Bow priest passes a lighted reed filled with native
tobacco to the flutists, one after the other ceasing to play to take a
puff. Ten mi'wachi bearers now pass in line before the ᶜkĭa'potiikwe
and ᶜkĭa'punakwe, each drawing her mi'li three or four times before
the mouth of each dancer, after which they approach the flute players
and repeat the passing of their mi'wachi before the mouths of the
flutists; and, beginning with the Sho'ko'we choir, they draw their
mi'wachi before the mouth of each person in the häm'pone, always
with prayers for a pure heart, health, and long life, which comes from
A'wonawil'ona.

After the reed has been smoked by the flutists the elder brother
Bow priest stands on one side and the younger brother Bow priest
on the other side of the dancers, and they whirl the rhombi that
the rain-makers may gather together and water the earth. When the
rhombi cease the ᶜkĭa'punakwe sprinkle the dancers as heretofore
described, passing from the north end of the line; and, preceded by
the pe'kwĭn and elder brother Bow priest and followed by the younger
brother Bow priest, they leave the plaza by the eastern covered way
to visit He'patina,ᵃ a shrine (see plate XL) which is symbolic of the
Middle of the world.

He'patina has an under room 6 by 6 feet, measured by the feet of
the Indian placed one before the other. The floor and walls are of
stone. The shrine is roofed with beams some 6 inches in diameter.
These beams are filled in with twigs and the whole is covered with
earth to a depth equal to the distance from the elbow to the tip of the
middle finger. This roof has a hatchway sufficiently large to admit the
objects deposited within. The roof is level, and forms the upper floor
of the shrine, which is walled on three sides with stone slabs securely set.
The fourth slab on the east side is so arranged as to be readily removed.
This wall is roofed with slabs upon which are several curiously shaped

---

ᵃ He, from he'liwe, mud; pa'tina, to place; so named because it was discovered that the water had
soaked through the vases and made mud on the floor beneath.

stones. The center one has somewhat the form of the helmet mask, and is referred to as "the mask of the Säl'imobiya" (certain warrior gods and seed bearers). The upper story of He'patina is the size of the heart of the 'Kĭan'astepi (Hydrotrechus remigis). The under chamber is the size of the 'Kĭan'astepi with his legs spread. North of the shrine, and adjoining it, is a small inclosure in which the A'shiwanni deposit te'likinawe.

When the party arrive at He'patina they circle round the shrine four times toward the left, the elder and younger brother Bow priests whirling the rhombi, and then halt before it. The two 'kĭa'punakwe of the 'Hla'hewe side empty the water from their vessels into one of the cloud vases standing within the upper chamber of the shrine; the other two 'kĭa'punakwe empty their vessels into another cloud vase in the shrine. After most earnest prayers by all, the pe'kwĭn deposits the vases containing the water in the lower chamber. The ears of corn carried by the maidens are left with their emptied vases in the upper chamber, symbolizing the rains impregnating the earth, so that she sends forth the fruits of her being. The jugs, which are ancient, are carried away, being the property of the Kĭa'kwemosi. The two cloud vessels carried by the maidens are manufactured for the occasion, the one for the 'Hla'hewe side being made by a woman of the Dogwood clan and that for the Sho'ko'we side by a woman of the Corn clan.

On their return to the plaza the 'kĭa'punakwe, by request of the pe'kwĭn, take their places in the line of dancers, each 'kĭa'punakwe alternating with a 'kĭa'potiikwe. The youths have been relieved of the jugs and reed sprinklers. When all have danced a short time, the mi'wachi bearers pass their fetishes before the mouth of each dancer and afterward to each person in the häm'pone. At this time the elder and younger brother Bow priests leave the plaza through the eastern covered way.

But a single log remains of the fire which burned brightly throughout the night. The man of the Badger clan who brought the coals from the ki'wĭ'sinĕ to the plaza now lights a cedar stick, about 2 feet long, at the fire and carries the burning wood to a spring north of the ruin Ma'sakĭa, together with four ears of corn tied together, and one te'likinanĕ to A'witelin 'Si'ta (Earth Mother) and three to the deceased members of the Badger clan. As he leaves the plaza the Sho'ko'we choir sing: "Go with the fire and plant your plume offerings." He makes an excavation the depth of the lower arm to the elbow and deposits the te'likinawe, with prayers to the gods, including the ancients of his clan, to bless the Earth Mother with rain, that she may yield the fruits of her being; then he returns with the corn and what remains of the stick of cedar. He throws the wood into the smoldering fire and carries the corn to his home, where it is kept until the next planting time.

As stated before, when the sunlight falls upon the cloud symbol the

mi'wachi and lines of te'likinawe fall over at the command of the man
of the Frog clan, who has kept his seat by the meal painting and west
of it facing east. Although the writer is seated near the cloud symbol,
it is impossible to discover the clever trick of the falling of the mi'wachi
and te'likinawe. The A'wan a'mosi now fasten with delicate splinters
native black blanket wraps over the blankets and necklaces of the A'wan
a'mosono''kĭa; the other mi'laiiläpo'na rise, and all place their baskets
on their heads. A member of the ᵗHla'hewe choir stands at the right
of the A'wan mosono''kĭa of his side and a member of the Sho'-
ko'we choir and a flutist stand to the left of the A'wan mosono''kĭa
on the Sho'ko'we side. The men also have baskets on their heads.
The A'wan mosono''kĭa of the ᵗHla'hewe side is the only one of the
party who holds the basket without the aid of the right hand. All in
the häm'pone remain still until the seats of the mi'laiiläpo'na are
removed and the Shi'wanni of the West has sprinkled all the participants with meal. The A'wan a'mosono''kĭa and three musicians keep
time with the Sho'ko'we choir and flutists by a peculiar motion of the
body, and the ᵗkĭa'potiikwe and ᵗkĭa'punakwe continue the dance.
The picture presented at this time is one of the most pleasing and
striking to be seen during the entire drama.

It is after 9 o'clock when the flutists, still performing, form in line
facing east. Again the elder and younger brother Bow priests stand
at either end of the line of dancers and whirl the rhombi. In a short
time the flutists, who have played unceasingly since the opening of
the early morning ceremony, group themselves together and pray
aloud; after the prayer the baskets are removed from the heads and
placed in line in their former position. The A'wan a'mosono''kĭa and
the three musicians remain standing, the other mi'laiiläpo'na stoop
beside their baskets.

The ᵗkĭa'potiikwe, their powers of endurance having been severely
tested through the long hours of continuous motion, now return to
the häm'pone by the Sho'ko'we side, four of them passing around
to the ᵗHla'hewe side and are disrobed. The ᵗkĭa'punakwe take
their former places in the häm'pone, and the te'likinawe which fell by
command of the man of the Frog clan are returned to the baskets
and the kilts thrown over them. Medicine water is then administered by the Kĭa'kwemosi, who dips it from the medicine bowl
with a shell. The holy water is given in turn to the A'shiwanni,
the male participants, the females, and the spectators in the plaza,
a goodly number having gathered after sunrise, though during the
night there were but few present and the house tops were quite
deserted. All eject the medicine water upon their hands and rub
them over their bodies for physical purification. The pe'kwin stands
west of the cloud symbol, and facing east closes the protracted ritual
with long prayers for rains to fructify the earth, that she may yield

to them the fruits of her being. After the prayers the mi′wachi
are gathered from the cloud symbol by their owners, and the man of
the Frog clan gathers the meal of the cloud symbol in his blanket and
deposits it in the river, to be carried to Ko′thluwala′wa. The A′wan
a′mosono′‘kĭa, the other mi′laiiläpo′na, and the a′mosi of the three
choirs carry the baskets to their homes, the women placing the ‘hla′we
and ‘hle′we in the corn stacks in their houses to remain permanently.
The corn from the baskets is put away separate from the other corn
in the house, to be planted the coming year. After the morning meal
each woman plants her te′likinawe in the field. The he′kupowan-
hak′tona and sho′lipsimonthie′ona accompany the pe′kwĭn to a field
north of the village, where each deposits te′likinawe to the Council of
the Gods, imploring them to gather the rain-makers of the North to
water their fields. Again they visit a field west of the village, where
te′likinawe are deposited to the Council of the Gods that the rain-
makers of the West may gather and send rain to fructify the earth.
The same is repeated in fields south and east of the village. All persons who have officiated in any way in the drama deposit te′likinawe.

The flutists at this season make offerings at a shrine dedicated to Pa′yatämu which
is seldom visited. It is in the south wall of a mesa several miles east of Zuñi, and is
barely accessible. It is necessary to scale an almost vertical rock for 12 or more
feet. The Zuñis have a way of getting their toes and fingers into crevices in rocks
and appear to proceed with but little difficulty.[a]

When the directors of the Little Fire and Cimex fraternities delegated two members
of the Flute order, one being an officer, to accompany the writer to the sacred spot,
they were charged to observe great secrecy, that others might not be made aware
of the visit. Accordingly, with a few companions, they started off, ostensibly for a
pleasure ride, not venturing to go direct to the locality. The detour prevented them
from arriving at the base of the mountain in time to reach the shrine before the cave
(see plate XLIa) had become too much shaded to be photographed, the climb being
long and tedious. It was therefore necessary for the objects to be removed and
placed in the sunlight.

The aged officer was horrified on discovering the writer's intention and begged
that the images of Pa′yatämu be not taken from the place where they had rested
undisturbed for centuries of moons. But it had to be done, and the curious figures
were placed in line on a ledge below the shrine just as they stood in the cave (see
plate XLIb). There was no evidence of other images than those photographed having
been deposited. Quantities of te′likinawe, with plumes still beautiful, were found in
the cave and in crevices in the roofing rocks, and hundreds long since despoiled of
their plumes lay scattered about. After the sacred objects had been photographed,
the officer and the writer tenderly returned them to their places in the cave.[b]

The party was discovered when descending the mountain, and the information
was carried to the village, so that upon the return of the writer and her companions
there was great excitement. Had the people in general known of the temporary
removal of the images of Pa′yatämu their wrath would have known no bounds; but
these children of nature are like civilized beings of tender years, and can be controlled through kindness or firmness, as occasion requires, by those for whom they
entertain profound respect.

---

[a] The novel plan of making two Indians serve as a ladder, one standing upon the shoulders of the
other, was used in order to reach this shrine.

[b] Two of these images are now in the National Museum.

O'WINAHAI'YE, THANKSGIVING FESTIVAL FOR CROPS

There is no fixed time for this ceremony. It depends upon the harvest and occurs after the gathering of the crops. While it is an annual occurrence[a] of the A'pi⁼ᵗläshiwanni (Bow priesthood), others take part in it. The Ant fraternity necessarily does its share, owing to its relation with the Bow priesthood.

The elder brother Bow priest having decided on the time for the festival, requests a meeting of the first body of A'shiwanni with the pa'mosona (scalp custodian) and his deputy. On the morning after the notification the first body of A'shiwanni assemble in the house of the Shi'wano''kĭa (Priestess of fecundity), and each makes a cigarette as long as the distance from the metacarpus to the tip of the second finger. Each reed is filled with native tobacco, and each shi'wanni, having painted his cigarette the color of the region to which he is assigned, wraps it in a corn husk; two additional cigarettes are made by the elder and younger brother Bow priests and given to the pa'mosona and his deputy. The Kĭa'kwemosi now collects the cigarettes made by the A'shiwanni and hands them to the pa'mosona telling him to find good men, one from each ki'wiᵗsinĕ, to give notification of the coming festival, and to select the girls for the dance. The pa'mosona hands three cigarettes to his assistant, who selects a man from each of the three ki'wiᵗsiwe, those of the South, East, and Nadir, designated by the colors of his cigarettes, while the pa'mosona chooses a man from each of the other ki'wiᵗsiwe, those of the North, West, and Zenith. The pa'mosona and assistant retain their cigarettes in their homes seven nights, and on the eighth night they take them to the ki'wiᵗsiwe to which they belong, where, after lighting them, all present take a whiff. The other cigarettes are then distributed. On the fourth day following the distribution of the cigarettes the selected men notify the young women of the village that they wish them to assemble in the evening in the Chu'pawa (south) and Mu'he'wa (west) ki'wiᵗsiwe. Obedience to this request is optional, but there is never any lack of girls, though those of the élite usually go against the wishes of their parents,[b] so great is their love for ceremonial and dance. They gather for four nights in the ki'wiᵗsiwe, the first three nights until midnight and the fourth until sunrise. They dance each night, but do not sing, this being the special privilege of the men. For four nights following the notification the song-makers from the several ki'wiᵗsiwe gather in dwellings and compose songs. The best songs are adopted. Those for the present occasion are not only songs of thanksgiving for the harvest, but of thanks for respite from the hated Navaho. Prayers are addressed to

---

[a] O'winahai'ye was an annual ceremonial until after the year 1896 when this account was written. In 1902 the ceremony was held for the first time in several years, another instance of the gradual suspension of the ceremonials of these people.

[b] Implicit obedience of child to parent is the rule among all tribes with which the writer is familiar, and any exception to this rule is very rare.

the Gods of War that the enemy may be destroyed. The members of
the Bow priesthood gather in their ceremonial chamber, each bringing
his warrior wand, which in some instances is completed after the
arrival. As each warrior arrives those present greet him, asking him
to be seated. Those who have their wands ready place them at once in
an Apache basket, the feather ends radiating. The others are deposited there as they are completed. The foundation of the wand is a slat
about 2 inches square at the base and about 8 inches in length, zigzagged to symbolize lightning, and colored blue-green. This piece of
wood never receives a second coat of paint, consequently the color soon
vanishes. A daub of medicine, resembling piñon gum, is placed on the
side of the slat at the time of its completion. Two eagle plumes are
attached to the slat, the quill ends joining, the tips spreading in V-shape.
White fluffy eagle plumes and other feathers[a] are added until there is
no evidence of the lightning stick. The base of the stick is covered
with a bit of red or black cloth, which is heavily wrapped with cotton
cord. The wand of the elder brother Bow priest has red cloth at its
base, and two feathers, one from the wing of the kïäp'kona (swallow),
the other from the o'no'hlikïa (bird of the north, Icteria longicauda),
are attached with a cotton cord to one of the long eagle plumes of the
wand. When the elder brother Bow priest completes the wrapping
of his wand, he tucks the end of the cord into the wrapping with a
knife. That of the younger brother Bow priest is covered at the base
with black, and the cord wrapping is formed into two lines about one-
half inch wide, each tied in a single bowknot. Another wand has four
oval pieces of abalone shell, pierced at one end, attached to the base;
another has a bit of crystal attached. These wands, which are usually
worn on the top of the head and extend outward from the back,
symbolize the heart, or seat of life. A package of commercial tobacco
which was handed the elder brother Bow priest is placed by him in
the center of the basket containing the plumes. The A'wan 'Si'ta
(Great Mother), mistress of the ceremonial chamber, grinds meal for
the use of the warriors at a mill at the east end of the room.

At 4 o'clock in the afternoon the elder brother Bow priest, impatient at the nonarrival of some of the members of the Bow priesthood, leaves the chamber, and cries through the streets for the
warriors to come at once to their post of duty. When seven of the
members have arrived the younger brother Bow priest starts a song
to the accompaniment of the drum, which is held between the knees,
all singing in low tones. The drum, not more than 20 inches high,
is made of wood, with the ends covered with hide; a padded stick is
used. After a short time two of the warriors dance, each holding

[a] All plumes when not in use are kept carefully wrapped and laid away in the medicine box, the same plumes being used year after year; many of them, even with all the care observed, bearing evidence of age.

a SHRINE

b IDOLS REMOVED FROM SHRINE TO BE PHOTOGRAPHED

CAVE SHRINE OF PA'YATÄMU

KĬA'NAKWE GODS CROSSING BRIDGE AT ZUÑI

SAYATASHA AND HÚTUTU (RAIN PRIESTS) AND TWO YÁ̆MU̇HAKTO (WARRIORS)

Mary Wright Gill, 1900

SHÁ´LÁKO (GIANT COURIER GODS OF THE RAIN MAKERS)

a war club.[a] The elder brother Bow priest, who has been sitting on
a low stool, now seats himself with the others upon the south ledge of
the room near the fireplace keeping time with the song and drum.
He holds his war club under his left arm and a pistol in his right hand.
At times the little ones gather in from the streets and listen most
attentively. After one song the elder brother Bow priest lays aside
the pistol and war club and beats time with his right hand, while he
holds in the left a lighted cigarette, from which he now and then
takes a whiff. Commercial tobacco is smoked incessantly.

The second song closes at 5 o'clock, and one of the men appointed
by the scalp custodian leads in a girl, who takes her seat on the
north ledge of the room, his alternate following, accompanied by a
second girl, who sits beside the first. The A'wan 'Si'ta appears from
an inner room with a shovel of live coals and proceeds to make a
fire in the fireplace. The girls' dresses are embellished by the men
whom they accompany, without removing the black woven gown. A
mi'ha (white embroidered blanket) is folded lengthwise and passed
under the right arm and fastened over the left shoulder. The arms
and legs are bare. The women as well as the men are never unmindful
of their adornments at such times, and a man is dispatched in haste
for the forgotten bracelets. The friends of the dancers are usually
willing to contribute fine blankets, ko'hakwa (white shell), coral and
turquoise necklaces, and earrings to add to the beauty of their dress.

As the fire burns up brightly the songs of the warriors become more
hilarious, growing louder and louder as they appeal to the Gods of
War to give them the lives of their enemies, that they may have rain
and bountiful crops.[b] They now leave the house and form into two
lines. After dancing before the ceremonial chamber the elder brother
Bow priest leads the north line, followed in succession by a young
girl, provided with an arrow, the younger brother Bow priest, a warrior, and another girl and warrior. The south line is headed by a
warrior, followed by women and warriors. Two virgins, each holding
an arrow, dance back and forth between the lines, the drummer walking in front north of the lines. Their number is increased by young
men and boys, some not older than 6 or 7 years. One boy carries
a stuffed horse's leg over his right shoulder, another a stick of wood
in the right hand and a drumstick in the left, and a third carries a doll.
The lines halt and dance vis-a-vis. After the first song the dancers
advance westward sidewise; and after a second dance they proceed in
the double file. The third song is prefaced with the war whoop as
they enter te'wita 'hlan'na (large plaza) from the northeast. The
house tops are crowded with spectators and the plaza is walled by
them, many on horseback. After dancing in the plaza for an hour

---

[a] These instruments of torture hang on the walls of the ceremonial room, ready for use.
[b] The spirit of the scalped enemy becomes a friend.

all disperse, and the elder brother Bow priest passes through the town, calling for all to gather later in the ki'wi'siwe to be happy and thankful.

The choir of the ᵗSän'iakïakwe (Ant fraternity) is assembled on the east side of the ceremonial chamber which extends north and south, singing to the accompaniment of rattle and drum. A bowl of medicine water is in the northwest end of the room. A man and a woman of the fraternity begin dancing, and the man appears to grow wilder and wilder as he growls and jumps about nearly as possible like the bear he represents. He wears a black breechcloth and carries an eagle-wing plume in each hand; a salmon-colored fluffy eagle feather is tied to his forelock. Every little while the man grabs at the legs of some of the members of the choir. The dancing continues nearly an hour, when the A'piᶜˡläshiwanni, with their nude bodies zigzagged in white kaolin, representing lightning, enter in single file and form into an ellipse. All wear deerskin skull caps, but Nai'uchi (elder brother Bow priest), who wears a fur cap instead. They carry their bows and arrows and war clubs. Nai'uchi now and then indulges in animal-like performances, and he also holds a live coal in his mouth, afterwards running an arrow down his throat, dancing about with it in that position. He is very graceful, and there is no member more enthusiastic and energetic than this old man, who has fought in many engagements with the Navahos.

At the close of the dance the A'piᶜˡläshiwanni stand aside to make room for a party personating Navahos, the songs being in the Navaho tongue. After one dance this party leaves the chamber for the Chu' pawa ki'wi'sinĕ, and the warriors sing another song and dance with even more enthusiasm than before. The dance is begun in an ellipse, but after a time they break into a promiscuous group, and after dancing a while they again form into an ellipse. These changes are repeated several times.

After the warriors leave the chamber, another party representing Navahos make their appearance and form into two files, the principal dancers being two boys, one personating a girl, who would deceive the closest observer, they are so like the Navahos. The girl wears a black velvet waist and a full red calico skirt, which falls below the knees. The tips of her moccasins are painted red, and her hair is done up in Navaho style. A red spot of the size of a silver dollar is on either cheek. The boy has his body spotted in white.

The choir of the Ant fraternity remains quiet during the presence of both parties personating the Navahos. When the lines cease dancing, the boy and girl take their position vis-a-vis and some distance apart. Bending slightly forward, they run until they almost meet, and then dance, the boy raising first one foot and then the other as high as possible by drawing the knees nearly to the chin. The girl's step is the same but not so high or violent. Their arms are kept in constant motion, and they carry in either hand triangular pieces made of slender sticks ornamented with white fluffy eagle plumes. Passing one another, they go some distance and turning repeat the figure. There is no variation from this figure during the dance. The others of the party sing in Navaho while the two dance between the lines. The men wear artificial mustaches of black goat's wool.[a] A ridiculous character appears with these dancers, wearing an old pair of American trousers and coat, an ash-colored mask with prominent nose, and a bushy wig; he carries an old pistol.

The Kĭa′kwemosi with others of the first body of A′shiwanni are in in the Chu′pawa ki′wiᵗsinĕ, while the Ko′mosona, pe′kwĭn, and others are in the Mu′he′wa ki′wiᵗsinĕ to receive the dancers. After dancing in the chamber of the Ant fraternity, the party representing Navahos proceeds to the Chu′pawa ki′wiᵗsinĕ, which is by this hour crowded, most of the north ledge being occupied by girls wearing black wraps over their heads and shoulders so as to conceal their faces. One sparkling eye only is to be seen through the folds of the blanket. They resist all efforts to make them expose their faces. The circular opening in the floor of the ki′wiᵗsinĕ, symbolic of the entrance to the innermost world, is exposed, and later, food and plumes are deposited within.

The dancers form, as before, into two files, running lengthwise down the room facing west, and dance. The queer-looking creature wearing a mask crouches at the west of the fire altar and keeps up a violent motion with the pistol which he carries, moving his head in time with his hand. He makes many jokes and the men joke with him. When the two lines cease dancing, the boy and girl dance between the lines, as before, to repeated encores. Finally some one cries: "Let them stop; they are tired." Others say: "Let them go on." They dance thirty minutes. The men of the ki′wiᵗsinĕ pass lighted cigarettes to the dancers, who indulge in a social smoke. The following dialogue between Nan′nahe, a Hopi Indian married to a Zuñi woman, and the creature wearing the mask, causes great merriment:

"Where did you come from?" "Over there," pointing to the east. "Have you a father?" "No." "Have you a mother?" "No; they died long ago." "Have you brothers or sisters?" "No." "Do you know how to weave?" "No." "Do you know how to do anything?" "No." "Do you have anyone to work for you?" "No." "You must have stolen your beads; you must have stolen your pistol." "I found an American sleeping and killed him and took his pistol. I would like to trade this red ribbon on my pistol for a watermelon." A boy brings some melons, which the man grabs and tucks under his blanket, handing the ribbon to the boy. "How did you get the wristlet you wear?" "I was lousy and a woman combed my hair; when she left I found this on my wrist." He endeavors to discharge the pistol by pushing the trigger forward, which creates much amusement.

---

[a] The mustache is worn in ridicule of the Navahos, as some of these people have slight mustaches. The Zuñi regard such growth of hair as most disfiguring, and a man of the tribe who has any signs of a mustache is jeered at by the others.

After the Navaho dancers leave the ki'wi'sinĕ the person wearing the mask is requested to dance. He falls at his first attempt, but afterward he burlesques the dancers who have just left. He is received with great enthusiasm, being called out a second and a third time. When responding to the encore he pretends to be quite lame from his fall. After taking his seat he says a few words in Hopi in a squeaky voice, upon which a member of this tribe who is present calls out: "Why, you are a Hopi." When he is leaving the ki'wi'sinĕ his foot misses a rung of the ladder, and the leg projects between the rungs, much to the enjoyment of all present. He is again called to the floor, when he produces general laughter by his ridiculous dancing. After he leaves, a choir composed of the young men of the ki'wi'sinĕ, stationed at the west end of the room, sing. The leader of the choir selects certain girls to dance. They protest, but without avail. The wrap which covers the face must be thrown aside during the dance, but at the close of the dance the face is quickly concealed again. There is an interval of some minutes, when other girls are selected to dance.

After a time three young men, who appear to be present for the purpose, select several youths from a group of young men who sit on the south ledge opposite the girls, leading them over to the girls. Some of the youths resist, apparently as bashful as the maidens appear to be. A youth on being presented to a girl addresses her in a few words. Her reply decides whether he shall sit at her feet or hurriedly return to his former place. Several of the girls persistently refuse to make a choice, while others discard many before the fortunate one is chosen. When the youth remains with a girl a bowl of water is passed to him, and he in turn hands it to the maiden, who bathes her face, hands, and legs, the young man remaining at her feet until she chooses a second youth, when the girl in company with the two leaves the ki'wi'sinĕ. The girls return to the ki'wi'sinĕ with their faces more closely veiled than ever.

This is the only occasion, excepting that recorded in connection with the closing ceremonies of the 'Hle'wekwe fraternity, in which there has been any evidence of licentiousness observed among the Zuñi women, and but comparatively few young women leave the ki'wi'sinĕ at this time. While they are permitted to go, such a course is considered most improper and a shadow of disgrace clings to every girl who does so, no matter how innocent she may be.

A visit was made to the home of one of these young women the morning following an evening spent in the ki'wi'sinĕ. A young girl was seen to approach timidly the family group at their morning meal; but she was ordered away by both parents, who were weeping bitterly, while the elder daughter was severe in her condemnation of her sister. The writer upon inquiring into the trouble was answered by the mother, who, weeping afresh, says: "My daughter stole from her home last night and joined the wicked set in the ki'wi'sinĕ, and she will never again be like my daughter." The girl at first refused to notice the writer, but being assured of her sympathy, she gratefully raised her eyes, filled with unshed tears, and said: "I am not guilty, but they will not believe me." This girl was severely whipped on her return from the ki'wi'sinĕ, a punishment inflicted only for a grave offense.

CEREMONIES OF THE SECOND DAY

The first body of A'shiwanni meet again on the morning following the first evening's festivities, in the Shi'wano'‛kĭa's house, and gathering around a small bowl of native tobacco they pray and smoke. Two reeds are filled with the tobacco and placed by the bowl, with a bunch of corn husks to be used for cigarettes. The Kĭa'kwemosi, holding two corn-husk cigarettes, clasps the hands of the scalp custodian, praying that he may clasp the hands of the A'shiwanni of all the world, from where the Sun Father comes up to where he goes down; praying that the Sun Father shall give to his people and to people of all the world, from where he comes up to where he goes down, all things good—food, raiment, and prosperity; that the priests of old and his other selves (his deceased predecessors) shall send the rain to water the earth that the crops may be bountiful; and that his people may have power to destroy the enemy. At the close of this prayer the hands of the Kĭa'kwemosi and scalp custodian are reversed, and the latter repeats a prayer, after which the two reed cigarettes are lighted and passed around, each shi'wanni taking a whiff. With a husk cigarette in his hand, the scalp custodian now departs for the house of the A'kwamosi (maker of medicine water) of the Ant fraternity. After the smoke, the A'shiwanni with bowed heads whisper most solemnly a prayer, after which a meal is served by the mother of the Shi'wano'‛kĭa; each one gathers bits of the food on a piece of bread, which is afterward thrown into the fire, with a prayer to the ancestors and a call to them to eat. The scalp custodian stands with the A'kwamosi of the Ant fraternity, their hands clasped, he retaining the cigarette, and they offer a prayer. Their hands are afterward reversed, and the A'kwamosi repeats a prayer. Both bow and smile to the white visitors who enter, but do not speak until after the prayers, when the A'kwamosi clasps Dr Tylor's[a] right hand with his left. Passing the hands in a circle over the Doctor's head and bringing them to his lips, the A'kwamosi draws a breath and passes the hands around his own head and then to the lips of Dr Tylor, to draw a breath, that all that is good may be drawn from the one to the other. The scalp custodian performs the same acts with him, and finally the ceremony is repeated by both the A'kwamosi and the scalp custodian over the writer.

The A'kwamosi of the Ant fraternity, who is a very old man of the Sun clan, now hastens to a large chamber opening upon the large plaza, where the A'pi‛läshiwanni are assembled, to officiate in the

---

[a] Dr E. B. Tylor, the distinguished English anthropologist, was present at these ceremonies, and during his short stay he won the confidence and affection of all the priests and theurgists of the tribe. The writer is much indebted to him for his valuable suggestions in regard to her investigations.

ceremonies. A few members of the priesthood sit in the south end, busying themselves making moccasins, shirts, etc. Later the A'pi⁺ꞏlä-shiwanni gather in a semicircular group on the east side of the room toward the north end, the A'kwamosi of the Ant fraternity, with flowing white locks, sitting just south of the group. Another old man, holding the ceremonial cigarette-lighter, a staff charred at one end, sits back of the choir on a quaint chair of Zuñi manufacture. The first body of A'shiwanni, excepting the Shi'wano'ꞏkĭa and the Kĭa'kwemosi (Shiwanni of the North), who remains in the house of the Shi'wano'ꞏkĭa during the day, stand in line at the north end of the room, on the east side, and members of the Ant fraternity stand on their right. An Apache basket, ornamented with cloud designs and arrow points woven into the dark straw, and containing feather wands, having each a streamer of red and green ribbons, radiating from the center of the basket, is deposited on the floor on the west side at the north end of the room. A second basket is placed near by, containing a small leather pouch of arrow points and two bunches of reed cigarettes filled with native tobacco, the reeds being colored red and wrapped with corn husks. On the floor are two bowls of medicine water, portions of several hawks' breasts, and a quantity of kaolin, red pigment, and a small jar of bear's grease.

When the choir has its complement of members, the song begins, each member holding and brandishing in time with the song a pistol, bayonet, or war club. The song embraces a long history of the valorous deeds of the Gods of War and of their people of old, down to the times when their fathers fought the hated Navahos, the invaders of their homes, recapitulating the instructions given by the Gods of War to go out to battle with brave hearts, the routes they must follow, and the means they must adopt in order to master the enemy. The gestures accompanying this portion of the song are specially graceful and pleasing.

When the song is begun, the elder brother Bow priest and three other members of the Bow priesthood take their positions on the west side of the room, and are prepared by four members of the Ant fraternity for the outdoor ceremony. The hair is separated into strands and rolled on burs, forming knots, half the size of a pigeon's egg, all over the head. The cotton shirts and trousers are not removed, and moccasins and leggings are worn. The war pouch, suspended across the shoulder, completes the dress. The face is given an application of bear's grease and red and black pigment. A paste of kaolin is applied to the chin, upper lip, tip of the nose, and eyebrows, and forms a circle on the top of the head, and hawk down, symbolic of the clouds of the world, is applied to the paste. The A'kwamosi

of the Ant fraternity removes arrow points from the sack and places
one in the mouth of each man, with a prayer. The arrow point must
remain in the mouth until the return of these warriors to the chamber.
Their decoration being completed, the four take seats on the ledge on
the west side of the room, two with heads erect, while two bow their
heads. A bow and arrow are laid before each man after four equidistant lines of kaolin paste have been applied to the bow, and hawk
down is attached to each line. Two A'pi‧ᵗläshiwanni now stand before
them chanting a low ritual, while the song of the choir rings through
the long chamber. At the close of the prayer the A'kwamosi of the
Ant fraternity gives a draft from the medicine bowl to each of the four
warriors by dipping a shell into the bowl, and he gives a reed filled
with tobacco to each. Each warrior now takes the bow and arrow
which lie before him and one of the feather wands from the Apache
basket and leaves the chamber, two going to Up'ᵗsannawa ki'wiᵗsinĕ
and two to Chu'pawa ki'wiᵗsinĕ, each couple being preceded by a
member of the Bow priesthood clad in ordinary dress. The scalp custodian is in the Up'ᵗsannawa ki'wiᵗsinĕ, which represents the side of the
elder God of War, and his fellow is in Chu'pawa ki'wiᵗsinĕ, which
stands for the younger God of War, to receive the warriors.

At the same time young men in the ki'wiᵗsiwe are adorning girls
about 10 years of age for the dance. The girls wear their moccasins
and black woven gown embroidered top and bottom in dark blue.
A white cotton embroidered kilt is fastened on the left shoulder,
passing under the right arm. The wands received by the members
are attached to the heads of girls in upright position by fastening the
lower ends to the dress at the back of the neck and tying them to the
top of the head with shreds of the maiden's hair, the loose hair, which
has been braided over night that it may be wavy, hiding all traces of
the mode of securing the wand. A leather band encircles the head,
the front of which is concealed by a long bang which covers the face.
A horn of carved wood is attached to the left side of the leather band
and an artificial blossom of the squash flower, woven of red and yellow
yarn, to the right. A red fox skin hangs from the right wrist and blue
yarn, tied in a tassel, is attached to the left. The left arm is encircled
almost to the elbow with rare beads, and the breast is covered with
coral, turquoise, and ko'hakwa necklaces. A spread turkey tail is
attached to the back of the waist. Each girl carries an arrow in her
right hand, which she gracefully manipulates between the thumb and
forefinger during the dance, the significance being that the arrows of
the Zuñi may destroy the hated Navahos.

Robes and blankets upon which to seat the warriors have been laid
upon the ledge on the south side of the ki'wiᵗsiwe near the west end. One

of the warriors in the Up′ᵗsannawa hands the reed cigarette he carries to the scalp custodian and the other hands his to the warrior who accompanies them. The scalp custodian's fellow fills his place in the other ki′wiᵗsinĕ. The cigarettes are lighted and returned to the donors, who draw the smoke into their mouths, and, puffing it out in clouds, wave the cigarettes around their heads; then they are again handed to the others, who wave them twice round the heads of the donors and then throw them on the floor. Two of the warriors, preceded by a choir of gaily dressed young men of the Up′ᵗsannawa and followed by two girls, proceed to the plaza and stoop upon the ground, the choir grouping themselves behind them, facing north; the girls dance before them, facing south. The motions of these young dancers remind one of humming birds hovering over blossoms. With their arms spread out, they seem to be winged creatures, their feet scarcely touching the earth. The length of time they keep their arms extended is remarkable. They constantly pass one another in the dance, always keeping their faces southward. A short time after the arrival of the party from the Up′ᵗsannawa ki′wiᵗsinĕ the warriors from the Chu′pawa ki′wiᵗsinĕ, with two girls, preceded by a choir formed by members of the Chu′pawa, take similar positions in the plaza, sitting a little apart from the others. This ceremony is repeated until all the warriors have taken part, sunset closing this feature of the day.

During the ceremony performed by the last four warriors a hideous object, representing the buffalo, appears in the plaza. His face and body are colored black, and he wears an enormous wig of black sheepskin. His only clothing is a kilt of brownish-red deerskin fringed with tiny bells, held on with an embroidered Hopi sash tied at the back. When the warriors leave the plaza for the last time, the four little girls form in two lines about 10 feet apart and dance. The buffalo man dances up and down between the lines for awhile, then darts off, shaking the rattle held in the right hand, and clasps one of the girls in an obscene manner.[a] He returns and dances between the lines, and finally leaves the plaza amid great enthusiasm of the spectators.

CEREMONIES OF THE SECOND NIGHT

By 9 o'clock those interested in the ceremonies of the night are busy preparing for them. While the Chu′pawa and Mu′he‘wa are the only ki′wiᵗsiwe in which the warriors assemble, members of the other ki′wiᵗsiwe, wearing the dress of the anthropic gods, dance in a number of dwellings during the night, singing songs composed for the occasion.

---

[a] This character, which has been adopted from the Hopi Indians, plays no part in the rites of thanksgiving, and is merely introduced for amusement, like the character in the night ceremonies in the ki′wiᵗsinĕ.

The picture presented in the chamber of the Ant fraternity, in which the men and women are preparing for their dance, and in two other rooms, where parties are being decorated for the dance, is not unlike the greenroom of a theater. Paints, robes, and ornaments are scattered about the rooms. The men of the Ant fraternity are painting their bodies in white to represent animals, snakes, and the heavens. The parts which they can not reach, such as their backs and shoulders, are painted by one another. The women paint their lower legs and arms in white. All have their hair done up in their usual style and wear yucca wreaths tied in rosettes at the side of the head and a fluffy eagle plume attached to the forelock. The portion of the wreath passing over the forehead of the women is covered by the long bang. Men place the wreaths and feathers on the women's heads. Both sexes wear elaborate necklaces, and the women have strings of turquoise in their ears.

When all are ready, two parallel lines are formed lengthwise of the room, which extends north and south. The choir is grouped on the east side and sings to the accompaniment of the rattle and drum. As soon as the dancers are on the floor they form into an ellipse, a woman to the left of each man, and dance from left to right. The men sing but the women are silent. After dancing thirty minutes the dancers pass in file out of the house to the Chu'pawa ki'wi'sinĕ. After entering they form in an ellipse and pray aloud, and, dancing around for a time in the ellipse, they form into two lines and dance again.

During the dancing a noise is heard on the roof, and on investigation there are found a number of men and one 5-year-old child, representing Navahos. All but the child carry rattles, and they are richly dressed, the best figure being the tiny boy, who personates a Navaho girl. Now and then they call through the hatchway to the dancers below, who reply; and in a short time they leave for the roof of the Mu'he'wa ki'wi'sinĕ.

A number of young women with their heads covered with blankets, as on the previous evening, are in the Chu'pawa ki'wi'sinĕ. Several of these are compelled to lay aside their wraps and dance back and forth between the lines of the Ant fraternity. Three youths, appearing as decrepit old men, personating the Zuñi when they lived on To'wa yäl'lännĕ (Corn Mountain), hobble around with the aid of staffs. Their clothing is ragged and their long, shaggy hair is unkempt. One carries a stone ax, and another has a pair of large tin tweezers hanging from his neck, and both carry bows and arrows.

Crowds that pour into the ki'wi'sinĕ indicate the approach of the Navaho dancers, who are evidently the stars of the evening. Coming down the ladder one by one, they form into double file and repeat the dance of the previous evening, the child appearing as interested as the elders. At the conclusion of the dance and song—the latter being a prolonged burlesque of the Navahos—the party leave the ki′wiᵗsinĕ, and the trio of old men from To′wa yäl′lännĕ take the floor and make efforts to dance; their joints appear to be so stiffened from age that they move their limbs with great difficulty. They utter a number of comical, innocent jokes. One, addressing the writer as "mother," causes a roar of laughter at her expense.

The A′piᵗläshiwanni, led by the elder brother Bow priest, are the next to appear. Their bared limbs are painted white and they wear cotton-embroidered or buckskin kilts. Some of them, including the elder brother Bow priest, have their heads ornamented with feather wands, while others wear the skullcap of buckskin with an aigrette of hawk feathers on the top. They, too, repeat their dance of the previous evening. One of the girls present has her blanket taken from her and is made to join in the dance.

After the warriors leave, the choir of the Chu′pawa ki′wiᵗsinĕ sings, and the scenes between the young men and women of the previous night are repeated. Musicians, dancers, and personators of the gods pass in and out of the covered ways and streets throughout the night, as they go from house to house to dance.

The ceremonies in the Mu′he‘wa ki′wiᵗsinĕ are the same as those observed in the Chu′pawa. At daylight all assemble in the plaza to offer prayers to the rising sun, and nothing of further interest occurs until afternoon, when the ceremonies of the previous day are repeated. The bodies of the warriors are now painted white to represent animals, snakes, and the heavens, and they wear white embroidered or buckskin kilts, held on with white cotton fringed sashes tied at the right side. A fox skin is pendent at the back of belt and the war pouch is worn over the shoulder. The hair is dressed as on the previous day, and their faces and heads are adorned with the hawk down. The Kĭa′kwemosi, who was absent on the previous day, is now present and stands at the right of the pe′kwĭn (sun priest). After the war song and the other ceremonials in the house where the warriors are assembled the plaza ceremonies are repeated. An hour before sunset the first body of A′shiwanni take seats upon a ledge outside, which has been covered with robes and blankets for the occasion. The terraced house tops are now a mass of color from the bright blankets and robes worn by the spectators, who crowd together to witness the closing scenes. Many Navaho visitors, also clad in rich attire and mounted on their horses, add to the gay setting of the plaza. Objects of various kinds are thrown by the crowd on the house tops to the people below, which occasions great scrambling and wrestling, but good humor is invariably preserved. The Navahos make but few attempts to get possession of the gifts, but occasionally they contend for them, and when it is done fairly the Zuñi make no resistance; but when there is any attempt to take advantage by tripping or the like, they are hustled off the plaza by the police, who are ever alert to preserve order when there are a number of Navahos in the town.

The dancing girls who accompany the warriors dance on, apparently unconscious of the hilarity around them. As each set of warriors appears in the plaza, the women of their families and women of their clans and their wives' clans bring baskets laden with various articles of food and deposit them on the ground at the back of the warriors, whom they sprinkle with sacred meal. As soon as each couple of warriors are through with the sacred ceremonies in the plaza, they don the ordinary clothing and throw the contents of their respective baskets to the crowd. The number and quality of the gifts of each warrior depends upon the wealth and extravagance of his family and clan connections, many of them throwing quantities of calico and ribbon. Nai′uchi, elder brother Bow priest, is lavish with his gifts. After throwing yards of calico, ribbon, and quantities of food, he leaves the plaza, to return in a short time clad in new black cloth trousers and vest, with a fine long silk scarf wound round his head. All of these are removed and thrown to the crowd. He is fully attired under this suit. Nai′uchi's gifts are eagerly sought.

The girls continue their dancing until the evening shadows fall over the plaza, when two warriors, with the choir of the Up′tsannawa ki′witsinĕ, leave the plaza, going toward the east, and two warriors, with the choir of the Chu′pawa ki′witsinĕ, going to the west. The writer follows the latter and sees the party divide in the street before the Chu′pawa ki′witsinĕ, forming into vis-a-vis lines. Rows of men and women, each holding a bit of cedar bark, stand on the roofs of the houses near by. A theurgist of the Ne′wekwe (Galaxy) fraternity walks back and forth between the two lines of warriors, passing down the body of each, to carry off disease, two eagle-wing feathers, while he repeats an inaudible prayer. At intervals during this ceremony those on the house tops expectorate three times upon the cedar bark and carry it in the hands from left to right around the head, simultaneously repeating a prayer. Then all separate, each having his head washed in yucca suds by the appropriate woman.[a] The writer accompanies one of the warriors, whose head is bathed by the wife of the elder brother Bow priest. The woman afterward bathes the head of the warrior's mother, and then all the members of the family have their heads washed.

QUADRENNIAL DANCE OF THE KĬA′NAKWE

The dance of the Kok′ko ko′han (white gods) is so called from the Kĭa′nakwe[b] having been clothed in white and having slept under white

---

[a] The top of the head is slightly washed, and then a forelock is vigorously bathed, the one doing the washing repeating a prayer for health, prosperity, and a good heart. Each hand and arm to the elbow is also thoroughly bathed.

[b] See Destruction of the Kĭa′nakwe, and songs of thanksgiving.

blankets. These blankets, which at present are made principally by the Hopi Indians, are supposed by the Zuñis to have originated with the Kĭa'nakwe. These ghost people are angry with the Zuñis for their destruction; hence the ceremony of propitiation, which occurs quadrennially and which is one of the most important as well as one of the most elaborate in Zuñi.

The part of this ritual that is performed in the Si'aa' te'wita, sacred dance plaza, was first witnessed by the writer in 1884. In comparing notes made on two later occasions with those made then, it was found that the outdoor ceremonials are identical in all details.

The personators of the Kĭa'nakwe are always members of the Corn clan and Chu'pawa ki'wi'sinĕ. Ten days previous to a ceremonial the masks, which are made of hide and cover the head, are taken from storage, filled with damp sand to soften them and bring them into shape, and placed along the north ledge of the large room, vacated for this purpose by the family, in the dwelling of the priest, or director, of the Kĭa'nakwe organization. Five days later the decoration of the masks begins. Four days are consumed in decorating the masks and attending to various details connected with the paraphernalia. This work, which is performed by the men who are to take part in the ceremony, is begun each morning and stops at sunset. Great secrecy is observed throughout the preparation for this ceremonial, and no one but those who have duties to perform may enter the room.[a]

The twelve songs that are sung during the ceremonies are archaic, the Zuñis say, though they admit that these songs are in the Sia tongue, which was the language of the Kĭa'nakwe. A newly appointed person requires much time to learn the songs; therefore, during the summer, when the day's work in the fields is over, those who are to take part in the Kĭa'nakwe ceremonial frequently meet and rehearse them. The rain priest and his associate have the same relative positions as the Kia'kwemosi and the pe'kwĭn of Zuñi.

When the Kĭa'nakwe are about to appear, those who are to personate them and their prisoners assemble 2 miles south of Zuñi. After painting their entire bodies with the pinkish clay used by the personators of anthropic gods, which is applied so thin that the color is scarcely to be discerned, they dress themselves in their mi'hawe[b] and masks and return to the village. Plate XLII shows them crossing the bridge over the river. The house tops are filled with men, women, and children, all eager to have the first look at the gods as they approach from over the southern hills singing a low chant. The priest leads, followed by his deputy. They wear white cotton shirts, white embroidered blankets, each having four dark fluffy eagle plumes attached, front and back, in the form of a square. They wear leggings

[a] The writer was present by special invitation of the priest of the organization.
[b] Mi'hawe is plural for mi'ha, sacred embroidered blanket.

of white cotton, knit in fanciful designs, and dance moccasins. A tortoise-shell rattle is carried in the right hand and a pottery meal basket and te′likinawe are carried in the left. Each mask is finished at the base with a collarette of spruce tipped with popcorn (see plate XLIII).

The other members of the Kĭa′nakwe, except the two directors of the warriors of the six regions, are dressed like their leaders, except the four feathers on the front and back of blankets. The directors have dressed deerskins instead of the mi′hawe, and they wear bow wristlets and carry tortoise-shell rattles in the right hand and bows and arrows in the left. The first captive to be seen is the Ko′thlama;[a] he wears the woman's dress of black, embroidered in dark blue, and caught at the waist with a red woven belt. A white embroidered sash passes from the left side of the waist to the right shoulder, where it is tied, the embroidered ends falling. A piece of white commercial cotton hangs over the back. The neck and arms, which are exposed, are painted white; the hair is parted from the forehead down the back of the head, and one side is done up over a wooden form, while the other side is tied with red and blue yarn and left hanging. The mask (see plate XLIV a) covers only the face. A rattle of deer scapulæ is carried in the right hand, and three ears of corn, tied together with yucca ribbons and te′likinawe, are carried in the left.[b]

The Sa′yaᵗhlia, another captive, wears a large deerskin, dyed reddish-brown and elaborately ornamented with various colored designs, an emblem of the sun being on the back. A white cotton embroidered sash is tied round his waist under the deerskin and falls at the side. The mask of the Sa′yaᵗhlia is of native cotton cloth, colored with paint made from the pinkish clay. The mouth of the mask is bearded with lynx skin, and the projecting teeth are made of corn husks. Gray goat's wool falls over the top of the head and forehead, and padded eyeballs are conspicuous beneath the wool. A red fox skin is worn around the neck at the base of the mask (see plate XVI). The Sa′yaᵗhlia carries a tortoise-shell rattle in the right hand and a bow and arrows and te′likinawe in the left.

The last captive to be seen in the line is It′sepäsha (game-maker), one of the ten Ko′yemshi;[c] he wears the seldom varying dress, the short, ragged skirt of native black cloth, and the three-cornered piece of the same at the base of the mask, the body and mask being colored with the pinkish clay. The ten Ko′yemshi masks differ in detail. There are six warriors of the Kĭa′nakwe for the six regions besides the two directors. The masks are of the appropriate colors, yellow for the North, blue-green for the West, and red for the South (plate XLV a, b, and c); white for the East. The white masks are the same as those of

---

[a] See Destruction of the ‘Kĭa′nakwe, and songs of thanksgiving.

[b] On one occasion the Ko′thlama had a quiver of arrows over his back and he carried a bow and arrows in his left hand.

[c] See p. 33.

the priest and deputy of the Kĭa′nakwe without the tadpole and dragon-fly decoration (plate XLIII); variegated for the Zenith, and black for the Nadir (plate XLVI a and b). The mask of the directors of the warriors of the six regions is blue-green on the face with a decoration of black, dotted white, on the back (plate XLVI c).

After each god crosses the bridge over the river that flows south of the village he halts, and when all have reached the bank they are greeted by nine Ko′yemshi. They afterward pass down the street on the south side of the village, then up on the east side to another street running east and west, and up this street to the Si′aa′ te′wita, then out by the western covered way to the street on the north side of the village, and down on the west side to an inner one leading to the Chu′pawa ki′wi⸱sinĕ, which they enter. Nine Ko′yemshi, the tenth being with the party of dancers, spend the afternoon entertaining the populace by going from house to house playing in primitive comedy.

After prayers, the masks, with the spruce wreaths, are removed and laid on a sheepskin spread on the floor in a room adjoining and north of the ki′wi⸱sinĕ, the doorway being about 2½ feet above the floor of the chamber, though on a level with the floor of the room in which the masks are placed. The Kĭa′nakwe now disband and return to their respective homes for refreshment. Later in the evening they return to the ki′wi⸱sinĕ, the priest taking his seat in the northwest corner and the two directors of the warriors sitting at his left; the others are grouped on the north side of the chamber. The priest and the two warriors by his side deposit broken he′we (wafer bread) in two basket trays. Soon afterward the song begins. The pe′kwĭn (deputy) of the Kĭa′nakwe arrives, but before taking his seat on the west ledge, he empties a quantity of he′we, brought in a soiled cloth, into one of the basket trays. During the first song the priest occupies himself making four flat packages of corn husks, each about 3½ inches long and 2 inches wide. Twelve songs are sung, there being a few moments intermission between each song. The director of the song sits at the east end of the group. Some move the right hand and some both hands in time with the song, which is at no time very loud. Rattles are not used until the beginning of the dance. The singing of the twelve songs requires a little over two hours, each stanza averaging two minutes. At the close of each song a prayer is repeated aloud by all, and the sacred breath of A′wonawil′ona[a] is inhaled. There are many members of the ki′wi⸱sinĕ present, who take no actual part in the ceremonies, they being privileged to come to their own ki′wi⸱sinĕ; in fact they assist the personators of the Kĭa′nakwe in various ways. At their own request and for protection against bad dreams, two are whipped with yucca across each arm and ankle by a warrior of the Kĭa′nakwe.

[a] See Classification of higher powers.

KÍA'NAKWE GODS DANCING IN PLAZA

BUREAU OF AMERICAN ETHNOLOGY

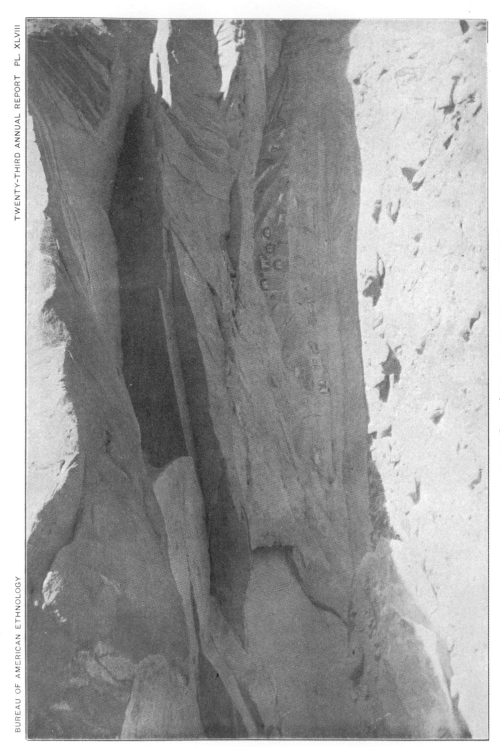

SHRINE AT PI'KĬAIA'KĬANA (WATER-CRESS SPRING)

MASK OF U'WANNAMI' (RAIN MAKERS)
front and rear views

a MASK OF NA'TÁSHKU b, c MASK OF NA'WISHO
front and side views

A bunch of deer scapulæ and thirty-five tortoise-shell rattles lie in a group on the floor near the two basket trays, and several packages of plumes, etc., wrapped in old cloths, are on the ledge near the priest. Two hours before midnight the priest empties the contents of one basket tray into the other, prays, and, placing his mouth very close to the food, puffs smoke over it from his cigarette of native tobacco. Though he prays aloud, the singing drowns his voice. After a prayer of five minutes he divides the food into three parts, returns it to the soiled cloths in which it was brought, hands a package to each of the chiefs of the warrior gods and one to his deputy, and afterward one of the corn-husk packages to each. The three wrap their blankets around them, go to the river, and deposit in the water the contents of their packages as food for the departed Kĭa′nakwe. These men are absent an hour. In the meantime one of the singers hands to a young man several pieces of green paint, a mixture of copper ore and boiled piñon gum. A large and beautiful paint stone and pestle are then placed on the floor on the south side and two young men proceed to grind the paint. First a piece is pounded into a powder, then water and squash seed are added, bits of the paint being placed on the stone as the grinding proceeds. Fully an hour is required for the proper mixing of the paint. The two take turns, one grinding while the other scrapes the paint toward the center of the paint stone.

The last song closes as the three officers return from depositing the offerings in the river, and immediately one of the singers jumps up and endeavors to open the door on the north side of the room. Finding it fastened, he goes to the window in the west end, which communicates with a room, and calls to the man of the family, who is sleeping, to open the door in the north wall. Soon this door gives way to the push of one of the singers, and they all disappear through this quaint little doorway. They soon return, each bearing a pair of dance moccasins, which are handed to the paint-grinders. The two grinders and a third man repaint thirty-six pairs of dance moccasins. This work is done very rapidly. A quantity of paint put into the mouth with the finger is thrown out through the teeth over the moccasin; then the tongue serves as a paint brush. The sight is most repulsive. One man becomes very sick from the effects of the paint. During the painting of the moccasins the Kĭa′nakwe rehearse for the dance of the coming day. They remove their cotton trousers, or roll them up, so that they are not seen below the white shirts which fall over them. All but the Ko′thlama hold tortoise-shell rattles; deer toes are attached with buckskin thongs to the tortoise shell. He holds the rattle of deer scapulæ. Then they form into an elongated horseshoe, the apex being toward the west end of the room, the directors of warriors at each end.

After all have taken position, one of their number examines each tortoise to see that the number of deer toes attached is correct. The dance begins with the priest and his pe'kwĭn walking abreast toward the west in slow steps, bending the knee with a stiff motion. When near the apex of the horseshoe they stop and face each other. The priest bends both knees and exclaims: "Hu'_____hu_____hu _____." The pe'kwĭn repeats the same. The priest again cries: "Hu'_____ hu_____hu_____," and it is again repeated by the pe'kwĭn, when they simultaneously bend their knees and call together, "Hu'_____hu_____ hu_____hu." Immediately the dancers' voices are heard in rich minor tones. Then the rattles sound and the dancers form in file, facing north, the one at the south end of the horseshoe now being at the east end of the line. In a moment they all turn and face east, and so they continue to reverse while the priest and pe'kwĭn walk stiff-kneed back and forth. Every time the two meet midway the line of dancers they halt and bow. After the priest and pe'kwĭn pass back and forth four times the dance ceases, and the two, facing each other, cry: "Hu'_____hu_____hu _____hu." The dance is repeated, and the song continues. After dancing an hour they leave the ki'wi⸱sinĕ and visit the house of Awan täᵗchu (Great Father) Ko'yem-shi, where they dance.

After the return of the Kĭa'nakwe to the ki'wi⸱sinĕ the night is spent in smoking and talking. At daylight the masks are brought from the inner room and placed on a sort of hanging shelf previously prepared for them. They don their paraphernalia at sunrise and dance before the dwelling of the priest of the Kĭa'nakwe, which is on the west street, and again in the plaza on the west side of the town, each dance being like the one in the ki'wi⸱sinĕ. The dress, however, is now complete. They return to the ki'wi⸱sinĕ, remove their masks, and smoke.

This particular ceremony of dancing at different points and passing around the village is repeated four times; each time they return to the ki'wi⸱sinĕ. The last of these dances closes about an hour before noon. In the meantime twelve women of the Corn clan, the supposed descendants of the Kĭa'nakwe, assemble in the ki'wi⸱sinĕ, taking seats on the ledges on the east and south sides of the room. Two bowls of yucca suds are provided, and the priest advances to have his head washed. Each woman dips a handful of the suds, and when all are supplied each one rubs them down the forelock of the priest. · An ear of corn is now rubbed on the top of his head four times. The other officers are washed in turn, and all the Kĭa'nakwe pass through the same ceremony.

After the washing of the heads, bowls of food and coffee are carried to the entrance of the ki'wi⸱sinĕ by the wives and daughters of the personators of the Kĭa'nakwe and are received by members of the

Chu'pawa ki'wi'sinĕ. The women who carry the food to the ki'wi'sinĕ must first wash their heads, although they go only to the entrance and return home immediately after depositing the food; they wear their best moccasins and dresses for the occasion. This elaborate feast in the ki'wi'sinĕ is particularly enjoyed by all, including the twelve women of the Corn clan, as a fast has been maintained by the personators of the gods since the previous evening.

After each man finishes his meal he collects a bit from each bowl upon a large piece of he'we (wafer bread) and, folding it lengthwise, wraps it at each end with yucca and forms a handle. This package is carried in the left hand in the outdoor dance and is afterward deposited in the river for the Kĭa'nakwe.

At the close of the meal one of the Chu'pakwe fills an Apache basket with grains of corn of various colors from a cloth that lies toward the west end of the room on which the corn is piled. He carries it to the east end of the room and gives to each of the twelve women of the Corn clan about a pint of corn to be planted the coming year. The women now leave the ki'wi'sinĕ, but before they depart the priest advances to the middle of the room and, with his te'likinanĕ clasped in his hands, repeats in a most impressive manner a litany. The others appear weary enough, except at the moments when they make responses, in which they never fail. When the priest returns to his seat the eating bowls are removed. Personators of the Kĭa'nakwe put on their masks and proceed to the Si'aa' te'wita, where the dance of the previous night is repeated (see plate XLVII).

Contributions for the first body of A'shiwanni begin to pour into the ki'wi'sinĕ during the dancing. The offerings are brought in blankets, the men carrying theirs on their backs while the women hand theirs through the hatchway. They are received principally by an aged man of the ki'wi'sinĕ. There are deer and antelope, some that have not been flayed, but simply drawn, with corn and other small offerings placed inside; others are flayed and the skins brought separate from the flesh; about 300 watermelons, many of them covered with a netting of yucca containing a number of feathers, and a large quantity of corn on the cob. Several men are busy tying the corn together in bundles containing four to ten ears, and a handle is formed of yucca over the top ear. A large number of birds are brought, the plumes of which are used by the A'shiwanni for their te'likinawe that are deposited at the winter solstice, that food may be abundant the coming year. The birds are laid apart from the general heap at the west end of the room, of light bread, which is strung together in fanciful shapes, dried deer meat, corn, melons, and pieces of calico. The unflayed game and skins are deposited at the east end of the chamber. As the dried deer meat, melons, and seeds are required to fill the game and skins, they are brought to the east side of the room.

The unflayed game and skins are sewed up with yucca threads. It is a busy time for the few who work. Others who crowd the room look on and give their opinions. Contributions continue to a late hour, and the packages, when completed, are carried to the ceremonial house of the keeper of the ᵗsuᵗʰlan'na (great shell), so as to have them near the scene of action and to make room for other donations.

After dancing four times in the plaza, the Kĭa'nakwe return to the ki'wiᵗsinĕ and remain about twenty minutes, and then go again to the plaza and dance four times more.

In the absence of the Kĭa'nakwe from the plaza, nine of the Ko'yemshi, the tenth dancing with the Kĭa'nakwe, amuse the audience. When playing the harlequin these men are sometimes obscene, but they rarely do anything more than amuse the populace with their jokes. Hearing the roars of the men, women, and children, one unacquainted with the language might infer that something had been said with at least a double meaning, but this is not often the case. They mimic the dancers, make fun of one another's masks or faces, pretend to be frightened at some child in the crowd, and call one another old and strangers who are known to no one, etc. They appear to greatly enjoy the games of wool bag, hopping on one foot, and ring-around-a-rosy, which they play during the intervals of the dancing.

At 4 o'clock the Kĭa'nakwe return to the plaza, their backs laden with gifts for the A'shiwanni, and form a broken ellipse, the apex being to the east side of the plaza. The priest carries a basket of loose corn of various colors, and his pe'kwĭn a basket tray of feathers artistically arranged on a bed of raw cotton. At this time the A'shiwanni, including the Shi'wano'ᶜkĭa, who have been in the ceremonial chamber of the Kĭa'kwemosi, form a line, facing east, at the west side of the plaza. The Kĭa'kwemosi stands at the south end, with the pe'kwĭn beside him, the Shi'wano'ᶜkĭa standing just back of them. The Shiwanni of the Nadir (also elder brother Bow priest), with the younger brother Bow priest by his side, stands next. The A'shiwanni of the West, South, and East complete the line. As soon as the Ko'yemshi, who stand on the north side of the plaza when the dancers come, relieve those on the north side of their burdens, the members of the Chu'pawa ki'wiᵗsinĕ remove the loads from the backs of those on the south side of the ellipse. The basket trays carried by the priest and deputy are taken and held by the A'wantä'ᶜchu Ko'yemshi and his pe'kwĭn, as these baskets must not touch the ground. Should the baskets be deposited on the ground the seeds would be unfruitful.

The A'shiwanni appear like so many statues during the dance, which begins after the loads are removed from the dancers. When the dance ends the burdens are returned to the backs of the priest of the Kĭa'nakwe and his deputy by two warriors of the Kĭa'nakwe, and the baskets are handed to them. The priest of the Kĭa'nakwe now stands before the

Kĭa′kwemosi, and his deputy before the pe′kwĭn (sun priest), who receive the basket trays. These trays are now transferred to the Shi′wano′ʻkĭa, who retains both, the basket of feathers being placed on top of the basket of corn. The burdens are now removed from the backs of the priest and his deputy and laid upon a blanket spread for the purpose. The directors of warriors advance and stand before the Shi′wanni of the Nadir and younger brother Bow priest, and their burdens are removed. Long prayers are repeated by the four personating the Kĭa′nakwe as they stand vis-a-vis to their prototypes in Zuñi. These prayers continue until all the offerings are deposited. The priest and deputy speak in the Sia tongue, which they refer to as archaic Zuñi, but the warriors talk in the modern tongue, as only the former are familiar with these prayers of the Kĭa′nakwe.

Two blankets are laid side by side, with a space of several feet between, and each dancer deposits his burden on a blanket. As soon as the Ko′yemshi perform their share in relieving the dancers of their burdens, they busy themselves bringing in the watermelons from the house of the keeper of the great shell, which they deposit in a heap near the ladder leading to the ceremonial chamber of the Kĭa′kwemosi. When all the dancers have made their offerings, the Kĭa′nakwe priest, his deputy, and the directors of warriors turn and face the dancers, and each dancer in unison grasps his rattle with both hands, the priest and deputy holding theirs in the same way. The priest offers a prayer, and all wave the rattle, still holding it with both hands, in a circle from right to left, and inhale a breath. Then the rattle is held in the right hand and shaken for a moment, and the song and dance begin.

The A′shiwanni now adjourn to their ceremonial chamber, but return to the plaza after the dancers leave and carry the gifts up the ladder on their backs. It is all Nai′uchi, the old Shi′wanni of the Nadir, can do to carry up a large buck. He fails to lift it by placing the yucca strings, which are attached to the fore and hind legs, across his breast, but is able to bear it after it is raised to his back by others. The offerings are spread on the floor of the ceremonial chamber of the Kĭa′kwemosi. The Shi′wano′ʻkĭa[a] at once begins collecting the birds and plumes from the packages. The A′shiwanni sit smoking in a group in the southeast corner of the room. Baskets of te′likinawe made during the afternoon are on the floor, to be offered to the deceased predecessors of the A′shiwanni and to the priests of the Kĭa′nakwe.

After all the birds and plumes are collected, and there are many of them, the question arises regarding the allotment of the buck. It seems that no special package goes to any particular shi′wanni, but that the whole mass is divided; yet in this case it is agreed that the buck

---

[a]The Shi′wano′ʻkĭa, the wife of the Kĭa′kwemosi, and the writer were the only women present.

must belong to the Kĭa'kwemosi. The Shi'wanni of the Nadir proceeds to flay the animal. The younger brother Bow priest holds the right hind leg, the Shi'wanni of the South holds the left foreleg, the wife of the Kĭa'kwemosi the left hind leg. The knife is run down the throat, then out the right foreleg, then down the paunch, and out the right hind leg, out the left foreleg, then out the left hind leg.

When the dancers retire from the plaza they are burlesqued by the Ko'yemshi, the jester having the same privilege in this rude life that was accorded to him in the courts of Europe.

During the afternoon, the time when the house tops and the plaza are crowded with spectators, two Ko'yemshi, one carrying a doll and the other a basket containing a doll and ears of boiled corn tied together with yucca ribbons, approach a little girl, whose mother places her arms around the child as they come near. The two hold a conversation with the child, asking her many questions. She seems quite interested and eager to receive the gifts. One Ko'yemshi presents to her the doll he carries, and the other hands the basket containing the doll and corn to the mother; the mother and child then leave the plaza.

Great excitement and amusement are caused by the Ko'yemshi throwing blankets over a dog. First one and then another throws a blanket until the howling of the dog is completely drowned and he can not move. The excitement reaches the highest point when this bundle is lifted by one of the Ko'yemshi. The greatest enthusiasm prevails over the return of the dancers, who are completely covered with gifts for the populace, including bread of fanciful shapes, strung together with yucca ribbons and calico tied into balls with long ends like kite-tails. The people of all ages are eager to catch the articles that are flying through the air. It is astonishing how dextrous the Zuñis are in throwing these objects. It is well-nigh dusk when the last gift is thrown. One of the dancers, requesting a Ko'yemshi to help him to remove the white shirt he wears, waves it, when off, until the male spectators are fairly wild when he tosses it into the air. No controversy or ill feeling is displayed between the Zuñis at these times.

The dancers and Ko'yemshi now leave the plaza and, passing out over the western road for a mile or so, they disrobe. A number of members of the Chu'pawa ki'wiᵗsinĕ follow on the south side of the river, apparently unconscious of the maskers; they carry ordinary apparel secreted under their blankets, and return with the masks and other paraphernalia covered from view. With this act the festival, which has been all-absorbing for days, closes, to be repeated in four years. The gifts to the A'shiwanni are carried at night to their homes. Small portions of the game, after it is cooked, are deposited by each shi'wanni in the river as offerings to the deceased Kĭa'nakwe, who are angry gods, and must be appeased with ceremonies and gifts.

ANNUAL FESTIVAL OF THE SHA'LÄKO

It was mentioned in treating of the winter solstice festival that those who are to personate the Council of the Gods, the Sha'läko (giant couriers of the rain-makers) and the Ko'yemshi, and those who are to entertain these gods are decided upon during the winter solstice ceremonies. One of the eight new or reconstructed houses is blessed by the Council of the Gods, six each by a Sha'läko, and one by the Ko'yemshi.

The large te'likinanĕ given in the ki'wi'sinĕ at the winter solstice to each man who is to entertain the Sha'läko is kept in his house, and is brought out from its resting place by him at intervals when the members of his and of his wife's clan gather in the house with his family while he holds the te'likinanĕ and prays. The prayer, which is long, is a supplication for life, health, and happiness.

At the close of the festival of the Sha'läko the Ko'yemshi collect these te'likinawe from the different houses and deposit them, except the one given to the host of the Council of the Gods, which is carried by Sa'yatäsha to his home and afterward planted by him.

When the ceremonial house of the Kĭa'kwemosi is to be repaired the work is done by the people of his clan, the workmen being appointed by the pe'kwĭn (sun priest), some member of the governor's staff calling from the house top each morning the names of those selected to labor during the day. Several gods are present at this time to see that all hands keep at work. Each ki'wi'sinĕ is repaired by its members. As the ceremonial chambers of the fraternities are general living rooms of families at all other times than when the ceremonials occur, there is no special building or repairing of these aside from the general house structure. The walls are whitened and sometimes decorated for ceremonials, the whitening being done by the women of the house and the decorating by members of the fraternity; in some cases decorations remain permanently on the walls.

In building or reconstructing houses the wor'li (manager) details members to work on the house in which his ki'wi'sinĕ is to be represented by a Sha'läko. Personators of the Council of the Gods and Ko'yemshi direct men of their ki'wi'siwe to work upon the houses in which they are to appear. Their wives and daughters and the women of their clans wait upon the builders.

Houses of either a domestic or a religious character that are to be constructed or remodeled must be in order before the coming of the Sha'läko. Such work is often delayed from day to day, and toward the end must be expedited to be ready at the prescribed time.

Zuñi, like a beehive in its peculiar construction, is most like one when house building is in progress. The streets near by are filled with men, women, and children.

In 1884 the reconstruction of a house of more than ordinary importance occupied attention.   It was the ceremonial house of the Kĭa'kwe-
a'mosi (first body of A'shiwanni), usually referred to as the house of
the Kĭa'kwemosi (Shiwanni of the North).   It was not his place of
residence, however, the custom of the husband going to the wife's
house applying to the Kia'kwemosi also.   His sister occupied the
house until its destruction by lightning, which also caused her death.
The Zuñis say she had no love in her heart for the Kĭa'kwemosi, her
brother; that lightning never destroys the good of heart.   The
A'shiwanni rejoiced that the room of the ĕt'tonĕ[a] of the Kĭa'kwemosi,
which is immediately over the center of the world, was not disturbed.

On this occasion there are present two Sa'ya'hlia (see plate XVI), three
A'toshle (two males and one female), four Ko'yemshi (see plate VA);
and three members of the Ne'wekwe (Galaxy fraternity), each carrying
his bauble.   Each Sa'ya'hlia wears a white cotton embroidered kilt,
with a sash of the same material and a woman's red belt tied on the left
side.   A finely dressed deerskin is fastened on the right shoulder, passing under the left arm.   Bands of leather, painted blue-green and edged
with three points of unpainted leather, ornament the upper arms.   A
leather thong several inches long, tipped with a turkey plume, is
attached to each point.   Bunches of native blue yarn with long tassels
encircle the wrists and are also worn below the knees.   Dance moccasins
complete the costume.   The entire body is painted with the pinkish
clay before referred to.   Bows and arrows are carried in the left hand,
and in the right tortoise-shell rattles and bunches of giant yucca.
Two of the A'toshle are similarly dressed.   The female wears ordinary
woman's dress, and a white cotton blanket bordered with red and blue
stripes is tied at her neck, falling over the back.   The Ko'yemshi
have their nude bodies and masks colored with the pinkish clay.   The
ragged kilt is worn, and a three-cornered piece of the same native
cloth is tied to the base of the mask.

The Ne'wekwe, attired in cast-off uniforms of the United States
Army, are supposed to lend assistance to the laborers, but they do
little else than eat filth and play the fool.   The Ko'yemshi scamper
about over the house tops and indulge in jokes and other nonsense,
while the Sa'ya'hlia go about the village with bunches of yucca, driving
the delinquents to work.   The A'toshle also carry giant yucca, which
they use without the slightest hesitancy, and they are supplied with
large stone knives with which they threaten to cut off the heads of
naughty and disobedient children.

While there is much work in the house building there is also much
pleasure.   The women chatter the gossip of the day, men pass their
jokes, youths and maidens laugh joyously at one another's expense,

---

[a] See A'shiwanni (rain priesthood).

and children vie with each other for the praise of their elders. Women
are busy preparing a feast for those laboring on the ancestral house of
the Kĭa'kwemosi. One group of maidens grinds at the mills, keeping
time to a choir of young men who are accompanied by the drum, while
at two fireplaces aged women, looking more like mummies than living
creatures, sit toasting the meal after it has passed through the coarsest
mill; after the toasting, it must again go through finer mills. On
another side of the room a group of half-grown girls sits husking corn,
their bodies keeping rythmic time with their voices. At another
fireplace two women are busy baking he'we, while in the room beyond
maidens are engaged over great pots of stewing meat, corn, and chili.
Two meals are served to the workers, one at midday and one at sunset.
Late in the afternoon the A'toshle and Ko'yemshi together visit a
number of houses to learn if the inmates properly perform their
duties. They make inquiries regarding the behavior of husbands,
wives, and children. In one house a wife accuses her husband of
being lazy and unwilling to work, whereupon he is brought up for
judgment. He pleads his own cause and finally succeeds in getting
the gods to accept his statement. In another house the mother
complains that her daughter will not grind. The girl declares that
grinding makes her very tired and her arms refuse to move. The
female A'toshle commands the girl to accompany her to the mills and
kneel beside her to be taught to grind so that her arms will not become
tired. The two gods lecture a boy of 4 years, while two younger
children of the family are held close in the arms of their parents, who
cover the little ones' eyes with their hands. The boy receiving the
lecture clings to his mother, and his knees shake as he replies to the
questions of the gods. The fear of the child is great as the gods wave
their stone knives above him and declare that if he is naughty they
will cut off his head. A father complains that his boys are uncleanly
and will not bathe, whereupon they are commanded by the gods to
proceed at once to the river, where the Ko'yemshi join the boys, and
dropping their kilts, jump into the water and bathe. In a short time
they make their brief toilet and return to the house and join the
A'toshle. Then all stand in line and repeat a long prayer, the members of the household observing the greatest reverence. At the completion of this prayer the family sprinkle the gods with meal and
pray.

After leaving the house the gods meet a man returning from his
peach orchard, his burro heavily laden with fruit, the master urging
him along with a heavy stick. The man is stopped by the gods and
held up for trial for working in his orchard instead of assisting in the
building of the house of the Kĭa'kwemosi. It is finally decided he

shall be allowed to go unpunished after supplying the party gener-
ously with peaches, which the Ko'yemshi carry to their house.   The
other gods now return to the ki'wiᵗsině, where they remove their masks
and apparel and put on their ordinary clothing, which has been brought
by young men, who convey the masks and paraphernalia closely concealed under their blankets to their proper places.   Such are the daily
scenes during the exterior building of the house.

The richer class is likely to entertain the Sha'läko most frequently, as they are better able to remodel and enlarge their houses
from time to time, yet those who are very poor sometimes aspire to
this honor.   In order to do so the house must undergo the necessary
improvements.   One of the entertainers of the Sha'läko in 1896
was tried and condemned as a wizard while engaged on his house
improvements.   It was with difficulty that the writer had this man
released, the whole village crying out against him, yet after being
exonerated he proceeded with his house building without further
obstacles.

Each family that is to remodel a house for the Sha'läko festival has
at harvest time a corps of men detailed to work in their fields by the
chief wor'li of the ki'wiᵗsině whence the personators of the gods are to
come.   These men leave the village in a body, usually on horseback,
at early morning, returning at sunset.   They enjoy a repast at the
house of those for whom they have labored.   Great preparations are
made for this occasion by the women of the household, their clan, and
the clan of the man of the house.   Grinding is again done as described,
with ceremony and song.

On August 16, 1896, the wor'li of the O'he‘wa (East) ki'wiᵗsině visited
the house where the Sha'läko of his ki'wiᵗsině was to appear the coming
autumn, and informed the matron of the house that his people would
work in the fields.   The fields worked on this occasion were those of
the man and woman of the house and of their two sons-in-law, the
products of all going to the household use.

On the return of the workers at sunset, those who were to personate
a Sha'läko, his fellow, and the Ko'mosona being of the number, a
feast was served them on the roof of the house.ᵃ   The food was placed in
a line and twenty-one persons were seated on each side of it.   The wives
of those who chanced to be of the clans of the inmates of the house were
assembled, with their babies, on the roof to receive their husbands and
aid in serving the meal.   The fathers whose babies were present seemed
very much more interested in the wee ones than in the elaborate meal
that awaited them, and the babies, who exhibited great delight at the
presence of their fathers, were taken and tossed about and played with
before the food was tasted.   Those men whose wives and babies arrived

───────────────

ᵃ These people enjoy being out of doors in the cool of the evening.

after they were seated took the little ones in their arms and played with them, to the interruption of their meal. At the close of the meal food wrapped in corn husks was handed to the man who was to personate the Sha'läko and to his fellow by the member of the household to whom the te'likinanĕ was given at the winter solstice. The food was carried to the river and deposited to the Kok'ko A'wan (Council of the Gods).[a]

The Sha'läko festival is the great autumn celebration, and is of more general interest to the Zuñis, and also to the Indians of the surrounding country, than all the others. At no other time is there such feasting among them. The larders are kept filled. The poorer class of Zuñis often give all they possess to their welcome and unwelcome guests, regardless of the suffering in store for them when the festival will have closed and the visitors, who have satiated their appetites at their expense, will have gone. Among these unwelcome guests are the Navahos, for whom, except in a few instances where a friendship has sprung up, the Zuñis have scant amity. The Navahos have not the slightest hesitancy in riding up to a house, unsaddling their horses, walking in, and remaining as long as it may suit their pleasure; and the Zuñis accept the inevitable as graciously as possible.

MINOR CEREMONIES

Though the great festival takes place in the autumn, minor ceremonies occur each month following the winter solstice, at which time the personators of the gods who are represented in this festival are appointed. They meet twice each month to rehearse their songs, and each month in the last quarter of the moon te'likinawe are deposited at some shrine to these gods.

In January the chosen Sa'yatäsha[a] visits the house of the new A'wan tä'ᵗchu Ko'yemshi, and the two remain together until far into the night. The following morning the personator of Sa'yatäsha goes on horseback to Nutria (a farming district) to gather cottonwood, returning as early as possible. After reaching his home and depositing the bulk of the branches, he carries a small bundle of them to the house where the masks of the Ko'yemshi are kept and where the Great Father Ko'yemshi awaits him. The two talk together for a while. The six personators of the Sha'läko also gather cottonwood for their te'likinawe. Early in the following morning the Great Father Ko'yemshi, having selected his nine fellows, requests them to assemble at his house.

Those who are to personate the Council of the Gods go to the house of the personator of Sa'yatäsha, who inquires of Shu'laawiᵗsi whom he has chosen to be his ceremonial father. The latter replying, Sa'yatäsha requests him to bring the father, who may be of any clan; in 1896 he belonged to the Corn clan. On his return Shu'laawiᵗsi holds the

[a] See p. 33.

te'likinanĕ given him by the pe'kwĭn in the He'iwa ki'wi'sinĕ during the winter solstice ceremonies and repeats with his chosen father the ceremony said by the pe'kwĭn over him. The Ko'yemshi assemble at the same time in the house of the Great Father Ko'yemshi, who repeats with each of his nine fellows the ceremony with his plume offering that the pe'kwĭn held with him. The te'likinawe are then returned to the basket tray from which they were taken.

On the following morning the Ko'yemshi again gather in the Great Father's house, and those who are to personate the Council of the Gods and father of Shu'laawi'si assemble in the house of the personator of Sa'yatäsha, the alternate of each man who personates a Sha'läko going to his principal's house. All are busy preparing te'likinawe. Each man makes four, except A'wan tä'tchu Ko'yemshi, who makes only three, having the one already given him by the pe'kwĭn. The sticks of all the Ko'yemshi are colored black, each having three eagle plumes, one from the back of the neck, one from under the tail, and one banded one, and feathers from the birds of the six regions. The te'likinawe made by the personators of the Council of the Gods have the sticks colored black. The one given to Sa'yatäsha by the pe'kwĭn is painted yellow. Each stick of these gods has three turkey plumes, one fluffy eagle plume, and feathers of the birds of the six regions. Each Sha'läko and his alternate prepare te'likinawe similar to those made at the house of Sa'yatäsha. When the offerings are completed they are laid in basket trays. The men return to their homes, where the head of each is washed by the wife or some female member of the family. Returning for the te'likinawe, they all proceed to U'hana 'kĭanakwi (Moss[a] spring), where Sa'yatäsha makes an excavation with an ancient corn planter the depth of his arm to the elbow, and sprinkles in meal combined with turquoise, ko'hakwa (white shell beads), and abalone shell until the place is thickly covered, when each man deposits his te'likinawe in the excavation, sprinkles them with meal, and prays. The excavation is carefully covered with earth by Sa'yatäsha. Continence must be observed during the four following days, the personators of the Council of the Gods spending each night until midnight in the house of Sa'yatäsha. The Ko'yemshi deposit their te'likinawe in an excavation by a spring. There are many concretion fetishes at this spring. The Ko'yemshi spend these four nights until midnight in the house of the Great Father, each alternate of a Sha'läko going in the same manner to the house of his Sha'läko.

The spring visited in February is some 6 or 7 miles south of Zuñi, in a most retired spot. The writer was there in the company of the elder brother Bow priest, who claimed that no one who was not a member of the Ko'tikili (mythologic fraternity) had before visited this

---

a U'hana is also the Zuñi name for wool.

shrine, Pi'kĭaiaᵗkĭana (Water-cress spring). (See plate XLVIII.) A
short, steep climb above the spring brings one to a cave rock, about
30 feet wide, with a projecting ledge at the base, the deepest place being
10 or 12 feet, the roof of stone projecting over the base. At each end
of this arch, on the roof, are impressions of hands, made by placing the
hand on the rock and spattering a brownish-red paint. There are seven
of these hand impressions at the north end, more at the south end, and
some near the center. A number of masks of anthropic gods are represented on the rock with black paint, the more recent ones having in
many cases been made over older ones. A central figure on the rock
wall represents a Ko'yemshi mask. An outline is formed by cutting
the rock, and three pits, colored black, each large enough to hold a
marble, denote the eye and mouth holes of the mask. The Ko'loowisi
(Plumed Serpent) extends nearly the whole length of the rock, its
head to the south. The teeth are large and of black paint. Many
other figures are on the rock, including several cougars, game animals,
and the god O'lolowĭshkĭa, with conspicuous generative organs. The
older markings on the rock are cuttings; the more recent are paintings
in black. Near each end of the rock are twelve pits, indicating different springs of the Council of the Gods. It was impossible to secure the
whole scene with the camera, which failed to bring out distinctly the
markings of this most elaborate and interesting shrine. A separate
stone near the middle of the rock, which has the mask of Sa'yatäsha
cut on it, is a seat for the personator of this god. There are stone
seats in line for the others, but these have no carvings. The stone
where the Sha'läko sit is large and has a square, smooth surface,
upon which is a geometrical figure composed of small pits.

In March A'ᵗsina ᵗkĭa 'nakwi (Stone-picture-place spring), not far
south of Zuñi, is visited. In April they go to Pi'shukĭaia ᵗkĭa'nawki
(Poison-oak spring), which is at the base of No'ponia yäl'lännĕ (Face
mountain). In May ᵗKĭan'uhl ᵗhla'kwi (spring coming from mesa
wall), situated at the base of Ke'ya'ᵃ yäl'lännĕ (Whitewash mountain),
is visited. In June they go to To'loknana ᵗkĭa'nakwi (Bulrush, Scir-
pus occidentalis, spring), at the base of a mountain bearing the same
name. In July ᵗKĭa'techikwi (ill-smelling water), at the base of I'tiwanna (middle) yäl'lännĕ, is visited. In August they visit O'pompiakwi
(Sack of meal hanging place).[b] In September they go to A'yaya-
kĭaᵗkĭanakwi (Blue-jay spring), at the base of a mountain of the same
name. In October Häl'on kwa'ton[c] ("Ant entering place"), is visited,
near which is a spring well protected by a wall and roof of stone
(see plate XLIX).

[a] It is from this mesa that ke'chipa, the material used by the Zuñi for whitewash, is obtained.
[b] Mountain of the Gods of War (see Bow priesthood).
[c] This shrine is on the site of the ruin Kĭakĭi'ma, at the southwest base of Corn mountain.

The shrine which symbolized the Middle of the world to the A'shiwi when they lived on To'wa yäl'lännĕ is a cave in the rocky wall just above Hä'lon kwa'ton (see A plate L). It appears impassable, but it can be reached by expert climbers.

The first body of A'shiwanni, the Ko'mosona, Ko'pekwĭn, and two Ko'pi⁽ʻläshiwanni assemble in the ceremonial chamber of the Kĭa'kwemosi at sunrise forty-nine days previous to the coming of the Sha'läko. The pe'kwĭn and Ko'pekwĭn each tie forty-nine knots in a white cotton cord, denoting that the gods will come in forty-nine days, including the day on which the knots are made. The cord is as long as the reach of the maker's extended arms, and is composed of four strands of cotton slightly twisted. The first knot is made about 8 inches from the end, and a turquoise or ko'hakwa bead is placed at this point. One string is given to the personator of Sa'yatäsha, the other to Great Father Ko'yemshi. The two go to Ku'shilowa (red earth), a short distance east of the village, and pray. The same evening Hä'lon kwa'ton is visited by the Council of the Gods, Ko'yemshi, and the Sha'läko, who deposit te'likinawe.

From this time till the coming of the Sha'läko there are constant meetings and rehearsals of songs and prayers.

In 1896 there was a serious discussion between the pe'kwĭn and the personators of the Council of the Gods, with the elder brother Bow priest on the side of the latter. The pe'kwĭn insisted that the others had miscounted and that some days should be dropped, while the others were strong in their opinion that the proper time had been chosen for the coming of the Sha'läko. The pe'kwĭn, however, carried his point.

Another trouble also occurred about this time over a scandal that caused much excitement and nightly discussions. The whole village was horror-stricken over a report concerning the man chosen to personate Shu'laawi⁽ʻsi; he was accused by the elder sister of the wife of the present pe'kwĭn of improper conduct after his appointment to office. A council, formed of the first body of A'shiwanni and those who were to personate the Council of the Gods and the Sha'läko, discussed the matter. The woman, being present, accused the man of approaching her at night with undue familiarity, he being her guest at the time. The man was tried, found guilty, and expelled from office; another was found to fill his place.

When ten days have passed after the visit to Hä'lon kwa'ton the same party goes to the shrine Pä'nitonin'kwĭ in the afternoon and deposit te'likinawe. They return to the village by early moonlight, the Council of the Gods, who proceed quietly, preceding the others a short distance. The songs of the personators of the Ko'yemshi and Sha'läko with their alternates, each party forming its own group, are heard some time before the men are visible. In ten days the same party visits A'ne ⁽hlawa an te' kĭapoakwi, a shrine on a mound southwest of Zuñi; and ten days later they go to Sus'ki a'shoktakwi (coyote stone drinking place). After ten more days they visit A'kohanna ti'nakwi (white rocks sitting), a group of white sandstone pinnacles perched on a knoll which are sacred to the Council of the Gods.

HÄL'ON KWATON (ANT ENTERING PLACE) SHRINE

HE'PATINA, SHRINE SYMBOLIC OF THE CENTER OF THE WORLD. A, POSITION OF SHRINE WHEN THE ZUÑI LIVED O
TO'WA YÄL'LÄNNE (CORN MOUNTAIN)

MASK OF MŪ́LUKTÄ́ᵏKIA: FRONT, SIDE, AND REAR VIEWS

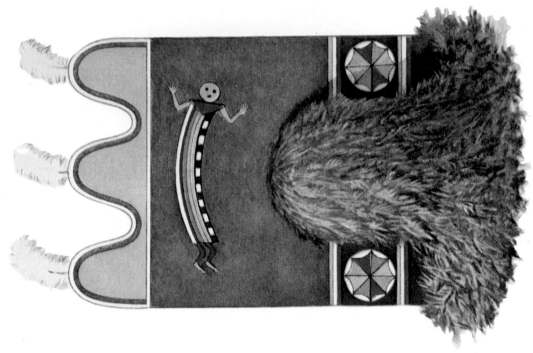

MASK OF HÉMISHIIKWE, WITH TABLET: FRONT AND REAR VIEWS

Two of the rocks are marked with perpendicular lines cut in the rock, one having twenty-nine the other twenty-eight lines. It was stated that these lines denote the number of years the late Ko'mosona and Ko'pekwĭn held office, a statement that requires substantiation.

The Ko'yemshi are chosen annually alternately from the fraternities enumerated below. It will be remembered that the Great Father is designated at the winter-solstice ceremonial, he in turn choosing his fellows. The clans given are not those of the men personating the Ko'yemshi, but the clans of their paternal parents. It makes no difference to what clan each man who personates a Ko'yemshi belongs, but his father must be of the clan mentioned. The Ne'wekwe (Galaxy), Sho'wekwe (Arrow reed), ᵗKo'shi'kwe (Cactus), and Maᶜᵗke ᵗhlan'nakwe (Great fire) fraternities follow annually in regular succession.

Ko'yemshi	Ne'wekwe	Sho'wekwe a	ᵗKo'shiᶜkwe	Ma'ᵗke thlan'na-kwe
1 A'wan tä'ᶜchu (great father)	Sand-hill Crane	Dogwood	Tobacco	Turkey
2 Pe'kwĭn (deputy to great father)	Dogwood	Corn	Dogwood	Badger
3 Pi'ᶜᶜläshiwanni (warrior)	Corn	Sun	Corn	Eagle
4 E'shoᵗsi (bat)	Bear	Coyote	Badger	Frog
5 Mu'yäpona (small horns)	Eagle	Badger	Frog	Dogwood
6 Po'sokĭi (small mouth)	Sun	Sand-hill Crane	Eagle	Bear
7 Na'thläshi (old grandfather)	Badger	Eagle	Turkey	Sand-hill Crane
8 It'sepäsha (game-maker)	Coyote	Frog	Sand-hill Crane	Sun
9 ᵗKĭa'luᵗsi (water-drinker)	Frog	Turkey	Coyote	Badger
10 Sa'thläshi (old youth)	Badger	Dogwood	Sun	Dogwood

The Ko'yemshi appear in the village the night of the day the plumes are planted at A'kohanna ti'nakwi. They are supposed to come from Ko'thluwala'wa,[b] but their starting point is He'patina, a shrine symbolic of the Middle of the world, situated a short distance south of Zuñi. They cross the river at the southwest corner of the town and announce the coming of the Council of the Gods in four days and of the Sha'läko in eight days. The village is illuminated not only by fires in the houses, from which each window is aglow, but by the ovens out of doors, the fire tongues issuing through the oven doors. The Ko'yemshi pass first to the te'wita ᵗhlan'na (large plaza) and stand in a group. Sa'thläshi is the first to speak: "Eight days everyone must go to the Navaho country and fight." ᵗKĭa'luᵗsi speaks: "In eight days my people come. You boys must look around for nice girls and stay with them." It'sepäsha speaks next: "To-night these men dragged me from my house, and I am lonesome without my wife. When they go to sleep I will run away and return to my wife." Na'thläshi speaks: "To-night this man [referring to the Great Father Ko'yemshi] picked out nine men; pretty soon they will fight." Na'thläshi says but little. Po'sokĭi speaks: "In eight days we will have the big dance; then you will have plenty to eat." He continues for a time with obscene jokes. E'shoᵗsi says: "To-night I come; all of you come to see me; all of

---

a Since the degeneracy of the Sho'wekwe the aged director of this fraternity selects his nine fellows from the people at large.

b Abiding place of the Council of the Gods.

you boys have a good time and do not be angry." Pi'"läshiwanni speaks: "I come to tell you to-night that in eight days everyone will be happy and have a good time; men should trade wives."[a] There are further remarks of obscene character. The pe'kwĭn (deputy to Great Father) closes with the following speech: "Night, my father, night, my mother, you have come a little near." He means that it is early in the night. Addressing the Zuñis, he continues: "In eight days my people will come [referring to their ancestors]. All will come from Ko'thluwala'wa and A'witĕn te'hula (fourth world). Even the old men too feeble to walk will come leaning on a cane, the mother with her son walking before her, her child led by the hand, her younger child carried on her back, the infant in her arms, and her unborn child—all will come hither to see you. They will see you, but you will not see them; they will not be in the flesh, but in the ghost self."

In the old time the people from Ko'thluwala'wa and A'witĕn te'hula appeared in the flesh, but their presence caused great mortality among the A'shiwi, which distressed the A'shiwanni, and therefore they of the ghost world decided to come thereafter only in the spirit, and so the gods instructed the people to wear masks like those worn by themselves, when they would come in spirit and abide for a time in the personators of themselves. The Zuñis have their mediums, gifted with superior sight, who see the ghosts.

The pe'kwĭn continues: "You must all work; the houses must be completed; you must bring much wood. Make your moccasins and clothes. Tell the women to whiten the walls and make their houses beautiful for my people, the gods who are to come. The Council of the Gods will come in four days, and in eight days the Sha'läko will come." After a few jokes from the others, they start for the Si'aa' te'wita, sacred dance plaza, where they again form into a circle, with two in the ring, and repeat what was said in the large plaza. From the Si'aa' te'wita they go to the ko'china te'wita (rat plaza), and from there to the He'kĭapawa te'wita (back-wall plaza). The same speeches are repeated in all the plazas.

On leaving the He'kĭapawa plaza the Ko'yemshi disappear on the western road, but they soon return with masks, etc., under a covering of blankets and go into the ceremonial chamber of the fraternity of which the Great Father Ko'yemshi is a member. They do not leave the house for eight days, except to make certain announcements at night regarding the coming of the gods and to collect wood. Each morning nine of them go for wood, one always remaining in the chamber.

A member of the fraternity to which the Great Father belongs is designated to secure the burros each day to bring the wood, each of the nine men having one burro. The men ride the burros in going

[a] Such practices are not common among the Zuñis.

for the wood, but on the return at sunset the little animals are loaded with the wood and are driven by the Ko'yemshi. The wood is deposited before the new house that is to be dedicated by the Ko'yemshi, and the women of the house and members of their clan stack it.

There is no altar erected during the eight days' retreat of the Ko'yemshi and they do not dance. The one remaining indoors spends his time principally in sewing his personal apparel. In the evening there are prayers and songs. They may eat anything, the food being served by women of the fraternity to which the Great Father belongs, but they must observe continence and not even touch the hand of a woman.

At this time the chief wor'li of each ki'wi\[t\]sině with his associates meets the people of his ki'wi\[t\]sině and of the fraternity which is to take part in the ceremonies of the Sha'läko. The members of the fraternity rehearse their songs and te'likinawe are prepared. At sunset the wor'we (plural of wor'li) proceed to the shrine of the Sha'läko and deposit the offerings. This shrine, called the house of the Sha'läko, is about 1½ miles southwest of Zuñi, at the base of A'kohanna tinakwi. It is a low-walled, rectangular inclosure in which stones are placed for seats. Here the personators of the Council of the Gods and Sha'läko hold a council previous to the Sha'läko ceremonial. Formerly the personators of these gods attired themselves for the festival at this place, but as the influx of Americans and others has rendered this spot liable to intrusion, a house some distance east of this point now serves for their dressing room. There are a number of stones piled together at A'kohanna ti'nakwi to form a special shrine for Sa'yatäsha, and about 12 feet south is what is known as the shrine of Shu'laawi\[t\]si. Quantities of te'likinawe are to be seen at the shrine of Sa'yatäsha and in and about all the crevices of the larger rocks.

On the same day that the Sha'läko wor'we visit the Sha'läko shrine the chosen father of Shu'laawi\[t\]si deposits two heaps of he'sho (piñon) wood at the western base of I'shäna an te'kĭapoa (Grease knoll), six piles about equal distance apart between this knoll and A'kohanna ti'nakwi, and another heap on the knoll at the shrine of Shu'laawi\[t\]si. At noon of the same day the Ko'mosona and Ko'pekwĭn visit A'kohanna ti'nakwi and make two sand mounds, symbolizing the two mountains near Ko'thluwala'wa, one on each side of Sa'yatäsha's seat or shrine, the one on the north being symbolic of Ko'yemshi mountain, and that on the south symbolic of Kor'kokshi mountain, the seat itself being symbolic of Ko'thluwala'wa.[a] The mounds are made of sand and covered with prayer meal. The Ko'mosona extends a line of meal outward from the shrine several feet to the east and crosses the line with meal four times, denoting the four regions, and sprinkles meal over a considerable surface, and the two return to the village.

---

a See p. 154.

At 10 o'clock at night a party visits A'kohanna ti'nakwi in the following order: Ceremonial father of Shu'laawi'si, Shu'laawi'si, Sa'yatäsha, Yä'muhakto, Hu'tutu; second Yä'muhakto, Ko'mosona, Ko'pekwĭn, and elder and younger brother Bow priests. The father of Shu'laawi'si carries a vessel of live coals from the house of the personator of Sa'yatäsha. Shu'laawi'si lights the wood at his shrine which is near by with the coals brought by his chosen father and ignites his cedar brand.

After the ceremonies at A'kohanna ti'nakwi the party proceeds in regular order across the plain to I'shäna an te'kĭapoa, Shu'laawi'si lighting with his fire brand each of the six heaps of wood and also the two piles at this knoll. It is midnight before the party reaches He'patina, where prayers are sung. From here they go to the village, and, after announcing the coming of the Sha'läko in four days, those who are to personate the Council of the Gods and the ceremonial father of Shu'laawi'si retire to the house of the personator of Sa'yatäsha and remain there four days in retreat, except when they go each morning for wood, leaving on burros provided for them and returning on foot driving the laden burros. They, too, must observe continence and not look upon the face of a woman during their retreat. On the morning of the arrival of the party from A'kohanna ti'nakwi a member of the governor's staff calls from the house top that all must offer food to the dead. Each member of a family deposits a quantity of food in the flames in the fireplace.

Work is being hurried on the new houses. One of the characteristics of these people is to delay their building until they find it necessary to hurry in order to complete their houses in time.

Each day wagonloads of corn of varieties beautiful in color are brought from the farming districts. Those who are to entertain the personators of the gods are already busy in their homes. While nearly all ceremonies are attended with feasts, there is no other time in Zuñi when festal preparations are made on such a scale as for the Sha'läko festival. In each house that the gods are to dedicate, the women of the house, those of their clan, and those of the clan of the male head of the house are as busy as bees. Sometimes women of the clans of those who are to personate the gods lend helping hands. As many maidens are invited to grind as will form two sets of grinders for the mills. The mills vary from three to eight in number, according to the wealth and pretensions of the family.

The following is a description of a scene witnessed in 1891 in the wealthiest house in Zuñi, in which preparations were being made to entertain the Sha'läko. All preparations for feasts, while more or less elaborate, are virtually the same, being controlled by the same customs.

As there are eight mills in this house, there are sixteen grinders. An aged woman, said to be the only one living[a] who knows the two original grinding songs[b] by heart, sits before the mills and leads the grinders in the song; that is, teaches them the song. While one set of maidens grind, the others dance in the same room to the music of a choir formed of eight young men, one of whom beats on a drum while the others use rattles in accompaniment to the song. The dancers are led by a young man standing in the middle of the line. His dress of cotton trousers and shirt is embellished by a leather belt that has many tiny bells attached. The girls wear their ordinary dress. A crone places in each hand of a dancer as she leaves her seat an ear of corn, which she takes from a basket beside her. She also gives two ears to the male dancer. She repeats a short prayer with each presentation. The dancers form in file up and down the room, the maidens keeping their feet close together and balancing themselves on their toes as they raise their heels. They partly turn their bodies from left to right, moving in a sort of shuffle, as they proceed in an ellipse to the starting point, where they reverse the movement from right to left. The song, in which they join, is a supplication for much rain and bountiful crops. At the close of the dance each maiden returns her corn to the crone, who draws from it a breath and presents it to the lips of the dancers, who also draw the sacred breath from the corn. The grinders, resigning their places at the mills to these girls, repeat the dance, which in this way continues until sunset.

Two aged women are busy before the fireplace in the same room toasting the corn after it has been passed through the first mill, the meal, which is in two bowls, being stirred with bunches of slender sticks. After it is slightly toasted it passes through two more mills, or perhaps three, until it reaches the required fineness, when it is as impalpable as wheat flour. Two women in an adjoining room are busy baking he'we (wafer bread), while in another room stews of mutton, hominy, and chili are simmering in great caldrons. A young mother, with an infant born the night before by her side, sits near the fireplace in the room with the grinders and dancers. All day she stays in the deafening noise of the rattle, the drum, and the song, and must not leave until the close of the feast that follows the dance, by which time she seems thoroughly exhausted and glad to retire to an adjoining room for rest. There is a cessation at midday, when coffee is served, a luxury to be found in such quantity only in a rich man's house. Before sunset the western door of the house is opened, and just as the

---

[a] Since deceased.

[b] The Zuñi priests and others versed in their lore declare there are but two original grinding songs. These were given to the Zuñi when the Corn maidens first danced at Shi'pololo. There are many grinding songs borrowed by the Zuñi from Acoma, Laguna, and other Pueblos at times when the Zuñis were driven to these places by failure of their crops.

last rays of the setting sun sink behind the mountain the grinders and the dancers simultaneously stop and a prayer to the setting sun is offered.

The party is now invited by the hostess of the house and her daughter into the great room, where a feast is spread, bowls of mutton stew, stewed peaches, and baskets of bread being placed along the center of the floor. On each side skins and blankets are spread for the guests to sit upon, and the youths and maidens have a merry time. The vessels are never allowed to become empty; they are speedily replenished by the hostess and her young daughter, who stand by the fireplace, where the large pots are balanced on stones. As each female guest prepares to depart after finishing the meal a large bowl of steaming stew is handed her to carry home. The young men are not so favored. Before leaving the house each guest takes a pinch of ashes from the fireplace in the mill room and passes it three times round the head of the newborn babe, and on leaving the house throws the ashes out with a prayer for the health and long life of the wee one.

When the day of the great festival has arrived Zuñi is astir with anxious expectancy. The streets are carefully swept—an unusual occurrence[a]—and six excavations about 12 inches square and 15 inches deep are made in different sections of the town and one under the ladder way of each house that is to be consecrated. The loose earth is made into a mound beside the opening, and a stone slab large enough to cover it is placed to the west of each excavation. Fires are blazing in every house, which denotes an occasion of importance, these people being most economical of firewood. As the afternoon wanes the house tops become crowded with gaily dressed men and women, not only the Zuñis, but those from other pueblos near and far, for nothing seems to be of such general interest to the Indians, not even the snake ceremonial of the Hopi, as the Sha'läko festival of the Zuñis. Many Navahos, most of them unwelcome guests, but treated nevertheless with courtesy, are scattered about the south front of the village in groups on horseback, all anxious to have the first glimpse of the gods.

The personators of the Council of the Gods and the Sha'läko, with their fellows, leave Zuñi at the rising of the morning star for A'kohanna ti'nawki, where a fire is lighted. They spend the day there and at the Sha'läko house at the base of the knoll, rehearsing prayers and songs. They cross the plain later in the day to the cabin used as the dressing room, to which place the masks and paraphernalia are conveyed under cover of blankets. Masks, when not in use, are stripped of their plumes, and, as the Zuñis have not the art of applying paint so as to make it permanent, they are repainted previous to being worn. The preparation of masks is attended with great solemnity, and only the initiated are present at such times. If anyone chances to

_____

a The streets and houses of Zuñi are kept in much better condition at the present time.

enter the room while the masks are being prepared, he must receive severe chastisement, extending first the right ankle, then the left, then the right arm, and then the left, to be struck with bunches of giant yucca. This is specially necessary in connection with the masks of the Sha'läko, for should they be seen while in course of preparation, and the offender not be punished in the way described, the Sha'läko would surely fall when running. Another danger is when the Navahos force their way too near to the Sha'läko on the ceremonial ground opposite the village. When a Sha'läko falls while running, if one of the preceding reasons can not be given to account for the accident, it is certain that the representative of the god has spoken to some woman, and no personator of this god must speak to a woman from the time he enters Zuñi until he leaves. If such be the case, then the representative of the god receives a severe whipping at the hands of four Sa'yaᵗhlia, each one giving him four severe strokes across his nude back with bunches of giant yucca.ᵃ

The time for this festival is in November, though occurring on different days. The ritual varies but little from year to year, and such few variations as do occur will be mentioned. Scenes from the ceremonials of 1879, 1891, and 1896 will be described.

NIGHT CEREMONIES OF THE COUNCIL OF THE GODSᵇ IN 1879

Shu'laawiᵗsi, preceded by his ceremonial father, leaves A'kohanna ti'nakwi on the afternoon of November 30 for He'patina, the shrine symbolic of the Middle of the world, and deposits te'likinawe in the lower chamber of the shrine.ᶜ After planting the plumes he follows his ceremonial father to the village, crossing a bridge of rock and earth made for the occasion. The ceremonial father of Shu'laawiᵗsi wears white cotton trousers and shirt, held in at the waist by a white embroidered sash tied at the right side, with a dressed deerskin hanging back from his shoulders; a streak of micaceous hematite extends across his nose and under the eyes. He carries a basket tray of te'likinawe, composed of eagle plumes taken from the under side of the tail, and other feathers, a mi'li, and a sacred meal basket, from which he sprinkles meal. Shu'laawiᵗsi, who on the present occasion is a young man,ᵈ is nude, wearing only a small breechcloth. The entire body is colored black and spotted over in yellow, blue, red, and white. The mask (see plate LI) is similarly decorated. A fawn skin filled with seeds, supported by a strap over his shoulder, hangs in front; two cottontail rabbits, with a fringe of rats (neotoma), which are procured by

---

ᵃThe workers on these masks were intruded upon, but the four strokes of the yucca which were allowed to be given allayed their fears of accident.

ᵇSee p. 33. Pau'tiwa and ᵗKïäklo do not appear on this occasion.

ᶜSee p. 201.

ᵈOn two occasions it was observed that Shu'laawiᵗsi was personated by a boy about 10 years of age; at ɔther times an adult filled the place.

Shu'laawiᵗsi's father and paternal uncles, hang over the back. He is adorned with many necklaces of ko'hakwa, coral, and turquoise. He carries te'likinawe in his left hand, and in his right is an unlighted fire-brand of cedar fiber, which has been burning.

As the two proceed through the village Shu'laawiᵗsi sprinkles meal into the six excavations which have been made to receive the prayer plumes; then, preceded by his attending ceremonial father, he recrosses the river and joins the other personators of the Council of the Gods at He'patina. The Council of the Gods on arriving at He'patina are met by the first body of A'shiwanni, the Ko'mosona, the Ko'pekwĭn, and the two Ko'piᶜᵗläshiwanni, who pray and sprinkle the gods with meal. Those who personate the gods deposit te'likinawe in the lower apartment of this shrine.

In a short time Shu'laawiᵗsi returns to the village, preceded as before by his ceremonial father, and is joined on reaching the town by three He'hea gods. There are two styles of He'hea masks, which are colored with the pinkish clay previously referred to. Two masks have a tuft of sheep's wool dyed reddish-brown, with red peppers on the top (see plate LII). The third mask is black with tuft of black sheep's wool (see plate LIII). The lines running from the eyeholes are symbolic of rain and do not, as has been stated, indicate that these gods are weeping. Each mask has a lynx skin at the base. Shu'laawiᵗsi visits each excavation, deposits te'likinawe, and sprinkles meal while he prays. The excavation first visited is in the street on the south side of the village. Here the offerings are made to the u'wannami (rain-makers) of the South; the plume sticks are colored red. The second excavation is also on the river front, but much nearer the eastern side of the village. The plume sticks deposited here are white, for the u'wannami of the East. The third excavation is in the second street from the north of the village, before the ceremonial chamber of the Shu'maakwe fraternity. The fact that the excavation is in front of the house of the Shu'maakwe is not regarded by the writer as having any significance. The sticks deposited here are yellow, for the u'wannami of the North. The next excavation visited is in the large plaza. The sticks deposited here are white, dotted in colors, to the u'wannami of the Zenith. Proceeding to the Si'aa' te'wita, Shu'laawiᵗsi deposits te'likinawe with sticks painted black for the u'wannami of the Nadir, and he plants others with sticks colored blue, for the u'wannami of the West, in an excavation in the He'kĭapawa te'wita on the west side of the village. It will be observed that in this instance the Zuñis have not visited the six regions in the order usually followed—north, west, south, east, zenith, and nadir.

Shu'laawiᵗsi is closely followed by the others of the Council of the Gods, Sa'yatäsha (see plate LIV), his attendant Yä'muhakto (see plate

LV a), Hu′tutu (see plate LV b, c), and his Yä′muhakto (see plate LV a), a Säl′imobiyaᵃ for the Zenith (see plate LVI), and a Säl′imobiya for the Nadir (see plate LVII). Both masks have collarettes of raven's plumes, and ʻHle′lashoktipona (Wood ears). These gods visit each excavation in the same order as that observed by Shu′laawiᵗsi. Sa′yatäsha wears a white cotton shirt, and over the right shoulder, passing under the left arm and falling below his waist, a dressed deerskin almost as white as the shirt. A mi′ha is sometimes folded and worn in place of the deerskin. An embroidered kilt, fastened at the right side, held on with an embroidered sash tied at the right side, is worn under the deerskin. He wears white-dressed deerskin leggings fringed at the sides, dance moccasins, anklets embroidered in porcupine quills, a silver bow wristlet, and a profusion of rare necklaces, to one of which is attached an archaic pendent, a red shell (Spondylus princeps), a portion of the shell being set with turquoise.ᵇ A war pouch is worn beneath the shirt, and a cougar-skin quiver hangs over the back, held on by a broad band of the skin. The dress of Hu′tutu is the same as that of Sa′yatäsha.

Both Sa′yatäsha and Hu′tutu carry bunches of deer scapulæ in the right hand and a bow and arrows and te′likinawe in the left. Among the latter is a miniature ʻsi′kon-ya′munĕ ti′kwanĕ, a game of the Ko′yemshi, consisting of a slender stick and a ring. The ring is the world symbol and also the symbol of longevity. It is large enough to loosely encircle the thumb, and is colored blue for A′wọnawilo′na (see p. 22). A la′showannĕ (one or more plumes attached to cotton cord) is tied to the ring, depending from the stick, which is also blue.

The exposed portions of the bodies of the two Yä′muhakto are dyed purple with the berry of Berberis fremontii. A white dressed deer-

---

ᵃ The above masks and those of the Great Father Ko′yemshi, Pau′tiwa, and Sa′yaᵗhlia were procured in 1896, after years of effort, and deposited in the National Museum. As the Zuñis have no duplicate masks of the Council of the Gods, and as the writer wished these particular masks, she finally induced two priests, whose duty it is to look after them, to duplicate them for her. Those secured are made of rawhide prepared by the priests, and throughout the long process of making and decorating them every ceremony associated with their preparation was religiously observed. In order to obtain these specimens it was necessary for the writer to provide a house about 50 miles away from Zuñi, where the priests could feel entirely safe from intrusion and also where they would not hear a word of "Mexican" spoken. For many years past the Zuñi masks have been made almost exclusively of rawhide prepared in a peculiar manner instead of deerskin, owing to the scarcity of the latter. When the deerskins are secured they are reserved for ceremonial dress. However, it was the good fortune of the writer during her investigations among the Zuñis in 1902 to obtain a mask of ʻKianil′ona (owner of springs), made of deerskin. She obtained also a mask of Ko′mokätsi, great mother of the anthropic gods, ʻChakwena, warrior goddess of the Kiä′nakwe, and several others.

ᵇ The shell has been freed from the thorns or projections and rubbed smooth. About two-thirds of the turquoises replace older ones. The modern work is not nearly so delicate as the original. The cement used in the older work is said to be a preparation of piñon gum, the same as that now in use by the Pueblos. The shell was secured for the United States National Museum. The writer has never seen another with similar setting except the one found by Dr Walter Hough, of the United States National Museum, in Chavez pass, 30 miles south of Winslow, Arizona, during one of Dr Fewkes's archeological expeditions. This rare specimen is in the form of a toad.

The Hopi Indians set turquoises on thin slabs of wood which they use as earrings by boring a hole in the slab and attaching it to the ear by means of a string. The Zuñis wear strings of turquoises in their ears instead of the slabs. These earrings are worn only on ceremonial and dance occasions.

skin hangs from the waist and dance moccasins are worn.   Both carry
a large collection of te′likinawe in each hand, and a ᵗsi′kon-yä′munĕ
tikwanĕ and small deer antlers in the left.   Strings of black and white
stone beads hang across the body over the right shoulder.

Two Säl′imobiya are nude excepting the breechcloth.   They represent the Zenith and Nadir, the one for the Zenith having the upper
portion of the body blocked in the six colors, each block outlined in
black.   The knees and the lower arms to the elbows have the same
decoration; the right upper arm is yellow, the left blue; the right leg
is yellow, the left blue.   Wreaths of spruce are worn around the ankles
and wrists.   The war pouch and many strings of grains of black and
white Indian corn hang over the shoulder, crossing the body.   The
upper half of the body of the Säl′imobiya of the Nadir is yellow and
lower half black; the lower arms and legs and the feet are yellow, the
upper arms and legs black.   He wears anklets and wristlets of spruce,
a war pouch, and strings of black and white corn.   Each of these gods
carries bunches of yucca baccata[a] in each hand with the points held
backward.[b]

ᵗIlle′lashoktipona (wood ears, so called from the serrated projection
of wood on either side of the mask) wears a white embroidered kilt
fastened at the right side with an embroidered sash and a woman's belt.
A fox skin is pendent at the back.   The mask which covers the head
is similar to that of Pau′tiwa; it has black goat's wool hanging over the
back, with two strings of unspun white wool falling over it.   The
mask is wreathed at the base with spruce dotted over with snow-white
popcorn.

The gods proceed to the excavations in the order observed by
Shu′laawiᵗsi.   Sa′yatäsha tramps back and forth by the excavation in
a kind of trot, depositing te′likinawe in the excavation, and then
resuming his step.   Hu′tutu plants his plumes, and resumes his stride.
They both sprinkle meal over the plumes and in the street about the
excavation.   The two Yä′muhakto stamp the meal which has been
sprinkled in the street.   Sa′yatäsha and Hu′tutu pass one another back
and forth.   As they meet, they stop and stamp, crying "Hu′_____
tu tu, hu′_____tu tu, hu tu, hu tu, hu tu, hu tu tu tu."   This is
repeated at each of the six excavations where the plumes are planted.
In the meantime the other gods run and tramp about by the excavations.   After leaving the sixth excavation, they proceed to the house
where they are to spend the night, Shu′laawiᵗsi and his chosen father
preceding the others.   The former plants plumes in the excavation
under the ladder, ascends to the roof, and enters the house through

---

[a] Yucca baccata is also referred to as giant yucca.

[b] In 1896 the Säl′imobiya of the North and West were represented.   The body of the one wearing
a yellow mask for the North was nude except the breechcloth, the lower arms and the legs were colored
yellow, the paint extending 5 inches above the knees.   The body of the one wearing the blue mask
for the West was painted in the same manner, the color being purpish blue, from corn husks.   There
was a wreath of spruce at the base of his mask.   The Säl′imobiya sometimes wear the embroidered
kilt in addition to the breechcloth.

the hatchway. The lower doors leading to the street are barred on
such occasions. The plume planting at the ladder and the other ceremonies are repeated by Sa'yatäsha, Hu'tutu, and the Yä'muhakto, after
which they ascend the ladder.[a]

The first body of A'shiwanni, the Ko'mosona, the Ko'pekwĭn, and
two A'pi'ᵗläshiwanni remain at He'patina to receive the Sha'läko, who
follows after the Council of the Gods; then hasten to the house of the
Kĭa'kwemosi, where the Council of the Gods are closing the ceremonies over the excavation in front of the house.

Crowds have gathered before the Kĭa'kwemosi's house to see the
last of the gods before they retire from the streets. On ascending to
the roof the Council is met by the Kĭa'kwemosi, his wife and
daughters, and the mo'sona (director) of the U'huhukwe (Eagle down)
fraternity (this fraternity having been invited to assist in the ceremonies), who pray and sprinkle meal upon the gods, each member of the
family first sprinkling meal through a small opening in the roof. The
family and the mo'sona, who carries his mi'li and meal basket, precede
the gods to the chamber below.

While the white visitors are hastening to enter a side room in the
hope of reaching the ceremonial chamber, they are ordered by a hundred or more voices to come away. One man, more persistent than
the others, follows, declaring that no American shall enter. The Kĭa'-
kwemosi,[b] hearing the disturbance, leaves the ceremonial chamber by
the side entrance, and, reproving the man in severe words for intrud-
ing upon forbidden ground, escorts the guests to the chamber and
seats them by the altar which stands in the west end of the long room
and then returns to his place with the other A'shiwanni. The altar
(see plate LVIII) shows the following objects:

1, cougar of cream-yellow sandstone; 2, bear of black lava; 3, bison of black lava;
4, badger of red sandstone; 5, white wolf of white quartz; 6, medicine stone 12
inches long and 2 inches in diameter of highly polished lava; 7, bear's foot, with
claws, north side of altar; 8, bear's foot, with claws, and two eagle-wing plumes
south side of altar; 9, flute; 10, sacred meal basket; 11, medicine bowl with two
eagle-wing plumes; 12, food; 13, human image in stone; 14, Apache basket of te'likinawe. The number of mi'wachi[c] at the altar shows the large membership of the
order of O'naya'nakĭa (Mystery medicine) in the U'huhukwe fraternity. The altar
itself is constructed of slabs and tablets of wood. The latter are supported by two
solid bars of wood laid upon the floor. The tablets are surmounted by faces of
Ku'pĭshtaya (lightning-makers), the lower portion of the face symbolizing black
rain clouds. Symbols of cumulus clouds, a bird resting on each, surmount the faces.
The yellow cougär of the North and the red cougar of the South, each having the
heart and the breath line indicated, decorate the two front tablets. Two lightning

---

[a] The entrance of this group of gods into the house and the ceremonies within are always the same
in their main features. Elaborate preparations were made for the reception of these gods in 1879 in
the dwelling of the Kĭa'kwemosi.

[b] Too much can not be said in praise of this Kĭa'kwemosi, who has since died. In dignity, courtesy, and graciousness he could not be surpassed by any civilized man, and the writer owes him a
debt of gratitude for his aid, which was at all times cheerfully given, in acquiring knowledge of the
most sacred rites of the Zuñis.

[c] See p. 416.

symbols, carved of wood, stand between the front and back tablets. The lower slab is carved with symbols of cumulus clouds, the sun, and the morning and evening stars. The slab above shows black rain clouds, with white clouds beyond. The upper slab represents the rainbow. The yellow face of the moon surrounded by the house of the clouds designed in black and white blocks rises above the rainbow. Ä′chiyäla′topa (the being with wings and tail of knives) and the figure of the star of the four winds are suspended above the altar. An eagle's tail plume is attached to the point of each star, which is decorated with cumulus clouds and the house of the clouds. The blue-green color of the altar symbolizes the firmament (see page 24).

A line of meal extends from the altar to the ladder on the south side of the room and thence to the east end. This line is crossed in three places at intervals of 3 feet, each cross line being about 15 inches long. A number of finely dressed deerskins lying one upon the other are on the floor north of the altar. The ledge on the north side of the room at the west end is covered with robes and blankets upon which the gods sit.

A number of members of the U′huhukwe fraternity, forming a choir, are grouped on the south side of the room near the west end. The flutist of the fraternity sits back of the altar. The A′shiwanni stand in line and sprinkle the gods as they pass up the line of meal to the altar. The Kĭa′kwemosi and pe′kwĭn each hold a flat basket. Shu′laawi⁺si empties the contents of his fawn skin into the basket of the pe′kwĭn and lays the rabbits and rats over the basket. Each of the other gods in order removes a quantity of seeds from his belt and deposits them in the basket held by the Kĭa′kwemosi. The two A′shi′wanni wave their baskets to the six regions and deposit them before the altar. Sa′yatäsha and Hu′tutu stamp back and forth as they did about the excavations. In a short time Sa′yatäsha takes meal from his belt and with it marks four lines on the north wall of the chamber by running his four fingers downward. Yä′muhakto runs his bunch of yucca downward over the lines. Sa′yatäsha and Yä′muhakto repeat the same action on the west, south, and east walls. After marking of the walls, Sa′yatäsha mounts a low platform arranged in the middle of the room and attaches te′likinawe—one blue for the Sun Father, the other yellow for the Moon Mother—wrapped together at the ends, to a unique device carved of wood and painted in various colors and secured to one of the rafters. This little structure, the making of which is not restricted to any special person, is symbolic of the house of the clouds and is to be found in every house which has been blessed at the Sha′läko festival.[a] During the placing of the te′likinawe the choir sing to the accompaniment of the rattle and drum, the flutist plays back of the altar, and a warrior of the fraternity stands before it and whirls the rhombus.[b]

[a] On this occasion it is made by the brother of the pe′kwĭn's wife.

[b] In 1896 the Council of the Gods met in the pe′kwĭn's house, where a ladder held by six men was used instead of the platform, an evidence of improvement in Zuñi house structure, these walls being much higher. The ambition of the Zuñis is to have one very large room with a high ceiling in the dwelling, and the houses are improved in this respect from year to year.

The plumes are placed, with prayers for rains, good crops, health and long life to the family of the house, and all good which can come to man through the pure breath of the breath of life, the breath of A'wonawil'ona, who pervades all space.   As Sa'yatäsha steps from the platform, Yä'muhakto takes his place and sprinkles the te'likinawe with meal, the other gods shaking their rattles at this time.   Yä'muhakto is followed by the others, who sprinkle the te'likinawe with meal, and pray, after which Sa'yatäsha deposits offerings through a circular opening about 4 inches in diameter, beneath the stone floor directly under the cage, the excavation being as deep as the length of a man's arm to the elbow.   These circular openings are symbolic of the entrance tó A'witĕn te'hula (fourth world) and are so carefully covered, when not open for such occasions as described, that one would not suspect their existence.   A diminutive game of ᵗsi'kon-yä'munĕ ti'kwanĕ with la'showawe attached, grains of corn of the colors of the six regions, sweet corn, squash, watermelon, and muskmelon seeds are deposited as seeds in the earth, the offerings placed below being symbolic of the seeds of life, those placed above of life itself. Prayers are offered for the seeds to grow into life, and for rains, much corn, and that the children of the house may grow to manhood and womanhood without disease; may grow old, not die, but sleep to awake in Ko'thluwala'wa.   After every god has sprinkled meal into the opening and prayed, the music of the choir and flute ceases and the warrior lays away his rhombus.   Sa'yatäsha and each god in succession stands with the left foot on a small package wrapped in corn husks and prays that their enemies may succumb to their children, and they again stamp about the floor before taking seats.   Each god is seated on the north side of the chamber by the Kïa'kwemosi, who places his hands on the shoulder of each one, beginning with the Sa'yatäsha, and motions him to the six regions.   Shu'laawiᵗsi remains on the floor a short time after the others.   The following diagram gives the position of the first body of A'shiwanni and gods as they are seated vis-a-vis:

1	Ceremonial father of Shu'laawiᵗsi, seated next to the altar.		
2	Shu'laawiᵗsi	2¹	Shi'wanni of the Zenith (sun priest)
3	Sa'yatäsha	3¹	Shi'wanni of the North (Kïa'kwemosi)
4	Yä'muhakto	4¹	Associate Shi'wanni of the North
5	Hu'tutu	5¹	Shi'wanni of the West
6	Yä'muhakto	6¹	Shi'wanni of the South
7	'Hle'lashoktipona	7¹	Shi'wanni of the East
8	Säl'imobiya	8¹	Shi'wanni of the Nadir and elder brother Bow priest
9	Säl'imobiya	9¹	Younger brother Bow priest
10	Ko'mosona		
11	Ko'pekwïn		
12	Ko'piᵗᵗläshiwanni		
13	Ko'piᵗᵗläshiwanni		

The two baskets are removed from the altar and held by the Kĭa′kwemosi and pe′kwĭn, while prayers are offered. The pe′kwĭn passes his basket by the Kĭa′kwemosi to the associate Shi′wanni of the North, and the Kĭa′kwemosi passes his basket to the Shi′-wanni of the West, and in this order the baskets are passed down the line. One basket is not passed over the other, but around and before it. As each shi′wanni receives a basket he draws a breath of the contents and prays for much rain, all seeds, rats, rabbits, and other game. The gods say: "To-morrow I go to Ko′thluwala′wa, but I leave my children [referring to other gods] with you for five days. They will dance in your houses [the new ones]; they will then go to the homes of the gods in the east, where they will spend one night and leave te′likinawe, which you shall give to them, and they will return to Ko′thluwala′wa. Give us food that we may eat, and next year we will bring you all kinds of seeds." The pe′kwĭn passes to the end of the line of A′shiwanni, receives the basket containing the gifts of Shu′laawi′si, places it before the altar, and, returning, receives the basket containing the gift of Sa′yatäsha, and places it beside the other. The rats and rabbits are offerings to the host. They are cooked by the women of the house and eaten as delicious tidbits by the A′shiwanni and others in the morning after the sunrise ceremony.

A young man clad in pure white, with a red silk scarf around his head, sits by the large fire holding a rod of cottonwood root, with which he furnishes light for the ceremonial reed cigarettes, which are constantly smoked by the personators of the gods and A′shiwanni.

For two hours a litany is intoned in low notes by the gods and responded to by the A′shiwanni while two members of the A′pi‘′läshi-wanni (Bow priesthood) stand before the altar and whirl rhombi. There is much repetition in the prayer, at the close of which the six A′shiwanni take their seats near the fire and the personators of the gods remove tneir masks and place them upon the dressed deerskins. Afterward fifty-six large bowls filled with meat stew, containing corn, beans, and chili, several varieties of bread, stewed peaches, and sliced watermelons are brought in by women and placed in lines down the north side of the room; for the want of space, some are placed on the opposite side. After the food is set down, the wife of the Kĭa′kwemosi, accompanied by a male member of her family (filling the place of the host, who must remain with the A′shi-wanni), advances to the altar, the man preceding the woman. He wears cloth trousers, a red calico shirt, a red silk scarf around his head, and another around his waist. The woman wears her ordinary dress, with the white pi′toni, a piece tied in front and falling over the back. After sprinkling meal upon the altar they turn toward the food, and the man in half whispers offers a long grace. Every

DEERSKIN HOOD OF THE SHA'LÄKO, GIANT COURIER GODS OF THE RAIN
MAKERS

NAI'UCHI PERFORMING A FEAT IN LEGERDEMAIN

a MASK OF GOD ACCOMPANYING HE'MISHIKWE b,c MASKS OF GODDESSES
ACCOMPANYING HE'MISHIKWE FRONT AND REAR VIEWS

MILI (EAR OF CORN COVERED WITH PLUMES) INSIGNIA OF
THE ORDER OF O'NAYA'NA̱KIA (LIFE GIVERS)

little while the woman repeats in a most impressive manner: "Athlä" (amen). The grace is repeated over the food on the south side of the room, and, addressing the people, the two say: "I'tonawe" (eat). The Shu'laawi^tsi, taking from one of the bowls a piece of he'we as big as his two hands, places upon it a bit of food from each vessel and disappears through the hatchway in the roof, followed by Sa'yatäsha and Hu'tutu. The large assemblage now revels in the feast.

Shu'laawi^tsi deposits the food in the excavation under the ladder before the house, Sa'yatäsha plants plumes in the opening and scatters meal, and Hu'tutu stamps upon the meal about the excavation. The prayers offered by the gods at this time are uttered in tones so low that it is impossible to hear a word. The excavation is afterward covered with a slab and with earth until no evidence of it remains.

The three gods return to the chamber and join in the feast. After all the food is consumed, the empty vessels are removed. The personators of the Council of the Gods having donned their masks, Sa'yatäsha and Hu'tutu stride up and down the floor until the rising of the morning star, after which Sa'yatäsha and the pe'kwĭn proceed to the roof, where they remain half an hour, chanting a prayer.

Returning to the room, they approach the altar side by side. The pe'kwĭn carries a meal basket and throws meal before them as they proceed up the room. Sa'yatäsha carries his bow and arrows in his left hand and a rattle of deer scapulæ in his right. On reaching the altar the two sprinkle it with meal and, turning about, slowly retrace their steps, repeating the prayer they chanted on the house top as they stride up and down the long room three times, Sa'yatäsha with every step waving the scapulæ downward. They halt midway for some thirty minutes until the close of the prayer, when Sa'yatäsha places his right foot forward, facing east, and extends his right hand toward the eastern heavens and his left backward and toward the earth; at the same time he sprinkles meal from both hands. This motion is repeated by the pe'kwĭn, and then Sa'yatäsha turns to the choir, repeats a prayer, and, going to the altar, offers a short prayer, which concludes the all-night ceremonial.

The mask is removed by an attendant and placed on the deerskins by the altar. A morning repast similar to the one spread during the night is enjoyed, and the personators of the gods rest and sleep until nearly 10 o'clock in the morning, when the ceremonies are resumed.

It has been stated that the Sha'läko are met on the opposite side of the river by the first body of A'shiwanni, the Ko'mosona, and the Ko'pekwĭn, who pray and sprinkle meal upon the gods. Each Sha'läko goes to the house he is to dedicate.

Night Ceremonies of the Sha'läko Gods in 1891.[a]

Before sunset the altar of 'Sän'iakĭakwe (Hunters Fraternity) was erected at the west end of the large room. (Plate LIX shows altar divested of its accessories.) The mo'sona of the fraternity prays over a bowl of meal and proceeds to make a cloud design of meal before the altar. The symbol is formed by making two scallops and filling them in with meal. A line of meal is extended from between the scallops a short distance, and the mo'sona places six mi'wachi in line between the two front tablets of the altar. He afterward continues the line of meal down the floor to the ladder and crosses it with the meal eleven times, the cross lines being about 3 feet apart. He then places the meal basket by the altar. The maker of medicine water consecrates the water with the usual ritual. The chamber is now ready to receive the gods.

The effigy worn by the Sha'läko is so ingeniously arranged that the wearer has only to step under the hoop-skirt structure and carry it by a slender pole, which is supported by a piece of leather attached to the belt. The top of the blanket skirt has a triangular opening through which the bearer of the effigy sees. A fox skin and a collarette of raven plumes complete the base of the mask. The personator of the Sha'läko and his fellow wear deerskin hoods (see plate LX) and white cotton shirts with native black woven shirts over them. The open sleeves of the wool shirts, which are fastened only at the wrists, expose the white sleeves beneath. They wear black woven kilts, embroidered in dark blue. White dressed deerskins having the appearance of sleeveless jackets are wrapped about the body. Each wears a white embroidered sash, and around the waist, over the deerskin, a woman's belt tied at the right side. An ancient stone hatchet, with handle, and a quantity of prayer meal are carried in the belt. The legs are bare and painted yellow, the color extending above the knees. They wear bunches of native blue yarn tied in tassels below the knees and dance moccasins.

The effigies are not carried by the personators of the Sha'läko when these gods come to the village in the evening, but by the Sha'läko wor'we (managers), who also have their legs painted yellow and wear dance moccasins. Each personator of a Sha'läko and his fellow, with other members of the ki'wi'sinĕ to which the personator of the Sha'läko belongs, accompany each effigy. The six Sha'läko, with their attendants, stop on the site of Häl'ona kwi (Ant place). Here they are met by the first body of A'shiwanni, who pray and sprinkle meal over the gods. The A'shiwanni return to the village and the Sha'läko run back and forth for a time, then proceed to the ceremonial ground, situated on the south bank of the river, already prepared

---

[a] The writer was unable to observe the indoor ceremonies of the Sha'läko gods in 1879, as she was housed with the Council of the Gods.

for them which was the last camping place of the Zuñis during their migrations in quest of the Middle of the world. This ground which is about 200 feet from north to south and 150 feet from east to west has been watered and stamped until it is level and smooth. Two Sha'läko stand on the left and two on the east side of the ground, while the other two run back and forth, starting from opposite sides, and return. Each Sha'läko takes his turn in running. They remain on the ground until after dark, then proceed to the village, each Sha'läko, with his attendants, going to the house where he is to remain during the night. On reaching the house the personator of the Sha'läko, not the present bearer of the effigy, deposits te'likinawe in the excavation under the ladder. His alternate repeats the act, and both sprinkle meal while the effigy bearer and others stand by, the attendants singing to the accompaniment of the rattle. As they ascend the ladder the rattle, drum, and song are heard within. The attendants remain on the roof and sing, while the effigy bearer, the personator of the Sha'läko, with his fellow, descend into the house. They are led by the master of the house, his wife and daughters, and the mo'sona of the fraternity which is to officiate, who carries his mi'li and his meal basket, from which he sprinkles meal as he proceeds. The room in which the ceremony here described is held is 60 feet long and over 20 feet wide. The maker of medicine water sits by a medicine bowl at the north side of the altar. The members of the fraternity are grouped on the south side of the room toward the west end. As the Sha'läko and party enter the room the effigy bearer, with the personator of Sha'läko and his fellow, pass to the west end of the room, where the figure is placed on a blanket rug north of the altar, there being a small circular opening in the stone floor to hold the pole to which it is attached. A large blanket is held so as to screen the figure while the bearer slips out and stands it in position. While the effigy is being placed by the Sha'läko wor'li, the personator of the Sha'läko, deposits seeds, a gift to the host, from his belt into a basket by the altar, and he also takes meal, from his belt and marks four lines on each wall—north, west, south, and east—by carrying the meal with his four fingers 2 feet down each wall. His alternate follows and strikes the meal lines four times with a bunch of giant yucca. A ladder is now held by five men, and the personator of the Sha'läko ascends and repeats the ceremony of Sa'yatäsha, attaching two te'likinawe to the symbolic house of the clouds that is fastened to the rafters. The choir of the Hunters fraternity, accompanied by rattles and drum, the flutist playing and a warrior of the fraternity whirling a rhombus, begins as soon as the personator of the Sha'läko steps upon the first rung of the ladder. The depositing of offerings in the floor beneath and the act of standing on the corn-husk package is also repeated here. His alternate follows each time and sprinkles meal, and the maker of medicine water beats time with two eagle plumes that he holds in each hand.

After this ceremony the personator of the Sha'läko and his alternate seat themselves by the male head of the house in the same manner as in the seating of the Council of the Gods, and repeat, in substance, the same litany. The Sha'läko, too, says: "I leave my children with you for five days. They will dance in your houses; they will then go to the home of the gods in the east and leave te'likinawe which you shall give to them, and they will return to Ko'thluwala'wa. Give us food that we may eat, and next year we will bring you all kinds of seeds." When the prayer closes the maker of medicine water dips his plumes into the water and sprinkles toward the north. This is repeated for each of the six regions. Again dipping the plumes into the water, he touches them to the lips of the personator of the Sha'-läko. The same is repeated with the alternate, who now rises and dances for a time, when he is joined by four members of the Hunters fraternity, who are nude except as to breechcloths. The personator of the Sha'läko slips into the effigy, behind a blanket, then the blanket is dropped and the giant god joins in the dance. He is observed by all present with the most solemn interest. Although the walls of this chamber are the highest in Zuñi, the man bearing the effigy is compelled to dance with bended knees, which he does with much difficulty. As he can not peep through the opening in the blanket, constant attention is required on the part of the attendant to prevent such accidents as stumbling, falling down, or knocking against others.

The six ki'wi⁺siwe furnish dancers to assist in the great celebration. Each director of a dance vies with the other in having his dancers perfect in the dance and song. Each personator of a god is supposed to⋅ have the spirit of the god he represents abiding with him for the time being. "Have the gods not said: 'We will all be with you in the spirit?'" When the visiting dancers are absent from the house the Sha'läko dances.

The Sha'läko houses are crowded at all times during the night. Each set of dancers is followed from house to house by a number of men, who pack the already overfilled chamber, leaving barely space enough for the dancers, and hang on to the inner ladder as long as there is standing room. Every one who enters the room, except the dancers, goes immediately to the altar and effigy to pray and sprinkle meal, passing the line of dancers for this purpose.

Zuñi, like more civilized places, has its exclusive set, and at no time is this more in evidence than at festivals, some women especially holding themselves aloof from others, whom they esteem less fortunate. Here also are many whose birth would justify but whose poverty prevents the exclusiveness in which they would indulge, their houses not being sufficiently spacious when ceremonials are held. In the present instance this, the largest house in Zuñi, has a private hallway and several inner rooms where the elect gather to observe the ceremonies through large openings in the wall, which are kept closed except on such occasions. Thus with this primitive drama there is to be found a primitive theater, with pit and boxes. The observers who watch through the openings are principally women and children, seated on chairs and boxes. If there be attractive maidens in these inner rooms, young men are sure to be found there, indulging in merrymaking with the girls in the intervals of the dances. The custom among men of visiting the theater box may have originated with the primitive drama. There are also in these rooms men seated on the ledge or on their wadded blankets on the far side of the room smoking and chatting in company with the male members of the house. They take turns in advancing to the openings to observe the dance over the women's heads or to spend a time in the ceremonial room. Such are the scenes early in the evening; but as the night advances drinking is indulged in until the scene becomes disgusting in the extreme. No whisky is served in the ceremonial chamber, and great care is observed that none but Indians shall know the sources of the intoxication.

In 1879 whisky was rarely if ever used by the Zuñis; but with the advance of civilization intoxicants are producing demoralizing effects on these people. While there is a law forbidding the sale of liquor to Indians, this law is not executed; at least it was not up to 1896. The peddling of whisky is begun weeks before the Sha'läko festival. The liquor is usually carried in kegs, not too large to be secreted under the blanket, and gallons are brought in this way to Zuñi by the Rio Grande Indians. The largest peddler of whisky during several seasons was a returned Carlisle student, who had spent five years under the influences of this school. When discovered by the writer his excuse was: "I am a saddler by trade. On my return from school I endeavored to get employment in Albuquerque, near my home—Laguna. On applying to the two saddlers there I received the same reply from both: 'White men are good enough for me.' What was I to do? You know my people make their own harness and saddles. I wanted money, so I engaged to carry whisky to Zuñi for a German." This Indian could not be induced to betray the name of the lawbreaker.

Every man in Zuñi spends what money he can obtain on whisky, not only for his own use and that of his friends, but to dispose to the Navahos, who come in large numbers to the dances. The whisky is usually taken from the kegs, bottled, and sold at exorbitant prices. The Navaho is a close trader, but the Zuñi is closer. The writer has observed many trades in which the Zuñis came out the better. One Navaho, crazy for liquor, trades a fine pony for a gill of whisky. Another exchanges a valuable necklace of coral, turquoise, and ko'hakwa for the same quantity. Those who are able to buy the liquor in any quantity usually make use of the time of the Sha'läko festival to replenish their stock of horses from the Navahos, who demand fair prices in their early stage of intoxication, but become so crazed with drink that they let their ponies go for any amount of whisky the shrewd Zuñi is willing to give. While the younger men of Zuñi drink as much as the Navahos, the older men and more clever traders keep their heads clear enough to get the best of the bargain. This trading of liquor goes on in the inner rooms, which are supposed, as has been stated, to be for the use of the elect; but the Zuñis, being no exception to those who are demoralized by the liquor traffic, indulge their love of gain at any cost, and send out emissaries from these inner rooms to bring in those who wish the liquor. The drunker the man the more eager the emissary is to get him, as he is sure that the trade will be in favor of those of his house.

After each dance the participants have medicine water administered to them with a shell from the bowl by the maker of medicine water. These dancers are no sooner outside of the house than the Sha'läko appears on the floor.

Dancing is suspended at midnight, when an elaborate feast is spread, in which those present indulge to the fullest extent. This supper is served with the same ceremonies as those observed over the feast in the house of the Sa'yatäsha, food being deposited under the ladder outside of the house by the personator of the Sha'läko and his alternate. After the feast the dance continues until daylight, when the ceremonies close to be resumed at a later hour in the morning.

NIGHT CEREMONIES OF THE KO'YEMSHI IN 1896

In 1896 the ten Ko'yemshi as usual closely follow the Sha'läko on their arrival at the village. They wear white cotton trousers, white dressed deer skins, or white embroidered blankets wrapped about them, and ordinary moccasins. Each one carries a fawn skin containing seed, the skin being sewed for the purpose. A miniature gaming ring of the Ko'yemshi, with a la'showannĕ attached, hangs from the mouth of the fawn skin carried by the Great Father Ko'yemshi, pe'kwĭn, and Pi'ᵘläshiwanni of the Ko'yemshi. Each carries a gourd rattle colored pink. They form into a group at the base of the outer ladder of each house entertaining a Sha'läko and sing. Now and then a joke is passed between them. After their tour through the village they go to the house which they are to dedicate. The Great Father Ko'yemshi deposits te'likinawe in the excavation under the ladder and his pe'kwĭn sprinkles meal over them. Ascending the ladder they are met by the master of the house, his wife, and daughters, and the director of the Ma'ᵗke 'San'nakwe (Little Fire) fraternity, who precede them to the room where the choir of the fraternity is singing to the accompaniment of the rattle and drum. This room, contrary to the Zuñi method of building, extends north and south. The altar, which is most elaborate—this fraternity being one of the largest and wealthiest organizations in Zuñi—is in the north end of the long room. The fraternity is grouped on the east side. The Ko'yemshi, led by the director of the fraternity, are sprinkled with meal as they proceed down the room. Each Ko'yemshi empties the contents of his fawn skin into a basket by the altar as a gift to the host of the house. The Great Father takes meal from his belt, and with it runs his four fingers down each wall of the room, beginning with the north wall. His pe'kwĭn follows and strikes the lines with a bunch of yucca baccata.

A ladder is held by six men while the Great Father ascends and attaches two te′likinawe to the symbol of the house of the clouds. When he descends the pe′kwĭn goes up the ladder and sprinkles meal over it and the plumes. The deposition of plumes and seeds, the sprinkling of meal in an opening beneath the floor, and the standing upon a package covered with corn husks are repeated, with prayers similar to those offered by those dedicating the other houses.

The Ko′yemshi are seated by the master of the house, who places his hands on the shoulders of each god, motioning him to the six regions before seating him. The Ko′yemshi sit in line on the west side of the room, and ten men of the Pi′chikwe (Dogwood) and Tä′kiakwe (Frog) clans, the master of the house being of the former clan, his wife belonging to the latter, sit opposite the Ko′yemshi, as shown in the following diagram:

Ko′yemshi		Vis-a-vis	
1	A′wan tä′ᵗchu	1¹	Man of the house
2	Pe′kwĭn	2¹	Tä′kĭakwe (Frog clan)
3	Pi′ᵘläshiwanni	3¹	Pi′chikwe (Dogwood clan)
4	E′shoᶦsi	4¹	Pi′chikwe (Dogwood clan)
5	Mu′ÿapona	5¹	Pi′chikwe (Dogwood clan)
6	Po′soᶦki	6¹	Tä′kĭakwe (Frog clan)
7	Na′thläshi	7¹	Pi′chikwe (Dogwood clan)
8	It′sepäsha	8¹	Pi′chikwe (Dogwood clan)
9	ᶜKĭä′luᶦsi	9¹	Tä′kĭakwe (Frog clan)
10	Sa′thläshi	10¹	Tä′kĭakwe (Frog clan)

Ten sticks for holding live coals are made from the center stalks of giant yucca by a man of Pi′chikwe clan, each stick being the length of the bended elbow on the inner side to the tip of the middle finger. After the men and gods are seated vis-a-vis, a coal of fire is placed between the split ends of each of the fire sticks by the man who made them and passed to the ten men, each man lighting a reed cigarette filled with native tobacco. These cigarettes are prepared by the male head of the house. Each one takes six whiffs from his cigarette and waves it to the six regions, and whirling it in a circle he passes it to his vis-a-vis, who repeats the smoking and waving. The masks of the Ko′yemshi are now put back so as to expose the face.

The Great Father consumes two hours reciting a litany. The others, including those opposite, respond: "A′thlu" (amen). This prayer is much the same as those repeated in the other houses, differing only according to the different versions of the Sa′yatäsha, the Sha′läko, and Ko′yemshi concerning the migrations of the A′shiwi from Ko′thluwala′wa. The Ko′yemshi also say: "I leave my children with you for five days; they will dance in your houses; they will then go to the home of the gods in the east and leave te′likinawe which you shall give them, and they will return to Ko′thluwala′wa. Give us food that we may eat, and next year we will bring you all kinds of seeds."

A feast is served after the long prayer, and a smoke with commercial tobacco is enjoyed. The Ko'yemshi, on finishing their smoke, begin dancing. Each one holds two te'likinawe, as long as from the inner side of the bend of the elbow to the tip of the middle finger, wrapped together at the end, one stick being colored blue for the Sun Father, the other yellow for the Moon Mother. After dancing some time in a promiscuous group to the song of the Little Fire fraternity, all but the Great Father, his pe'kwĭn, and Pi'ꞌꞋläshiwanni visit the houses of the Sha'läko and dance. During their absence the members of the fraternity, who have their nude bodies elaborately decorated in white with kaolin, continue dancing. The dancing begins in earnest after midnight, each man seeming to throw his whole soul into it.

MORNING CEREMONIES OF THE SHA'LÄKO IN 1891.

Morning brings an additional influx of visitors. Every house of any pretensions has guests, welcome or otherwise; nearly every pueblo is represented, and large numbers of Navahos are here to enjoy the lavish hospitality of the Zuñis. The house tops on the south side of the village are crowded with men, women, and children, while the streets are filled with pedestrians and equestrians, many being Navahos of both sexes.

It would be difficult to find a more revolting picture than the one presented during the day and night. The scene of debauchery in the morning is shocking, but as the day wanes it becomes disgusting in the extreme. The mad desire for drink among many of the Zuñis is too great for them to remain sober enough to observe the ceremonial of their gods, to which they have looked forward for many days. Many of these staggering Indians are not over 14 or 15 years of age. Numbers of Navahos are fighting with one another or with the Pueblos, drawing knives and pistols. The wonder is that some of the disturbers of the peace are not trampled to death, for many fall from their saddles during their quarrels; others lie motionless in the streets, too drunk to move away from approaching hoofs. Native police are kept busy in their efforts to quell disturbances and to clear the streets for the processions.

Before midday the first Sha'läko with his retinue comes forth from the house where he spent the night. The participants in this procession are, first, the members of the order of Pa'yatämu (god of music), ten in number; next those of the Little Fire fraternity. Each man plays upon his sho'konna (flute) which is as long as the muzzle of a gun. The noise from these instruments is deafening. This group is followed by an officer of the fraternity carrying his mi'li,[a] and meal basket, from which he sprinkles meal. He leaves his position now and then to sprinkle meal on the Sha'läko of his party. The alternate of

---

a See p. 416.

the Sha'läko follows next, carrying a quantity of te'likinawe; and after him comes the Sha'läko.   Thirty or more members of the ki'wi'sinĕ to which the personator of the Sha'läko belongs follow later, singing, the four Sha'läko wor'we (managers) being foremost in the group.   As the Sha'läko passes through the village those on the house tops throw meal upon the effigy, while both sober and intoxicated men crowd forward to sprinkle the gods with meal.   The procession crosses the river to the south bank.

After the first Sha'läko crosses the river with his retinue, another follows, attended in like manner by the order of Pa'yatämu belonging to the Pe'shä'silo'kwe (Cimex) fraternity.   The other Sha'läko are

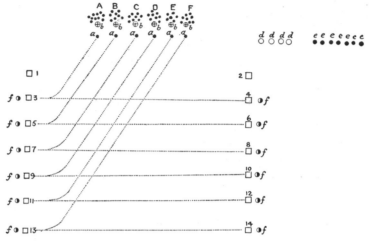

FIG. 8—a, personators of Sha'läko with effigies; b, alternates of the Sha'läko; A, B, C, D, E, F, groups from the ki'wi'siwe; d, Ko'mosona, Ko'pekwïn, and two Ko'pi·'läshiwanni; e, first body of A'shiwanni; f, Sha'läko managers; 1, 2, square excavations in which the Council of the Gods deposit te'likinawe; 3, 4, 5, 6, 7, 8, 9, 10, 11, 12, 13, 14, square excavations in which the Sha'läko deposit te'likinawe.   The ki'wi'siwe a are paired as elder and younger brother, and the excavations are visited in the following order: A, People of the He'iwa ki'wi'sinĕ; B, people of the Mu'he'wa ki'wi'sinĕ; C, people of the Chu'pawa ki'wi'sinĕ; D, people of the O'he'wa ki'wi'sinĕ; E, people of the Up'sannawa ki'wi'sinĕ; F, people of the He'kïapawa ki'wi'sinĕ; 3, 4, excavation for the Sha'läko of He'iwa ki'wi'sinĕ (elder); 9, 10, excavation for the Sha'läko of O'he'wa ki'wi'sinĕ (younger); 5, 6, excavation for the Sha'läko of Mu'he'wa ki'wi'sinĕ (elder); 13, 14, excavation for the Sha'läko of He'kïapawa ki'wi'sinĕ (younger); 7, 8, excavation for the Sha'läko of Chu'pawa ki'wi'sinĕ (elder); 11, 12, excavation for the Sha'läko of Up'sannawa ki'wi'sinĕ (younger).

attended in the same way except that they have no order of Pa'yatämu to furnish music.   The Sha'läko parties follow each other in close succession.   Plate LXI shows a Sha'läko on his way to the ceremonial field.[b]   Upon reaching the ceremonial ground above referred to, the bearers of the effigies stoop on blanket rugs and face the village, six blankets having been spread for the purpose in line from east

---

[a] The ki'wi'siwe are relegated to the six regions, as follows: He'iwa (North), Mu'he'wa (West), Chu'pawa (South), O'he'wa (East), Up'sannawa (Zenith), He'kïapawa (Nadir).

[b] Formerly, temporary bridges of stones and earth were constructed, but in 1896 the bridge built for the use of the writer became the way of crossing the river, not only for the people at large but for the personators of the gods until carried away by a freshet.

to west, their fellows standing back of them, and behind each fellow the group from the ki'wi^tsinĕ to which the Sha'läko belongs. In addition to these groups two of the Sha'läko have the flutists of the order of Pa'yatämu behind them. The Ko'mosona, the Ko'pekwĭn, and the two Ko'pi"^tläshiwanni stand in line immediately west of the Sha'läko, and the first body of A'shiwanni, not including the Shi'wano'ʻkĭa, and first associate to the Kĭa'kwemosi are in line west of these. The accompanying diagram (figure 8, page 257) shows the positions of the Sha'läko and other participants on the ceremonial ground.

The excavations, which are each 12 inches square, are made after the Sha'läko take positions on the rugs. Of these, 12 are made by the Sha'läko wor'we, who remain back of the excavations, ready to rearrange the paraphernalia of the Sha'läko when necessary. The two excavations at the south end of the ground are made by a wor'li from the ki'wi^tsinĕ to which the personator of the Sa'yatäsha belongs. The Sha'läko are in position before the Ko'mosona with his associates and the first body of A'shiwanni take their places. The Council of the Gods, Shu'laawi^tsi going in advance, follow after the Sha'läko. (Plate LXII shows Shu'laawi^tsi preceded by his ceremonial father.[a] Plate LXIII shows other members of the Council of the Gods.) The personator of Shu'laawi^tsi passes up the east line of exacavations and deposits te'likinawe to Shu'laawi^tsi in excavation 1 and, passing before the line of Sha'läko, he deposits similar offerings in excavation 2. Passing down the west line of excavations and up the east line, he sprinkles meal over the te'likinawe in excavation 1; again crossing to the west, he sprinkles meal over the offerings in excavation 2, and, passing by the A'shiwanni, he retires from the ceremonial ground. Sa'yatäsha and his Yä'muhakto and Hu'tutu with his Yä'muhakto proceed up the east line of the excavations. Sa'yatäsha with his Yä'muhakto cross before the Sha'läko to excavation 2, where they deposit te'likinawe to these gods. Hu'tutu with his Yä'muhakto deposit te'likinawe at the same time in excavation 1. Sa'yatäsha and his Yä'muhakto continue down the west line, and, crossing the ground, they pass up the east line and deposit te'likinawe in excavation 1. Hu'tutu with his Yä'muhakto deposit te'likinawe in excavation 2 and then pass down the west line and up the east. While Sa'yatäsha and his associate cross over to excavation 2 and sprinkle the offerings with meal, Hu'tutu and his associate sprinkle the offerings in excavation 1. The two couples exchange places by crossing directly before the Sha'läko. Sa'yatäsha and his Yä'muhakto sprinkle meal into excavation 1 while Hu'tutu and his Yä'muhakto sprinkle it into excavation 2. The two couples now meet midway in the line of Sha'läko and face the village, Yä'muhakto to the east, Sa'yatäsha next, Hu'tutu next, and the other Yä'muhakto at the west end of the line. Sa'yatäsha cries "Hu‑‑‑‑‑‑‑, hu‑‑‑‑‑‑‑, hu‑‑‑‑‑‑,

---

[a] "Ko'thluwala'wa" on the plate is an error. For "deputy" see p. 33.

hu_____, hu_____." The couples cross, Sa′yatäsha and his alternate
going to excavation 2, while the others go to excavation 1. They bend
and motion over the excavations, and again they meet midway in the
line of Sha′läko and face the village. Sa′yatäsha is now west of Hu′tutu
and beside him. Hu′tutu exclaims: "Hu′tutu_____, Hu′tutu_____,
Hu′tutu_____, Hu′tutu_____." The four now pass in file down the
east line to the north side of the ground, where they are joined by two
Säl′imobiya, who run back and forth over the north end of the ground
during the ceremony of the Council of the Gods. The Council of the
Gods return up the east line of excavations, followed by the two Säl′i-
mobiya, and pass by the Sha′läko and on by the Ko′mosona, Ko′pe-
kwĭn, the two Ko′piᵗläshiwanni and the A′shiwanni. Each shi′wanni
holds a basket of prayer meal, from which he sprinkles the gods as
they pass. The Ko′mosona, with his associates, and the A′shiwanni
leave the field in company with the Council of the Gods. The two
Säl′imobiya soon return to their former place and repeat the running
back and forth. The Ko′mosona, with his associates, and the A′shi-
wanni return to the village after accompanying the gods a short distance. The Council of the Gods deposit te′likinawe in a cornfield a
south of the village, and near by, in an excavation about 4 feet in
diameter. The depth of the hole is the distance from the feet to the
waist of the wor′li who made it. They proceed to the cabin previously
referred to, where they remove their masks and paraphernalia.

The personators of the Sha′läko rise with the effigies, each as his
turn comes. The one from He′iwa ki′wiᵗsinĕ runs to excavation 3,
and, drawing a te′likinanĕ from his belt, thrusts his hand through
the opening in the blanket and deposits it to the Sha′läko of the North;
then, rapidly crossing to excavation 4, he plants a second te′liki-
nanĕ to Sha′läko of the North [a] and returns to his position in the line
of Sha′läko, when the group from his ki′wiᵗsinĕ sprinkle the effigy
with meal. He then slips from under the effigy, his alternate taking
his place, while the personator of the Sha′läko occupies the former
position of his fellow. This proceeding is followed by each Sha′läko.
As soon as the Sha′läko from He′iwa ki′wiᵗsinĕ starts for excavation 4,
the one from O′he′wa runs to excavation 9 and deposits a te′likinanĕ
to the Sha′läko of the East, and, crossing the ground, he deposits
another in excavation 10. He is no sooner off for excavation 10 than
the one from Mu′he′wa ki′wiᵗsinĕ runs to excavation 5; and, after
depositing a te′likinanĕ to the Sha′läko of the West, he runs to excavation 6 and deposits another te′likinanĕ. The Sha′läko from He′kĭapawa
ki′wiᵗsinĕ closely follows the one preceding him and deposits a te′liki-
nanĕ in excavation 13, and, crossing to excavation 14, he plants another.
The Sha′läko from Chu′pawa ki′wiᵗsinĕ follows next. He runs to

_____

a Much skill is required by the bearer in manipulating the beak that is attached to the mask
which he keeps in a constant chatter while he runs rapidly with the effigy.

excavation 7, where he deposits a te'likinanĕ and crosses to excavation 8, where he plants another. He is no sooner started for excavation 8 than the Sha'läko from Up'ᵗsannawa runs to excavation 11, where he plants his offering, and, running to excavation 12, he deposits another. Before he is fairly on his way for excavation 12 the alternate of the Sha'läko from He'iwa ki'wiᵗsinĕ proceeds to excavation 3, where a te'likinanĕ is deposited, and he runs to excavation 4 to deposit another. The changing of places by the Sha'läko and their alternates to and from the effigies is most dexterously managed. The planting of the te'likinawe is repeated by each alternate in the regular order mentioned above. When the fellow from Up'ᵗsannawa starts for excavation 14, the personator of the Sha'läko of He'iwa ki'wiᵗsinĕ, having taken charge of his effigy, runs to excavation 3 and sprinkles the te'likinawe with meal, which he also carries in his belt, and, crossing, he sprinkles the te'likinawe in excavation 4. The sprinkling of the plume offerings with meal is conducted in the same manner in which the plumes are deposited. All the Sha'läko now appear on the field at once (see plate LXIV), running as rapidly as possible, after which they leave the field in single file to return to their dressing room above referred to. Each Sha'läko is accompanied by his wor'li and alternate. The groups from the ki'wiᵗsiwe and the flutists return to the village. The Sha'läko are followed by a number of gaily dressed young men, and when these gods are a distance from the village they run as rapidly as possible and are pursued by the young men. When a Sha'läko is caught, the bearer of the effigy throws it upon the ground amid great excitement. The one who catches the effigy exclaims: "I have killed the deer." He sprinkles it with meal, praying that he may be successful in the hunt. The catching of the effigy is indicative of success in the coming hunt, and great efforts are made to get ahead of one another to capture the so-called deer.

Each personator of a Sha'läko and his alternate deposit te'likinawe in the same excavation in which the Council of the Gods planted offerings. This opening is filled in by the Sha'läko wor'we, who proceed to the cabin a little farther off where the effigies are taken apart and the masks and paraphernalia are brought to the village by them under a covering of blankets.

This elaborate ceremonial is to bring rains to fructify the earth. The rapid running from one excavation to another is a dramatization of the services performed by the Sha'läko, the couriers of the A'shiwanni u'wannami (priest rain-makers) of the six regions, who, when wishing to communicate with one another, employ couriers for the purpose. The A'shiwanni u'wannami of the North, wishing to send rains upon some particular land, communicate with their younger brothers, the A'shiwanni u'wannami of the East; and the A'shiwanni u'wannami of the West send their courier to their younger brothers, the A'shiwanni u'wannami of the Nadir; and so also the A'shiwanni u'wannami of the South dispatches their courier to the A'shiwanni u'wannami of the Zenith. Any one of these couriers may also be sent to any other or all of the regions when it is desired that the rain-makers of all the regions should lend their aid in watering the earth. The prayers of the personators of the Council of the Gods and Sha'läko at this season are for rains from all quarters, that the rivers may be great and come dashing through the canyons; that the streams may swell like rivers, flooding the water courses; and that the lakes may grow large and the wells be filled to overflowing, so that the earth may give to them the fullness of her being. These prayers are accentuated by the drama on the ceremonial ground.

The last participants in the ritual have no sooner left the field than it is filled with those who may not come when the gods are here. Numbers of Navahos, wrapped in their best blankets, their horses resplendent in silver bridles and silver-mounted saddles, make a brilliant picture as they dash across the stream to the recently forbidden ground, now free to all. But far more exciting is the race of 200 or more Navahos, mounted on their fleetest ponies. After their return the afternoon is consumed in equestrian and foot racing with the Zuñis, the latter winning in almost every instance, leaving the field with ponies, fine blankets, and silver and coral beads. Though the streets are filled with men too drunk to move, others are sober enough to participate in the pastime which delights the heart of aboriginal man as well as his more civilized brothers.

This is indeed a gala time for the Zuñis. After the last of the Sha'läko have disappeared over the hills the ten personators of the Ko'yemshi appear in daylight for the first time since their appointment to office, except when they leave their retreat for wood. Their absence during the ceremonial of the Sha'läko is noticeable, as the Ko'yemshi appear on most occasions of the coming of the gods, acting as their attendants, arranging any portion of their dress which may have become disarranged, and playing the clown or fool during the intervals of the dance. After emerging from their ceremonial chamber the Ko'yemshi visit every house top in the village, sprinkling meal, singing, dancing, and acting, in primitive comedy. They are supported in these plays by women inside the houses, whose voices can be heard through the hatchway in the roof.

CEREMONIES FOLLOWING THE SHA'LÄKO FESTIVAL OF 1891.

An elaborate display is supposed to be made for five consecutvie nights, by order of the gods, by representatives from all of the ki'wi⁺siwe. There is little or no difference from year to year in the main features of these ceremonies. Each o'taikĭa mo'sona (dance director) makes every effort to have his dance excel the others. The number of dances varies from time to time. Jugglery differs as it is performed by the different fraternities, depending on the one to which the Great Father Ko'yemshi is associated at the time of the festival. There is but little done the first night following the disappearance of the Sha'läko, the men being too much engrossed in debauchery to attend to obligations to their gods. Liquor is the only thing that prevents these Indians from performing their religious duties.[a]

The dances described occurred in 1891 on the fifth night following the arrival of the Sha'läko in the house of Roman Luna, a hardy old Indian, as brave as a lion, yet as gentle as a child. Masks of the 'Cha'kwena (certain anthropic gods) hang against the west wall of the large room toward the north end. They are covered with a strip of calico, the tips only of the long beards showing beneath the covering. At an early hour the ledge around the room, which extends north and south, is well filled with spectators. One group of young men not familiar with the songs of the 'Cha'kwena, which are in the Laguna tongue, are receiving instructions from a Laguna Indian but recently returned from Carlisle, for this song is a prayer to the gods of his people. He seems as fully absorbed in his native worship as though he had not been instructed for years at the expense of the Government. The song is very low at first, but it gradually swells into louder and louder bass tones, which are very pleasing.

The large openings in the wall which divide the front and back rooms, through which the Sha'läko ceremony was observed, are left for the convenience and pleasure of the Zuñi aristocracy, principally the younger members of this set, who wish to observe apart from the mass of people who crowd the room. During the dances many of the older women and children and the more sober maidens of the elite occupy seats with the more common people on the east side of the large room, but the privileged ones adjourn to the back room during the intermissions. Two Acoma Indians in this room, teaching three Zuñis song prayers in their tongue, draw about them a few listeners. The writer observes that several elderly women are the most interested, except those receiving instruction. The scene through the openings in the wall is most pleasing. Lights and shadows, according to the freaks of the fire in the back room, play about the faces of the dusky maidens and youths, who are seated on chairs and boxes. Occasionally merry laughter is heard when the young men say pleasing or amusing words to the girls.

---

[a] Since Mr Douglas D. Graham has had the Zuñi Indians in charge there is much less dissipation among them. It is certain that he will see that the law is executed if it be within his power, and that liquor is kept from them.

KO'YEMSHI GODS IN PLAZA

CANVAS PACKS OF PERSONATORS OF THE KO'YEMSHI GODS

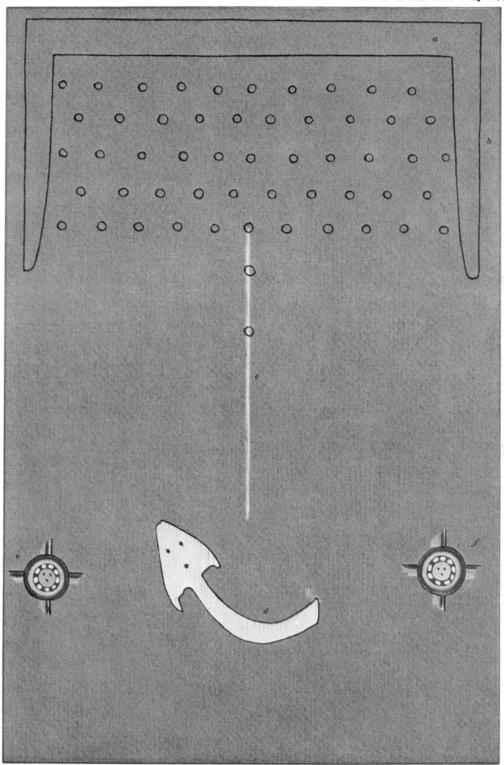

DRY PAINTING IN FRONT OF ALTAR OF SHI'WANNAKWE

a MASK OF KOK'KO⊤HLAN'NA (GREAT GOD) OF NE'WEKWE FRONT AND REAR VIEWS
b MASK OF MI'TOTÄSHA FRONT AND SIDE VIEWS

A small side apartment is used as the greenroom for the personators of the 'Cha'kwena to adorn themselves for the dance, the elder son of this house being dance director of this body. It is in this room that heads of the dancers are washed after their dance, and the dancers wash off the paint from their bodies. The merrymaking becomes general here and in the back room; and while the hair washing is going on even the women who perform this service, which is a part of their ritual, enjoy the jokes of the others. This apartment serves another purpose. It is the barroom, where are served Isleta wine, and also whisky obtained from the whites. Some intoxicated men are made to leave the house early in the evening at the demand of the women in the back room. These men becoming too practical in their jokes with them, the elder son of the house is called to the rescue from the front room. With but few words he quickly dispatches the offenders, who are all Zuñis of quality. As they pass through the front room in file each one endeavors to say in his most polite manner, " So'anni kets'änishi to'o än'tiwatu (Good-by; all good come to you)."

About 9 o'clock the group learning the Laguna song separate and take seats in line on the west side of the room at the north end. In a short time the approaching rattle and drum are heard, and twenty-one men personating the He'mishiikwe enter the room in single file, led by a man carrying his mi'li and meal basket.

In all religious dances the plaza or chamber is entered in file, led by a man or woman who will be termed the leader of the dancers. The woman leader wears conventional dress, always her newest and best, and, if necessary, articles are borrowed from her family or members of her clan for the occasion. Special attention is given to the moccasins and leggings, which are of the whitest dressed deerskins, with glossy black soles, an entire skin being used for the purpose. The larger the skin the more desirable, for the ambition of a Zuñi woman is to have her legs so wrapped from the ankle to the knee that the feet, naturally small and beautiful in form, shall appear as diminutive as possible. The white blanket bordered in red and blue is worn over the back. Sometimes, but rarely, another blanket is worn in its place. A fluffy eagle plume is tied to the forelock of the female leader, and she carries her mi'li and meal basket. While silver beads of native manufacture are the only necklaces used as the daily adornment of the women, the ko'hakwa, turquoise, and coral beads—the necklaces of the men—are added to the silver ornaments when the women appear in ceremonials, as many as can be secured from members of the family or intimate friends, until the breast is covered with the precious beads. Borrowing of finery is not confined to the women, the men being equally as anxious to adorn their persons; yet it is always done in the most secret manner.

The man is less conventional in his dress, so there is greater margin for variety in costume. He frequently wears velvet knee breeches lined on the outer sides with silver buttons, a native woven black wool shirt, elaborately trimmed with red and green ribbons, over one of white cotton, the sleeves of the other being open so as to expose the undersleeve of the white shirt. Sometimes a silver belt is worn; at other times a red silk scarf is tied around the waist. Ordinary moccasins, always the best ones, are worn with leather leggings ornamented with silver buttons and tied on with red garters. While this is the usual dress of the male leader, any apparel which suits his taste, and is not directly associated with the dress of the anthrophic gods, may be worn.

In cold weather the leader frequently has a blanket in addition to his other dress, worn with the grace with which only an Indian can wear the blanket. A line of micaceous hematite crosses his face below the eyes, denoting office, and a fluffy eagle plume is tied to the forelock. He carries his mi'li and meal basket.

It will be understood that in all ceremonials where men and women act in the capacity of leaders of dancers or serve to secure dancers for the festivals, the dress is similar to that described above. Any exceptions will be noted. The leader is never included in the number of dancers.

The He'mishiikwe are met at the entrance by the host of the house, who carries a meal basket and throws out a line of meal before him as he leads the dancers down the room. Each He'mishiikwe has his body and limbs colored purple with dye from the berry of Berberis fremontii. He wears a white embroidered kilt held on by a white fringed sash and a woman's red belt tied in loops at the right side, a fox skin pendent at the back of the waist, and a tortoise-shell rattle attached to the calf of the right leg. Bunches of blue yarn with sleigh bells attached are tied in tassels below the knees, and dance moccasins are worn. No masks are worn on this occasion by those dancing in line, though a few maskers appear with each party of dancers. Each He'mishiikwe carries a spruce twig in the left hand and a gourd rattle, colored pink, in the right. The drum, rectangular in form and wrapped with rope, is made of undressed hide, the hair on the inner side. The dancers enter in single file and proceed down the room raising the right foot high and balancing on the left, the heel only of the left foot being raised from the floor. This is a common step in all dances where the anthropic gods are personated. On reaching the north end of the room on the west side they remain in file, and, facing north, the left arm of each dancer is slightly bent and held at the side; the right arm is also slightly bent, but less than the left. The movement is with the right foot, the left one being used to balance. Four boys, who are masked, accompany the He'mishiikwe and take seats on the west ledge by the dancers, two of them playing on notched sticks during certain portions of the dance, the lower sticks resting on boxes. After shaking the rattle the He'mishiikwe wave both hands to the left, then to the right, and repeat the motion, the rattle being kept in constant action. The body is now bent forward to the left, the left hand being held to the side and the right hand hanging, as a long, rapid, even musical shake of the rattle is given. All now turn and face the east and give a long, steady shake of the rattle. The first movement is repeated, the right foot is raised high, and they stamp four times very quickly while the rattle is held low and shaken. But this time the sound is altogether different; it is loud, while the other is like the shaking of many seeds. After the stamping the hands are waved to the left and then to the right five times; then the body is bent still lower and the stamping repeated eight times. Raising the body, the first movement is repeated as they all turn, facing the north, and in a moment they continue around toward the left until they again face the east, the rattles held above their heads.   Turning entirely around, they face the north and bending low, first to the right, then to the left, shake the rattle.   The first two figures are again repeated, and when all are facing north they stoop and with a quick step, bending the knees and leaning toward the right, pass around toward the left, the song changing from a major to a minor key, with considerable variety of tone.   The motions in the dance are rhythmic.

The next dancers to appear after the He'mishiikwe depart are seventeen Mu'luktäkïa (tall thin gods).   They carry in their left hands long slender staffs ornamented at the top and middle with plumes, and in their right gourd rattles.   The dance and songs of the Mu'luktäkïa, though pleasing, are far inferior to those of the He'mishiikwe.   The dress of both parties is similar.   A boy, 10 years of age, wearing a bearskin wrapped about his body and falling to his knees, accompanies the Mu'luktäkïa.   Skins of bears' legs with the claws are drawn over his feet.   He carries a stone hatchet in his right hand and giant yucca in his left.   He gesticulates and growls, animal-like, as he dances back and forth east of the line of dancers.

Having made their toilets in the side room, the 'Cha'kwena gods are the next to appear, the returned Carlisle student being one of the number.   The leader of these dancers is a boy not more than twelve years of age.   He carries his mi'li and meal basket in the left hand and sprinkles meal with the right.   The limbs of the dancers are painted white and their bodies are zigzagged in white, symbolic of lightning. They wear white dressed deerskins as kilts, which fall below the knees, held on by white fringed sashes and red belts tied to the right side, and a fox skin pendent from the back of the waist.   The bodies and upper arms are colored black, a yoke is designed in yellow paint, and the lower arms and hands are yellow.   In one case the yoke is pink instead of yellow, and the hands and lower arms are white.   A scalp knot is painted on each scapula and each breast.   Some of these are in yellow and some in white.   Dressed deerskins worn as skirts, held in place by an embroidered sash and a red belt fastened at the right side, fall nearly to the ground; a fox skin is pendent at the back.   They wear dressed deerskin leggings, fringed at the outer sides, and dance moccasins with anklets embroidered with porcupine quills.   Leather armlets colored blue-green, each having three points to which pendent-banded turkey plumes are attached by buckskin throngs, encircle the upper arms.   Spruce twigs stand around the upper side of the armlets, and gourd rattles, painted blue-green, are carried in the right hand; bows and arrows are in the left.   A quiver containing arrows hangs over the back.   Each carries giant yucca in the left hand.   The hair is done up in a knot at the back, and a fluffy white eagle feather is attached to the forelock.   A yucca ribbon is tied around the head.   One of the number wears a black skull cap covered with the skin of a duck so well mounted as to appear as if a duck had just perched there.   A black wool cap is used when the masks are not worn.   Two others wearing masks accompany these dancers.   One hideous mask has padded eyes; another has a long white beard.   The 'Cha′kwena form in line north and south, and the other two dance violently east of the line, which faces west quite as frequently as east during the dance.   Before this party complete their song and dance, the 'Cha′kwena of another ki′wi'sinĕ arrive, the dancers making room for them.   The newcomers also form in line on the west side of the room.   Their dress and masks are similar to those worn by the 'Cha′kwena who precede them.   The 'Cha′-kwena, like most of the Zuñis, are beautiful in form, and the sight of their bodies swaying from side to side in rythmical motion, while they gracefully manipulate the rattle in accompaniment to the song, gives real delight.

A boy of five or six years and a man representing a bear, the latter wearing a mask, dance in front of the line.   The child wears a black woven breechcloth, buckskin leggings, and a tortoise-shell rattle tied to the calf of his right leg; a yucca ribbon is tied around his head, and his breast is covered with necklaces.   He carries in his right hand a gourd rattle which is almost as large as himself, and in his left a bunch of giant yucca.   The child seems as much interested in the dance as his elders.   The man representing the bear has his lower legs painted black and spotted white.   He wears armlets of uncolored leather.   A bearskin covers the body and a portion of the lower limbs and skins of bears' legs with the claws are drawn over his feet.   A tortoise-shell rattle is attached to the calf of his right leg.   He carries a wooden hatchet, with goat's wool, significant of a scalp lock, in his right hand and yucca in his left; yucca is also tied around his legs below the knees.   These two remain a short time after the 'Cha′kwena leave, running about the room like animals.[a]

Next to appear are seventeen Wa′tĕm'la (all herds), seven of the number being boys.   They are led by a man carrying his mi′li and meal basket.   Their bodies are nude, marked thus)(in yellow on each scapula and breast.   The legs are painted white, and they wear various styles of kilts and wrappings about the loins and legs.   Each carries a gourd rattle in his right hand, with a bunch of giant yucca in his left.   Forming in line on the west side of the room and facing east, they stamp three times with the right foot and begin the dance, which is like the former, though the song is quite different.

After these dancers leave, a Hopi dance is introduced, led by Nan′-

---

[a] At this point in the ceremony four spectators are severely whipped across the ankles and arms for speaking a word or two of Spanish, for a word in this language must not be uttered in the presence of the personators of the anthropic gods.

nahe, a Hopi Indian married to a Zuñi woman. The feature of this dance is the enthusiasm exhibited by Nan'nahe, who, being conscious that his associates are but partly drilled in the song, makes every effort to prevent failure. Their costume is a Hopi kilt, a silk scarf passing over the right shoulder and tied on the left side, dance moccasins, and anklets embroidered with porcupine quills. There are two others outside of the line of dancers, and they wear improvised Hopi masks.

After these dancers leave, the Ko'yemshi arrive, wearing masks and having blankets around them tied at the waist. Goatskins with the wool inside cover their feet. A fawn skin hangs over the shoulder, the head peeping up from under the blanket, and a quantity of te'liki-nawe are held in the blanket, two are longer than the others, one stick being colored blue for the sun and the other yellow for the moon. Each carries a gourd rattle in the right hand. The masks are so covered with meal from the sprinkling they have received at other houses that they appear as though they had been in a heavy snowstorm. They are preceded by sixteen male members of the Ant fraternity led by the female head of the house dedicated by the Ko'yemshi. She wears ordinary dress, with a white blanket striped blue and red and many silver beads. The members of the fraternity wear black native breechcloths. Their bodies are painted white to represent stars and animals. The hair hangs down the back, a wreath of yucca is worn, and a salmon-colored fluffy eagle plume is attached to the forelock. They are led down the room, as usual, by the host of the house. The woman, following next, carries her mi'li and meal basket in her left hand and sprinkles meal with the right. The pe'kwĭn (deputy director) of the fraternity, carrying an eagle plume in each hand, is next to her. The director comes next, he being a member of the Sun clan. He wears over his left hand the skin of a bear's leg with the claws attached. He carries an eagle plume in each hand and holds with both hands a basket containing six disks of wood about $2\frac{1}{4}$ inches in diameter, painted blue-green and edged with black and white blocks, symbolic of the house of the clouds and four fluffy white eagle plumes are attached to the periphery. Three black lines on the disk indicate the mouth and eyes. All the others, with one exception, carry two eagle plumes in the left hand and a rattle in the right. The third man following the director has a bear's leg skin over his left arm, and the quill ends of his eagle plumes are stuck into it on the top of the arm. The male head of the house dedicated by the Ko'yemshi follows at the end of the line of the fraternity, also carrying his mi'li and meal basket. They all pass down the west side of the room and around to the east, forming an ellipse which is left open by a gap of 3 or 4 feet. These circles must never be closed, the opening being symbolic of the road of life, of rain, and of the sun—everything suggestive of life. After dancing around once, everyone waving his plumes or whatever he has in his hands up and down, the director, first handing his basket containing the disks to his pe'kwĭn, takes meal from the basket of the host of the house. He drops six pinches of meal on the floor north of the center of the ellipse, indicating the six regions; over this he forms a disk about 6 inches in diameter and extends a line of meal, 9 feet in length, south from the disk and taking the mi'li from the woman who leads the party dances about with it, waving it to the six regions. Then raising it up and down six times to the music of the rattle and drum, he places it on the meal disk, and taking his basket from the pe'kwĭn, removes one of the disks and returns the basket. Then, after many gesticulations and incantations, throwing his body at times almost prostrate upon the floor in his animal-like gestures, he lays the disk on the meal south of the mi'li. The host of the house, removing his moccasins, enters the circle and standing to the left of the director, leans his head toward him while the director whispers to him. The dance is suspended during this performance. The picture is striking. The director says: "Take this yä'tokĭa ʼsan'na (small sun) [handing him the disk] and place it next to the heart of the warrior," referring to the warrior of the Ant fraternity, who now leaves the circle and stands at the end of the meal line. The latter waves his plumes, held in each hand, up and down, moving his beautifully formed body most gracefully. The director says to the host of the house: "When you place the disk over the warrior's heart, and it remains there, then your heart and your wife's are good and you will have much corn and other things in the coming year. Should it fall, then the heart of the wife desires another than her husband." After receiving the disk, the host manipulates it before the mi'li for a time, and then, passing down the meal line, puts the disk to the warrior's heart, who does not cease his dancing and gesticulation at this time. The disk is no sooner placed than it drops to the floor. The director hastens to pick it up, and the host leaves the circle with the belief that his wife is unfaithful to him, at least in her heart.

As a Ko'yemshi is led into the circle by the director, he hands his rattle to the companion at his side. The Ko'yemshi makes the effort with the disk, manipulating it before the mi'li, and puts it to the heart of the warrior, with the same result as that which befell the host of the house. The Ko'yemshi exclaims: "My wife has been with another, and I think I will run off to-night." This causes general amusement, especially among his fellows, who are passing their jokes, paying little or no attention to what is going on before them.

The director now selects a member of his fraternity and hands him a disk. He acts wildly, cowering and leaping about with bended knees, and in this posture jumping up and down the meal line, all the while keeping his eyes fixed on the mi'li. Finally he rises suddenly and places the disk to the heart of the warrior, and the warrior dances more violently than ever, the disk remaining in place. The man who places the disk returns to the circle, and in a moment or two the director removes the disk from the breast of the warrior, but after an instant replaces it. In a short time, however, he returns it to the basket and raising the mi'li, repeats a long prayer over it; then, facing south, he waves it to the six regions, and returning it to its owner, takes his position with the dancers. The warrior also joins the circle and they all dance around twice and leave the house in file.

One of the cleverest tricks was observed in 1879 in the house dedicated by the Ko'yemshi that year. At the time the writer was not sufficiently familiar with this Zuñi ceremonial to know that it was the fraternity furnishing the altar and songs for the Ko'yemshi that performed the trick. She was invited by a member of the Galaxy fraternity to visit the house dedicated by the Ko'yemshi. The Ko'yemshi and the members of the fraternity were in the midst of their preparations for the coming ceremonial. The members were painting each other from a large bowl of kaolin, while the Ko'yemshi rubbed their bodies over with a paint of pinkish clay. Two hours were consumed in perfecting the toilets, consisting only of the paint which covered their bodies and the breechcloth. The hair was parted in the middle and done up in the usual knot in the back, with a single ribbon of yucca, scarcely an inch wide, tied around the forehead at the edge of the hair and fastened on the side in a bowknot. Feathers were attached to the forelock of the members of the fraternity. The altar, as usual, stood at the west end of the room, and the masks of the Ko'yemshi lay on dressed deerskins behind the altar. The inner rooms were covered with sheepskins and blankets, which were occupied by those privileged to be present. Many of the women had their infants with them. All chatted merrily while they awaited the opening of the ceremony. The bowl of medicine water was in its usual place in front of the altar; also a basket tray containing grains of corn, and another containing white fluffy eagle plumes. The Ko'yemshi, having completed their toilets, except the masks, sat in line along the south ledge of the room.

The writer tied a silk head-kerchief around the head of a youth sitting by her, and the next moment one of the Ko'yemshi approached her and gracefully bent on one knee and bowed his head to receive a similar gift. Having a second head-kerchief she tied it around his head. He arose and bowed in acknowledgment of the gift. When the hour arrived for him to don his mask, he looked toward the giver and expressed with his eyes that which could not be said by the lips—his regrets that the head-kerchief must be removed.

The evening festivities opened with fourteen dancers from one of the ki'witsině, led as usual by a man carrying his mi'li and basket of meal. They danced to the accompaniment of the rattle and drum for thirty minutes, the variations in the dance consisting in the motions of the body and not in the step. As all the dances which occurred in this house have been previously described, the writer will not repeat the descriptions, but will depict the scene after the last group of visiting dancers departed.

When the Ko'yemshi donned their masks behind the altar they were immediately metamorphosed from attractive-looking men into hideous, unnatural objects. The members of the Galaxy fraternity formed into an ellipse before the altar, and the Ko'yemshi stood in line south of them. A curious old pottery lamp was produced by a woman of the house and placed on the mantel. The fire, which burned brightly during the early evening, had been allowed to die out, leaving a heap of bright coals.

Of the Ko'yemshi four were very old, and there were sixteen aged men of the fraternity. The writer has never seen as large a number of men so advanced in years actively associated with any of the other fraternities. One or two appeared to be at least 85. It was most interesting to see these men imbued with all the vigor and vitality of youth, their shapely limbs as nimble as those of the younger men who danced before them.

The director of the fraternity left the ellipse and advanced to the center. After a time the A′kwamosi (maker of medicine water), who retained his seat by the side of the altar up to this time, carried the basket containing the eagle feathers, tied in twos, to the director, who took one bunch, singing all the while, and, holding it up, danced about in the most fantastic manner, the plume in his own white hair bending with the breeze. After a time he handed the feathers to one of the Ko′yemshi, who danced in the center of the ellipse with him, and, running to the lamp, which had been lighted, he passed the feathers through the flame, bringing out two charred bits. Returning to the circle he danced and sang, pressing the crispy atoms to his breast, making desperate efforts to accomplish something, the writer could not imagine what. Failing in his efforts, he returned what remained of the feathers to the director, who continued to dance. After a while a member of the fraternity left the ellipse and drew near to the director, who handed him the charred bits; he immediately ran to the lamp and passed them through the flame with curious antics and returning to the ellipse, pressed them to his nude body. After dancing and singing a short time, all the while pressing the atoms to his breast, two beautiful white plumes appeared.

A similar trick was performed in 1896 by the Little Fire fraternity in the house dedicated by the Ko′yemshi. All altars have been removed from the houses except the one dedicated by the Ko′yemshi. Here the altar remains intact with the mi′wachi. Two bowls of medicine water and two large flat baskets of grains of corn of all colors are by the altar, and the small flute of the fraternity is immediately before it. The Ko′yemshi sit in line on the west side of the room wrapped in their blankets; they wear their moccasins. At half past 8 in the evening twenty-four members of the fraternity retire to an adjoining room to prepare for the dance. When they reappear, their bodies are elaborately decorated in white kaolin to represent the heavens, prey animals, and lightning; the only ones privileged to use the lightning symbol being such members as belong also to the A′pi‘‘läshiwanni (Bow priesthood) and the order of the Arrow in the Great Fire fraternity. Each wears a native black breechcloth embroidered at the ends in dark blue. Each member of the Bow priesthood wears his war pouch, and his wand which is usually attached to the bandoleer near the shoulder. Yucca ribbons are worn around the head, and their breasts are covered with a profusion of necklaces. The director is the first to enter the room. He takes his seat before the altar on the east side, facing south, and the others, who closely follow, group themselves near him and, after a prayer, indulge in a smoke. The Ko′yemshi now remove their moccasins, put on their masks, and throwing off their blankets expose the ragged black kilt. The members of the fraternity form in a file, led by a woman of the fraternity. Her necklaces are numerous and rare, and her moccasins are of the finest quality. She carries a meal basket in the left hand and her mi′li in the right. The last man in the line is

also a member of Shu'maakwe, of which fraternity he is pe'kwĭn
(deputy) to the director.   He carries his mi'li of Little Fĭre fraternity
in his right hand and a meal basket in the left.   An eagle plume thrust
through the septum of his nose, the quill end protruding through the
left side, is a badge of his high office in the Shu'maakwe.   Nai'uchi,
the elder brother Bow priest, who is warrior guardian of the Little
Fire fraternity, carries a small basket tray, on which is a hemispherical
gourd, the concave side down.   This gourd is painted white and capped
with a tuft of raw cotton, colored red, in the center of which are a
number of white fluffy eagle plumes; he also carries his two eagle-wing
plumes.   All the men, including the Ko'yemshi, have gourd rattles in
the right hand.   After passing once around the room, the Ko'yemshi
following after the fraternity, they form an ellipse and dance for
a short time, after which they visit the six houses blessed by the
Sha'läko.   In the first house visited is observed the following trick:

The drummer precedes the dancers, who, to the music of the rattle
and drum, pass down the room, the host of the house leading.   The
female leader and the member at the rear end sprinkle meal in the
usual manner as they proceed.   An ellipse is formed, and after dancing around once they halt, and the Great Father Ko'yemshi secures a
blanket from one of the spectators and spreads it in the center of the
ellipse.   Nai'uchi now makes a small disk of meal in the center of the
blanket and forms a cross by extending four lines outward from it and
places the basket tray on the disk.   One of the Ko'yemshi performs
about the basket tray with his two eagle plumes.   Returning to his
place, Nai'uchi and another member of the fraternity, the pe'kwĭn of
Shu'maakwe, stand side by side by the basket.   After the pe'kwĭn
whispers in the ear of the Nai'uchi he moves about in the ellipse
like an animal, stooping and growling, while the others cry out
as though they were giving warning of the presence of some wild
beast.   Finally he plucks the plumes from the gourd and dashing to
the fireplace, passes them through the flames.   Returning with the
charred bits, he dances wildly about, part of the time in a cowering
posture, making great efforts apparently to draw something from his
breast, all the while holding the charred bits between his fingers.
Finally the plumes reappear.

The director of the fraternity and the Great Father Ko'yemshi stand
side by side before the basket, facing east, and pray.   At the close of
the prayer Nai'uchi takes the basket, and the Great Father, after shaking the blanket slightly to remove the meal, returns it to its owner.   All
dance around once and leave this house to visit another.   In the second
house the gourd is turned concave side upward in the basket.   After
several futile attempts of the Ko'yemshi to raise the gourd with their
eagle-wing plumes, a member of the fraternity, touching the gourd
with the quill ends of his plumes, gracefully holding them at the feather

ends, raises it some distance above the basket. This feat calls forth the wildest encores from the spectators. Though the writer is near and closely observing, she fails to discover the trick.

The Little Fire fraternity give such delight during the evening that they are requested to appear in the te'wita (plaza) the following day. All are decorated as they were the previous night, excepting two members, they being the director of the Shu'maakwe fraternity and his pe'kwĭn, who are also members of the Little Fire fraternity. Each has two eagle plumes passed through the septum of the nose, the plumes being about 8 inches long, and the quill ends put in from opposite sides. The Ko'yemshi follow the fraternity in file, each one having a rattle. As on the previous night, the members of the fraternity are led by a woman carrying the mi'li and meal basket. After passing once around the Si'aa' te'wita the party form in a broken circle, and a Ko'yemshi procures a blanket from one of the spectators and places it upon the ground. The wind is blowing so hard that the blanket must be secured with heavy stones. Nai'uchi, warrior of the fraternity, proceeds to make a small cross of meal upon the blanket, and placing the mi'li upon it and securing the fetish to its position with small stones, lays a large gourd rattle, painted white, by its side. The Ko'yemshi who procured the blanket selects two men from the crowd of spectators, who approach, first removing their own blankets. Nai'uchi hands the mi'li to one of the men, whispers something to him, hands his rattle to the second man, whispers to him, and returns to his place with the dancers, who proceed to shake their rattles and dance. The second man, holding the white rattle close to the blanket, shakes it in time with the others. The other man, holding the mi'li with the tip pointing to the ground (see plate LXV), taps it with two eagle plumes. He continues this for some minutes and returns the mi'li to the warrior, who also takes the rattle. The mi'li and rattle are placed on the blanket, a Ko'yemshi brings two other men, and the performance is repeated. Nai'uchi now calls a member of the fraternity and hands him the mi'li, and a Ko'yemshi takes the rattle. All dance and sing to the accompaniment of the rattles. As soon as the man with the mi'li begins tapping it with his eagle plumes, grains of wheat pour out from the plumes until fully a quart is deposited on the blanket, much to the delight of a large number of spectators. This trick, which the writer has observed on several occasions, is a clever one. After dancing a short time the fraternity, followed by the Ko'yemshi, leave the plaza.

Personators of the gods from different ki'wi'siwe appear in the Si'aa' te'wita five consecutive days in full ceremonial attire, including masks. Although at times the wind blows like a hurricane, carrying so much dust that one not accustomed to these storms finds it almost impossible to exist, the dances go on. The thermometer is never too low or the

winds too piercing for these devotees to take part in the outdoor
ceremonial. Such windstorms are not considered favorable, and for
this reason the dance is all the more vigorously performed and the
songs the more fervently sung, the singers hoping in this way to appease
the wrath of the gods. A rain priest gave the following as a reason
for the continued windstorms in 1891: "The Kok'ko A'wan (Council
of the Gods) are angry, and send the winds because the Ko'yemshi are
personated this year by the Ne'wekwe (Galaxy) fraternity, who do not
speak the old language. Some years ago, when the Ne'wekwe represented the Ko'yemshi, similar hard winds came, and the Kĭa'kwemosi,
who has since died, declared that the Ko'yemshi must never again be
personated by this fraternity; but his successor, being a member of the
Ne'wekwe, this fraternity continues to take its turn in representing
the Ko'yemshi, and therefore the gods are very angry. Other personators of the Ko'yemshi bring rain and good crops, for they speak their
prayers in the old tongue."

RETIREMENT OF THE KO'YEMSHI AND ACCOMPANYING CEREMONIES

The day following the ceremonies described the first body of A'shiwanni gather in the ceremonial chamber of the Kĭa'kwemosi in the
early morning and prepare te'likinawe. The Ko'mosona, Ko'pekwĭn,
and two Ko'pi‘‘lăshiwanni assemble in the He'iwa (North) ki'wĭ'sinĕ,
where they remain throughout the day, except at such times as they
appear in the plaza. Each prepares te'likinawe. After the A'shiwanni complete their te'likinawe, the offerings are grouped into a
kĭa'ĕtchinĕ, and the Kĭa'kwemosi carries it in a flat basket to the
He'iwa ki'wĭ'sinĕ, where it is placed on the floor on the cloud symbol
of meal made by the pe'kwĭn. The te'likinawe prepared by the
Ko'mosona and his associates are also made into a kĭa'ĕtchinĕ and
deposited on the meal painting.

Baskets of all sizes containing meal are carried by the women and
children of the paternal clans of the Ko'yemshi to the house where
their masks are kept, and where they are to be entertained at a feast.
These offerings are to furnish bread for the occasion. Some are
diminutive, coming, as they do, from children three or four years of
age. These little tots carry their baskets on their heads as their
mothers do. The meal is stacked high, as smoothly as possible, every
care being taken in the arrangement of it; yet it hardly comes into
the house before it is emptied from the vessel in which it is brought
into one belonging to the woman of the house. Before the transferring of the meal, the one who brings it takes a pinch from the apex
and reserves it to sprinkle upon the Ko'yemshi.

At 9 o'clock in the morning fourteen members of the Little Fire
fraternity wearing ordinary dress and moccasins, each having his

mi'li and two eagle-wing plumes, precede the Ko'yemshi in file to
the Si'aa' te'wita, led by a woman of the fraternity carrying her mi'li
and meal basket. The Ko'yemshi are wrapped in heavy blankets,
and wear moccasins. Each has a large roll of canvas on his back and
carries te'likinawe, including those given to the male head of each
house dedicated at the coming of the Sha'läko, except the te'likinanĕ
of the male head of the house visited by the Council of the Gods.
This one was carried by the personator of Sa'yatäsha to his home
and is afterward planted by him. Each has also a fawn skin filled
with seeds, to be distributed to those in the ki'wiᵗsinĕ. They pass
four times around in a circle, when the Kĭa'kwemosi, who awaits
them in the plaza, forms a cross of meal (symbolic of the four regions)
on the ground at the west side of the plaza, and the Great Father
Ko'yemshi standing east of the cross the Kĭa'kwemosi places a hand
on each shoulder, motions him to the four regions, and then seats him
on the cross. The forming of the cross is repeated as many times as
there are Ko'yemshi to be seated. The other Ko'yemshi are in line
on the north side of the plaza; all of them except the Great Father
are to be seen in the illustration (plate LXVI).

The members of the Little Fire fraternity stand in an irregular line
during the seating of the Ko'yemshi. The Kĭa'kwemosi, returning to
the Great Father Ko'yemshi, draws a line of meal upward over the
mask and prays, repeating the same with each Ko'yemshi; and the
members of the fraternity, with a prayer, sprinkle each mask with
meal, and leave the plaza. The Ko'yemshi now rise, leaving their
rolls of canvas in place on the ground, and group themselves by the
man who is at this time completing an excavation in the ledge in front
of the ki'wiᵗsinĕ. When he retires, each Ko'yemshi stands his te'likinawe in the opening. They remove them late in the night, and still
later plant them in an excavation west of the village. This excavation
is as deep as from the breast to the feet of the man who makes it.

The Kĭa'kwemosi comes from his ceremonial chamber and, sprinkling
meal upon the Ko'yemshi, throws a line of meal up the ladder and
leads the Great Father and the other Ko'yemshi into the chamber. The
canvas packs are left in the plaza (see plate LXVII). Men and women
soon begin to crowd the plaza, bearing offerings to the retiring
Ko'yemshi (see plate LXVIII). The first donations are made by women,
who bring baskets of corn and wheat flour and light bread. White
chalk lines across the blanket wraps show that they are fresh from the
weavers' hands. A Zuñi woman is as eager to exhibit the line on her
blanket as a civilized woman is to display the marking on her India
shawl. Later men come to the plaza with dressed sheep, watermelons,
and other food.

At half past 11 the Ko'yemshi descend to the Si'aa' te'wita and,
unrolling their canvases, deposit bread which they have received

upon the cloth. The first dancers to appear in the plaza are the Wa'tĕm'la (all herds; see plate LXIX), who come from the newly dedicated house which faces the east.

Among the gods in this group are the u'wannami (rain-makers; see plate LXX),[a] Na'täshku[b] (see plate LXXI a), and Na'wisho (possessor of many deer; see plate LXXI b, c), also called O'lolowĭshkĭa. This god is supposed to sweeten bread by micturating upon the meal (" His urine is sweet like honey "). The penis is represented by a gourd with white fluffy eagle plumes attached pendent. During the dance of the Wa'tĕm'la the Ko'mosona approaches the O'lolowĭshkĭa and most reverently prays while he sprinkles the mask and artificial penis with sacred meal.

The Mu'luktäkĭa are among the most attractive of the gods who appear. They wear white embroidered kilts held on by sashes tied at the right side, fox skins are pendent at the back, sleigh bells are fastened to the blue yarn which is wrapped around the legs below the knees, strings of black and white corn hang over the right-shoulder, and they wear elaborate necklaces of ko'hakwa, turquoise, and coral, each necklace having an abalone shell pendent at the back. Each carries in the left hand a slender staff ornamented with plumes and spruce twigs, and in the right a gourd rattle (see plate LXXII). Plate LXXIII shows mask of Mu'luktäkĭa. The He'mishiikwe follow the Mu'luktäkĭa to the plaza. Their dress is similar, but their masks are altogether different. All the He'mishiikwe masks are alike, but the tablets which surmount them are different, not so elaborate usually as one shown in plate LXXIV. The disk on the front of the tablet denotes the sun; the small figures on each side symbolize squash blossoms. The varicolored geometrical figures represent corn of different colors. The rainbow is represented on the back of the tablet. Plate LXXV shows masks of a god and goddesses accompanying the He'mishiikwe.

The plaza is constantly changing in aspect. It is a kaleidoscope for hours, the lines of dancers varying from one to six, and when the full number are present in their picturesque costumes and the house tops are crowded with gaily attired spectators the scene is most brilliant. Each party of dancers brings ears of corn to the plaza, which are collected by the A'shiwanni, who are present at times in the plaza, and carried into the ki'wi'sinĕ. The Kĭa'kwemosi, his associate, and the

---

[a] The bear's claws on the mask symbolize the footprints of the bear in the soft earth, indicating the desire of the A'shiwi (Zuñis) for the earth to be well watered that the feet of all animals may sink into it—another expression to indicate the desire of these people for the fructification of the earth. The zigzag each side of the face of the mask denotes the lightning shooting from the house of the clouds of the north, yellow symbolizing the north and the black and white blocks the house of the clouds. The blue-green shown each side of the back of the mask indicates the house of the clouds of the west, this color symbolizing the west. Eagle down on the top of the mask represents clouds. The dragon flies on the back are suggestive of rain.

[b] Na'täshku, the Zuñis assert, was adopted from the Hopi Indians, and a sketch secured by Dr J. W. Fewkes shows that the Hopi have the identical mask.

Shi'wanni of the West sprinkle the Wa'tĕm'la with meal and pray before returning to the ki'wi'sinĕ.

Large quantities of corn are collected from the dancers during the day and carried into the ki'wi'sinĕ. The pe'kwĭn, the younger brother Bow priest, and the Ko'pekwĭn receive several ears of corn from the dancers, and each repeats a long prayer to the donor. The Ko'pekwĭn receives corn also from the O'lolowĭshkĭa. They, too, return to the ki'wi'sinĕ after they have prayed and sprinkled the gods with meal.

The performances of four men and three boys of the Galaxy fraternity add to the amusement in the plaza. All but one wear trousers; those worn by the men are from cast-off uniforms of the Army. Their bodies and faces are painted ash-color. The entire body of the nude man is painted ash-color. All wear the ash-colored skullcap, with bunches of ribboned corn husks on each side. The drum used on the present occasion is of hide, folded with the hair inside, and wrapped around with rope. The one who leads the others in mimicry of the dancers carries a piece of goat's hide as a mi'li (see page 416). After passing around the plaza they all join in a Navaho dance and afterward burlesque the personators of the Zuñi gods. The dance breaks up in a regular mêlee between the Ko'yemshi and the members of the Galaxy fraternity. The youthful members of the fraternity deem it wise to keep somewhat aloof at this time. The Ko'yemshi snatch the skullcaps from the men of the fraternity, throw them down, and rob them of their trousers. At one time during the excitement one of the boys runs to the scene and kicks the hide drum against a Ko'yemshi, who falls down, and a member of the fraternity calls upon members of the 'Ko'shi'kwe (Cactus) fraternity, who are spectators, for aid. Finally one of the 'Ko'shi'kwe leaves the plaza and returns with a bunch of long willows and, removing his clothing to the breechcloth, divides the willows with the one who called for aid, and there is a general switching. A woman throws another bunch of willows from a house top to the plaza for the use of the Ne'wekwe, and the scene becomes exciting. The Ko'yemshi apparently have the best of it for a time. During this excitement the drum never ceases. Some of the Ko'yemshi take seats on the ledge, but they are not allowed to retain their seats for any length of time, the switches being used to bring them to their feet. Finally the elder brother Bow priest gathers all the willows in his right hand, waves them to the six regions, and carries them from the plaza through the eastern covered way.

The Ko'yemshi now examine the man who was foremost in the fight and say: "Oh! ho! I see nothing is the matter." The man replies: "No, I was not hurt." Much merriment is shown

WOMEN BEARING OFFERINGS TO THE PERSONATORS OF THE KO'YEMSHI GODS

WA'TĔM'LA (ALL HERDS) GODS IN PLAZA

ALTAR OF THE NĚ́WEKWE (GALAXY FRATERNITY)

DRY PAINTING, FETISHES, AND WALL DECORATIONS OF HLE'WEKWE
(SWORD SWALLOWER FRATERNITY)

over the wool-bag game played by the Koꞌyemshi and Neꞌwekwe during the absence of the dancers, who retire from the plaza after each dance. When the dancers return for the last time to the plaza they are laden with cooked sweet corn, rabbits, and sliced watermelon, the ears of corn tied together with yucca string braided in fancy shape and hung over their shoulders.

BIꞌᵗSIᵗSI[a] WITH THE MOꞌLAWE, FRUIT AND SEED BEARERS[b]

About half an hour after noon, while the plaza is alive with dancers, Biꞌᵗsiᵗsi comes alone from the eastern covered way. He wears a gray-and-white-striped blanket and has a strip of rabbit skin tied around his throat and hanging in front. A line of white paint runs across his nose and under his eyes. Another line crosses the lower part of his face, passing over his lips. These lines, about three-fourths of an inch wide, extend entirely across his face. His arms have several bands of white above the wrist and one around the upper arm. White fluffy eagle plumes are attached at the bands by means of a thread around the arm. His hair is done up in a long knot extending out beyond the forehead, to which corn-husk ribbons are attached. Bunches of the same are on both sides of the head. He wears ordinary moccasins and carries two eagle-wing feathers. His Neꞌwekwe baton is stuck in his belt at the back, the large blanket he wears being belted in. With great dignity he crosses the plaza with even strides. His presence does not interrupt the dancing in the plaza. He ascends the ladder and enters the kiꞌwiᵗsinĕ to announce the arrival of the moꞌlawe[c] at Kuꞌshilowa (red earth). The first body of Aꞌshiwanni, the Koꞌmosona, Koꞌpekwĭn, two Koꞌpiꞌᵗläshiwanni, the ceremonial father of Biꞌᵗsiᵗsi, and others, are gathered in the kiꞌwiᵗsinĕ to receive him. Live coals are on the fire altar, and a cloud symbol of meal is on the floor in the west end of the room. A number of miꞌwachi (plural of miꞌli) extend along the west side of the meal painting. A bowl of medicine water stands by the painting. The medicine water has been consecrated by the Koꞌmosona, who deposits six aꞌthläshi concretion fetishes sacred to the fields, in the bowl and forms a cross and circle on the water with a powder made from a root ground by his wife. A line of meal extends from the cloud symbol to the ladder.

---

[a] Biꞌᵗsiᵗsi was the original director of the Neꞌwekwe (Galaxy) fraternity (see p. 408).

[b] See Rediscovery of the Corn maidens and recreation of corn.

[c] To spare the women the long exposure to the cold, the moꞌlawe are, on the occasion described, personated by men from the six kiꞌwiᵗsiwe, who are supposed to be young, although such is not always the case, the chief worli of each kiꞌwiᵗsinĕ making the selection. Each worli is supposed to supply four moꞌlawe, but on the occasion described there are but fifteen; on another occasion observed by the writer there were twenty-three. An equal number of women are chosen by a man of the Aiꞌyahoꞌkwe (a plant) clan, whose office is for life. At his death the clan gather together and the parent, or elder, of the clan selects a successor. The present representative is an albino.

After Bi‴si‘si goes to the ki′wi‘sinĕ the Ko′mosona and the Ko′-
pekwĭn leave the plaza, where they have received corn from the
Mu′luktäkĭa gods, and return to the ki′wi‘sinĕ.   The plaza, kaleido-
scopic with the various dancers until half past 3 o’clock, forms a
striking picture, especially when several lines are dancing simultaneously in their brilliant dress, their bodies swaying in rhythmic
motion.   Each time they come they bring corn, which is received by
some of the officiating priests and carried to the ki′wi‘sinĕ.   When
the dancers leave the plaza for the last time, they are supposed to
go to Chi′pia,[a] in the east, to visit the anthropic gods who live there
and then return to Ko′thluwala′wa by a northern route.   In fact,

FIG. 9—Depositing prayer plumes at Ku′shilowa.

they visit Ku′shilowa, just beyond the eastern side of the town,
where they deposit their te′likinawe.   All the members of the Ko′ti-
kili (mythologic fraternity) visit Ku′shilowa sometime during the
afternoon, each carrying his Kor′kokshi mask and eight te′likinawe,
of which four are planted to Kok′ko A′wa (all the gods) and four to
Ko′yemshi (see figure 9).   Those who are absent from Zuñi or are
unable to go must have their masks and offerings carried by others.

While the personators of the mo′lawe gather at Ku′shilowa, the
chosen women (see note c, p. 277) congregate at the southeast point in
the village, each carrying on her back, held on by a blanket around her
waist, an offering of a watermelon and seeds to be made by a mo′lawa
(singular of mo′lawe), each donation having been supplied from the

_____
a See p. 407.

house of the woman who carries it.   When all is in readiness, the man of the Ai’yaho‘kwe clan who has chosen them throws out a line of meal toward Ku’shilowa and commands the women to run.   Off they go as rapidly as possible, each one trying to outrun the other.   On reaching Ku’shilowa the women deposit the baskets containing the offerings in line on the ground, just where the Corn maidens are supposed to have taken their places (see page 52).

B‘’ᵗsiᵗsi, coming from the He’iwa ki’wiᵗsinĕ, descends the ladder, face forward, with the ease and grace of a Roman (see plate LXXVI), and disappears through the eastern covered way, followed by the pe’kwĭn (sun priest).   The two return at sunset, accompanied by Pau’tiwa (director-general of the gods), elaborately dressed in white embroidered blankets, wearing the mask, and carrying a gourd jug of water, the neck of the jug being filled with grass, and by the fifteen mo’lawe, each carrying a basket on his head containing a watermelon and seeds.   These wear white embroidered kilts, sashes, and dance moccasins, and the hair, which had been tightly braided to make it wavy, hangs loosely over the shoulders.   A bunch of yellow parrot plumes is attached to the fore part of the head.   Each carries te’liki-nawe in the right hand and a mi’li in the left.   They are met at the entrance of the eastern covered way by the Great Father Ko’yemshi, and the procession advances in file across the plaza.   It presents one of the most attractive pictures to be seen in Zuñi.

The pe’kwĭn retires immediately to the ki’wiᵗsinĕ, sprinkling meal as he proceeds.   Bi‘’ᵗsiᵗsi follows him to the roof, where he remains until Pau’tiwa ascends.   While the latter prays at the hatchway Bi‘’ᵗsiᵗsi stands behind him and pats him on each side with his eagle-wing feathers, which are unusually long and sharp at the ends.   Bi‘’ᵗsiᵗsi remains standing at the hatchway for a short time and then follows Pau’tiwa into the ki’wiᵗsinĕ.   When Bi‘’ᵗsiᵗsi enters, he stands, with his arms crossed, north of the meal line near the ladder and points to the east.   The pe’kwĭn now takes a cigarette, proceeds to the fire altar, and igniting a roll of cedar fiber at the coals lights the cigarette; then, stooping before Pau’tiwa, he takes six whiffs from the cigarette, blowing the smoke over Pau’tiwa’s mask; next, passing to the jug of water, he blows smoke over it six times, and after depositing the remains of the cigarette upon the grass he returns to his seat by the side of the Ko’pi‘’läshiwanni, and all present sprinkle meal over Pau’-tiwa’s mask (see plate XXVIII).   Each one now sprinkles meal over the jug of water, and Pau’tiwa, passing south of the meal painting, ascends the ladder from the west side; descending into the plaza, he leaves it by the western way.   All present sprinkle his mask with meal as he crosses the plaza.   After Pau’tiwa’s exit from the ki’wiᵗsinĕ, Bi‘’ᵗsiᵗsi, passing north of the meal line and stepping over the heaps of corn, stands before the place vacated by Pau’tiwa.

The pe′kwĭn places his hands upon Bi‴ᵗsiᵗsi's shoulders, turns him to the six regions, seats him, and makes a prayer over him.   At this time the Shi′wanni of the Nadir, who is also elder brother Bow priest, leaves the ki′wiᵗsinĕ, followed by a man of his clan (Eagle) whom he calls younger brother, who carries the jug brought by Pau′tiwa, and by the younger brother Bow priest, who carries a lighted brand of cedar fiber about 1½ inches in diameter and several feet long.   The Shi′wanni of the Nadir whirls the rhombus as they proceed to He′patina, where the water is emptied from the jug into one of the rain vases on the upper floor of the shrine (see page 201).   Each one also deposits te′likinawe in the inclosure on the north side of the shrine, after which the party returns to the ki′wiᵗsinĕ.

As soon as Pau′tiwa disappears from the plaza, the Great Father Ko′yemshi leads the fourteen mo′lawe around in a circle, stopping four times as he proceeds.   They afterward form an arc of a circle, which vanishes as they leave one by one for the ki′wiᵗsinĕ.   As

FIG. 10—Whistle used
by Bi‴ᵗsiᵗsi.

Pau′tiwa crosses the court the Great Father Ko′yemshi sprinkles the ladder with meal and the first of the mo′lawe ascends and passes to the northeast corner of the roof of the ki′wiᵗsinĕ, and still holding his basket on his head stands on a cross of meal facing north, the Great Father Ko′yemshi having made a cross in each of the four corners of the roof.   Bi‴ᵗsiᵗsi, having come from the ki′wiᵗsinĕ, stands at the back of the mo′lawa and blows a tiny whistle,ᵃ which is secreted in his mouth (fig. 10 shows whistle of Bi‴ᵗsiᵗsi).   He taps the mo′lawa with his eagle-wing plumes on each side, at the same time blowing his whistle, and the latter turns completely around from right to left and then on until he faces west.   Bi‴ᵗsiᵗsi does not change his position until the mo′lawa throws out a line of meal toward the west and passes to the northwest corner of the roof, when Bi‴ᵗsiᵗsi follows.   The ceremony is repeated at each of the four corners, the southeast corner being the last one.   The mo′lawa faces west at the second corner, south at the third, and east at the fourth.   After he has turned on the fourth cross the Kĭa′kwemosi comes from the ki′wiᵗsinĕ and, approaching the mo′lawa, sprinkles the plumes he carries with meal, receives from him the basket, which he hands to his associate, who awaits on the inner ladder, and, throwing meal upon this ladder, descends to the ki′wiᵗsinĕ.   The mo′lawa, retaining the te′likinawe in the right hand and the mi′li in the left, leans forward with bended knees and catches hold of each side of the ladder that leads into the ki′wiᵗsinĕ, just below the roof, and jumps upon it while he is whipped on both sides

---

ᵃ A whistle used by Bi‴ᵗsiᵗsi was secured and deposited in the United States National Museum. Fig. 10 gives top, side, and end views of the whistle, which is of vegetable matter and less than an inch in length.

with the feathers by Bi‘'ᵗsiᵗsi, who at the same time blows his whistle. Bi‘'ᵗsiᵗsi afterward stands west of the hatchway, facing east, and offering a short prayer follows the mo'lawa into the ki'wiᵗsinĕ. The Kĭa'-kwemosi, and his associate holding the basket of fruit and seeds, stand east of the ladder at the end of the meal line. The pe'kwĭn, advancing, sprinkles meal on the gift and passes up the meal line, sprinkling meal as he goes. The associate shi'wanni, following him and also sprinkling meal, deposits the basket containing the watermelons and seeds on the meal line near the mi'li of the Kĭa'kwemosi. The Kĭa'kwemosi follows, sprinkling a line of meal, and upon reaching the basket throws meal over the offerings. The Kĭa'kwemosi and his associate then return to their places back of the cloud symbol; the pe'kwĭn returns to his seat on the north side of the room. The mo'lawa passes from the east side of the ladder around north of the meal line and takes his seat to the left of the pe'kwĭn. Bi‘'ᵗsiᵗsi follows, passing up north of the line, and, stepping over the heap of corn, takes his former place immediately back of the meal painting. He does not speak on this occasion, but expresses much as with folded arms he looks upon all those present. If anyone should sleep or doze while Bi‘'ᵗsiᵗsi is in the ki'wiᵗsinĕ he must remain seated until the sleeper awakens. Such a delinquent usually receives a shake from some one. No one in the ki'wiᵗsinĕ speaks during this ceremonial, when heart speaks to heart. When a cigarette is to be lighted, the younger brother Bow priest ignites the cedar fiber at the fire altar and hands it to the one wishing to smoke.

When all the mo'lawe have entered the ki'wiᵗsinĕ,[a] Bi‘'ᵗsiᵗsi, passing south of the meal line, joins his ceremonial father at the east end of the room and stands with crossed arms; his father rises from his seat, and Bi‘'ᵗsiᵗsi deposits his whistle from his mouth into the palm of the right hand of his father, who on this occasion is director of the Ne'wekwe fraternity. The father prays for rain and the fruits of the earth, waves his hand in a circle symbolic of all the world, and draws in common with the others present the sacred breath of A'wonawil'ona (see page 22). Then Bi‘'ᵗsiᵗsi, speaking for the first time, utters the greeting given after sunset: "Ko'naton sun'hakĭanapkĭa." The others reply: "Kets'-anishi (All good come to you, or be with you)." After Bi‘'ᵗsiᵗsi takes his seat by his ceremonial father the general silence is broken. The mo'lawe now rise and remain standing while the pe'kwĭn removes each offering from the basket, returning it to the owner. After the return of the basket the Ko'mosona administers the consecrated water, dipping it with a shell to each mo'lawa, beginning with the one at the west end of the line. As soon as the draft is swallowed the recipient says: "Tä'ᵗchumo" (Father). The Ko'mosona replies: "Täl'lemo"

---

a The scenes in the ki'wiᵗsinĕ at this time are a dramatization of the rediscovery of the Corn maidens and re-creation of corn (see p. 54).

(Younger brother) or younger one. After the mo'lawe are helped, the Ko'mosona administers the water to the others in the following order: First, Bi⸱''ᵗsiᵗsi; second, his ceremonial father; third, the younger brother Bow priest; fourth, the elder brother Bow priest; fifth, sixth, seventh, eighth, ninth, tenth, the A'shiwanni in order; then the Ko'pekwĭn, and finally the two Ko'piᵗläshiwanni. The Ko'mosona makes a different reply to the Bow priests from the one that he gives to the others. They say, like the others, "Täᵗchumo." The Ko'mosona replies, "Na'namo" (Grandfather). When all have been supplied with the consecrated water, the Ko mosona takes a mouthful and throws it out through his teeth over those present and then takes a draft himself. Bi⸱''ᵗsiᵗsi now advances to the west end of the room, passing north of the meal line, and stands west of the meal painting while he offers a prayer, after which he leads the mo'lawe from the ki'wiᵗsinĕ and through the eastern covered way to Ku'shilowa to deposit te'likinawe. Those of Bi⸱''ᵗsiᵗsi are offered to A'towa e'washtokĭi (Corn maidens), each stick being colored for one of the six regions. These offerings, which are tied in a group, are separated before planting. The mo'lawe offer te'likinawe to all the ancestral gods.

Bi⸱''ᵗsiᵗsi and the mo'lawe no sooner disappear from the plaza than the work begins of removing the offerings to the Ko'yemshi, which would fill several large wagons. These donations are carried away in blankets or canvas on the backs of members of the clans of the paternal parents of the Ko'yemshi, each Ko'yemshi assisting with his own gifts. This work continues until far into the night, and though much labor is involved in filling large sacks with flour or meal from the baskets in which it is brought and assorting numbers of dressed sheep, melons, corn, etc., still all seem to be having a good time generally, and the air resounds with merry voices.

After the te'likinawe are planted, the mo'lawe separate and go to their homes, where their heads are washed in yucca suds by women of their clans. Bi⸱''ᵗsiᵗsi returns to the ki'wiᵗsinĕ, taking his seat by his ceremonial father. The pe'kwin now distributes the offerings of the mo'lawe. He presents the group nearest the meal painting to the Kĭa'kwemosi and the next one to the first associate Kĭa'kwemosi. The third one is given to the Shi'wanni of the West, the fourth to the Shi'wanni of the South, and the fifth to the Shi'wanni of the East; the sixth he takes for himself; the seventh is given to the elder brother Bow priest, who is also Shi'wanni of the Nadir; the eighth to the younger brother Bow priest; the ninth to the Ko'mosona; the tenth to the Ko'pekwĭn; the eleventh to the Ko'piᵗläshiwanni of the Ko'mosona; the twelfth to the Ko'piᵗläshiwanni of the Ko'pekwĭn; the thirteenth to Bi⸱''ᵗsiᵗsi; the fourteenth to the ceremonial father of Bi⸱''ᵗsiᵗsi.[a] The corn collected from the personators of the gods

---

[a] The fifteenth was given to a party unknown to the writer.

during the dancing in the plaza is next distributed in the same order. The ceremonial father now takes down Bi‴si⁺si's hair, removing the husks. The hair is left hanging.

The mi'wachi are collected and given to their owners, and after the other objects are removed from the meal painting the Ko'mosona brushes the meal of the painting together with his hands and deposits it in the small circular opening in the floor of the ki'wi⁺sině, symbolic of the opening through which the A'shiwi came to this world from interior worlds. The A'shiwanni and others carry their gifts to their homes, and then they may indulge in a repast, no food having been taken since the previous day by any in the ki'wi⁺sině except Bi‴si⁺si and Pau'tiwa, who were not obliged to observe the fast.

HISTORY, ARTS, AND CUSTOMS

Chronologic Summary of Historical Events Connected with Zuñi
1539–1800

Zuñi history, as recorded by the Spanish invaders and others, has been so fully exploited that little space need be devoted to it in the present paper. Mr F. W. Hodge, of the Smithsonian Institution, to whom the writer is much indebted, has furnished the following synopsis of historical events:

1539, May.　Fray Marcos of Niza visited Cibola in this month and viewed Hawikuh, one of the Seven Cities, from a neighboring height. This pueblo was the scene of the death of his negro companion Estevan at the hands of the Zuñis about May 20. Niza here took possession of the province in the name of the King of Spain.

1540, July 7.　Francisco Vasquez Coronado, after a conflict in which he was wounded, captured Hawikuh and applied to it the name Granada. It had 200 warriors. On July 11 the Indians retired to Toaiyalone (To'wa yäl'länně). This is the first reference in history to the use of this mesa as a place of refuge, although it may have been used as such in prehistoric times.

1540, July 15.　Coronado sent Pedro de Tovar from Cibola to the province of Tusayan (the Hopi country).

1540, July 19.　Coronado journeyed from Granada to Toaiyalone and returned the same day.

1540, August 3.　Coronado wrote his celebrated letter to the Viceroy Mendoza, dated "from the province of Cevola, and this city of Granada."

1540, August 25 (?).　Coronado sent Lopez de Cárdenas from Cibola on a journey which resulted in the discovery of the Grand Canyon of the Colorado river.

1540, August 29.　Hernando de Alvarado was sent eastward from Cibola to the buffalo plains.

1540, September.　The army of Coronado reached Cibola with sheep and cattle. This doubtless marked the beginning of the sheep and cattle industry and of the use of horses among the Southwestern tribes. Twenty days later the army started for Tiguex, on the Rio Grande, where it established winter quarters.

1542, spring.　Coronado and his army passed through Cibola on their way back to Mexico, leaving some natives of Mexico among the Zuñis.

1581, summer.　Francisco Sanchez Chamuscado, with a small force, visited the province of Zuñi (misprinted Cami in the records), which comprised six pueblos; one village having been abandoned subsequent to Coronado's visit.

1583, —. Antonio de Espejo, with Fray Bernardino Beltran and an escort of fourteen men, visited a group of six pueblos; one of them named Aquico (Hawikuh), "which they call Zuñi, and by another name Cibola." Here crosses were found erected near the pueblos and three Christian Mexican Indians who had been left by Coronado forty-one years previous. Fray Bernardino remained at Hawikuh for several weeks, while Espejo made a tour to the west.

1598, September 9. The province of Zuñi became a parochial district under the new governorship of Juan de Oñate, the colonizer of New Mexico, and Fray Andrés Corchado was assigned to it, but he never was an active missionary there. In the records Fray Juan Claros is also assigned to this parish, through misunderstanding.

1598, November. Juan de Oñate visited Zuñi, and on November 9 the natives made their vows of obedience and vassalage. Oñate mentions the six villages by name: Aguicobi, or Aguscobi (Hawikuh); Canabi (Kyanawe?); Coaqueria (Kyakima); Halonagu (Halona); Macaqui (Matsaki); and Aquinsa (Apinawa?). Crosses were found and also children of the Mexican Indians left behind by Coronado. Here Oñate spent only a couple of days.

1598, December 10 (?). Oñate passed through Zuñi on his way back to the Rio Grande from the Hopi country.

1604, October. Oñate again visited Zuñi, or Cibola, on his way from the capital of New Mexico, San Gabriel, on the Rio Grande, to the Gulf of California. The province consisted of six villages containing about 300 houses. Hawikuh was the most important village at this time, its houses numbering 110. In Coronado's time it was said to have more than 200 houses or 500 families. From thence Oñate proceeded to the Hopi country, the province of Tusayan.

1605, April. Oñate probably passed through Zuñi on his way from the mouth of the Colorado to the Rio Grande, as he carved an inscription April 16 on El Morro, or Inscription Rock, 35 miles east of Zuñi.

1629, June 23. A band of missionaries under Fray Estevan de Perea, accompanied by the governor, Don Francisco Manuel de Silva Nieto, started westward from Santa Fé for the purpose of planting missions among the Acomas, Zuñis, and Hopis. They evidently reached Zuñi late in July, as Nieto's first inscription on El Morro is dated July 29. Fray Roque de Figueredo, Fray Agustin de Cuellar, and Fray Francisco de la Madre de Dios, together with three soldiers, one of whom was Juan Gonzales, remained at Zuñi. A house was bought for religious purposes at Hawikuh, which became the first mission established in the Zuñi country. Possibly the Hawikuh church, the walls of which are still traceable, was built by these missionaries, and they may also have erected the church the ruins of which still stand at Ketchipauan, on a mesa southeast of Ojo Caliente, as well as the one which formerly existed at Halona. These three missionaries disappear from Zuñi history before 1632. They were succeeded by Fray Francisco Letrado, who arrived in New Mexico in 1629 and was first assigned to the Jumanos east of the Rio Grande.

1632, February 22. The Zuñis killed Fray Francisco Letrado at Hawikuh and fled to Toaiyalone, where they remained about three years.

1632, February 27. Some Zuñis, having followed Fray Martin de Arvide, murdered him and his escort of two soldiers on their way from the Zuñi villages to a tribe called Cipias, or Zipias, who lived toward the west.

1632, March 23. The maestro de campo, Tomás de Albizu, was at El Morro on his way to Zuñi with some priests and a small detachment, to reduce the Zuñi stronghold. They were admitted to the summit of the mesa, and the Zuñis promised to be peaceful thenceforth.

1635. Some of the Zuñis left the mesa and began the resettlement of their villages in the valley.

1636. No missionaries at Zuñi because the governor at Santa Fé refused an escort. There appears on El Morro the inscription: "We pass by here, the lieutenant-colonel and the captain Juan de Archuleta, and the lieutenant Diego Martin Barba, and the ensign Augustin de Ynojos, in the year of 1636."

1643. Missionaries were probably again established at Zuñi about this time.

1670, October 7. The Apaches (or Navahos) raided Hawikuh, killing the Zuñi missionary, Fray Pedro de Avila y Ayala, by beating out his brains with a bell while he was clinging to a cross. The priest at Halona, Fray Juan Galdo, recovered Fray Pedro's remains and interred them at Halona. The mission of La Concepcion de Hawikuh was henceforth abandoned, but the pueblo was occupied by the Indians for a few years.

1680, August 10. A general revolt of the Pueblos against Spanish authority took place. The Zuñis murdered their missionary, Fray Juan de Bal, of the mission pueblo of La Purificacion de la Virgen de Alona (Halona), burned the church, and fled to Toaiyalone, where they remained for more than twelve years. At the time of this rebellion the Zuñis, who numbered 2,500, occupied, in addition to Halona, the villages of Kiakima, Matsaki, and Hawikuh. Two villages (Canabi and Aquinsa) had therefore been abandoned between Oñate's time (1598) and the Pueblo revolt (1680).

1692, November 11. The Zuñis were found on the mesa by Diego de Vargas Zapata Lujan Ponce de Leon, to whom they submitted, and about 300 children were baptized.

1693, April 15. Vargas consulted with a Zuñi chief at San Felipe with a view to transferring the pueblo of Zuñi to the Rio Grande, but no definite action was taken.

1696, June 29. An expedition was sent by the Spaniards against the Jemez and their allies from the Navaho, Zuñi, and Acoma tribes. The Indians were defeated, and the Zuñis returned home frightened.

1699, July 12. The pueblo of La Purisima de Zuñi (evidently the present Zuñi village, which meanwhile had been built on the ruins of Halona) was visited by the governor, Pedro Rodriguez Cubero, to whom the inhabitants renewed their allegiance.

1700, June. Padre Juan Garaicochea was priest at Zuñi.

1702. In the spring the Hopis tried to incite the Zuñis and others to revolt. Captain Juan de Uribarri was sent to investigate and left Captain Medina at Zuñi with a force of 19 men as a garrison. This force was later reduced, those who were left treating the natives harshly.

1703. Padre Garaicochea, who was still missionary at Zuñi, complained to the governor at Santa Fé, and the Indians, receiving no redress, on March 4 killed three Spaniards who were exiles from Santa Fé and who had been living publicly with native women. Some of the Zuñis thereupon fled to the Hopis, others took refuge on Toaiyalone. Captain Roque Madrid was sent to Zuñi to bring away the friar, leaving Zuñi without a missionary.

1703, November (?). Padre Garaicochea urged the reestablishment of the Zuñi mission, but no action was taken.

1705, March–April. Padre Garaicochea returned to Zuñi as missionary early in the year; he induced the Indians to come down from Toaiyalone, where they had been since 1703, and again settle on the plains. On April 6 they renewed their allegiance to Captain Roque Madrid.

1705, September. The Spaniards found a knotted cord, probably a quipu (calendar string), which reminded them of the days of 1680, when a similar device was employed to notify the revolutionists and to fix the day of the rebellion.

1706, April-May. The Hopis had been raiding the Zuñis, who were now baptized Christians; therefore Captain Gutierrez was sent with eight men for their protection. The Zuñis made an expedition against the Hopis in May, killing two and recovering seventy animals. Later the Zuñis aroused suspicion by asking that the garrison be removed from their pueblo. Fray Antonio Miranda, now resident missionary at Acoma, occasionally ministered to the Zuñis.

1707. Governor José Chacon Medina Salazar y Villaseñor, Marquis de la Peñuela, sent an embassy of Zuñis to the Hopis to exhort them to peace and submission, but refugee Tanos and Tewas, who lived among the Hopis, responded by making a raid on Zuñi. At this time Fray Francisco de Irazábal was missionary at "Alona," indicating that the old name was still sometimes applied to the new pueblo.

1709, June 5. The following inscription occurs on El Morro: "On the 5th day of the month of June of this year of 1709 passed by here, bound for Zuñi, Ramon Paez Hurtado." He was lieutenant-general of the province and acting governor in 1704–5. The expedition here noted was probably sent against the Navahos, who were hostile this year.

1713, May. Padre Irazábal reported that a Zuñi Indian attempted to instigate the Acomas and Lagunas to kill their missionary, Fray Carlos Delgado.

1713, December. Two Zuñis were granted permission to visit the Hopis, who expressed eagerness for peace and alliance with the Zuñis, but not with the Spaniards.

1716, August 26. The governor, Don Feliz Martinez, carved his inscription on El Morro on his way to conquer the Hopis, by way of Zuñi. The custodian, Fray Antonio Camargo, and the alcalde of Santa Fé accompanied him. Native commissioners were sent forward from Zuñi, which was still called Alona.

1726, February. The ensign, Don José de Payba Basconzelos visited Zuñi, leaving his inscription on El Morro dated February 18 of this year.

1736–1738. General Juan Paez Hurtado (son of Ramon), official inspector, visited the pueblo in 1736; Bishop Elizaecochea of Durango visited the pueblo in September 1737; and Governor Enrique de Olavide y Michelena in 1738.

1744–1748. Zuñi is reported by one authority as having a population of 150 families, and by another 2,000 souls. It had two priests, one of whom was Padre (Juan José?) Toledo.

1760. Bishop Tamaron reported the population of Zuñi to be 664, but this number is smaller by nearly 1,000 than that reported by Ilzarbe in 1788.

1774–1778. Fray Silvestre Velez Escalante was missionary at Zuñi.

1779–1780. Fray Andrés Garcia was missionary at Zuñi.

1788. Fray Rafael Benavides was missionary at Zuñi, also Fray Manuel Vega. Ilzarbe reports the population to be 1,617.

1792. Fray Daniel Martinez was missionary at Zuñi before this date.

1793. Revilla Gigedo reports the population at 1,935.

1798–99. The population of Zuñi is reported at 2,716. (In 1820–21 it had apparently dwindled to 1,597.)

NATIVE ACCOUNTS OF THE REVOLT OF 1680

Accounts of the revolt of the Zuñis against Spanish rule in 1680 were obtained by the writer from a shi'wanni (rain priest) and from Tu'maka, a theurgist of one of the esoteric fraternities. The shi'wanni's account is as follows: When (in 1680) the Pueblo Indians as a body planned the revolt, the Zuñis went to the mesa called by them To′wa yäl′länně (Corn mountain) and prepared for defense. On their way they poisoned a number of the springs. They also deposited stones near the brink of the mesa, for use as missiles. The Spanish priest who was with them at the time accompanied them to the mesa. When the Spaniards came to avenge the supposed death of this priest, who had long since adopted the dress of the Zuñis, having none other to wear, they were met with missiles hurled from the mesa and with small shells filled with magic medicine, that could not fail in its purpose, ejected from the mouths of the keeper of the ᵗsuᵗʰhlan′na (great shell) and his deputy. Finally the rain priests scraped a buckskin and requested the foreign priest to write upon it telling the Spaniards that he was safe and beloved by the Zuñis. This he did, and a large stone was fastened to the rolled skin and thrown down into the valley. Learning of the safety of the priest, the Spaniards retired.

A more detailed account of the revolt was given by the theurgist Tu′maka, as follows: "After the old church was built in I′tiwanna, a Spanish priest resided permanently at the village. After a time the Zuñis came to believe that they were to be destroyed by the Spaniards, and they planned a revolt. They told all their women and children to refrain from attending services on a certain day, and the men, providing themselves with bows and arrows, which they hid under their blankets, started for the church. The leader of this revolt was the keeper of the great shell, who said that he was not afraid, as he had plenty of medicine to destroy the enemy. The Indians found only a few Spaniards in the church. They locked the doors and killed all but the priest and one other who escaped through the roof. The priest was stripped of his vestments and made to wear Zuñi dress. The keeper of the great shell declared that it would be best to return to To′wa yäl′länně to protect themselves better from the enemy.

While on To′wa yäl′länně they noticed one night a fire in the distance, and several men, perhaps six, were sent to find out what it meant. A party of Laguna Indians had made the fire, and they told the Zuñis that in a short time many Spaniards and many Indians would attack them. The Zuñis returned with the news and were again dispatched to the Lagunas, who joined the party of Zuñis. The Lagunas said that they had been compelled to accompany the Spaniards in the march against the Zuñis, but had escaped. They were instructed by the Zuñis to fill hides with water and not to touch water from any spring in the Zuñi country, as they would all be poisoned, and also to take a bit of cedar twig into their mouths to protect them from the poisoned shells which would be shot by the keeper of the shell. When the enemy was discovered approaching the keeper of the great shell and his deputy were in their house. Three times they were called upon to come out and help the people, but they did not appear.

When they were called the fourth time and came forward, the enemy was well up the mesa. The keeper and his deputy were nude except a breechcloth, their bodies and limbs were painted red, and they had anklet and wristlet wreaths of yucca. The face of each was painted black, the forehead and chin covered with eagle down, and a red, fluffy eagle plume was tied to the scalp lock. They had been preparing medicine, which had to be obtained on the mesa, and therefore could not appear sooner. Each theurgist filled a tiny shell with the medicine, put the shell into his mouth, and approached the edge of the mesa unarmed. The people were alarmed and cried to them not to advance. The theurgists said: 'We are not afraid.' They blew the shells containing the medicine toward the enemy, who were immediately affected by it. The enemy at first appeared to be intoxicated. One would try to catch the other as he fell, and then both would stagger and soon fall. Nearly the whole army was destroyed. The survivors retreated. All the Rio Grande pueblos except the Lagunas fought the Zuñis. Those of the Lagunas who accompanied the Spaniards did not shoot an arrow. About six months after this attack the Lagunas again appeared and made a fire, and information was given to the Zuñis that another attack was expected. The keeper of the shell prepared his medicine, but the Spanish priest, who was still with them, being anxious to prevent further destruction of the Spaniards, looked about for something on which to send a message. He finally wrote with charcoal on a piece of deerskin, saying that he was safe and that he loved the Zuñis and wished to remain with them, and threw it down the mesa side, calling to the Spaniards to receive it. After the message was read and the Spaniards learned of the safety of their priest, they made no attack, but sent clothing and other things to him.

An associate of the keeper of the great shell fell sick about a year after the Spaniards came the second time, while the Zuñis were still living on the mesa. A sorcerer went one night to this man's house and, ascending to the roof, put his medicine all around it; but when he attempted to descend through the hatchway into the house, he found that his strength was gone and that he could not move. At daylight the father of the sick man, discovering the sorcerer on the roof, said: 'You had better come into the house. If anyone should see you here you would get into trouble.' He helped the man into the house. The sick man asked: 'What were you doing on my roof?' 'I put medicine there because I wished you to die.' 'You must not try that again. I can easily find you out and destroy you.' The sister of the sick man said to her brother: 'I shall put away your medicine. You find out too many bad men and kill them.' She placed the medicine, including all the tiny shells, in a water vase, dug a hole about 2 feet deep on a knoll at the base of the mesa, and buried the vase. And so those little shells are all gone; only the great shell is left for the Navahos. This shell would be used with the medicine if an attack were made upon the Zuñis, but at the ceremonials it is only blown, for if the medicine were used it would kill all the people."

After dwelling a long time on To'wa yäl'länně (Corn mountain), the Zuñis again descended and scattered over the valley, but raids of the Navahos and Apaches forced them to build the present village upon the remains of old I'tiwanna, which stood on a knoll containing 15 acres, considerably elevated above the north bank of the Rio Zuñi. This village has a population of about 1,600. It consists principally of groups of houses, compactly built, one upon another, the highest portion being five stories. The roof of the lower houses furnish the front yards for the houses above. Generally the interior is so arranged that the inhabitants can readily communicate with one another. These remarkable structures served as fortifications, the ladders for ascending to the roofs being drawn up in case of attack. A church was built in Shi'wona, the name of this new village, and after a time the Zuñis became interested in the Catholic ritual, especially as they were allowed to make use of their own symbols in decorating the churches. So far as the writer has been able to discover, the religious and social institutions of the Zuñis have been but slightly affected by the teachings of the Spanish priesthood, and their mode of thought is practically what it was before the arrival of Coronado more than 350 years ago.

GOVERNMENT

The government of Zuñi is hierarchical, four fundamental religious groups, the A'shiwanni (Rain priesthood), the Ko'tikilli,[a] the A'pi‘tlä-shiwanni (Bow priesthood), and the other esoteric fraternities being concerned. The dominant authority, however, is what the writer terms the first body of A'shiwanni, composed of eight men and one woman.[b] A governor with four assistants and a lieutenant-governor with his four deputies constitute the civic branch. These men are all nominated by the first body of rain priests, though much influence is brought to bear for or against the various men supposed to be in favor with this body. The public notification to the governor of his appointment takes place in the te'wita ‘hlanna (large plaza), when the governor's cane, a gift from President Lincoln (formerly a native staff was in use), is handed to the new appointee. Though the governor is elected for one year, he may be reelected one or more times. He may, for proper cause, lose his office at any time, and this is also true

---

[a] Organization directly associated with anthropic worship.

[b] The rain priests are designated by terms which indicate freedom from secular work, the six A'shiwanni directly associated with the six regions, the Shi'wano'‘kla (Priestess of fecundity), and the elder and younger Bow priests, the two latter being A'shiwanni ex officio, as they are the earthly representatives of the Divine Ones, constitute the first body of A'shiwanni.

of any member of his staff. The governor and his staff attend to such secular affairs as do not require the judgment of the first body of rain priests or of the Bow priests. Capital punishment comes within the jurisdiction of the latter body.

A case came to the notice of the writer in 1891, when a conference was held between the Kĭa'kwe'mosi (rain priest of the North) and an associate rain priest, who was, however, not connected with the first body of rain priests. It was interesting to note the determination of the young associate priest in his attempt to convince the rain priest of the North that the governor was unworthy to fill the position, and he succeeded so far as to receive directions to inform the other members of the first body of rain priests that a meeting to discuss the situation would be held on the following night in the house of the Priestess of fecundity. Seven days after this meeting a hundred or more men, most of them past middle life, gathered in the large plaza. The elder brother Bow priest sat upon a ledge extending across a house on the north side of the plaza, with the governor's assistants on either side, the governor sitting opposite the elder brother Bow priest. A Mexican who had been captured by the Zuñis when a child and afterward adopted into the tribe accused the governor of having stolen Zuñi horses and traded them to Mexicans for sheep. The governor with great dignity resented the charge and made a rather lengthy speech, in which he exhibited independence and determination. The elder brother Bow priest spoke next. His voice was low, but every word was distinct, and he was listened to with profound interest as he set forth the reason why the governor should be dismissed. During his speech one of the younger men ventured to address a word to a neighbor, upon which the elder brother Bow priest stopped and without uttering a word stared at the offender. The fellow ceased suddenly, as though struck dumb, and the elder brother Bow priest continued his speech without further interruption. Both sides were earnest in their arguments for and against the governor, but the whole affair was conducted with great dignity. and when the judges, the first body of rain priests, announced that the governor was deposed, he, with his friends, left the plaza without speaking a word, the others following in silence.

PROPERTY

The Zuñis are an agricultural and pastoral people. The fields are not owned by clans, and the Zuñis claim that they never were so owned. A man may cultivate any strip of land, provided it has not already been appropriated, and once in his possession, he has the right to transfer it to whomsoever he pleases within the tribe. Land is obtained from the owner by trade, and houses are disposed of in the same manner. The sale of a house came under the observation of the

Mary Wright-Gill

INCIDENT IN RETIREMENT OF KOYEMSHI: MU'LUKTĀKÏA GODS IN LINE FOR DANCE AS WA'TĔM'LA GODS RETIRE

PERSONATOR OF BI''SI'SI, ORIGINAL DIRECTOR OF NE'WEKWE (GALAXY
FRATERNITY) CROSSING PLAZA

SWORD OF ꞎHLE′WEKWE (SWORD SWALLOWER FRATERNITY)

BOXES OF ᵀHLEWÉKWE (SWORD SWALLOWER FRATERNITY)

writer in 1896. An old woman owning two houses, one immediately in front of the other, sold the one in front, to the great annoyance of her female children, who feared that a story would be added to the house, thus cutting off the view of the street from their upper floor.

Much generosity is exhibited by these people regarding property left to them. According to the law the landed property of a married man or woman goes after death to the daughters. The sons are supposed to be able to acquire their own fields, but if there are no girls the sons are the next heirs. In case a man has sisters or brothers, especially sisters who are poor, his children are apt to give them part of their property or permit them to enjoy some of the benefits received therefrom. Disputes arising over the distribution of property are usually settled by the civil authorities, although occasionally they are carried to the first body of A'shiwanni, who have the higher control of civil affairs.

After a man is married, the products of his fields are carried to the house of his wife's parents (his home after marriage), and, though it is understood that these products are for general household use, there is an unwritten law that the property of each man may be removed from its storing place only by his wife and himself. The wife's grain—the produce of fields given her by her father or mother—is placed with that of the husband. On the death of the owner, horses, cattle, sheep, and blankets are divided among the girls and the boys of the family; the silver beads and turquoise earrings of the mother go to the daughters; the coral, white shell, and turquoise necklaces and earrings of the father go to the eldest son. The little gardens about the villages, which are tended exclusively by the women, are inherited by the daughters.

LIST OF CLANS

The Zuñi tribe is divided into clans (a'notiwe). While descent is through the maternal side, the offspring is also closely allied to the father's clan. The child is always referred to as belonging to the mother's clan and as being the "child" of the father's clan. It should be borne in mind that "child of the clan" throughout this paper refers to its relation to the paternal clan. In the family the child is under the control of both parents. The clan plays an important part in ceremonials. Many ceremonial offices are filled either by a member of a given clan or by a "child" of the clan—that is, either the mother or the father must belong to the particular clan. In some cases offices are filled annually, in rotation, first by a member of a particular clan and secondly by a "child" of the specified clan. Some offices are always filled by a particular clan; in other cases the offices must be filled only by a "child" of a designated clan. The list of clans here presented has been collected with the greatest care. If there were other clans at any period of the past, the knowledge of them is lost to the sages of the present time.

The existing clans are as follows:

Pi′chikwe	Dogwood clan
To′wakwe	Corn clan
Yä′tokĭakwe	Sun clan
To′nashikwe	Badger clan
Äiñshikwe	Bear clan
Sus′kikwe	Coyote clan
ꞌKoꞌꞌloktakwe	Sandhill-crane clan
Kĭäkĭälikwe	Eagle clan
Tä′kĭakwe ꞌ	Frog clan
A′naꞌkwe	Tobacco clan
Ai′yahoꞌkwe	—— (a plant)
Po′yiꞌkwe	Chaparral-cock clan
To′nakwe	Turkey clan
Sho′hitakwe	Deer clan
Taꞌhlupꞌsikwe	Yellow wood (Berberis fremontii) clan
Ma′wikwe ᵇ	Antelope clan

The extinct clans are as follows:

Ta′wi	Wood clan
A′poyakwe	Sky clan
Ok′shikokwe	Cottontail-rabbit clan
Kwĭn′ikwakwe ꞌ	Black corn clan

SOCIAL CUSTOMS

THE HOUSEHOLD

Though some Zuñi houses have as many as eight rooms, the ordinary house has from four to six and a few have only two. Ledges built with the house extend around the rooms, forming seats and shelves. The largest is the general living room, where the entire household works, eats, and sleeps, and where guests are entertained. When the room is required for the use of some fraternity, the family adjourns to other quarters, moving all its belongings. In this room the family wardrobe hangs on a pole suspended from the rafters. The more valuable things, especially the ceremonial paraphernalia, are carefully wrapped and deposited in the storage rooms. As a rule the mills for grinding meal are set up in the general living room. They consist of three or more slabs of stone, of different degrees of fineness of grain, set side by side at an angle of about 45° and separated by upright slabs, the whole surrounded by other slabs, making an inclosure for each mill.

Most of the rooms are provided with fireplaces, of which there are several varieties. One style is formed by a wall several feet high and

---

ᵃ See p. 168, note ᵇ.

ᵇ One man has been the only member of this clan for the past ten or twelve years.

ᶜ This clan became extinct in 1902 by the death of an aged shi′wanni.

of equal breadth extending at right angles from one of the longer walls of the room, the projecting wall being so placed as to protect the fireplace from the doorway. A commodious mantel usually extends over a part of the fireplace, and on it rests the masonry chimney, reaching up through the roof, while the exterior chimney is composed of old pottery vessels with perforated bottoms. Cooking vessels are set on stones in the fireplaces; food is also cooked in the coals and ashes. One room of every dwelling of any pretension has a fireplace of peculiar construction. It is from 6 to 12 feet wide and has a projection above like a Chinese awning. When the great ceremonial caldrons are used for the feasts, they are balanced on stones in this fireplace. He'we (wafer bread) is also baked in this fireplace upon highly polished stone slabs. The room, however, is not exclusively set apart for this cooking. Like most of the rooms, except the general living room and the one immediately adjoining, it is used largely as a storage room.

Candles are never used in a Zuñi house nor are lamps used for ordinary lighting. A lamp made of baked clay and somewhat resembling a Roman lamp is employed on the occasion of certain ceremonials. It gives very little light.

The domestic life of the Zuñis might well serve as an example for the civilized world. As has been stated, the husband lives with his wife's parents, and it is common to find several families, under the same roof. The Zuñis do not have large families, and the members are deeply attached to one another. The writer found great enjoyment in her visits to the general living room (see plate LXXVII) in the early evening, after the day's labors were over and before the elders were called away to their fraternities or elsewhere. The young mothers would be seen caring for their infants, or perhaps the fathers would be fondling them, for the Zuñi men are very devoted to their children, especially the babies. The grandmother would have one of the younger children in her lap, with perhaps the head of another resting against her shoulder, while the rest would be sitting near or busying themselves about household matters. When a story was told by the grandfather or some younger member of the group, intense interest would be depicted on the faces of all old enough to appreciate the recital.

The Zuñi child is rarely disobedient, and the writer has known but one parent to strike a child or to use harsh words with it. The children play through the livelong day without a quarrel. The youngest children never disturb or touch anything belonging to others. In years of experience with the Zuñis and other Indians the writer has never lost an article through them, either of food or otherwise.

The boys have many childish amusements, which they greatly enjoy. One of their especial delights at night is to run about with burning brands made of balls of fiber attached to slender poles. The boys and girls do not play much together. In fact the girls seem to have little

time for things which delight other children.   They carry the younger
sister or brother on their backs, often tottering from the weight. They
seem ever ready to look after the younger ones, and when they are
free from this care they imitate all that their mothers do.   They make
pottery, weave belts (see plate LXXVIII), make bread, and at times they
may actually be found playing with dolls instead of the living babies.
The children are as punctilious as their elders in attending to ceremonial observances.

Games and impromptu dances are the favorite pastime of the young
men.   Though they never wear their ceremonial masks in these dances,
they do wear masks copied after those of the Navahos (see plate
LXXIX).   The dog dance (plate LXXX), in which the performer picks
money and silver buttons from the ground with his mouth, always
draws a large audience and leads to considerable betting.   Girls
occasionally join in some of the pleasure dances (see plate LXXXI).

The older girls do not usually go about the village unattended.   The
only place they are free to visit alone is the well (see plate LXXXII),[a]
where the youth may be found lurking in the early evening, waiting
for an opportunity to speak a word to the pretty girls, and to some
special one if he has settled his affections.   Those who state that the
Zuñi maiden makes advances to the man are in error.   The writer has
observed many cases of love-making, and they have never differed
essentially from the experiences of our own youths and maidens.   The
conduct of a girl who shows her preference for a man before he has
shown his for her is looked upon as indelicate.   While parents are
inclined to look to the marriages of their children, there are many
love matches in Zuñi.

NATAL CUSTOMS

Previous to the birth of a child, if a daughter is desired, the husband
and wife, sometimes accompanied by a doctress or a female relative,
visit the Mother rock,[b] on the west side of To'wa yäl'länně (Corn
mountain).   The pregnant woman scrapes a small quantity of the
rock into a tiny vase made for the purpose and deposits it in one of
the cavities in the rock (see plate XII a), and they all pray that the
daughter may grow to be good and beautiful and possess all virtues, and
that she may weave beautifully and be skilled in the art of making
pottery.   If a son is desired, the couple visit a shrine higher up the
side of the mountain, in a fissure in the same rock, and sprinkle meal
and deposit te'likinawe, with prayers that a son may be born to them
and that he may be distinguished in war and after death become great
among ancestral gods.   Should the prayers offered at the shrines be

---

[a] This picturesque well will soon become an object of the past.

[b] The base of this rock is covered with symbols of the a'sha (vulva) (see pl. XII b) and is perforated with small excavations. The Zuñis are not an exception among aboriginal peoples in respect to phallic worship.

not answered, it is believed that the heart of one or other of the couple is not good. There is also another shrine most sacred to the Zuñis to which parents desiring sons resort. This shrine is on the summit of a low mound in a narrow valley and consists of a stone slab about 1 foot square, slightly raised from the ground by loose stones. Three stones, two round and one several inches long, symbolizing the male generative organs, are placed upon the slab, the long one pointing to the east.

Another resort for women in this condition is a queer-looking inclosure by the side of the trail leading to the peach orchards of To'wa yäl'länne. It is formed by a stone wall some 2½ feet high at the west end, the space within being 2½ by 6 feet. Two of the largest stones of the wall project into the interior. The wall slopes unevenly on each side and is only a foot high at the east end. When a daughter is desired, one or other of the couple or both visit this place and the woman, passing into the inclosure, breaks off a bit from each of the projecting rocks. These bits are afterward powdered and put into water and drunk by the woman. It is believed that a daughter is sure to be the result if the heart is good.

A pregnant woman suffering from a cough and a pain in the right side of her abdomen was relieved by the writer with simple remedies; but the celebrated Nai'uchi, surgeon and doctor, had to be sent for, as the family was sure the sufferer had been bewitched. Nai'uchi came and appeared to draw from the abdomen two objects which he claimed were the mother and child worms. One was about the length of the second finger of the hand; the other was smaller. Of course this showed that the woman had been bewitched and that it was well that he was sent for in time, as these worms would have eaten the child and caused its death. It was afterward reported that when the woman was grinding at Nutria some weeks previous, a sister of a witch, who ground by her side, touched the pregnant woman on the side of the abdomen, and it was then that the worms were "cast" in.

A pregnant woman while at her farm at Ojo Caliente became alarmed at the retarded action of the fetus, and she and her husband returned to Zuñi to consult Nai'uchi. On learning that the woman had been drinking water from the sacred spring of the Ko'loowisi (Plumed serpent), he declared that she was not carrying a child but a serpent. The following day the husband came to the writer in great distress and begged her to go to his wife, who was in such a wretched mental state that he feared she would die. After examining the abdomen the writer declared that Nai'uchi was mistaken; but his words had sunk into the sufferer's mind, and hours were spent with the distracted woman before she was convinced that her doctor was in error. After several days a slight color took the place of the death-like pallor of the woman, and she slowly improved, but it was many days before she was like herself again.   In less than six weeks from that time a healthy boy was born. The writer named the child at the request of the mother, but the nickname of Little Ko'loowisi will cling to him for many a day.   The gratitude of the husband to the writer for saving, as he thought, the life of his wife and child was very marked and was shown in every way possible.   Each week the best products of his fields and garden were brought to her from his farm, 15 miles away.

It is believed that if the Sa'ya'hlia or Säl'imobiya (certain anthropic gods) strike a pregnant woman with their yucca switches parturition will immediately result.   Therefore all women in this condition are careful to keep out of the reach of the yucca when these gods appear in the village.   A spiral shell is worn in the belt of the woman when a boy is desired, and another variety of shell when a girl is wished for. After childbirth a white pebble is taken into the mother's mouth, and the teeth are pressed against it in order that the child's teeth may be white and strong.   It has been reported that Zuñi women during childbirth are segregated in houses specially set apart for the purpose.   Such is not the fact.   Nai'uchi would not visit his granddaughter for some days after her confinement because of wounds he had received from arrows years ago, as he feared that the wounds would frighten the infant, causing it to cry all the time and not sleep.   It is declared by all the Zuñi theurgists, both men and women, that ten months are required for the gestation of a male child, but only nine for a female child. Twins are not common; triplets are very rare; they are attributed to embraces in immediate succession.

A young pregnant woman, becoming alarmed, called in the theurgist.   He examined the abdomen, and declared that she was carrying three children and that should they reach full development she would surely die.   He produced premature birth; and it was claimed by the doctor that the first two born breathed a few times and that the third was stillborn.   Abortion is rarely practiced on married women; but it is not uncommon among the fallen women, who are always pointed at with the finger of scorn, except when they are on a bed of illness; they then receive the same consideration as others.   Their infants are not discriminated against in any way.

Women complain but little previous to parturition, performing their duties as usual until the actual presence of labor.   The feet and hands are frequently swollen to a painful degree, and it is not unusual to find the face affected in the same way.   This swelling does not often exist except during the ten or twelve days immediately previous to accouchement, and in most cases observed by the writer the swelling disappeared rapidly after confinement.

Laceration of the perineum is of frequent occurrence.   It is a natural result of the method of childbirth as practiced by the Zuñis. In three labor cases observed by the writer in 1896–97 laceration occurred. At such time high fever is apt to be present, though in one of the cases referred to the pulse never rose above 90. Milk leg is very rare, but abscess in the breast is not uncommon. When the doctresses fail to bring relief, the surgeon is called in.

The only case of operation on the breast observed by the writer was performed by Nai'uchi, who administered a native narcotic (Datura stramonium) before using the lancet. After making the incision he squeezed out the pus, and then, without having previously washed his hands, inserted his index finger and pulled out the remaining pus. A powdered medicine was sprinkled sparingly over the wound, and a soiled cloth was afterward bound over it. The patient returned to consciousness in much the same manner as one gradually arousing from a natural sleep. She afterward told the writer that she knew nothing of the operation, but had beautiful dreams. The powdered medicine was applied for several days, and in a week the breast was entirely healed.

The writer has never discovered among any Indian tribe a case of blindness after confinement, nor has she ever known a woman to suffer from convulsions before or after confinement. The Zuñi women sometimes suffer from uterine trouble after bearing children, though such troubles are uncommon. In some instances observed by the writer the uterus had protruded. In such cases the surgeon is called in to replace it. There are but two or three theurgists who undertake such cases, and these are men. Nai'uchi is the principal man in such troubles, but his charges are so high that some of the poorer women are obliged to call upon less distinguished practitioners.

Sore nipples are unusual. The child is placed to the breast within ten hours after birth, every effort being made to make it draw the milk. Constipation is carefully guarded against, and is therefore uncommon. A hot tea made of toasted juniper twigs and berries steeped in boiling water is constantly drunk from the beginning of labor for the purpose of relaxing the system, and afterward to induce copious lochial discharge. Should this tea be drunk in earlier stages of pregnancy, it is believed that the child would be very dark. The writer has never known a case where catamenia continued longer than four days, and the Zuñi doctors and women declare that it seldom continues for a longer period. Though hemorrhage is uncommon, it sometimes occurs, and for this trouble a tea is made by pouring boiling water over the fungus commonly known as corn smut (Ustilago maidis), which has the same effect as ergot of the pharmacopeia.

The childbirth ceremonies of the Sia tribe, described in the Eleventh Annual Report of the Bureau of Ethnology, are very much more elaborate than those of the Zuñis.

A typical labor case observed by the writer occurred at midnight, October 20, 1896. A child wife, not more than 15 years old, gave evidence of approaching parturition. She suffered from that time until 6 o'clock in the following evening, when she was delivered. Owing to the absence of her mother in Ojo Caliente, a farming district, the girl was confined in her mother-in-law's house. She wore only the camis, which leaves the arms exposed, and was covered with a heavy blanket. She lay most of the night on sheepskins spread on the floor near the south end of the room, pressing her feet during the pain against the ledge at the south wall of the room. She changed position from her side to her back and often lay face downward. The mother-in-law, who was a doctress, had no professional part in the treatment of her daughter-in-law, but took a seat on the floor beside the girl, offering no assistance. The two grandmothers of the girl were present and were much concerned over her suffering. The father, the father-in-law, and a paternal uncle were in an interior room. Their faces expressed anxiety, and they spoke in whispers. The husband of the girl, not expecting the birth of the child for several days, was absent at his farm in Ojo Caliente. The pains increased, and at 4 o'clock in the afternoon, two doctresses having been summoned, the kneading of the abdomen began. Each doctress took her turn, bestowing much strength and energy on the manipulation. With each pain the girl turned on her right side and caught the belt of the doctress before her, while the second doctress pressed hard upon the back, the girl pressing her feet against the ledge. The labor being prolonged, a doctress held the nostrils of the patient and blew into her mouth, occasionally releasing the pressure upon her nose for an instant. This heroic treatment appears cruel in the extreme, but it is supposed to force the child into the world. The girl wept continually. The sympathy expressed by the relatives and doctresses was enough to unnerve the sufferer. The juniper tea was frequently drunk and the girl occasionally stood over the urinal during the day, but did not leave her bed after 4 o'clock. Rupture of the membranes occurred an hour and a half before the birth of the child. Half an hour previous to delivery, one of the doctresses made an examination by inserting her hand. Apparently discouraged and alarmed, she notified the mother-in-law of her intention to call upon the officers of the Great Fire fraternity to come and sing their songs. This fraternity has four songs addressed to the Beast Gods for hastening delayed delivery. Should the child be born after the first song, the singing ceases, and so on. Should the child not be born soon after the fourth song, the heart of the patient is bad; the songs are not repeated, and the theurgists leave the house. Accordingly, the mother-in-law provided the doctress with a quarter of mutton and many yards of cotton and calico as an advance payment to the theurgists. For a long time the doctress was unsuccessful in her efforts to find the men, but she persisted in her search and finally returned with them just as the girl was being delivered of a male child. The four theurgists departed at once with the medicine of the Beast Gods and their rattles. As soon as the child's head was exposed, the girl was at once turned upon her back and most vigorously kneaded. Her drawn knees were held by two women and a doctress took her seat upon the ledge between the girl's knees and, pressing her hands to the sides of the infant's head, assisted the birth by slightly shaking the child as she pulled it to her.[a] Another doctress severed the umbilical cord with a steel knife, while the doctress holding the child pressed the cord close by the umbilicus until a cotton cord as thick as a lead pencil was procured and wrapped around it several times. In the meantime the abdomen of the young mother was manipulated until the placenta passed. It was held by the umbilical cord and hastily taken from under the blanket on the left side, dropped into a bowl, and carried from the house by the girl's maternal grandmother, who deposited it in the river with a prayer that the young mother might be blessed with many children. While this was happening the mother bit upon a white pebble, that the child's teeth might be strong and white. There seemed to be no evidence of life in the child for

---

[a] Though it is the aim of each doctress present at childbirth to bring the child into the world in order that if it be a boy, he will enter the ki'wiꞏsinĕ of her husband, there is no evidence of unfairness toward one another.

an hour after birth, still the doctresses and the paternal grandmother of the girl never ceased their efforts to produce respiration by pressing the nostrils, blowing into the mouth, manipulating the chest, and moving the arms, held outward and above the head. Warm clothes were kept around the body and over the head. There was great rejoicing when the faintest sign of life was discovered, but it was fully another hour before respiration was such as to give real hope of life for the child. The writer was surprised at the success of these patient efforts, as the case seemed to be a hopeless one. When no further anxiety was felt for the little one, the doctress called for piñon gum which had been boiled and, chewing it until it was white and pliable, mixed mutton grease with it, and then the paternal grandmother of the girl rubbed it on the stone floor until she produced a roll one-half inch in diameter and about 4 inches long. A blanket was now folded over the upturned feet and the extended legs of the doctress, who laid the child upon the blanket, its head resting against her feet. Opening the wrappings about the child, she raised the umbilical cord, which was about 2½ inches long and heavily wrapped with the cotton cord previously referred to, and encircled the umbilicus with the roll of piñon gum; then fluffing some carded wool and making an opening in the center, she drew the wrapped umbilical cord through, patting the wool over the piñon gum. This dressing, which was very clumsy, protruded more than an inch. The abdomen was covered with a bit of soiled cotton cloth, laid on warm, and the child's head was kept covered with a warm cloth. The paternal grandmother of the infant now dropped water upon its scrotum, and the doctress rubbed it over the parts, manipulating the penis until its form could be seen. The child's nose was frequently pinched, and the mouth and eyes were delicately manipulated. The latter when closed resembled the eyes of a frog, the lids protruding to a remarkable degree. The child's arms were now placed by its side and it was wrapped in a piece of cotton cloth and a tiny blanket, and these were held in place by strings of yucca over the shoulders, breast, and lower portion of the legs. The child was then laid upon a folded blanket. Meantime the young mother stood unassisted over the urinal, wrapped her belt around her to hold in place a heated stone, and took her seat on the ledge. Two women removed the sheepskin on which was a pool of the lochial discharge; this the maternal grandmother covered with sand, and the sand was then swept into a cloth and carried out. The girl then drank a cup of commercial tea without sugar,[a] which she enjoyed. After the young mother had taken this nourishment the father-in-law and mother-in-law brought a quantity of damp sand and deposited it upon the floor. One of the doctresses divided the sand into two portions, placed a hot stone slab under one portion and another slab on top of the sand, and worked the sand about the stones until it was thoroughly dry and heated, when she removed the stones and placed them with the other part of the sand, which was heated in the same manner. The second portion of sand was made into a circular mound, in which an elliptic depression was formed and made perfectly smooth. A circular depression to fit the child's head was made west of the ellipse, and a ridge of sand was raised between the two depressions to support the child's neck. Over the sand a heated cloth was laid. At this time much disappointment was felt that neither of the ears of corn which were brought by the mother-in-law was a ya'pota (perfect ear). One ear had three plumules, symbolizing fecundity; the other was a single ear. The latter[b] was held, pointing upward, back of the child's head by the mother-in-law, who also held the child. A basket of prayer meal was deposited at the head of the sand bed by the doctress who received the child into the world, and the latter offered a long prayer to A'wona-

---

[a] There is great prejudice against the use of sugar at such times. The Zuñi doctors forbid the sweetening of tea or coffee.

[b] For a boy the single ear of corn, called the father, is used; a divided one, called the mother, is placed by a girl.

wil′ona for long life and health to the child.[a] After the prayer the doctress raised
the cotton cloth and sprinkled a line of meal from east to west over the sand bed,
symbolic of the straight path the child must follow in order to receive the blessings
of A′wonawil′ona and the Sun Father.   The cloth was then returned to its place, the
child was laid upon the bed, and the single ear of corn was placed at its left side.
The maternal grandmother covered the child with a small blanket, which was a
gift from herself.   The doctress then struck the sides and ends in turn of a quaint
little stool against the floor at the head of the bed, and placed it finally on its side
at the head of the bed, with the seat next to the bed.   An Apache basket tray was
inverted over the child's head, one side resting on the edge of the stool, the other
on the blanket covering, so as to raise from the face a cotton cloth which was thrown
over the head. A small blanket was placed over the cotton covering. An occasional
faint sound was to be heard from the infant, which caused genuine delight to the
family and friends.   The mother-in-law next proceeded to prepare the mother's
bed with the second portion of sand, first heating the sand in the manner described.
The ear of corn having three plumules was placed to the left of the bed, and when
the young mother took her seat upon her bed, a bowl of mutton stew, a basket of
mush boiled in corn husks, and a basket tray of wafer bread were deposited on the
floor beside her. A number joined in the meal, none eating with more relish than
the young mother, who sat up an hour and a half.   During the meal the paternal
grandfather of the infant came from the inner room.   At this moment the child
gave its first vigorous cry, which delighted all present, especially the grandfather.
One hour after the birth of the child the mother's pulse was 80.   At the first peep
of the sun on the morning following the birth, the doctress who delivered the
young mother, having been supplied with a vase of warm water, a gourd, and a
basket of ashes, proceeded to bathe the infant. Dipping a gourd of water, she
filled her mouth, and pouring the water from her mouth over the head of the
child, washed its face and head, rubbing quite vigorously, after which ashes were
rubbed over the face, a quantity adhering to the skin. [b] The infant's paternal
grandmother now folded a blanket and laid it over the extended legs of the doctress,
who placed the infant upon the blanket, its head against her upturned feet.   The
doctress sprinkled the breast of the infant with water, using her right hand, with a
prayer for long life and health of the child; and, dipping her hand into the vase of
water, she proceeded to bathe the child.   After the bath the child's entire body was
rubbed over with ashes. [c] The cloth which had previously wrapped the infant was
changed for another, which, however, was neither new nor clean. A blanket that
had been previously warmed by the fire was afterward placed around the child.
The young mother observed the bathing and wrapping of her infant with great
interest.   The infant was next laid upon a fresh sand bed prepared by the paternal grandmother, and the young mother walked to her bed and lay down, while
a doctress bathed the lacerated perineum with warm root tea and afterward sprinkled the affected parts with a powder, [c] after which she manipulated the abdomen
for thirty minutes. The young mother then sat upon the ledge by the fire while
a fresh sand bed was prepared for her. After a time the child was placed to the
breast, but it failed to get nourishment, though it made persistent effort. The
hot juniper tea was drunk constantly after the confinement for the purpose of

---

[a] The Zuñis believe that the span of life is marked out at birth, This belief, however, does not
prevent their incessant prayers to A′wonawil′ona (the supreme power; see p. 22) for health and a
long life.

[b] The Zuñis declare that in four days from the putting on of the ashes exfoliation occurs and a new
skin appears. Ashes are used throughout the first year to render the face and other parts of the body
depilous. With rare exceptions, these people are depilous, except on the scalp.

[c] In aggravated cases of laceration certain male theurgists are called in. In the case here mentioned the parts appeared to be entirely healed after the eighth day. The tea and powder were used
only four days. The powder secured by the writer was not of sufficient quantity to admit an analysis.

hastening the close of the lochial discharge, which ceased after the fourth day. On the second day, October 22, the pulse of the mother was 78. Though several efforts were made through the day to nourish the child from the mother, the milk did not appear. On the 23d the pulse was 79. Mother and child were doing well. The lacerated perineum was much improved. The same treatment was continued. Though the feet and ankles were excessively swollen for days before parturition, they rapidly returned to their normal condition after the birth of the child. On the 24th the pulse was 79. Though the milk came, it appeared like pus, and the child refused it. The infant was so weak from lack of nourishment that the writer prepared condensed milk, upon which it was fed for some days, and its improvement was marked. On the 25th the pulse was 90. The infant was placed to the breast several times, but refused the milk. At the first light of day on the 26th, a line of meal, symbolic of the path of life, was sprinkled from the house to the point where the child was to observe for the first time the Sun Father. The doctress who had received the child when it came into the world, accompanied by the young mother and the paternal grandmother, carried the infant, with the ear of corn which had been by its side since its birth held close to its head. The doctress stooped and held the child to face east while she offered a prayer for the health and happiness, goodness of heart, and long life of the child. At sunrise the doctress dipped up several gourdfuls of water in which juniper had been steeped and emptied it into a bowl near the fireplace; then the paternal great-grandmother of the child pounded yucca root and handed it to the doctress, who made suds of it by beating it in the juniper water. As the bowl became filled with snowy froth, she took off the suds, putting them into a second bowl, and when this bowl was filled, the suds were warmed with hot juniper water. The paternal grandmother held the child until the doctress had removed her moccasins and was seated on a blanket spread on the floor. The physician held the infant, its head to the east, supporting it with the left hand. The great-grandmother and the paternal grandmother stood one on each side of the bowl. The doctress first dipped a handful of suds, and then the others took suds with their right hands. The young mother sat on the ledge near by, but took no part. The suds were held while the doctress offered a long prayer to A′wonawil′ona, the Sun Father, and the Earth Mother, that all blessings might come to the child. At the conclusion of the prayer the doctress placed the suds she held on the top of the child's head, and then the other two patted the suds on the head; and the head was then held over the bowl and thoroughly washed by the doctress. Great care was observed in bathing the eyes; they were smoothed over and over, and the nose was pinched many times. A blanket was folded and spread over the extended legs of the doctress, in the manner heretofore described, a wad being placed before the upturned feet where the child's head was to rest. The dressing was removed from the umbilicus, which was found entirely healed. The child was then bathed from a bowl containing only warm juniper water. The paternal grandmother was careful to warm the cloths in which the child was to be wrapped. Nothing was used to dry the child aside from the ashes which were rubbed over its entire body. The infant, still refusing its mother's milk, was fed with condensed milk from a spoon. It smacked its lips with satisfaction, much to the delight of the paternal grandfather and the others present. The child was then held by the grandmother, while the doctress worked up anew the yucca suds. The young mother's hair was loosed, and she bent her head over the bowl while the doctress, the mother-in-law, and the latter's mother and young niece dipped suds with their right hands and held them while the doctress prayed. After the prayer the doctress applied to the head the suds she held, and the others did the same; after which the doctress thoroughly washed the head and long hair. The young mother then took her seat while the doctress removed the remainder of her sand bed, which was carried in a blanket to the far end of the room and deposited in a heap. The doctress afterward placed by the sand heap the bowl of juniper water, in which the yucca suds had been deposited to bathe the infant, and proceeded to bathe the young mother, who was now at the other end of the room. The girl kept on her camis, which soon became thoroughly wet. The doctress poured water over her by the gourdful. The girl washed her own legs, standing while she did so. Twenty minutes were consumed in this bath, though the large room, except near the fire, was very cold. No cloth was used to dry the body. A soiled camis was slipped on her as she dropped the other, and, wrapping a heavy blanket around herself, the young mother walked over the cold stone floor in her bare feet, which were still swollen, and took her seat by the fire. Within twenty minutes after the bath the mother's pulse was 82. She seemed perfectly well and declared that she felt so. An excellent meal was served, but the grandfather was too absorbed to leave his work of attaching buckskin thongs and loops to the new cradle, which was a present from the paternal uncle Mauretio. On the cradle, just where the head of the infant should rest, was a perfectly round turquoise of excellent color. Inlaid below and close to the neck rest were three turquoises. When the cradle was completed, the child was strapped to it. In folding the wraps around the child care was observed first to bring around the piece of cotton from the right side of the child so as to prevent the arms from coming in contact with the body, the cloth passing under each arm. The other side of the cloth was then brought over both arms. The blanket was folded around and tied in two places. On the 27th the mother's pulse was 82. She was sitting up, dressed, and apparently perfectly well. The infant took the mother's milk for the first time. The pulse was the same on the 28th and 29th. The mother was up and sewing on the 29th, and the child took much notice and appeared brighter and more observing than any civilized child of the same age known to the writer.

Another obstetrical case observed was that of an unmarried girl of 16. She received the same attentions as if the child had been born in wedlock, and the writer did not detect any difference in the ceremonies because of illegitimate birth. The parents of this girl were dead. The relatives with whom she lived were very tender with her, though they expressed deep regret at her misconduct. Her brother, who was an associate shi'wanni (rain priest), acted kindly toward her and was as pleased with the infant as if it were his own. This girl was in labor twenty-four hours, but most of the pains were slight and she had a comparatively easy delivery. Her pulse immediately after the birth was 96. During the day following her confinement she sat up for two hours. She had no dropsical symptoms. On the second and third days after confinement her pulse was 96; after that it was normal.

The worst of a number of cases of laceration observed was that of a girl about 18 years of age who lived at a farming district 15 miles from Zuñi. The infant, her first child, was strangled by the umbilical cord at its birth, which occurred on October 18, 1896, and on the 22d the father of the young mother was notified that she could not live. On the 23d he and his father, Nai'uchi, went at once for the girl and brought her to Zuñi through one of the severest rain storms of the season. They traveled in a covered wagon without springs, the young mother lying on blankets spread in the bed of the wagon. They arrived late at night, and in the morning Nai'uchi made an examination in the presence of the writer. The patient was very low, the pulse being 125. The perineum was terribly lacerated and the labia majora were swollen to enormous size, the flesh being almost black. As the labia majora were depilous the condition was the more readily observed. Nai'uchi pulled off the sloughs, some 2 inches in length and as thick as the finger. The invalid showed no signs of suffering at this time, except to frown as the diseased flesh was removed. The writer had the parts bathed in a solution of carbolic acid, five drops in a cup of boiled water, and it was with the greatest difficulty that she induced the doctress to use fresh aseptic gauze instead of a filthy cloth for the bathing. Nai'uchi sat beside the patient and deposited fetishes and medicine bags in a basket tray; after his prayers over the fetishes and the medicines he took a pinch of a powder and, as he prayed, ran his fingers that held the powder down the inner side of the arm, seeming to understand that the blood and lymph circulation is more abundant on the inner side of the arm and therefore more easily affected. He afterward held a pinch of the powder to each shoulder and to the top of the head, and then sprinkled what he held sparingly upon the parts affected.[a] On the 25th the pulse was 98, and the parts appeared to be slightly improved. Applications of the carbolic acid were made morning and night and the powder was afterward sprinkled on. Although the patient was very ill, it was with difficulty that she was induced to remain in bed. On the 26th the pulse of the patient was 102. The affected parts were slightly improved. The treatment of Nai'uchi and the writer was continued. The patient was anxious to get up, though still very ill. On the 27th the pulse was 98. The parts continued to improve, though the right side was still considerably swollen and discolored. The improvement of the patient seemed remarkable. The same treatment was continued. On the 28th the pulse was 113, but nearly all the swelling of the labia majora had disappeared. The patient sat up and claimed to feel quite well. The same treatment was continued, and on the 29th the pulse was 98. The parts were almost normal in size, and there was no appearance of sloughing. The treatment was continued, and on the 30th the pulse was 90 and the parts had become normal in size. On the 31st the pulse was 78, and the parts appeared perfectly healthy. The patient was up and at work, sweeping the floor with a native broom which compelled her to bend almost double. At this time treatment ceased, and a few days later the patient was going about everywhere. She went with bare feet and legs, giving no thought to protecting herself from the rain or the cold. She performed all her duties and declared that she was perfectly well and strong. The only evidence of delicate health was extreme pallor which continued until the writer left Zuñi in January.

PUBERTY CUSTOMS

With the Zuñis marriage usually occurs at very tender years, girls frequently marrying two years before reaching puberty. Should one not be married at the time she arrives at womanhood, her mother goes to the house of the paternal grandmother or, if the grandmother is not living, the paternal aunt, and informs her of the event. The grandmother returns with the mother, and the girl accompanies her grandmother to her dwelling, where she labors hard all day grinding corn. When the girl returns to her home in the evening, she carries a bowl of meat stew prepared and presented by the paternal grandmother, who returns with her to her house. The belief is that if a girl works hard at the dawn of her womanhood she will not suffer pain at this period; but should she be idle on the first day, she will always suffer from dysmenorrhea. This is the only occasion when a woman makes a point of exerting herself during menstruation. As a rule, the women walk but little at this time. They are not expected to bring water from the well. This, however, is not due to any particular weakness at this period, though the women do suffer to some extent. They employ themselves with indoor work, usually weaving

---

[a] Dr Washington Matthews suggests that this powder is probably a mixture of piñon gum and red willow. It was certainly a most effective antiseptic.

or grinding, and sit or kneel over heated sand that is spread thickly on the floor. Their robes are caught up around their waists and blankets are fastened around their shoulders, falling loosely to the floor, covering all the sand. This custom has been largely discontinued since the writer secured the confidence of the women. Extreme delicacy is observed by the women at this period. A heated stone is worn in the belt and a hot juniper tea is frequently drunk. The menses usually continue four days, but in some cases they cease at the expiration of the second or third day. The Zuñi women are not segregated during this period. It is claimed that a certain root tea, which is drunk hot, will permanently suspend the menses at the expiration of four months. For two months the flow is said to be copious and of a very dark color; in the third month the color is normal, and in the fourth month the discharge is almost colorless. This root is kept by certain old medicine men and women, who carefully guard the secret, that the young women may not procure the medicine and thereby render themselves incapable of becoming mothers. Specimens of the root referred to were collected during the summer of 1904 and are now with the remainder of the plant collection in the National Museum.

MARRIAGE CUSTOMS

The marriage ceremony of the Zuñis is very simple. When a man is pleased with a girl, he manages to meet her on the road and tell her of his admiration, asking permission to go to her house. If she favors the suitor, she replies: "Wait until I speak to my father and mother." Another day he meets the girl and inquires what the father and mother have said, and if the parents are willing, he accompanies the girl to her home. The mother asks him to be seated and directs her daughter to bring food and place it on the floor before the guest. Should the girl hesitate either from lack of interest in the man or from love of coquetry (for the Zuñi maidens are all coquettes), she is admonished by one or both of her parents. After bringing the repast the girl takes her seat facing the visitor. While he eats, the parents sit on one side and talk to the man about the duties of a husband to a wife. When the repast is finished, the father calls the man to him, the wife sitting by the husband's side; the girl remains on the other side of the room. The father says: "You are about to marry my daughter. You must work hard; you must watch the sheep and help to cut the wood and plant grain and cut it." The mother tells him he is to be kind and good to his wife. He remains at the house five nights, sleeping alone outside the general living room, working for the family during the day. The sixth morning he goes to his parents' house. They inquire where he has been, and when he tells them, they ask if the girl's parents are willing. If they themselves are pleased with the match, they say, "It is well." When the groom returns from his visit to

ZUÑI LIVING ROOM

LEARNING TO WEAVE BELTS

MASK OF KO͘KKO̍ ͭHLANN̍A̍ (GREAT GOD) OF MA̍ͭKE ͭHLANNAKWE (GREAT FIRE FRATERNITY)
FRONT AND SIDE VIEWS

ALTAR OF MÁ́KEᵀHLANꞮNAKWE (GREAT FIRE FRATERNITY)

his parents on the sixth morning, he carries a dress as a present from
his mother to her intended daughter-in-law. The bride receives the
dress and then grinds a lot of corn into flour, and the following day
the groom returns to his mother's house in company with the bride,
who carries the meal in a basket on her head. She presents it to
her mother-in-law, saying: "Mother, this is for you." The mother
says: "My child, thanks; be seated." She then hands bread and
meat, if she has it, to the girl, who sits alone while she eats. She
takes but a few mouthfuls. Before she leaves the house, the father-
in-law folds a deerskin and, laying it before her, says: "This is for
your moccasins." The girl then rises and places upon her head the
basket in which she brought the flour, which has been filled with wheat
by the mother-in-law, and upon which the folded deerskin is laid, and
with the groom returns to her mother's house, where they make their
permanent home.[a] The couple do not sleep inside the living room
for a year or until the birth of the first child.

The Zuñis are monogamists, polygamy being looked upon with
abhorrence, but divorce is quite common. They would rather separate than live together inharmoniously.

MORTUARY CUSTOMS

The Zuñis claim that they always buried their dead. They insist
that should they incinerate the bodies, there would be no rain, for
their dead, are the u'wannami (rain-makers). Incineration, they
believe, would annihilate the being. Infants that are buried with
their ears unpierced are not supposed to help water the earth, but
are believed to carry baskets of toads and tadpoles on their heads
and to drop them to the earth while the rain-makers are at work; and
it is believed that they must wear toads attached to their ears instead
of turquoise earrings. It is looked upon as a misfortune that this
should occur, and an infant's ears not previously pierced are therefore
pierced after death.

Immediately after death the body is placed with its head to the
east, bathed in yucca suds, and rubbed over with corn meal. It is
then dressed in the best clothes available, a gash being cut in each
garment that its spirit may escape to serve the spirit of the dead.
The body is next wrapped in one or more blankets and is usually
buried soon after death. There are more elaborate preparations for a
deceased rain priest and other officials.

A death is usually announced as soon as it occurs by a woman of the
immediate family to a member of the clan of the deceased and to one
of the clan of the spouse, and they in turn spread the news among

---

[a] The same customs are followed when the match is made by the parents, the man being invited by
them to come to the house. The more progressive Indian takes great pride in providing a house of
his own for his family, and it is only a matter of time when the family groups will become separated.

the clans and intimates of the family.   Unless the death is sudden
the fraternity father (see Esoteric fraternities) of the deceased has
been present and he notifies the fraternity, especially the fraternity
children of the deceased.   On such occasions the writer has never
observed other members of a fraternity present than the fraternity
father or mother, except when the deceased is a prominent member
of the tribe.   The mourners begin arriving before the body is fully prepared for the grave, and as each woman enters she looks at the corpse
and at once sets up a hideous howl, taking a seat on the ledge which
extends around the room.   The howl is continuous, except when the
women stop from exhaustion, until some time after the remains are
buried.   Members of the immediate family of the dead and others
connected by strong ties of friendship remain quiet during the funeral
rites, exhibiting the keenest grief.   Sometimes the devoted relatives
linger over the remains, loth to have the dear one carried away.   The
bodies of distinguished persons lie in state for a time, in order that those
privileged may view the remains, but they are always buried within a
couple of hours.   Prayers are always offered by all present, and meal
is sprinkled over the body.   The body is seldom accompanied to the
grave by mourners.   The less prominent people occasionally follow
as far as the burial ground and then return, leaving the bearers of the
corpse to go alone to the grave.   Interment is a disagreeable duty and
is concluded as soon as possible.   Having been compelled during the
Spanish conquest to bury their dead in the churchyard, this place
became sacred to the Zuñis, and they have continued to use it as a
burial place in order that they may not be separated from their own.
They adhere also to the old custom of placing the men on the south
side of the burial grounds and the women on the north, with their
heads to the east.   The churchyard is so packed with bodies that when
a grave is dug the bones thrown out seem as abundant as the soil.
The immediate male members of the family, not including the husband
or father, dig the grave, which is not more than 5 or 6 feet deep,
and bury the dead.   The numerous objects of art found in graves on
prehistoric sites show that in the past it was customary to bury valued
possessions with the dead, but this is not done at present, although
occasionally one or two trifling articles are placed in the grave.

After the burial of a husband or a wife the body of the surviving
spouse is bathed by female relatives.   There must be but little fire
in the fireplace at the time, however cold the weather.   If the survivor is a man, he is nude, except a cover over the loins; a woman
wears her camis.   The head is washed first.   Several women stand about
a bowl of yucca suds and each one dips a handful; when all are supplied, each woman places the suds on the head, then one of them thoroughly washes it.   Afterward the spouse is led to the under side of a

ladder, which passes through the hatchway of the room, and his entire body is bathed in cold water.

If the burial occurs sufficiently early for the Sun Father in his journey over the world to receive the prayers wafted from the plumes, the immediate members of the family go a short distance west of the village, by the river bank, and make an excavation, in which the extra clothing and other belongings of the deceased are deposited. Nearly all the objects belonging to the dead are either destroyed or buried. If the deceased is a member of the Ko'tikili (mythologic) fraternity, the mask received at voluntary initiation into this organization is heavily sprinkled with meal and buried, with prayers, in a small excavation made near the large one. A third excavation, about 12 inches square and the same in depth, is afterward made near the river, and te'likinawe, prepared by a male member of the family, of which each adult has four and the children one or two, are planted in this excavation, the hands of the infants being guided by their mothers. After the plumes are placed, all sprinkle meal upon them, and on the following day the excavation is filled with earth. After returning to the house all except the infants take from one to three large gourdfuls of warm water as an emetic for their physical purification.

It is believed that the ghost hovers about the village four nights after death and starts on its journey to Ko'thluwala'wa (abiding place of the Council of the Gods) on the fifth morning. During the spirit's stay in the village the door and hatchway of the house must be left ajar that it may pass in and out at will; should the door be closed, the ghost would scratch upon it and not be satisfied until it was opened. These shadow beings can be observed by seers and by others under certain conditions.

A shi'wanni (rain priest) related the following:

Once when the 'Hle'wekwe (sword swallowers) held their ceremonies at my house (the ceremonial chamber of this fraternity happens to be in the dwelling of this rain priest). the sword swallowed by one of the women must have touched her heart, as the blood came so fast. We laid her on the roof of the house and endeavored to stop the flow, but we could not, and in a little while she died. Her spirit troubled us so much with rapping that we placed live coals in the center of the room and added piñon gum; the room was soon filled with smoke, which effectually rid us of the spirit.[a]

Parents or sisters of a deceased person sleep at the side of the surviving spouse during the four nights that the spirit is supposed to remain in Zuñi. A grain of black corn and a bit of charcoal are put under the head of the mourner to insure against dreaming of the lost one, whose ghost would appear should the sleeper awake.

When a husband or wife belonging to the Ant fraternity dies the

---

[a] The Chinese go through their houses after sunset with firebrands to drive out evil spirits.

survivor, accompanied by the father or brother, goes the morning following the death over the southern road to an ant-hill, and standing before it facing west, sprinkles prayer meal. The mourner then steps over the ant-hill, putting the left foot first, and starts for his home, and a relative obliterates the ant-hill with his feet. The spirit is fed each day with food thrown into the fire, and on the morning of the fifth day, when the spirit starts on its journey to Ko'thluwala'wa, a large bowl of different kinds of food is cast into the fire for its use during the journey of two days and nights. Upon reaching the lake, in the depths of which is Ko'thluwala'wa, the spirit descends the mystic ladder to meet the Council of the Gods, and thence passes on to the undermost world, the place of Zuñi nativity. There are mediums who have seen the deceased Zuñi dancing in Ko'thluwala'wa. The exhibition of grief of a parent over a child or of a husband or wife over the deceased partner is touching in the extreme. One scene observed by the writer was particularly affecting. A girl wife had just died. The body lay wrapped in a blanket on the floor, the head to the east, a piece of white cotton cloth spread over the face. The young husband sat by the head, on the right side of the corpse; the mother sat on the opposite side, and the father by the side of his wife. The nearer friends were silently weeping, while others crowded the room keeping up a continuous howl. The young husband raised the covering from the head, placed his cheek against that of his dead wife, and throwing his arms over the body murmured lamentations. Every little while the sobbing mother caressed the cheek of her dead child, and the father's bent form completed the picture of abject despair.

The body of a woman of one of the poorer families was brought from Nutria, a farming district 25 miles distant, wrapped in a blanket secured here and there with yucca strings. In less than an hour after the body reached the house, the son and grandson of the deceased proceeded with hoe and spade to dig the grave. Previously, however, the daughter-in-law of the deceased had made a fire of chips in the fireplace of the room in which the remains lay and had brought from an inner room a basket containing four large cakes of bread, a large fold of wafer bread, four ears of corn, a quantity of dried peaches, and some unground wheat. The cakes were first laid on the pyre, and the wafer bread added, then the ears of corn were stuck about, and the peaches and wheat were thrown over all. The daughter-in-law then made yucca suds in a large bowl near the head of the corpse, and the husband of the deceased untied the yucca knots in the blanket. When the blanket was opened a fresh outburst of grief was heard. Such relatives and friends as were present remained while the body was being prepared for burial. The daughter-in-law covered the head and face with yucca suds.[a] Then the hair was loosed and washed

---

[a] The root of yucca glauca is employed to make the suds.

thoroughly; the eyes were closed, but the mouth was left open. The face was much swollen and nearly black, though death had occurred but six hours before, and the day was cool for July.[a] There was a clot of blood about an inch in diameter upon the forehead, caused, they said, by a lancet wound. The mouth was also covered with blood. After the face and head had been washed they were covered with meal by the daughter-in-law, who tore off the calico garment, leaving the camis. She then passed her hand under the camis and rubbed meal over the loins, and proceeded to wash the entire body, going down from the neck. No cloth was used for drying the body, and the loins were bathed by rubbing with the dampened camis. The body, which was not swollen, was then covered with meal, not sprinkled, but rubbed on. At one time the husband requested that the camis be brought up a little so as not to expose so much of the body; extreme modesty was observed throughout. The soles of the feet, which were very dirty, were cleansed with a corncob in addition to the suds. When there was the slightest indication of discharge at the mouth, corn meal was laid heavily on the face. One of the women scattered a quantity of dry sand by the side of the corpse to catch the water with which it was bathed. Two small locks of hair were cut from the head of the corpse and laid separately in a niche in the wall. A superstition exists that if a person takes a bit of hair of a deceased friend, burns it, and inhales the smoke he will have good health and not die, but go to sleep and thus pass on to Ko'thluwala'wa. After the body was bathed the daughter-in-law and her assistant proceeded to dress the corpse amidst the greatest weeping and wailing. Holding the head and feet, they moved the body to one side, out of the water, after which they put on a calico shirt, a cotton under garment, a woolen dress, and a belt; then the rest of the basket of meal was scattered over the face. The knit blue leggings were put on last, and the body was again moved. A blanket was spread diagonally on the floor; several yards of red calico and white cotton were placed upon this, and over these a white cotton camis was laid; the body was then lifted and laid on the camis and covered by folding the fabrics over it. The daughter-in-law, who apparently first thought of placing a pair of knit shoes on the feet, laid them beside the corpse. As soon as this was done, the blanket being left slightly open at the head, all hands dipped meal from a small bowl and sprinkled it through the opening upon the face, the youngest child being led by the grandfather to perform this rite.

As soon as the son and the grandson returned from preparing the grave, they also sprinkled meal through the opening in the blanket. The son then proceeded to close the opening with two yucca strings,

---

[a] All that could be learned about the cause of death was that the woman died from vomiting.

and the two young men carried the body to the grave. The burden was so heavy that the bearers were compelled to stop and let it rest on the ground for a few moments. The head was laid to the east in the grave; then the blanket was opened and earth was thrown in. No one accompanied the bearers to the grave, and only a few outside of the immediate family visited the house before the body was removed. The eldest grandchild, a girl of 12 years, had to be sent for. She seemed much afraid at first, but her grief appeared to allay her fears, and the picture of the grandfather bowed with grief with the two little girls and a boy, the latter being about five years of age, clasped in his arms was one not soon to be forgotten. The only men present at any time were the husband, the son, and the grandson. After the body was buried the husband, quite prostrated from grief, was compelled to lie down. The other members of the family had their forelocks and hands bathed in yucca suds, and when the husband recovered sufficiently he was also bathed. His elder female relatives were most sympathetic and devoted to him, one woman holding his head in her arms. The daughter-in-law proceeded with hoe and native broom to remove the earth which had been placed on the floor to catch the water used in bathing the corpse. She first threw more earth upon that which was wet and then scraped all together, putting it into a cast-off blanket. She was careful to scrape every particle of earth from the stone floor, taking great pains to get it from the crevices; not an atom was allowed to remain.

A death which caused universal regret and distress in Zuñi was that of We'wha, undoubtedly the most remarkable member of the tribe. This person was a man wearing woman's dress, and so carefully was his sex concealed that for years the writer believed him to be a woman. Some declared him to be an hermaphrodite, but the writer gave no credence to the story, and continued to regard We'wha as a woman; and as he was always referred to by the tribe as "she"—it being their custom to speak of men who don woman's dress as if they were women—and as the writer could never think of her faithful and devoted friend in any other light, she will continue to use the feminine gender when referring to We'wha. She was perhaps the tallest person in Zuñi; certainly the strongest, both mentally and physically. Her skin was much like that of the Chinese in color, many of the Zuñis having this complexion. During six months' stay in Washington she became several shades lighter. She had a good memory, not only for the lore of her people, but for all that she heard of the outside world. She spoke only a few words of English before coming to Washington, but acquired the language with remarkable rapidity, and was soon able to join in conversation. She possessed an indomitable will and an insatiable thirst for knowledge. Her likes and dislikes were intense. She would risk anything to serve those she loved, but toward those who crossed her path she was vindictive. Though severe she was considered just. At an early age she lost her parents and was adopted by a sister of her father. She belonged to the Badger clan, her foster mother belonging to the Dogwood clan. Owing to her bright mind and excellent memory, she was called upon by her own clan and also by the clans of her foster mother and father when a long prayer had to be repeated or a grace was to be offered over a feast. In fact she was the chief personage on many occasions. On account of her physical strength all the household work requiring great exertion was left for her, and while she most willingly took the harder work from others of the family, she would not permit idleness; all had to labor or receive an upbraiding from We'wha, and nothing was more dreaded than a scolding from her.

In the fall of 1896 a Sha'läko god was entertained at her home. Although at this time We'wha was suffering from valvular heart disease, she did most of the work, including the laying of a stone floor in the large room where the ceremonial was to occur. She labored early and late so hard that when the time came for holding the ceremony she was unable to be present. From this time she was listless and remained alone as much as possible, though she made no complaint of illness. When a week or more had passed after the close of the great autumn ceremonial of the Sha'läko, and the many guests had departed, the writer dropped in at sunset to the spacious room in the house of We'wha's foster father, the late José Palle. We'wha was found crouching on the ledge by the fireplace. That a great change had come over her was at once apparent. Death evidently was rapidly approaching. She had done her last work. Only a few days before this strong-minded, generous-hearted creature had labored to make ready for the reception of her gods; now she was preparing to go to her beloved Ko'thluwala'wa. When the writer asked, "Why do you not lie down?" We'wha replied: "I can not breathe if I lie down; I think my heart break." The writer at once sent to her camp for a comfortable chair, and fixed it at a suitable angle for the invalid, who was most grateful for the attention. There was little to be done for the sufferer. She knew that she was soon to die and begged the writer not to leave her.

From the moment her family realized that We'wha was in a serious condition they remained with her, ever ready to be of assistance. The family consisted of the aged foster mother, a foster brother, two foster sisters with their husbands and children, and an own brother with his wife and children. The writer never before observed such attention as every member of the family showed her. The little children ceased their play and stood in silence close to their mothers, occasionally toddling across the floor to beg We'wha to speak. She smiled upon them and whispered, "I can not talk." The foster brother was as devoted as the one related by blood.

During two days the family hoped against hope. Nai'uchi, the great theurgist, came three times and pretended to draw from the region of the heart bits of mutton, declared to have been "shot" there by a witch who was angry with We'wha for not giving her a quarter of mutton when she asked for it. We'wha appeared relieved when the theurgist left. She knew that she was dying and appeared to desire quiet. After Nai'uchi's last visit, the foster brother, with streaming eyes, prepared te'likinawe (prayer plumes) for the dying, the theurgist having said that her moments on earth were few. We'wha asked the writer to come close and in a feeble voice she said, in English: "Mother, I am going to the other world. I will tell the gods of you and Captain Stevenson. I will tell them of Captain Carlisle, the great seed priest,[a] and his wife, whom I love. They are my friends. Tell them good-by. Tell all my friends in Washington good-by. Tell President Cleveland, my friend, good-by. Mother, love all my people; protect them; they are your children; you are their mother." These sentences were spoken with many breaks. The family seemed somewhat grieved that We'wha's last words should be given to the writer, but she understood that the thoughts of the dying were with and for her own people. A good-by was said to the others, and she asked for more light.

It is the custom for a member of the family to hold the prayer plumes near the mouth of the dying and repeat the prayer, but this practice was not observed in We'wha's case. She requested the writer to raise the back of the chair, and when this was done she asked if her prayer plumes had been made. Her foster brother answered "Yes," whereupon she requested him to bring them. The family suppressed their sobs that the dying might not be made sad. The brother offered to hold the plumes and say the prayers, but We'wha feebly extended her hand for them, and clasping the prayer plumes between her hands made a great effort to speak. She said but a few words and then sank back in her chair. Again the brother offered to hold the plumes and pray, but once more she refused. Her face was radiant in the belief that she was going to her gods. She leaned forward with the plumes tightly clasped, and as the setting sun lighted up the western windows, darkness and desolation entered the hearts of the mourners, for We'wha was dead.

Blankets were spread upon the floor and the brothers gently laid the lifeless form upon them. After the body was bathed and rubbed with meal, a pair of white cotton trousers were drawn over the legs, the

---

[a] At the time of We'wha's visit to Washington Hon. John G. Carlisle was Speaker of the House of Representatives. The Speaker and Mrs Carlisle were very kind to We'wha, and upon her return to Zuñi she found a great sack of seed which had been sent by the Speaker.

first male attire she had worn since she had adopted woman's dress years ago. The rest of her dress was female. The body was dressed in the finest clothing; six shawls of foreign manufacture, gifts from Washington friends, besides her native blanket wraps, and a white Hopi blanket bordered in red and blue, were wrapped around her. The hair was done up with the greatest care. Three silver necklaces, with turquoise earrings attached and numerous bangles, constituted the jewels.

We'wha's death was regarded as a calamity, and the remains lay in state for an hour or more, during which time not only members of the clans to which she was allied, but the rain priests and theurgists and many others, including children, viewed them. When the blanket was finally closed, a fresh outburst of grief was heard, and then all endeavored to suppress their sobs, for the aged foster mother had fallen unconscious to the floor. The two brothers carried the remains unattended to the grave. The sisters made food offerings to the fire. The foster brother on his return prepared prayer plumes for each member of the immediate family, and also the writer. The little procession, including the foster mother, who had recovered sufficiently to accompany the others, then made its way to the west of the village and on the river bank deposited the clothing, mask, and prayer plumes in the manner heretofore described. Upon the return to the house the foster mother had the rest of We'wha's possessions brought together that they might be destroyed. All her cherished gifts from Washington friends, including many photographs, were brought out; all must be destroyed. This work was performed by the mother, who wept continually. All was sacrificed but pictures of Mr and Mrs Carlisle, Mr Stevenson, and the writer. These were left in their frames on the wall. With another outburst of grief the old woman declared they must remain, saying: "We'wha will have so much with her. I can not part with these. I must keep the faces of those who loved We'wha and whom she loved best. I must keep them to look upon."

The death of Nai'uchi, rain priest of the Nadir, and for many years elder brother Bow priest, occurred during the writer's visit to Zuñi in 1904. She saw Nai'uchi but once after her arrival, still in possession of the bright mind that would have marked him as a superior man in any community. When the writer called upon Nai'uchi at his request two days previous to his death, which occurred June 26, 1904, the old man held her hand while he begged her to remain with him: "I have waited and waited for you; you will not leave me; you will remain by me." These were the last sentences uttered by Nai'uchi. Two theurgists of the Little Fire fraternity, one a woman, sat by the pallet watching the patient with the keenest anxiety. Children, grandchildren, and others dear to Nai'uchi were near him. The writer had not been long present when she observed that the patient appeared to be suffering in one or both of his extremities, and insisted upon exposing the feet. The doctress protested against uncovering the right foot, but was quite willing for the left foot to be seen, which was found to be much swollen. The right foot was bandaged. It was learned that it had been lanced by the doctress some days before to relieve the swelling and that she had also cut the scalp and "extracted two small green peaches which had been shot in by a witch," and had applied the powdered wood of a tree that had been struck with lightning to relieve Nai'uchi from an attack of vertigo. This doctress is a member of the Lightning fraternity, which possesses the specific for relieving those who become unconscious and fall. The writer sent at once for the Government physician, and when he arrived not only the theurgists, but the family declared that it was the left foot, not the right, which troubled the patient, but the doctor insisted upon examining the right foot, which he found on removing the bandage to be ulcerated to the bone. There was a great cry when he consigned the filthy wrappings to the flames: "They should be kept as long as Nai'uchi lived." His death on the same evening was attributed to the American doctor's treatment of the foot. The doctor, who diagnosed Nai'uchi's trouble as Bright's disease, had been treating him for weeks, not dreaming that the patient was never permitted to take a drop of his medicine, which was always left, with instructions for administering it, in the care of Nina, the granddaughter, who had spent years at the Government school at Zuñi, and who has a remarkable command of the English language. Nina, who has all the cunning of the Indian, combined with a great deal absorbed from the whites, practiced every deception upon the doctor, who found the bottles untouched after Nai'uchi's death. Nina's excuse for not giving the medicine was: "I am young and I could not do that to which my elders objected."

When only the two theurgists and the family were present, the writer managed to have her own way with the patient; but as approaching death became more evident, several other doctresses appeared and took seats by the pallet with the determination that their ancient customs should not be interfered with. When Nai'uchi exhibited the restlessness which comes with approaching death, a doctress crossed his hands under the blankets and held them firmly, and the expression of the old man's face told plainly the suffering he endured, which was only the beginning of his torture. Hä'lian, the son, prepared a mush of white corn meal, and a doctress fed it to the dying man by the spoonful. With each dose she said: "Father, take this; it will feed you on the road." He was continually stuffed with the mush, which he swallowed with great difficulty until too far gone to make the effort. The doctress then held the nostrils and blew into the mouth until it was concluded that life could no longer be prolonged; then another

doctress began a violent kneading of the stomach to assist the spirit
to free itself from the body, and still another doctress and Nina began
pressing the lips and eyelids.   It was horrible to observe the tortures
inflicted upon the dying man, who struggled for breath.   The writer
was powerless to contend with such numbers as were present.   Finally,
seeing an Indian who was visiting the pueblo pass the house, she
hurried him for the physician, who came in time to aid her to force the
torturers away by his stern demeanor and physical force, and the last
sparks of life were permitted to pass quietly away.   The special crock-
ery used by Nai'uchi was broken and deposited upon the coals which
were afterwards gathered into a bowl by In'nocita, a stepdaughter of
Nai'uchi, and carried out and set close beside the house, and upon
returning In'nocita made a fresh fire and threw Nai'uchi's war
club into the flames.   Then Nina brought to the fireplace a vessel
containing piñon gum which had been boiled; taking a quantity with
a spoon, she deposited it on a bit of wood in the fireplace.   Hä'lian,
Nai'uchi's son, lighted the gum and held his hands over the smoke,
and then rubbed them over his face and his breast that he might not be
touched by the spirit.   Others were meantime preparing the remains
for burial.   The body was stripped of its clothes, bathed, and rubbed
with meal.   A pair of new white cotton trousers and a red calico shirt
were put on it.   It is usual for burial clothes to be new, and the red
calico for the present occasion was selected because of Nai'uchi's fond-
ness for that color.   A lock of hair was cut from the head and laid
away.   Four blankets, two black and two red, gifts of the son, the
son-in-law, and the writer, were placed one upon the other, first a
black one, then the red ones, and again a black one, the gift of the
writer, which was placed next to the remains as an expression of
Nai'uchi's close ties with her.   A corner of the blanket, which was
placed within 2 feet of the north ledge of the room, pointed to the
east.   The body was lifted and gently laid upon the blankets, the head
sufficiently far from the corner to admit of the blanket being turned
over the face.   Hä'lian and Nai'uchi's nephew measured the corpse
for the grave by extending a rope by the side of it.   They then went
in company with another man to dig the grave, which required but a
short time.

Me'she, younger brother Bow priest, came in after Nai'uchi was
prepared for the grave and tied his warrior's wristlet on his right
wrist and arranged his beads around his neck.   It was most affecting
to see Me'she kneeling beside the remains of the man with whom he
had been intimately associated for years.   The associate rain priests
of the Nadir gathered around the head of their beloved late superior,
sitting perfectly still while men, women, and children sprinkled meal
on the remains and prayed.   It was necessary for the daughter to be
supported while she stood by the remains.   The blind grandson, too,
was led to the body of the grandfather, who had ever been devoted to

him, and it was distressing to observe this poor afflicted man sitting apart
from the others, overwhelmed in his silent grief. The stepdaughter
was almost beside herself with grief, while Hä'lian struggled to keep
back the tears which he deemed unmanly. Nina was the only member
of the family who showed little feeling; she busied herself ironing the
clothing of strange Americans until the last moments of Nai'uchi's
life, when all the rest were grief-stricken, and yet the love of the old
man for his favorite grandchild was supreme. The warrior who had
been so powerful in his tribe was a gentle subject for her to manage.
Nina fully appreciated her power over the old man and never failed to
make use of it. In justice to her, it must be said that she was often
seen to caress her grandfather during his life.

There was a fresh outburst of grief when Me'she began to cover the
remains with the blanket; at the same moment a member of the family
placed two pairs of soiled cotton trousers and two shirts beside the
corpse. The lower corners of the blankets were first drawn over the
feet, then the corners each side were wrapped tightly around the body
and secured by passing a cord through the blanket at intervals of
about a foot and knotting it. When the body was covered up to the
neck, Me'she returned to his seat on the ledge, and the associate rain
priest, who sat north of the remains, proceeded to decorate the face
and head. He first dipped a wad of raw cotton in a bowl of water,
and delicately washed the face, then drew a line of black over the
face, passing across the upper lip, and then painted the chin black
down to the throat. Corn pollen was stippled on with a mop of raw
cotton over the upper portion of the face, great care being observed
to place it evenly. The priest then removed raw cotton from a basket,
soon formed it into a sheet, and with dextrous manipulation made a roll
on one side, and then placed the cotton over the head, with the roll next
to the face. This cotton hood is the same in form as that worn by the
Sha'läko bearers (see plate LX). Then the immediate family prayed
over the remains and sprinkled meal upon the blanket over the
breast. The writer was requested to be very careful not to drop a
particle of meal upon the face. This would have been a terrible
calamity. Many last farewells were taken before the family was willing to part from their beloved. Me'she covered the face by folding
over the blanket and fastening it as described. The remains were
carried to the grave and buried by the son and nephew, one holding
the head, the other the feet. After they reached the grave the knots
in the blanket were cut so that the spirit might pass out. Soon after
the remains were carried out, each member of the family had his front
hair and hands washed by each female clan relative present.

The lateness of the hour prevented the burial of Nai'uchi's belongings and the prayer plumes the day of the death, as the Sun Father
would have passed over the road of day and could not receive the

prayers. In'nocita, the stepdaughter, gathered together the belongings of the old priest into two bundles, which were deposited on the roof for the night; on the following morning Nina carried one and In'nocita the other, both having their prayer plumes, to the burial place. The associate rain priests, including Hä'lian, and the writer carried their plumes. Hä'lian dug an excavation sufficiently large to bury the articles. A smaller excavation was made for the prayer plumes and the war pouch. All prayed and sprinkled meal over the plumes, and the party returned to the village.

No mask was buried, as Nai'uchi had never worn his mask or danced with the personators of anthropic gods since his hair had been cut while a prisoner in a Territorial jail for having hanged a supposed witch. His mask will go to a male member of his family and he will not dance in Ko'thluwala'wa. In'nocita begged the writer to remain with her during the night, as she was sure the witch who destroyed Nai'uchi's life would be about the house. While it was still light enough to see, In'nocita made a careful survey of the exterior of the premises, and finding several stones by the outer door, which she believed to have been placed there by the witch, threw them off with an expression of satisfaction that she had discovered the diabolical attempt to harm the household. When the writer insisted that all should retire, In'nocita wanted the door and windows securely fastened. She preferred to hear the scratches of the spirit to running the risk of witches entering the house. The only way in which the writer secured fresh air was by declaring she would not remain unless a window could be open, and finally the household, consisting of In'nocita, Nina, her husband, the blind boy, and the man wearing female apparel, retired to the pallets in the far end of the room, while the writer kept watch by the open window.

GAMES

Among enlightened peoples games are usually associated with sport and recreation. With some primitive peoples games are played primarily for divination, but the ceremonial games of the Zuñis are for the bringing of rain, and they constitute an important element in their religious and social life. Each game has its regulations and limitations, and there is deep meaning underlying such of the games as are supposed to have come from the gods.

The games (i'koshnawe) here recorded embrace all that are of importance to the grown people. Although the children have a variety of sports exclusively their own, they may be found on any pleasant day enjoying some of the games of their elders, and like their elders they indulge in betting, for this habit is developed in the North American Indian while he is still in his infancy. The younger Zuñi children play the ceremonial games, however, with little or no understanding of the occultism associated with them.

Aside from personal observations of the games, the writer's investigations have been made through the rain priests, elder and younger brother Bow priests, personators of the Ko'yemshi (see page 33) and the theurgists. As the elder and younger brother Bow priests are the earthly representatives of the Gods of War, they are supposed to have intimate acquaintance with all things connected with these deities.

Many of the sages of Zuñi, including Nai'uchi, assert that the first eight of the seventeen games mentioned in the following list belong to the Gods of War. One, they say, was originated by the Zuñis, four are the games of the Ko'yemshi gods, one was adopted from the Navahos, and three came from Mexico. Others say that five games belong to the Gods of War, three originated with the Zuñis, five are the games of the Ko'yemshi, two came from the Navahos, and two came from Mexico. Where there is any question as to the origin of these games, both sources will be given. The origin claimed by Nai'uchi and other sages is mentioned first in cases where other derivations are given. The games are as follows:

Ti'kwanĕ, plural ti'kwawe (racing stick); sho'liwe (arrow reeds); i'yänkolo'we (hidden ball); ho'kĭamonnĕ (yucca ball); la'pochiwe (crossed feathers); ha'poännĕ pihl'kwanawe (bundle of reeds), Gods of War, Zuñi; sa'yat'laknawe (horns kill), Gods of War, Zuñi; sho'wi-yaltowe (arrow reeds one on the other), Gods of War, Navaho; po'kĭi ännawe (jack-rabbits hit), Zuñi; 'si'kon-yä'munĕ ti'kwanĕ the rain-makers' game, Ko'yemshi; po'pone (wool bag) Ko'yemshi, Mexican; po'pone kĭap'nanĕ (ball whipping), Ko'yemshi; ya'chuni sa'wanni, Ko'yemshi; 'kĭash'tuwiwi, Ko'yemshi; ta'-sholiwe (wood arrow-reeds), Navaho; tän'kalawe, Mexican; a'wet'laknawe (stones kill) checkers, Mexican.

Ti'kwanĕ. There are but two exclusively religious games of ti'kwawe played annually. In one members of the ki'wiᵗsiwe[a] play; in the other the clans take part. Both of these games are for rain to water the earth that the crops may grow. They take place some days previous to corn planting, which usually occurs from May 10 to May 15. These religious games must precede the betting games of ti'kwawe, which may occur at any time afterward when not prohibited by the retreat of the rain priests for rain.[b]

Ti'kwanĕ race of the ki'wi'siwe. The A'piᵗläshiwanni (Bow priesthood) convene six days previous to the race and remain in session throughout the night. On the following morning they prepare prayer plumes to the Gods of War, the Säl'imobiya, warrior gods and seed-gatherers of the six regions, and to the deceased members of the Bow priesthood. A portion of these offerings are deposited at noon the

---

[a] See p. 62.
[b] Ti'kwanĕ has been described by Mr F. W. Hodge in the American Anthropologist (July, 1890) and also by the late Mr John G. Owens, in connection with other games, in the Popular Science Monthly (May, 1891). Both of these gentlemen have visited Zuñi, but they fail to give a systematic

ZUÑIS IMITATING THE DANCE OF THE YE'BI'CHAI GODS OF THE NAVAHOS

DOG DANCE

ALTAR OF HÄ´LO´KWE (ANT FRATERNITY) BEFORE FETISHES ARE PLACED ON IT

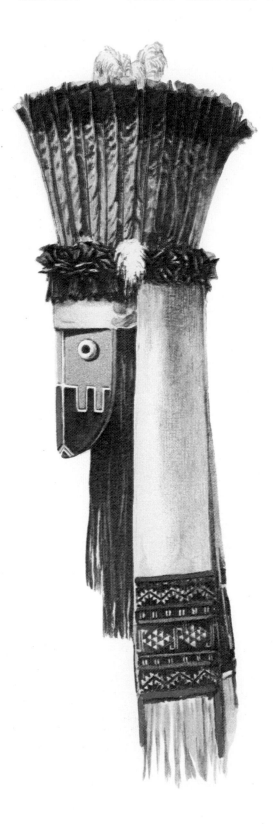

MASK OF THE SHUMAI'KOLI OF THE ZENITH

same day at Shop'ᵗhlua yäl'läkwi, a shrine north of the village and on the ground supposed to have been occupied as the home of the Gods of War during their stay at I'tiwanna (the site of the present Zuñi). The remainder of the prayer plumes are made into five kĭa'ĕtchiwe (groups of prayer plumes bound together at the base). The sticks of four groups are colored black and are offerings to the deceased members of the Bow priesthood. The fifth group consists of six prayer plumes, one for each of the six Säl'imobiya.

The kĭa'ĕtchiwe to the deceased members of the Bow priesthood are deposited at midnight on the four sides of the village, by such members of the organization as may be designated by the elder brother Bow priest, in excavations carefully concealed by stone ledges, which extend along the exterior of houses, furnishing seats for those who like to sit out in the balmy afternoon of a New Mexican winter, or to enjoy the cool breezes after sunset in summer. The depositors of the plumes know just which slab to remove in order to have access to the depository. The fifth kĭa'ĕtchinĕ is planted in an excavation, also concealed by a slab seat, on the west side of the Si'aa' te'wita (sacred dance plaza). After the placing of the plumes the Bow priests continue their songs and ceremonies in the ceremonial chamber until sunrise, and soon afterward the elder brother Bow priest announces from a housetop that the people of the ki'wiᵗsiwe will run in four days.

The director of each ki'wiᵗsinĕ gives formal notice to his people, and the young men who wish to take part in the race appear at the appointed time. Those from the He'iwa (North), He'kĭapawa (Nadir), and Chu'pawa (South) ki'wiᵗsiwe represent the side of the elder God of War, while those from the Mu'he'wa (West), O'he'wa (East), and Up'ᵗsannawa (Zenith) ki'wiᵗsiwe represent the side of the younger God of War. After an early breakfast, the runners having exercised before the meal, nothing more is eaten during the day but crushed wafer bread in water.

In the afternoon the first body of rain priests,[a] except the woman, proceed about a mile south of the village over the road leading to the present home of the Gods of War, and here the elder brother Bow priest lays upon the ground a la'showannĕ (one or more feathers attached to a cotton cord), composed of two upper wing feathers of a bird called sho'kĭapiso,[b] and the younger brother Bow priest places a similar la'showannĕ on the ground west of the other, the distance between the two la'showawe being as long as from finger tip to finger tip of the extended arms. The rain priests stand west and the Bow priests east of the plumes, the elder brother Bow priest standing with his fellows of the Bow priesthood, the younger brother Bow priest

---

[a] The writer designates the rain priests of the six regions, the elder and younger brother Bow priests, and the Priestess of fecundity as the first body of rain priests. There are a number of other rain priesthood groups in Zuñi.

[b] A bird, the Zuñi say, which flies, but never tires.

with the rain priests.   A line is made south of the plumes by drawing, or rather pushing, the foot over the earth from west to east.

Six members of the Bow priesthood selected by the elder brother Bow priest have each a gaming stick made by himself.   Three of the sticks are colored black at each end and midway, as were those of the elder God of War, and three are painted black midway only, as were

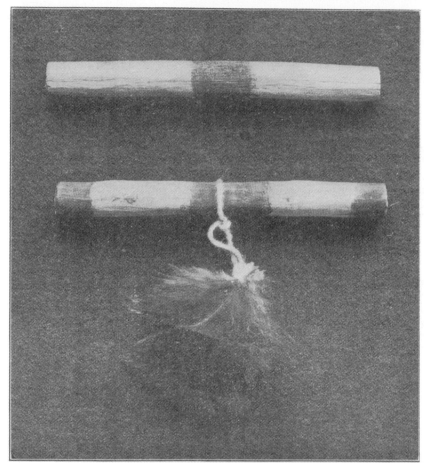

FIG. 11—Ti′kwawe of the Bow priests.

those of the younger God of War (figure 11).   The plumes are attached only when the sticks are made as offerings to the Gods of War.ª The six warriors, clad only in breechcloths, stand by the line, the one at the east end having a stick of the elder God of War, the man at the right having one of the younger God of War, and so they alter-

---

ªBoth Mr Hodge and Mr Owens say that these sticks are placed on the trail three or four days previous to the race.   It would be very difficult to find these bits of wood after four days on a trail frequented not only by men, but by burros and other beasts.

nate down the line.   Each warrior places his right foot on the line and lays the stick across the foot near the toes; he then sprinkles meal upon the stick and prays for rain and for success in the race.   The rain priests also sprinkle meal and pray for rain.   Meantime the runners gather at the base, which is south of the pueblo, just across the river which flows by the village,

The racers, the number of whom is not limited, wear only kilts, and the long hair is drawn back and tucked into the banda or head-kerchief at the back, the hair being brought over the band and tucked in from the top.   A member of the Bow priesthood marks off in the way described the line on the earth upon which the runners take position, facing south.   The warrior who stands some feet beyond the line carries a bow and arrows in his left hand and an arrow in his right. He directs the runners the course they are to take, and, facing east, prays and sprinkles meal eastward.   The meal is thrown four times, the fourth being the signal for the start.   No word is spoken.   The course is south to the group of rain priests and Bow priests, a course that must never be deviated from in these races, as this is the road of the Gods of War.   On reaching the body of priests awaiting them, each runner passes between the two la'showawe previously described. Bending and extending his hands toward the plumes, he brings his hands to his mouth and draws in a breath from the plumes that he may run like the sho'kĭapiso, which flies but never tires.   The runners do not halt, but pass right on.   Each Bow priest in the line calls out the name of the ki'wiᵗsinĕ he represents as he kicks the stick into the air. The runners of each ki'wiᵗsinĕ at once look to their appropriate sticks. They are followed by the first body of rain priests and Bow priests, except the elder and younger brother Bow priests.   The rain priests and Bow priests, however, do not attempt to keep pace with the runners, who move in a circuit, and return to the la'showawe, which are guarded by the elder and younger brother Bow priests, and pass between the latter and on to the village.   On their return the runners kick the sticks into the river so that they may go to Ko'thluwala'wa (abiding place of the Council of the Gods), and hasten to their homes. The ceremony of washing the hair of the runners occurs before the race and also on the morning after the race.   The younger brother Bow priest makes an excavation the depth of his arm and the two la'showawe are deposited therein, with prayers by the elder and younger brother Bow priests to the u'wannami (rain-makers) for rains.   These two now proceed to the base, where the large crowd gathered to greet the returning runners still remains.   At this point, before leaving, the elder brother Bow priest cries out that the a'notiwe (clans) will run in four days.

The race of the clans may occur simultaneously at Zuñi and one or more of the farming districts, where most of the Zuñis at this season are gathered, provided a Bow priest is present to start the racers, but it is usual for the men to gather at Zuñi for the race. The observances previous to the race of the clans are much the same as those for the race of the ki'wiꞏsiwe. A member of each clan makes the stick to be used by the racers of his clan and he is free to select that of either one of the Gods of War. The runners dress as on the previous occasion, and their hair is done up in the same manner. The clan symbol is painted on the breast of each runner, and that of the paternal clan is painted on the back. Those of the Pi'chikwe (Dogwood) clan have a conventional design of dogwood, including the roots, on the breast, and below a macaw or a raven with the head pointing to the left, according to the division of the clan to which the man belongs.[a] The gaming stick is also decorated with the totem.

The Bow priest makes a line south of the village by drawing or pushing his foot over the earth, as has been described, and the runners stand on the line, facing the south, members of each clan being together and the runner at the west end of each clan group placing the stick across his foot, as before noted. The Bow priest stands in advance of the runners, and facing east, prays and throws the meal four times eastward, the fourth throw, as before, being the signal for starting. The same course is followed as that pursued by the people of the ki'wiꞏsiwe. Each of these races covers about 4 miles.

No thought of betting is in the Zuñi mind when these races for rain occur, yet deep interest is exhibited by the women as well as by the men in the purely religious races, but the real enthusiasm occurs at the time of the betting races, when about 25 miles are covered.

When a man wishes to become fleet of foot for the race or to be sure of the winning side of a race, he calls upon the rain priest of the west or south (he may not consult any of the others) and requests to be instructed what to do to insure success in the races. The rain priest tells him to meet him the following night at the house where his ĕt'tonĕ[b] is kept. When the man arrives at the place of meeting, the rain priest with his associate priests and their families are gathered, the priests sitting about a cloud symbol embellished with fetishes, the most sacred of which is the ĕt'tonĕ, and offerings from the women who are present (see plate XXXIV). The rain priest rises to meet the man, who hands him four ears of corn tied together. The whole night is spent in offering song prayers to the u'wannami (rain-makers), and at sunrise the rain priest gives the man a te'likinanĕ (prayer plume) half the length of the middle finger measured on the under side. The stick

---

[a] The writer adopted Cushing's translation of Pi'chikwe, "macaw," until a more familiar acquaintance with the Zuñi tongue led her to discover that the word comes from pi'chiko, dogwood; kwe, plural ending denoting a people or body of people. This clan has two subdivisions, the macaw and the raven (see p. 40).

[b] See A'shiwanni (Rain priesthood).

is black with soft feathers from the leg of the turkey and birds of the
six regions; a la'showannĕ of a soft turkey-leg feather is attached to
the prayer plume, and an old ko'hakwa bead is strung on the cord of the
la'showannĕ.   After the presentation of the prayer plume, a bowl of
yucca suds is prepared by the wife of the rain priest, and each person
present takes a handful of the suds, and when all are supplied the
rain priest, his associates, and the others present place the suds upon
the man's head, with prayers; then the wife of the rain priest washes
his hair.   The man is instructed by the rain priest as to the course he
is to follow to insure success either as a runner or at the stakes.
One of two mesas must be ascended at this time; there are rock
markings on each. ˙The man never begins to run until he is a half
mile or more from the village and on his return always stops running about the same distance from the town so that the people may
not suspect him of starting or returning from a run.   The mesa north
of the village to which the runner resorts was the one visited by the
writer.   A rocky, picturesque trail leads to the mesa top.   A few feet
below the summit there is a stone heap 6 to 7 feet high and fully 15
feet at the base, and just before reaching this spot the runner takes
a small stone in each hand; he expectorates on the one in the left hand
and carries it two, three, or four times around his head from left to
right or the reverse and throws it upon the stone heap that he may be
rid of his tired breath so that he can start the run with new breath
and not lose it.   There is an exposure of rock surface 125 by 60 feet
about half a mile north of the stone heap on the summit of the mesa.
A running course is cut or worn upon the surface of the rock.   The
course has six loops, symbolizing cumulus clouds of the six regions.
All but one of these loops are to the east; the first one winds to the
west.   The distance between the first two loops is 24 feet; between
each succeeding two 12 feet.   The line extends 6 feet beyond the last
loop, making a total distance measured in a straight line of 78 feet.
A second stone heap stands a short distance beyond the line.   The
stone carried in the right hand is deposited on the near end of the line
and is pushed over the course beneath the right foot.   As the man
must move rapidly and the stone can not be restarted when once it gets
from under his control, not infrequently the stone is left behind, in which
case it is moved with the foot a short distance off the line to make room
for other stones and runners, where it must remain until the runner
makes another attempt at passing over his "luck line," as this marking
is called, for one is never sure of success until one has carried one's
stone to the end of the line with one's foot and cast it upon the second
stone heap.   When this has been accomplished a man may be sure of
winning the race or may risk high wagers on the races, as he has gone
over his luck line to the end; but when he has passed with his stone

only partly over the line, he is very cautious in betting.[a] The run continues across the mesa to a shrine where prayers are offered and meal mixed with crushed turquoise, ko'hakwa, and abalone shell is sprinkled to the Gods of War for good luck in the race. Then on he runs, down the mesa over a regular course directed by the rain priest over the Ojo Caliente road and around to the south and back to Zuñi, the distance covered being about 25 miles.

The betting race is not confined to the ki'wi'siwe or to any section of the village, although statements to the contrary have been made. A man approaches another with his plan for a race, and if it be acceptable to the other, a race is arranged. It is heralded from the house top by a civil officer of the village, who shouts: "To-morrow there will be a race!" Those wishing to take part in the race gather at the houses of the two managers. The swiftest runners are sure to be present. After some discussion the originator of the race visits the house of the other manager and learns from him how many runners he will have in the contest. He then returns to his house and selects the same number for his side. The number varies from three to six on a side, one side representing the elder, the other the younger, God of War. Each manager calls at the house of one of the first body of rain priests, those of the North and Zenith excepted, and announces: "My boys will run to-morrow. You will come to my house to-night." The friends of each party gather at the two houses, the runners being on one side of the room and the friends on the opposite side. When the rain priest arrives, bearing a basket tray of broken wafer bread, he takes his seat on his wadded blanket, the manager sitting opposite him. The rain priest places the basket upon the floor and asks for corn husks. Preparing as many husks as there are runners for the side, he sprinkles prayer meal into each husk and after adding bits of white shell and turquoise beads, folds it and lays it on the bread in the tray. Raising the tray with both hands to his face, he prays for success, and drawing four breaths from the contents of the tray, says: "Si!" (Ready!). The runners approach; the rain priest deposits a handful of broken bread from the tray in the blanket, supported by the left arm of each runner, and hands a corn-husk package to each. The body of runners who represent the elder God of War go to a point north of the village; the others go south. An excavation to the depth of a man's arm having been made by an ancient bean planter at each point, each runner opens his husk package, deposits the contents in the excavation, and drops in the bread as offerings to the Gods of War and ancestral gods. The one who prepares the earth to receive the offerings covers the opening, leaving no trace of the excavation. All now sit perfectly still and listen for sounds from the departed. When they hear any noise which they suppose comes from the dead, they are

[a] Photographs were secured of these very interesting rock markings.

gratified and say: "El'lakwa, na'nakwe" (Thanks, grandfathers). After walking a short distance they halt and wait again for some manifestation. Should they hear a few notes from the mockingbird, they know the race will be in favor first of one side and then of the other, uncertain until the end. If the bird sings much, they will meet with failure. If they hear an owl hoot, the race will be theirs. The runners return to the houses which they left and retire for the remainder of the night in the large room, the family having withdrawn to another apartment. Sometimes a runner goes to an arroyo and deposits offerings of precious beads to the Gods of War; or he goes to a locality where some renowned runner of the past was killed by an enemy and there, after offering food to the Gods of War with a prayer for success in the race, he sits and eagerly listens for some sound from the deceased. After a time he moves a short distance and listens again. He then moves a third time and listens, and if he hears anything from the dead he is almost sure of success. If he hears the whistling of the wind, he is also likely to meet with success; if he hears an owl hoot, his success is assured. In this event he imitates the owl during the race, which annoys the opposite side, for they know the reason for the owl-like cries.

At sunrise each runner carries a corn husk containing bits of precious beads and meal a distance from the village and sprinkles the offering to the u'wannami pi'"läshiwanni, the lightning makers of the six regions for success.

It is the custom of the runners to exercise for the race in the early morning, returning to the houses of the managers, where they eat a hearty breakfast; but they must not drink coffee, as this distends the stomach. After this early meal nothing is taken except a small quantity of wafer bread and water. They remain at the managers' houses until the hour for the race.

By afternoon the betting and excitement have increased until every available possession of the bettors is placed in the large plaza. Crowds gather around the managers, who are busy looking after the stakes. Everything is wagered, from a silver button to a fine blanket. Yards of calico are brought out, silver belts, and precious beads; in fact, all the effects of many are staked, especially those of the old gamblers, who have lost heavily perhaps in the gambling den and hope to regain their fortunes. The objects are stacked in two heaps, the two managers having charge of arranging the articles. A blanket from one heap finds its counterpart in the other, and both are placed together, forming the base of a third pile. Drawing in this way from the two piles is continued until they are consolidated into one great heap. Much of the forepart of the afternoon is consumed in this work. When the managers return to their houses and announce to the runners that the task of arranging the stakes is completed, the latter remove their clothing and after donning a kilt of white cotton or some other light material take medicine of the Shu'maakwe fraternity in their mouths, eject it into their hands, and rub their entire bodies, that they may not be made tired by running. A piece of humming-bird medicine, a root (species undetermined), is passed around; each runner takes a bite, and after chewing it ejects it into his hands and rubs his body that he may be swift like the humming bird. The hair is brought forward, and a bow priest forms a long knob by folding the hair over and over and wrapping it with yarn; he then places an arrow point in the knot to insure fleetness; lifting ashes with two eagle-wing plumes, he passes them down the sides of each racer and sprinkles ashes to the six regions for physical purification.

Medicine is sometimes put into the paint used on the stick, which for the betting races is painted red instead of black, and a bit of this paint is slipped under the nail of the index finger of the right hand. If a runner is seen to keep his thumb pressed to his finger, it is known that he has medicine under the nail, and those making the discovery are apt to bet high on that side, for they believe the medicine will bring success. Failure in such cases is attributed to the bad heart of the runner.

The wives of the two rain priests who were present on the previous night each go to the house visited by the husband, where they remain during the absence of the runners. Several parcels, including two blankets, are removed from the heap in the plaza and carried to each house and deposited beside the woman for good luck to the runners. The runners are accompanied to the base by their managers and the bow priests. Crowds gather; every man who can obtain a horse is mounted. All is excitement, the women's enthusiasm being almost equal to that of the men, for each wife is interested in the side her husband has chosen, and every maiden is eager for the success of her favorite admirer. While the men gather about the runners preparing for the race, and follow them, the women must content themselves in the village.

The two sticks designating the sides of the elder and the younger God of War are made by the bow priests of the side of the second manager and are carried by a runner of this party to the base, where he holds the sticks out to the opposite side, one of the party taking the stick of his choice. The racers do not form in regular line. Each leader places the stick across his foot near the toes and sprinkles it with meal; they then cry out "Si!" (Ready!) The stick must not be touched with the hand after it is placed on the foot. It is often thrown a long distance, and no matter where it may rest it must be managed with the foot.

There is nothing more exciting to the Zuñis, except the scalp dance, than this game of ti'kwanĕ. Those on horseback urge their ponies on-

ward to keep pace with the racers, who run southward over the road
of the Gods of War for a distance, then around to the east, crossing
the river. On they go toward the north, keeping to the foothills.[a]
Recrossing the river several miles west of Zuñi, they continue southward then veer round to the east and return by the southern road to
the base, when the members of the successful party vie with one
another in reaching the great plaza, for he who is first to pass around
the heap of wagered articles is the hero of the hour. As they run
around this heap, they extend their hands toward it and bringing
them to the mouth draw in a breath and pass on to the house of
the manager whence they started, where the victor deposits the stick
of his side in a basket of prayer meal, while all present place offerings of bits of precious beads in the basket. The wife of the rain
priest takes the hands of the victor and standing brings her clasped
hands four times before his mouth. Each time he draws a breath.
The waving of the hands four times is repeated before each runner, who
draws as many breaths. After the prayers the victor empties the contents of the basket, which includes the meal and bead offerings and the
stick, into a corn husk and carries it to his home. After each runner
returns to his home he drinks a quantity of warm water as an emetic, and
when relieved he retires for the night. It is not uncommon for a runner
to be so affected by the race that the manipulations of a masseuse (the
Zuñis being expert in massage) are necessary to restore him. The
following morning the head of each runner is washed in yucca suds,
and he bathes. After the morning meal the stick of the elder God of
War and the contents of a corn husk carried by the runner from his
manager's house are deposited at a shrine on U'hana yäl'länne (Wool
mountain), while the stick of the younger God of War and offerings
are deposited on To'wa yäl'länne (Corn mountain).

The most prominent religious positions do not debar men from taking part in these betting races. One of the fleetest as well as most
enthusiastic runners of the present time is the Ko'mosona (Director-
general) of the ki'wiᵗsɪwe.

There are many informal games of ti'kwanĕ in which young men
hurriedly gather for sport, and sometimes a considerable stake is
raised. One of these races observed by the writer, in which great
enthusiasm was exhibited, began at 5 o'clock in the afternoon, the parties returning after 7. There were three runners on a side, of whom the
Ko'mosona was one. Though considerable interest is manifested in
the informal races, there is little or no ceremony associated with them,
and the excitement is as nothing compared with the more formal
affairs. Each runner bets on his side. Outside parties bet with one

---

[a] There are six stone heaps which direct the runners in their course. These monuments, which
are about 4 feet high, are supposed to have been made by direction of the Gods of War. Vases
containing medicine of these gods are believed to be buried beneath the mounds, though these
objects are too sacred to be commonly referred to.

another, one holding the stakes, or, more frequently, a third party has charge of the stakes, which are heaped in the large plaza. Sometimes the articles are afterward carried to the ki'wi'ᵗsinĕ to which the successful party belongs, while again they may pass to the winner in the plaza, who in turn divides the profits among the runners of his side.

It is interesting to see the very young boys engaged in their foot-races (plate LXXXIII) and to observe how closely they follow their elders in the rules governing the stakes. Wagers are always made, as the races would be of little interest even to the younger boys without the element of chance associated with them. Beginning at so early an age, these people develop naturally enough into swift runners. The writer has never known the Zuñis to loose a footrace with other Indians or with the champion runners of the troops at Fort Wingate, who sometimes enter into races with them. It is rather common for the Zuñis and Navahos to race. Though these races are always informal, the stakes are often large, and the Navahos frequently depart from the pueblo, leaving their precious beads, silver belts, bridles, and valuable blankets in the hands of the Zuñis.

Sho'liwe (*arrow reeds*). The lot game of sho'liwe is second on the list of the games of the Gods of War and is the great indoor gambling game of the Zuñis. The implements are four split reeds, a bowl-shaped basket, a buckskin, a blanket, bits of pith or the central core of a corncob, straws for counters, and chips which are usually silver buttons. Legend says that this game was played for rain by the Gods of War and the rain priesthood while the A'shiwi (Zuñis) were at Hän'-ᵗlipĭnkĭa (see page 34). The rain priests thought the reeds used for the game were too long, so their length was measured from the tip of the thumb to the tip of the middle finger, both extended.

The rain priests considered this game so efficacious in bringing rain that they organized a fraternity, which they called Sho'wekwe (Arrow-reed people), for the express purpose of playing the game for rain. Ten men were designated by the rain priests as the original members of the Sho'wekwe. The prayers of this fraternity were sure to bring rain.

When the gods visited I'tiwanna (Middle place, the site of the present Zuñi), eight days after the first appearance of ᵗKĭäklo (see page 65) in I'tiwanna, certain ancestral gods gathered in the ceremonial chamber of the Kĭa'kwemosi where the first body of rain priests, the Galaxy fraternity, and the ten members of the Sho'wekwe were assembled. The Ko'yemshi at this time gave their songs and prayers to the fraternities present, after which the Ne'wekwe and Sho'wekwe alternated annually in personating the Ko'yemshi (see page 33).

The Great Fire and the Cactus fraternities are more recent accessions to the personators of the Ko'yemshi. The four fraternities now personate these gods in turn (see page 235); at least such was the case until the Sho'wekwe became so degenerated that the director of the fraternity preferred to choose the personators of the Ko'yemshi from the fraternities at large rather than to call on the men of his own. The fraternity no longer exists in its original purity, having degenerated into a body of professional gamblers which bears no relation whatever to the one organized by the rain priests; but the game is still played by the priests and others in all sacredness for rain.

The reeds used for ceremonial occasions are rarely brought out at other times. Such reeds are old and are preserved with care, and it is considered a great privilege when one having lost heavily at the game may secure, as indicated in the succeeding paragraph, a ceremonial set of reeds through which to recover his possessions.

The following was related by a celebrated player of sho'liwe.

The only rain priests who have the game of sho'liwe are those of the south, west, and the one who goes last into retreat for rains.[a] Long ago the rain priest of the west and the one last mentioned possessed the game, but the rain priest of the south having great desire for the game presented a fine buckskin and many turquoise to the priest of the west, requesting the game in return. The request was complied with, and the priest of the south became the happy possessor of the game. This occurred long before the birth of my uncle, the rain priest of the west, who is now an aged man. The medicine given the priest of the south with the game is all gone, but he pretends that he still has some, but we know that he has not, as he always loses the game.

I gambled with new reeds and lost beads, blankets, and other things, and in my distress I went to the house of my uncle, rain priest of the west, where an original set of reeds belonging to the younger God of War is kept. I told him of my trouble and begged him to let me have the precious reeds to play with in order to win back my valuables. I visited my uncle's house the night of the day I lost my things. It was in the month of May. He said: "Come to me at the winter solstice." I did as he bade me, going to him at night. He gave me the reeds, a klĕm'tutu'nuni' (rhombus), and two prayer plumes which he had prepared for me, the sticks being of the length of the middle finger measured on the underside. A la'showanně, composed of a turkey-leg feather, a duck plume, and a wing feather from each bird of the six regions, was tied pendent to each stick, with several precious beads strung on the cord, the length of the cord from the stick to the plumes being measured by the four fingers crosswise. My uncle also gave me medicine, which was a little black and a little white, to rub on my hands when I should be ready to play. It appeared like grease, but I do not know what it was. I spent the night with my uncle while he taught me four old songs. He said, after I had learned the songs by heart: "Before you play the game shut your mouth and sing the songs with your heart. After singing the songs once you may speak with the man with whom you are to play, but you must again shut your mouth and sing the songs with your heart, and then you may play." At sunrise the wife and the daughter of my uncle came into the room where my uncle and I had spent the night. The girl prepared a bowl of yucca suds and placed it immediately before me. I sat facing east and the wife stood behind me, placing a hand on each shoulder. The girl stood south of the bowl and faced it. My uncle was the first to dip two eagle-wing plumes four times into the suds, each time

---

a See A'shiwanni (Rain priesthood).

drawing them forward over the top of my head. This was repeated by all present except the girl, who prepared the suds. After the others had rubbed suds over my head with the plumes, she washed my hair thoroughly from the bowl, standing before me, and my uncle's wife also washed my hair while I was still in my seat. My uncle gave me four ears of corn, yellow, blue, red, and white, tied together, and enough calico for a shirt. In giving me the corn and calico he said: "I give these to you that you may receive such things from the man with whom you play. Carry the plumes (reference being to the four prayer plumes given the previous night) a long distance to an arroyo where you find débris has collected from running water and plant them to the Gods of War." When I was within a few feet of the place I had selected for depositing my plumes I whirled my rhombus until I reached the spot.

I afterward returned the rhombus to my uncle, but kept the sho′liwe[a] until the anniversary of the loss of my possessions.[b] I won back my lost articles, after which I returned the sho′liwe to my uncle.

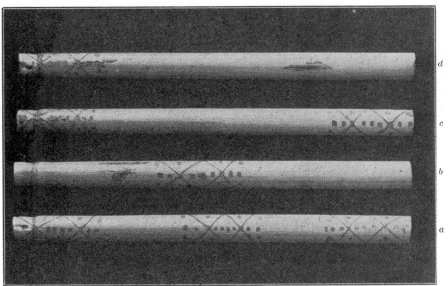

FIG. 12—Split reeds used in sho′liwe.

Each player takes the side of one of the Gods of War. There are four pieces of split reeds, two representing the side of the elder and two the side of the younger God of War. The reeds shown in figure 12 may be described as follows: *a* and *c* belong to the elder and *b* and *d* to the younger God of War; *a*, kwĭn′na (black), has the concave side of the reed colored black, indicating the whole day, and three sets of markings on the convex side denoting the three periods of the day, morning, noon, and sunset; *b*, a′thluwa (center), has a daub of black in

---

[a] It was the writer's good fortune to have two sets of ceremonial reeds presented to her by the elder and the younger brother Bow priests. They are now in the National Museum.

[b] One must begin to play on the same day of the month that the loss occurred. Playing may be continued until the summer solstice, but no games must be played while the rain priests are in retreat for rains. If success does not come to the player with the ceremonial reeds, he may ask for them again and try his luck another year, in the meantime purifying his heart, for if the heart is good, these reeds are believed to bring success.

the middle of the reed on the concave side, denoting midday, the markings on the convex side also denoting noon; c, ko'hakwa[a] (white medicine), has a daub of black paint at each end of the concave side, indicating morning and evening or sunrise and sunset, markings on the convex side denoting the same; d, pahl'to (mark on the end), has a daub of black paint on the concave side of the joint end denoting sunrise, which to the Zuñis is the first light of day, or the white light which comes first, and markings on the convex side indicate the same, while three dots sometimes found on the joint of the reed, not shown here, indicate eyes and mouth of the face; other reeds have only two dots, which stand for the eyes.   The player representing the elder God of War holds c in the right hand with the convex side exposed, the joint end pointing toward him, and slides the septum end of b into the groove c, leaving the septum of b an inch within the end of c; d is then run into b in the manner described, the septum of d being an inch within the end of b. The three reeds are then transferred to the left hand and reversed, and a is placed at right angles, the concave side exposed, the septum end pointing to the left, as shown in figure 13. The game is passed in this position back to the right hand and rests upon the first three fingers with the thumb on the top.

FIG. 13—Method of placing reeds in playing sho'liwe.

When the representative of the younger God of War plays he runs c into the groove of b and a into c and crosses them with d. The reed which crosses the others is designated as the thrower, but the same reed, as stated, is not used by both players. In this position the reeds are thrown upward against an inverted basket, 10 or 12 inches in diameter, covered with a piece of blanket or cloth and suspended from the ceiling. The reeds strike the cloth over the basket and fall to a blanket spread on the floor to receive them. If played out of doors, which is not usual at the present period, the basket is suspended above the blanket from the apex of three poles, arranged tripod fashion, with sufficient space beneath for the blanket and players.

---

[a] The fine white shell beads which are used not only as ornaments and as money, but also as offerings to the gods, have the same name.

When the representative of the elder God of War throws, and the concave side of *a* and the convex sides of the others are up, the trick is won; or if *a* is convex side up with the others concave up, the trick is won. If *a* crosses *c* or vice versa convex sides up, the trick is won, even should one cross the other by but a hair's breadth. If *b* and *d* should be crossed as described, the trick goes to the opponent. If all convex sides are up or vice versa, the trick is lost. If the convex side of *b* is up and the others have the concave sides up, the trick belongs to the opponent. Silver buttons are the favorite chips for the game.

Though sho'liwe is a favorite of the lot games, it being the game of the professional gamblers[a] of the pueblo, there is no thought of personal gain when it is played by the rain priests for rain.[b] At such times great ceremony is observed and buckskins are used in place of the cloth covering over the basket and of the blanket on the floor. The skin on the floor has the head to the east. A portion of a circle, a quadrant, or octant, is drawn on the skin.

The gambling den of Zuñi was as notorious and was regarded with the same aversion as a place of similar character is in civilization. The more profligate characters, who depend upon gaming for their livelihood, spent much of their time in this den, which was one of the old interior rooms of the pueblo. The room was reached by a ladder through a hatchway, and, if the memory of the writer is correct, the room was dimly lighted with a small window of selenite near the ceiling. The hatchway was covered with a straw mat, upon which an eye was kept that there might be no intruders. The writer first visited this den in 1896. Her unannounced arrival was a surprise to the eight or ten men present, who appeared to be much annoyed; but when they were informed that she had come to observe the game and not to denounce them for their profligacy a sigh of relief escaped them.

There is but little ceremony associated with the game when played by the professional or other gamblers. The most abandoned, however, would not dare to play without first offering prayers to the Gods of War, invoking their blessing, and breathing on their reeds. The professional gamblers show in their faces deep lines and other indications of dissipation, although they lose no more rest than the rain priests and the theurgists. The inveterate gamblers, like other people not altogether lost to a sense of right, must have the conscious-

---

[a] After an absence of six years the writer found on her return in 1902 that the Zuñi gambling house was a thing of the past and that the game of sho'liwe was not so frequently played as formerly, either ceremonially or for pleasure.

[b] The reader who has perused "Chess and Playing-cards," by Mr Stewart Culin (Report of the United States National Museum, 1896), will note the difference between the explanation of sho'liwe found in that publication and that given here. For example, Mr Culin says: "Formerly sho'liwe was exclusively a game of war divination and was played only by the priests of the Bow and members of the esoteric society of the war shamans." According to Zuñi belief sho'liwe was played by the Divine Ones (Kŏw'wituma and Wats'usi) and the rain priests for rain soon after they reached this world, long before the creation of the Bow priesthood.

PLEASURE DANCE

MAIDENS AT THE WELL

Mary Wright Gill.

ALTAR OF SHU'MAAKWE

ALTAR OF PḖSHĀTSILŌ̈KWE (CIMEX FRATERNITY)

ness of doing wrong, while, on the other hand, the rain priests and
theurgists have the satisfaction of realizing that they are propitiating
their gods, not only for their own good but for the good of all; not
only for their own people but for all the world.

I'yänkolo'we—Implements of the game. Four cups of quaking aspen
wood, 12½ inches high, 2¾ inches across at the opening, and slightly
less than 2¼ inches at the bottom, are hollowed to the depth of 2½ inches
to accommodate a stone ball. There is a stone disk painted white on
one side and black on the other, and 106 straws. The cups are painted
white with kaolin. The bottom of each cup is covered with black paint,
which extends up the side 1½ inches. This paint, which is said to
have come from the undermost world, is first mixed with water and
then a medicine is added. Powdered 'suhapa (micaceous hematite) is
also added. The hematite bears the same name as the fixed stars and
is referred to as the star medicine. The finger is dipped into the white
paint and touched to the gaming ball, which is afterward wrapped in
cotton cord, or the entire ball is painted white. The Zuñis say that
the game originally had instead of the cups four deer carved of wood,
with an opening in the side of each large enough to contain the ball.

I'yänkolo'we is played only in January, February, and March, but
mostly in February, and when once begun must be continued without
intermission to the close. In February, 1904, a game was begun the
evening of the 10th and continued through the 12th. When a man
wishes to play a game of i'yänkolo'we he calls upon a rain priest of
either the West, East, Zenith, or Nadir (the other rain priests have nothing to do with this game), at sunset and makes known his wish. The
rain priest asks him where his he'we (wafer bread) is, his precious beads,
his prayer meal, and tells him to return at night with these things.
The rain priest then goes to a storage room and brings out an ancient
u'linně (gaming ball). After his wife or some female member of the
family has swept the floor of the inner room, the rain priest makes,
with prayer meal, four parallel lines running north and south by the
north wall of the room, the length of these lines measuring from the
tip of the middle finger to the tip of the thumb, with fingers extended.
He then places the ball midway on the most western line and says
to it: "You will remain here through the night." Then he gives to
the man some wafer bread in a piece of cloth, a corn-husk cigarette
of native tobacco (Nicotiana attenuata), a sack containing powdered
te'na'säli (mythical medicine plant), and a piece of banded gypsum, 2½
or 3 inches in length, slender, round, and tapering. When the time
for the game has been decided upon by the rain priest and player, a
member of the governor's staff calls from the house top that the game
of i'yänkolo'we will be played the following night, giving the name of
the leader, and another group is then formed to play. The players are
not confined to particular clans, ki'wi'siwe,ᵃ or sections of the village.

ᵃ See Ki'wi'siwe and their functions.

After carrying the articles to his home the leader of the game selects his three associate players and four watchers (the seers who choose the hidden cups) and returns with them to his house, where a number of friends interested in the game have gathered. The leader is always careful to choose players whom he may trust and who will not indicate to the watchers of the opposite side where the cup with the ball is placed. The players and watchers sit upon the floor midway of the room, the head player having by his side a basket tray containing the wafer bread, cigarette, and sack of te'nas'säli given him by the rain priest whom he consulted. The leader and the head watcher each deposit four corn husks upon the floor and all present, beginning with the leader, deposit turquoise, ko'hakwa (white shell beads), micaceous hematite, red hematite, and corn pollen in each corn husk. Each places a reed cigarette in one of his packages and they fold each husk, with the offerings, into a rectangular package.

The leader's prayer is addressed to the Gods of War, rain-makers, the sun, moon, stars, and A'wonawil'ona[a] that he may be successful in the game and have long life, that the other side may have bad luck, and that his playing may bring much rain, many crops, and all things to eat, and horses and sheep. The buckskin sack of te'nas'säli is then opened and a corn husk is placed beside it. A gourd of water is now handed the leader. He dips a little water with his first three fingers and drops it into the corn husk; then dipping a bit of the te'nas'säli with the tip of the banded gypsum, he mixes the powdered plant with the water in the husk. If a rain priest chances to be present, he dips the stone into the mixture and places it in the left ear, then runs it across the face under the eyes, and puts it in the right ear of the leader of the players, who repeats the same with the rain priest and then with the others of the group. The placing of the te'nas'säli in the ear and under the eyes is to insure seeing and hearing unusual or mysterious things and sounds. All now sit perfectly still for a few minutes and then the leader hands his corn-husk package containing the cigarette to the first watcher, who is instructed to visit the most eastern shrine of the elder God of War and ask him to come with him. On reaching the shrine the man opens the husk given him by the head player and depositing the offerings prays: "I pray you, A'hayuta, come with me at once to te'wita 'hlann'a kwi (large plaza place), for we begin our game to-morrow and we wish you to remain with us until the game closes." A line of meal is then sprinkled, suggestive of the road over which the god is to pass from the shrine to the point in the plaza where the game is to be played, and then the man says, addressing A'hayuta: "Sit here until to-morrow, when we will come and be with you. Wait for us." The

---

[a] See Classification of the higher powers.

man then returns to the house of the leader of the players. The other three watchers may visit whatever cardinal point they wish, but they must keep together. Each one carries a corn-husk package prepared by the head watcher, the leader of the party having the one containing the cigarette. They usually go about 2 miles from the village, where one of the party makes an excavation the depth of the arm in which to deposit offerings. They then pray to the deceased i'yänkolo'we players. The offerings are made that success will follow them in the game and that the game may bring rains and all things good. The excavation is covered and the three go a short distance and sit down and listen attentively. Then they move on a little farther and sit and listen again. This is repeated four times, each time a little farther off from the excavation. One must never turn around nor look back if he hears any steps and knows that there is something unusual. If he sees a star move, or sees the lightning, a mysterious fire, or bright light on the earth, he knows his side will win the game. If he hears an owl or coyote, he knows the other side will win. If he hears a summer bird, the success will come to his side. If he hears a mocking bird or snow bird, he knows there will be trouble, perhaps the two sides will have a fight and one will be hit with the ball of the game. The watchers now return to the house of the leader.

After the head watcher departs for the shrine, the leader of the players hands three of his corn-husk packages to each of the other three players. Then taking wafer bread with both hands from the basket tray, he places it in the blanket over the left arm of each man, putting the remainder of the bread in his own blanket over the arm. He carries the sack of te'na͡tsäli and the cigarette. The fourth corn-husk package of the leader of the watchers is given one of the men present by the leader of the players with the following instructions: "You will go to-morrow to the house of the rat man. Give these offerings to him and ask him to help you to collect the straws that are to aid us to win the counters in the game." The leader of the players with his three associates then visits the house of the rain priest, removing their moccasins and head-kerchiefs on entering. They deposit the wafer bread, which they carry in their blankets, and the husk packages in a basket tray, which the rain priest extends to them without rising from his seat on the floor in the middle of the room. The leader of the players returns the sack of te'na͡tsäli to the rain priest, who lays it in the basket. The rain priest sings four songs to certain rain priests of the four regions, calling each by name: "Here is your Ko'hakwa, 'Suhapa, [etc.], take these and give me much rain, many seeds, all things good, give me long life that I may not die, but sleep to awake in Ko'thluwala'wa." The rain priest makes no mention of the game. These songs belong especially to the rain priests, all of whom have the same songs, which are purely for rain and fructification of the earth. The rain priest prays again over the basket tray, raising it to his face, and repeats the ceremony of placing the te'nas⁺säli, mixed with water, in the ears and across the faces of the four players, who stoop before him; they then receive the wafer bread, husk packages, and cigarette from the rain priest in their blankets over the left arm. The gaming ball, which remains in place in the inner room, is not seen at this time by any of the players. The players leave the house of the rain priest at midnight without speaking a word and go to the old church, built by the Spaniards and now a ruin, where the leader makes an excavation the depth of the lower arm and deposits the offerings to the deceased players of i'yänkolo‘we. After depositing the offerings with prayers within the walls of the church, they pass to the south of the cross in the center of the graveyard. The leader of the players removes several handfuls of earth and places it in a cloth. He carries it to the rain priest's house and deposits the earth outside the door, when they return to the leader's house, where a rain priest (not the one, however, whom the leader has visited) says to the leader: "Your great 'Moon Mother' and stars who are out saw you come from the dead. What have you to say? What do you know about your Moon Mother or the stars or A'wonawil'ona? What have they told you? If you know nothing it makes no difference." The leader tells the rain priest what he heard while visiting the dead in the graveyard and the rain priest replies, "That is well. I hope you will have a good time and win, that we shall have much rain and many crops." If one is touched by the dead he is sure to win the game.

All sit down, and with a slender rod of cottonwood root that has been lighted in the fire the shi'wanni lights a corn-husk cigarette of native tobacco. A match must not be used to light this cigarette. Puffing it, he blows the smoke and motions the cigarette to the six regions, forming a circle symbolic of the whole world. He then hands the cigarette to the leader, who repeats the form and hands it to the next man, who does the same. The cigarette is then passed to some of the friends present who are going to bet on the game. When only a bit of the cigarette remains, it is placed in a basket tray for the night (the players and watchers sleep in the house of the head player) and in the morning it is cast into the river, to go the abiding place of the Council of the Gods.

After the cigarette is laid in the basket tray, the leader of players and his associates put on their moccasins, and the rain priest, still sitting, lifts the basket tray and prays again for rain, food, etc. After this prayer the four men go to the summit of Corn mountain. When they all return they crush ko'hakwa, turquoise, a'hoko (a red stone said to come from the far south), and black turquoise (so named because this black stone is found in the locality of the turquoise), which they mix with corn meal and corn pollen. This mixture is placed in a corn husk with small feathers from a bird secured from the neighborhood of Santa Anna. This package is afterward carried to the large plaza where the game is played.

Later in the morning the kotchi (rat) man returns to the house of the head player for the corn-husk package given him the previous evening and carries it to the house of the wood rat (Neotoma). After depositing his offerings, with prayers to the rat to aid his side in winning the straw counters by collecting many twigs and stems, he proceeds to the shrine of the younger God of War on the summit of Corn mountain, where he makes offerings and prays for success in the game. Descending the mountain, he goes to the cactus bed belonging to the Cactus fraternity and secures a piece of cactus (Opuntia arborescens) about 12 inches in length and prays: "When I place you in the plaza do not let anyone touch you. Give us good luck in the game; give us much rain and all things." Then he deposits bits of precious beads and prayer meal at the base of the plant which is known as the father of the cactus bed. He afterward visits a bed of flat-leaf cactus (Opuntia filipendula) and collects several pieces, saying: "When I place you in the plaza do not let anyone touch you. Give us much rain, all things to eat, all things to wear." He then goes to a yucca glauca plant and pulling a central stalk says: "Give me good luck in the game; give me much rain, all things to eat, etc." A plant of kïapuli (not classified) is then visited, and he repeats the prayers and breaks off a small twig with several branches. All the plants are wrapped together in a cloth and carried to the house of the leader, where he joins the watchers and players. On entering the house the rat man says: "May the day go well with you." The others reply: "All good come to you." The leader advances to meet him and receives the bundle of plants, depositing it on a ledge in a corner of the room where it will be secure from view. He then calls the three players and requests them to help him arrange the plants, which are grouped together. Turquoise, ko'hakwa, abalone, meal and corn pollen, and a quail feather, to which is attached a cotton string with one black archaic bead strung on it, are bound to the base of the bouquet with buckskin, which is carefully tied over the end and wrapped with a buckskin thong. While the plants are being prepared the four watchers each bind an arrow to the center of the sole of his foot with a cotton cloth (either foot may be used), the arrow pointing toward the toes, and the moccasin is drawn on. No secrecy is observed in binding on the arrow. A fine meal is then served by the leader's wife and family, who are assisted by female members of her clan; they all eat heartily. Coffee and water are freely indulged in. The leader addressing his players, watchers, and the rat man, says: "You must eat much now, for you must neither eat nor drink while the game is being played." Should the leader of the game on the opposite side come to him and ask if he did not wish to eat or drink with him, he replies, "Yes, we will eat with you," if he thinks it is best, but usually the invitation is refused. After the repast the four players and four watchers gather near the fireplace and apply bear or cougar grease under and above each eye and then place red hematite over the grease. The leader then asks, "Are you ready?" and they reply "Yes," and the players and watchers go to the plaza. The leader takes his place on the west side of the plaza with his party; the players of the other side sit on the east side of the plaza by the old Spanish church. The game, which is carried by the

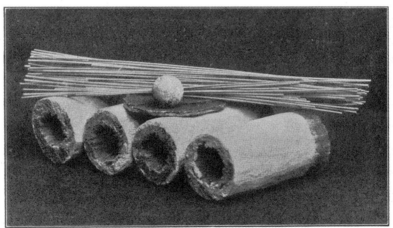

FIG. 14—Implements used in i'yänkolo'we.

leader, is deposited on the west side of the plaza, the open ends of the cups to the east. The stone disk, ball, and straw counters are laid upon the cups (see figure 14). A party from each side is dispatched for sand, and the first leader visits the house of the rain priest to secure the gaming ball which was left on the west line of meal. If it has moved to the most eastern line, the leader knows that his side will win, but if it has moved only to the second or third line, he can not tell anything about it. He lifts the stone while he stands by the side of the rain priest, and, drawing a breath from it, places it inside his shirt, and saying to the rain priest "So'anni" (Good-by), returns to the plaza. He requests one of the watchers to remove the disk from the cups and carry it to the head player of the opposite side and ask which side of the stone disk he will choose—black or white. When the side is chosen, the watcher

stands with the stone beside the stakes which are piled in the plaza
and throws it up, and if the side exposed is that chosen by the opposite
party, the watcher carries the game over to that side; otherwise the
game is carried to the first leader, who hands a cup to each of the three
players and keeps one himself, each player facing a cardinal point.
The cup may be held in either hand. In addition to the cup, the leader
holds the disk, the ball, and straws. While the four players sit by the
sand pile, which is 6 or 7 inches high, they are covered with a large
blanket held by a man. The sand is brushed to one side and the
leader orders one of his men to dig a hole about 1½ feet in depth in the
center of the place where the sand was placed. Any implement may be
used for this purpose. The bunch of plants is deposited in the excavation, the tops being just even with the earth, so that when the hand
is rubbed over the earth the cactus and other things are detected.
Each of the four players then makes a small excavation immediately
before him and about 1½ feet from the plants and deposits a small
corn-husk package of precious offerings, including a la'showannĕ.
The openings are then covered with earth, and the sand is brought
back to its original place. Then the leader who sits on the east side
digs a hole 1½ inches in depth to the right of him and deposits one
ancient ko'hakwa bead. He then digs a similar hole an inch or so
east of the other and deposits a bit of fine turquoise; then the excavation is covered. The turquoise must be of the best quality obtainable and of sufficient size to be of real value. The ko'hakwa and
the turquoise must be upright, not laid flat in the excavation. Again
another hole is drilled with a stick or iron rod to about the depth
of the hand an inch or so east of where the turquoise is placed.
The leader runs the point of a slender pencil-shaped stick through
the black stone bead and then puts the point of the stick to the
hole which has been drilled and works the stick until it goes as far
as the depth of the hole, when he withdraws it, leaving the black bead
in place, and covers the hole with earth. Then each player holding
his cup to his mouth offers a silent prayer. The lips do not move.
The explanation is "We sing with our hearts, not with our lips."
The song is to the crow and owl. The former can hide corn in
the mountains and find it long months after, and the owl could
carry the ball in his claw and jump about and no one know that he
had it.[a] Songs are also addressed to the Gods of War. After the
songs the leader takes from his shirt the ball which the rain priest
gave him, rubs it in his hands with the ball of the game, draws
a breath from the two balls, returns the one given by the rain
priest to his breast, and places the other immediately over the

---

[a] It is claimed that there are balls in Zuñi marked with the owl's foot, the owl having stolen a
ball and hidden it in his claws when the Zuñis were at Hän'ᵈlipinkla. (See p. 34.)

buried plants. He then stands one of the cups over the ball, and the other cups are placed where he chooses. He brings the sand up well around them, and lighting a husk cigarette puffs the smoke over the cups, waving the cigarette to the North, West, South, East, Zenith, and Nadir, that the rain-makers of the six regions and all the world will send rain upon Zuñi. All this is done under cover of the blanket. The blanket is now withdrawn, and the head watcher of the opposite side goes over to choose the cups. The cups are touched with the hand. If the second cup touched contains the ball, six straws are lost, and the players are again covered with the blanket. The cups are taken from their place, the small package of corn-husk offerings is moved a little nearer to the center, the cups and ball are again placed, and the blanket is removed. Then one of the watchers from the opposite side comes over and asks for the bunch of straws (there must always be 106 straws) and carries it to his side and hands it to the rat man. Then the head watcher returns and pays six straws for his first guess, which was not successful, and again he touches the cups. If he touches the one with the ball at the first guess, he has to pay ten straws, and accordingly returns to the rat man and gets the straws. The four players are covered again to change the cup and ball, and the corn-husk offerings are again moved a little closer to the plant bunch, which is always in the center, and the ball is always immediately over this spot, but the three cups are so moved and the sand so changed that it is impossible for one to know the center. The head watcher from the opposite side then brings his ten straws and again chooses.

If the fourth cup he touches contains the ball, he must pay four straws. Again the blanket covers the players, the cups and corn-husk package are changed, the man returns with the four straws which he received from the rat man, and once more he chooses the cups. If the third cup he touches contains the ball, he carries the game over to his side, and the playing is reversed. The game is not won until one side or the other is in possession of all the straws. When the game goes back to the first party, and the leader places the ball, he says to it: "If you wish to move about, go outside to your mother, Ko'hakwa [referring to the bead planted near by], but do not go to your father, 'Hli'akwa [Turquoise]; go to your mother and soon return." The game sometimes continues four days and nights. It has been known to last five days. One must never sleep, eat, or drink during the game, which goes on no matter how cold the weather or how heavy the storm. The first leader of the game, whether he is successful or otherwise, removes all the deposits but the black archaic bead, which remains permanently in the ground, and carries them with the game to his home. He still has the ball given him by the rain priest in his shirt. The wagers are also carried to his house, placed on the floor, and afterward given to the winners. He places the game and offerings in a basket tray with the money and silver articles offered at the stakes. Prayer meal is sprinkled over the basket and also over the other wagers with prayers to the Gods of War, rain-makers, A'wonawil'ona, and the deceased gamesters.

The game (which is not always the property of the one who plays) is returned to the owner, if borrowed, and the leader carries all the offerings made by his side, except the la'showannĕ, to Corn mountain in a small corn-husk package, and deposits them at the shrine of the younger God of War. He places the la'showannĕ in his medicine box, and on his return from Corn mountain carries the gaming ball of the rain priest to him and at the same time presents a string of precious beads large enough to encircle the left thumb, considered the

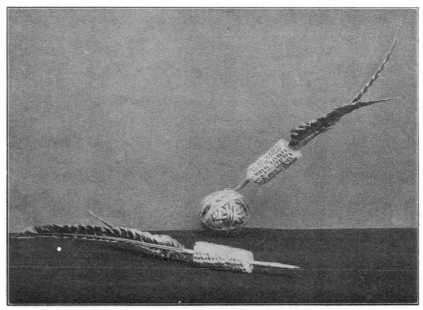

FIG. 15—Implements used in ho'kĭamonnĕ.

lucky one in this game. The rain priest adds these beads to those which wrap his ĕt'tonĕ (see Rain priesthood).

Ho'kĭamonnĕ. The implements of this game are a ball of yucca ribbons and two slender sticks, each sharpened at one end and passed through a piece of corncob having two hawk plumes inserted in the other end (see figure 15). The yucca ball is placed on the ground and the sticks are thrown at it from a short distance. The object is to penetrate the ball. If the first player strikes the ball, the stick is allowed to remain in place until the other party plays. If both sticks strike the ball, it is a draw. If the second stick fails to strike, it remains where it falls, and the first player removes his stick from the ball and throws again. The one who strikes the ball the greater number of times wins the game.   Ho'kĭamonnĕ is a precious game of the Zuñis, being one of those offered to the Gods of War at the winter solstice.   The game is frequently played for rain, and when played in this connection sacred meal is sprinkled on the ground before the ball is placed; the one who first penetrates the ball lifts it by the stick and, drawing a breath from it. offers thanks to the gods that the rains are soon to come.

La'pochiwe.   The implements used for this game are three pencil-like sticks; three reeds of the length of the sticks, one of them with

FIG. 16—Plumed sticks and reeds used in playing la'pochiwe.

a sharpened stick projecting from one end, and one longer reed, designated the "chief," also having a pointed stick attached to the end.   Two fluffy feathers are attached to each reed and stick (see figure 16).[a]   Three sometimes play with the number of reeds and sticks mentioned, but when more than two play, it is usual to increase the number of sticks, although in the genuine game of the Gods of War the number does not exceed seven.

The one proposing the game divides the six smaller reeds and sticks between his opponent and himself, and throws the "chief."   The game

---

[a] The string tied to the second stick from the right in the figure has no significance.

is played like sho'wiyaltowe, described further on, except that the players are seated and throw a comparatively short distance. La'po-chiwe is one of the favorite indoor games.

Ha'poännĕ pihl'kwanawe. The implements of this game are a bow and arrows and an oval wad of green corn husks. Any number of

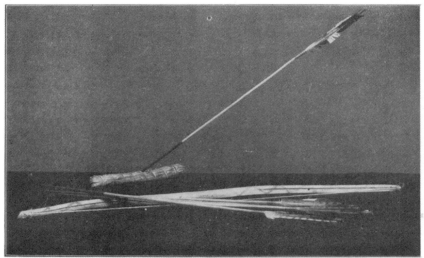

FIG. 17—Implements used in ha'poännĕ pihl'kwanawe.

players may take part. A ha'ponnĕ (roll of husks) is placed upon the ground and arrows are shot at it from a distance of 40 or 50 feet (see figure 17). While the others turn their backs, the first player to strike the wad covers it with a mound of earth very much larger than the wad

FIG. 18—Implements used in sa'yat‘laknawe.

itself. The one who places the roll of husks is almost sure to remember the exact location of it; accordingly he resorts to various devices to mislead the players. A favorite mode of deception is to leave the mound low where the roll is actually buried, but more elevated at some other point. The players aim to shoot their arrows into the roll of husks, and the one who strikes it wins the game. The winner draws the husk from beneath the earth with the arrow. When the arrow strikes the mound, but does not touch the roll of husks, it is removed by the one who secretes the object, and a second player shoots his arrow. Each player takes his turn until the wad is struck. The one who had the arrangement of it is the last to shoot, and naturally the most frequent winner. The game affords great amusement to the younger men.

Sa'yat'laknawe (horns kill, or killing the rabbit). Six goat horns are placed in line on the ground at equal distances apart (in figure 18 only four appear), and the players stand some rods away. The game

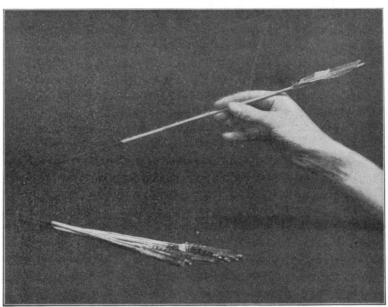

FIG. 19—Method of holding arrows in playing sho'wiyaltowe.

begins by a player starting to run and at the same time throwing a rabbit stick toward the horns. He is entitled to as many horns as he strikes and may continue to throw the stick as long as he is successful in striking a horn. The one who strikes the largest number of horns wins the game.[a]

Sho'wiyaltowe. Sho'wiyaltowe may be played by any number of persons, each one being provided with several arrows. Holding an arrow between his index and middle fingers and thumb, the first player throws it a distance of 10 or 12 feet (see figure 19). Then a second player throws, aiming to have the feathers on his arrow shaft touch

---

[a] Dr Walter Hough, of the United States National Museum, observed the Indians in Mexico playing this game.

those of the one already on the ground.   If he is successful, he takes both arrows and proceeds to make another throw, after which the next player throws at the arrow on the ground; if he fails, the arrow remains in place, and another player throws, and so on, each man taking the arrows which are touched by his own.   Sometimes disputes arise as to whether the feathers are really in contact, and the men stoop and examine the arrows with the closest scrutiny.   The taker of all the arrows wins the game.   If all the arrows fall apart, each player takes his own from the ground and a new game is begun.

   Po'k'ri ännawe (jack-rabbits hit).   The implement of this game is a neatly interlaced pad of corn husks with two delicate feathers projecting from the center (see figure 20).   This game is so named because the sound produced by one of these shuttlecocks coming in contact

FIG. 20—Implements used in po'kïännawe.

with the palm of the hand is similar to the noise of the tread of the jack-rabbit upon frozen snow.   It is played as frequently by the younger boys as by their elders, and always for stakes.   One bets that he can toss the shuttlecock a given number of times.   While ten is the number specially associated with the game, the wagers are often made for twenty, fifty, and sometimes one hundred throws.   In case of failure, the other player tries his skill, each party alternating in the game until one or the other tosses the shuttlecock the given number of times, only one hand being used, thus winning the game.

   'Si'kon-yä'munĕ ti'kwanĕ.   The implements of this game are a slender rod longer than an arrow shaft, zigzagged in black, symbolic of lightning; a ring about 2½ inches in diameter, composed of yucca ribbons, and a ti'kwanĕ (racing stick).

This game (see figure 21) is played only by order of the Great Father Ko'yemshi, and is used exclusively to bring rain.

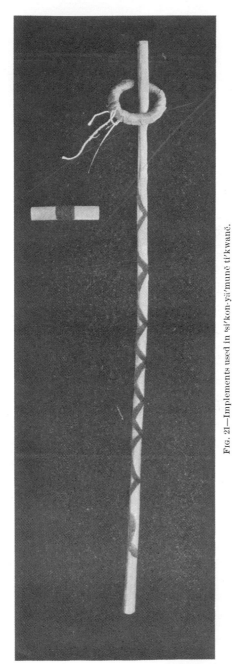

FIG. 21—Implements used in ʦi'kon-yä'muně ti'kwaně.

A chosen number of women, each supplied with a rod, stand in line to the left of a number of men. The latter are provided with a racing stick, which they kick; and the women who play against the men use the yucca ring, tossing it from the ground with their sticks. Though the distance covered is short, the latter seldom win. This game is rarely played at the present time. The writer observed it from a distance and can not describe it in detail.

Po'pone (stuffed bag or ball). This game is also played by the Ko'yemshi and members of the Ne'wekwe (Galaxy) fraternity during the intermission of the dances of the anthropic gods in the sacred dance court. Two sides are formed in line, and a man runs out from one side and turns his back to his opponents, one of whom advances and throws a small bag filled with wool. If he succeeds in striking the one who has his back turned, the latter must join the side of the one who strikes him; but should the one endeavoring to strike be hit from the other side before he returns to his ranks, he must pass to his opponents' side.

These children of nature appear to derive as much real enjoyment from this game as the children of civilization do from their game of tag.

Po'pone ǩap'naně (ball whipping). This game is the same as shinny, or bandy, and is a favorite betting game. The ball is usually made of buckskin.

M. Wright Gill.

YOUTHFUL RUNNERS

MARY-IRVIN-WRIGHT·

GAME OF TA'SHOLIWE

ALTAR OF MÁʼKE ꞋSANꞋNAKWE (LITTLE FIRE FRATERNITY)

PLUME OFFERINGS MADE AT SHRINE OF PAI'YAT'YAMO, GOD OF MUSIC

Ya'chuni sa'wanni. This game, equivalent to our ring-around-a-rosy, is one of the games played in the sacred dance court by the Ko'yemshi and the Galaxy fraternity between the dances. A circle of men with hands clasped is formed about one in the middle, who aims to catch one of the others as they jump around. He is frequently whispered to as to whom to choose. When one is caught, he takes his place within the circle, and his predecessor leaves the game altogether. When the number is reduced to three, the amusement increases, and it reaches its height when only two are left. These two hop about, each on one foot; the one becoming exhausted first joins his fellows, now grouped on one side of the plaza, and then in order to win the contest the remaining one must hop to the group before placing his other foot on the ground. At times all the players hop on one foot, each endeavoring to outdo the others and remain longest in the field. The song accompanying the game is a repetition of words which the Zuñis themselves appear not to understand, but which they believe to have come from the Ko'yemshi gods. The words are: Ya'chuni sa'wanni, ya'chuni sa'wanni, ya'anni ku'ya, ya'anni ku'ya, shi'ki, shi'ki, shi'ki, shi'ki, a'mashu'.

'Kĭash'tuwiwi. Two files of men hold each other around the waist, the leaders of the two files clasping hands, and in this position they jump about the plaza. At times the men separate and form into opposing lines, and, clasping hands, jump back and forth. The songs sung by the leaders tell stories of youths of old—how their fathers fell in love with their mothers. One begins by telling of how he came from his mother, and when he was old enough his grandfather made him a bow and some arrow reeds, and attaching fine arrow points he went off to hunt game. The game came close to the cornfield and he killed many deer. He was hungry and wished to cook some of the meat, but his success in the hunt had brought such heavy rains that he was compelled to fast until his return home. The story of another youth is sung by the other leader. He gives his experience previous to his birth, how finally he is able to peep out and see a little light, and discovers that there is a road by which he may come out into the world; he decides then that he will no longer remain in his mother's womb. His parents and grandparents rejoice over his birth, and as soon as he is old enough his grandfather supplies him with a bow and arrows, and he goes off on a hunt, and finding many deer near the cornfield he kills them, and the rain comes in torrents and waters the earth. The chorus, which is sung constantly throughout the game, compares the rupture of the membranes to violent rains which cause the springs to flow out through the holes in the rocks. The words of the chorus are as follows: "'Kĭash'tuwiwi, 'kĭash'tuwiwi käl'iyän, kwa'chi, käl'iyän kwa'chi kwa'chi, kwa'chi chi chi chi chi."

Ta'sholiwe (wood reeds). The implements of this game are three staves, colored red or black on one side and white or uncolored on the other; forty small stones, a stone disk, and straws or slender strips of wood. This game is played out of doors. The stones are laid in a circle, broken into four segments, with a disk in the center. From two to four persons generally play, but the number is not limited to four. The staves are held vertically over the disk and thrown downward with force (see plate LXXXIV). The three colored sides coming up entitles the player to move his marker by ten of the stones. The three uncolored or white sides coming up gives the player five moves; two uncolored and one colored up gives the player three moves; two colored and one uncolored up entitles the player to two moves. The markers, being moved in opposite directions, sometimes meet. In such case the last player is said to be killed and must begin again at the starting point. The first one around the circle wins the game, provided his count does not carry him beyond the starting point, in which event he must continue going around until his counter reaches the doorway, or spring, as the opening is often called.[a]

Tän'kalawe. This is similar to quoits, and is played as frequently by young boys as by their elders. Any number may play. The stakes are placed on a corncob or sometimes on a stone planted in the ground. The players throw a stone disk, aiming to strike a line marked on the ground. The one coming nearest has the privilege of throwing first at the stake. If the corncob is knocked over and the disk remains by it, the thrower has another chance; if the disk goes beyond the corncob, he loses; if it falls short of the cob, he wins.

A'wet'laknawe (*stones kill*). The implements of this game are a number of small flat stones, having a different color for each side, and a stone slab with geometrical markings. An improvised board is sometimes marked on the ground. There is no specified size for the board, this being larger or smaller, according to the number of angles. The stones are placed on all the intersections of the geometrical drawing except the central one. The first player moves to the center, where his man is jumped by his opponent. The stones may be moved in any direction so long as the lines are followed.[b]

---

[a] Ta'sholiwe (ta from ta'we, wood; sho'liwe, arrow reeds) is played extensively by the Zuñis, although the writer has never observed prominent men playing it. Notwithstanding the Zuñis claim that they adopted the game from the Navahos, the Sia Indians, who call it wash'kasi, regard it as one of their oldest games. Instead of the circle, they form a square with ten stones on each side (see The Sia, Eleventh Annual Report of the Bureau of Ethnology). Dr E. B. Tylor, in his paper on "American lot games as evidence of Asiatic intercourse before the time of Columbus," refers at length to this game, giving a diagram of it as played by the Apache Indians, which is identical with the form of the game as played by the Zuñis. Mr Culin, in Chess and Playing Cards, calls attention to a form of ta'sholiwe known as "tem thla nah na ta sho li we (of all the regions wood canes)." The writer has not discovered any such form as is described by Mr Culin, but a Zuñi will sometimes, when he wishes to play sho'liwe, refer to the canes as tĕm'¹la na'nakwe sho'liwe (all grandfathers' arrow reeds, i. e., reeds of our forefathers).

[b] The Zuñis also make the checkerboard within a circle, and in this case they have the advantage of resorting to the periphery when cornered. Some of the older men of Zuñi declare that this game, when it came originally to Zuñi from Mexico, was played with a set of stones for one side and a stick

The first three games ti'kwanĕ, sho'liwe and i'yänkolo'we have been described as associated with elaborate ceremonies.   It is probable that the other games of the Gods of War when played under certain conditions are attended with more or less ceremony which the author has not observed.

ARTS AND INDUSTRIES

HOUSE BUILDING

A Zuñi pueblo resembles a great beehive, with its houses built one upon another in a succession of terraces, the roof of one forming the floor or yard of the one next above, and so on until in some cases five tiers of dwellings are successively erected (see plate LXXXV); only a few houses, however, are over two stories in height.   Among the Zuñis, as among more civilized peoples, riches and official position confer importance upon the possesssor.   The wealthy class live in the lower houses; those of more modest means, next above; while the poorer families, as a rule, content themselves with the uppermost stories.   No one, naturally, would climb to the garret who had the means to live below.   The houses, which are built of stone and adobe (sun-dried bricks composed of earth and straw molded in wooden forms), are clustered about three plazas, or squares, and a fourth plaza is on the west side of the village.   There are three covered ways and several streets.

The women delight in house building, especially in plastering the houses.   They consider this their special prerogative and would feel that their rights were infringed upon were men to do it.   Men lay the stone foundations, build the walls, and place the huge logs which serve as beams to support the roof.   These logs are brought from a long distance and are dressed by the Zuñi carpenter.   After the logs are placed (see plate LXXXVI), carefully selected willow boughs are laid crosswise upon rafters, brush is spread over these, and the whole is covered with earth, forming a roof substantial enough for this climate. Little girls assist in bringing the water used in mixing the mortar, working industriously, and trudging from the river with their diminutive water vases on their heads in a fashion quite Egyptian.

The lower houses, as well as those above, have outer doors; hatchways in the roof, through which ladders pass, serve as other entrances. The doorways are so small that in many instances it is difficult to squeeze through, yet they are an improvement on the more ancient

---

for the opposite side, and that the use of the double set of stones is an innovation of their own.   The writer observed the Africans at the Buffalo Exposition, in 1901, playing on a rude slab of wood marked in squares, each alternate square being colored black.   This game was identical with the modern game of checkers, with the exception that twenty men are used on each side.   One player, who spoke English well, told the writer that his people had always played the game, the board with them being marked by having alternate squares excavated on a heavy slab of wood.

entrances, which were in some cases circular openings in round stone slabs of considerable thickness, just large enough for one to pass through by assuming a horizontal position. These doorways were closed with round stone slabs held in place by props of strong poles.[a] The houses are so provided with interior doors that almost the entire older portion of the village can be put in communication without passing outside the communal structure. Small openings made in the walls to admit light are filled with irregular pieces of selenite. The chimneys are composed of cooking utensils with perforated bases, placed one upon another and cemented together. When a cooking pot can no longer serve its original purpose, it is stored away for future use in the chimney. After the house is constructed, the exterior and interior walls are covered with a reddish-brown plaster made of earth and water. It is applied with the hand, which is swept over the wall in semicircles (see plate LXXXVII). In working the plaster the woman keeps her mouth filled with water, which is skillfully applied to the wall, when necessary, in the manner in which a Chinese laundryman sprinkles clothes. The inner walls are whitened, and for this purpose a white clay is dissolved in boiling water and applied with a rabbit-skin glove. The gloved hand is dipped into the liquid and then rapidly passed over the wall. The color of the outer walls is usually of the dark color.

AGRICULTURE AND HORTICULTURE

Assistance in the fields is obtained as follows: A member of a fraternity asks the mo'sona (director) for help, and he designates a certain number of the fraternity to assist their fellow. The female head of the house or the daughter or perhaps both go to the people of their clan asking the assistance of the sons of the families; the paternal heads of these houses also give their services, so that the work is not confined to a single clan. The only time the people of a ki'wiᵗsinĕ [b] are called upon for such work is when a house is to entertain a Sha'läko.[c] The laborers are entertained at an evening meal after the return from the fields each day by the family for whom they work. The clans of the heads of the house also aid in the entertainment.

These primitive agriculturists have observed the greatest care in developing color in corn and beans to harmonize with the six regions— yellow for the North, blue for the West, red for the South, white for the East, variegated for the Zenith, and black for the Nadir. They

---

[a] Although the Zuñis are perfectly aware that stone doorways were in early use among their people, the only perfect specimen to be seen in this village belongs to an aged theurgist who mourns the fact that his people have not preserved these objects of their ancient architecture. In the Eighth Annual Report of the Bureau of Ethnology, 1891, in a paper entitled "A Study of Pueblo Architecture," by Mr Victor Mindeleff, is a most interesting pen picture, on p. 192, containing a reference to stone doorways discovered in ruins.

[b] See Ki'wiᵗsiwe and their functions. p. 62.

[c] See Annual festival ot the Sha'läko, p. 227.

have all shades of yellow and blue, and of red from the deepest cardinal to the most delicate pink.   The white corn is intensely white, and there are remarkable varieties of variegated corn.   There are several shades of purple corn, and black corn.   The same variety of shades is to be found in the beans, which are grown in the cornfield.   Much of the corn and all of the wheat is raised in the farming districts of Nutria, Pescado, and Ojo Caliente.   The cornfields also spread over the land near Zuñi and elsewhere.   In most instances the fields remote from the farming districts are not irrigated.   The corn is grown in clusters so as to give a better chance for development in this arid land.   The three farming districts are each irrigated from a spring.   The description of one will answer for all.   The spring To'seluna, at Ojo Caliente, is at the base of a low limestone mountain.   The body of the spring, which is deep, is between 35 and 40 feet long, 18 by 20 feet wide, and is a beautiful, clear sheet of water.   The Zuñis say that a man may sink to his neck, but the force of the water as it comes from the earth is so great as to prevent his touching bottom.   It is said that a woman returning to Ojo Caliente with a burro loaded with milling stones, about twenty-five years ago, allowed the little animal to go into the spring to drink.   The weight of the stones carried him to the bottom, and he disappeared forever from sight.

Two ditches extend in different directions from the spring for irrigating the fields.   The main ditch waters an area about $3\frac{1}{2}$ by $2\frac{1}{2}$ miles, while the other does not irrigate so large a surface.   Since the main ditch is lower than the other, it often becomes necessary to dam it in order that a greater force of water may go from the spring into the higher ditch.   To accomplish this, earth is banked between a number of tree boles which stand in line where the water of the spring flows into the ditch.   The damming is done by the master of the ditch at the request of those who desire water from the higher ditch.   No stick or board or any other kind of water measure is used by the Zuñis, and there is no history or legend among them of the employment of such articles.   Disputes over the water seldom occur; when one does occur the governor of Zuñi settles the question.   It is the business of the governor to see that the water is fairly distributed.

When the writer visited To'seluna spring in 1904, she found men making, under the direction of the master of the ditch, a temporary ditch to enable a woman to water her garden, which was on an elevation immediately above the spring.   In order to have the water reach this garden it was necessary to dam both of the main ditches.

Muskmelons, watermelons, squashes, and gourds are usually grown near the cornfields.   When the corn and melons begin to ripen the fields are constantly guarded, and for this purpose rude shelters are erected (figure 22).   The country is so infested with ravens that the Zuñis have become expert in the construction of scarecrows.   The

majority of the Zuñis leave the village and settle in comfortable houses
in the farming districts for the summer, remaining as late as possible
in the autumn. Some few have found the country home so greatly
preferable that they have taken up their permanent abode at their
farms, but this does not prevent their prompt attendance at ceremonials held in Zuñi.

When the corn has been gathered it is brought home and spread on
the roof. After the husk has been removed, the ears are stacked with
great precision and care in the storage rooms. Corn husking is as
much of a frolic with the Zuñis as it was with the youths and maidens
of our own country districts in the past. Wherever corn is seen on
the roof one is pretty sure to hear the merry voices of the huskers,

FIG. 22—Shelter for the field guardian.

though the red ear does not suggest the kiss. The Zuñis are not much
given to kissing, though they are not entirely free from it; the young
men kiss their favorite girls on the sly, and fathers are fond of kissing
their infants.

The soil is harrowed with primitive implements, and the wheat is
threshed in the farming districts where it is raised, goats and occasionally horses taking the place of threshing machines. The wheat is
winnowed by tossing it in baskets made for the purpose. It is stored
either in large bins constructed of stone slabs or in immense pottery
jars in the storage rooms. A Zuñi storage room (figure 23) contains a
promiscuous mass of material ranging from objects of the most sacred
character to those of little or no value.

The Zuñis aim to keep a year's supply of grain on hand untouched to provide against failure of crops. They have learned this lesson from experience. Starvation has sometimes compelled them to seek relief from other pueblos. Neighboring tribes have also sought aid from the Zuñis for the same reason.

Onions, chillis, a species of amarantus (used for imparting a red color to the wafer bread[a]), and a variety of herbs used as condiments are raised exclusively by the women in little gardens in the farming districts and at Zuñi. In Zuñi these gardens, which are protected by adobe walls, are at the southern edge of the village on the river front. The energetic little women may be seen at daybreak carrying vases of

FIG. 23—A storage room.

water from the river and watering their gardens, which require constant care in order that they may not be parched by the burning sun.

Watermelons, muskmelons, beans, onions, and chillis, which are raised in great abundance, are grown not only for summer consumption, but are preserved for winter use. The watermelons and onions are laid away in the storage rooms without preparation; the muskmelons are seeded from the end, pared, and hung on crotches of low trees which are found at the farming districts. Squash is cut into long strips, as one would pare an apple, formed into hanks, and dried in the sun. Chillis, which are gathered when red, are strung together and hung on the outer walls to dry. The brilliant red against the somber adobe wall gives a pleasant bit of contrasting color. All edible

---

[a] This red coloring is rarely used by the Zuñis; it is the Hopis who glory in brilliant red bread.

plants[a] are cured for winter use, most of them being tied in bunches and hung in the storage rooms, as are also the medicinal plants.

Peaches are raised in the foothills, where there is more moisture than below. The trees are low, many of them not over 3 feet in height, some even less. Their spreading limbs are laden with fruit when the season is favorable, but the crop is plentiful only every other year. When the fruit is ripe, all families that have orchards, or some of the members of each family, move to the orchards and remain in temporary huts or permanent structures until the fruit is gathered, in many instances until it is dried. Though the fresh fruit is greatly enjoyed, and even green peaches stewed and sweetened are a treat, care is taken to dry large quantities for the winter. The Palle family, the richest in Zuñi, dry their fruit on the top of a great rock which appears to be inaccessible to any but an Indian. A man of this family, now deceased, who wore female attire placed the peaches on this rock at the time when the writer visited the orchard. This is a delightful season for the Zuñis, and especially for the children, who spend their days eating peaches and rolling over the sand hills.

SALT GATHERING

The annual journey to the Zuñi salt lake[b] for the purpose of gathering salt is an important event with the Zuñis, as it is with the other pueblos, and is accompanied by elaborate ceremonies. In July the first body of A'shiwanni (rain priests) gather together in the ancestral chamber of the Kĭa'kwemosi (rain priest of the North and high priest of Zuñi) to arrange for the annual journey, and early the following morning the elder brother Bow priest announces from the house top that those in need of salt must be ready to start in four days, inclusive of that day, for the home of the Salt Mother.[c] The women never go. On this occasion each man of the first body of rain priests[d] takes his turn in regular order in leading the party. He is accom-

---

[a] In 1902 the writer collected a large number of edible and medicinal plants, which were placed in the hands of Dr F. V. Coville, curator of botany, National Museum, for classification, and will be described in a later publication.

[b] The following facts regarding this lake are kindly furnished by Mr N. H. Darton, of the United States Geological Survey:

The Zuñi salt lake is situated on the south slopes of the valley of Carrizo Creek, 42 miles south by east from Zuñi pueblo. Sinking abruptly below the sloping plain of the surrounding valley is a round, crater-like depression about a mile broad and 200 feet deep. In its center rise two symmetrical volcanic cinder cones about 150 feet high, to the north of which is the salt lake, and to the south a nearly smooth plain floored with wash from the slopes. The lake is an oblong body of water extending east and west across the northern end of the depression, with a length of about 4,000 feet and a breadth somewhat less. Apparently the lake occupied the entire floor of the depression at one time, but by evaporation and the deposition of mud it has greatly diminished in size. The waters of the lake are saturated with common salt, containing 26 per cent, according to Professor C. L. Herrick. As the natural evaporation progresses salt is deposited. Although no deep borings have been made the depression appears to contain a salt deposit of considerable thickness, mixed with a small amount of mud washed from the surrounding slopes and dust carried by the wind.

[c] See Zuñi version of Origin of the salt lake, p. 58.

[d] The first body of rain priests comprises the rain priests of the six regions, the elder and younger brother Bow priests, and the Priestess of fecundity.

panied by the elder and younger brother Bow priests and personators of the Ko'yemshi. Every man who is to visit the lake prepares plume offerings to Ma'lokät'si, the spiritual name for mawe (salt), and carrying them to the rain priest who is to visit the lake presents the offering with the words: "I wish to go to my Salt Mother. I wish to ask her for a part of herself." The rain priest receives the offerings with expressions of thanks. The salt-gatherers, including the three priests, prepare plume offerings to the Salt Mother, the Sun Father, the Moon Mother, and the Corn Mother. The elder and younger brother Bow priests also make offerings to each of the Gods of War. The personators of the Ko'yemshi[a] make others to the Council of the Gods.

At sunrise of the morning on which the journey is to begin the heads of those who are to make the pilgrimage are washed in yucca suds and their entire bodies are bathed. The women of the family see to it that the men are provided with a sufficient quantity of jerked meat and wafer bread—in fact the larders are emptied of their choice things for the occasion. All Zuñi is in the streets and on the house tops to witness the departure of the salt-gatherers, each one offering a prayer for their success and safe return. The rain priest who makes the journey carries the plume offerings given him by the men upon their announcement that they wished to visit the Salt Mother. Nai'uchi, elder brother Bow priest, carries in his right hand a rhombus, which consists of two slats about 6 inches long, oval at one end, each attached to end of a cord, and in his left hand offerings consisting of plumes and a diminutive shield and bow and arrows for the elder God of War. Me'she, younger brother Bow priest, carries a rhombus and similar offerings to the younger God of War. The three proceed on foot and are followed by the A'wan tä'chu (Great Father) Ko'yemshi, who sprinkles meal as he proceeds. The rhombi are whirled for the rain-makers to gather over Zuñi. The rest of the party, mounted on burros, follow a short distance behind and manage the extra burros that are to bring back the salt. The salt lake, according to Mr Darton, is 42 miles south by east from Zuñi,[b] and is reached before sunset on the second day. Several ranges of mountains are crossed, but the trail is good, running largely through long stretches of timbered country, the one drawback being the absence of water. There are several shrines between Zuñi and the lake, at which plume offerings to the Sun Father and Moon Mother are deposited.

When Mr Stevenson and his party visited the salt lake, the Kǐa'kwemosi appointed a prominent man of the tribe as guide. The first night a dry camp was made, where not only the animals but the men suffered for lack of water. As Mr Stevenson learned on the following morning that he was within 4 miles of fine springs, his chagrin was great. When he called the Indian to task for not having led him to

a See p. 33.
b Mr Darton evidently refers to the Indian trail, as the distance by the road is much farther.

the water, the old man exclaimed: "These springs are at the house
of the Kok'ko ko'han (white gods[a]), and a Zuñi would not dare to
camp near by." Thus the guide had purposely led the party from the
main trail in order that the sacred spot should not be desecrated.

The party had not proceeded far on the following morning when
the old Indian came close to the writer, and, pointing to an extensive
ruin, whispered: "There is the house of the Kǐa'nakwe; I will take
you to see it." The writer suggested that they await the others, who
were but a short distance behind. This was a mistake. It is never well
to give an Indian too much time to think. The gods communicated
with him and warned him that if he should visit the house without
the permission of the director of the personators of the deceased
Kǐa'nakwe, Zuñi would be in imminent danger of destruction. Therefore the party found it necessary to visit these ruins without the presence of the guide, who remained behind and grieved much because
the horses were permitted to tread upon the sacred soil. The writer,
however, hoping to induce the Indian to accompany her to the ruin,
remained behind and persuaded him to do so. It was necessary for
him to dismount and leave his animal at a respectful distance from
the sacred spot, and while he pointed out the various sacred springs,
many of which were so covered that one would not dream of the
presence of the living water, the corral in which Ku'yapäli'sa, a female
warrior bearing the name of 'Cha'kwena (see page 35), and the mother
of all game, kept game, and other points of interest to the writer, he
uttered lamentations that he must die within four days for offending
the gods by visiting the forbidden spot.

After camping on the second evening, it was with difficulty that the
Indian was prevented from continuing his journey to the lake. The
old guide said: "You are Americans and can follow in the morning,
but I am a Zuñi, my mother (referring to the Salt Mother at the lake)
calls me, and I must go and sleep contentedly by her. Many years have
passed since I have seen her,[b] and I can not rest until I have reached
my mother."

Before the stars had ceased their twinkling in the early morning, the
writer was awakened by the old guide addressing her: "Mother, I do
not care to eat, I must go, and you can follow later." He was again
with difficulty restrained. Before sunrise the guide and the writer
started from camp ahead of the party. For a time he chatted gaily,
telling many stories of interest, until he had the first peep of the home
of the Gods of War, which is a volcanic peak rising from the lake (see
plate LXXXVIII), when he immediately removed from his head the kerchief and, taking out his prayer-meal bag prayed and sprinkled meal

---

[a] So named because these people, who were the Kǐa'nakwe wore white cotton blankets. The
house referred to is an extensive ruin (see Destruction of the Kǐa'nakwe and songs of thanksgiving).
[b] No Zuñi visits this lake except by permission of those who have authority.

until the lake was reached.   Not a living thing was to be seen; all was somber gray except a patch of grass here and there and the salt lake with its clear waters and the two peaks reflected therein.[a]   Two circular walls, about 5 feet high and 15 inches thick, with an aperture in each, stand in the lake.   These walls are composed of the blue clay of the lake bed and are respectively the houses of the rain priests and Ko'yemshi.   As but little time is required for these walls to wear away, they must be rebuilt when occasion requires.   Similar structures in the southwestern portion of the lake are the property of the Hopi Indians, and are used by them when they visit the lake to collect salt.[b]

It has been said that the Zuñis claim the salt lake exclusively and demand tribute from the other tribes, but such is not the case.   In fact, the records tend to show that this locality has been from time immemorial the great source of salt supply for the Indians near and far.   The writer has made careful inquiries on several occasions when the Hopi caravan stopped at Zuñi on their return from the salt lake.   The Zuñis made no demands upon the Hopis whatever, but on the contrary treated them as distinguished guests.   The Navahos and Apaches also collect salt here, each tribe being accorded complete freedom in collecting the salt, although the lake is claimed as the special mother of each of the various tribes.

The place is neutral ground, and in times of war one was safe from the attacks of the enemy so long as one remained within the recognized limits of the lake.   Many thrilling stories are told by the Zuñis of their efforts in the past to anticipate the hated Navahos in reaching the lake, knowing that by so doing they would be preserved from harm.

The volcanic peaks which rise 150 or 200 feet above the waters of the lake are quite symmetrical.   The interior of the cone of one descends at an angle of 45° to an elliptical basin, 150 by 200 feet in diameter, filled with saline water of a brilliantly green hue and bordered by a footpath of red lava, partly formed by débris from the slopes, but carefully remodeled by the Zuñis into a narrow, even path about 5 feet wide[c] (see plate LXXXIX).   The outer and inner sides of the peak are so covered with volcanic cinders that it is difficult to

[a] On a subsequent visit in 1902 there was found quite a Mexican settlement, earning a livelihood by dealing in salt.   The apparatus used in securing the salt from the lake bed is of the crudest type.

[b] In 1902 there was no evidence of these structures.   The presence of Mexicans at the lake prevents the ceremonies which were previously enacted within these walls.

[c] Though a number of soundings have been made, the depth of this lake is still unknown.   While the temperature of the water is cold, the bather often finds himself over jets of hot water.   It is impossible for him to sink.   There is a peculiar charm in the waters, and they are considered a specific for rheumatism by the few who have tested them.   Were it not for the scarcity of drinkable water, this most sacred spot of the Indians would become a resort of the white man from near and far.   On the occasion of a visit in 1902 two improvised dressing rooms made of stone were found on the shores of the lake.

ascend or descend.[a] Only those of the Bow priesthood who have taken four scalps may enter the crater. The warrior who has scalped but one enemy goes only part way up the mountain and deposits his offerings; when he has scalped two, he may go still farther up the mountain; after the scalping of three, he may ascend to the top and make his offerings; when he has scalped four enemies, he may descend into the crater and deposit his offerings in the sacred lake. At least such was the rule until the cessation of intertribal wars, during which only such men as brought back scalps were entitled to join the Bow priesthood.

Members of this fraternity who go down to the house of the Gods of War must descend over a certain path which was traveled by these gods when they descended to this crater lake. The elder and younger Bow priests, the living representatives of the Gods of War, when visiting this sacred spot descend by the path referred to and on reaching the water's edge separate and make the circuit of the lake, passing each other on the opposite side.

A shrine especially set apart for the offerings of the elder and younger brother Bow priests is located on the east side of the lake. It is 3 feet from the water's edge and is square, some 18 inches across, and formed of four slabs. Prayer plumes, miniature war clubs, batons, shields, bows and arrows, and various other objects were found at this shrine, while the rocks all about the shore were dotted with other offerings to the Gods of War.[b]

Many valuable beads have in the past been deposited along the shores of the lake and in a spring not far from the cone, but the coming of the whites has compelled the Zuñis to refrain from making offerings of commercial value. Some years ago an American found in the spring a rare necklace of antique black stone beads.

The guide refused with alarm to descend into the crater, saying he could not go as he was not a member of the Bow priesthood, but he was finally persuaded and added to the interest of the visit by his description of the objects found there. Upon reaching the lake of the crater the Indian gave meal to Mr. Stevenson and the writer, requesting them to breathe a prayer and scatter the meal upon the waters, and he sang a long, low chant. The prayer was addressed first to the Sun Father, then to the Gods of War, asking them not to be angry with him for entering their house. Again he prayed to the Salt Mother and ancestral warrior gods of the six regions to intercede for him with the Sun Father and Gods of War that they be not angry with him. His prayers also invoked the good health and prosperity of his people and the people of all the world.

---

[a] In 1902 a substantial path of gradual slope, made by Americans or Mexicans, was found. The Zuñis, who deplore the intrusion of strangers, continue to visit this lake by the old Zuñi path.

[b] Many interesting specimens from this region secured on this trip were placed in the National Museum.

At sunrise on the morning following the arrival of the salt-gatherers at the lake, the elder and younger brother Bow priests, with the additional warriors of the party, visit the home of the Gods of War, which is supposed to be in the depths of the crater, where they deposit offerings to these gods. The rain priest deposits in his house in the lake plume offerings to the Salt Mother, and the Great Father Ko'yemshi, having received prayer plumes for the Council of the Gods from each person present, plants them in his house, which is near that of the rain priest.

After the ceremonial of plume planting and prayers they all pass into the lake, each provided with a blanket or a piece of cloth in which to gather salt, which is scraped from the bed of the lake where the crystals are deposited. When thoroughly cleansed the salt is white and most excellent. Each man has two ears of corn, Father corn and Mother corn, which he covers with clay containing salt from the bed of the lake. These ears are afterward placed with plume offerings amid the stacked corn in the house, where they remain until the cobs have lost all of the grains, when they are deposited in the river to go to Ko'thluwala'wa and others are substituted, for no corn heap must be without the Father and Mother corn. No Indian would dare part with the parent corn, fearing the wrath of the Salt Mother, " whose ghost self is ever about the Zuñis," though death would befall the one who endeavored to see her. An ear of corn having a direct line of grains is of special significance for the parent corn, as it is symbolic of the straight path of life its possessor should follow.

As soon as the salt-gatherers are sufficiently near home, they always make signal fires to notify the people of their return. In 1902, smoke from the first fire was discovered at half-past 7 in the morning, and the villagers at once began the watch. Several fires were lighted, each one nearer the village, before the voices of the salt-gatherers were heard. Their song grew more and more distinct as the party drew near. The party was greeted warmly by all, especially by the religious and civil officers of the town. As the beasts of burden were driven to the doors of the dwellings they were surrounded by those eager to assist in unloading the salt and conveying it to the houses. The three pedestrians carried the two ears of corn (Father Corn and Mother Corn) in husks covered with mud from the salt lake, together with a slab of salt crystal, closely wrapped in cloth, in deep baskets on their backs. The other members of the party were on burros and were kept busy managing the little animals laden with sacks of salt. Each man of the party went directly to his own door on reaching the village; those on foot entered the house at once; the others proceeded to unload the animals, assisted by members of their families and by neighbors. The salt is not only necessary to their physical comfort, but it has a sacred value to them beyond price.

A nephew of Nai'uchi, elder brother Bow priest, after unloading all but two of his animals and depositing Father Corn and Mother Corn on a heap of salt in the living room of his house, drove the two remaining burros with the packs to the home of the elder brother Bow priest. The daughter of the house spread a large piece of canvas on the floor of the spacious living room, and the salt-gatherer deposited the salt upon the canvas without ceremony. The two ears of corn, which were removed from a sack before the salt was emptied, were laid upon a slab of salt crystals that was placed at the southwest corner of the canvas. In a short time the daughter of the house formed the salt into an oval mound, made a depression lengthwise on the top, and placed the salt slab and the ears of corn in the center. An old ear of yellow corn, A'wan ᵗsita (Great Mother), was deposited south of the slab; two others, Awan ho'ta (Great Grandmother), and an charli (the child), were placed north of it, all the tips of the ears pointing to the east. The daughter of the house covered the corn and a portion of the salt with a woman's woven wrap, but removed it for a time while they all stood around and prayed. A blind grandson of Nai'uchi was led forward, and his hand was directed to the prayer-meal basket, from which all present sprinkled the sacred objects with meal. After the morning repast all infants of the families in the houses where salt had been brought were carried to the salt heaps, where the mothers spat upon their limbs and rubbed them with the salt, in order that the children might be strong, and adults rubbed the salt over their own hands; then the salt was again covered. The head of each salt-gatherer was afterward washed in yucca suds, and then the entire body was bathed by a female member of his family. The salt was later packed away in jars and the ears of corn were placed with the stacked corn in the storage room.

A very pleasing scene is the appearance in Zuñi of Ma'lokätᵗsi, who is sister to the Sun Father, in company with Ko'hakwa (white-shell bead), Mother of the Sun,[a] whose home is in the great waters of the West, and the Sun with his two heralds, the Morning and the Evening stars. The home of Ko'hakwa is the house to which the Sun journeys each day to rest at night. The mask of Ma'lokätᵗsi, or Mawe, is of hide, covering the head. Formerly much difficulty was found in making the salt adhere to the mask; finally native cotton was placed over the hide; on this was spread a paste made of wheat flour boiled in water, over which the salt crystals were scattered, and the mask was set near the fire until the crystals combined with the paste. The face is white, with a red spot on each side over the cheeks. An ear of corn which has been covered in clay from the salt lake is attached upright to the

[a] It should not be inferred from this expression that the Sun was supposed to have been born of Ko'hakwe.

VIEW OF THE HIGHEST SECTION OF ZUÑI

PLACING RAFTERS

back of the mask.   An embroidered white-cotton scarf is tied around the mask at its base.

The Ko'hakwa mask also covers the head and has a white face with a red spot on either cheek.   The top of the mask is covered with turquoise and Ko'hakwa beads attached in loops, and necklaces of the same hang from the neck to the waist of the wearer of the mask. Strings of the same precious beads encircle the arms from the wrists nearly to the elbows.

The face of the Sun mask is painted blue-green and encircled with yellow, red, white, and a design in black and white blocks, symbolic of the home of the clouds.   A tablet which is attached to the top of the mask is decorated in front with the sun symbol and in the back with the rainbow.   A wig of black goat's wool covers the back of the mask, falling over the shoulders of the wearer.   The masks of the heralds, or warriors, of the Sun are colored white in the back and blue-green in front and have a long beak.   They are surmounted with a decorated tablet cross, each end tipped with a star, symbolic of the stars of the four regions.

Ma'lokät'si approaches the village in the morning from the south over the road leading to the salt lake.   After reaching the river she is carried across by a Ko'yemshi (the great fathers of ancestral gods). At the same time Ko'hakwa comes from the west and the Sun with his heralds, or warriors, the Morning and the Evening stars in advance, appear from the east.   They remain until sunset, when Ma'lokät'si returns over the southern road and the Sun with his heralds accompany Ko'hakwa over the western road.

FOOD AND DRINK

Bread making.   The women of Zuñi take special pride in having good bread, of which there are several varieties.   He'we (wafer bread), is a household staple.   It is baked on slabs of gray sandstone, cut from the quarry at the base of To'wa yäl'länně (Corn mountain),[a] some 3 miles east of Zuñi, by men or boys who bring them home, after which the women take charge of them.   They vary in size from 24 inches in length by 20 in width to 38 inches in length by 30 in width.   When the cut side has been rubbed smooth with a stone, the slab is supported on two parallel walls, 8 or 10 inches high, built of small stones laid in plaster on the hearth in the broad fireplace, which is capped with an awning resembling those of the Chinese.   The slab is gradually heated by a small fire of cedar wood built under the stone, and afterward a greater fire is made.   When it has reached the proper degree of heat, native squash seeds with the husks removed are chewed and ejected

---

[a] Thunder mountain has been erroneously accepted as the translation for To'wa yäl'länně. The error may have arisen from the similarity between to'wa (corn, archaic), and to'wawa (thunder), the last two syllables of which are pronounced rapidly.

from the mouth over the slab. When the fire is burnt out, the slab is seen to be black from the oil of the squash seeds. The greater portion of the bed of coals is removed, and a flat stone is placed across the end of the walls supporting the slab to keep the drafts from fanning the remaining coals. A pound or more of raw piñon gum in pieces of good size is rubbed over the slab, and when this is melted the rubbing is continued as long as the stone will absorb the gum. Pine twigs are employed to brush off the surplus gum, each twig or bunch of twigs being passed but once over the stone. After a few such sweepings, twigs are held firmly in the hand and rubbed hard over the stone. The pine twigs are finally discarded for juniper, which are used until the slab has the appearance of polished black lava. A quantity of juniper twigs is crushed and sprinkled over the stone to remain until needed for baking.

No word must be spoken above a whisper from the beginning to the completion of the dressing of the slab. Should the voice of anyone present be raised above a whisper, the stone would crack in the polishing process. The writer once observed a stone cracked in two places, and as no one had spoken aloud the conclusion was reached that the worker had a bad heart.

The corn to be used for the he'we is first crushed on the coarsest milling stone and then toasted in a bowl placed on stones in one of the right-angle fireplaces and stirred continually with a bunch of slender sticks or osiers. When the meal leaves the fire it is placed in a mill of the next degree of fineness, and afterward it passes through the third and last mill, in which it is ground to a fine flour. A quantity of this flour is mixed with cold water and stirred into a pot of boiling water; the mixture is stirred constantly during the cooking. When the mush is done and so far cooled that the hand may be introduced without scalding it, the pot is placed at the side of the maker of the he'we. A thin batter of uncooked meal made with cold water is placed in one side of a large bowl. If the bread is to be of bluish-green color, lime is slaked and the water poured from it into the batter. A double handful of mush is dipped from the pot and deposited in the bowl on the opposite side from the batter; then a handful of batter is added to the mush, and when they are thoroughly mixed, a quantity is dipped with the hand and swept thinly over the heated slab, which is always placed at one side of the fireplace. The hand passes from right to left, beginning at the far side of the slab, until the whole slab has received a film of the mixture. By the time the spreading is complete the gauzy sheet is baked, and it is lifted and laid to one side on a mat, where it soon cools and becomes somewhat crisp. After a number of sheets are baked they are placed on the hot slab, and on becoming warm may be rolled or folded without breaking. The bread is now piled in baskets and is ready to be eaten. Occasionally the Zuñis color he'we red, using for that purpose amarantus, which they grow sparingly in the gardens.

A variety of this bread is sometimes made as follows: Cold, boiled beans are pounded and made into a paste by adding cold water and mixed with the batter in place of the mush; salt is added to this mixture. Sometimes the he'we is made of untoasted meal; in this case salt is added. The bits of he'we which necessarily accumulate are carefully laid away, for not an atom of food is wasted by the Zuñis, and when there is a sufficient quantity of these bits, they are deposited in a bowl placed over the fire and stirred with a bunch of osiers until thoroughly toasted. The bowl is then removed from the fire, and the bits are crushed in the hand and deposited in a basket tray. This bread is warmed in grease or moistened with water before it is eaten.

He'yahoniwe is a bread in common use at Zuñi. A small quantity of mush is made of corn which has been passed through mills of the first two degrees of coarseness by mixing with cold water; salt is added, then water from slaked lime to give a greenish color to the bread. A handful of this mush is added to a quantity of the batter previously referred to, and this mixture is baked, two cakes at a time, on a stone similar to the he'we stone. These cakes are about 10 by 12 inches, and many times thicker than the he'we. As the cakes are removed from the stone they are laid in a basket or bowl.

Mu''kĭapawe is a favorite mush. Meal ground through the first two mills is mixed with boiling water to a stiff dough, and water from slaked lime is added to give color; cold water is then supplied in sufficient quantity to give the mush the proper consistency; this is then shaped into large oval balls, which are dropped into a pot of boiling water. Mu''kĭapawe is eaten cold.

Mu''kĭaliwe is another variety of mush. It is prepared in the same manner as he'yahoniwe, except that the mush is rolled into rope-like strips, from which bits are broken and made into balls an inch or more in diameter. These are dropped into just enough boiling water to cook them; the water becomes thickened from the mush balls, and the whole is eaten with a ladle or spoon.

He'pachiwe[a] (singular, he'pachinĕ) is a favorite bread of the Zuñis. The stone slab on which this bread is baked is 8 or 10 inches in diameter, only large enough to bake one cake at a time. The slab is thoroughly washed and is supported on stones in one of the smaller fireplaces over a low fire. It is constantly rubbed with mutton grease while heating. The natural color of the stone is gray, but it becomes black from treatment similar to that given the he'we stone. Flour, properly salted, is put into a bowl, and warm water is added to make a dough, which is worked only long enough to mix

---

[a] Tortillas.

the ingredients thoroughly. The woman sits beside the fireplace and performs the double duty of tending the fire and making the bread. A bit of dough is broken off and fashioned into a ball, and the ball is hollowed with the hand into a deep bowl, which is placed inverted upon a round, flat stone especially fashioned for the purpose, flattened, and worked with the hand[a] into a symmetrical round cake. The fingers are placed close together and the nails zigzagged over the cake so that it may brown in ridges. This furrowed side is placed next to the baking stone. As air bubbles form they are pricked with a wooden pin. While one cake is baking another is prepared for the stone. As the cakes are removed from the fire they are laid in a flat basket. He'pachiwe is made in great quantities when gifts are to be thrown to the populace. On such occasions many show much dexterity in sending cakes through the air.

Chu'ᵗsikwanawe (corn without skin) he'pachiwe is made by pouring diluted lye over corn and leaving it until the hull is shed. It is then thouroughly washed, dried, and afterward ground. The meal is mixed with water, no salt being used, and made into cakes 6 or 8 inches in diameter and about two-thirds of an inch thick. It is baked on he'pachiwe slabs.

Mu'loowe (light bread) is made at feasts, seldom at other times, and is baked in ovens outside the house. A bit of dough is reserved from each baking for the next, being sometimes kept a month or six weeks, or even longer; when the leaven is to be used, it is soaked in water, cold or warm, to soften it. A small quantity of flour is added to make a soft batter, which is well beaten with the hand. The batter is covered with a cloth and set to rise over night. The bread making begins about 10 o'clock in the morning. The sponge is emptied into a large bread bowl; warm water is gradually added while the sponge is constantly kneaded until the bowl is half full; salt is put in; then flour is added, the kneading process going on all the while. The bread-maker runs her arms into the dough halfway to the elbow, but as it becomes firmer from additional flour, only the fists sink into it. In kneading the dough it is brought from the outside over the center, broken off, and pushed down into the mass. When the dough has had sufficient kneading, a quantity is separated from the mass and manipulated for a time on a beautifully finished wooden slab some 3 feet in length and 18 inches wide, used exclusively for this purpose. If turnover rolls are to be made, which is the common form, a batch of dough is shaped into a round cake equal in size to a small loaf of bread; a depression is made across the center with the ulnar edge of the hand; melted mutton grease is spread over the cake; and then the turnover is formed. As each roll is made it is laid upon a cotton cloth spread on the floor. The dough is sometimes made into various fanciful

---

[a] The Mexicans use a diminutive rolling-pin.

shapes, such as animals and birds, and some of the old women delight in making portions of their dough into obscene characters.

The oven (see plate xc) is mound-shaped, built of stone, and plastered on the exterior and interior, and when not in use for baking purposes serves as a kennel for dogs. The opening through which the bread is passed is rectangular and near the base, while the vent for the smoke is near the top on the opposite side. A fire of cedar wood is made and the lower opening is securely closed until the oven is thoroughly heated and the wood reduced to coals. The coals and ashes are sprinkled with water and removed with long-handled wooden shovels made for the purpose. Some of these shovels are decorated with symbols of the ancient ladder made of a notched log. The floor of the oven is carefully swept and afterward washed with a mop of cedar twigs supplied with a long handle. This work must be done rapidly that the oven may not become cooled. The heat of the oven is tested by scattering bran over the bottom. One or two pieces of the dough are placed upon a wooden shovel and deposited in the oven with great accuracy so that there shall be no waste room. When the oven is quite filled, the doorway is covered with a piece of sheep-skin, the wool outside, held in place by a stone slab. A number of bakings can be done with one heating of the oven. Economy is observed in the use of wood because it comes from a distance. It is brought in wagons by those who are the happy possessors of them, otherwise on the backs of burros or of men; the women rarely act as beasts of burden, and only occasionally has the writer observed a woman bringing wood to the village (see plate xci). Wood used in ceremonials is usually transported on burros.

He'palokĭa is made from wheat or corn, a quantity of wheat is placed in a bowl and cold water poured over it. It is then left to stand twenty-four hours, when it is washed and placed in a basket tray, sprinkled with water, and covered with a cotton cloth. The tray stands in the sun during the day and is set in a warm place during the night. This process of sprinkling and placing the wheat in the sun is repeated until the wheat has sprouted and become sweet. A handful of the sprouted wheat is ground and added to a soft batter of wheat flour, and the mixture is worked with a stick made for the purpose; some-times a bunch of slender sticks is used. Nine or ten slabs, about 10 by 10 inches, are stood on end in an excavation in the same fire-place used for baking the he'we, and cedar wood is placed between them. The wood is then lighted; when it is reduced to coals, and the excavation is properly heated, the slabs are laid to one side, while the coals are removed, and the surface where they rested is thoroughly swept. A number of dried corn husks, sufficient to cover the space occupied by a slab, are dampened and flattened, and the mixture is spread over them. Husks are now laid around the edge of the stiff batter to such depth that the stone which is placed over it will not touch the batter. The arranging of the stones, depositing of the batter, and placing of the husks are repeated until all the slabs are employed. A stone slab is laid over the whole, and a fire is made upon it. The coals produce sufficient heat with that below to bake the he′palokĭa, which remains all night in the slab oven. In the morning it is ready to be eaten, and is regarded as a great delicacy.

Another process is to fill a large pot with the mixture and place it on a deep bed of coals in a permanent excavation made for the purpose outside the house. A small fire is built around the pot; the batter is stirred until it begins to boil; a slab is then laid over the excavation and a fire is built upon it. This process, which also requires the pot to remain in place overnight, has never been in such favor as baking in the house, because when the food is baked out of doors it is believed to be more or less exposed to the witches, who are ever ready to destroy people, not only by directly "shooting" bad medicine into their bodies but by the indirect method of affecting the food when it can be reached.

A more modern way of baking wheat he′palokĭa is to fill an iron pot with the mixture, deposit it in the oven used for light bread, the oven having been properly heated, and let it stand overnight. This method has grown in favor during the past few years.

Though wheat he′palokĭa is considered a delicacy, that made of corn is dear to the Zuñi palate. Usually yellow or black corn is selected. This is ground through the first and second mills, and the meal is sifted through a fine sieve. About a cupful of the meal is chewed, several girls usually performing this part of the bread making. Each mouthful is chewed several minutes and then ejected into a small bowl. A quantity of the unchewed meal is placed in a large bowl, boiling water is added, and the mixture is stirred in the manner before described; the chewed meal is afterward added, and the whole is well stirred. The batter is baked in the manner observed with the wheat he′palokĭa in slab ovens.

He′palokĭa is sometimes made into pats, wrapped in corn husks, and baked in the outdoor oven, which is heated as for light bread. A comparatively short time is required to cook the bread in this form, and it is regarded as a mere makeshift.

Scraps which are left of both the wheat and corn he′palokĭa are spread on cloths and dried in the sun, or, should it be raining, the cloth is spread by the fire. When thoroughly dried they are ground in the finest mill and the meal is mixed with cold water and drunk. The meal of the corn he′palokĭa is also eaten dry as one eats bonbons. The older men may be seen with a small bowl of the dry meal beside them taking a pinch every now and then while they work on their beads or moccasins.

Mu'ᵗsikowe (doughnuts) were adopted from the Mexicans. A soft dough is made of salted wheat flour and cold water. A bit of dough is broken from the mass, flattened, and shaped into square cakes, about 4 by 4 inches. These are dropped into a pot of boiling beef or mutton grease, or lard when it can be secured. A slender stick that is used to manipulate the doughnuts is punched through each piece to turn it over in the grease, and is also used for lifting the bread through the opening previously made; the doughnut is held over the pot for a moment or two to allow the grease to drip from it and then is deposited in a bowl. There are other varieties of bread not mentioned in the list given.

Chu'ᵗsikwanawe[a] (hominy) is one of the staple articles of food. To prepare it a quantity of ashes wet with cold water is placed in a large pot of cold water, and corn removed from the cob is deposited in the pot. After the corn has boiled awhile it is stirred with a stick. The boiling and stirring continue upward of three hours, when the corn is removed from the pot and carried in a basket or bowl to the river, where it is thoroughly washed, and then the hominy, which does not require soaking, is ready for use. Hominy is not kept on hand, but is prepared as it is desired for a meal. It would be impossible to find hominy that is whiter or of better quality in any respect than that prepared by the Zuñi housewife.

Mi'lo‘we (roasted sweet corn) is a favorite food. An excavation 10 or 12 feet deep and 3 or 4 feet in diameter is made in the cornfield. After cedar branches have been thrown into the opening, coals from a fire previously made are heaped on the branches and cedar wood is placed upon the coals. When about a quarter of the depth of the excavation is filled with live coals, the corn still in the husks is thrown in; stones are placed thickly over the corn, and coals are heaped upon the stones. The corn remains in this oven from late in the afternoon or about sunset until after sunrise the following morning, when it is ready to be eaten. What is not consumed while fresh is hung in the storage rooms to dry, each ear having the husks pulled back exposing the corn. Roasted corn is preserved in this way for months, and when it is to be eaten the husks are severed from the cob and the ear is boiled. If this corn is to be distributed in ceremonials, however, the husks are allowed to remain on when it is boiled. It is thrown to the populace by holding the pulled-back husks.

Ta'kunawe (bead corn) is popped corn. The grains of corn are toasted in bowls balanced on stones over coals and are constantly stirred with slender cottonwood sticks until they pop and become white as snowflakes. One is sure to find all the youngsters hanging about waiting, ready for the first mess of corn, which is the most delicious that the writer has found anywhere. It is sprinkled with salt while hot.

---

a See p. 364.

Among vegetables the squash is the only one that receives particular attention in preparation, the others being used principally in combination with other things. The favorite way of preparing fresh squash is to roast it whole in the ashes, after a small opening in the rind has first been made. It is delicious after cooking all night. Fresh squash is also stewed; dried squash is broken in goodly pieces and placed in a pot of cold water to boil.

The native fruits, including that of one of the cacti (opuntia filipendula), both fresh and preserved, are used extensively. A very pleasant conserve is made from the fruit of yucca baccata which serves on occasion to sweeten either fresh or dried peaches when stewed. Nuts from the piñon cone are gathered in great quantities.

The flesh of animals forms a large element in the Zuñian dietary. The Zuñis have large numbers of cattle, goats, and sheep,[a] and a limited number of hogs and chickens. Chickens are kept for the eggs, the whites of which are used for mixing paints to be applied to wooden objects. The whole egg is sometimes eaten by men to bring them larger families. The Navahos have the same superstition. Pork is regarded as a great delicacy. There is nothing that so tickles the palate as bacon, and whenever possible it is secured from the trader. Mutton is the everyday meat. Beef is usually cut into strips and sun-dried for winter use, although fresh beef is greatly enjoyed. There is a regular frolic over the flaying and dressing of a beef (see plate xcii). Only small portions of the beef and mutton are cast aside as unfit for use; chitterlings are a delicacy; the liver, heart, and lights are eaten; and the head with the brains remaining is roasted before the fire, the brains especially being esteemed choice morsels. The blood is made into a pudding. Meat is usually stewed; when only a few are to be served, it is sometimes fried in mutton grease; in either case it is cut into pieces. When a stew is to be made the meat is placed in a pot with cold water over the fire on stones; white corn is removed from the cob, washed, cracked in the coarser mill and in the next broken into finer bits, and put into the stew; salt, the condiment kulantu (a Mexican name),[b] and chilli are added, the latter making the dish look as though tomatoes formed an ingredient. In camp, meat is roasted before the fire.

Large game is always enjoyed, but is becoming scarcer every year. Jack-rabbits and little cottontails are abundant. Most game is stewed, if served in the village; in camp it is roasted. Game is a necessary offering to the Beast Gods to induce them to act as mediators between the Zuñis and the anthropic gods. Deer meat is cut into strips, sun dried, and preserved for ceremonials and for guests who are present

[a] The sheep and goat corrals, which are within the town and close to the houses, render the air in moist weather offensive in the extreme.
[b] A fuller description of plant food will be given in a later publication.

at such times from other pueblos, for the best must always be placed before strangers.

While the Zuñis do not eat horses, they sometimes eat a burro which has died from hunger or abuse. They raise large numbers of horses, but keep them exclusively for riding.

A native drink, which the Zuñis claim is not intoxicating, is made from sprouted corn. The corn is moistened and placed in the sun until it sprouts. Another drink which the Zuñis enjoy is ta'kuna'kïawe (bead water), made of popped corn ground in the finest mill. The powder is put into a bowl and cold water is poured over it. The mixture is strained before it is drunk. This beverage is also used in ceremonies and during fasts of the rain priests.

Coffee with sugar is greatly relished, the Zuñis obtaining it at any cost within their means. Tea is also enjoyed by these people. Whisky is rarely, if ever, used.

The Zuñis have only two meals daily. Breakfast is served about 11 o'clock, after the men and women have done a good morning's work; the other meal is taken after sunset. The family sit around the food, which is set on the floor in separate vessels, large or small as may be required, either of pottery or basketry. Bread is usually served on basket trays. Though small ladles are in use for dipping the stews, the general practice is to take a piece of bread and dip up the stew with it. Fingers take the place of knives and forks. Before partaking of the food, bits of the different viands are gathered by each adult and thrown into the fire with a prayer as an offering to the dead. In the presence of strangers this grace is omitted, but the Zuñis covertly put by food close beside them on the floor.

DRESS AND ADORNMENT

The everyday dress of the men is not attractive. White cotton or calico shirts are worn outside the loose cotton trousers, which are formed of two straight pieces joined at the top, leaving the breech-cloth to complete the covering. The calico shirt is a folded slip with two cuts midway, one crosswise, the other lengthwise from the center of the crosscut, through which the head passes. As the gusset has not been introduced into Zuñi tailoring, only the upper portion of the sleeve is attached to the shirt, the under side being left free, exposing the axilla. The shirt is fashioned after the native woven garment, the difference being that the calico sleeve is sewed from the hand to the top while the woven sleeve is fastened only for a short distance from the hand upward. The woven shirt is now used exclusively for cere-monial occasions. The shirt is frequently belted in with a leather strap, on which silver medallions are strung. The moccasins are of deerskin, well tanned, and colored reddish brown, or occasionally black; they have rawhide soles, and are fastened on the outer side with silver buttons. To afford additional warmth the foot is often wrapped in a piece of cloth before drawing on the moccasin. In wet weather the moccasins are usually left off, and for snow on the road and in very cold weather pieces of goatskin or sheepskin are tied over the feet, the wool inside. The deerskin leggings, which extend from below the knee to the ankle, are usually of the same color as the moccasin. They have a line of silver buttons down the side, and are wrapped around the leg, and held in place by red woven garters. A knit stocking leg of blue yarn is worn under them. A silk kerchief or a banda, wrapped in the Turkish fashion around the head, is worn by those who can afford the extravagance, others wear a cotton head-kerchief. A leather bow wristlet, ornamented with silver, is commonly seen on the left wrist. Necklaces of white shell, turquoise, and coral beads, more or less elaborate, according to the wealth of the wearer, are the principal adornments. Turquoise bead earrings, tipped with bits of coral or a red stone precious to the Zuñis, are attached to the necklaces, unless they are removed for ceremonial occasions, when they are worn in the ears. The well-dressed Zuñi seldom appears without his blanket unless the thermometer is unusually high, and every man who can secure one possesses a Navaho blanket, which he wears in preference to the coarser and less ornamental weave of home manufacture. Rabbit-skin blankets, woven of strips of the skins, though much used in the past, are now very rare.

The women's dress is picturesque and is donned when the girl is about four years of age, before which the children of both sexes wear little or no clothing in warm weather. The gown is of black diagonal cloth, woven in one piece,[a] embroidered at top and bottom in dark blue.[b] The cloth is folded once and sewed up to within a short distance of the top, and again the top edges are caught together for a few inches, draping gracefully over the right shoulder. The arm passes through the opening, while the gown is carried under the left arm. A long belt of Zuñi or Hopi manufacture is wrapped several times around the waist. It is generally tightly drawn by the younger women and tucked under, with the ends falling a few inches, one end of the belt having a deep fringe. A cotton camis, similar in shape to the dress, is worn beneath, and a high-necked and long-sleeved garment is also worn under the dress and next to it; this is left off for ceremonials. The neck and wrists of this garment are finished with bands, which are fastened with silver buttons. A pi'toni, which is a piece of white cotton or of calico, tied in the front at the neck and falling over the back, is an indispensable article of dress. The woman whose hus-

---

[a] Navaho dresses are woven in two pieces.
[b] This style of finishing is exclusively Zuñian. The Hopi Indians weave in their blue borders and the Rio Grande Indians have red mixed in the borders of their gowns.

band or father has brought her a shawl of foreign manufacture from
Santa Fe or Albuquerque, which on state occasions she wears as an
extra pi'toni, for the cotton one is never laid aside except for ceremonials, is envied by the other women. When the Government school
closes for the day, the children hasten to their homes to add the pi'toni
to their school uniform before joining their playmates. The Zuñi
woman must be poor indeed who does not wear a silver necklace and
bangles. These necklaces are made of coin-silver.beads with pendent
crescents; occasionally a number of crosses or other forms are added.
Silver rings are also worn by the women. Turquoise earrings, which
are worn only in ceremonials, are the same as the men's, and the women
borrow the men's bead necklaces to wear at such times.

Knit stocking legs with moccasins complete the toilet (see plate
XCIII). The women's moccasins are elaborate according to the wealth
of the wearer, the more deerskin used the handsomer the moccasins.
After the white moccasin with polished black sole is drawn on the
foot, the skin is wrapped around the leg giving it a clumsy look but
causing the foot to appear much smaller than it really is. In summer
the women and girls usually have their feet and legs bare. All moccasins are made by the men, and men also do the sewing for the female
members of the family as well as themselves. They sew from instead
of toward themselves. The men knit the stocking legs and also knit
shoes of bright colors for women and little girls, who wear them in
moderate weather.

The woolen garments of home manufacture are washed occasionally
in suds of the root of the yucca glauca on the river bank, the Indians
appreciating the necessity of sometimes cleansing them in order to
preserve them; but cotton clothing is worn, not only by the poorer,
but by the better class, until it falls apart from decay caused by filth.
If these garments are replaced by fresh ones for ceremonial occasions,
they are put on again and worn until full service has been rendered.

No one dresses his own hair. Women comb the men's hair and one
another's, unless a lover or a bridegroom greatly enamored of his
bride sometimes plays the part of hairdresser. One of the favorite
pastimes is to sit outside the house and search in the hair for vermin; and
as each specimen is found the hairdresser cracks it between her teeth
with an expression of genuine satisfaction. The vermin are not eaten
as has been stated, but are thrown from the mouth. The hair is parted
from ear to ear over the crown of the head, a fine straw being used for
the purpose of making the part perfectly clear. The front of the hair
is allowed to fall in heavy bangs over the forehead, while the back
hair is carefully brushed. A bunch of broom corn tied about 4 inches
from the cut ends serves a double purpose, the longer portion being
the broom, the shorter the hairbrush. When every hair is in its place,
a long string is wrapped once around the hair and tightly drawn at

the nape of the neck. A person whose hair is being dressed holds each end of the string while the hair is brushed again; and it is frequently spat upon as it is folded over and over. The hair-dresser, taking first the right-hand string, wraps it tightly around the hair, which is formed into a bow. The other end of the string is also wrapped around the hair, and the string is firmly tied. The tongue is frequently used in smoothing every hair into its place. The bow is now wrapped with a red woven garter or with red yarn. When the hairdresser has finished, the man separates the bangs, which fall to the eyebrows, and brushing both sides back with the hands, he ties a head-kerchief or a silk band around his head. The woman's hair is done up in a similar manner in the back. Instead of a bow she wears a queue, so wrapped with a garter or yarn as almost to obscure the hair, except in certain ceremonies when the hair, which has been previously braided to render it wavy,[a] falls down the back. After the hair is dressed the woman or girl, by a peculiar manipulation of the fingers, separates her bangs, which fall to the lower lip, on one side and catches up the hair behind the ear. In dancing, grinding, and all other ceremonies the bangs fall over the face. Bangs are worn for the same reason that Turkish women veil their faces. The Zuñis say, "It is not well for a woman's face to be exposed to the gaze of men."

WEAVING

The Zuñis depend upon their native blankets for bedding and to a large extent for wraps, though the Navaho blankets are worn by men and boys, and are used as saddle blankets. Commercial wool cards are in general use. The Zuñis spin with a primitive spindle, a slender stick passed through a wood or stone disk.[b] Their blankets, as a rule, are made of wool of its natural colors—white, gray, brown, and brownish-black—woven in stripes; but they also dye the wool in two shades of blue, using indigo, and urine as a mordant, mahogany red, yellow, and green.[c]

It is the opinion of the writer that the pueblo blankets in the past were more elaborate in design than now, and that the Navahos learned to weave from the pueblos. It is further believed that as the progressive Navahos became greater experts in weaving, the art of the Zuñis deteriorated: they came to depend on the Navahos for the better grade of blankets.

In 1881 a young boy about 12 years of age became jealous over the writer's admiration for the Navaho blankets and determined to see

---

[a] Two men were observed to have naturally wavy hair.

[b] Dr Washington Matthews, U. S. Army, in the Third Annual Report of the Bureau of Ethnology, gives an exhaustive account of Navaho weaving. In stating that the Zuñis employ a different method from that of the Navahos in handling the spindle, Dr Matthews is in error. The method shown on plate XXXIV of Dr Matthews's paper is a favorite one with the Zuñis.

[c] A full description of the preparation of yarn for weaving will be given in a forthcoming paper Specimens of native-dyed yarn were secured in 1904 after prolonged efforts.

what he could do. Going to work with no design before him, he produced a saddle blanket of exceptional beauty. The elaborate figures were woven in various colors on a red ground. In 1902 a Zuñi priest presented the writer with a blanket of his own weaving, which, though not fine, was elaborate in design and color. It was made in order to show the writer that the Zuñis possess the art of weaving blankets in the Navaho style even though they do not practise it. They prefer to purchase blankets of the more elaborate kind from the Navahos and give their time to other things.

Men's shirts, ceremonial kilts and breechcloths, and women's dresses and wraps are woven of black or dark blue native wool in diagonal style. These articles have embroidered borders of dark blue. Commercial needles take the place of bone. The woman's belt is generally woven of red yarn, bordered in green, with designs in white cotton thread. Before commercial yarn was obtainable, these belts were woven of native yarn dyed mahogany red and green. Plate XCIV shows We'wha, who was one of the important characters of Zuñi, employed in weaving. The picture was made during We'wha's visit to Washington. The dress is inappropriate, being ceremonial.

BASKETRY

The Zuñis make for ordinary use a variety of coarse baskets of willows, dogwood, and a plant, Chrysothamnus graveolens, which grows profusely over the country. Many of these baskets are deep and are carried in the hand or suspended on the back by a strap passing over the forehead. They also serve as saddle bags. There are winnowing baskets, and small, deep receptacles for collecting grasshoppers, these insects being sometimes eaten as a delicacy. All the finer bread baskets and ceremonial trays are purchased from the Apache, Hopi, and other Indians. Those of the former are especially prized. It is not that the Zuñi women can not make the fine baskets, but it happens in aboriginal life as in civilization that different peoples have their specialties, and objects of foreign manufacture are prized

POTTERY

The manufacture of pottery is one of the most interesting industries of the Zuñis. Most of the women are potters, the art being learned at an early age, the wee ones working bits of clay by their mothers' sides and the mother often stopping her work to instruct the child; few, however, fully understand the meaning of the symbols depicted on the modern ware, and the wisest of them are unable to decipher many of the symbols on the ancient pottery found in the ruins near by. In like manner the people are unable to understand many of the rock carvings which cover the mesa walls in New Mexico and Arizona.

The black clay used in the manufacture of pottery is obtained on Corn mountain. It is also collected from mesas near the farming districts of Ojo Caliente and Pescado as occasion may require. The same clay is found in many localities, but so strictly do the Zuñis adhere to custom that they could not be induced to use clay for such purposes from any other than the localities here mentioned. They declare that the clay will never become exhausted, as Mother Earth will supply them as long as they remain pure of heart.

On one occasion Mr Stevenson and the writer accompanied We'wha to Corn Mountain to obtain clay.[a] On passing a stone heap she picked up a small stone in her left hand, and spitting upon it, carried the hand around her head and threw the stone over one shoulder upon the stone heap in order that her strength might not go from her when carrying the heavy load down the mesa. She then visited the shrine at the base of the mother rock and tearing off a bit of her blanket deposited it in one of the tiny pits in the rock as an offering to the mother rock (see plate XII a). When she drew near to the clay bed she indicated to Mr Stevenson that he must remain behind, as men never approached the spot. Proceeding a short distance the party reached a point where We'wha requested the writer to remain perfectly quiet and not talk, saying: "Should we talk, my pottery would crack in the baking, and unless I pray constantly the clay will not appear to me." She applied the hoe vigorously to the hard soil, all the while murmuring prayers to Mother Earth. Nine-tenths of the clay was rejected, every lump being tested between the fingers as to its texture. After gathering about 150 pounds in a blanket, which she carried on her back, with the ends of the blanket tied around her forehead, We'wha descended the steep mesa, apparently unconscious of the weight.

The only implements used in making pottery are the bottom of a discarded water vase and a sort of trowel made of a gourd or a suitable fragment of pottery. No wheel is used, nor is any kind of lathe or revolving support known to these people. The clay is ground to a powder and mixed with a small quantity of pulverized pottery, fragments of the latter being carefully hoarded for this purpose. The powder thus compounded is mixed with water enough to make a pasty mass, which is kneaded like dough. The more care taken in pulverizing the material and the more time spent in working it the finer becomes the paste. When the mass reaches such a state of consistency that the fingers can no longer detect the presence of gritty particles it is still more delicately tested with the tongue, and when found to be satisfactory it is

a The men who collect clay are the few who adopt woman's dress and do woman's work, and these are always referred to as women.

WOMEN PLASTERING A HOUSE AND FIRING POTTERY

THE ZUÑI SALT LAKE

placed in a vessel and covered with a cloth, where it will retain the moisture until wanted for use. In beginning the work a sufficient quantity is first made into a ball and then hollowed out with the fingers until it assumes a conventional bowl shape, which serves as the foundation to be afterward built up and elaborated into any desired shape. The vessel is then formed by the successive additions of strips of the paste long enough to encircle the bowl, each layer being pressed on the brim with the fingers and accurately fitted, the trowel being then skillfully used to finish the joining and to remove all traces of the original separation of the strips. Most of the work of modeling the vessel into its final shape is done on the inside with a trowel, this implement being used on the outside chiefly to smooth the surface. The clay, if it has been properly worked, possesses sufficient tenacity and plasticity to admit of being pressed and scraped without cracking.

The completed utensil is placed in the sun for a day to dry, after which it must be handled carefully until after it is baked. This is nevertheless the state of manufacture in which it is to be decorated. The modern ware is usually painted white, except the cooking vessels, which are unpainted. A white clay is dissolved in water and then made into cones which are dried in the sun. When required for use these cones are rubbed to powder on a stone, again mixed with water, and applied in the liquid state to the object with a rabbit-skin mop. Polishing stones are used to finish the surface. After a thorough drying of this foundation, the designs are painted with brushes made of yucca needles, the pigments having been ground in stone mortars and made into a paste with water to which a sirup of yucca fruit is added. Water from boiled Cleome serrulata (Mexican name waco) is mixed with black pigment (a manganiferons clay containing organic matter) in decorating pottery. Ferruginous clays which on heating burn to yellow, red, or brown are employed for decorating.

These potters do not use patterns in molding or decorating their work. In many of the pueblos the pottery is undecorated, the surface being finished in plain red or black. The ware is made of a yellowish clay, in the manner heretofore described, and the vases are placed in the sun, where they remain for some hours. They are then washed with a solution of red ocher, and while wet the process of polishing begins, the woman with untiring energy going over the surface again and again with her polishing stone, every little while passing a wet cloth over the vessel to keep the surface moist. When the polishing is completed, the vessel is again placed in the sun for a short time before receiving its final baking in the oven. When the baking is completed, the vessels that are to retain the reddish color are removed, while those that are to be black remain in the ovens, which are then covered with a quantity of loose manure. The fire is so smothered by this process as to produce a dense smoke, and it is this smoke absorbed into the pottery that produces the black coloring, no black pigment of any kind being used. While there is no attempt at surface decoration, many pretty and curious shapes are modeled by the clever potters. There are water jars and bowls with fluted edges, imitations of birds and beasts, and many queer figures.

When the Zuñi potter has completed the decoration, the articles are ready for baking. A suitable spot out of doors is selected, and if possible a day is chosen when there is no wind to interfere with the

FIG. 24—Old Zuñi vase.

process, unless it be the regular time for baking pottery during the summer solstice ceremonies. The pieces to be fired are placed upon stones to raise them a few inches from the ground, and an oven of dried manure from the sheep and goat pens is built around and over them. The fire is carefully managed in order to produce a gradual heating, after which the entire mass is subjected to an intense heat until the baking is completed, the process usually requiring one or two hours. A bit of wafer bread is deposited in each vase, so that the spirit of the vase may be fed with the spiritual essence of the bread.

It is believed that should a pregnant woman look upon a piece of pottery while in process of firing, it will be marred with a black spot. Thus the Zuñis account for the blemishes caused by the smoking of the pottery.

Much of the modern pottery is decorated with animal forms, with an attempt to depict them as such, while birds and animals in the ancient ware are so highly conventionalized that only the initiated can determine the original of the motive. Figure 24 shows a very old vase decorated with conventionalized butterfly and cloud and rain symbols, while the more modern style of vases[a] are presented in figure 25.

FIG. 25—Modern Zuñi vases.

SILVERSMITHING

The Mexican dollar, owing to its purity, is employed by the silversmith in preference to the silver dollar of the United States. Native silver is not known to the Zuñis, at least at the present time, and Zuñi sages claim that their people never worked in silver or copper before the presence of the Spaniards. With crude implements are manufactured elaborate ornaments for bridles, silver belts, and buttons for men, and silver beads, bangles, and rings for women. The furnace, bellows, dies—everything pertaining to the workshop of the silversmith (see plate xcv)—are of home manufacture, except the files and hammers, and these are carpenters' tools. The silversmith is also the blacksmith and general utility man of the village.

---

[a] Symbolism will be described in a later paper devoted to the subject.

BEAD MAKING

The more precious beads of the Zuñis of shell, black, red, and white stone are antique, and are not manufactured at present. They still make beads of turquoise, white shells, preferably the olive-shell, and spondylus princeps. They also color shells red in imitation of the last-named shell. Though the turquoises are sometimes ground to correspond to the white shell beads, the stones are usually left in the form in which they are secured. Coral beads are purchased from traders and vary somewhat in form, though they are generally cylindrical or round. The ancient stone beads are as a rule cylindrical; some few are flat. The white shell beads are flat.[a]

The process of bead making is long and tedious. Shells are broken into bits and each piece is rubbed on a stone slab until it is of the desired thinness. The more delicate the bead the more valuable it is. After each piece has passed through the rubbing process it is laid to one side until there are enough pieces to form a string of beads; then the boring is begun (see plate xcvi). As each stone is pierced it is usually slipped on a string for safe-keeping until the boring is completed, when the irregular pieces are rubbed separately on the stone to form them into symmetrical disks less than one-eighth of an inch in diameter. From four to six strings form a necklace. The coral beads are sprinkled among the turquoise and the more numerous white shell beads. The beads never reach the end of the string; a finger's length is left bare of beads. The older necklaces, which were more carefully made than the modern ones, are very valuable, a single string bringing a number of horses.

WAGON MAKING

The only commercial wagon in Zuñi is owned by Mr Graham, the agent. The Indian wagon is of home manufacture, although of Spanish origin (see plate xcvii). The wheels are heavy blocks, carved in the rudest fashion; the bed is composed of beams or poles and the sides of slender poles. The structure is lined, when necessary, with hide. It is drawn by oxen, and the whole is of the most primitive character.[b]

AUCTIONEERING

Auctioneering with the Zuñis is quite as much of a feature as it is with civilized people, and the auctioneer is a conspicuous character. When the larder becomes overstocked with some varieties of food and is deficient in others, the head of the household looks anxiously for

---

[a] A fine specimen of a cylindrical turquoise bead three-fourths inch in length, found at a ruin near the Zuñi salt lake, was secured for the National Museum.

[b] Mr Stevenson secured one of these wagons from a Rio Grande pueblo for the National Museum at Washington

the announcement that the auctioneer is to give his services to those in need of them. The time being arranged for the sale, the auction occurs in the great plaza (see plate XCVIII). The following is a description of an auction which lasted three days, observed by the writer in 1896: Early in the morning the auctioneer placed a bunch of yellow blossoms in the center of the plaza and covered it with a conical cooking vessel, no one being present but the auctioneer and the writer. What was under the vessel was a secret, and the flowers were not removed until everyone had left the plaza in the evening. At 10 o'clock in the morning the women began bringing in their wares. Bowls and baskets were deposited about the inverted cooking vessel. These contained wheat flour, dried peaches, beans, squash which had been cut into strips and dried, and other articles of food. Burros sometimes found their way to the sale and got their noses into the baskets before they could be driven away. Though only the women were supposed to be interested in the auction, a number of men sat about with their knitting. The auctioneer set forth the good qualities of the article for sale, stated what the owner wished in exchange for it, and with his ready tongue soon enticed a purchaser. He frequently sold an article within thirty seconds after it was brought to the plaza. Payment was made at once, and the traders left the plaza to return in a short time with the vessels, which go back to their owners.

The auctioneer, an aged man with white hair, had served long at the business and would have been considered a model one in any community. He was kept busy on this occasion from morning until night. He received no compensation for his services except innumerable invitations to eat.[a]

RECENT CHANGES IN ARTS AND INDUSTRIES

Mr Stevenson, during his first visit to the Zuñis in 1879, inaugurated many changes for the better. Window panes, candles, lamps, and silversmiths' implements were introduced, and larger doors were made. Each Indian who aided in making boxes for packing the Government collection received enough lumber to make a door, the Indians being taught to make the doors and hang them. Improvements progressed slowly from that time to 1902, since which date great strides have been made in certain directions; but in 1904 the people were found to be in a deplorable condition morally.

While the ceilings of the older houses are low, those of the newer ones, or of such as have undergone renovation, are high. The finer houses are now built entirely of stone, quarried a few miles from Zuñi. An ax and chisel are the only means adopted for quarrying,

---

[a] This system of trading is said by the Zuñis to have existed long before the invasion of the Spaniards, and it is practiced in all the pueblos.

sometimes the ax alone being used. Shingles made by the Zuñi carpenter take the place of the willow boughs across the beams of the ceiling, and the rooms are much larger. The women still do much of the work in the construction of houses.

Large, sometimes double, windows with curtains, doors with locks, and china closets are much in fashion at present. Enameled iron bedsteads are to be found in a few houses, while a number of families have chairs and tables. The table is introduced rather as an ornament, as they prefer to serve their meals in the old-fashioned way on the floor. The writer has observed but two families eating from tables. A number of small heating and cooking stoves are in use, and yeast-powder bread baked in the stove is fast taking the place of bread prepared in the native manner.

Soap was introduced in 1879 in the hope that the Zuñis would wash their cotton clothes, and the writer undertook the task of instruction. She selected as a pupil a man who had adopted woman's dress and who was known to be the strongest, most active, and most progressive Indian in the tribe; but he was averse to the work, and at first refused to wash. He looked on in silence for a time while the writer worked. Never having had any experience in that work herself, she soon had most of the water from the tub on the floor and was drenched to the skin. The pupil exclaimed: "You do not understand that which you would teach. You do not understand as much as the missionary's wife; she keeps the water in the tub and does not make a river on the floor. Let me take your place." Ironing time came, only to find the pupil still more averse. He declared he had learned enough and would never learn to iron. But he was finally persuaded to go on with the work. Many weeks passed, however, before he would wash and iron without constant urging. Finally he began to realize that he was accumulating silver dollars from the members of the expedition. Then he declared that he would become a good laundryman and would go to Fort Wingate and wash for the captains' families. This man ultimately became as celebrated as a Chinese laundryman, his own cleanly apparel being his advertising card, and was called upon not only by the officers' families at the garrison, but by the white settlers near and far. Others of the tribe concluded that they, too, would wash their clothes, and consequently a great change for the better took place.

Laundering, which is carried on extensively at the present time, is not confined to either sex; the men wash their own clothes, and the women launder for their children and themselves. Only a few work for the whites, the men wearing female attire being preferred to the women on account of their strength and endurance.

The Zuñis sell their wool and buy blankets and quilts, so that the bed blankets so extensively woven by them in past years are no longer to be seen. Weaving needles made of tin cans are used instead of the bone needle of earlier days.

The art of dyeing is virtually lost.   Gussets in sleeves and trousers have been introduced, and whenever the men can raise money for the purpose, they have come to wear European dress, including hats and shoes.   Now even the baby boy who has not a hat is quite out of the fashion.   Aboriginal women are much slower than the men to adopt new styles, but in 1902 many of the Zuñi women were to be seen wearing a full cotton skirt and blouse waist, such as the Navaho women have worn in warm weather for years.   The women now do much of the sewing, and some few are the happy possessors of sewing machines.   The artistic pottery is supplanted to a great extent by stone china washbowls, used for serving food as well as for bathing, and by cheap china and glass dishes.   The pottery made at present is very inferior, and is ordered in large quantities by traders to supply the demands of trade.   The modern pottery collected by Mr Stevenson in previous years for the National Museum can well be regarded as belonging to the past.   In addition to their poor pottery the Zuñis are making baskets colored with diamond dyes in imitation of the fine basket work of the Hopi pueblo of Oraibi, and sad to relate the beautiful coloring of the Hopi baskets has been supplanted by diamond dyes. No one in Zuñi who can buy flour now grinds wheat.   Lard, yeast powder, coffee, and white sugar have become staple articles with the Zuñis.

While the people themselves are slowly but gradually improving their condition of living, they are having a hard struggle to preserve the live stock which they labored so industriously to secure.   The goodly supply of horses and cattle found in Zuñi in 1879 dwindled to a small number, owing to the deprepations not only of Navahos and Mexicans, but also of some of the white settlers in the country. They have been more fortunate with the sheep and goats, as the ever-watchful eye of the herder has prevented inroads upon them except from time to time by the Navahos.   More recently their horses and cattle as well as sheep have increased.

The wheat fields are now largely protected by barbed-wire fencing, and when the dam now being constructed by the Government is finished the Zuñi problem of living will be settled; but alas, the Zuñi as a man and good citizen has fallen far below what he was before he came into intimate contact with civilized man.   In 1879 no amount of money could have purchased a genuine Zuñi mask, and not for the world would they have manufactured a bogus specimen, so great was their dread of offending their gods.   It was not until 1896 that the writer was able to collect any of the masks of these people. Through her long acquaintance with the priests and their attachment to her she then succeeded in securing nine choice specimens.   At present the less orthodox men will manufacture almost anything a collector may desire.   Spurious ancient fetishes are made by the sackful and passed off as genuine.   So it is also with masks and altars. Any number of fraudulent objects may be obtained at the prices set by the clever Indians.

The village as a whole has undergone considerable change since 1879.   The corrals which were immediately around the village, almost at the doors, have been removed to a distance.   The walls of the old Spanish church are nearly gone.   In 1879 the walls of this church were in a fair state of preservation and partly roofed.   The two bells, rung by striking with stone hammers, which hung in the belfry are in the care of one of the Zuñi theurgists.   The lone cottonwood tree which long stood in the village has disappeared.   The streets are now kept in much better condition than formerly.   The general improvement in living is due principally to additional trading stations scattered through the country.   The adoption of foreign ways, however, has brought with it the evils of intoxication and trickery in dealing with the white man, whom they delight to lie to and cheat, though among themselves the Zuñis are still honest.   They are as secretive as ever concerning their religion and rituals, and they are as far from Christianization as before the Spaniard set foot in their land.   The few who attend the Christian services do so with no real understanding of what the services mean.   One marriage has been solemnized by a Protestant minister.   The girl is Nina, the granddaughter of Nai'uchi formerly elder brother Bow priest.   Though Nina at one time showed with much pride her marriage certificate given her by the minister who performed the marriage ceremony, realizing that it was something her Zuñi sisters did not possess, she had no real conception of Christianity.   In 1904 the certificate was destroyed, that both Nina and her husband should be rid of Christianity.

The writer named Nina when she was 4 years of age, and started her to school, exacting a promise from Nai'uchi that he would compel her regular attendance.   This promise was solemnly kept, though Nina many times begged to be allowed to leave school.   After several years of regular instruction she understood considerable English, and later grew to have remarkable command of the language, which she still retains, though she has come in contact with Americans but little since she left school.   When asked by the writer in 1902 how she remembered English so well when she saw so few Americans, she replied: "I make two people of myself and I talk to myself." [a]

Although there had been a school at the pueblo since 1876, the few other Zuñis who spoke any English in 1896 were men who had acquired a meager knowledge of the language as they came into communication with explorers and others, and the adopted child of a teacher.   The

---

[a] Tu'maka, a man who was taught when a boy by Mr Graham, many years a trader at Zuñi, and now agent to these people, has a good understanding of English.

writer observed a great improvement in 1902. Many of the school children could make themselves understood in English, and the men, from more frequent association with the whites, had made sufficient progress in the language to protect to some extent, their rights in trading. In 1904 a still larger number of Zuñis had more or less command of English.

PHYSICAL CHARACTERS[a]

As a rule the forms of the Zuñis are symmetrical and their carriage graceful. The women are small, with shapely limbs, hands, and feet. Many are handsome in their youth, but they grow corpulent at an early age. When the laughing eyes of youth become somewhat dimmed by years, they acquire a kind, motherly expression. In 1879 seven albinos were found amond the Zuñis. Mr Stevenson with difficulty gathered six of the albinos in a group and secured a photograph of them (see plate XCIX). The mother of an infant albino could not be prevailed upon to allow her child to be photographed. Indeed, these people are so sensitive of their condition that they avoid the presence of strangers, and while the men may stand their ground, the women and children, especially the latter, flee from the "Americano." The writer has seen several of the children grow to girlhood and womanhood. A birth of an albino child occurred in 1896. These people have light, decidedly yellowish hair and complexions of decided delicacy. They all have weak eyes, and their vision is so affected by the absence of choroid pigment that they are obliged to protect their eyes, which always become inflamed from ordinary daylight. When out of doors the albino men wear hats, when they can be secured, and the women cover their faces with blankets and peep through the smallest openings. The statement that albinos are compelled to live apart from the others of the tribe is erroneous, and none of them are debarred from religious or social privileges. In no instance has an albino parent an albino child, and no two of them belong to the same family. The adults are each married to a dark-haired Indian, and they have healthy offspring.

The writer is under obligations to Dr Ales Hrdlicka, curator of physical anthropology in the United States National Museum, who in 1900 visited and examined many of the Zuñis, for the following notes, in the proportions and features of the peoples:

The Zuñis show a considerable variation in stature, but may be described as below medium height. Among 60 adult men, 5 per cent measured 150 to 155 cm. in height; 23.3 per cent, 155 to 160 cm.; 26.7 per cent, 160 to 165 cm.; 31.7 per cent, 165 to 170 cm.; and 13.3 per cent, 170 to 175 cm.

Among 49 men with undeformed heads only 5 had a cephalic index below 77; in 12 it was between 77 and 80, and in 32, or 65 per cent, it was above 80. Thus the tribe may be considered as predominately brachycephalic, with a considerable varia-

---

[a] The extreme isolation of the Zuñis has preserved a strong individuality.

tion. There are indications that this variation is largely due to an early admixture
of a dolichocephalic people.

The face is usually of moderate dimensions, with more less prominent cheek bones.
The average bizygomatic breadth in the men is 14.3 cm.; average height from chin to
nasion, 11.5 cm.; average height of forehead from nasion to hair line, 7 cm.   The
nose is rather short, with an average nasal index of 82.   The nasal bridge is mostly
moderately convex or concavo-convex.   The mouth is rather large; the lips vary
from medium to well-developed, in the European standard.   Alveolar prognathism
is mostly pronounced, but facial prognathism is small.   The angles of the lower jaw
are often quite prominent in the male.

The body is generally well developed, and shows more uniformity than in whites.
In 3 out of the 60 men examined there was a tendency to obesity.   In women this is
more frequent, but the corpulence very seldom reaches a degree at which it would
become uncomfortable.   The average chest diameters in men, at nipple height, are:
Depth, 21.4 cm.; breadth, 32.9 cm.   The limbs show ordinary muscularity.   The arm
expanse in men exceeds the height on the average by 4.7 cm.   The sitting height is,
in males, on the average, 52.3 per cent of the stature.   The calf is generally smaller
than in whites, and the hands and feet are of moderate dimensions.

The physical characteristics of the Zuñis identify this tribe closely with the Hopis
and the majority of the other Pueblos.   There is also some physical relation to the
Navahos, and, farther south, to many of the peoples who spoke the Nahuatlan
language.

The several albinos who were examined showed nothing abnormal in their measurements.

MEDICAL PRACTICE

The belief held by some students that the therapeutics of the North
American Indians is associated altogether with occultism is erroneous.
Though the practice of the Zuñis is to a large extent fetishistic, it
is rich in legitimate drugs.   Some of these drugs are employed in
conjunction with theurgism; but frequently medicines are administered
both internally and externally in the most matter-of-fact way without
prayers or incantations, not only by the old women, who know various
plant medicines, but also by the professional man or woman, who is
always a theurgist of some esoteric fraternity.

Some of the Zuñi medicines are administered in accordance with the
doctrine of signatures, in conjunction with prayers and other ceremonies.   Others are the medicines of the Beast Gods of the six regions,
snake medicine, ant medicine, medicine of the feathered kingdom, and
te'nas'säli, the mythical medicine plant which is said to bear blossoms
of the colors of the six regions.   While these medicines, which are
mainly plants, are used in conjunction with fetishes of the animals to
which they belong, they are generally of real medicinal value.   Massage is extensively practiced, and the masseur or masseuse is most
proficient.

For any complicated or mysterious trouble, or one which does not
yield readily to legitimate medicine, some higher power than man must
be called upon to eradicate the disease "shot" into the person by
witchcraft.   In such cases the Beast Gods act through their agents, the

theurgists, who have great influence, the patient and the family showing every confidence in their doctor, who selects some one against whom
he harbors animosity as the destroyer of the health of his patient.
The patient also, or a member of the family, may accuse some man or
woman as the witch who "shot" the medicine into him.   The practices
of the theurgists are fully described in the section relating to witchcraft and esoteric fraternities.

There can be no doubt of the use of antiseptics among these primitive
people antedating the modern practice of surgery.   What the scientific man learns through investigation and experiment, aboriginal man
discovers by accident and chance experience.   The Indian's treatment is blindly empiric.   He does not understand why his medicine
cures; he simply knows that it does cure, and he attributes the cause
to some divine power.   He applies the antiseptic without bathing his
hands or the parts affected, and the wound is usually covered with a
soiled cloth.   He does a part, however, and nature completes the work.

Bacteriology teaches that disease is to a large extent the result of
microbes; the Zuñi theurgists declare disease generally to be caused
by foreign life "shot" into the body by witches.   Roentgen learned
to illuminate the bones and viscera with X rays; the Zuñi theurgist
holds a crystal in the light immediately before his patient that he may
see into the flesh and locate the disease.   It can not be said whether
the Zuñi women ever had a struggle to enter the field of medicine, but
to-day some of the most successful practitioners, both in legitimate
medicine and in theurgy, are women, though they are much fewer
than the men.   Some of the male theurgists are successful in certain
kinds of surgery, especially in the treatment of fractures and disloca-
tions.

In 1879 the writer discovered that the Zuñis employed a narcotic,
but she failed to secure specimens of the drug until 1902, which was
then found to be Datura stramonium, jimson weed.   The mention of
the original discovery caused remark at the time, some ethnologists
declaring that though the North American Indians had intoxicants,
they were entirely ignorant of narcotics.   Mr James Mooney, of the
Bureau of American Ethnology, who observed the use of the peyote
plant with ceremonial forms among the Kiowas and other tribes of
the southern plains southward into Mexico, was the first to bring, in
1891, the plant and ceremony to scientific attention.   He supplied the
late Dr D. W. Prentiss with a quantity of this plant, and after many
careful experiments with it Doctor Prentiss administered it to his
patients as an anesthetic with most favorable results.   The Zuñis do
not know the peyote, but they use the jimson weed, which they
call a'neglakya, both as a narcotic and externally for wounds and
bruises.   The blossoms and root ground to a powder are applied
externally.   This plant is of still further value to the Zuñis, for when

the rain priests go out at night to commune with the feathered kingdom they put a bit of this powdered root into their eyes, ears, and mouth that the birds may not be afraid and will listen to them when they pray to the birds to sing for the rains to come. A small piece of the root is chewed when one wishes to commune with the spirits of the dead that rains may come. The following is the legend associated with this plant: "In the olden time when the A'shiwi were near Ko'thluwala'wa (abiding place of the Council of the Gods) a brother and sister—the boy's name was A'neglakya, and the girl's name was A'neglakya'si'sa—were always walking about the country and looking everywhere and seeing everything, and were always telling their mother what they saw. This was not pleasing to Kŏw'wi- tuma and Wats'usi, the Divine Ones, and the two were banished into the earth and they became the plant which bears their name. They have many plant children. Some of the blossoms are all white, others are tinted with blue, while others are edged with yellow, blue, or red."

A'neglakya belongs to all of the rain priests and to the directors of the Little Fire and Cimex fraternities. Only those to whom the plant belongs are privileged to collect it. Four prayer plumes are made by one who is to gather the plants. One offering is to A'neglakya, one to A'neglakya'si'sa, and two to ancestors. The four prayer plumes are planted the depth of the arm in an excavation made with an ancient bean planter at daylight on the morning the plant is to be collected.

The writer observed Nai'uchi, the celebrated theurgist of the Little Fire fraternity, administer the narcotic previous to operating upon a woman's breast. The abscess was cut with a flint lancet, the wound was probed with the index finger and the pus forced out. The patient slept placidly through the operation, which would otherwise have been most painful, and when she awoke there was no evidence that she had been under the influence of a drug.

A'neglakya is sometimes administered by a rain priest when one wishes to recover stolen property. The rain priest is received at night in an inner room in the house of the man who lost his property. He sits alone without fire or light, and the room is dark. The man wears a new white cotton shirt and trousers and new blue knitted leggings. No head-kerchief or moccasins are worn. His hair is done in the usual style. A pallet is spread on the floor. The rain priest sits before the man, and taking a bit of the root of a'neglakya from the palm of his left hand places it in the man's mouth with the words: "I give this medicine to my child that he may become häli'shoti (intoxi- cated)[a] and see the one who has robbed him." The man then lies on the pallet, and the rain priest retires to a front room and sits by the com- municating door, which he closes, and continues to listen attentively during the night. He does not smoke, as A'neglakya does not like

---

[a] The Zuñis use the same word for insanity.

smoking at this time, and he is all alone. He hears the man walking about at intervals and is careful to catch every word he utters. The name which the man calls during the time he is under the influence of the medicine is that of the thief. At daylight the rain priest returns to the inner room to find the man either lying down or walking about. He wakens the man by grabbing his arm and leads him into the front room, where they sit side by side facing east, and the rain priest relates what he heard during the night and tells the man that the name he called is that of the thief. The man denies all recollection of what passed during the night. He is instructed by the rain priest to call upon the rogue and demand his property. The rain priest then makes a fire and heats water and has the man drink a quantity, which induces vomiting. The dose of warm water is repeated four times with the same results, that all the a'neglakya taken the previous night may be thrown up. The rain priest then leaves the man alone, but returns in a short time with his wife and other female members of the family who prepare yucca suds and wash the man's head, while he kneels on a blanket, and the rain priest sits behind him with a hand on either shoulder. The man's family may be present at this ceremony, but they take no part in it. After the head is washed, the rain priest gives four ears of corn tied together, calico, and other presents, according to his wealth or generosity. The corn is planted the coming season separately from other corn. The women return to their house and bring food which they prepared during the night, which is eaten by all present. After the repast, the loser of the property goes to the house of the person whom he named when intoxicated and demands his property, saying: "I saw you when I was drunk with a'neglakya." If the accused is guilty, he returns the property, for he would be afraid to keep it and thus offend A'neglakya.

For treating a patient outside the ceremonial chamber the Zuñi doctor is paid according to his reputation, but there is no charge when the patient is treated during a meeting of an esoteric fraternity. Like the civilized physician, the Zuñi doctor does not practice in his own family, except in rare instances when the theurgist has great faith in his ability and feels that he can save the life of the dear one.

A case of pneumonia developed on October 20, 1895, and continued six weeks, with severe fever, leaving the man very weak, and with an ugly cough. He was anxious to be placed in the care of the writer, but the jealousy of the officiating theurgist prevented any other treatment than his own. The theurgist, on his arrival, took a seat by the patient and requested that a basket tray be brought to him. He then took the hand of the patient and made inquiries regarding his condition. He removed a cougar fetish and several small bags of medicine from his pouch and deposited them in the basket; then, holding the fetish between his hands, which he carried close to his lips, he made a long prayer, so low as not to be heard. Laying the fetish in the basket, he took a minute quantity of medicine from two of the bags and deposited it in a bowl of cold water, stirring the water with a hollow reed; then he held the bowl close to the patient, who took six swallows of the medicine through the reed. The blanket covering was then turned down, exposing the chest of the patient. A small quantity of the medicine was again taken from each bag and this was run in four perpendicular lines over the chest and down the lymphatics; then both ears were touched with the medicine. The theurgist did not cease praying while handling the medicine. Continuing to pray for power to restore his patient to health, he took the fetish and medicine bags into his right hand and touched them to the right shoulder, the head, and the left shoulder of the patient. The diet was confined to a small quantity of bread and commercial tea without sugar for the first four days, during which time the Beast Gods of the four regions were appealed to and the fetish medicines were used. After this the patient was permitted to eat as he chose. For the first ten days the pulse was 120; and afterward it was never less than 110 during the six weeks of the fever, and the cough with constant expectoration caused the patient great suffering and almost reduced him to a skeleton.

The body was usually exposed to the waist, as it is not considered well to be covered when the skin is hot. During rainy and cold weather the sick man was often left without fire, especially at night, when the room, which was small, became intensely cold. On November 2 the patient was carried in a blanket through the snow to his mother's house, where he could have a larger and more comfortable room; and the mother had Na'iuchi and others of the Little Fire fraternity called in to use their efforts in curing her son. The ceremony was similar to that held by the Kĭa'kwemosi and other members of the U'huhukwe fraternity over a smallpox patient.[a] The day following the fourth and last night of the ceremonies of the members of the Little Fire fraternity the patient claimed to feel much improved, though the pulse was 105; eight days later the pulse was 90, the cough slightly better. After six weeks of this low condition the patient began to mend, and at the end of the eighth week he was able to be about, but the cough remained when the writer left in January.

A most distressing case of hysteria was witnessed by the writer. A beautiful young girl, about 12 years of age, had suffered for five weeks, the cause being suppression of the menses. Her family attributed the trouble to witchcraft, and no sooner was the girl brought from her mother's farm at Ojo Caliente to Zuñi than a prominent theurgist was summoned, and no time was lost in bringing the accused

---

aSee p. 527.

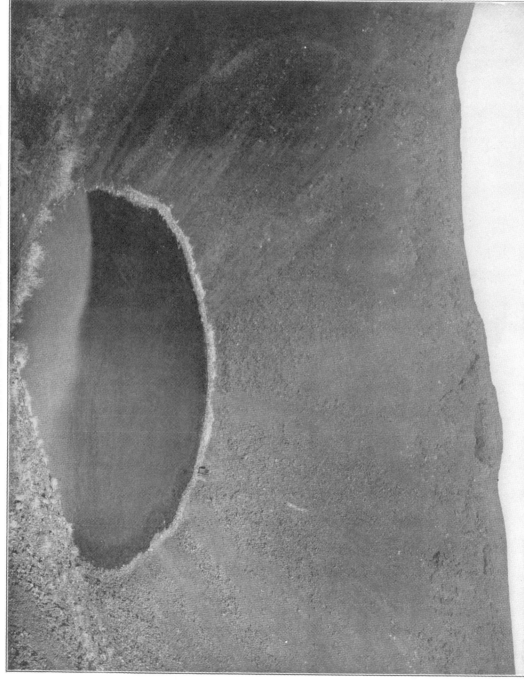

LAKE IN THE DEPTHS OF VOLCANIC CONE, HOME OF THE GODS OF WAR

M. Wright-Gill

BREAD MAKING FOR THE FEAST

wizard to trial. The tribunal met on the night of the arrival of the child. This trial is fully described in the section on witchcraft. The writer, who was called to the house of the invalid soon after her arrival, endeavored to take the pulse, but found this impossible, though the little sufferer, who was rational and deeply attached to the writer, made every effort to keep the emaciated arm quiet. She rolled and tossed, pulled at her hair and throat, and threw her arms wildly about, her legs moving as violently as her arms. Her head was never quiet for a moment. The loving family took turns in gently holding her on the pallet. First the mother, then the father at intervals appealed to the writer to help their poor child. After many efforts the writer succeeded in taking the pulse of the girl on the third evening after her return to Zuñi, and found it to be 110. It was still necessary for her to be held on the bed. She slept but little, and the liquid nourishment prepared by the writer was given to her from the mouth of her mother in small quantities until the eleventh day, when there was a slight change for the better. The pulse was now 90, but on the twelfth day it rose to 100. On the night of that day the writer found the patient eating cold boiled potatoes, and on the following day she was indulged with unripe watermelon, which she seemed to enjoy greatly. The menses appeared on the thirteenth day, and the pulse was reduced to 80. The patient continued gradually to improve until her health was fully restored. The writer could not discover that any other than fetishistic medicines were administered to this girl.

Once, while the writer was deep in the mysteries of theurgism with Na'iuchi, an elderly woman hurried into the room and with streaming eyes and trembling voice urged the great theurgist to come to the bedside of her dying grandchild. Not a moment was to be lost if the life of this wee one, so precious to the parents and grandparents, was to be saved. The writer accompanied Na'iuchi, who closely followed the grandmother, and they found the infant, who was 18 months old, lying on a pallet in a comatose condition. The fond mother, half reclining by its side, looked the picture of despair. With tears rolling down her face she greeted the doctor and implored him to save the life of her child. Na'iuchi at once began his work. Taking his seat at the left of the child, he manipulated the entire body in the most heroic manner, giving special attention to the stomach and abdomen. The infant was not exposed to the air, as is usually the case during such treatment, Na'iuchi seeming to understand that the body must be kept warm with the blanket covering. In a few seconds after he began his treatment a faint wail from the child was heard, and later the groans from the little one were distressing to listen to; yet the mother sat by without saying one word to the theurgist,[a] and there was not even an expression of concern on his face for the pain he was inflicting upon the child. No medicine was used in this case, which appeared to the writer, on entering the room, to be an entirely hopeless one. Within an hour the patient was restored to its normal condition of health, and on the following morning the writer observed the infant on the back of its mother eating green watermelon, which seems not to have induced a return of cholera infantum.

In another case treated by Na'iuchi the child, though very low, was not in a comatose state. He remained but a short time with the little one, manipulating it as described above, and then left, saying: "I must go now to my fraternity, but will soon return." After an hour he went to his home, and securing medicine, made another visit to the infant. He mixed the medicine, which was an emetic, with warm water and administered a small quantity at a time by dipping a reed into the water and putting it to the child's mouth. After doing thus several times, Na'iuchi again left, giving instructions to the mother about repeating the dose. About two hours after the doctor departed, the infant, after copious vomiting, was found much improved and enjoying nourishment from the mother's breast.

Massage is the treatment for rheumatism, and sheep chips heated before the fire and sprinkled with water, which are used for any trouble that may be relieved by steady heat, are applied externally, one cake of the manure being kept by the fire while another is in use.

In 1896 the writer became interested in a child of 9 years afflicted with curvature of the spine. This child fell from a ladder when she was 5 years old, injuring her back, and she had been growing worse since the accident. She had a beautiful face and was so patient and gentle that she won the heart of the writer, and the two became fast friends. At this time there was no appearance of abscess. In 1902 the writer returned to Zuñi and found her little friend, who was then 15, suffering from a large lumbar abscess with probable caries of the vertebræ. The girl's face, though still beautiful, bore evidence of great suffering. She was colorless and emaciated, but with it all a most patient little sufferer. Her sad face and ever gentle bearing were profoundly touching. An incision had been made for the purpose of drainage, beginning in the lumbar region about 1½ inches above the crest of the pelvis at the outer side of the spinal column and running diagonally downward and forward to the inner side of the anterior superior spine of the ilium and continuing forward along the groin for nearly its entire extent. The wound was packed with a mix-

---

[a] The writer has never known a member of a family to interfere in the slightest degree with the treatment of the theurgist. It may be here stated that no precaution whatever is taken to prevent cholera infantum among the Zuñi children. As soon as an infant is able to hold anything in its hand the probability is that it will be sucking or biting on something not less harmful, perhaps, than a piece of unripe watermelon.

ture of piñon gum, kernels of squash seeds, and mutton grease, and a cotton bandage of many thicknesses was wrapped around the body. The writer, wishing to render such relief as was possible, called upon Doctor Wood, of the Indian Service, who had been sent from the Indian school at Albuquerque to treat diphtheria.[a]

After a short call upon the child the doctor left her to visit the diphtheria patients while the writer attended to having the wound cleansed for his inspection. The work assigned her was not an easy task. The parents of the child, who were in great distress over her suffering, were ready to obey instructions, but other members of the family feared to give offense to the doctor who was treating her. Their opposition was finally overcome by the suggestion that the Zuñi and American doctors meet and discuss the case. The father of the invalid at once hastened for the medicine man, who, on his arrival, made positive objection to any interference on the part of the American doctor. His scruples were overcome, however, and he placed the little sufferer over his knee, face downward. A doctress who was present heated water, and the process of cleansing the wound began. After applying the crushed kernels of squash seeds moistened in the mouth to soften the piñon gum, the doctor inserted his forefinger into the wound and drew out the gum. Some time was required to remove all of the packing, and a heart of stone would have been touched at the sound of the feeble moans and cries of the child. It seemed as if she must succumb to the supreme agony. Doctor Wood on his return found that the wound had been thoroughly freed of the gum and bathed with warm water and soap. He knew that the patient was beyond even temporary improvement and that all he could hope to do was to make the remaining hours as comfortable as possible. He sprinkled the wound with boracic acid and wrapped it with aseptic gauze. After a time a faint smile brightened the face of the sufferer as she whispered to the writer: "I feel as if I had never been sick, the pain is so little now." And so this little soldier, who had endured so much, lay in comparative comfort and peace for two days, when she fell into her everlasting sleep, leaving her "Washington mother" to tell of her beauty of person and soul.

Another interesting case of primitive surgery was that of a Hopi Indian who had been married many years to a Zuñi woman. He fell from a wagon and broke his left jaw. The inferior maxillary bone was removed, leaving a fistular opening in the cheek opposite the lobe of the ear, the rim of the opening having completely cicatrized when

---

[a] Doctor Wood's use of antitoxin soon brought the diphtheria under control. Too much cannot be said in praise of Miss Palen, the field matron, for her untiring work in carrying out the doctor's instructions. As the medicine man must be liberally compensated for his services, many of the Zuñis are glad to save the expense of the doctor's fee in cases of slight troubles by going to Miss Palen, in whom they have great confidence; at least this is the case with the more progressive Indians. Miss Palen professes to know but little about therapeutics, but her heart is in her work, and the Indians would hate to part with her.

seen by the writer. The man in conversation or when eating pressed his hand against the opening.

The writer has observed one case of dislocated kneecap for which splints and bandages were used—that of a child 6 years of age. In plate C a mother and two children are shown. The elder child with the right leg in splints is the one suffering from dislocated kneecap.

The Ne'wekwe (Galaxy) fraternity are famous for curing the bite of the rattlesnake. A man suffering from a wound must remain alone in a room, for should he chance to see a woman nourishing her infant he would surely die. A combination of three roots is chewed by the medicine man and applied to the wound. The patient also chews the roots. It is believed that if clouds gather after one is bitten, he is more likely to die, for then the snakes go about vigorously and the limbs swell to the heart; but if the sun shines hot, the snakes are lazy, and in four days the one bitten will be well.

WITCHCRAFT

Belief in witchcraft seems to be universal among the Indian tribes, and no great advance in civilization can be made among them until the beliefs and the accompanying practices are rooted out. It can not be hoped that this will be accomplished at once, at least if strangers to the religion and social customs of the people undertake the task. When it is remembered how recently reputed witches were put to death among our own people, and how persistently the negroes and the more ignorant whites still cling to the belief, what can be expected from peoples in that stage of culture where superstition is the prime factor in their lives?

Primitive man is less happy in his philosophy than enlightened man, because the latter has left behind many of his superstitions. The primitive man's world abounds in perplexing mysteries. All that his untutored mind fails to comprehend is associated with some occult power. This is the condition in which we find the North American Indians. These people are in constant terror of being conjured. Young mothers especially are solicitous for their infants, since these are the targets for the venom of diabolical beings. The child's head and face are always covered when a supposed witch approaches. Again, no man or woman who is reduced to poverty or has some physical deformity, especially any peculiarity that might be taken for the evil eye, or has made an enemy of a prominent member of the tribe, feels safe from accusation. The owner of fine beads and other adornments experiences much bitter with the sweet of possession because of the fear that some witch, prompted by jealousy, will strike him with disease. Moonlight is a great boon to those who must go about at night, for it enables them to identify suspicious objects. They say that witches love the night and lurk in shadows and darkness. Witches are believed to be able to assume the shape of beasts, and the domestic cat, on account of its stealthy habits and its ability to pass through small openings, is a favorite form.

The philosophy of these people is such that though the witch may be regarded as all powerful, none but the poor and unfortunate are condemned. Few others are even brought to trial, for although it may be whispered about that certain ones are witches, their prominence prevents public accusation. Several years ago the droughts were very serious, and a retired sun priest was suspected and impeached, and his place was filled by another. The people whispered among themselves, "He is a sorcerer." This man was in fact far superior in intelligence to his successor, who miscalculated altogether the winter solstice in 1894, and consequently threw the winter ceremonies out of time, much to the disgust of the wiser heads in Zuñi, who, in spite of the assumed infallibility of a sun priest, felt sure that this one had made a mistake. The previous incumbent, who had filled the office for many years, never miscalculated so far as the writer ever knew or heard.

While there are always among these people certain despised creatures who are referred to as witches or wizards, it remains for some direct cause, such as the illness or death of some resident of the village, to bring the supposed witch to trial. The attendant theurgist or some member of the invalid's family makes search for the person who has caused trouble, and alas for the poor creature who has offended the theurgist or who has an enemy in the house of the invalid, for he is sure to be pounced upon. In rare instances a member of the family of a deceased person takes the matter into his own hands. Such a case occurred some years ago, and was witnessed by Mr D. D. Graham, at that time trader at Zuñi. A man shot and killed a woman whom he accused of having bewitched his child and caused it to die. The man was not brought to trial, the court being satisfied with the declaration of the murderer that the woman was a witch. As witches are believed to be the direct cause of death, on conviction they suffer capital punishment.

The usual procedure is for a member of the family to make known his suspicion to the attendant theurgist, or for the theurgist himself to decide upon the person to be accused. One is seldom brought to trial unless death has actually taken place or the patient is near death. The theurgist must account for his inability to cure the patient, and this he does by bringing to trial the supposed guilty person whose malevolence defies the powers of the theurgist. In ordinary cases of sickness patients are relieved by the theurgist, who pretends to extract foreign matter "shot" into the body, and the sorcerer or witch is thus left unmolested, with only whispers against him.

The following stories of witchcraft were told by a prominent member of the Badger clan:

I spent some days with the missionary's wife. She gave me a good bed to sleep in and blankets to keep me warm. She was very kind to me, and I was happy in her house, but after a time I grew very ill and had to return to my mother's home. A shaman [a] was sent for and, through the power of the Beast Gods, he was enabled to discover the cause of my illness by placing pinches of sacred meal upon me, which opened to him the windows of my body. He discovered the disease and declared that I had been bewitched, and commanded the material which had been thrust into my body to come forth. He said he saw within me bits of the blankets I had slept between during my stay in the missionary's house, and bits of yarn and calico which the missionary's wife had given me. All this he commanded to come up through my mouth. The material ejected by me was so putrid that my mother and I could not distinguish the bits of blanket, yarn, and calico, but they were apparent to the all-powerful eye of the shaman. I do not know, but I think it was the old one-eyed woman who bewitched me. She was jealous of the good times I had at the mission.

At one time I had a very bad throat, which was much swollen and very painful. The theurgist came and soon discovered the cause of my suffering. A witch had shot a stone into my throat. The theurgist had to repeat many prayers to the Beast Gods before power was given him to extract the stone. He had to place his hands hard upon my throat and call with great power; but, obedient to his command, the foreign matter finally appeared. It was, he averred, a large, ugly stone, and he immediately cast it into the fire, as unfit for my mother and me to see.

A certain wizard painted his body red, and the scalp knot was painted in white on his breasts and knees. He placed wreathes of yucca around his wrists and ankles, and then entered the whirlwind, which is the friend of witches, headforemost. He traveled to the great river of the west and returned to Zuñi in one day. He went to the great river to steal the plume offerings deposited by the rain priests near Zuñi and carried by the butterflies attached to the plume sticks to the great river. [The spirit of the butterfly is supposed to carry the spirit of the plume offering.]

The whirlwind becoming weary dropped the wizard a short distance from Zuñi, and as he fell, a youth passing by exclaimed: "Aha, where have you been? Man, you are a sorcerer or you would not be traveling in the whirlwind." And the youth followed the wizard to the village and told his story, and it was discovered that the man was a wizard and had stolen the plume offerings of the rain priests. This wizard belonged to the Dogwood clan. He was tried by the Bow priesthood and was convicted and hung by the arms. No food was given him, and at the end of one night and a day he died. [b]

A wizard attached crow and owl plumes to his head that he might have the eyes of the crow to see quickly the approach of man and the eyes of the owl to travel by night. He flapped his arms and left Zuñi after the people were asleep. He visited the Apaches and told them to come in four days and destroy the Zuñis. At daylight a Zuñi man was on his way to gather wood; hearing a cry like an owl, yet human, he looked about him and found a man whom he recognized as a Zuñi. "Aha!" said he, "Why have you those plumes upon your head? Aha, you are a sorcerer." "Do not betray me," said the sorcerer, "and I will give you many blankets and all my precious beads, and in four days, when the Apaches come, as I have told them to do, I will go out and have them kill me." "No," was the reply, "I do not wish

---

[a] See p. 567.

[b] Accused witches are hanged by suspending them by the elbows, which are brought back as far as possible, from a beam of the old church built several centuries ago by the Spaniards. If death does not occur at the time desired by the Bow priesthood, the unfortunate is struck on the head with a war club and so relieved of prolonged suffering.

your things; but if you will allow the Apaches to take your life when they come, I will not tell." The man, thinking that perhaps the sorcerer had lied and that the Apaches were already on their way to Zuñi, hastened to a place near by, gathered such wood as he could, and returned home. His wife chided him for the poor quality of the wood: "You always bring good wood and a large back load; now you bring but little, and that very poor." But he did not betray the secret; and on the fourth morning he listened attentively, and when he heard the ax striking upon the rock, which was the signal given by the witch, he hurried from the village and found that the Apaches had indeed been met by this man and that they had killed him, not knowing him to be a sorcerer and their friend. The Apaches had gone, leaving the body of the sorcerer lying upon crossed arrows. A Navaho, whom the Zuñi met on the road, and who accompanied him to where the body lay, exclaimed: "The Apaches have killed a friend." "How do you know?" inquired the Zuñi. "Because," said the Navaho, "it is their custom and ours when we kill a friend through mistake to place the body upon crossed arrows that all may know that a friend and not an enemy has been killed." "But how is it the Apaches value this man, who is one of your people?" asked the Navaho; and the Zuñi replied, "He was a sorcerer."

All the crops of the Zuñi farming district of Pescado were destroyed one year by grasshoppers, which came so thick that they made the air black. It was discovered by a man digging in the field that this misfortune was brought upon them by a witch or wizard, who had mixed together some blue and red beans, a grasshopper, finely ground corn meal, some wheat, and other varieties of seeds. These he wrapped first in a piece of white cotton cloth, afterward in red calico and buckskin, and buried 3 feet in the ground.

The following story was related by a young mother:

I was sleeping alone in the large upper room. My brother slept on the roof near by. I was awakened by the approach of a creature like a large cat; but it was not a cat; I knew at once that it was a witch. It came close to my bed and looked at my little one, and then hastened from the room. It went out through the broken window pane. In a short time my baby died.

A young man came to the writer's camp one morning in a state of great excitement. He had a very sick wife and related that upon leaving his house on the previous night to attend a meeting of his fraternity he noticed a queer looking burro lurking before the house. Upon his return he was told by those who sat with his wife that a large cat had entered the house, and he knew at once that a witch or wizard had been there. He hastened from the house to discover a man wrapped in a blanket, but not in the Zuñi fashion; his head was sunk low in the blanket. Accosting this creature, whom he knew to be a wizard, he told him that if his wife died, he should inform Nai'uchi, the elder brother Bow priest, and have him hanged. Fortunately for the accused the wife soon recovered her health.

The vice pa'mosono'kĭa (female assistant to the scalp custodian) was debarred from office in 1889 by the elder brother Bow priest, who declared her to be a witch. Her son was first brought to trial as a wizard upon the ground that he had caused the death of many children, and while he hung by the arms from a beam in the old church he declared that his mother knew more than he and that he acted only under her influence. The vice pa'mosono''kĭa was then summoned and hung by the arms. At first she asserted her innocence, but finally the elder brother Bow priest declared that her only chance for life was in divulging the secrets of her craft by producing medicine and showing how it was obtained. One of this woman's accusers was a neighbor, who stated that she had stolen a buckskin sack from his house, had killed his mi'li (see page 416), and had deposited excrement in his house. Her only protection being the ready invention of falsehoods, she told how she had sent her son to the neighbor's house to steal the sack, cut the heart (the various seeds) of the mi'li, and deposit the excrement. All this was intended to lend efficacy to her medicine and bring death to the people of the house. She combined the heart of the mi'li with the hearts of the rattlesnake and toad, and this mixture she shot into the children. Her story had its effect upon the warriors, who listened attentively. They concluded that she must indeed know much of medicine, and upon her promise that she would never again destroy the life of another, they released her, but the son was killed.

Hundreds of times the writer has observed the theurgist working over his patient, pretending to extract substances "shot" into the body by witches. Objects of great variety, such as bits of yarn, a charred goat's horn, etc., were produced, and though the observer was usually by the side of the theurgist or on the opposite side of the patient from him, she was never able to discover where or how the object supposed to be taken from the body of the patient had been secreted and produced until, in 1904, she observed Nai'uchi practice (for sore eyes) upon his last patient. The old man was led to the invalid's house by his granddaughter, Nina. There he pretended to extract pebbles from the eyes of his patient, but his hands were feeble, and he was so awkward that it was readily seen that he carried the pebbles in his mouth and dropped them into the palm of his hand while pretending to breathe upon it.

A singular feature associated with witchcraft is that accused persons are permitted to be conspicuous in religious entertainments and sometimes to aid in religious festivals. A man belonging to the 'Hle'wekwe (Wood) fraternity or Sword swallowers, which is one of the most important in Zuñi, was regarded by a majority of the people as a wizard, yet he was not debarred from membership in his fraternity. During the last visit of the writer to Zuñi this man entertained one of the Sha'-läko (giant gods) at the annual ceremonial, at which six of these gods are personated, though it is regarded as a high privilege to prepare one's house, which must be thoroughly renovated for the reception of the Sha'läko. This poor fellow, who was poor also in worldly goods, after having the honor accorded to him, made every effort at his meager command to have his house suitable for the reception of the god he was to entertain. He labored hard and long each day, for he was so much despised for his poverty that few would aid him. During his labors upon the improvement of his house, a favorite patient of Nai'uchi's died; but he was not allowed to die in peace. He was interrogated regarding the cause of his trouble and implicated the member of the Sword swallowers above referred to, and while the invalid lay dying, the accused man was summoned and tried by the Bow priesthood in his presence. The accused declared he knew nothing of witchcraft, but his judges pressed him to tell what he had done to the sufferer. Finally, realizing that pleading innocence would be of no avail, he declared that he injured the man by touching his throat with the tips of his fingers, hoping by this statement to inspire the jurors with his supernatural power and thus save himself from torture; but he was condemned, and returned to his home to await the hour of execution.

Near midnight the writer was notified that this man was to be put to death. It seemed too terrible to believe, and hastening from her camp to the village she met Nai'uchi as he was returning from the deathbed of his patient. The great theurgist and elder brother Bow priest was urged to withdraw his verdict on the ground that he might be mistaken. Since he was obdurate, he was told that the United States Government would certainly punish him. He retorted: "I am your friend. Friends do not betray one another. Would you betray me to the soldiers?" "I have not said I would inform upon you," was the reply; "I am too much your friend to wish to see you suffer." "I shall hang this wizard, even though I displease you," he declared. "I shall hang him though the United States Government put me in prison for one month, six months, a year, or forever. He has killed my child, and he must die." The writer and the theurgist soon reached the house of the latter and stood by a lamp attached to the wall of the large living room. The light fell upon Nai'uchi's face and the expression, usually so kind, was now set and stern. There was nothing of rage expressed, only the firm determination of a man bent upon doing his duty though he lost his life by the act. "Do you care for me at all?" asked the writer. "I have told you I am your friend." "Will you do one thing for me?" "Anything but what you have just asked." "I wish that you would delay hanging the man until to-morrow night." "So that you can send to Fort Wingate and have the soldiers come for me?" "No, I will not send for the soldiers, nor will I inform anyone upon you." "Then, I will wait until to-morrow night; but the wizard shall then be hanged." The position of the writer was a delicate one. The man must be saved, but she must not make an enemy of a tried friend and one of the men most important to her in her studies. All work was suspended on the improvement of the house of the accused. On entering a miserable apartment on an upper floor of his house early on the morning following the writer's conversation with Nai'uchi, a sad scene was presented. The accused sat upon the floor, leaning against the wall, a picture of abject despair, though perfectly calm. His wife, who was ill, sat on one side and his young daughter, ready to become a mother, on the other. The eyes of both women were swollen and inflamed from weeping, and they continued to weep as they clung to the man they loved. It would not do for the writer's presence in this house to become known. Taking the man's hand she said: "Have faith in me; I will save you." His face became radiant for a moment; then the stoical sadness returned, and, smiling faintly as he thanked her, he said: "No, mother; you wish to save me, but you can not. Nai'uchi has spoken." Adding another word of assurance the writer hurriedly left the house without being discovered. Before night came she held a court of her own, Nai'uchi, the younger brother Bow priest, and the accused being present, and the result was that the unfortunate was released. This was brought about by a declaration on the part of the writer that she had deprived the man of his power of sorcery; and he was soon at work upon his house, fitting it for the reception of a Sha'läko god.

One must witness a trial for witchcraft to appreciate all the horrors associated with this superstition. The writer has never seen anything else in aboriginal life which so thoroughly aroused her indignation as did a trial for witchcraft in which a child of 12 years, the girl previously referred to as suffering from a severe case of hysteria, and a youth of not more than 17 were involved. She had been brought from a farming district to Zuñi to be placed under the care of a theurgist. Her illness must be accounted for, and upon inquiry it was learned that on the morning before the attack she was seen romping with a young man, who held her hands, and this was sufficient evidence to bring him before the court for trial. The grandfather of the girl, himself a member of the Bow priesthood, went to inform Nai'uchi, but he was then with a very sick patient and must not be disturbed, so the younger brother Bow priest was notified, and he called together such members of the Bow priesthood as were in Zuñi. Then the old grandfather came for the writer, who was engaged in important work with a rain priest. The hour was late, the night cold, and they seemed quite safe from intrusion, but one should never be surprised however sudden the appearance of an Indian in Zuñi or in any other Indian land. Often they seem to rise from the earth or to drop from the clouds. On hearing approaching footsteps, the rain priest declared he must not be caught talking, and disappeared behind a portière just as the grandfather of the sick girl stepped into the camp. He had come to ask his mother to go with him to his house that he might prove to her that his granddaughter had been bewitched. They had the culprit in custody and the court was assembled to try him. There was nothing left for the writer to do but to leave the priest without formality and accompany the grandfather. Not a word was spoken when the house was entered. The members of the court and the others bowed their heads in greeting. Near the east end of the long room five members of the Bow priesthood formed a semicircle. The accused, a handsome youth, sat slightly back with a warrior on either side of him. The patient lay on a pallet on the opposite side of the room, every member of her body in violent motion. Her mother attempted to keep the head quiet, while the brother clung to her legs. The poor little arms were thrown wildly about until an aunt essayed to control them. The writer passed to the pallet and sat by the sufferer. The custom of trying the accused in the presence of the afflicted is barbarous, and is likely to have a most unhappy effect on the patient. In the present case the result was most disastrous. A theurgist of the Galaxy fraternity sat on a low stool, some 15 feet west of the group of warriors, and faced east. He sprinkled a line of meal 3 feet in length before him, then placed his mi'li (see page 416) at the east end of the line, and deposited a crystal about 2 inches high midway down the line. A medicine bowl and a basket of sacred meal were by his side. A woman of the household deposited a vase of water and a gourd at the right of the theurgist, who lifted a gourd of water as he began his prayers, in scarcely audible tones, and emptied it into the medicine bowl. Six gourds of water were poured into the bowl as prayers were addressed to the Beast Gods of the six regions to give the theurgist, who is simply the agent of these gods, power to see the disease and heal the patient. Medicine was afterwards sprinkled into the water, six fetishes were dropped in, and a cross, signifying the four regions, and a circle, the world symbol, were formed on the surface of the water with sacred meal. After the water had been consecrated, the theurgist rose and dipped ashes from the fireplace with the eagle plumes and deposited them near the meal line and north of it. In a moment he lifted some of the ashes with the two plumes and sprinkled them to the north; again dipping ashes, he sprinkled them to the west; and then continued the sprinkling to the four regions for physical purification. Then he dipped the feather ends of his eagle plumes into the medicine water and put them to his lips. Again dipping them into the water, he sprinkled the invalid, who was held in sitting posture by her father, whom she had asked to stay by her in this trying ordeal. The tenderness of those about the little sufferer was most pathetic. The faces of both parents bore evidence of intense mental suffering. The theurgist rubbed the girl's body with the medicine water and prayed. He then placed his lips to her breast, pretending to draw material from her heart; this he deposited on the floor and covered with the meal.

Again he took ashes from the fireplace and deposited them as before by the meal line; and again he sprinkled them to the four regions. After the sprinkling of the ashes, he compelled the girl to drink four times from the medicine bowl, though she almost strangled in the effort. At other times the mother took a mouthful of water and placed her lips to those of the child, thus relieving her feverish thirst. The theurgist, having completed the treatment of the patient, lifted the material supposed to have been extracted from her heart with his two eagle plumes, deposited it in a corn husk, and carried it from the room. As soon as the theurgist left, the accused was made to sit closer to the group of warriors, and the trial began. The first accuser was the grandfather of the invalid, who declared that the boy accosted the child a short distance from her house and that she returned in a demented condition. The boy most earnestly denied the accusation, declaring that he knew nothing of witchcraft. The grandfather appealed to the invalid, begging her to tell all she knew, to talk without fear: "Hota (granddaughter), tell us." The child, held up by her grandfather, told her story with great difficulty in broken sentences. The spasms made it almost impossible for her to articulate, and her head was not still for an instant. Her story was soon told: "When a short distance from my house this boy wanted me to go with him, and when I refused, he grabbed my hand. As soon as he touched me, I began to tremble, and I ran home." The parents added: "And in a short time our child was crazy, as you see her now." The fact is, the child was perfectly rational, but her nervous condition induced them to think her mind was not right. Again the grandfather sat before the accused and demanded that he tell what medicine he used on the girl. The boy made no response. Others of the court commanded him to speak, threatening him with punishment if he remained silent. One who was a theurgist of the fraternity to which the boy belonged drew near and urged him to speak, using persuasion rather than threats. Again and again he was menaced, but for half an hour no word escaped his lips, and his head was bowed. The writer observed that he was closely watching every movement of the girl. Finally he spoke in low and measured words: "Once, when I visited the pueblo of Santo Domingo, I was asked by the mo'sona (director) of the Galaxy fraternity of that place if I wished to learn the secrets of witchcraft. Then he asked the same of my companion, a Santo Domingo boy. We told him we should like to know his secrets. We followed him at midnight, when all slept, to his house and to an inner room. The director placed two round cases of hide beside him, and from these he took many medicines. He had every kind of medicine. He asked me what I most desired. I told him love philters, that I might captivate girls as I wished. Then the director asked my companion, and he chose the same. The director deposited root medicine in two bowls; the medicine in one was for me and that in the other for my companion. He directed us when intending to use it to bite off the smallest quantity, chew it, and spit it into our hands, then to rub them together and shake hands with the girl we wished to control. He also gave us a root medicine to counteract the effect of the other. He prepared two plume offerings for each of us. At daybreak he placed a root medicine in a bowl and poured water over it, and as he stirred the water with his reed, suds rose high, like a mountain. He did not sing, but talked low while he made the suds. He then bathed our heads and entire bodies in the medicine suds, and directed us to take our plume offerings to the fields and plant them under a ledge of rock, so that the eyes of the plume sticks should look west, not to the sun, as that would offend the Sun Father. Returning to the village and seeing two maidens bearing water vases upon their heads, we chewed our medicine, rubbed our hands together and approached them. We shook hands with the girls and they went on to their homes, and after depositing the water vases, seated themselves, for they felt their hearts flying around. Each girl sat still a minute, then jumped up and turned around like a top, then slept a moment, and then threw her arms wildly about. They could not keep their heads or legs still. They jumped up and ran about the streets. We did not make these girls our wives. They were too crazy. In a short time they died." It was evident to the writer that the boy had made use of his observations of the girl in weaving his story, and it was a clever thought which prompted him to claim to possess a medicine which would counteract the effect of the other. His tale was no sooner told than the warriors declared in one voice that they must have proof of what they had heard: "We must see the medicine. You must produce it." Whereupon the grandfather of the girl was detailed to accompany the accused to his home for the medicine. On his return he drew two kinds of roots from his pocket. That which would produce insanity was in one piece; that capable of counteracting its effect was in three pieces. He claimed he could make himself crazy and well again at will, according to the root he used. His description of these roots as he presented them for the inspection of his judges was dramatic. The warriors had become so absorbed by their interest in the narrative of the boy that they seemed entirely to have forgotten the cause of his appearance before them. In one voice they demanded a manifestation. The boy removed his head-kerchief and trousers, leaving on only his beads and breechcloth, the moccasins having been removed on entering the room. He asked for a basket of sacred meal and sprinkling some on the floor, covering a space about 4 inches square, he examined the roots: first the piece that would produce insanity, which he laid south of the meal, then the three bits of good medicine, which he deposited north of the meal. He now sang in so low a voice that it was impossible for the writer to understand what he was saying. Taking a bite from the root south of the meal, he chewed it, ejected it upon his hands, and rubbed his body. In a moment he distorted his face, spun around, and jumped about; then, shaking his body violently, rushed to the invalid, pulling at her arms and running his hands over them. The spectacle was so harassing that it was with difficulty the writer retained her composure. The child's efforts to scream as she endeavored to release herself from the grasp of her father and brother who held her, her terror each time the boy approached her, the cries of the women, and the tears of the men, except the warriors, who were absorbed in what was going on before them, presented a scene never to be forgotten. When the boy had preyed upon the credulity of the warriors as long as he deemed wise, he swallowed a small quantity of the other medicine and became perfectly rational in his demeanor. He now touched the girl's lips with his own and pretended to draw disease from her heart, while she was almost thrown into convulsions by his touch. He ejected into his hand what he pretended to have drawn from her heart, and deposited it upon the meal; he then compelled the girl to swallow three bits of the good root medicine. She nearly strangled in the effort, but the parents insisted that she swallow it, in hopes of her restoration. After this the boy coolly took meal from the basket, stood and offered a long prayer, sprinkled meal upon the material supposed to have been extracted from the girl, asked for a corn husk, gathered the meal together into his hands and deposited it in the husk, and left the chamber, accompanied by the grandfather of the girl. They went west of the village, where the boy buried the husk, and returned within thirty minutes; then the two occupied their former seats and the warriors interrogated the boy until 2 o'clock in the morning. The child was in such an alarming condition of nervousness that the writer decided that the farce must end. After a few words with the warriors, they agreed to retire and release the boy, with the understanding that he should accompany two of them to the writer's camp later in the morning. While the writer was breakfasting, the grandfather of the little invalid appeared and informed her that the boy had escaped, news which was most gratifying to her, but which enraged the Bow priests. The elder brother Bow priest at once ordered the grandfather of the girl to mount his horse and capture the boy. After some miles of hard riding the boy was overtaken and brought back to Zuñi and to the house of the poor little sufferer, who was subjected to another ordeal, while Nai'uchi gratified his thirst for the marvelous by subjecting the boy to a second trial, himself now acting as chief justice of the court.

AGED WOMAN CARRYING FAGOTS

FLAYING A BEEF

When the boy repeated his story, Nai'uchi declared it to be a lie: "You did not get your knowledge of witchcraft from Santo Domingo, and I am here to see that you speak the truth. I shall keep you talking until you do speak the truth." Losing all faith in winning belief for his story, the wretched boy invented another, which he hoped would satisfy his judge: "Yes; I lied. I lied because I loved my father and mother and sister, and did not wish to speak of them. They are witches. I belong to the family of original witches. All my grandfathers were wizards. I have the plume offerings brought to this world by my witch ancestors." "Where? Where?" exclaimed the warriors in one breath, as they bent eagerly forward, so as not to lose one word. "In my mother's house. There at the winter solstice witches gather from all over the country to prevent the rains and snows." "You lie," cried one of the warriors. "We would know of this if it were true." "How?" inquired the boy. "Some one would see the strangers come." "No; they would not. Ancient plume offerings held to our hearts and yucca strings crossed over our breasts, while we jump through a hoop made of yucca, empower us to make ourselves into dogs, cats, coyotes, hawks, crows, and owls, so that we pass quickly and unknown about the country. We gather in an inner room of my mother's house where four ancient lamps hang, one on each wall, and by this light we sit and talk and make the rain-makers angry, so that they will not work. I can assume the form of a cat and pass through the smallest hole to enter a house. I can fill my mouth with cactus needles and shoot them through windows and destroy life. I have killed two infants, three girls, and two boys. I have packages of ancient prayer plumes, and I have two others that are used to convert us into other forms than our own." "We will see them! We will see them!" exclaimed the warriors. The boy had not anticipated this in weaving a story which he thought might make his accusers fear to take his life. "Alas! I can not show them; they are in my mother's ancestral house, and she is absent at the farming district and has the keys." Nai'uchi, not to be thwarted, exclaimed: "I have keys!" He left the house to procure them, and in a short time returned with a bunch of keys and commanded the accused to proceed to his mother's house.

The assembled warriors and the writer, who was always provided with candles and matches, accompanied Nai'uchi and the boy. Ascending a ladder from a court the party, led by the accused, climbed over several roofs to reach the house. The door was locked, but it yielded to the first key. The warriors have great authority and are not delicate about using or abusing it, and it may be presumed that if the keys had failed, the doors would have been forced. The boy maintained remarkable composure as he entered the house. He declared that the prayer plumes were secreted in the wall of the adjoining room,

and that he feared his mother's anger should he break the plaster.
The warriors cried "Expose them! Expose them!" One handed an
ax to the boy and commanded him to go to work. With the first
stroke a large quantity of plaster fell crumbling to the floor. The
room was almost dark, the faintest light penetrating through the
door. The writer lighted a candle and held it so as to throw the best
possible light upon the worker. After a quantity of plaster had fallen
the boy stooped to examine it. Again he used the ax and more plaster
fell, and again he stooped and looked for the prayer plumes, while the
warriors watched eagerly to see that nothing escaped them. The
scene was weird in the extreme. The handsome youth was clearly
visible by the candle held near him as he worked, apparently calmly
and leisurely, stopping to examine the plaster each time it fell, thinking to weary the watchers and accusers. When the west wall was
half robbed of its plaster and the prayer plumes were not found, the
warriors became impatient. The dust in the room was stifling, and
when the warriors accused the boy of having deceived them he declared
that the plume sticks were deposited two years before and that he could
not remember the exact location of them. The impatience of the
accusers becoming greater, they said: "You have lied! You have
lied!" The boy made no reply, but led them into an adjoining room,
thence through a hatchway so small that all passed through with difficulty into a room below. This room was very small and low, and
would have been absolutely dark but for the candle. After passing
on into a room still deeper in the heart of the great beehive, a strange
scene occurred. The youth was closely followed by the writer, and
when he stooped in the dungeon-like room all gathered about him and
discovered two packages of old prayer plumes on the floor beside a
concretion fetish that was some 6 inches in diameter. There was consternation among the warriors, who exclaimed in one voice: "What
does this mean?" Now they felt assured that the youth had spoken the
truth. The accused separated the packages and explained each prayer
plume. The concretion is a fetish for corn, and was placed here by the
witches, declared the boy, that the crops might be destroyed. The
examination of the prayer plumes by the warriors was thorough and
the explanation by the accused deemed most complete. But the warriors were not to be satisfied until the prayer plumes used to transform
the witch into beast form were produced. In despair, the boy declared
they must be in a room below, but as there was no ladder it would be
impossible for him to descend. The warriors decided to let one of two
young men who followed the party to the house descend into the lower
chamber. He was held by the arms and lowered. The candle was then
reached to him by his companion, who went headforemost through the
hatchway and was held by his feet. A diligent search was not rewarded
with success, and the man was with difficulty dragged back through the

hatchway. Again the warriors gathered about the two packages and listened to the marvelous tales told by the accused; then Na'iuchi took possession of them and the party ascended to the upper floor, where the boy was set to work to remove more plaster, in the hope that the much-coveted prayer plumes might be found. After another hour's work an old prayer plume appeared among the plaster, which the boy declared to be one of those he was looking for. This plume stick, he asserted, when planted in the ground the top down, or when worn in the belt in the same position, so offended the rain-makers that they refused to water the earth. It must be worn over the heart to convert one into animal form. If the boy tricked the warriors with the plume stick, supposed to be found in the plaster, the deception was well done. There was great rejoicing among them, but they were not to be satisfied with the one prayer plume; they must have the other, and they did not leave the room until driven out late in the day by the intense cold and the dust from the plaster. At the suggestion of the writer, the accused now accompanied her to her camp under guard of Na'iuchi and the grandfather of the girl. She was not sure what Na'iuchi intended to do with the boy, but was determined that the poor fellow should not be hanged. The boy was seated with a warrior on either side of him, and the writer talked to him and doctored him a little, and finally convinced Na'iuchi that the boy would never again be able to practice his diabolical art, and that therefore it was not necessary to hang him. He was not yet freed, however, but was conducted to the large plaza, where Na'iuchi called the warriors to assemble. The populace, in the meantime, crowded into the place, people of both sexes and all ages. When the warriors did not respond promptly, Na'iuchi called in loud and angry tones for their immediate presence. They were not long in obeying the second command of their chief. A wagon in the plaza was filled with women and children, who took advantage of the elevated position. The sun had set and the shadows of night were gathering. The accused looked weary and he leaned against the wagon, as if sadly in need of support. The warriors gathered closely about him, and the writer stood by the side of Na'iuchi. The eager spectators apparently understood that the boy was about to speak, and there was a profound silence. As the night advanced several lanterns were brought forth, the writer placing hers in the hand of a warrior who stood by her side so that she could direct the light as she chose. The appetite of the warriors for marvels was not yet satisfied. Na'iuchi called upon the already exhausted youth to confess his crimes before the people. He was kept talking until midnight, when the prayer plumes and medicines produced by the accused earlier in the day were placed by Na'iuchi upon the ground immediately before the youth, whereupon the people moved in a great wave toward the spot to peer at the mysteries.

The longer the boy talked the more absorbed he became in his subject. He added many wonderful statements to those made during the day. At times his face became radiant with satisfaction at his power over his listeners. His final stroke made it evident that he intended to protect himself against all further persecution, for he closed with the remark: "I did possess all the power of my wizard forefathers. It came to me through many generations. I have been all-powerful in witchcraft. But since visiting my mother's camp this evening I have lost all power. While with my mother, and while she talked to me, I felt my eyes change from black to blue, and then turn from blue to black, and then I felt that all my power of witchcraft was gone, not only for a little while, but for all time. Alas! No more shall I be great among my people. I shall be one of them no more. My power is all gone! all gone forever!" Hundreds cried out: "Good! Good! Thanks, mother! Thanks!" Na'iuchi took the writer's hand and expressed his gratitude and that of his people, with regrets that she could not remain among them and rob all witches of their power to destroy. This incident is mentioned simply to show that it is possible, if these people are managed in the right way, to overcome their miserable superstitions.

Na'iuchi presented the complete set of prayer plumes and medicines to the writer, requesting her to show them to the President as proof that witches do exist in Zuñi; for these people had had threats from the United States Government regarding their practice of hanging persons accused of witchcraft. These threats, however, were never carried into execution until after the writer had left Zuñi in 1896, when Na'iuchi and several others were arrested for hanging a woman they had accused of witchcraft. Help came in time to save the woman, and troops were stationed in Zuñi to protect the Government teachers while Na'iuchi and others were in prison in Albuquerque, awaiting their trial. During this period the words of the writer's poor misguided, but dear and tried, friend, Na'iuchi, came often to her: "They may imprison me for one month, six months, a year, or forever, but I shall hang the witch who destroys the life of my child."

Primitive man must be approached according to his understanding; thus the prime requisite for improving the conditions of the Indian is familiarity with Indian thought and customs. Those possessing superior intelligence and a love for humanity, and only such, may lead our Indians from darkness into light. The Indian will never be driven.

ESOTERIC FRATERNITIES

ORIGIN AND FUNCTIONS OF THE FRATERNITIES

Previous to the coming of the A'shiwi (Zuñis) to this world through Ji'mi⁺kĭanapkĭatea, certain others appeared coming through the same place, which the Zuñis locate in the far northwest; and these others, by direction of the Sun Father, traveled eastward, crossing the country by a northern route to Shi'papolima[a] (place of mist).

After remaining four years (time periods) at Shi'papolima, this party of gods—for such they were or became—moved eastward and southward a short distance, and made their home at Chi'pia, located by the Zuñis in Sandia (watermelon) mountain, New Mexico. This mountain is believed by the Sia to be the home of their gods of war, who bear the same names as the Zuñi gods—U'yuyewi and Ma⁺sai'lema.[b]

The gods of Chi'pia compose the group known to the Zuñis as Kok'ko⁺hlan'na (great God): Shits'ukĭa, Kwe'lele, and six Shumai'koli for the six regions, with their Sai'apa (warriors).

Just four years after these gods came to this world another party appeared through Ji'mi⁺kĭanapkĭatea, consisting of Po'shaiyänki, his associates, and the possessors of the secret of O'naya'nakĭa (Mystery medicine), Po'shaiyänki, who figures as the culture hero of the Zuñis, being the leader. These also followed a northern route to Shi'papolima, where they remained. This place is held sacred by the Zuñis as the home of their culture hero and of the Beast Gods. The Zuñis believe the entrance to Shi'papolima to be on the summit of a mountain about 10 miles from the pueblo of Cochiti, N. Mex. Two crouching lions, or cougars, of massive stone in bas-relief upon the solid formation of the mountain top guard the sacred spot. The heads of the animals are to the east. A stone wall some 4 feet high forms an inclosure 18 feet in diameter for the cougars. Additional stone walls, also about 4 feet in height and 14 feet in length, mark a passageway 3 feet wide from the inclosure. A monument of stones stands 12 feet before the middle of the entrance, which faces east or a little south of east. It is remarkable that these wonderful pieces of aboriginal sculpture should have no legends associated with them by the Indians who live in comparatively close proximity. The Jemez, Sia, San Juan, Santa Clara, San Ildefonso, and Cochiti Indians have been closely questioned regarding

---

[a] Dr Fewkes gives the Hopi name as Si'papu, which is, according to Hopi lore, their place of nativity, or coming through to this world. Bandelier gives the Keres name as Shi'papu, the place of nativity of that people. The writer found the Sia Indians, who are Keres, using the form Shi'papo. Among the Zuñis the name is Shi'papolima and its signification is quite different; Shi'papolima is not the place of their nativity, but the home chosen by Po'shaiyänki (Zuñi culture hero) and his followers.

[b] Ma⁺sai'lema is the term used in ceremonials for the younger God of War, but in common parlance he is called Ma'asewe. These names are used only in reference to war or combat; at other times both the elder and younger Gods of War are referred to as A'hayuta.

these carvings, and while they have no history associated with them other than that the lions were converted into stone at the time the great fire spread over the earth, the Zuñis believe them to be the guardians of the place chosen by Po'shaiyänki as a home for himself and his followers. The writer visited this spot in 1904 and found these carvings to be just as the Zuñi theurgists had described them to her, other than that the heads of the lions had been defaced by the vandalism of sheep herders. When Mr Stevenson visited Shi'papo-lima in 1880 these carvings were in perfect condition.

In four years from Po'shaiyänki's nativity the A'shiwi came through Ji'miᵗkĭanapkĭatea, and soon after their reaching this world the Divine Ones organized four fraternities.

The following account was given to the writer by the mo'sona (director) of the Ne'wekwe ti'kili (Galaxy fraternity) and verified by a number of other priests and theurgists:

While the A'shiwi were yet in the undermost world, two men and two women, married couples, rubbed the epidermis from their bodies and, rolling it into a ball, placed it on the ground; and the four sat around it and sang, each one shaking a rattle. After a time a youth appeared dancing in place of the ball, and this youth, who was named Bi'ᵗsi'si, was held in high regard by the people. Soon after the creation of Bi'ᵗsi'si the A'shiwi began their ascent to the outer world. [a]

The first organization was composed of one of the couples who created Bi'ᵗsi'si, these two being the original members of the fraternity which the Divine Ones named Shi'wannakwe.[b] The membership of the Shi'wannakwe was immediately increased by the original male member selecting a pe'kwĭn (deputy), a Pi'ᵗläshiwanni (warrior), and others, and initiating them into the secrets which Kŏw'wituma and Wats'usi had intrusted to him and his wife. The songs for rain given to the Shi'wannakwe at that time have special influence upon the Council of the Gods, who direct the rain-makers.

The second fraternity organized by the Divine Ones was the Ne'-wekwe, the original members being the other couple who assisted at the creation of Bi'ᵗsi'si; of whom this man too initiated others. Bi'ᵗsi'si, owing to his special qualifications, was chosen to be musician and entertainer, or harlequin, to the fraternity, bearing the name

---

[a] The following is a bit of Sia cosmogony:

He, Sus'sĭstinnako (creator), drew a line of meal from north to south, and crossed it midway with one from east to west, and he placed two little parcels north of the cross line, one on each side of the line running north and south. These parcels are very valuable and precious, but the people do not know to this day of what they consist; no one ever knew but the creator Sus'sĭstinnako. After placing the parcels in position, Sus'sĭstinnako sat down on the west side of the line running north and south, south of the cross line, and began to sing, and in a little while the two parcels accompanied him in the song by shaking like rattles. The music was low and sweet, and after a while two women appeared, one evolving from each parcel. (The Sia, Eleventh Annual Report Bureau of Ethnology, 1894.)

[b] Shi from shi'li; plural, shi'we, meat. Kwe is a plural termination referring to people, the word ti'kili (fraternity) being seldom used in referring to a fraternity. Kwa tesh'kwi (not forbidden), though not expressed in words is understood, and the full meaning of Shi'wannakwe is, people who do not fast from animal food.

Pa'yatämu.[a]   The Shi'wannakwe and Ne'wekwe, owing to the close
relation of the two original couples, are allied to one another, the
Shi'wannakwe being regarded as the elder brother of the Ne'wekwe.
The Divine Ones named the third fraternity they organized 'Sän'ia-
kĭakwe (Hunters).   This fraternity is also called Sus'kikwe (Coyote).
The fourth fraternity they named 'Hle'wekwe (Wood people).   The
Divine Ones gave medicines and songs to each fraternity.

After the A'shiwi had settled at Häl'ona (Ant place), the Divine Ones
visited Shi'papolima and there met Po'shaiyänki, his associates, and the
body of men holding the secrets of Mystery medicine.   Po'shaiyänki
and his associates were already initiated into the mysteries of O'naya'-
nakĭa before the arrival of the Divine Ones, who declared to him
that they must have guardians for the six regions of the world and
for the whole world, but that man could not fill these places: they must
have some one with cunning of scent and sight.   They thereupon
changed the men possessing the secrets of Mystery medicine into
beasts.   One, becoming the cougar, was dispatched to the North to
guard that region; another was changed into the bear and made guardian of the West; another, changed into the badger, was sent to the
South; another, transformed to the white (gray) wolf, was sent to the
East; another, made into the eagle, was sent to the Zenith; still another,
converted into the shrew, was sent to the Nadir.   Others were converted into rattlesnakes that they might preside with wisdom over the
six regions; others into ants that they might scatter their houses over
the earth, these becoming the zoic gods of the A'shiwi.

The Divine Ones, when leaving Shi'papolima, requested Po'shaiyänki with his associate Na'ke'e and others to accompany them to
Häl'ona and initiate the A'shiwi into the mysteries of O'naya'nakĭa
(Mystery medicine).   On reaching Häl'ona, the A'kwa a'mosi (makers
of medicine water) of the Shi'wannakwe and Ne'wekwe fraternities
were initiated into the order of Mystery medicine, and these afterward
initiated the others of their fraternities.   The Divine Ones wishing
more fraternities, formed one composed of Na'ke'e and his wife and
another man.   These initiated others into the mysteries of O'nay-
a'nakĭa and also of eating large coals of fire.   This organization the
Divine Ones named Ma''ke 'Hlan'nakwe (Great Fire fraternity),
Na'ke'e becoming the original director.   Having received the knowledge of sword swallowing from Ä'chiyälä'topa (a being with wings

---

[a] Pa'yatämu of the Ne'wekwe fraternity must not be confounded with Pa'yatämu, the god of music,
flowers, and butterflies, who lives in the spring Shun'te'klaya, and is conspicuous in the myth of the
Corn maidens.   The flute of the former is unlike that of the latter.   Pa'yatämu of the Ne'wekwe plays
the part of jester as well as that of musician, and he is represented on the altar in a dress of stripes in
party-color.   Baubles ringed in party-color are the insignia of membership in the Ne'wekwe.   The
earliest published mention of the harlequin that the writer has found is in "Sakuntala," an Indian
drama by Kalidasa, translated into English by Monier Williams.   Organizations similar to the Ne'-
wekwe exist in the other pueblos.   The Keres name is Ko'shairi, which Bandelier translates delight-
makers.

and tail of knives) at Shi'papolima, Na'ke'e initiated members of his fraternity into the secrets of sword swallowing, which order he named 'Hle'wekwe (Wood people), the swords being fashioned of wood.

The 'Hle'wekwe, one of the original fraternities, traveled northward, then eastward, finally reaching the home of Po'shaiyänki.[a] While there the 'Hle'wekwe were initiated into the secret of sword swallowing by Ä'chiyälä'topa.[b]

After the 'Hle'wekwe had remained four years at Shi'papolima they started to return to their people, not, however, until those possessing the secrets of Mystery medicine had been converted by the Divine Ones into beasts. The details of the migration of the 'Hle'wekwe will be given in the account of the ceremonies of this fraternity.

Another man was called by the Divine Ones, and he was initiated into Mystery medicine and into the mystery of playing with fire, but not that of eating it; and he in turn initiated others, forming a fraternity which the Divine Ones named U'huhukwe (from u'kĭa, down,[c] in reference to eagle down).

Again, Kŏw'wituma and Wats'usi desiring to increase the number of fraternities chose two men, whom Po'shaiyänki initiated not only into the mystery of medicine which cures disease caused by witchcraft of man, but also into the secrets of healing disease caused by angry ants; and these two initiated others. This fraternity was named Hä'lo'kwe, but it is also called Ä'chiya (Stone Knife), from the order of this name. The secrets of fire were not given to the Hä'lo'kwe.

Some of the officers of this fraternity declare that the Knife order originated in this wise: A stone knife, descending from the gods above into the ceremonial chamber through the hatchway, indicated that such an order should be created. This order does not swallow the knife, but the knife is passed before the lips at initiation. In old times this order had many stone knives which they used in the ceremonials, much as eagle-wing plumes are used at the present time.

Po'shaiyänki distributed the beast god medicines, also the tablet altars and sand or dry paintings to the fraternities. One night, while a man of Po'yi'kwe (Chaparral cock) clan sat in his house, one of the Shumai'koli gods and his sai'apa (warrior) appeared to him without masks. They told the man that their present home was Chi'pia, which is near Shi'papolima, but that they originally came from the undermost world; that, traveling by the northern route eastward, they reached Shi'papolima, afterward going to Chi'pia. The gods remained but a short time with the man and returned to their home.

The pe'kwĭn (sun priest) was notified on the following morning of

[a] The 'Hle'wekwe insist that their fraternity started for the north from the vicinity of Ko'thluwala'wa, while all other priests and theurgists declare that this fraternity started from Hän''lipĭnkĭa after receiving their totems. All agree, however, that the 'Hle'wekwe had departed before the engagement of the A'shiwi with the Kĭa'nakwe (see p. 36).

[b] The 'Hle'wekwe insist that their initiation into the swallowing of the sword occurred previous to that of the wood order of the Great Fire fraternity.

[c] U'kĭa means also down of other birds, and of cotton.

the visit of these gods and he was so anxious to see them that he visited Chi'pia. He invited the six Shumai'koli, with their warriors, to Häl'ona. The invitation was accepted, and on the occasion of the second visit the gods wore their masks. During their stay they initiated the man of the Po'yi'kwe clan whom they first visited into the secrets of their medicine, which is the panacea for convulsions and cramps in the limbs,[a] and they taught him the songs given them by the Sun Father. These gods left their masks with the man, and he initiated others, forming a fraternity, which was named Shu'maakwe.

A short time afterward, when the Great Fire fraternity were assembled in their ceremonial chamber, the three gods, Kok'ko'hlan'na (great god—that is, of this particular group of gods), Shits'ukĭa, and Kwe'lele, appeared from Chi'pia. Each god initiated a man of the fraternity into the secret of his medicine, which is the specific for swellings of the throat, body, or limbs. The gods left their masks with those they initiated, and these men in turn initiated others.

The Ma''ke 'San'nakwe (Little Fire fraternity), though one of the important fraternities, was not embraced in those organized at Häl'ona or I'tiwanna, and it is generally believed by the sages of Zuñi that this fraternity was adopted by them from the Hopi Indians.[b]

The main body of Mu''kwe (Hopis) left the Corn clan and, after various vicissitudes, settled on three mesas. The Corn clan remained for a long period where they first settled, and while at this first village they were visited by two A'shiwi (Zuñis), one a member of the Badger clan, the other belonging to the Frog clan, whose members could kill deer and antelope by simply throwing the medicine of the 'Sän'iakĭakwe fraternity upon the game. The A'shiwi at this time were living at Hän''lipĭnkĭa, and they had not as yet learned the secrets of Mystery medicine from Po'shaiyänki. The two A'shiwi were warmly welcomed by the Mu''kwe of the Corn clan and were permitted to observe the marvelous feats of the members of the Little Fire fraternity. They had never before seen anything like it, and said: "We wish to be initiated into your fraternity." The mo'sona replied: "Very well; if you wish it so." He received them into the order of It'sĕpcho (Jugglery). This fraternity was too covetous to divulge the secrets of more than one order, for which the two A'shiwi paid nothing. On their return to Hän''lipĭnkĭa eight others were initiated into the secrets of It'sĕpcho, making ten members in all. This order, transmitted from the Hopi Indians, existed, according to Zuñi belief, among the A'shiwi before the organization of the fraternities by the Divine Ones at Häl'ona.

[a] The limbs are rubbed with one kind of medicine and another medicine is drunk.

[b] After long and careful investigation it was found that the sages are correct; that the members of this fraternity were among those Zuñis who separated at a remote period from their people, going to live with the Hopis. This separation may have taken place previous to the occupation of Häl'ona by the Zuñis. During Mr Stevenson's first visit to Zuñi he was informed by many of the priests of the pueblo that the middle village on the first mesa of the Hopis was known as a Zuñi settlement. This was subsequently confirmed by information from the people of this Hopi village.

When certain of the A'shiwi removed from To'wa yäl'länně (Corn mountain) to Shun'te͏ʻkĭaya, situated near by, those who had been initiated by the Corn clan of the Mu'ʻkwe into It'sĕpcho danced in the plaza in Shun'te͏ʻkĭaya in the presence of all their people.

The director of the order held an unlighted torch and four red-colored fluffy eagle plumes while he danced and called for the presence of the Cougar of the North. Looking in that direction, he cried: "Hai_____i, hai ____i, hai ____i, hai ____i, hai_____i;" and the cougar, hearing, obeyed the call. The director then tied one of the plumes he held to the back of the cougar's neck, saying: "I give you a plume, and I pray you will make intercession with the u'wannami (rain-makers) for rain." Then the cougar returned whence he came. The director called in like manner for the Bear of the West, and when the bear appeared, he attached a plume to the back of his neck, begging that he would intercede with the rain-makers for rain. Again he danced and called upon the Badger of the South, and when the badger appeared, he tied a plume to the back of his neck, asking that he would intercede with the rain-makers. And on the badger's return to his home the director called upon the White Wolf of the East, and attaching a plume to the wolf's neck, asked that he would make intercession with the rain-makers for rain. When the wolf returned to his home the director transferred the unlighted torch from his left to his right hand and danced. After a time he chewed some of the Corn clan's medicine and lighted his torch by blowing a strong breath of medicine upon it. Extending the blazing brand toward the north, he lighted a fire at a great distance, and a fire was made in the same manner in the three other regions. The people, looking on, were greatly annoyed, and after much discussion they decided that this man and his followers were sorcerers. The director of the order of It'sĕp-cho with his fellows were indignant at the accusation, and declared: "We are not sorcerers; our Mu'ʻkwe fathers of the Corn clan taught us this." These A'shiwi were so offended that they left their people and joined the Corn clan of the Mu'ʻkwe. After the A'shiwi and the Mu'ʻkwe of the Corn clan had been together four years (time periods) they traveled to where the other Mu'ʻkwe had settled and built a vil-lage on the most eastern of the three mesas, by the side of the pueblo of Walpi. The A'shiwi named this village Shi'wona, after the village of their own people that was built in the Middle place of the world.[a] During their stay with the people of the Corn clan the A'shiwi were initiated further into the rites of the Little Fire fraternity. When the A'shiwi returned to their people after their long absence they were received with great ceremony, and the ceremonials of the Little Fire fraternity were observed with the greatest interest. The above account is generally believed, though a different version is given by some. It

---

[a] I'tiwanna was also called Shi'wona.

is as follows: A party of Mu'ʻkwe came to the A'shiwi country in search of their god Le'lentu.[a] This long-looked-for god was found at the spring Shun'te'kĭaya, at the base of the mesa bearing the same name, and near Corn mountain. The A'shiwi Gods of War also discovered Pa'yatämu at this place. The music which the Mu'ʻkwe heard before reaching the spring guided them to their god Le'lentu. This god of the Hopis and A'shiwi is supposed to be short in stature, his head crowned with the flowers of the te'nasʻsäli (mythical plant which bears six-colored blossoms). While these Mu'ʻkwe, who were members of the Little Fire fraternity, were with the A'shiwi they initiated some of the latter into their secrets, thus organizing a Little Fire fraternity at Häl'ona as at Shi'wona. The Mu'ʻkwe having brought cotton with them, the A'shiwi women spun it and wove it into shirts, which were presented by the novices to the Mu'ʻkwe.

Chi'kĭalikwe (Rattlesnake) fraternity is a branch of the U'huhukwe. Pe'shäʻsilo'kwe (Cimex) is a branch of the Ma'ʻke ʻSan'nakwe. ʻKo'-shi'kwe (Cactus fraternity) is declared by theurgists and others to have been adopted long since from the Hopi Indians.

The A'piʻʻläshiwanni (Bow priesthood) was created by the Gods of War at Häl'ona, they becoming the original directors; and the elder and younger brother Bow priests, who fill the places of the Gods of War in this fraternity, having followed them in direct succession, are supposed to be as infallible through their initiation as were the gods who preceded them.

Membership in the fraternities mentioned, except the ʻKo'shi'kwe and A'piʻʻläshiwanni, is open to Zuñis of both sexes and of all ages above 4 or 5 years. Besides the fraternities mentioned, there is the Ko'tikili (Mythologic fraternity).

Though the fraternity of Sho'wekwe (see Games, page 329) still exists, it is now not considered worthy of mention by the Zuñis. Men make use of it to waste their lives in casting lots instead of working.

There is still another organization, the Struck-by-lightning fraternity. This fraternity has its standing among the others, and no less a personage than Nai'uchi, the greatest of the Zuñi theurgists, was treated by a woman of the fraternity just previous to his death. It is interesting to the writer on account of its very recent origin, giving her an insight into the manner of creating a Zuñi fraternity. The following was the story related by the director of the Struck-by-lightning fraternity:

In the summer of 1891, at the village of Nutria, five men, one a Navaho, and two women, all in one house, were made senseless by lightning. The first to recover was a man, the husband of Catalina, one of the women present. He thought his companions were dead, and at first could not inquire into the circumstances of this catastrophe. Presently one of the women, this man's sister, began crying, and then

---

[a] Le'lentu of the Hopis is the same as Pa'yatämu of the Zuñis. The description by both peoples of their god of music, butterflies, and flowers, is the same.

one after another returned to consciousness without medical aid, except Catalina and the Navaho guest. This man's body had been badly burned, and, though he lived, his reason was gone. They all agreed that the shock was like a severe stroke on the head with a club. The news was at once dispatched to Zuñi, and a man who had been struck by lightning in the previous year hastened to Nutria. He administered medicine to all who had been stunned. Catalina was restored by a piece of wood from a tree which had been struck by lightning. The charred wood was powdered and applied to the affected part, and an arrow point was then bound over the charred wood powder. They all returned to Zuñi and remained four days in the lower room of the house of Catalina, observing a strict fast, taking nothing but a little prayer meal in water. After the heads of the afflicted were washed in yucca suds, te′likinawe (prayer plumes) were made and deposited in the fields to the lightning-makers on the morning after the fourth night; and so the Struck-by-lightning fraternity was organized.[a]

It is a natural impulse of the human mind to seek for truth and to endeavor to account for the phenomena of nature, and thus philosophy grows. Mythologic philosophy is the fruit of the search for the knowledge of causes. The reasoning of aboriginal peoples is by analogy, for at this stage of culture science is yet unborn. So the philosopher of early times is the myth-maker. The philosophy of primitive peoples is the progenitor of natural religion. Religion was invented through long processes of analogic reasoning. The Zuñi is in this stage of culture. He is conscious of the earth, but he does not know its form; he knows something of what the earth contains beneath its surface, of its rivers and mountains, and of the sun, moon, and all celestial bodies which can be seen without optical instruments; he sees the lightning, hears the thunder, feels the winds, and knows the value of rains and snows; he is acquainted with the beasts of the forests, the birds and insects of the air, the fishes of the rivers, and knows that these living things possess attributes not attainable by himself, so he endows these animals with superior or supernatural qualities. When one becomes ill from any other cause than that of a wound, he may be treated in a most practical manner with legitimate drugs, but if the disease does not yield readily to treatment, then it is attributed to some foreign element thrust into the body and beyond the power of man to overcome. Nothing is left but to appeal to the creatures of superior qualities, and thus a system of theurgism develops. Religion and medicine become a dual system. The animals that are worshiped become healers, acting through the agency of the theurgists. These theurgists have no power in themselves to avert the evil of sorcery; they must first pass entirely under the influence of the Beast Gods.[b] In order that the theurgist should heal his patient,

[a] Though this fraternity had developed into a well-recognized organization in 1904, it is doubtful, owing to the rapidly changing environment, whether the Struck-by-lightning fraternity will ever be classed with the older esoteric fraternities.
[b] The belief that beasts of prey employ human agents is not confined to the Zuñis; it seems that the same belief is held by the Cœur d'Alène Indians. "The medicine man was considered a very powerful being by his tribe. He could take away the life of a man at his word or cure a sick or dying person. His power depended on the wild beasts that are fierce and powerful." (Extract from a letter written by Lieutenant Campbell E. Babcock, U. S. Army, to the United States National Museum.)

this foreign object in the body must be extracted, and the method usually adopted is curious. Extravaganza before the altar and the animal fetishes induces the spirit of the animal to enter the body of the theurgist, giving him the power to discover the afflicted part, which is often done by holding a quartz crystal before the patient; the lips are then applied to the flesh, and the disease is drawn out by sucking.[a] A theurgist may be of either sex, but must be a person regularly initiated into the order of Mystery medicine. Though young children of both sexes enter this order, they do not practice healing until, in the opinion of elder theurgists, they have reached years of discretion, when they become members of the first degree. A dry painting is one of the prominent features at the ceremony of initiation. A ground color in sand is laid on the floor before the tablet altar and made perfectly smooth, and upon this figures are delineated by sprinkling powdered pigment with the thumb and index finger. These paintings, of more or less elaborateness, are common among all the pueblo Indians, the Navahos, the Mission Indians of California, and tribes of the north, and are all used in connection with medicine practices.[b]

The mode of joining the different esoteric fraternities in which the sick are healed through Mystery medicine is substantially the same. Although those restored to health usually join the fraternity to which the theurgist called upon belongs, to do so is not obligatory. The aim of the one restored to health is to become a member of the Mystery medicine order, but the expense of the necessary gift to the fraternity father often deprives the person of his heart's desire, and so another order is joined until such time as the requisite gift is secured. When a restored patient desires to join the order, a small quantity of sacred meal, composed of white corn, turquoise, and micaceous hematite, coarsely ground, the last being specially acceptable to the Beast Gods, is deposited in a corn husk. It is then folded in rectangular form, tied with the greatest care, and carried in the right hand of the restored invalid to the theurgist who effected the cure. In case the patient is a young child the offering is carried by a parent. A similar offering is made when the theurgist is called upon to visit the sick. It is also made by those desiring to join the Sword and Fire orders of a fraternity. The theurgist carries the package at night to one of the points of the compass, makes an excavation, and sprinkles the contents of the husk into it as an offering to the Beast Gods.

[a] This process of sucking to cure disease is not confined to the Zuñis, but is common among the aboriginal peoples of the world, differing only in minor details.

[b] The writer can not say how widespread is the observance of sand painting, but the low-caste people of India design their gods in sand on the ground by sprinkling in the manner described, and they also have sprinkling cups for this purpose. Dr Fewkes has several interesting specimens of sprinkling cups, supposed to have been used in the dry paintings, in his collection of ancient ceramics from Arizona. The writer has never observed the use of the cups among the Indians of the Southwest. Unlike our Indians, the natives of India do not have a ground color of sand, but spread the surface with diluted chips of the sacred cow. The high castes have greatly elaborated the sand paintings, which are used by them purely for decoration. This same feature is to be found in the Renaissance, when the tables of the French were bordered in elaborate designs with powdered marble.

Anyone acceptable to the fraternity may join the Fire and Sword
orders, whose ceremonials are for rains and snows and have nothing to
do with healing the sick.   The father of the chosen fraternity presents
a gift of a blanket to a male and of a woven dress to a female novice.
A member of the Mystery medicine order may ask his fraternity father
in this order to act for him in the other orders, but it is not uncommon
for the fraternity father to reply: " It will be well for you to choose
another father, as I have no gift to make to you."

The order of It'sĕpcho, the ceremonies of which are also for rains,
can be joined only after membership has been gained in the Fire and
Sword orders, unless one is already a member of Mystery medicine.
The fraternity father gives to the novice a woman's belt, which is
worn by men during ceremonials.   The order of Pa'yatämu exists only
in the Little Fire and Cimex fraternities and may be joined only by
male members of the Mystery medicine order.

For four days previous to initiation each novice of a fraternity wears
a fluffy eagle plume attached to the hair, and if a man, woman, or
child accidentally touch a member of the Fire and Sword orders of
a fraternity when that person is wearing a plume, the one commit-
ting this offense must join the order; or if one step upon or within
the meal lines which are drawn at ceremonial times on the roof of the
ceremonial chamber, the offender must join the Fire or Sword order.
If the wearer of a plume of the Mystery medicine order of the
Ne'wekwe be touched on the no'line (penis) or breast, the offender is
compelled to join the order.   This rule is also observed in relation to
the Shu'maakwe fraternity, which, however, does not practice Mystery medicine, their medicine having come to them from the Shumai'-
koli (certain anthropic gods) and not from the Beast Gods.   The novice
of the order of Mystery medicine presents his fraternity father with
a finely dressed deerskin, and the fraternity father in turn gives a
mi'li[a] to the novice.

While the fetish ĕt'tonĕ, a most sacred object of the A'shiwanni,
symbolizes Earth Mother, rains, and vegetation, including all that supplies physical nourishment to man, the mi'li symbolizes the life-giving
or soul power which comes from A'wonawil'ona, the supreme bisexual power, who is the breath of life and life itself.   And when the
breath of the plumes, which are a part of A'wonawil'ona, is inhaled,
one receives that life which is the great mystery and which when
given by the Supreme Power defies all life-destroying agencies.
Beneath the plumes of the mi'li are an ear of corn and other seeds,[b]
symbolizing the widespread power of A'wonawil'ona.   The Earth
Mother, even though she be embraced by the rains of the u'wannami
(rain-makers), could not yield to the people the fruits of her being for
physical nourishment without the all-pervading power of A'wona-

---

[a] See p. 416.   [b] See p. 22.

ZUÑI MATRON

WE'WHA WEAVING BELT

wil'ona.　The healing of the body also must come by the will of the
Supreme Power.　All the medicine of the Beast Gods would be of no
value unless blessed by the mysterious life-giving power of A'wonawil'ona.　Therefore each person initiated into the order of Mystery
medicine, or the mystery of healing through the Beast Gods, possesses
a mi'li, which is constructed by the fraternity father in the ceremonial
chamber while singing five songs in the presence of members of the
order.　The songs are addressed to A'wonawil'ona, the Sun Father, the
Moon Mother, the Beast Gods of the six regions, and Ä'chiyälä'topa
(being with wings and a tail of knives).　When completed, the mi'li is
placed by the altar, where it remains until given to the novice.

There are several fraternities to which the preceding rules do not
apply.　The ʻHle'wekwe has a Sword order, but it has no order
of Mystery medicine.　It has one mi'li, composed of an ear of corn,
eight turkey-tail plumes, with a few smaller bird feathers, and a
po'nepoyanně,[a] and it possesses an ět'toně.　The manner of joining
this fraternity is given in the ceremonial of the ʻHle'wekwe.

ʻSän'iakïakwe has no order of Mystery medicine, but each member
has a mi'li, composed of an ear of corn surrounded by eight turkey tail
plumes.　Though this fraternity was organized specially for the chase,
it was initiated into the mystery of playing with fire.

Shu'maakwe has no order of Mystery medicine, but such members
as have the septum of the nose pierced possess a mi'li, though this is
quite different from that of Mystery medicine.　It is built up over an
ear of corn, which is also completely covered with plumes; but these
plumes, which are elaborate, are first attached to four slender sticks,
each one constituting a te'likinaně (prayer plume), this having a
la'showanně (one or more plumes attached to cotton cord) hanging
from its tip.　A stick with zigzag marking, symbolic of lightning,
some 4 inches higher than the prayer plume, its upper portion colored
blue and tipped with a white fluffy eagle plume attached with a cotton
cord, stands in the center.　These mi'wachi (plural for mi'li) are not
so high as those associated with Mystery medicine.　All mi'wachi are
associated with A'wonawil'ona.　The base of the Shu'maakwe mi'li is
heavily wrapped for 4 inches or more with white cotton cord.　The
one which the writer examined had two spiral shells over 1 inch long,
with a piece of abalone shell the size of a silver quarter between them,
strung on the cord at the upper portion of the wrapping.　These
adornments are referred to as the necklaces of the mi'wachi.

---

[a] The po'nepoyanně (from po'ne, to place; poyanně, bundle) is composed of an ear of corn surrounded by a number of reeds the length of the middle finger.　Each reed contains pellets of the epidermis secured by persistent rubbing of the body.　The reeds are closed at the ends with raw cotton.
They are securely wrapped together with cotton cord and are surrounded with eagles' wing feathers.
These plumes must be dropped by wild eagles and found by members of the fraternity.　They are
given to the director of the fraternity, who attaches the plumes to the fetish, which gradually
becomes larger by the addition of the plumes as they are found from time to time.

On the fourth morning after the death of a member of the Mystery medicine order, the director having taken the mi'li of the deceased apart, each member of the order prepares a prayer plume from the plumes of the mi'li. As each prayer plume is completed, the maker prays to the Beast Gods to intercede with the rain-makers for rains, and draws from the plumes the breath of A'wonawil'ona, the breath of life. He also prays for happiness for all, and that they may not die, but live to old age, and that they may sleep to awake in Ko'thluwa-la'wa. The prayer plumes are handed to the director, who, after receiving them, makes them into a kĭa'ĕtchinĕ (a group of plumes wrapped together at the base) and deposits it in the river that the spiritual essence of the plumes and prayers may be carried to the gods. The same process is observed with the mi'li of a deceased Shu'maakwe, the prayers being offered to the Shumai'koli gods for rains, happiness, and long life.

When a mi'li is disintegrated, the seeds are taken from the cavity of the corn cob and the grains from off the cob, and they are distributed among members of the order, who plant them in their fields in the coming year.

The Shi'wannakwe do not destroy their mi'wachi. The mi'li of the deceased is kept in his house until his son is old enough to join the fraternity, when it is presented to him. If there is no son, or should the son not wish to join the fraternity, the director of the fraternity presents the mi'li to whomever he chooses. Although the writer has never allied herself with any of the fraternities, several of them have presented to her sacred objects of their organizations; among these is a mi'li[a] of the order of Mystery medicine (see plate CI) prepared by Nai'uchi, the elder brother Bow priest and warrior of the Little Fire fraternity, which was presented with the same prayer and ceremony as over a novice. Nai'uchi also allowed her to have his own mi'li for a few days, with the promise that no one, unless it be his own son, should see it.

The ear of corn for the fetish must be perfect in form and every portion of the cob must be covered. Should the ear be irregular, and it often occurs that a straight ear can not be found, it is held by the fire for a while, the breath is blown on it for a few minutes, and then it is securely bound to a rod and left for a couple of days. When removed from the rod the ear of corn is straight. Should one or more grains be lacking to make the ear a ya'pota (perfect ear), grains are taken from another ear of corn and attached by the use of cement. After the portion repaired is dampened with the mouth, several mouthfuls of water are thrown over the ear to cleanse it thoroughly.

The son, an associate shi'wanni and a theurgist of no mean standing in the Little Fire fraternity, who, being fraternity father to several persons, had constructed

---

[a] This fetish was deposited in the United States National Museum.

mi'wachi, was induced, after long persuasion extending through several days, to take the mi'li of his father and that of the writer apart and reconstruct them. Great secrecy was observed in this work. When he set about removing the seeds, which were in a cavity in the corn cob, he brought an ancient pot containing a paste of blackish earth that is supposed to have been brought from the undermost world. With this earth and a cement of piñon gum and yucca fruit he closed the cavity upon returning the seeds to their place. Depositing the jar and cement before him, he removed his head-kerchief and moccasins and silently prayed to A'wonawil'ona and the Beast Gods that he should not be punished for desecrating the sacred mi'wachi. To prepare a mi'li without the appropriate ceremony is sacrilege. This devotee to his ritual shed tears while he clandestinely pulled apart and repaired the mi'wachi.

His father's mi'li was first handled. The string containing the beads was removed, then the straw covering at the base, after which the plumes, one by one, were displaced and laid on the floor beside the worker. The ear of corn was now taken from the buckskin cup which held it; the cotton cloth was loosened from the base of the corn; the clay which sealed the cavity in the cob was broken from the base of the corn, and the seeds were removed. Other seeds were emptied from the buckskin cup. All these objects were laid down in order with the tenderest care. The writer's mi'li passed through the same form of disintegration, and the objects were laid a little apart from the others.

In the reconstruction the theurgist worked first on the writer's mi'li. He ran four fresh lines of paint, made by diluting some of the earth paste, lengthwise over the lines which were made when the mi'li was originally fashioned. These are symbolic of the four regions. He then refilled the cavity in the heart of the cob with the seeds, which include corn grains of the six colors—wheat, squash, watermelon, and muskmelon seeds, beans, and piñon nuts. When the cavity was closed with the earth paste, the cotton cloth was tied over the base of the cob, symbolic of the apparel of the Mother Corn. The theurgist showed how the buckskin cup in which the base of the ear rested was made, placing it, after removing the thong lacing, in a small bowl of warm water, and leaving it there until it was thoroughly pliable. This piece of dressed buckskin, which was dyed black and rectangular in form, was laid on the floor while wet. A disk of raw deer hide was held at the base of the ear of corn as it stood in the center of the piece of buckskin. It seemed difficult to form this rectangular piece of leather into the desired shape. ·The left hand held the corn in place while the real work was performed with the right hand. The moist leather was pulled and fitted to the corn, the left thumb doing its share in the way of pressing the leather into shape. Holes were punched in the laps of the leather, and moist thongs were used to lace the laps together. Various seeds were dropped into the cup before the lacings were tightened, after which the cup was securely wrapped with the thong and tied. At the present time some of the cups used for mi'wachi are cut from blocks of wood, this process being much easier than the shaping of the leather; but the leather cup is the genuine and original kind. The cup containing the ear of corn was set aside while the plumes were being arranged in proper order, each variety of feathers being placed in a separate row. Each of the four long parrot, or macaw, plumes was first attached to a slender stick, and afterward cotton cord was tied to the ear of corn and held in the mouth two fingers' length from the corn. One of the macaw plumes was now attached to the ear by binding to it the end of the slender stick to which the plume was attached, the plume extending far above the top of the corn. A similar plume was bound at the opposite side of the corn by wrapping the end of the stick. A third was placed between the two, and a fourth opposite the third, thus symbolizing the four quarters. The four sticks were now wrapped together where they were attached to the plumes, which drew the four plumes close together. Figure 26 shows the mi'li at this stage of reconstruction. Six white o'wa (dove) plumes from the tail of the male bird followed next, each one being wrapped on separately.

The mi'li was now placed for a few minutes beside the low fire, while the theurgist sat in silence, his lips moving in prayer. Then six mai'ya (Cyanocitta macrolopha) tail plumes, representing eyes, were added. Three green macaw plumes followed these; next twelve wing feathers from the male duck's shoulder; then six male dove wing plumes; following these fifteen duck feathers from under the wing; after these twenty small red parrot feathers; and then three white fluffy eagle plumes were attached, representing the feather adornment on the head of the Corn Mother. A band of fourteen small turkey feathers, from the top of the neck of the male bird, completed the plumes of the mi'li. The plumes were arranged with the greatest precision. The cord, still held in the mouth, was wrapped loosely around the feathers to the tip of the long macaw plumes, where it was secured, and the mi'li was stood on the floor while the case for the base, which was made of wheat straw, was moistened and delicately manipulated into shape. It was set aside for a

FIG. 26—Theurgist reconstructing the mi'li.

few moments and then drawn over the mi'li from the top; hence the extra wrapping of the plumes with the cord. The case was carefully fitted to the base, and the outer wrapping of cord, being now removed from the plumes, was used to secure the top edge of the straw. After the cord was wound many times around, it was carefully fastened by tucking it under the wrapping. Bits of shell and beads tied around the top of the straw with a cotton cord completed the mi'li of the order of Mystery medicine. The theurgist repeated a long prayer while he held the mi'li; then, after passing it four times over the writer's mouth, that she might draw in the sacred breath from the fetish, he handed it to her, saying, "Receive your father." To a male he would say, "Receive your mother." The same procedure was observed in rebuilding the father's mi'li, except that the buckskin cup was not disturbed. When the father's fetish was completed the young theurgist, with tears on his cheeks and with a deep sigh, said, "I have pleased my mother, but I have offended my gods."

The ʻKoʼshiʻkwe and Aʼpiʻʻläshiwanni are not divided into orders like the other fraternities. Those who have performed valorous deeds, such as killing an enemy, may join the ʻKoʼshiʻkwe; one must not only have killed the enemy, but must have brought in the scalp, to entitle him to membership in the Aʼpiʻʻläshiwanni—at least such was the custom until more recent years. The cessation of intertribal wars, with the consequent absence of scalps, has so depleted this organization, in many respects the most powerful in Zuñi, that men who have never been in an engagement with the enemy are received into the fraternity, and the ceremony of initiation occurs exactly as if they were genuine victors, an old scalp from the scalp house, without a vestige of hair, being used in place of the fresh scalp.

All the fraternities except the ʻHleʼwekwe, ʻKoʼshiʻkwe, and Aʼpiʻʻläshiwanni hold synchronal meetings for eight days and nights at the winter solstice (see page 112), when the sick are healed, swords are swallowed by those belonging to the Sword order of the Great Fire fraternity, and playing with fire and jugglery are practiced. There is no initiation at this time. Suds to symbolize snow clouds are made by the deputy aʼkwamosi (maker of medicine water), who whips in a bowl of water with a reed, such as arrow shafts are made of, a crushed or broken root, praying meantime for cold rains and snows. At other times meetings of these fraternities do not continue longer than one day and a night unless there is to be an initiation, when the fraternities must convene during four days—for three nights until midnight, for the fourth until sunrise.

The ʻKoʼshiʻkwe meets on the first day and night only of the festival of the winter solstice. The members of the Aʼpiʻʻläshiwanni meet separately at this time with the fraternities to which they are allied as warriors or guardians of the altars and fetishes. The fraternities having the order of Mystery medicine meet in January for initiation and to heal the sick. They may or may not practice jugglery. Such fraternities as have the Fire order meet in February. As a rule, only the Little Fire and Cimex fraternities meet in March, and their meetings occur but once in four years, the Cimex alternating quadrennially with the Little Fire in the Great Fire dance. The fraternities do not convene in April and May. There are synchronous meetings of the fraternities at the summer solstice, to invoke the Beast Gods to intercede with the rain-makers for rain, when the Aʼpiʻʻläshiwanni act as warriors and guardians of the altars, as they do at the winter solstice. No ceremonies of the fraternities are held in July. The fraternities, except the ʻHleʼwekwe and Aʼpiʻʻläshiwanni, convene in August and September to prepare their plant medicines, at which times there are elaborate ceremonies. These fraternities meet again in October and November for initiation, when the sick are healed and fire eating and jugglery are practiced. Meetings may be held at other times at the discretion of the director for initiation, but this is done only in extreme cases. Though concurrent meetings of elaborate character occur only at the winter and summer solstices, it may happen that two or more fraternities convene at the same time, the date for the meetings being fixed by the director, who has direct control over the fraternity, the exception being the Shu′maakwe; the director of this fraternity is under the jurisdiction of the pe′kwĭn (sun priest) and it may convene only at his command, and the sun priest is usually punctual in his notices to the director that the fraternity meet with the others.[a]

The 'Ko′shi'kwe hold but three meetings annually, and the novices must wait for a regular meeting to join the fraternity. The A′pi''läshiwanni have the scalp ceremonial for initiation once in three or four years, at the will of the elder brother Bow priest. It is depended on to bring rains in case of severe drought. This fraternity also has an annual festival of thanksgiving, known as the "Harvest dance." The 'Hle′wekwe hold but two regular meetings annually, in January and February, and a name presented for membership must be held over for a year before the person can be received into the fraternity. The Wood order (Sword swallowers) of the Great Fire hold synchronous meetings with the 'Hle′wekwe in January and February, each fraternity having its warrior or warriors from the A′pi'läshiwanni. Except the 'Hle′wekwe and Shu′maakwe, each fraternity is notified of a meeting to be held by one of its warriors, who goes from house to house saying to the members: "Our father (referring to the director) wishes the fraternity to meet." The party addressed replies: "It is well." The members of the 'Hle′wekwe are notified through the Kĭa′kwemosi, rain priest of the North, and, as has been stated, the Shu′maakwe are notified by the sun priest.

The members of all the fraternities gather semimonthly in the ceremonial chamber to prepare prayer plumes, which they offer to their gods. The tablet altars are often placed for these occasions. The men prepare offerings for their fraternity children of the opposite sex and for boys not old enough to have received voluntary initiation into the Ko′tikili.

When a woman loses a fraternity father she must choose another to fill his place, because women can not prepare prayer plumes unless they are members of the Ko′tikili. A male member of her fraternity father's clan presents a quantity of meal wrapped in corn husk; laying this in the palm of a man's hand, he prays and announces to him that he has been chosen to fill the place of the deceased fraternity father. The only case, so far as the writer has been able to learn, in which

_____

[a] The pe′kwĭn having been a little tardy in 1892, the director of the fraternity complained to the writer that he had not yet been notified to hold the ceremonial which should occur in February. On the following day his mind was set at rest by the notification from the sun priest.

women not associated with the Ko'tikili make prayer plumes, though they sometimes color the sticks to which the plumes are attached, is after a woman has severed her connection with the U'huhukwe[a] fraternity. She must then prepare plume offerings, having been instructed by her fraternity father, and must deposit them as though she were still a member of the fraternity.

Prayer plumes are made and deposited at the new and full moon of each month by the members of all the fraternities except the ʇHle'wekwe; also at the winter and summer solstices, upon the death of a member, and at meetings of the fraternity. The plumes are deposited in the fields, at shrines of the various fraternities and in other places. The Great Fire, the Little Fire, the Cimex, the Eagle Down, and the Rattlesnake fraternities plant prayer plumes in April at a shrine south of Zuñi dedicated to the rattlesnake, where they invoke the snakes to intercede with the rain-makers to send rains upon Zuñi. The sticks of these offerings are colored red, with black lines at one end to indicate the rattle. Figure 27 shows the shrine. Prayer plumes made semimonthly are deposited in the cornfields or melon patches. In the autumn, fruits and all edible seeds are also buried in the fields as offerings of thanksgiving, with supplications for abundant supplies in the coming year. At the full moon of October the altar is erected in the ceremonial chamber, where the members sing until midnight.

The ceremonials of the fraternities, the Ko'tikili excepted, are held in large chambers on the ground floor, which are ordinarily used as the general living rooms for the families. Whenever possible, these rooms must extend east and west, and almost invariably they do, in order that the altar may face east and the first light of day enter through the eastern window.

Each fraternity asserts that it has occupied its present ceremonial chamber since the founding of Zuñi, except the branch fraternities, which had to find for themselves other rooms where, when once located, they have remained. The rooms have been enlarged and improved from time to time. Prior to the occupation of a room by a fraternity the household moves out and gives the room a general cleaning. They do not remove, however, until just previous to the convening of the fraternity. Their presence in the chamber does not interfere with the meeting of the members to rehearse their songs and talk over matters. The men and women of the house, who are not members of the fraternity, converse or go to bed with the children without paying the slightest attention to the group present or their songs. The songs are not begun, however, until the non-members are supposed to be asleep.

---

[a] See U'huhukwe fraternity.

The fraternities do not confine themselves to songs in the Zuñi tongue.   The Shi′wannakwe and Ne′wekwe sing in the Zuñi and Santo Domingo languages, the ᵗSän′iakĭakwe in Zuñi and Laguna, the ᵗHle′-wekwe in Zuñi and Acoma, the Ma′ᵗke ᵗhlan′nakwe in Ke′pachu,[a] the Hä′lo‘kwe in Zuñi and Santo Domingo, the U′huhukwe and Chi′kĭalikwe

FIG. 27—Shrine dedicated to the Rattlesnake.

in Zuñi and Tewan, the Shu′maakwe in Pima, the Ma′ᵗke ᵗSan′nakwe in Zuñi, A′pachu (Navaho), and Mu′‘kwe (Hopi).   The Mu′‘kwe are said to have learned the A′pachu songs from these people soon after they came to this world; the ᵗKo′shi‘kwe sing in Zuñi and Hopi; the Pi′‘ᵗläshiwanni in Zuñi and Laguna.   According to the legend, the

---

[a] The Ke′pachu are said by the Zuñis to be a people living far north of their Zuñi country.   These people are said to live in tents of deerskin and wear clothing of the same skins (see Great Fire fraternity).

A'pachu were friendly with the Zuñis and Mu''kwe when they first came through Ji'mi'kĭanapkĭatea, but they did not attach proper importance to the a'mosi (directors) of the Zuñis, who resented the slight and insisted upon going to war. The A'pachu did not wish to fight, but the Zuñis attacked them and drove them to the north.

The pottery drums of the fraternities are curled at the mouth, which prevents any slipping of the rope that fastens the deerskin which is stretched over the opening. These drums are vase-shaped, and have a ground color of white or cream, and are generally decorated with cougars, bears, and snakes. The beasts are usually represented in combat with one another; the snakes likewise. Some rare old specimens of these drums were secured by Mr Stevenson and deposited in the National Museum at Washington.

The tablet altars of the fraternities are made in sections, and when not in use are stored away. They are freshly decorated for ceremonials, as the Zuñis have not acquired the art of permanent coloring. The altars and dry paintings which appear in the ceremonials are referred to as tĕsh'kwi (not to be touched). The number of officers varies in different fraternities. The a'kwamosi (maker of medicine water) sits north of the altar, and his pe'kwĭn (deputy) sits south of it. The flutist, with rare exceptions, sits behind the altar while he plays.

Great care is observed in washing the hair in yucca suds and bathing for ceremonials, since an unclean person is most offensive to the tutelary gods. The bath is repeated in the morning and evening of each day during the meetings, the men frequently taking their morning baths in the river, at other times disrobing to the breechcloth and bathing in the general living room. Women of the family wash the men's hair and one another's.

The process of the women's bath is tedious. The woman goes to a corner of the general living room and bathes without removing the cotton camis. If this garment is to be worn after the bath, great care must be taken to prevent it from getting too wet; if it is to be changed, it is used as a towel for the lower portion of the body, and the pi'toni (the cotton piece worn over the shoulders) is used to dry the remainder of the body. It is astonishing how adroitly the women manage not to be exposed during the bath, yet this precaution seems unnecessary, since the men present appear not to have the slightest concern in the ablutions of the women.

The high-necked and long-sleeved cotton garment is discarded by the women for ceremonials, and their necks and arms are bare. Men wear their cotton shirts and trousers in the ceremonial chamber, but afterward discard them, wearing, except on rare occasions, only a woven breechcloth in the dances. The moccasins of both sexes are always removed on entering the chamber. The strictest etiquette is observed in these ceremonials. No one enters the chamber without giving and receiving a greeting of welcome, the newcomer being asked to be seated. No one is allowed to fall asleep in the ceremonial chamber except such members as are held almost sacred on account of their extreme age. The offender is at once touched in no gentle manner by some member. Pregnant women and young children are held as severely to account as the others. After the close of the ceremonial the head of each member is washed in yucca suds. Continence is observed during the ceremonials and the four days following, for all carnal thoughts must be dispensed with at this season.

The plume which is worn for four days by the novice, during which time he must observe continence and abstain from animal food and grease (the fast continues for four days after initiation), is removed the morning previous to initiation (the initiatory ceremony as a rule occurs during the fourth night of the ceremonial) at Ku'shilowa (red earth), a short distance east of Zuñi, by the fraternity father, who ties the plume mentioned to a blade of yucca, sprinkles it with meal, and then, with a prayer for long life and a true heart for the novice, deposits the plume on the ground. A similar plume is tied to the hair when the person is decorated for the initiation ceremonies. Ku'shilowa is a great repository for these plumes and te'likinawe, and hundreds of plumeless sticks are to be found there.

On returning, the member elect goes to the house of the fraternity father, where the wife or daughter bathes his head. Afterward he is entertained at a feast at which no animal food must be taken. When the members of the fraternity have completed their toilets for the evening, the novices take their seats in line on the north side of the room near the altar until the fraternity fathers are ready to prepare them for the ceremony, when they cross to the south side of the room, standing usually near the fireplace, where each fraternity father adorns the person of his fraternity child. For Mystery medicine the face, body, upper arms, and legs of the males are colored brownish red. The feet, the legs halfway to the knees, the hands, and the arms halfway to the elbows are colored with a white paint made of kaolin. A black woven breechcloth, embroidered at the ends, is worn. With females only the feet, the lower portion of the legs, the hands, and the arms are painted, kaolin also being used for this purpose. They wear the usual woven dress. An owl and a raven feather, held in place by yucca ribbons, are crossed on the top of each wrist, the owl feather pointing outward, the other pointing inward. Similar feathers are also crossed on the outside of each leg below the knee, the owl feather pointing to the knee, that the child of Mystery medicine may be up early with the raven and go about at night, without fear, like the owl. The chin and the upper lip are covered with a paste of kaolin, a circle of which is put around the top of the head, and hawk or eagle down is dotted over the kaolin, symbolic of the clouds of the world. After the adornment of their person the novices return to their seats on the ledge, and their hands are held in turn by the invited female guests. In some instances the wife of the fraternity father sits on the left of the novice and the elder sister of the fraternity father on the right. This custom is also followed by the 'Hle'wekwe.

The closing ceremonies at sunrise are substantially the same with all the fraternities having the order of Mystery medicine. Boxes or low stools are placed in line near the center of the floor and are covered with blankets. The novices are led by their fraternity parents and seated upon these boxes, facing east. The wife or sister of each fraternity parent stands behind the novice, resting a hand on each shoulder. A vase of water and a bowl containing yucca root are set before each novice, and the makers of the suds stand beside them. Each fraternity parent now takes the gifts for his child from the altar and stands east of thé bowl and before his child. Each novice receives a mi'li, four ears of corn tied together with yucca ribbon, prayer plumes, of which each member of the order has made two, wrapped together at the ends with corn husks, and two eagle-wing plumes, one of the plumes having a fluffy eagle feather colored red, emblem of Mystery medicine, attached to its tip. Before the presentation of each gift it is drawn four times across the left side of the head, four times over the crown of the head, then across the right side, and then before the mouth of the candidate, who inhales the sacred breath of A'wonawil'- ona. The gifts are held in the left arm of the novice, and they are about as much as a child can manage.

After the women prepare the suds they rise, and the fraternity parents, being in line outside of where the makers of the suds stand, pass before them, starting at the south end, and dipping their plumes into each bowl they deposit the suds on the novices' heads. Then each member of the order of Mystery medicine repeats this act, also passing from the south end, the members of the choir returning to their places. The head and hands of each candidate are afterward thoroughly washed by those who prepared the suds, and the hair is wiped by the mother or sister of the fraternity parent. Each fraternity parent now removes his mi'li from the altar and passes it four times in line downward before the mouth of each novice while the sacred breath is drawn. The mi'li is put to the left side of the face, to the crown of the head, and then to the right side of the face. As the members do not afterward return to their positions, the choir becomes gradually reduced, until only one besides the drummer remains, and his voice and the drum die away when they come forward with their mi'wachi. The bowl that the head is bathed in is a gift to the novice. The women of the fraternity father's family and of the family of the candidate exchange gifts of flour, cornmeal, etc." The women of the fraternity and the families of the male members furnish and prepare the food consumed during the ceremonial days.

---

^aExceptions to these rules will be mentioned in the description of the ceremonials.

SHI'WANNAKWE[a]

The Shi'wannakwe and 'Sän'iakïakwe are the only fraternities which do not observe the fast from animal food at the winter solstice festival, these two fraternities having at the time of their origin received direct instructions from the Divine Ones not to observe the fast. The Shi'wannakwe must not, however, touch jack rabbit as food at any time. This fraternity has three orders—O'naya'nakïa (Mystery medicine), It'sĕpcho (Jugglery), and Ma'ᵗke (Fire). The novice usually does not appear before the fraternity until the fourth night, when the fraternity father escorts him from his home to the ceremonial chamber.

The writer failed to get a sketch of the tablet altar, which is similar to those of the other fraternities. Plate CII shows the dry painting which is made at the time of initiation. This painting is not directly associated with the worship of beasts of prey, but with celestial worship. a, Outline of tablet altar; b, mi'wachi of the order of O'naya'nakïa; c, line of meal; d, Yu'piaᵗhlan'na[b] (Galaxy), formed of meal and outlined in charred corncob; e, sun symbol; f, moon symbol. The sun and moon are formed of corn pollen, burnt corncob, crushed turquoise, and other mineral colors. These two emblems are about 5 inches in diameter. The lines extending from the disks denote the sun's rays.

At an initiation into the Shi'wannakwe fraternity the meal from the symbol of the Galaxy is rubbed on the novice, as the sands are in initiatory ceremonies in orders associated with Mystery medicine.[c] The meal is afterward gathered in corn husks and carried with prayer plumes to the shrine of the Shi'wannakwe on a knoll southeast of Zuñi, where there is a stone slab containing etchings of the sun and moon. The novice, accompanied to this shrine by his fraternity father, plants his prayer plumes, which are offerings to u'wannami A'shiwanni (rain priest rain-makers), u'wannami pe'kwĭn (sun priest rainmakers), Yu'piaᵗhlan'na, and the Beast Gods, these latter being supplicated to intercede with the others. The plumes are planted a few feet southwest of the slab, which rests on four elevations several inches high.

When initiation into the Fire order occurs, the novice sits for a time in the center of the floor, and he rises when the fraternity father is ready to place coals in his mouth. The medicine, achillea millefolium (yarrow), taken beforehand "to prevent burning" is put into the novice's mouth directly from the mouth of the fraternity father.

The Shi'wannakwe possess a rude carving in stone of a female,

---

[a] Those who do not fast from animal food.
[b] The male gender is applied to the Galaxy.
[c] To be described in connection with other fraternities associated with zoic worship.

some 10 inches high, which is reverenced as the A′wan ᵗSi′ta (Great Mother). This image is said to have been in their possession since the organization of the fraternity. In fact, they declare they had two, but one was long since stolen and, they think, carried off to another pueblo. Since this catastrophe the remaining image has been guarded by an old woman of the Eagle clan, who never allows it to see daylight except when placed by the altar or when offerings are to be made. A theurgist standing near the altar moves his two eagle-wing plumes for a time with weird incantations until the image appears to catch the tip ends of the plumes with each hand, when the theurgist apparently raises the image with the assistance of the plumes. The illusion is perfect. The offerings to the image are strings of precious beads large enough to encircle the thumb of the donor.

> The old creature who guards this image, and who seemed very much in love with her husband, was induced to bring it out for the inspection of the writer, only, however, after threats by the husband that he would leave her for all time if she refused.

The director of the Shi′wannakwe holds in sacred trust a dressed deerskin containing pictorial writings in color describing the coming of the A′shiwi to this world, how they appeared with their tails and webbed hands and feet, and their migrations from the far northwest to the Middle place, which is the site of present Zuñi. The old theurgist claims that his fraternity was the happy possessor of two such documents, but that a student from the East to whom he showed them carried off one, and since that time the other has not been allowed to be brought from the sealed vase in which it is kept, except at the time of an annual ceremony, when it is exhibited to the members of the fraternity. The Shi′wannakwe is especially revered as having on one occasion brought rains upon Zuñi when all other efforts had failed. A great calamity caused by a drought brought about at that time by the elder brother Bow priest, who proved to be a witch, was averted by the songs of the Shi′wannakwe.

NE′WEKWE (GALAXY FRATERNITY)

The Ne′wekwe fraternity embraces the orders of O′naya′nakĭa and It′sĕpcho and has a Kok′ko ᵗhlan′na (Great god) (see plate CIII a), as a patron god. Two other gods (plate CIII b shows mask of one of these gods) also appear at times with the Ne′wekwe, but the writer is not sure what their relation is to the fraternity. It has been stated that the Ne′wekwe was one of the four original fraternities organized soon after the A′shiwi came to this world, and that Bi·″ᵗsiᵗsi, having special qualifications, was appointed musician and jester to the fraternity. Bi·″ᵗsiᵗsi remained with the Ne′wekwe during the migrations of the A′shiwi until they reached ᵗKĭap′kweñä (Ojo Caliente), a farming district of the Zuñis 15 miles southwest of the village. Here the

Ne'wekwe visited Lu'kĭana 'kiai'a (Ashes spring), where Kok'ko-'hlan'na[a] appeared to them. The god inquired of the mo'sona (director): "What medicine have you?" Upon being told, he said: "Your medicine is good, but not good alone. Should you give it alone, it would destroy the intestines, for it is very hot. I will give you medicine which must be taken to allay the burning qualities of the other." Kok'ko 'thlan'na instructed the Ne'wekwe to use human excrement in conjunction with their medicine.

Since that time the Kok'ko 'hlan'na is personated at the initiatory ceremonials of the Ne'wekwe. He administers the excrement not only to the initiates but to others of the fraternity. While the Ne'wekwe are considered great theurgists, one of the organization is seldom called upon except in extreme cases, from the fact that the invalid, if cured, is expected to join the fraternity and one naturally hates to indulge in its filthy practices; but after joining, the new fellow seems as eager as the others to excel in their disgusting acts.

The excrement is not given to invalids, but is administered on the occasion of an initiation, when every member of the fraternity must receive it, so that their bodies may be kept in condition for the other medicine. Kok'ko 'hlan'na talked much to Bi⁗ˡsiˡsi, who told him of the mi'wachi (see plate CI), of the te'likinawe, and of the bauble of his fraternity; and Kok'ko 'hlan'na said: "That is well; that is well. Come and live with me and you shall be musician and jester to the Sun Father." Before Bi⁗ˡsiˡsi disappeared in the waters of the spring he told his fraternity that whenever they needed him they should notify him with te'likinawe and he would come to them. Since that time Bi⁗ˡsiˡsi has borne the name of Pa'yatämu. The ground for a considerable distance about this spring is marshy and so covered with tall, rank grass that it was with difficulty the writer followed Nai'uchi[b] to the place. Very little water was found in the spring, and it was dark and disgusting to taste. The spring is walled on three sides, the walls, about 2 feet high, being made of the gray soil (from which the spring takes its name) and stones. Slender poles placed across the spring, with brush and soil, make the roof. The soil about this spring is used by the Ne'wekwe to decorate their persons and skull caps for their ceremonials.

To add to the amusement of the spectators, members of the Ne'wekwe frequently appear in the plaza with the Ko'yemshi between the dances of the gods, and whenever this occurs they play the fool generally; but it is when the Ne'wekwe appear in large numbers that their conduct is shocking.

The writer was first present at a meeting of the Ne'wekwe in 1884.

---

[a] The Kok'ko 'hlan'na of the Ne'wekwe is quite different from the patron god of the same name of the Great Fire fraternity.

[b] Elder brother Bow priest, since deceased.

Mary Wright Gill —

SHOP OF SILVERSMITH

a BEAD MAKING

b BEAD-MAKER'S FAMILY

On the evening of October 28 she happened to be passing the ceremonial chamber and was attracted by a half circle of white meal before the ground entrance to the chamber.   She immediately stepped

FIG. 28—Hopi Indian married to a Zuñi woman carving an image of Pa′yatämu for Ne′wekwe (Galaxy fraternity).

to the door, and although many Indians protested against her entering, she passed through the doorway before their cries and threats could be heard inside. The members of the fraternity looked up from their repast with surprise, but the writer was made welcome and invited to be seated and to join in the meal. An elaborately decorated tablet altar stood at the west end of the long room and a bar representing the Galaxy, on which stood two figures of Pa'yatämu (Bi‴ᵗsiᵗsi), extended across the room above the altar. Figure 28 shows a Hopi Indian carving an image of Pa'yatämu (see also plate CIV). The central portion of the bar is composed of cloud symbols with seven stars representing Ursa Major. The sun's face is shown by a disk of blue-green, surrounded by blocks of black and white, which denote the house of the clouds. The carved birds, suspended from the blue-green serrated clouds of the bar, represent the eshoᵗsi (bat). "If a man sees a bat when he is on his way at night to plant prayer plumes, he is happy, for he knows that in four days there will be much rain." The birds perched on the clouds of the upper portion of the bar represent the kĭa'wuloᵗki bird of the Zenith (Progne subis, purple martin). Lightning is symbolized by zigzag carvings at each end of the bar upon which figures of Pa'yatämu stand. The pendent eagle plumes symbolize the breath of life, which is A'wonawil'ona (see page 22), the supreme power. The tablet altar is composed of cloud symbols, the sun surrounded by the house of the clouds, the morning and evening stars carved on the tops of the rear posts and painted in white each side of the sun. The yellow lion of the north and blue-green of the west are represented on the two front posts, each of which has two hawk plumes standing from the top. Three small stone prey animals stand in line before the mi'wachi. A dark stone animal about 2 feet high is sejant before the altar. The flute of the fraternity, a medicine bowl, and a prayer-meal basket are placed before the altar. The star of the four winds, each point decorated with a star and cumulus clouds (the serrated ends) from which eagle cast plumes hang, is suspended above the altar (see description of plate LVIII, page 245).

On entering the chamber the writer observed at once an object which in their surprise at her entrance had for the moment been forgotten by the fraternity. It was the large stone animal. This fetish stood before the altar on the north and was partly covered with a lynx skin. But a few moments elapsed before they remembered with consternation that the sacred object was exposed to the eye of the visitor, who, appreciating the situation, appeared unconscious of any objects beyond the group of men about the food. Expressions of relief escaped their lips and on the instant several large blankets were thrown over it. Those whom the writer afterward questioned regarding the fetish at first denied all knowledge of it, but finally they admitted it to be their great father of Mystery medicine, and stated that the animal was converted into stone at the time when the great fire spread over the earth (see Origin of animal fetishes). After the meal the men formed into groups and prepared plume offerings, which are quite different from those made by other fraternities, spears of grass being combined with the plumes. Figure 29 shows the method of combining plumes and grass. As there was to be an initiation, a parallelogram was outlined in white meal on the floor near the altar,

FIG. 29—Method of combining plumes and grass.

and was afterward filled in with the meal. A line of black inclosed the whole, and segments of circles, symbolic of rain clouds, were formed in black upon the white ground. The black coloring is made from charred corncobs. A black line was run transversely across the parallelogram. Two figures were delineated also in black on the

ground color, one representing Bi⁗ˢsiˢsi and the other his younger
brother or fellow, and horizontal black lines crossed these figures from
the top of the head to the feet.

After the completion of the prayer plumes each man lighted a reed
filled with native tobacco and drawing a mouthful of smoke puffed it
through the feathers. The smoking of the cigarette was repeated
three times, and the prayer plumes were then gathered by one of the
fraternity and deposited in a basket tray, which was placed by the altar.
At 10 o'clock the members of the choir grouped themselves in the
southwest end of the room, the women sitting on the north side. The
large animal fetish now stood behind the altar.[a] The flutist had his
usual place behind the altar. The a′kwamosi, who sat on the north
side of the altar, proceeded to prepare the medicine water (see page
492). The consecration of the medicine water is virtually the same as
in all orders of Mystery medicine. After the water was consecrated the
a′kwamosi took each plume offering separately from the basket and
sprinkled it with water. He then dipped the water with a shell and
taking it into his mouth threw it in a spray over the plumes. After
the offerings were all sprinkled, the director wrapped them in corn
husks in groups of twos and fours and returned them to the basket
tray.

During the long ritual there were several interludes, when such
jokes as the following were introduced: "I know a girl; her name is
Manuelita; she is very good and pretty; she has many horses and
fine clothes; her father and mother are rich and are very nice. Who
desires Manuelita?" Some one in the choir calls the name of a member of the choir and the whole party joke him. Then again they call
the name of another girl and say: "She is ugly and poor, with mean
and despised parents." One of the choir is named as her lover, which
causes great merriment. The Catholic priest is mimicked and the
paternoster repeated with all seriousness to its close, when the assemblage indulges in wit at the expense of church and priest.[b]

After such an intermission the choir would take up the thread of
their ritual. The following are terms employed in one of their songs:
Käsh′ita ˡsi′ponipon (fish with bearded mouth); Käsh′ita chu′tape
(spotted fish); Käsh′ita ′hlan′na (great fish, or father of all fish).

The healing ceremonies of the order of Mystery medicine are similar to those described in connection with the Great Fire fraternity
(page 493). All night the weird performances continue, and at sunrise
the Kok′ko ′hlan′na appears in order to administer his medicine to the
novices—a man, a woman, and a girl 6 years of age. The latter is the

---

[a] When the officers of the fraternity and the writer became better acquainted no effort was made
to seclude the sacred fetish from view. This fetish, however, is usually partly covered with a
lynx skin or a sacred white embroidered blanket, so that it is necessary to raise the covering to see it
clearly.

[b] No other fraternity indulges in any such hilarity during their rites.

daughter of the Kĭa'kwemosi (rain priest of the North), who is a member of the fraternity and is as much of a buffoon when acting with the Ne'wekwe as any of the others. Though the child does not flinch from the ordeal, it is apparent that the noxious dose is taken with aversion. They must eat of the offal and drink the urine, that their intestines may not be destroyed by the hot medicine. This dose is given and received with the same seriousness that Christian churches observe with their most sacred sacraments. Later in the morning, when the

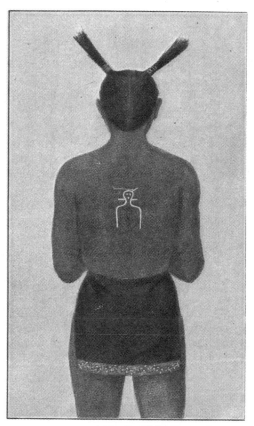

FIG. 30—Markings on back and arrangement of hair of the Ne'wekwe.

fraternity adjourns to the Si'aa' te'wita, the Kok'ko 'hlan'na administers another dose. He wears a cotton shirt, the sleeves of which are tied to the wrists with blue yarn. A Hopi embroidered blanket is worn as a skirt; it hangs from the waist and is fastened at the back. An embroidered cotton sash is tied at the back of the waist and a fox skin is pendent at the back. The lower portion of the legs is wrapped with white cotton cloth of Hopi weaving, and the feet are covered with dance moccasins. Ko'hakwa and turquoise beads hang in profusion over the breast. He carries in each hand large bunches of giant yucca, each

spear being split into fine pieces.   It is observed that the yucca sprays
are always held horizontally except when they are being used over the
back of some one.   He also carries in his left hand a feather wand wrapped with corn husks.   There are thirty men and five boys, all but one
having their bodies painted in ash color; the one exception has his
body painted black with bands of white.   All wear the black woven
breechcloth embroidered at the ends in blue.   A bust of Biʺ'ˢiˡsi,

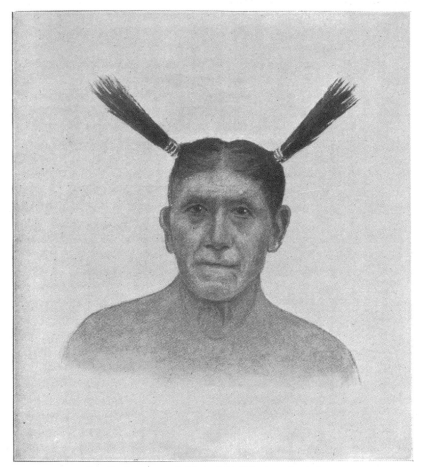

FIG. 31—Arrangement of hair of the Ne'wekwe, front view.

made by scraping off the paint from the body, is outlined on the back
of each man.   Figure 30 shows markings on the back.   Four of the
men wear skullcaps of cotton cloth painted in ash color, with bunches
of ribboned corn husks on top and on each side near the ears; the
others have their hair parted and tied in bunches.   Figure 31 shows
arrangement of hair.   Each carries a baton (see plate XVII) about 10
inches long and 1 inch in diameter wrapped closely with cotton cord,

which is afterward colored in circles of blue, green, and yellow, with black lines between, and finished at the top with banded turkey plumes. A single grain of corn, symbolic of the heart of the baton, is attached to the other end of the stick by wrappings of corn husks. The women and girls wear the conventional dress, with white Hopi blankets, bordered in red and blue, around their shoulders, and their best moccasins; their hair is done up like the men's.

The Kok'ko 'hlan'na administers the wretched morsel while moving in a peculiar dancing motion, reminding one of a humming bird hovering about a blossom. He advances to a man and whips him with the yucca switches, and then hands the dose to one of the Ko'yemshi gods (see page 33) in attendance, who in turn gives it to the person designated by the god. None of the older members of the fraternity seem to shrink from the dose, while some receive it with apparent relish. Occasionally the one receiving the morsel divides it with a man, woman, or child by placing his lips to the other's lips and forcing it into the mouth. The children accept it as a religious duty, but it is evident that they do not relish it. The god leaves the plaza at intervals and during his absence there is great revelry, the principal amusement being the wool-bag game, played between the Ne'wekwe and Ko'yemshi, and the emptying of vessels of urine over one another.

While the scenes at the closing of the initiatory ceremonies are disgusting, the acme of depravity is reached after the Kok'ko 'hlan'na takes his final departure from the plaza. The performances are now intended solely for amusement. The women and girls of the fraternity leave the plaza after the ceremony and take no part in the debauchery. The one who swallows the largest amount of filth with the greatest gusto is most commended by the fraternity and onlookers. A large bowl of urine is handed by a Ko'yemshi, who receives it from a woman on the house top, to a man of the fraternity, who, after drinking a portion, pours the remainder over himself by turning the bowl over his head. Women run to the edge of the roof and empty bowls of urine over the Ne'wekwe and Ko'yemshi. Each man endeavors to excel his fellows in buffoonery and in eating repulsive things, such as bits of old blankets or splinters of wood. They bite off the heads of living mice and chew them, tear dogs limb from limb, eat the intestines and fight over the liver like hungry wolves. It is a pleasure to state that the Ne'wekwe is the only fraternity that indulges in such practices.

The Ne'wekwe are great mimics and all strangers are subjects for their ridicule, especially the Catholic priest and the army officer. A youthful member is picked up by one of the fraternity, who declares him to be a "Católico santo," and the others form in line and carry the quasi saint about in procession. Finally a small blanket is spread on the ledge which extends across the north side of the plaza, and another is pinned to the wall behind it, in imitation of a church altar; two of the fraternity disappear, to return with two torches, which they place upon the mock altar, and then they seat the "santo" between these.   So the day passes until the evening shadows fall upon the most ridiculous and revolting sights that are to be seen in the pueblo of Zuñi.

'Sän'iakĭakwe (Hunters Fraternity)

The 'Sän'iakĭakwe, also called Sus'kikwe (Coyote), fraternity has two orders—Hunters and Fire.   The members of the latter order do not eat fire, but they play with large live coals and rub them over their bodies.

The painting made at the time of the initiation into the order of 'Sän'iakĭakwe is a disk with a ground color of white, and around the periphery two concentric circles in black which are blocked in white, symbolic of the house of the clouds.   A spread eagle painted in the center of the disk is surrounded by game, and groups of grains of corn are scattered over the surface.   The tablet altar is similar to those of the other fraternities.   Plate LIX shows the altar of the 'Sän'iakĭakwe with its accessories removed.   This fraternity has a second altar which differs from any the writer has observed, in that it is capped with eagle's tail plumes.   The songs of the order of the 'Sän'iakĭakwe invoke the gods to give them power over the game when on the hunt, and there are also most attractive songs of thanksgiving after the capturing of game.   Songs, too, are addressed directly to such animals and birds as prey upon game.

The ceremonial chamber of the Hunters fraternity is one of the few that extends north and south, and on the occasion of a ceremonial the tablet altar is erected in the north end of the room.   The pictures on the walls are permanent; the writer has never seen the walls without them except when the chamber was undergoing repairs.   The bear plays no part in the 'Sän'iakĭakwe, for although it will devour flesh, it lives principally on vegetable food; but the cougar, the gray wolf, the lynx, and the coyote are represented upon the walls in the chase after elk, mountain sheep, deer, jack rabbits, and the cottontail, which are fleeing from their pursuers.   Certain birds are also represented in the decoration—the su'lulukĭa (butcher bird, Lanius ludovicianus), "which pecks at the deer's head when he sleeps until it kills the deer;" the kĭe'wia (Oreospiza chlorura), which kills the deer by pecking at his eyes; the pi'pi (a species of hawk), which surprises the deer when grazing and kills him by striking him with his beak first on one side of the jaw and then the other; and the kĭakĭali (eagle), which does the same, not only to deer but to mountain

sheep and other game. Posh′kwa, an eagle that the Zuñis say has
perfectly black plumage, destroys game in the same way.

The fetish used in the hunt is the property of the individual and
passes from father to son. It does not belong to the clan or fraternity. This fetish is carried in the head-kerchief, the belt, or whatever the hunter may fancy. Fetishes of the larger animals, such as
the cougar and wolf, are carried for elk, deer, or antelope, and of the
eagle for rabbits and other small game. The shrew is employed as a
protection from mice and various rodents destructive of corn and
other vegetation. The hunter carries for large game an owl's wing
feather, and when game is discovered he takes the feather into his
mouth, expectorates in the direction of the game, and advances slowly.
He is sure to meet with success if his heart is good. To insure success in the hunt, arrows are shot into a vertical fissure in an inaccessible rock on the west wall of To′wa yäl′lännĕ (Corn mountain).
A hundred or more arrows were to be seen in this cleft in 1879. The
happy possessor of a rifle carries it in preference to the bow and
arrows. There is a good drawing in blue-gray of a deer on the face
of a mesa about 30 miles southwest of Zuñi, which is shot at by all
hunters who pass that way, and success is inevitable for the one whose
arrow strikes the mark. The Zuñis say that their ancestors made
this pictograph, which is most sacred, during their migrations from
the far northwest when the world was new.

When skins are to be used for ceremonial masks or fetishes, the
game must be smothered, not shot. The process of securing game for
these purposes is as follows:

A deer drive of chaparral more or less extensive is constructed,
and at intervals of about 100 yards openings are left, and before each
of these openings a pit is dug sufficiently large to admit a deer.
Two poles are laid saltirewise between the entrance and the bottom of
the pit, which is finished at the top with poles laid as beams are placed
at the hatchway of a ki′wiᵗsinĕ.ᵃ Two poles extend across the opening at the top of the chaparral and so near the trap that should the
deer be able to extricate himself he has not room to jump the pole
beyond. Each huntsman deposits five prayer plumes in each trap,
three to Kok′ko A′wan (Council of the Gods), and two to ancestors.
Two of the hunters wear cotton shirts with sleeves to the elbow, the
front and back of the shirt being painted to represent as nearly as
possible the body of the deer; the hands and the arms to the elbow
and also the sleeves are colored to represent the deer's forelegs.
Each wears the skin of a deer's head over his head, held in place by
buckskin thongs. In this dress the two huntsmen imitate as closely
as possible, even to the browsing, the game they would catch. As
soon as a deer or herd is started these two men are assisted by the

ᵃChambers dedicated to anthropic worship.

others of the party to drive the deer to the chaparral and down it to an opening. As soon as a deer discovers a clear spot with only a pole to obstruct his flight he jumps, only to find himself caught in a trap. If the fall does not kill the deer, one or more men smother it by pressing the nostrils, at the same time offering the following prayer to A'wonawil'ona: [a]

Lu′kĭa yä′tonně yäm ′Kĭash′ima yäm to′shonaně yäm
  This   day   your   rains,   your   seeds,   your

O′naya′nakĭa ho′o   ä′nichiyanap′tu
  Mystery medicine   I   inhale the sacred breath of life.

Free translation: This day I give you my thanks for your rains, your seeds, and the mysteries of life which I inhale.

When a deer or an antelope is brought from the hunt, the hunter is announced by some of the villagers, whereupon the matron of the home of the hunter advances to meet him, carrying a basket of sacred meal, some of which she sprinkles upon the game, and as she returns she throws a line of meal before her, the hunter following immediately behind. After entering the house the hunter places the game temporarily on a sheepskin until the arrival of those who are to participate in the ceremonial. They comprise the members of the household, the order of the ′Sän′iakĭakwe, and the members of the Coyote clan. Another sheepskin is laid on the floor, to which the game is transferred, with the head of the animal toward the east near a small circular hole, symbolic of the entrance to the undermost world, in the stone floor in which prayer plumes to the te′nas′säli (mythical medicine plant), which is eaten by the game, are buried.

Prayer plumes can only be offered when the members of the household belong either to the ′Sän′iakĭakwe fraternity or to the Coyote clan. When the offerings are to be deposited, those which have been previously buried in the cavity are removed in order to make room for the new ones and are cast into the river to be carried to Ko′thluwala′wa (abiding place of the Council of the Gods). After the plumes are deposited the hole is plastered over—another illustration of the manner of concealing sacred objects in cavities in dwellings. The ′Sän′iakĭakwe possess the blossoms and the roots of the te′nas′säli because it is good medicine for game.

One of the most attractive dances in Zuñi has been adopted from the Hopi Indians, the masks for which represent the heads of different game animals, from the elk to the hare. The leader of the dances personates Le′lentu, the Hopi god of music, butterflies, and flowers, who bears a tray or bowl containing a flowering plant of the te′nas′säli. Nothing could seem more Chinese than the paper blossoms on this artificial plant. When it is set down in the plaza the dancers gather around to eat the flowers. The animal-like and graceful movements of the men personating the game present a beautiful picture (see plate cv). These dancers appear at intervals during the day, and the scenes close with a man shooting a little cottontail, which appears to give great grief to the other animals.

_____

[a] See classification of higher powers.

The medicine bag containing the te′nas′säli is placed by the side of the game. The fetish which was carried to the hunt, if the animal was shot, was dipped into blood of the game immediately after it was killed and was told to eat of the blood. This is now laid beside the game. The neck of the animal is elaborately ornamented with necklaces of ko′hakwe, turquoise, and coral. A cotton cloth is first laid over the unflayed body of the game, and upon this a white cotton embroidered sacred blanket. Plate CVI a shows a deer lying in state. The song of thanksgiving is then sung. After the song the father of the household, the family, and all present, including the youngest children, their mothers guiding their tiny hands, sprinkle sacred meal on the game.

The deer is now flayed. The first cut is made from the heart, or breast, to the mouth. The knife is then run from the heart out and down the right foreleg, then along the ventral line and down the right hind leg. This process is repeated on the left side of the animal. Prayer meal and corn pollen are sprinkled into the mouth of the deer and the prayer mentioned above is repeated. After the animal is flayed it is drawn. The fetish is dipped in the first blood drawn from a deer which has been smothered. If the game is not to be offered ceremonially to the A′shiwanni, it is consumed by the fortunate huntsman and his friends.[a] The heart and intestines are chopped and put into the paunch and are cooked in an excavation lined with slabs, which contains live coals. The skin is his unless the hunt was for the purpose of securing skins for masks or other religious purposes. If the skin of the head to be used as a mask by the huntsman, it is packed with hay in order that it may retain its shape while it is being cured. A hoop of white cedar is attached to the base, and buckskin thongs are secured on each side with which to tie the head to that of the hunter.

A portion of all game, whether it is used for ceremonial purposes or otherwise, is offered to the Beast Gods, with prayers that they will intercede with the Sun Father and the Council of the Gods for the A′shiwi. It is related that years ago the warrior of the ′Sän′iakïakwe threw large live coals of fire to the six regions in order that the game should hurry and come near. He threw to the North for the blacktail deer, to the West for the mountain sheep, to the South for the antelope, to the East for the whitetail deer, to the Zenith for the jack rabbit, to the Nadir for the cottontail rabbit.

RABBIT HUNT

Although the rabbit hunt described in anthropic worship occurs only by the order of certain priests, the one here recorded is by order of the governor. It also is of a religious character.

---

[a] After the flesh is eaten its spiritual life returns to the spirit home whence it came, saying: "I have been to my people and given them my flesh for food; they were happy and their hearts were good; they sang the song, my song, over me, and I will again return to them."

The hunt occurs in the three farming districts of the Zuñis—Pescado, Nutria, and Ojo Caliente—as thanksgiving for abundant crops, and takes place immediately after the gathering of the corn and wheat.

Mr Stevenson and the writer accompanied a party which went out from Zuñi to Ojo Caliente. Those who had not returned to Zuñi from their summer homes were found busy at this place preparing for the hunt. The men's hair was hanging loosely about their shoulders, having recently been washed in yucca suds, since no one can take part in any ceremony without first washing the hair in yucca. The women were busy arranging for the feast to be enjoyed after the hunt. A jack rabbit and a cottontail were suspended from the outer beams of one of the houses. These had evidently been there many days. Upon inquiry as to why the decomposed bodies were not cast away, the reply was: "They were caught some days ago by order of the Ko'yemshi [a] and hung there for good luck to hunters, and they must not be taken down until after the hunt."

At 1 o'clock the command was given, and in a short time every man in the village was mounted, with rabbit stick in hand, many of them carrying two, and a couple were handed to Mr Stevenson with the words: "You, too, must join in the hunt." The writer was wise enough to refuse the two that were offered to her, knowing the certainty of failure.

No Zuñi women were to accompany this party, but as a young man was taking leave of his bride her eyes expressed such a longing to accompany him that the writer insisted that the unspoken wish be gratified. It was not until after much persuasion, however, that the pretty little girl, bedecked in her best gown and jewels, seated herself behind her husband's saddle and rode off with him. The several hundred Indians, all gaily dressed, made a pleasing picture. The horses were kept in a walk until a knoll, about half a mile from the village, was reached. The A'wan tä''chu (Great Father) Ko'yemshi, his pe'kwĭn (deputy), and a man of the 'Sän'iakĭakwe fraternity sat at the base of a piñon tree at the summit of the knoll. The Great Father and his deputy were vis-a-vis, one facing east, the other west. The other man faced east. The Great Father clasped the hands of his deputy, his hands passing under those of the deputy.

The party of hunters dismounted and sat around the trio while the Great Father whispered a long prayer in a most impressive manner. At the close of every stanza "Athlu" (amen) was repeated by the deputy and the man of the 'Sän'iakĭakwe fraternity. At the close of the prayer the Great Father placed the clasped hands to the mouth of the deputy and, drawing them to his own mouth, inhaled from him a breath of all that is good. The deputy now repeated the prayer while he clasped the Great Father's hands. These prayers are a thanksgiving for the crops and good health to the people and a petition that in years to come the ancients may bless them with the same good crops, that their people may not die, but live, and sleep to awake as little children in Ko'thluwala'wa (abiding place of the Council of the Gods). The ceremony closed with a smoke, in which all joined. The two Ko'-yemshi and the man of 'Sän'iakĭakwe fraternity led the way on foot to a fire previously made by the Ko'yemshi that was burning in a low and symmetrical cedar tree, the flames spreading evenly and beautifully. They must walk, because when the world was new the A'shiwi had no horses. The three men stood near the fire, offering prayers to the dead and begging the intercession of their ancestors with the Council of the Gods that the rain-makers should water the earth. Bread was thrown into the flames, with a call to the fire to eat and convey the spiritual essence of the food to the dead.

The hunters now dismounted in couples, and receiving bits of bread from the Great Father, who had an armful, threw them into the fire, with prayers that the

---

a See p. 33.

spiritual part might be conveyed to the gods. After passing their rabbit sticks through the flames, asking the gods to crown them with success, they remounted their horses. The Ko'yemshi and member of the 'Sän'iakĭakwe led them for a distance; then they gave the order to proceed with the hunt. The party divided into squads. For a time there was considerable disputing in regard to the disposition of Mr Stevenson and the writer, each party claiming the company of the visitors. Finally it was agreed that they should be allowed to choose for themselves, and they accompanied the party composed of the more important men. They had not proceeded many steps when a little cottontail came skipping along, all unconscious of its fate. There was confusion as all hands rushed after the wee thing, surrounding it, each man intent upon being the captor. With the chivalry of a knight the happy man presented the rabbit to the writer. The Indians are very dexterous in the use of the rabbit stick. Not a single rabbit that appeared escaped the weapon. Mr Stevenson killed the second rabbit, which was the occasion of much rejoicing among the Indians, for they took his success as evidence that his heart was with them and their people. When the rabbit is surprised it starts off in one direction, but finding itself cut off from escape it darts to another point and there meets with a barrier, and so to all points until it becomes utterly bewildered, and it is not remarkable that one of the dozen sticks darted toward it should strike the mark. The Great Father Ko'yemshi remained with the hunters until the killing of the first rabbit, when he dipped his fetish into its blood. This was not repeated by any of the hunters and the writer understands that fetishes are not generally carried on the occasion of a ceremonial rabbit hunt. At sundown the party returned, some to Ojo Caliente and many to Zuñi, laden with rabbits. The back of the writer's saddle was fringed with them.

When one of these hunts is over, each hunter takes his rabbits to his home, where some member of the household, male or female, places them abreast on their sides, with their heads to the east and facing south. An ear of corn is placed between the fore paws of each rabbit, the upper end of the corn being even with the mouth (see plate CVI b), and each member of the household sprinkles meal and prays that the beings of the rabbits may return home and send many more rabbits. The game is afterward flayed. The skin is left on the fore paws, the tips of the ears, around the mouth, and around each eye, and a bit of it on the breast just below the neck; it is then cut crosswise in the middle of the paunch and is drawn; the forelegs are crossed, the hind legs bent upward at the joint, so that the feet meet upon the back; food, usually wafer bread, is placed under the left foreleg, and the rabbits are laid on the coals on their breasts with their heads to the east and remain in this position until the first crackling noise, when they are removed, for then the spiritual essence of the bread has left the body and gone to feed the rabbits. If this is not done, the rabbits will not appear, and hence can not be secured. The one who dresses the rabbits must wash the blood off his hands over the fire. For this purpose water is taken into the mouth and while the hands are held over the fireplace the water is poured from the mouth over them. This is to insure success in the rabbit hunt; if one fail to do this and should the blood be washed from the hands at a distance from the fire, the rabbits will go off, and can not be caught.

'HLE'WEKWE (WOOD FRATERNITY), OR SWORD SWALLOWERS

The 'Hle'wekwe separated from their people at Hän''lipĭnkĭa[a] to travel northward in quest of the Middle of the world. The great ones of the 'Hle'wekwe carried two ĕt'towe (rain and crop fetishes; see A'shiwanni, rain priesthood) with them—the 'hle'ĕt'tonĕ, the property of the fraternity; and mu'ĕt'tonĕ, the cherished possession of the 'Ko''loktakwe (Sand-hill crane) clan. Previous to the separation of the 'Hle'wekwe from the other A'shiwi these most precious of precious things contained only the seeds of water for rain and vegetation. Some time after the separation, the ĕt'towe being placed upon cloud forms of meal on the ground with te'likinawe (prayer plumes), and prayers being offered for rain, great was the consternation when snow came instead. Never before had the ĕt'towe brought snow; never before had the people seen snow; but henceforth these precious seed reeds of the 'Hle'wekwe were destined to bring the cold rains and snows of winter.[b]

Having proceeded as far north as the directors thought wise, a desperate dispute arose between a man and wife and the fraternity, the former declaring that the northern route should be continued, while the others declared that their course should now be changed and they should go a little southward and then eastward.

A large and conspicuous Triassic sandstone rock, about 1½ miles southwest of Zuñi, contained interesting markings that are declared by the Zuñis to be a map of the route followed by the 'Hle'wekwe after separating from their people, together with other roads, with certain mesas, and constellations. An associate rain priest, who was also a member of the 'Hle'wekwe, knowing the interest of the writer in the markings on this rock, decided that she should have them; with no other tools than two axes, a slab containing the pictographs was severed, and this was forwarded to the United States National Museum. (See plate CVII.)

This etching is believed by the Zuñis to have been made by the original director of the 'Hle'wekwe fraternity. The wavy line crossing the stone indicates the course of migration of the 'Hle'wekwe from Hän''lipĭnkĭa in the west to Shi'papolima in the east. After traveling a long distance northward, the 'Hle'wekwe turned south, and then proceeded to Shi'papolima in the east. The line crossing the bend in the road was followed by the fraternity to secure certain medicinal plants. They returned to the point whence they started for the plants and then resumed their journey. The pits north of the line of travel indicate mesas and mountain peaks. The significance of the hand symbol is not clear. The larger pit east of the hand is an extensive basin constantly filled with water from rains and snows. The dots surrounding the pit represent Ursa Minor. The short lines, no longer than an inch in the pictograph, indicate the number of years consumed by the 'Hle'wekwe in going from Hän''lipĭnkĭa to Shi'papolima and thence to I'tiwanna, the site of the present Zuñi. The human figure is an ancient Shi'wi before the tail and water moss had been removed

---

[a] See p. 34.

[b] While tradition points to the far northwest as the Zuñi place of nativity, the belief, not only of the 'Hle'wekwe but of the combined priesthood, that snows were unknown until brought by the ĕt'towe of the 'Hle'wekwe on their northern journey furnishes an interesting subject for investigation. According to the 'Hle'wekwe, the roots of grasses, after the snow disappeared, contained much moisture and furnished refreshment for them when thirsty.

ZUÑI WAGON IN 1879

AUCTIONEERING

and the webbed hands and feet cut. The dots about this figure denote hail, for the director of the 'Hle'wekwe fraternity desired much hail. The straight line extending east and west across the slab indicates the road leading from Hän'ʻlipĭnkĭa to the Salt Mother before she left her home east of I'tiwanna. The cross near the east end of this line and south of it symbolizes the morning star. The group of seven dots denotes Ursa Major; the group of four, the Pleiades. The short heavy line indicates the road followed by the Kĭa'nakwe on their way to the place where they were found by the A'shiwi.

The man and wife made themselves so offensive to the fraternity that when they were asleep in one another's arms on their blanket of ʻsu'le (a grass) the 'Hle'wekwe lifted them in the blanket and tossed them to the far north, where they remained and multiplied, becoming giants. These are the Su'ni-a'shiwanni.

Proceeding eastward, the 'Hle'wekwe drew near to Shi'papolima, home of Po'shaiyänki (Zuñi culture hero). The two chief officers of the fraternity conducted them to the presence of Po'shaiyänki, and through him they became known to the people of medicine and craft and were taught by Ä'chiyälä'topa (being with wings and a tail of knives) the art or secret of sword swallowing.[a]

When the 'Hle'wekwe started on their return journey they were provided with Beast Gods as warriors. It has been stated that the Divine Ones visited Shi'papolima and transformed the medicine men into Beast Gods as guardians of the world. The cougar, bear, badger, wolf, shrew, and six snakes for the six regions were appointed to accompany the 'Hle'wekwe. Long was their journey and many their stops ere finding the Middle place and their people. On reaching To'yakwi (Nutria)[b] they built a village and here, as elsewhere, they placed their ĕt'towe, with the sacred prayer plumes, on the ground upon cloud symbols of meal, and prayed, whereupon the earth was soon covered with snow. Then the people cried: "Let us hunt the rabbit." Two of the officers of the 'Hle'wekwe instead of hunting the rabbit went to the mountains for deer. Looking westward from the mountain top they discovered smoke, and exclaiming that their people must be there they hastened toward the point whence the smoke issued. When the two officers entered the village the people inquired of them who they were, and they replied: "We are A'shiwi, of the 'Hle'wekwe fraternity." The Kĭa'kwemosi (rain priest of the North) was notified and he gave them a warm greeting and said: "After ten days [time periods] bring your people hither." Upon their return to To'yakwi the two officers told of their meeting with the A'shiwi, and the 'Hle'wekwe, anxious to be again with their people, moved on nearer to

---

[a] The swords originally used by this fraternity are supposed to have been exactly like the one now used by the 'Hlĕm'mosona (sword director), which is asserted to be the original sword presented by Ä'chiyälä'topa to the original 'Hlĕm'mosona. This sword has a cylindrical handle about 3 inches in thickness, and there are no plumes attached. The zigzag sword carried by the warrior of the fraternity is also declared to be one of the original swords.

[b] Nutria is a farming district 25 miles east of Zuñi.

I'tiwanna, stopping at Top'apkwĭnna (black rocks). Here their original director disappeared in the spring, which has since been a most sacred spot to the 'Hle'wekwe, who assert that underground roads lead from it to Ko'thluwala'wa and A'witĕn te'hula (fourth or undermost world). Again the two officers visited their people at I'tiwanna and told the A'shiwanni (rain priests) that they wished to come to the Middle of the world. The Kĭa'kwemosi said: "You shall make te'likinawe (prayer plumes) for rain." They answered: "No; you have found the Middle; you shall make te'likinawe." Each party insisted that the other should prepare the plume offerings. Finally the A'shiwanni made te'likinawe and planted them, whereupon clouds gathered from the four quarters, rain fell for four days and four nights, and the rivers and lakes were full. Then the two officers of the 'Hle'wekwe made te'likinawe and planted them, and soon the smallest white clouds could be seen everywhere; then there came so many that they appeared as one great sheet, and snow fell for four days and nights. The snow was halfway up the ladders of the houses. The A'shiwanni were very angry, and the Kĭa'kwemosi visited the village of the 'Hle'wekwe and told them he did not wish them to be near. "Should you come and bring your ĕt'towe and songs for snows, we should have no corn."[a] The director of the 'Hle'wekwe replied: "If you have only warm rains your corn will fall over and die after it has come a little above the earth. The earth should be cooled part of the time with the snows; then the sun's rays will melt the snows and sink them into the earth, and when the warm rains come the corn will be strong." "It is well," said the Kĭa'kwemosi. Then the Shi'wanni of the West made ä te'likinanĕ and gave it to the director of the 'Hle'wekwe, who also made one and planted both at the spring, into which he afterward disappeared, and much rain fell. It rained for four days and four nights, so that all the rain roads (stream beds) were filled with water, and the people were happy and contented, being assured of the value of the ĕt'towe containing the seeds for snow. The Kĭa'kwemosi and other A'shiwanni desired that the return of the 'Hle'wekwe should meet with such a reception as became their exceeding greatness. Wishing that there should be more than two ĕt'towe for snows, the Kĭa'kwemosi chose one of those brought to I'tiwanna by the Kĭa'nakwe people of the Corn clan,[b] one belonging to the Badger clan, and one from the Ai'yaho'kwe (a certain plant) clan. He designated these ĕt'towe as mu'ĕt'towe. He also chose maidens as bearers of the ĕt'towe and 'hla'we (bunches of slender white stalks with beautiful silvery leaves resembling feathers, brought by the Corn maidens from the undermost world).[c] Reflecting on whom he should choose as leader of these, he decided

[a] Though the above legend is associated in the minds of the Zuñis with the site of the present pueblo, such a legend must have had its origin with a people unaccustomed to snow.

[b] See p. 44.

[c] See Discovery of the Corn maidens.

to select a man from his own clan, the Pi′chikwe (Dogwood). This man carried a sacred meal basket of the A′shiwanni, supposed to have been brought from the undermost world, and he was called the Mu′-chailihä′nona. The Kĭa′kwemosi also chose two maidens and a youth, virgins, whom he called the Mu′waiye,[a] to dance on the occasion, and the people of a ki′wi⸱sinĕ to accompany these dancers and sing for them.

The Beast Gods who accompanied the 'Hle′wekwe from Shi′papo-lima continued with them to I′tiwanna. The fraternity were met by the first body of A′shiwanni (rain priests), who had been apprised of their coming, and were conducted to Si′aa′ te′wita (sacred dance plaza), the fraternity grouping themselves on the west side. Of the beast warriors, two sat on the west side toward the north and played on notched sticks with deer leg bones, the sticks resting on inverted baskets, each basket being placed upon a cross of meal on the ground, while the other beast warriors sat in the center of the plaza, looking upward to the heavens. After the elaborate ceremonial in Si′aa′. te′wita, the ĕt′towe were placed in baskets partly filled with meal and the baskets were set in line on the floor of the O′he'wa ki′wi⸱sinĕ.[b] Then the shi′wanni of the mu′ĕttonĕ that belonged to the 'Ko''loktakwe clan, and the singing man, or leader, of the ĕt′towe-bearers that were chosen to accompany those of the 'Hle′wekwe in the ceremonial, prayed over the ĕt′towe, that they might bring snows and cold rains. After these prayers the director of the 'Hle′wekwe announced that for one night the ĕt′towe would countenance any amount of licentiousness,[c] the payment from each man being a string of beads large enough to encircle his thumb. This should be given to the woman of his choice, who in turn should deposit it with the ĕt′towe.

The 'Hle′wekwe has but two orders, the Sword and the Spruce (Pseudotsuga douglassii). The fraternity holds two regular meetings annually, one in January and the other in February.[d]

Should the 'Hle′wekwe fraternity dance or make te′likinawe in summer, the corn would freeze, as their songs and dances are for cold rains and snows. The medicines of the 'Hle′wekwe are especially good for sore throat. When a person is sick the father or mother of the patient or, should the parents not be living, the brother or a near relative, carries a quantity of prayer meal wrapped in a

---

[a] Mu′waiye has reference to the bending of the knees or body.

[b] See Ki′wi⸱siwe and their functions.

[c] There are no rites among the Zuñis or any other Indian tribe which the writer has studied that involve any conditions of unchastity, and it is only during the closing ceremonies of the 'Hle′wekwe fraternity, the night dances of the harvest festival, the frolics of Ko′yemshi, and one or two borrowed dances that any suggestion of improper conduct is made by men associated with the ceremonies. Immoral women in Zuñi are regarded with the same aversion as they are in civilization; at least such was the case until these people became demoralized by the environment of civilization.

[d] At the time the writer last observed the indoor ceremonial the fraternity had two directors. One having retired on account of age, another took his place as the active director, yet the aged man presided ex officio at the ceremonials and performed some duties.

corn husk to the doctor of his choice who is associated with the 'Hle'wekwe, who personally notifies the warrior of the fraternity, who in turn notifies each member of the organization to be present at night in the ceremonial chamber.   Later all go with their rattles from the ceremonial chamber to the invalid's house and sing.   The relatives of the invalid may be present.   A basket containing the corn husk of meal, presented to the doctor by the parent or relative of the invalid, is placed on the floor, and after one song by the fraternity the husk is opened and each member of the fraternity, even the youngest child, takes a pinch of the meal and, passing to the invalid, runs the hand containing the meal up the larynx to the tip of the chin.   Retaining the meal in the hand, he passes directly out of the house, and facing east prays to the Pleiades and Orion for the restoration of the invalid, and then throws the meal toward the east.   Three more songs are sung and then all return to their homes except the chosen doctor and one woman of the fraternity whom he selects.   The family also withdraw.   The two remain alone with the invalid.   Early in the morning. a member of the fraternity brings a white-blossomed medicine plant[a] which has been freshly gathered.   A woman of the fraternity brings the pot in which the medicine is to be boiled, and the woman in attendance prepares it for the invalid, who drinks three large gourdfuls one after the other.[b]   The throat is then tickled with a feather by the doctor, and copious vomiting is the result.   The material ejected is carried by the woman who prepared the medicine some distance from the house; it must not be emptied near by.   This treatment is repeated for four mornings.   On the fifth morning a tea is made from a red root and drunk warm, and is administered on the three succeeding mornings.   The family may now be present.   After the tea is drunk the doctor and the woman leave the house for a short time, going a distance from the village, and each deposits two prayer plumes, which were made by the doctor on the fourth day, to the deceased members of the fraternity.   The doctor and associate remain with the patient until after their morning meal on the eighth day.

When one has been restored to health by the 'Hle'wekwe, he may at any time go to his doctor and request permission to join the fraternity, handing him at the same time a small quantity of meal wrapped in a corn husk, with a fluffy eagle plume pendent from the white cord wrapping.   Should the request be made in summer one winter must pass and another come before initiation, as the 'Hle'wekwe fraternity holds only winter ceremonials.   It is common for a member of the fraternity to solicit new members, especially among his own clan. Certain clans are always represented in this fraternity.   The 'Hlĕm'-

---

[a] Plant not yet classified.

[b] No one not a member of the 'Hle'wekwe could be induced to enter the room of the patient while the medicine is there.   All the meals of the doctor and his associate during their stay with the invalid are served by the patient's family in a separate room from that occupied by the invalid.

mosona (sword director) must be of the ᵗKo′ᶜloktakwe clan and the
pe′kwĭn (deputy) of the To′wakwe (Corn) clan.   Other offices are
filled by the Pi′chikwe clan, while the warrior must be of the Äiñ′she
(Bear) clan.   This latter clan having few representatives in the fraternity, two children (a boy of 5 years and a girl his senior by three
or four years) were brought into the fraternity.   The boy begged
that he might be excused, but his mother was firm, being impressed
with the importance of the child's fulfilling his duty to this body.
Though this child had been a member of the fraternity but a year
when the ceremonial described occurred, there was no more enthusiastic member.   He had not learned to swallow the sword, but he
shook his rattle, which was but half as large as those of his elders,
with the others and kept perfect time in the dance, never exhibiting
the slightest weariness; nor did he flinch from the cold walks in the
snow from house to house at midnight in January and February.

Besides the method of entering this fraternity by reason of the success of the medicine doctor in the case of sickness, there is another
method, which is for a member of the fraternity to go to the house of
the person he desires to have join the organization and make the propo-
sition.   An adult is addressed directly; if a child is solicited, the child's
parents and not the child are addressed.   If this invitation is accepted,
the person invited gives to the solicitor a quantity of meal wrapped in a
corn husk, with a single white fluffy eagle feather attached by means of
white cotton cord, and the solicitor thus becomes his fraternity father.
Both the fraternity father and the novice stoop with bended knees.
The novice holds the husk containing the meal and plume in both
hands, the thumbs over the top and the fingers pointing to the fraternity father, who, holding the candidate's hands with his thumbs on
top, moves the hands to the six regions with a prayer and receives the
package of meal from the novice.

On the day previous to the opening of the ceremonial in the following year the fraternity father removes the eagle feather from the
package of meal, places it in another husk, sprinkles meal upon it,
folds the husk, tying it at each end with cotton cord, and leaves it for
the time being in his home.   He afterward visits the house of each
member of his clan and of the clan of his paternal parent, carrying the
husk of meal from which the feather was removed, and gives a pinch
to each female of both clans.   The fraternity father and each recipient
stoop in turn with bended knees, facing one another.   After a pinch of
meal is received in the palm of the left hand, the right hand is placed
over it, the man holding the hands with both of his while he offers a
prayer for the good health of the members of his fraternity and good
heart of the one receiving the meal, and the same for the child who is to
be received into the fraternity.   Meal is often given to girls not over 5

years of age. Each person wraps her pinch of meal in a bit of corn husk, tying it with a ribbon of the same, and lays the package away until the following morning, when it is sprinkled at daylight out of doors to the rising sun. All the recipients of the meal are expected to be present and take part at the all-night dance which occurs on the fifth night of the ceremonial.

Some days prior to the actual ceremony the fraternity gathers in the ceremonial chamber to practice its songs, which, however, never begin until near the approach of midnight, the early part of the evening being consumed in telling te'lapnawe (tales); at least, it was so in the past. Now, these Indians have so many grievances against the United States Government and the white settlers of the country that their present distressed condition is ever the subject of discussion, and no time is found at these gatherings for the old tales in which in former days they found such delight.

These gatherings for rehearsal bring no change of the family arrangements. Each woman of the household prepares in the same room her children's beds and her own when she chooses, and husbands, wives, and little ones retire at will. The elder ones frequently sit near the group of the fraternity and join in the discussion until the director is notified that the villagers are asleep or are engaged in other meetings, when the first stroke of the drum is the signal for the choir to begin.

In all Zuñi worship, feathers form a conspicuous feature. The 'Hle'wekwe make la'showawe (one or more plumes attached to cotton cord) of wing feathers of the 'hlai'aluko (Sialia arctica), which are not more than 2 inches in length, and the 'Hlĕm'mosona carries them to the He'iwa (North) ki'wi'sinĕ on the tenth morning of the winter solstice ceremonies. The Kǐa'kwemosi chooses two young men and two girls to serve as a'mosi (directors) and a'mosono'‘kǐa (directresses) to the Mu'waiye,[a] and two young men and two girls to act in the same capacity to the six members of the A'pi'‘lӓshiwanni (Bow priesthood), who make the tehl'nawe[b] to be carried in the i'kwǐnnakǐa, circle dance, and who lead the dance. The la'showawe referred to are given by the pe'kwǐn (sun priest) to the four amosi, and each one gives a la'showannĕ of a single plume to his associate directress and each director

---

[a] The Mu'waiye are two girls and one youth. Should they not be virgins, the snows for which they dance would not come.

[b] The tehl'nanĕ (singular for tehl'nawe) is a slender staff the length of the extended arms, the ends cut squarely off, and each painted for one of the six regions. Seeds are held in place at the lower end by a wrapping of corn husk extending 7 or 8 inches up the staff, bound on with yucca ribbons. An eagle plume, a buzzard feather, and four feathers from smaller birds are attached in a group midway on the staff, the center of the staff being supposed to lie directly over the heart, which is indicated by the center of the breast, when measured by the extended arms. A la'showannĕ of a tail feather and a white fluffy eagle feather hang by a cotton cord from the upper group of feathers. A miniature war club, a bow and arrows with a shell strung on the bowstring, and a shield formed of a slender hoop, filled in with a network of cotton, its circumference measured by bending it around the knee, are attached to the staff. The bow and arrows are colored red and the shield and groups of plumes are rubbed with a dry red paint. The la'showannĕ given to each maker of a tehl'nanĕ by the mo'sona who selects him is attached to the bow, and five fluffy eagle plumes, also rubbed over with the pigment, are tied to the shield. A stick as long as from the

keeps one composed of two feathers for himself. These plumes are worn attached to the hair from this time to the close of the ᵗHleʹ-wekwe ceremonial as an insignia of their office. The remainder of the laʹshowawe are afterwards distributed by the aʹmosi among those who are to form the choir for the Muʹwaiye, the kiʹwiᵗsinĕ, which is to furnish the singers having been selected by the Kĭaʹkwemosi, and among such members of the Bow priesthood as are chosen to make the tehlʹnawe. The peʹkwĭn also gives laʹshowawe of the ᵗhlaiʹaluko, made by the first body of the Aʹshiwanni in the house of the Shiʹwa-noʹᵗkĭa (Priestess of fecundity) to the ᵗHlĕmʹmosona as a notification that the swords of the fraternity shall be removed from his house to the ceremonial chamber in six days.ᵃ At the same time the Kĭaʹkwe-mosi gives two laʹshowawe to the ᵗHlĕmʹmosona for two women of the fraternity whom he chooses to hold the two ĕtʹtowe of the ᵗHleʹwekwe in the plaza on the fifth day of the ceremonial. These laʹshowawe are handed to the women with the words: " In ten days you shall bear the mother ĕtʹtonĕ."

A ceremony in 1892, initiating a youth and maiden, is here described.

When the first day of the real ceremony arrives, each male member brings a burro's pack of wood, which is deposited in the street before the house and carried to the roof of the ceremonial chamber, where it is carefully stacked, principally by the female members of the fraternity and the women of the house. This is quite a merrymaking time, when the girls and women are at liberty to play practical jokes on their elders.

The medicine to be used in the ceremonial is secured by one of the wood-gatherers, the fraternity father of the female novice being the collector on the occasion described, who secretes it near the village when he brings his load of wood, returning for it on the following morning. It can not be brought to the pueblo until the room is prepared to receive it on account of its infectious qualities, which are transmitted not only directly from the plant, but through anyone who has been near or has inhaled its fumes after it has been uprooted. By midnight the room is empty and the floor washed, the walls are whitened, and the doors and windows opening into the adjoining rooms are carefully plastered over so that not a crevice is left through which the fumes of the medicine to be prepared by the fraternity on

---

elbow to the tip of the thumb and 1 inch in diameter, colored red, with a single buzzard feather, is attached to the upper end of each tehlʹnanĕ, the lower end having seeds bound on in corn husks. The tehlʹnanĕ carried by the elder brother Bow priest is supposed to have belonged to the Gods of War. It is white, being freshly decorated whenever it is brought into use, and is tipped with a fine spearhead 4 inches long. A fringe of goat's wool, 5 inches deep, dyed a purplish red, with four eagle feathers attached at equal distances, hangs from the upper portion of the staff. This tehlʹnanĕ is kept in the house of the younger brother Bow priest.

ᵃ The blades only are left in charge of the ᵗHlĕmʹmosona, who keeps them, when not in use, in an old cougar skin with not a vestige of hair on it. They are made of juniper, the length from the tip of the middle finger to the elbow, three-fourths of an inch wide, slightly curved, and rounded at the end. They are rubbed with cougar or bear grease and red hematite (see pl. CIX). The elaborate feathered handles are stored away in the ceremonial house.

the following morning can penetrate and cause bad throats and perhaps death to the uninitiated. The fraternity convenes during the evening, when the swords are deposited in the ceremonial chamber and the choir sing; but they disband at midnight, returning to their homes. The two men who are to act as fraternity fathers to the novices bring in sheep from their herds on the following morning, taking them to their homes to be dressed for the coming feast; if they are not owners of sheep, they must purchase them. The richer the man, the more elaborate the feast.

The fraternity gather in the ceremonial chamber the night before the ceremony begins. On the following morning the fraternity father carries to the ceremonial chamber, still wrapped in its corn husk, the plume given him with the package of meal by the novice when he expressed his wish to join the ᵗHle'wekwe, and, sprinkling a little meal on the ledge at the west end of the room, lays the husk on the meal. The sword of the ᵗHlĕm'mosona is laid by the side of this package.

Before the morning is far spent all the members of the fraternity congregate in the ceremonial chamber. The medicine plant with white blossoms, which is an emetic, is boiling in a large pot, that is used for no other purpose, in the fireplace under the supervision of two elderly women of the organization. When the medicine has been boiled sufficiently it is removed from the pot and deposited on the ledge at the east end of the chamber. The tea is drunk warm by each member, and copious vomiting is the result. A single large bowl is the receptacle, and when all are relieved it is carried by a female member of the fraternity a short distance from the village, where the contents are emptied. This medicine is taken on the first four mornings to enlarge the throat and prepare the stomach for the reception of the sword.

A medicine made by boiling a reddish root is drunk hot each evening. It is regarded as quite harmless to the uninitiated and is a sovereign remedy for a deranged stomach or headache.

Each morning, at the first peep of day, the members of the fraternity ascend to the house top to pray. They appear in groups of twos and threes, each one offering a short prayer and covering a spot about the size of the foot with meal. As soon as the last group descends, the drum and rattle are heard, the song begins, and the dance soon follows. The sword is continually swallowed during the indoor dances. After one dance they ascend to the roof and sing, and after the song the men go to the river to bathe, if necessary, breaking the ice.ᵃ

ᵃ It is a common thing for members of the ᵗHle'wekwe, after dancing without cessation for an hour or more, to rush out of the house with the perspiration streaming down their nude bodies, go to the river, and finding a break in the ice, plunge into the water, afterward standing on the ice while they bathe their hands. During their night dances in other houses than their own they pass through the frozen streets barefoot after constant dancing in their ceremonial chamber.

The women and children bathe from large bowls on the roof of the chamber between 9 and 10 o'clock in the morning. The songs continue each night until the rising of the morning star.

When the men bathers return from the river they drink the emetic, and after vomiting take the morning meal. The food is brought to the hatchway by relatives of the members of the fraternity. Continence must be observed throughout the ceremonial and for four days following it, and all sweets, beans, squash, dried peaches, and coffee must be abstained from during the ceremonies.[a] Prayers are again offered on the roof between 9 and 10 o'clock in the morning.

No member of the fraternity must touch persons not members or be touched by anyone until after sunset of the fifth day. The women as well as the men, therefore, sleep in the ceremonial chamber. The women, however, go to their homes during the day, principally to prepare food for the fraternity. Even the children understand that they must keep at a proper distance at this time.

On the first morning the male members prepare te'likinawe after their morning meal, each one making six, one to the 'hle'ĕt'tonĕ and one to the mu'ĕt'tonĕ, the two being joined together, three to the deceased members of the fraternity, and one to Kok'ko A'wan (Council of the Gods). These offerings are carried on the same afternoon by two men of the fraternity and deposited in the spring at the black rocks into which the original 'Hlĕm'mosona is supposed to have disappeared, with prayers for snows and cold rains.

The west wall of the ceremonial chamber is decorated with the sun and moon symbols, Ä'chiyälä'topa (the being with tail and wings of knives), the Beast and Snake Gods, the Pleiades, and Orion. Ä'chiyälä'topa and the animals are painted on paper and afterward cut out and pasted upon the wall. The snakes and stars are painted directly on the wall, and a cloud symbol of meal is made on the floor.

After the early morning dance on the second day there is no more dancing until sunset, the time being consumed in preparing te'likinawe. After the sunset dance the time is spent in eating, smoking, and chatting until about 10 o'clock, when the dance is resumed to the music of the rattle and drum. After the morning meal on the third day each one makes five prayer plumes to the deceased members of the fraternity. Dancing occurs during the day and night. The 'Hle'wekwe dance on the third and fourth nights in the house where the Mu'waiye rehearse. On the fourth morning the male members again make prayer plumes and dance as before, and a woman of the fraternity makes a ha'kwani (a number of cotton loops symbolic of a mi'ha, sacred white blanket). The 'Hlĕm'mosona, the warrior, and six members at large, including

---

[a] The reason given for abstaining from the foods mentioned above is that during the journey of the fraternity over the northern route to Shi'papolima they subsisted on game, as it was too cold for all fruits of the earth.

two women, all of ʿKoʾʿloktakwe clan, later in the day go to the house of the ʿhleʾĕtʾtonĕ, where each man makes eight prayer plumes to the uʾwannami (rain-makers) and each woman makes a haʾkwani. A member of the fraternity, who must be of the Dogwood clan, visits the house of the Shiʾwanni of the West and receiving a prayer plume from him, carries it to the chamber of the ʿHleʾwekwe.

The ceremonials of the ʿHleʾwekwe and of the Sword order of the Great Fire fraternity are synchronous, and the two combine in most elaborate dances. An hour before sunset on the third day five members of the Great Fire fraternity, attired in their regalia, precede the warrior of the ʿHleʾwekwe, who has been visiting their fraternity, to the chamber of the ʿHleʾwekwe, where they dance and swallow their swords. After the dance the ʿHleʾwekwe who visit the house of the ʿhleʾĕtʾtonĕ now return, bearing the prayer plumes and haʾkwawe (plural of haʾkwani) which they have made. The ʿHlĕmʾmosona carries the ʿhleʾĕtʾtonĕ[a] resting in a flat basket partially filled with meal, two stone fetishes, and two ancient small bows and arrows which are kept with the ʿhleʾĕtʾtonĕ, covered with his blanket, to the chamber of the ʿHleʾwekwe. He sprinkles meal before him with his right hand as he proceeds from one house to the other. On entering the ceremonial chamber he removes the ĕtʾtonĕ from the basket and, after sprinkling a thick bed of meal on the west ledge of the room directly under the wall decoration, deposits the sacred fetish upon the meal. Plate CVIII shows the dry paintings and fetishes of the ʿHleʾwekwe. a, Ĕtʾtonĕ; b, corn husks containing the fluffy eagle plumes given by the novices to the fraternity fathers; c, skins of bears' feet; d, miʾli of the fraternity, composed of banded turkey plumes and feathers of the long-crested jay and the white dove; e, poʾnepoyannĕ of the fraternity; f, miʾwachi of such members of the ʿHleʾwekwe as belong to the order of Mystery medicine of other fraternities; g, ancient bows and arrows; h, stone fetishes; i, medicine bowls; k, archaic medicine bowl; l, prayer-meal basket; m, gourd water jug; n, water vase; o, vase of popcorn water. Since 1902 the ʿHleʾwekwe have added to the ritual group shown in the illustration a tablet altar similar to those used by other fraternities.

Each one having wrapped his own prayer plumes together, these are grouped by the ʿHlĕmʾmosona with the offering of the Shiʾwanni of the West into a kĭaʾĕtchinĕ,[b] and the haʾkwawe are wrapped around its base and held in place by a cotton cord. After the kĭaʾĕtchinĕ has been sprinkled with meal and prayed over by all the members of the fraternity, each of the four men who accompany the bearer of the kĭaʾĕtchinĕ to the spring in which it is to be deposited prepares eight

---

[a] The ʿhleʾĕtʾtonĕ is covered with native cloth, and an ear of corn is placed on it, the corn being completely obscured by prayer plumes, whose ends project beyond the package, and by elaborate wrapping of precious bead necklaces which almost covers the white cloth and teʾlikinawe.

[b] The Kĭaʾĕtchinĕ consists of a number of prayer plumes wrapped together at the base.

prayer plumes, which they carry to the spring on the same afternoon
in company with the bearer, a man of the ꞌKoꞌꞌloktakwe clan, who personates the original director.   The bearer of the kĭa′ĕtchinĕ wears black
trousers, ordinary moccasins, a cotton shirt, and a mi′ha (white embroidered blanket) wrapped about his body.   He carries a ꞌkĭa′pokatom′mĕ
(long-necked gourd water jug) in his left hand and the kĭa′ĕtchinĕ in his
blanket over his left arm.   He is followed in the proper order by the four
others, who represent the beast warriors of the four regions.   The first
warrior, who personates the Cougar of the North and who must be of the
Corn clan, there being no Cougar clan, carries his sword and eight prayer
plumes in his left hand.   These prayer plumes, which are as long as
from the inner side of the bend of the elbow to the tip of the middle
finger, are one-half inch in diameter, with the ends cut squarely off, and
are colored yellow for the North.   The feathers attached to the upper
portion of the sticks are from the buzzard, the duck, the long-crested
jay, and Ꞌsi′liliko (Falco sparverius).   Two la′showawe, each composed
of a feather from the duck, the long-crested jay, and the Ꞌsi′liliko, hang
from the upper feathers of the prayer plumes.   The second warrior,
who personates the Bear and must belong to the Bear clan, carries one
of the ancient bows and arrows previously referred to, and eight
prayer plumes like the former, except that the sticks of his offerings
are colored blue for the West.   The third warrior, who personates the
Badger, is of the Badger clan; he carries the other ancient bow and
arrows and the same plume offerings as the one who precedes him, the
sticks being colored red for the South.   The fourth warrior, who represents the White Wolf, may be of any clan.   The sticks of his prayer
plumes are colored white for the East.   They proceed in single file,
and when at a distance from the village they may change their offerings from one arm to the other.   Though these five alone go to the
spring, they are led for a short distance beyond the village by the
ꞋHlĕm′mosona, who wears a white cotton shirt and kilt of native
black cloth.   A large white fluffy eagle plume and a tiny wing feather
of the spurred towhee are tied to his hair.   The face is covered with
white meal, which is constantly applied throughout the ceremonial, the
meal and white plume being symbolic of snows.   His feet are bare,
and he carries a pottery meal basket and the mi′li of the fraternity
in his left hand, sprinkling meal with his right as he proceeds.   On
reaching the spring, 3 miles distant, the leader of the party deposits
the kĭa′ĕtchinĕ on a rock near the spring, and the party stand around
it and prays, sprinkling meal upon the plumes.   After the prayer
the leader lights a reed cigarette, colored black and filled with native
tobacco, with a small roll of cotton ignited by sparks from a flint;
puffing the smoke over the kĭa′ĕtchinĕ, he prays for cold rains and
snows.   When more than half the reed has been consumed, the
remainder is stuck into the bunch of plumes.   The four other men

attach suitable stones to the kĭa'ĕtchinĕ for the purpose of sinking it and they then deposit it in the middle of the spring. The other prayer plumes are deposited among the rocks.[a] The bearer of the kĭa'ĕtchinĕ fills his jug with water from the spring and the five men return to the ceremonial house.

After the five men have started for the spring those members of the A'pi"läshiwanni chosen to make the six tehl'nawe, accompanied by the elder brother Bow priest, each bearing a tehl'nanĕ, visit the ceremonial chamber of the 'Hle'wekwe and take seats on the north ledge of the room toward the west end, the fraternity sitting on the south side of the chamber. The elder brother Bow priest crosses the room and delivers his tehl'nanĕ to the 'Hlĕm'mosona, who remains seated, with a prayer, which is followed by one from the 'Hlem'mosona as he receives the staff. The bearer of the yellow tehl'nanĕ for the North now presents his to the 'Hlĕm'mosona; and all follow in order, prayers being repeated at each presentation, after which each warrior stands before the 'hle'ĕttonĕ, sprinkles meal and prays, and returns to his seat. The warriors, after presenting their tehl'nawe, remain and join in the feast. The same afternoon the elder and younger brother Bow priests deposit at Shop''hlua yäl'läkwi,[b] a shrine a short distance north of Zuñi, prayer plumes to the Gods of War, who are supposed to have lived at this place during their sojourn at Häl'ona and I'tiwanna. The younger brother Bow priest first visits the shrine, and after his return the elder brother makes his visit. Each carries the ancient tehl'nanĕ to the shrine. The party who carried the kĭa'ĕtchinĕ to the spring returns with a gourd jug filled with water. He hands the jug to the 'Hlĕm'-mosona, who deposits it with the other sacred objects by the meal painting, where it remains during the night, and in the morning the water is consecrated by the 'Hlĕm'mosona.

The work of grinding wheat and corn begins in the houses of the fraternity fathers and novices on the fourth morning of the ceremonial, which is the 10th of January. One of the fraternity fathers belongs to the house where the meetings of the fraternity are held. The corn is removed from the cob by the elder women, the crones toasting the meal after it has been through the first mill, girls taking turn at the line of eight or ten mills. The grinders sing under the directorship of an aged woman, who sits before them on the floor. At the same time some of the alternate grinders dance in the same room. The girls, when not dancing, are seated near by, waiting for their turn at the mills. Women of the household are busy stewing meat and peaches and making he'we (wafer bread) to supply the workers for the feast.

---

[a] It is claimed by the 'Hle'wekwe that this spring is very deep and that the place below is large enough to accommodate all the deceased 'Hle'wekwe and the beast warriors that were once directly associated with the fraternity, who receive the plume offerings at this point and convey them to Ko'thluwala'wa.

[b] See p. 57.

Comparatively little work is done by the grinders on the fifth day, as all go in the afternoon to witness the dances of the ‘Hle′wekwe and Great Fire fraternities in Si′aa′ te′wita.

After sunset on the fourth evening the novices are accompanied from their homes to the ceremonial chamber by their fraternity fathers. Soon after their arrival an emetic is given them, the women in charge of the medicine filling with it as many bowls of goodly size as there are candidates. Each fraternity father places a bowl of the medicine before his child, who sits on a stool in the middle of the floor, facing east. After the novices swallow the contents of the bowls the throat is tickled with a feather, causing violent vomiting. Another bowl is placed for the ejected matter. When the vomiting ceases, the fraternity father takes from the side of the ‘hle′ĕttone the husk containing the eagle plume with the meal given him by the novice and, opening the package, he picks the feather into bits, dropping them into the bowl with a prayer for good health, a pure heart, and long life for the novice. He then sprinkles in the meal from the husk and, lifting the bowl with both hands, waves it to the six regions with a prayer to the ‘Hle′wekwe rain-makers for snows and winter rains; then he carries it from the chamber, depositing the contents in the river, that the feather and the meal may go to Ko′thluwala′wa to be received by the ‘Hle′wekwe, who are constantly leaving the undermost world and passing back and forth from their spring to Ko′thluwala′wa.

The male members of the fraternity remain seated on the south side and the female members on the north side of the room; the two novices take seats between three women on the north ledge. All remain seated during the first song, for which rattles only are used, while the women and the novices, with their fingers interlocked, keep time to the music, with their hands held downward. After the song all present stand in two lines, the men remaining on the south side, the women and novices on the north. A fraternity father now requests the ‘Hlĕm′mosona to give him the ancient sword of the original ‘Hlĕm′mosona, at the same time calling for a certain medicine.[a] A young man belonging to the Corn clan removes from the group of fetishes a small sack from which he takes a bit of root, which he places in the fraternity father’s mouth, who, holding the ancient sword in his left hand, approaches the novice and, taking him by the hand, says: “My child, come with me.” He leads the novice to the middle of the room, where they both face the north, the novice standing at the right of the fraternity father. All the members of the fraternity now sing. When the second stanza of the song is begun, the fraternity father and the novice dance, and soon the fraternity father swallows the sword, having the root medicine still in his mouth. After the sword has been passed down the throat once he places his lips to those of the novice, giving him the medicine

[a] A plant not yet classified.

from his mouth, and the novice, taking the sword in his right hand, runs it down his throat and, withdrawing it with his left hand, hands it to his fraternity father. The two do not cease dancing while swallowing the sword. The novice and the fraternity father now return to their places. The fraternity father of the other novice, who is a woman, repeats the ceremony. She does not run the sword down her throat at this time, but merely puts it into her mouth,[a] the fraternity father running it down his throat in her stead. The song does not cease during the initiation. Afterward the candidate is accompanied to his home by his fraternity father. At daylight on the following morning he goes to the fraternity father's house, where his head is bathed in yucca suds by the wife or daughter of the fraternity father. After the head is washed the novice eats alone in the fraternity father's house. He may take meat and bread, but no peaches, beans, coffee, or sugar. The one who bathes the head accompanies the novice after the meal to his home, carrying the large bowl from which the head is bathed, which is a gift to the novice.

THE MU'WAIYE [b]

Before the drama of the 'Hle'wekwe is enacted the Mu'waiye dance must be rehearsed. The two maidens and youth who personate the Mu'waiye perform their part in the drama of the 'Hle'wekwe just as their prototypes are supposed to have done when the 'Hle'wekwe were received by the Kĭa'kwemosi upon their return after the long separation from the A'shiwi. The Kĭa'kwemosi selects from among the ki'wi'siwe[c] the one which is to furnish the choir for the dance of the Mu'waiye. The rehearsals occupy six nights previous to the drama, which occurs in the plaza at sunset, three nights in the house of one and three in that of another member of the ki'wi'sinĕ which furnishes the music. The people of the Chu'pawa (South) ki'wi'sinĕ appeared on the occasion described. The i'kwĭnnakĭa (circle dance) is also rehearsed in the same chambers. There seem to be no stated hours for such meetings in Zuñi. Punctuality is not one of the characteristics of these people.

About 10 o'clock the Chu'pakwe and others begin to saunter into the large room. The three Mu'waiye, attended by their a'mosi (directors) and a'mosono''kĭa (directresses), enter through the smaller room, the Mu'waiye taking seats on the north ledge midway down the large room. The choir assembles on the south side, opposite the dancers. The girls who are to perform in the circle dance take their

---

[a] It is said that this is invariably the case with women at initiation, whereas the men and elder boys of the 'Hle'wekwe seldom fail in their first effort to run the sword down the throat. New women members practice in the February ceremonial until they can swallow the sword with some degree of ease; but few women become as expert in sword swallowing as men.

[b] See p. 447, note a; p. 450, note a.

[c] See Ki'wi'siwe and their functions.

GROUP OF ZUÑI ALBINOS

CHILD WITH BROKEN LEG IN SPLINTS

seats on the ledge at the south side of the room, west of the choir, and the youths sit at the west end of the room. The only thing in the large chamber to indicate there is to be any unusual occurrence is the presence of two boxes toward the west end of the room, side by side, painted white and decorated with figures of the cougar, bear, shrew, wolf, Ä'chiyälä'topa (being with wings and a tail of knives), and stars.

It is 10 o'clock when the Mu'waiye begin dancing. The girls wear their ordinary dress, also the boy; but he soon removes his calico trousers and shirt, and a director places on him a black woven kilt embroidered in blue, and also furnishes each of the three with bunches of ribboned and curled corn husks. The three have their eyes obscured by their bangs.[a] The dance begins to the music of the pottery drum and song; no rattle is used. The first motion of the Mu'waiye is a lowering of the body without bending forward or raising the feet, the boy holding his upper arms out and forearms up, with his hands clasping the husks before him, the girls holding their arms out and upward, each hand clasping a bunch of husks. After two motions of this kind the bodies are bent forward, the arms extended straight before them, the boy keeping both hands clasped to the husks as they beat their hands violently toward the earth, at the same time raising their heels from the floor and returning them with a stamp. After one motion of this kind, the first is repeated three times, then the second twice, after which comes a pause, and then the two motions are repeated. After three repetitions of this figure, which consumes forty minutes, there is a pause and the time and the character of the music change. The girl to the west side is the first to begin dancing. First the right arm, then the left—the face following each time to the right or left in the direction of the extended arm—is thrown out from the side, the hand resting on the breast before it is extended, and a step is taken each time by raising squarely from the floor first the right foot, then the left. When the girl to the west has taken a few steps, the boy begins, and after he has taken a step or two, the second girl starts. When the three are dancing their motions are synchronous and rapid. They dance some distance to the west, then to the east, and so they move to the right and left several times, when the music again changes and the first movements are repeated for an hour, when the dance closes. One of the girls is compelled to rest a minute or two during the dance.

Although many witness this dance from the beginning, the room becomes crowded at its close, when preparations for the arrival of the 'Hle'wekwe are begun. The smaller of the two boxes referred to is placed immediately west of the larger one, four notched sticks and deer-leg

---

[a] When the writer was learning this dance, her instructor declared many times that unless her hair covered the eyes the snows would not come.

bones are laid upon it, and four musicians from Chu′pawa ki′wi'sinĕ take seats west of this box. At this time the crowd makes room for the members of the 'Hle′wekwe fraternity, who enter, led by a woman carrying in her left hand a pottery basket of sacred meal and her mi′li (insignia of the order of O′naya′nakïa), which she possesses through membership in another fraternity, and sprinkling meal with her right hand. She wears ordinary dress, with a white cotton blanket bordered in red and blue.

The 'Hlĕm′mosona, who follows the woman leader, is dressed in a white cotton shirt, white embroidered kilt held on with an embroidered sash and red belt, and dance moccasins. A large white fluffy eagle plume and a wing feather of the 'hlai′aluko are tied to the left side of the head, and several short yellow parrot plumes are attached to the forelock; the hair is flowing, and has been plaited to make it wavy. The sword supposed to have been used by the original 'Hlĕm′mosona is in his left hand and one with a feathered handle is in his right. He precedes the other officers, who are followed by the fraternity at large, each man preceding those for whom he acts as fraternity father. The bodies of the men are nude, except for the black woven kilt. Each wears his bow wristlet and elaborate necklaces. Hanks of dark-blue yarn, with sleigh bells attached, are tied around the legs below the knees, the yarn hanging in tassels at the side. Gourd rattles are carried in the right hand and swords in the left, a number of the men having two swords, two three, and one four. Plate CIX shows sword of the 'Hle′wekwe. The swords, which are of juniper (species unde-termined), are slightly curved, rounded at the end and are as long as from the tip of the middle finger to the elbow, this being the method of making the measurements. The aged warrior has a serpentiform sword, tipped with an arrow point 2 inches long and 1 inch wide. Though this sword is frequently swallowed to the handle, it is run very cautiously down the throat.

The women and the girls wear the usual dress, with the limbs and feet bare, and are adorned with many necklaces of silver, coral, and ko′hakwa (white shell beads). They carry two eagle-wing feathers in the right hand and the sword in the left; one woman has two swords. They hoot and make animal-like sounds as they enter the room, and as they proceed they shake their rattles and sing for a moment or two before the performers on the notched sticks and deer-leg bones begin their music. The party moves in single file with slow, even step, keep-ing perfect time with the music of the notched sticks. First one foot is raised squarely from the ground, then the other, the men raising their feet much higher than the women. The women hold their arms out and up, and the left arms of the men are held in the same way. They pass around the boxes and the musicians by the north side, and when the 'Hlĕm′mosona reaches the south side of the boxes he steps from the line and, waving his sword before and over the boxes, turns, facing

east, and swallows it. The rattle is usually transferred from the right
hand to the left, and the sword held in the right hand when it is run
down the throat; but occasionally it is put down the throat with the
left hand. The dancing does not cease an instant, and the wonder is
that the sword can be run with safety down the throat while the body
is in motion. The ᵗHlĕmʹmosona no sooner swallows his sword than
he returns to the line; but ere he has reached his place the man who
follows him is before the boxes swallowing his sword, and so the
swords are swallowed in succession. If a woman fails to swallow hers,
her fraternity father swallows it for her; in the cases of very young
children their fraternity fathers swallow the swords for them.

By the time the head of the line reaches the east end of the room all
the ᵗHleʹwekwe have entered the chamber and an ellipse is formed.
They pass around the boxes three times, the swords being swallowed each time. The ᵗHlĕmʹmosona stands before the boxes and,
facing them and clasping his sword with both hands, prays in an under-
tone, moving his sword, still held in his clasped hands, to the six
regions, then again over the boxes, and, drawing a breath, closes his
prayer, and the fraternity leaves the room.

During this dance the musician at the south end of line committed the grave offense
of accidentally touching one of the dancers. The elderly warrior of the fraternity
returned and an animated discussion ensued. Three other members of the fraternity
came, one being the man who was touched, the two others witnesses. They insisted
that the musician should consent to become a member of the fraternity, and finally
won his consent, thereby saving the unfortunate member of the fraternity from the
ills, perhaps death, which he would otherwise suffer. [a]

Soon after the departure of the ᵗHleʹwekwe the Sword order of the
Great Fire fraternity arrives in order similar to that of the ᵗHleʹwekwe,
a woman leading. Their step is like that of the ᵗHleʹwekwe, and they,
too, hold their swords in the left hand, the ᵗHlĕmʹmosona carrying
a crooked prayer plume (symbolic of longevity) instead of a rattle.
The men wear native black woven kilts and yucca wreaths. Unlike
the ᵗHleʹwekwe, two or three form a group before the boxes and
swallow their swords together. The choir does not sing during the
presence of the Sword order of the Great Fire fraternity.

After the Great Fire fraternity leaves the room the smaller box is
hastily placed to the north of the larger one. Then eight men arrive
from the Oʹheʻwa (East) kiʹwiᵗsinĕ, and six of them seat themselves
behind the boxes, and one at each end; they play on the notched sticks.
Before this music begins the aʹmosonoʹʻkĭa of the circle dance who
are girls of 10 or 12 years, clad in ordinary dress and the white cotton
pitoni (a piece of cloth tied together at the upper ends at the neck and
falling over the shoulders), stand before the boxes, sprinkle meal over
them, and pray. Some of the girls now form the circle and dance from

[a] This superstition of the ᵗHleʹwekwe is not entertained by the Sword order of the Great Fire
fraternity.

left to right around the two boxes. The circle is gradually enlarged by the addition of girls—the youngest being 8 or 10 years of age, the oldest not over 20—who often require persuading and in many cases are forced into their places by the a'mosi and others. When all the girls are on the floor the youths and young men join the ring, each taking his place by the side of the girl of his choice, and with clasped hands, which they swing backward and forward, they dance for more than an hour. Some of the girls try to drop out, but without success, as they are caught in a good-natured way and made to return to the ring. After this dance the girls flock together in the northwest corner of the room, where they have a merry time, the young men bringing them water to drink and chatting with them. The musicians at the boxes pray, each drawing in a breath from his stick and deer-leg bone, and then leave the chamber, closing the ceremonies for the night.

The 'Hle'wekwe repeat the dancing the last three nights of the rehearsals of the Mu'waiye, and the Sword order of the Great Fire fraternity appear on the fourth and sixth nights, remaining the fifth night in their own ceremonial chamber, where, in addition to swallowing the swords, they perform feats with fire. On the fourth night of the rehearsal the a'mosi of the Mu'waiye distribute the la'showawe, which they received from the sun priest, among the Chu'pakwe choir, breathing upon each la'showannĕ and placing it to the lips of the recipient, who remains seated, and then tying it to a lock of hair to the left side of the head, when a short prayer is repeated.

At daylight on the fifth morning of the ceremonies of the 'Hle'wekwe a man makes a picture of dry colors of Ächiyälä'topa on the stone floor of the ceremonial chamber, immediately before the cloud symbol of meal. Upon the completion of the picture, which is about 30 inches long, a broad line of meal, bordered with black, is extended from the head of the figure toward the east; eight arrow points are laid upon the line of meal, and a stone fetish is stood on a meal line that extends from the cloud symbol to the figure. A line of corn pollen extends from the heart of the figure to the mouth, symbolic of truth, and a crystal is placed at the lower end of this line, symbolizing purity of heart (see plate CVIII).

The figure of Ächiyälä'topa often performs wonderful things, but only when the fraternity is absent from the ceremonial chamber and dancing in the plaza. The aged man of the Bear clan who is left alone in the chamber sees the arrows, which are placed at equal distances apart, move, and on their return the fraternity finds them in closer proximity to one another, and strands of hair taken from heads of those destroyed by Ächiyälä'topa between the arrow points. Oracles are whispered by this figure to the lone watcher and wonderful disclosures are made. A strand of hair is always laid by the figure before it is consulted. On the present occasion the solitary watcher is told by the oracle that there is talk among the Americans of building a railroad through the Zuñi country, but the people must never consent to this, for the moving trains would cause the earth to tremble, and this would rouse the ĕt′towe from their perfect quiet, thus causing their anger, so that they would prevent the rains and snows.

The ᵗHlĕm′mosona ascends the ladder leading from the ceremonial chamber to the roof, and by aid of the faintest daylight runs a line of meal over that portion of the house top which forms the roof of the ceremonial chamber. The line is begun at the ladder which extends from the roof to the street, runs across the south side, then along the east, down the north side, and across the west, and around by the south to the opposite side of the ladder to that whence the line started. The ancient tehl′nanĕ with the six others, each with its accompanying stick, which were brought by the warriors to the ceremonial chamber the previous evening, are placed at a very early hour in the morning against an upper wall on the northeast corner of the roof outside of the meal line. The men bathe as usual, and later in the morning, after they have danced in the chamber, they go in couples to the roof and wash from a large gourd of water before decorating themselves for the outdoor dance.[a]

When the ᵗHlĕm′mosona, after drawing the meal line on the roof, returns to the chamber, he places the ancient medicine bowl and gourd jug of water from the spring near the middle of the floor and takes his seat facing the ĕt′tonĕ and other fetishes. The male members of the fraternity are grouped on the south side and the women on the north side. The ceremony opens with the ᵗHlĕm′mosona holding his sword, which is handed him by his deputy, in his left hand, while he deposits a′thlashi (concretion fetishes, sacred to vegetation) in the bowl. Each stone is held while the male members sing to the accompaniment of the rattle a prayer for snows and winter rains. A song is addressed to the Beast Gods of the six regions, imploring their intercession with the rain-makers for snows, and rains of winter. The Hlĕm′mosona has some fifteen small medicine bags containing plant medicine before him, and he deposits a pinch of medicine from each into the bowl. Water is poured six times from the gourd jug into the bowl, and after placing eight eagle plumes across the bowl with their tips to the east he sprinkles four lines of corn pollen over the feathers. The bowl and jug are placed by the cloud symbol, and all present take a drink of the red-root medicine previously referred to. In a short time the signal comes from the ᵗhle′ĕttonĕ to the aged ᵗHlĕm′mosona

a Although the writer occupied the upper story of the ceremonial house and her door opened upon the roof to which the members resort, on account of the superstitious dread of the powerful medicine of the fraternity, entertained by inmates of the house, great efforts were required to secure photographs on the roof and to enter the ceremonial chamber, in which the writer spent most of the time during the several days' ceremonies. We′wha, a conspicuous character of Zuñi, was untiring in her efforts to detain an old father below while the writer secured photographs on the roof, and several times released her when the father had barred the door of her room with heavy stones. The wrath and distress of the old man knew no bounds, and he declared that the writer would bring calamity not only to herself but to all the household.

that the hour has arrived for it to leave the chamber. The four other
ĕt′towe[a] appearing in the ceremonial were deposited the previous
night in the house of a member of the Badger clan. The ᵗHlĕm′-
mosona places the ᵗhle′ĕttonĕ in the hands of a maiden whose hands
have been rubbed with sacred meal. She is attired in ordinary dress,
with a mi′ha (white embroidered blanket) hanging from her shoulders,
the feet and lower limbs being bare. The ᵗhle′ĕttonĕ is carried by the
right hand and arm, and the left hand is used as an additional support;
two men, each carrying in his right hand one of the archaic bows
with arrows, accompany the girl from the ceremonial chamber to the
plaza. They proceed in single file, the girl between the men, and
are joined by four girls clad in ordinary dress, each with a black blanket over her shoulders, bearing the mu′ĕt′towe, each ĕt′tonĕ being
carried by a girl of the clan to which the ĕt′tonĕ belongs. Every
member of the household of each ĕt′tonĕ-bearer, every member of her
clan, and every member of the ᵗHle′wekwe fraternity must offer to the
ĕt′tonĕ four prayer plumes composed of eagle and turkey plumes and
feathers from the birds of the six regions, for snows, each individual
depositing an offering to each of the four regions. They proceed to
the plaza, where the two decorated boxes seen at the rehearsals of the
Mu′waiye are placed end to end east of the center of the plaza (see
plate CX).

There are six notched sticks on the boxes, each crossed with a deer-
leg bone, two of the sticks being on the smaller box. A tiny twig of
spruce, symbolic of vegetation, is planted by the a′kwamosi (maker
of medicine water) near the southeast corner of the larger box, with
prayers for snows and longevity for his people; he sprinkles meal over
the twigs while he prays.

A wicker basket without a handle, made by a female member of the
ᵗHle′wekwe and colored purple with the berries of Berberis fremontii,
is filled by the aged ᵗHlĕm′mosona with finely ground meal, the meal
being smoothed over in mound form and crossed with corn pollen, and
having a white fluffy eagle plume at the apex, is deposited under the
larger box. There are three men from the O′heʻwa ki′wiᵗsinĕ sitting on
wadded blankets west of the boxes. The ĕt′towe-bearers stand in line
before the boxes, facing east. The men with the bows and arrows stand
on each side of the bearer of the ᵗhle′ĕt′tonĕ. The girl next to the man
on the north side carries an ĕt′tonĕ of the Ai′yahoʻkwe (a plant) clan;
the girl on her left holds an ĕt′tonĕ of the To′nashikwe (Badger) clan;
the girl at the right of the man on the south side carries the ĕt′tonĕ
of the Kĭä′nakwe (people of Corn clan); and the girl on her right
carries an ĕt′tonĕ of the ᵗKoʻʻloktakwe (Sand-hill crane) clan. The
ĕt′towe-bearers and the two men throw a line of meal about 2 feet

---

[a] See p. 444. One of the four ĕt′towe referred to belonged to the Sand-hill Crane clan, who were members of the ᵗHle′wekwe fraternity.

before them as they take their positions in Si′aa′ te′wita, and the three
men behind the boxes play on the notched sticks.   This music is said
to be controlled by the Beast Gods, the musicians being merely their
agents.   Each player wears the upper leg skins of the bear or cougar
over his lower arms.[a]   Variation in the music is produced by different
movements of the bones over the sticks.   The three musicians, who
must come from the O′he‘wa ki′wiᵗsinĕ, as only the people of this
ki′wiᵗsinĕ sing these particular songs, draw the bones from the far end
of the sticks toward them.   After this motion is repeated four times
the bones are run from the near side of the stick to the far end,
this being repeated four times; then the bones are rapdily drawn
back and forth several times, after which they are again drawn to
the near side four times, beginning at the fourth notch from the
player; and then the bone is again run from the player over the four
notches, and afterward is moved very quickly back and forth over the
four notches, after which the first movement is repeated.   The songs
sung at this time are the same as those sung in the circle dance in the
closing scene of the scalp ceremonial, but the harmony of the songs is
destroyed on the present occasion by the grating noise of the bones
running over the sticks.   The ĕt′towe and bows and arrows are moved
downward in time with the song from dawn until sunrise, or until the
sunlight strikes the plaza.

When the music ceases the party leave the plaza in single file by
the western way, the bearer of ᵗhle′ĕttonĕ and the two men with the
bows and arrows returning to the ceremonial chamber of the ᵗHle′-
wekwe, the others going to the house whence they came.   As the
party of ĕt′towe-bearers leave the plaza the musicians draw the bones
lightly over the notched sticks and, bringing the bones to their mouths,
draw a breath from them, repeating a prayer aloud, and return them
to their position on the box.   The musician at the south end of the
line now rises and passes to the east of the boxes, when the others tip
the larger box toward them to allow him to remove the small basket
of meal from under the box.   Returning to his seat with the basket,
he offers a short prayer and, bringing the basket close to his lips,
draws a breath, inhaling all that is good from the meal; then he passes
the basket to the others.   When each man has repeated the prayer and
drawn a breath, the basket is passed to the man at the south end of the
line, who returns it to its place under the box while the others tip the
box toward them.   In a short time the ĕt′towe and bows and arrows
are again brought to the plaza.   This time, however, the ᵗhle′ĕt′tonĕ
is carried by another girl, the bows and arrows are in other hands,
and there is an additional musician at the boxes.   All the other

---

[a] It is claimed that these skins are very old, and from their appearance the truth of the statement
can not be questioned.

features of the second ceremony over the ĕt′towe are identical with those of the first.

As soon as the ĕt′towe-bearers leave the plaza the ᵗHle′wekwe appear. Their bodies are nude, and daubs of yellow paint about 8 inches long and 3 inches wide appear over each scapula and breast. The forearms, hands, feet, and the legs halfway up to the calf are also yellow. They wear black native wool kilts embroidered in blue, and yucca wreaths adorn their heads, the hair hanging and tied at the back with a red garter. The ᵗHlĕm′mosona wears a white cotton shirt with white embroidered kilt, held on by an embroidered sash and a red belt. All those belonging to the order of Mystery medicine of other fraternities wear the reddish eagle plume tied to the forelock; the others wear only the white plume. The ᵗHlĕm′mosona has a very large white fluffy eagle plume and a single feather of the ᵗhlai′aluko (Sialia arctica) tied to his forelock. All males wear the bow wristlet, and such members of the ᵗHle′wekwe as belong to the A′piˮläshiwanni (Bow priests) wear the war pouch.

The drummer of the ᵗHle′wekwe, who is a warrior to the fraternity, precedes the female leader of the dancers a short distance, beating on the wooden drum of the fraternity, and takes his position on the east side of the plaza. The leader, who has requested this position from the ᵗHlĕm′mosona, wears ordinary dress, with a white blanket bordered in red and blue falling over her shoulders, and carries the mi′li of the fraternity and a basket of meal in her left hand, using the right hand to sprinkle the meal, which she throws out before her as she advances. The ᵗHlĕm′mosona follows her, the deputy comes after him, the retired ᵗHlĕm′mosona is next, and the aged warrior of the fraternity follows. The plaza is entered from the western street, and the dancers, passing south of the boxes, continue around in single file by the east, north, and west, making the complete circle before swallowing the sword. Rattles are carried in the right hand and the swords with the feathered handles held upward in the left. The musicians play on the notched sticks, while the members of the fraternity sing. They proceed with measured step, raising first one foot, then the other, squarely and quite high from the ground. The women do not raise their feet so high as the men. The leader of the song and dance has his place, as usual, midway in the line of dancers. The ᵗHlĕm′mosona steps from the line just as he passes south of the boxes and, dancing before them, he turns and faces east and runs the sword once down his throat. In most instances the rattle is transferred to the left hand and the sword taken in the right before it is put down the throat, but occasionally a dancer manipulates the sword with the left hand. In no case does the dance cease during the swallowing of the sword. Soon after withdrawing the sword he joins the circle, and the next man steps before the boxes and repeats the sword swallowing.

A number of the men have two swords in their throats at the same time, running the second down the throat after the first has been swallowed; two swallow three and one even four swords in this way. Others run first one sword down the throat and, withdrawing it, run another down. Only one woman swallows two swords at once. Each fraternity father is followed by his children, and when a child fails to run the sword down the throat until the handle only is exposed, the fraternity father takes the sword and swallows it. He also swallows the swords of the juvenile members, there being no attempt on the part of these children to do more than place the tip of the sword between the lips. As the circle continues around there is a repetition of the sword swallowing, but in the third circuit the form of sword swallowing is changed; two or three now step from the circle at the same time, or rather in close succession, and swallow their swords.

When the ᵗHle′wekwe return to the ceremonial chamber after the early morning dance they group themselves around the painting of Ä′chiyälä′topa and, placing their hands near the figure, but not upon it, bring them to their lips and draw a breath. A female member now erases the figure by brushing the sand from the four cardinal points to the center with a tepi (native broom), and brushing the sand with the broom into her left hand, she deposits it in the blanket thrown over the left arm of a male member.[a]

The boiled root medicine of Ä′chiyälä′topa, which is taken from the pot the first four mornings of the ceremonial and laid on the east ledge of the room, and a la′showannĕ (one or more plumes attached to a cotton cord), composed of a white fluffy eagle plume and a feather from a bird of each of the six regions, the end of the cord extending 6 inches, with a single ko′hakwa (white shell) bead strung on it, are deposited with the sand in the spring at the black rocks where the original ᵗHlĕm′mosona is supposed to have disappeared, with the words: "Go to your home, I′amakwi (Zenith)," referring to the home of Ä′chiyälä′topa.

A feast is now enjoyed and the fraternity rest until about half past 9 o'clock, when the ᵗHlem′mosona goes to the plaza alone, where a number of spectators are gathered. The musicians again sit at the boxes and play and sing while the ᵗHlem′mosona faces the north and swallows his sword. The sword swallowing is repeated at the west, south, and east, and at the last point he swallows his sword three times, for the East, Zenith, and Nadir. Figure 32 shows ᵗHlem′mosona swallowing his sword. In making the circuit each time before swallowing the sword he stops at each of the cardinal points and stamps several times. The sword swallowing at the six regions is repeated,

---

[a] No one must cross the meal lines on the roof while the painting remains on the floor, and these people, entertaining great fear of such a calamity, allow no one but members of the fraternity on the house top, though there is no reason why one can not walk on any other portion of the roof.

and the 'Hlem'mosona stands facing the east and prays to the Sun Father, sprinkling meal toward the east before returning to the ceremonial chamber. After the 'Hlem'mosona leaves the plaza the musicians pray aloud, and waving the deer-leg bones over the boxes draw a breath from them.

Upon the return of the 'Hlem'mosona to the ceremonial chamber a woman of the fraternity ascends to the roof and securing the tehl'nawe[a] carries them to the outside ladder leading to the street and hands them to some one below. Soon afterward the elder brother Bow priest appears from the eastern covered way, leading six members of the

FIG. 32—'Hlem'mosona swallowing sword.

Bow priesthood, each having a tehl'nanĕ, while he himself carries the ancient staff. The musicians who perform for the 'Hlem'mosona now leave the plaza and others take their place at the boxes to play for the circle dancers. The tehl'nanĕ bearers and others form a circle, which must never be entirely closed, and as they pass, with slow, even steps from left to right, the tehl'nawe are waved up and down to the rich strains of the song of the choir. There is no singing by the dancers. The circle, which is small at first, is gradually joined by men, women, youths, and maidens until it is very large. All clasp one another's hands except those next to a tehl'nanĕ; in such cases the staff is held below the hand of the warrior who carries it.

a See p. 450, note b.

The waving of the tehl'nawe, an exceedingly graceful motion, never ceases during the dance.

The two a'mosi (directors) and two a'mosono''kǐa (directresses) having charge of this dance were energetic in gathering dancers. The a'mosi wear black velveteen trousers over white cotton shirts, black native wool shirts with plaited red and green ribbons over the shoulders and falling in streamers, and the ordinary moccasins. Yucca wreaths are worn and a fluffy white plume is tied to the forelock, and the la'showannĕ, made of two ᵗhlai'aluko feathers, hangs at the right side of the head. The hair is done up in the usual knot. Elaborate necklaces complete the costume. The a'mosono''kǐa have their hair done up as usual, with the white fluffy eagle plume attached to the forelock and the la'showannĕ at the right side. They wear the black wool dress embroidered at top and bottom in dark blue, a red belt, and about the shoulders a white blanket bordered at top and bottom in red and blue. The moccasins are white buckskin, with black soles. Long strings of turquoise beads hang from the ears and silver and other beads adorn the neck, while the left wrists are well covered with bangles. Each director carries a ball of yarn, colored light green from a native dye, with the end run through a large needle, for the purpose of fastening the blanket wraps of the girls who dance, that they may not fall from their shoulders.

The circle dance continues until the arrival of the ᵗHle'wekwe, when the dancers group themselves in the northeast corner of the plaza. The ᵗHle'wekwe enter the plaza from the western street and proceed as described in the account of their previous dance. They pass six times around the boxes, swallowing the swords each time after the first circuit. Several group themselves before the boxes and swallow their swords simultaneously. After the last circuit the ᵗHlĕm'mosona, on reaching the south end of the boxes, steps before them and facing them waves his swords over the boxes and prays aloud to the Cougar, the Bear, the Badger, the White Wolf, the Shrew, Ä'chiyälä'topa, the Rattlesnake, the Pleiades, and Orion[a] for their intercession with the Council of the Gods for cold rains and snows, and that the Sun Father may give to his people, referring not only to the ᵗHle'wekwe but the Zuñi in general, long life, that they may not die, but sleep to awake in Ko'thluwala'wa. During this prayer all hold their swords with the points upward, and as the prayer closes each one draws a breath—all that is good from his sword.

At this time the rattles and drum of the Sword order of the Great Fire fraternity are heard, and as the last man in the line of the ᵗHle'wekwe reaches the east side of the boxes the leader of the Great Fire fraternity arrives at that point. This fraternity follows in file after the ᵗHle'wekwe, the step of both fraternities being the same. After

---

[a] While the animal warriors labor for the Sun Father on earth, the Pleiades and Orion are his important celestial warriors.

every few steps both parties turn and face the boxes. The female leader of the ʻHleʼwekwe precedes her fellows from the plaza through the western covered way and the Sword order of the Great Fire fraternity form into a circle around the boxes. Hundreds of spectators, wrapped in their bright blankets, crowding the house tops and the south and west sides of the plaza, present a brilliant scene.

Two women of the ʻHleʼwekwe return to the plaza before the leader of the Great Fire fraternity has passed west of the boxes, and the musicians tip the larger box toward them while one of the women removes the basket of meal,[a] whereupon the musicians retire from the plaza.

Before the Great Fire fraternity leaves the plaza the male and the female novice of the ʻHleʼwekwe and their catchers, who are also referred to as their fathers, appear. The male novice wears a fine large white buckskin around him. The woman wears the ordinary black dress and blanket. They stand close to the wall of the Heʼiwa (North) kiʼwiʻsinĕ[b] on the north side of the plaza, and the catchers stand by the wall of the house on the west side of the plaza.

The Great Fire fraternity leave the plaza, but soon return to repeat the dance, and while they are dancing the ʻHlemʼmosona and a warrior of the ʻHleʼwekwe appear, the former carrying the sword of the original director in his right hand and his own with feathered handle in his left. The warrior carries his sword in his right hand and six swords in a cougar-skin quiver, supported by a broad band of the same skin which hangs from the left shoulder. The couple pass within the circle of dancers and pray. The ʻHlemʼmosona takes his position to the southeast and facing north swallows his sword; then turning to the west he swallows the sword of the original director, and withdrawing it hands it to the warrior, who having removed the swords from the quiver holds them in his left arm. The warrior gives one of the swords to the ʻHlemʼmosona, who, leaving the circle, runs to the six regions, the east representing also the Zenith and Nadir, stamping and hooting at each cardinal point. Again he makes the circuit, repeating the stamps and hoots, and returning to the west swallows the sword which was handed him within the circle of dancers by the warrior. Exchanging this sword for another and running twice around the circle of dancers, stopping at each cardinal point to hoot and cry, he stands facing south and swallows the sword. The ʻHlemʼmosona repeats the swallowing of the sword at the other regions in the manner described until the six swords from the quiver have been swallowed. He and the warrior now stand before the boxes and, facing west, swallow their swords. Withdrawing them, they wave them over

<hr>

[a] This basket is afterward carried by a male member of the ʻHleʼwekwe to Maʼtsakĭa, a ruin a short distance east of Zuñi, where he deposits it in an excavation the depth of his arm, which he makes at the base of the mound upon which the ruin stands.

[b] See Kiʼwiʻsiwe and their functions.

the boxes and pray, closing the prayer by inhaling a breath with their mouths close to their swords. The warrior now returns the six swords to the quiver. The sword swallowers of the Great Fire fraternity complete their dance and sword-swallowing and leave the plaza, and the circle dance is formed before the ‘Hlem′mosona and warrior of the ‘Hle′wekwe fraternity terminate their ceremony. As soon as the circle dancers begin to move, the melodious strains of the singers at the boxes are repeated.

When the ‘Hlĕm′mosona and the warrior reach the ceremonial chamber, the latter, who is a very aged man, dons a queer-looking mask, entirely unlike those worn by the personators of the gods but similar to our common falseface. He then returns to the plaza, where he causes general amusement. He is not in the plaza very long when six of the ‘Hlĕ′wekwe, including two women, come through the eastern covered way, each one carrying a bunch of slender willows 6 feet in length. This is the signal for the novices, who are still standing by the ki′wi‘sinĕ, to start on a run through the western street. They first hurriedly pass the right hand around the head three times and throw a la′showannĕ, composed of four fluffy eagle plumes, to the ground. The catchers start after them, those carrying the switches following. However, several of the latter delay long enough to use their switches right and left on those spectators who are not so fortunate as to escape to the house tops. The whipping of the novices ceases as soon as they reach the ladder leading to the hatchway of the ceremonial chamber, where the novices and catchers wait until the others have gone into the chamber, when they descend and take their places at the east end of the chamber.

The clans of the two fraternity fathers, one being the Dogwood and the other the Badger, and their paternal clans, both being the Turkey, crowd the north, east, and south ledges which extend around the wall. Many are standing for want of room. The fraternity forms vis-a-vis in lines at the west end of the room toward the north side.

The gifts for the novices lie folded on top of the ‘hle′ĕt′tonĕ, a fluffy eagle plume, dyed red, protruding from the folds of each gift, that for the man being a white cotton embroidered kilt and the woman’s a mi′ha (white embroidered blanket). The retired ‘Hlĕm′-mosona and the active one remove the la′showawe from the kilt and mi′ha and dance down between the lines of the fraternity, whose members at the same time gracefully wave the feathered handles of their swords up and down. The two pass on to the novices and tie the feathers to their forelocks. No prayers are offered when the plumes are attached, and the two return at once to the west end of the room. Each fraternity father taking his gift for his fraternity child holds it spread with both hands, with the right side next to him, and passing on to the novice he ties the upper corners at the back of the neck and returns to the west end of the room, while the other members continue to wave the handles of their swords. After the mi'ha and kilt are presented, the catchers stand before the novices and present them each with a bunch of prayer plumes and four ears of corn tied together with yucca ribbon and then return to their places behind the novices. The 'Hlĕm'mosona now stands before the male novice and prays, while he passes the 'hle'ĕt'tonĕ four times before the lips, the heart, the right shoulder, the head, and the left shoulder; repeating the ceremony over the female novice, he replaces the 'hle'ĕt'tonĕ at the west end of the room and passes his sword in the same way over the two novices. Each time he passes between the lines of the fraternity he is fanned gracefully by the handles of the swords.

Each member of the fraternity takes his turn in repeating the ceremony of the sword over the novices, the sword being swallowed by its owner before he leaves the line. When he is through with the novices, he hands his sword to the 'hle'pekwĭn (deputy) to the 'Hlĕm'-mosona, who stands at the west end of the room. When all the members have disposed of their swords the guests and people of the house crowd about the novices, each one having his or her mi'li, and, beginning with the male novice, repeat a prayer and pass the mi'li over each novice, just as the swords were passed. [a]

At the close of the ceremony a feast is enjoyed by the fraternity and guests, this being the first refreshment taken by the members of the 'Hle'wekwe since the previous night. After the feast the novices carry their gifts to their homes, but soon return with the corn and prayer plumes and take their seats on the north ledge of the room toward the west end, the woman sitting to the right of the man.

The Sword order of the Great Fire fraternity dances four times in the plaza during the indoor ceremonies of the 'Hle'wekwe, leaving the plaza after each dance, when the circle dancers dance until they return. At the close of the last circle dance in the plaza the tehl'nawe are carried from the plaza by the a'mosi of the dance, each carrying three; the a'mosono''kĭa walk to the right of the a'mosi, and they leave the plaza by the western street. The tehl'nawe are returned to the roof of the ceremonial chamber of the 'Hle'wekwe, where they remain over night.

The dancing of the Great Fire fraternity in the plaza ceases at sunset, and a member of the 'Hle'wekwe immediately arrives on the scene and forms two crosses of meal near the northwest corner of the plaza, the arms of the crosses being each 2 feet, two of the horizontal arms meeting, a disk of meal being made on each cross. The two

---

[a] The writer and a woman of the Dogwood clan who was not associated with a Mystery medicine order used the mi'li of the mother of the latter, the mother being a member of the U'huhukwe fraternity.

ZUÑIS IMITATING DEER DANCE OF THE HOPIS

a DEER LYING IN STATE

b PRAYER OVER RABBITS

boxes around which the musicians sit during the day are reversed and turned bottom up, which places the heads of the paintings on the boxes in an upturned position in accordance with a tradition that when the beast god warriors who accompanied the ᵗHle'wekwe to I'tiwanna sat in the plaza they looked upward to the heavens while the people passed around them. Next, two members of the fraternity who belong to the Bear clan, each carrying an old bowl-shaped basket about 6 inches in diameter, approach from the western street and sprinkle meal upon the notched sticks and deer leg bones, which are now inside the boxes. They are clad in white cotton shirts and trousers, embroidered kilts striped with blue-green, the stripe decorated with a conventional design of the game sho'liwe, a mi'ha over the shoulders, and dance moccasins. Stooping before the meal crosses, each takes a notched stick and a deer-leg bone, and facing northeast places his basket, inverted, on a disk of meal. Then twelve male members of the ᵗHle'wekwe and the novices and catchers, who are foremost in the group, the novices carrying the ears of corn and prayer plumes given them in the ceremonial chamber, stand back of the two men, all facing northeast. Those who form the group wear blankets wrapped around them and carry rattles in their right hands. The two men of the Bear clan, resting the notched sticks on the baskets, run the deer-leg bones outward over the sticks thirty-two times, then draw the bones toward them over the sticks the same number of times. This movement is repeated without variation until the cessation of the music.

As soon as the musicians rise the male members of the fraternity present begin singing to the accompaniment of their rattles, and the two men of the Bear clan take their position in front of the group, holding the notched sticks and deer-leg bones and baskets in their left hands, which they move to the time of the music. Their right hands are not visible under the large blankets worn around them. The warrior of the fraternity intones at intervals and the whole body joins in the song. Almost immediately upon the opening of this song the ĕt'towe and ᵗhla'we bearers, with Mu'chailihä'nona,[a] their leader, appear from the eastern covered way. The leader is chosen by the ᵗHlĕm'mosona from the fraternity and must be of the Dogwood clan, or his paternal parent must be of this clan (the same man can not act in the two ceremonials of January and February). The leader is clad in a white cotton shirt with full gathered sleeves, and a white cotton embroidered kilt, decorated like those worn by the men of the Bear clan, is fastened at the right side; he also wears an embroidered sash and a white fringed sash looped at the right side, blue knit leggings, and dance moccasins. A fine mi'ha tied at the upper ends hangs over the body, the long wavy hair falls over the back, and bangs cover the brows. A large white fluffy eagle plume and a bunch of yellow parrot feathers are attached to the

a See page 447.

forelock. The face is white with meal. The necklaces are elaborate.
He carries in his left hand a black bowl-shaped basket 5 inches in
diameter, three cords about 12 inches long and terminating in a knot
being attached equal distances at the rim. This basket is suspended by
the strings from a slender stick, 12 inches long, with a la′showannĕ
pendent from one end. The basket is filled with fine meal shaped into
a mound. A cross is formed over the mound with corn pollen and a
line of pollen encircles the meal, symbolic of the four regions (see
plate CXI). The basket and stick, which latter is never freshly painted,
are supposed to have come from the undermost world.

As Mu′chailihä′nona proceeds with majestic step and sprinkles meal
carried in his belt he is followed by eight maidens in single file, the first
four carrying in the right hand two ancient ʰhla′we, resting them
across the left arm, the sticks of which are claimed to have been
brought from the lower world by the Corn maidens[a] (see plate
CXII, a). The others carry each a mu′ĕt′tone resting on the left arm
and supported with the right hand. These girls wear the dark wool
embroidered dresses, white moccasins and leggings, and white blankets
bordered in red and blue, fastened at the upper ends and falling over
the shoulders. After advancing a short distance in the plaza, they
halt and stand for a couple of minutes in line, facing west, and then
advance, passing around to the north. When they have all reached
the north side of the plaza they again halt and face south.

At this time the Mu′waiye appear, dancing sidewise, from the eastern covered way. The girls each wear two mi′hawe (plural of mi′ha),
the under one having the deep embroidery at the neck, the outer one
the deep border at the bottom. In order to make the blanket serve as
the short skirt, it is folded over at the top and held on with an
embroidered sash, the upper edge, which is turned over, standing up
in a kind of ruffle. The sashes are tied at the back. They wear fine
white deerskin moccasins with black soles. The ʰhelh′pone (see plate
XXXVIII) is worn on the head. Elaborate necklaces of ko′hakwa, coral,
and turquoise, with turquoise earrings pendent from the necklaces, are
worn. The boy has his hair flowing, with two white fluffy eagle
plumes, one above the other, hanging down the center of the back, a
bunch of yellow parrot feathers and a white fluffy eagle plume being
attached to the scalp lock. He has a yucca wreath fancifully tied at
the side, and his hair falls in bangs over his eyes. He wears an
embroidered kilt, with a border of blue-green and the game of sho′-
liwe painted upon it, fastened at the right side. A white fringed sash
and a red belt are looped at the right side and a fox skin is pendent at
the back of the belt. He also wears earrings and a profusion of necklaces, a silver bow wristlet on the left arm, blue yarn leggings with

---

[a] The stems were originally white, with foliage of delicate silvery leaves resembling feathers. When
the leaves disappeared they were replaced by feathers of the ʰhlai′aluko (sialia arctica).

bunches of yarn tied around them below the knee, with sleigh bells hanging, and dance moccasins. The maidens hold a ᵗhlu′ᵗsipone*a* in each hand (see plate CXII b, c). The youth holds his mi′li between his hands.

The Mu′waiye advance like drilled soldiers, keeping perfect time with their heads, hands, and feet. This trio is closely followed by the a′mosi and a′mosono′ᶜkĭa of the choir, the drummer and choir, which consists of about 100 men of the Chu′pawa ki′wiᵗsinĕ, grouped immediately behind them. The a′mosi wear black velvet trousers, native-woven shirts of black, elaborately ornamented with red and green ribbons, and quantities of necklaces, the hair being done up in the usual way. The a′mosono′ᶜkĭa are dressed similarly to the ĕt′towe-bearers, all being adorned with as many necklaces as they can secure from relatives and friends. The air rings with the song, which is quite independent of the ᵗHle′wekwe choir on the western side of the plaza. The ĕt′towe and ᵗhla′we bearers linger in line on the north side of the plaza until the Mu′waiye are fully in the plaza, when they move on very slowly, circling round the boxes four times, each person frequently sprinkling meal into them. They leave the plaza by the western way, proceeding to a house of the Badger clan, where the ĕt′towe are received by their keepers, four aged women. They are deposited in flat baskets partly filled with meal, and placed in line from north to south in the center of the floor of the large room. The ancient ᵗhla′we are laid across the baskets north of the ĕt′towe, with the tip ends pointing east. Mu′chailihä′nona and each bearer of a fetish carries a pinch of meal held in the left hand four times around the head and sprinkles it over the ĕt′towe.*b* Meal is now taken in the right hand and sprinkled over the fetishes with a prayer for rains. The girls take their seats on the north ledge of the room, and Mu′chailihä′nona returns to the chamber of the ᵗHle′wekwe.

After the fetish-bearers and the leader leave the plaza they are followed by the ᵗHle′wekwe choir, and the Mu′waiye with their choir have the plaza to themselves. The Chu′pakwe do not proceed farther than the northeastern corner of the plaza until the Mu′waiye have passed four times around the boxes. The music, which is the same as that sung to the accompaniment of the notched sticks earlier in the day, and which is now to be heard free from the grating noises of the deer-leg bones rubbed over the notched sticks, is rich and melodious.

---

a The ᵗhlu′ᵗsipone is made like the ancient ᵗhla′we. The stems are painted white and white duck feathers take the place of the silvery leaves. The various seeds are wrapped in cotton at the ends of the ᵗhlu′ᵗsipowe. The ᵗHlem′mosona of the fraternity presented to the writer two ᵗhlu′ᵗsipowe (plural of ᵗhlu′ᵗsipone), having the white feathers and two ᵗhla′we with ᵗhlai′aluko plumes, which are now in the National Museum.

b "One failing to sprinkle the meal would be troubled with excrescences and swellings; perhaps one, perhaps many, would come."

The evening shadows are falling when the Mu'waiye complete the fourth circuit around the boxes and advance toward the western entrance. This movement is the signal for the spectators to hasten from the plaza and stand in lines facing each other on each side of the streets through which the dancers are to pass, their course being through the western entrance to a second plaza, thence to the north street and around to the west street, and down this street to the house where the ĕt'towe are deposited. The Mu'waiye dance every step of the way, as has been described, to the music of the Chu'pakwe, who follow closely. It is dark by the time the Mu'waiye reach the house. As each girl is relieved of her ʰhluʰsipone it is placed with an ancient ʰhla'we, and both are passed before her lips while she inhales all that is good from them, they being then laid across the basket from which the ancient ʰhla'we is taken.

An old woman removes the la'showawe of ʰhlai'aluko feathers from the hair of each of the Mu'waiye and it is tied to the ancient ʰhla'we with which her ʰhluʰsipowe are placed. The Mu'waiye and choir take in their left hands meal from the meal basket by the ĕt'towe and, carrying the hand from left to right around the head four times, throw the meal over the fetishes for physical purification. Meal is afterward taken in the right hand and sprinkled over the ĕt'towe, with prayers for food, raiment, and good health. The Mu'waiye now have their headdresses, mi'has, and other paraphernalia removed by the two a'mosi of the Mu'waiye, and they take their seats on the south ledge. The choir crowd around the fetishes and pray. Each man gives a la'showannĕ of the ʰhlai'aluko, which he received during the rehearsals of the Mu'waiye, to the old women, who attach them to the ancient ʰhla'we; by this means the ancient sticks are kept supplied with plumes. The masses gather from the street and repeat the performance with the meal, held first in the left hand, then in the right.[a] The ĕt'towe are now placed on the north ledge of the room and the ʰhla'we and ʰhluʰsipowe are stood against the wall, back of the ĕt'towe.

On the fifth morning of the ceremonial the plastering is removed from the doors and windows leading from the ceremonial chamber of the ʰHle'wekwe into the adjoining rooms, and stone slabs which block up spaces in the north and south walls when not required to serve as openings through which the elite observe the final ceremony, are also removed. The room immediately back of the ceremonial chamber is prepared for the reception of special guests. A smaller room beyond is devoted to the preparation of toggery by those who are to amuse the fraternity and guests previous to the night ceremonial.

At 9 o'clock in the evening the two novices take seats on the north

---

[a] Squads of drunken men and boys offering prayers and sprinkling meal over the fetishes present a revolting sight.

ledge of the chamber, toward the west end, the woman sitting to the
right of the man. The male members of the fraternity sit on the
south side, midway between the fireplace and the west end of the
room, in a group which forms the choir. The female members sit
west of the choir on the ledge and the floor. The women of the
To′nakwe (Turkey), To′nashikwe (Badger), and Pi′chikwe (Dogwood)
clans have the positions they occupied during the afternoon ceremony.
By 10 o'clock the room is crowded. The adjoining room is also filled
with the cronies of the old man of the family and others of the privileged clans, principally males. The interior windows and door leading
into the ceremonial chamber afford a view of what is going on, and a
group of the women of the family and their most honored guests sit
in a side room, looking through quite an extensive opening in the
wall that is made by removing a couple of large stone slabs plastered
in this space. At this time five masked characters appear in the ceremonial chamber, their dress rendering them as ridiculous as possible.
At one time they caricature the He′mishiikwe (certain anthropic
gods). Again, one plays upon a notched stick, caricaturing a scene of
the day. Their songs and performances draw constant applause from
the spectators. After remaining a few moments in the ceremonial
chamber this party visits the house in which the four ĕt′towe are
placed, where a large number of people are congregated besides those
especially designated to be present with the ĕt′towe.

The ceremonies in the chamber of the ᵗHle′wekwe begin shortly
before 11. The men wear breechcloths. All the women wear their
black wool dresses with red belts, their necks and arms uncovered and
their hair flowing, with the bangs over their eyes. Both the men and
women have elaborate necklaces and the women wear silver bangles
and rings. As the choir begins, the novices rise and the catchers stand
on the ledge behind them, with a hand on each shoulder of the novice.
An elderly woman and two young girls stand between and on each side
of the novices, clasping their hands, the forearms being held upward,
and in this position the hands are moved back and forth, while the
catchers slightly move first the right and then the left shoulder of the
novices. In a few minutes the three women are replaced by others,
and they take position on the floor according to their clan, the one of
the Dogwood clan dancing on the north side of the room and those
of the Badger and Turkey clans on the south side, each holding
two eagle-wing plumes in the right hand. On two or three occasions
it is noticed that the plumes are held in the left hand. The upper
arms are extended outward, the forearms upward. No one can dance
until she has stood by the side of the novices, and after the first two
groups have served women also stand at the backs of the novices in
the place of the catchers. There are usually ten female dancers on
the floor at one time, forming two lines. The motion is sidewise

to the east and then to the west, the dancers facing first south and then north. The members of the ꞌHleꞌwekwe dance between these lines. The ꞌHlĕmꞌmosona is the first of the ꞌHleꞌwekwe on the floor. He swallows his sword several times while dancing. He is followed by the aged warrior, who runs his sword, which has the arrow point, a number of times down his throat. The dancing is more violent on this occasion than in the plaza, and therefore the sword swallowing more difficult and dangerous. The officers of the fraternity are followed to the floor by all the members (except two or three young children), generally two at a time, sometimes three. Some hold the sword down the throat twenty seconds, others ten seconds, the usual time being five seconds. One man holds two swords at once in his throat seven seconds. On three occasions the swords are run down one another's throats during the most violent motions of the dance.[a] Toward the close of the dance a director of the Muꞌwaiye visits the ꞌHleꞌwekwe and joins in the dance.

The novices do not take their seats from the beginning to the close of the night ceremonial. The male novice becomes so exhausted during the night as to be in danger of fainting,[b] and a small blanket is laid under his feet as a rest for them. Popcorn water and the red medicine previously referred to are drunk frequently during the night, and one or two members of the choir are stimulated with whisky brought in by the old woman of the house. Shortly after midnight the drinking of whisky begins in the back room. It is dealt in by both male and female members of the family. One woman buys a horse with a small glass of whisky and a handsome string of beads with half a glass. The morning star is carefully watched for, and its appearance above the horizon is the signal for the ceremonies in the chamber to cease. The aged warrior closes the dance, holding the poꞌnepoyannĕ[c] in his right hand and a bow and arrows in his left.

The ꞌHleꞌwekwe and dancers now leave for the house where the etꞌ-towe were placed and those who are not too drunk to stand venture from the back room into the ceremonial chamber and join in drunken revelry. Though the conduct of many of the guests in the house of the ĕtꞌtowe during the night is, in a quiet way, most insinuating and indecorous, those associated with the fetishes perform their duties in great seriousness. The four ĕtꞌtowe are still side by side in their baskets of meal on the ledge on the north side of the room, about midway. The aged woman having charge of the ĕtꞌtonĕ of the Aiꞌyahoꞌkwe clan sits west of the line of ĕtꞌtowe, and the old woman having charge of the ĕtꞌtonĕ of the Toꞌnashikwe clan sits on her right; the bearers of

---

[a] While accidents seldom happen from swallowing the sword, death is sometimes the result. This is attributed to a bad heart or to the unfortunate having been touched by another.

[b] Such an exhibition of weakness, were he to succumb, would be unfortunate for his standing in the fraternity.

[c] See p. 417, note a.

these two ĕt′towe sitting next, and next to them two of the ᵗhlu′ᵗsipowe-
bearers.   The aged woman in charge of the ĕt′tonĕ of the To′wakwe
clan sits east of the ĕt′towe, the woman in charge of the ĕt′tonĕ of the
ᵗKo′ᵗloktakwe clan sits on her left, the two bearers of these ĕt′towe
sit next, and the other two ᵗhlu′ᵗsipowe-bearers are next to them.   The
Mu′waiye and their a′mosi and a′mosono′ᵗkĭa sit quietly through the
night on the ledge at the south side of the room opposite the ĕt′towe,
except when one of the a′mosi visits the ᵗHle′wekwe chamber.

On the arrival of the ᵗHlĕm′mosona bearing the ᵗhle′ĕt′tonĕ eight of
the ᵗHle′wekwe take seats east of the two boxes, which are now at the
east end of the room, and play on the notched sticks, the rest of the
fraternity grouping themselves near the boxes.   The four ĕt′towe are
lifted from the baskets by the old women and handed to the ĕt′towe-
bearers, and the ᵗHlĕm′mosona hands the ᵗhle′ĕt′tonĕ to a woman of the
fraternity.   The ĕt′towe-bearers are joined by two men having the
bows and arrows, and they form in line, facing east, just as they did in
the plaza in the previous morning.   The two novices stand before this
line, also facing east.   The wives of the fraternity fathers are behind
them, with a hand resting on each shoulder of the novice, the
shoulders being kept in slight motion.   The notched sticks with deer-
leg bones are played in accompaniment to the song and rattle while
the ĕt′towe are waved downward, with the same inclination observed
in the plaza.   They are never moved upward, as the prayers are for
cold rains and snows to fall to prepare the Earth Mother for the
embrace of the Sun Father.

At sunrise the singing ceases and the ᵗHlĕm′mosona receives the
ᵗhle′ĕt′tonĕ in the basket, and the two men hand him the bows and
arrows.   Each of the other ĕt′towe-bearers delivers her ĕt′tonĕ to the
old woman in charge of it, she receiving it in a basket.   The baskets
are deposited in line in the middle of the floor, and after the ᵗHlĕm′-
mosona prays over them the old women carry the ĕt′towe and the
Mu′waiye carry the ᵗhla′we to the houses where they are kept, two
of the ᵗhla′we being deposited with each ĕt′tonĕ.   The ᵗHlĕm′mosona,
accompanied by the members of the ᵗHle′wekwe, carries the ᵗhle′-
ĕt′tonĕ in the basket to the ceremonial chamber of the ᵗHle′wekwe,
but afterward removes it from the basket and lays it on the ledge,
upon which he first sprinkles meal.   He now removes the eight eagle
plumes from across the bowl of medicine water, shaking the pollen
from the plumes into the water, and administers the water from a
shell to each member of the household, including the infants.   The
drinker says: "Tä⁺chumo (father)."   The ᵗHlĕm′mosona replies:
"Cha′limo (child)."   Each one now takes meal in the left hand from
the pottery meal basket and, waving the hand around the head from
left to right four times, throws it upon the ĕt′tonĕ for physical purification and good health.   Meal is afterward taken with the right

hand and sprinkled on the ĕt'tonĕ, that one may not die, but grow old and sleep, to wake as a little child in Ko'thluwala'wa (abiding place of the Council of the Gods), where the Zuñis go for a time after death. During the prayers the women of the paternal and maternal clans of the novices are bringing large bowls of food, and the center of the floor soon bears evidence of preparation for an elaborate feast. At the conclusion of the prayers over the 'hle'ĕt'tonĕ, We'wha, not a member of the fraternity but a member of the house, addressing the assemblage, in the presence of the guests of the night, says:

"My children, those of you who would be members of the fraternity of the 'Hle'weke, prepare corn meal and choose a father, that you may become one of them. In five worlds below all was dark; in five worlds below all was unclean. The 'kĭa'ĕt'tonĕ, chu'ĕt'tonĕ, mu'ĕt'tonĕ, and 'hle'ĕt'tonĕ came up to the light of the Sun Father and passed to the land of the creation of the gods, our children becoming gods; but first those of the 'Hle'wekwe were water snakes, tortoises, frogs, and tadpoles. 'Kĭa'ĕt'tonĕ and chu'ĕt'tonĕ passed to Häl'ona, but 'hle'ĕt'tonĕ and mu'ĕt'tonĕ traveled with the 'Hle'wekwe by the far north road to Shi'papolima and the house of Po'shaiyänki, where we lived four years [time periods], and after that time we arose and traveled to the west and made our home at To'yakwi 'kĭai'akwi [Nutria spring place], where we lived four years, and again we arose and passed to the west to Top'apkwĭnna [Black rocks]. Here the 'Hlĕm'mosona spoke to us saying: 'I am old. I will go no farther. Here I shall make my home for all time. Now we are near I'tiwanna; I will go on farther with you.' Addressing his deputy, he said: 'I give to you my pok'ĕt'tonĕ [the ancient sword]. You [referring to others of his fraternity] will go to Häl'ona I'tiwanna [ant middle place], and when you wish snows and cold rains make te'likinawe and bring them hither [to the spring] and I will receive them and carry them to the Kok'ko A'wan [Council of the Gods], at Ko'thluwala'wa, for the road from my house here leads to that house."[a]

Thanks are now given for the food, and after making the proper offering to the dead of the fraternity all enjoy the feast. Then the ceremonies close.

The 'Hlĕm'mosona returns the 'hle'ĕt'tonĕ with its associated fetishes, including the bows and arrows, to its chamber in a house of the 'Ko'-loktakwe clan. He carries the sword blades in the cougar-skin sack to his home. The basket and slender stick which is attached, carried by Mu'chailihä'nona, the ancient bowl and bear's feet skins, the stone fetishes, and the sword handles are kept in a back storage room of the ceremonial house.[b]

---

[a] The writer has given such portion of the prayer as she was able to hear.

[b] A large stone cougar, brought out only in cases of severe illness, is secreted beneath plastering in a niche in the wall of the ceremonial chamber.

After the close of the morning feast the tehl'nawe are carried by such members of the fraternity as belong to the A'pi‘‘läshiwanni to their homes, and later in the morning they are taken to the shrines of the Gods of War, which are situated at the four cardinal points. Each shrine is about a mile and a half from Zuñi, the tehl'nanĕ for the north, with its accompanying stick, being deposited at the shrine by the aged warrior of the ‘Hle'wekwe fraternity. The names of these shrines are as follows: Äl'ahoimul‘hlakwi, north shrine; Ha'wikonakwi, west shrine; I'shäna an tekĭapoa ‘san'nakwi, south shrine (see plate CXIII); To'nashi an te‘kĭapoakwi, east shrine. These shrines are on elevated ground. They are built of rock, the opening being on the east side, covered by a stone slab. The south shrine is superior to the others. It is in horseshoe form, built of flat stones, with a dome-like top. On removing the slab at the entrance on the east side many prayer plumes are seen planted in the ground. The tehl'nawe for the Zenith and Nadir are deposited at the east shrine. The tehl'nawe, being taller than the walls of the shrines, are placed on the outside against the walls. The ‘Hle'wekwe deposit prayer plumes in January and February within the walls of these shrines, where they remain until it becomes necessary to throw them to one side to make room for others.

The la'showawe worn by the a'mosi and a'mosono'‘kĭa of the A'pi‘‘läshiwanni and those worn by the a'mosi and a'mosono'‘kĭa of the Mu'waiye are made into prayer plumes after the closing ceremonies, the paternal parents or brothers preparing those for the women. The plumes of the former party are planted in the fields with prayers to the u'wannam A'pi'‘läshiwanni (rain-maker warriors), deceased members of the Bow priesthood,[a] and those of the others are offered in the field to the A'wan ‘Si'ta (Great Mother) ĕt'tonĕ, which bring rains and fructification, with prayers for snows and winter rains. The two men and the women go separately to plant their plumes.

Four days afterwards each fraternity father dresses sheep for a feast to be given to his newly initiated child, while the women of his household bake the meal and flour previously ground. The families of each novice are also busy preparing meal and other gifts, which are to go to the house of the fraternity father. About the same time the newly initiated member accompanies the fraternity father a short distance east of the village and deposits the prayer plumes given at the time of initiation to the rain-makers of the ‘Hle'wekwe for snows and winter rains, that the crops may be plentiful, and that the people may have health and happiness. The four ears of corn given the novices at initiation are kept until planting time and then planted in the field

[a] The rain-maker warriors are lightning-makers who assist the rain-makers with their lightning arrows.

with the other corn.   On the return from plume planting the novice's head is bathed in yucca suds by the wife or female relative of the fraternity father, and a feast is enjoyed at the fraternity father's house.

FEBRUARY CEREMONIAL OF THE 'HLE'WEKWE

The January ceremonial is repeated in February with but slight variation.   If no members are to be received, the initiation ceremonies are omitted and the decorations are left off the west wall of the ceremonial chamber.   Instead of the black breechcloth seen in January, a white embroidered kilt held on by a white embroidered sash and a woman's red belt is worn, with a fox skin pendent at the back. The fraternity dance once in the plaza after the early ceremony with the ĕt'towe and return to the ceremonial chamber for their morning meal.   At noon the two a'mosi of the circle dance visit the plaza by the western street.   The leader carries a small purple wicker basket of meal, such as was used in the January ceremonial; the other carries the tehl'nawe.   The bearer of the tehl'nawe takes his position southeast of the boxes, and the leader places the basket in his right hand, and then removes the notched sticks and bones from the boxes, laying them upon the ground, reverses the position of the boxes, placing the larger one south of the other, and, taking the small basket of meal deposits it under the larger box, and leaves the plaza by the route he entered.   In a few moments three musicians arrive and sit by the boxes, and the 'Hlĕm'mosona, carrying the original sword and one with a feathered handle, appears through the eastern covered way and repeats the swallowing of the swords in the manner previously described.   After making the circuit he stops again at the north end and swallows first the sword with feathered handle and afterward the ancient sword.   The swallowing of the swords is repeated at the six points, but he makes the circuit each time before swallowing them.   After the sword-swallowing is repeated at the six regions the 'Hlĕm'mosona stands before the boxes and, facing them, waves the swords over the boxes to the six regions and prays.   At the close of the prayer the swords are carried in a circle over the boxes, brought to the lips, and all that is good in them is inhaled.   The musicians pray aloud at the same time.   The retired 'Hlĕm'mosona stands at the western entrance and observes the ceremony with the deepest interest.   As soon as the 'Hlĕm'mosona leaves the plaza the circle dance begins.

Before 2 o'clock the 'Hle'wekwe are assembled in the plaza to dance.   The women carry two eagle-wing feathers in the right hand, the sword in the left, except in the case of the most expert female sword-swallower, who has a sword in each hand.   The 'Hle'-wekwe dance three times in the plaza, and during the third dance the leader, who is midway the dancers, takes from his three frater-

nity children the swords and swallows them in succession. Finally
he runs four swords, one after the other, down his throat, allows the
four to remain several seconds and then withdraws them all at the
same time. The ceremony in the plaza closes with the 'Hlĕm'mosona
standing before the boxes and praying while he waves the swords over
the boxes and draws the sacred breath (see plate cxiv). After their
return from the last plaza dance the 'Hle'wekwe form lines vis-a-vis
at the west end of the room. running east and west. Each fraternity
father, after taking his sword into his mouth, places the end of it in
the mouth of his fraternity child that the child may not die, but live
to be old, and sleep to awake as a little child in Ko'thluwala'wa.

The closing outdoor ceremony now occurs which is described in the
January ceremonial, except that the two men of the Bear clan wear
white buckskins around them instead of the sacred embroidered blankets. The male novice, who stood in front of the group of singers in
January, now has his place among them and sings, and a different
member of the Dogwood clan leads the ĕt'towe and 'hla'we bearers.
The night ceremonial of the 'Hle'wekwe and the ceremonies in the
house of the ĕt'towe are the same as those described in the account of
the January ceremonial.

The ceremonies observed in January, 1897, corresponded, with few
exceptions, to those of former years. Owing to the death of an adopted
brother of a prominent member of the fraternity and also of the house
where the fraternity holds its meetings, there was no dancing in the
plaza, and the only sword-swallowing out of doors was done by the
'Hlĕm'mosona and his warrior. The 'Hlĕm'mosona first appeared
alone and swallowed his swords; afterward, in company with a warrior, both swallowed their own swords and others carried by the warrior. At 3 o'clock in the afternoon a man who took the place of catcher
sat on a chair in the east end of the room, and a novice, who was a
young girl, sat on a blanket spread on the floor at his feet; he had
his hands on her shoulders. The fraternity stood in two opposing
lines. The ceremony of presenting the mi'ha, corn, and prayer plumes
occurred exactly as before described. White embroidered kilts were
worn by the men instead of the dark ones. The novice accompanied
the group of 'Hle'wekwe who appeared in the plaza at the sunset
ceremony.

ORDER OF THE KĬÄ'LÄ'SILO [a] (SPRUCE TREE)

The ceremony of the order of the Kĭä'lä'silo occurs in February in
connection with the one described and for the purpose only of initiating a member. The ceremonial in which the initiation into this order
occurs is the same in all particulars as others described excepting the
variations here noted. A man is seldom long a member of the 'Hle'-

---

[a] Pseudotsuga douglassii.

wekwe before joining the Kïä′lä⁺silo. He is usually requested by the ⁺Hlĕm′mosona to join the order. If he consents, the ⁺Hlĕm′mosona, on the second day of the ceremonial, selects a director to conduct a party to collect spruce trees. The ⁺Hlĕm′mosona places meal in the palm of the man's left hand and directs him to go the same day for the trees. The man afterward wraps the meal in a corn husk. He is accompanied by six men of the fraternity, who assist in cutting and bringing to the ceremonial chamber the trees, which are always collected south of the village, since the distance in other directions to such trees as they wish is much greater. The leader or director ascends a tall tree and attaches a la′showannĕ of a single fluffy eagle plume to the tip of the top branch, saying: "I wish the kïä′lä⁺silo for the ⁺Hle′wekwe; in a little while we will dance. I ask that ourselves may not be made ill by swallowing the kïä′lä⁺silo. I pay you with this la′showannĕ." When he descends from the tree the men sprinkle its base with meal from the corn husk and look about for the best tree near it, since it is not necessary to choose the tree nearest the one with the plume. The selected tree is supposed to be cut down with an ancient stone ax, but it is not unlikely that a modern ax is also secretly used. The same ancient ax is supposed to be used in cutting the other trees, one for each member of the order and one for the novice. The trees, which are about 3 inches in diameter and 12 to 15 feet high, are transported crosswise on the backs of the men by ropes which pass around the forehead. Though the distance is several miles, they must always make this trip on foot.

During the absence of the tree-collectors the ⁺Hlĕm′mosona asks the novice, and if there be more than one he asks each one separately, whom he wishes for a fraternity father. He replies, "I do not know." Then one is chosen by the ⁺Hlĕm′mosona, who takes meal from the basket, places it in a corn husk, folds the husk, and, stooping before the chosen fraternity father, who remains seated, lays the package in his hands; clasping the man's folded hands he offers up a prayer. The fraternity father afterward distributes a pinch of this meal to each of the women of his clan, as mentioned in the description of the initiation into the Sword order.

At sunrise the work of making the sword at the butt of the tree begins. The first chip from each tree is cut with the stone ax by the man who acted as director to the tree-collectors, and the tree is passed on to the man who is to use it in the dance, and he fashions the sword. When the swords are completed each maker attaches to the top branch of the tree a la′showannĕ, composed of a turkey feather, an eagle plume, and feathers from the birds of the six regions. The tree director gives a bit of root medicine to each one, the same as that placed in the novice's mouth at initiation into the Sword order, and they chew this and draw their swords through the mouth four times to cover them with the medicine. The trees are now hung to the rafters, except the one made by the fraternity father for the novice, who also makes one for himself. This tree is laid in the middle of the floor with the sword end pointing west.

At sunset the fraternity, including, as before, the women who are on the north side of the room, stand and sing. After one song for snows and rains the tree director puts a bit of the root medicine into the mouth of the fraternity father, who stands before the collection of fetishes at the west end of the room. After receiving the medicine the fraternity father takes the novice by the left wrist and leads him close to the ladder, standing south of the novice, while both face west. Stepping to the middle of the floor, the fraternity father lifts the tree with the sword end pointing downward, passes the top out through the hatchway, and hands the tree to the novice, who, facing south, attempts to swallow the sword, but fails. The tree is returned to the fraternity father and he swallows the sword. After three songs for snows and rains the fraternity father places the tree with the others, and the men smoke, the novice joining the group.

The trees are carried to the plaza on the fifth day, when the sword ends are swallowed during the dances. After the dances the trees are placed in their former elevated position in the ceremonial chamber, and after the early morning ceremony they are carried on the backs of six men (different men from those who brought them) to a mesa about 4 miles north of the village, where the trees are laid upon the ground with the sword ends pointing to the west. Meal is sprinkled over the trees, and prayers are offered for snows, rains, and the general good health of the people. When the novice's head is bathed, on the fifth morning, the fraternity father presents him with a few yards of calico or some simple gift, this being the only gift from the fraternity father to the novice.

MA'ᵀKE ᵀHLAN'NAKWE (GREAT FIRE FRATERNITY)

The Ma'ᵀke ᵀhlan'nakwe (Great Fire fraternity), has three orders: Kok'ko ᵀhlan'na (Great god), which is under the patronage of three anthropic gods, Kok'ko ᵀhlan'na, Shits'ukĭa, and Kwe'lele; I'wenash'nawe (knowledge of sucking) or O'naya'nakĭa[a] (Mystery medicine), and Ma'ᵀke ᵀHlan'na (Great Fire). The latter order has several divisions—Pi'änniᵀhle (Sword), Kĭä'läᵀsilo (Spruce), Sho'tikĭanna (Arrow),[b] Pa'oti'we[c] (Navaho dance), and Po'sikishi[d] (commonly interpreted spruce tree). The officers of the Great Fire fraternity consist of a

---

[a] The officers of O'naya'nakĭa have valuable songs for relieving delayed parturition and are called in when the doctresses fail to relieve the patient.

[b] Sho' is from sho'li, arrow reed; ti'kĭanna is another expression for ti'kili (fraternity).

[c] Pa is from A'pachu (Navaho).

[d] Po'sikishi is the name of a bird which frequents the kĭä'läᵀsilo (Pseudotsuga douglassii). The sword swallowed in the Po'sikishi ceremony is fashioned at the base of a kĭä'läᵀsilo.

mo'sona (director) of the fraternity, pe'kwĭn (deputy) to the director, a'kwamosi (maker of medicine water), a'kwape'kwĭn (deputy) to the a'kwamosi, 'hlem'mosona (wood director; the order, however, is known as the sword, the blade being made of wood, hence the name), te'hai'-toy'nona (music-maker, flutist), pi'"läshiwanni (warrior), a'lunakwe (walking about), general managers, and couriers.

"Long, long ago" two members of the Great Fire fraternity, one belonging to the Eagle clan, the other to the Badger clan, went to the northeast and there met the Ke'pachu[a] (buckskin Navahos), whom they found to have a language similar to their own; and these people understood mystery medicine, it'sĕpcho, sword swallowing, and arrow swallowing. The two A'shiwi returned to their village, bringing songs from the Ke'pachu, and since that time the Great Fire fraternity have sung only the songs of the Ke'pachu, and the a'kwamosi has been of the Eagle clan or child of the clan[b] and his pe'kwĭn of the same clan. The sword director has been of the Badger clan or a child of this clan and his pe'kwĭn of the same clan.

The following stanzas are in the Ke'pachu tongue:[c]

SONG ASSOCIATED WITH PRACTICING OF MYSTERY MEDICINE

I

Eniniya' achu'yia tai'wayaia' tai'wayaia' Ta'kuluwaye tai'wayaia' eni'niya' eni'yaia'.

Ya'eniya eniyae'na ya'eniya' eniya' aha'ena' Hea' ya'eniya' hea'ena hea'ena hea'ena hea'ena hea'heya Hea'heya ena' ena' hea'ena'.

II

Eya' henia' eyaha' henia' eya' eya' he......na' Eyaha' eyaha' he......na' hena' eniya' yaha' ena' yaha'e......na'.

Eyaha' eyahena' eyaha' eyahena' eyahena' eyaha' e......yaha'hena'.

Eyaha' ahena' eyahena' eyahe......na'.

SONGS USED IN THE SWORD-SWALLOWING CEREMONY

I

Ai..yi'..yi..yi..yi ye..he..ena' ai..yi'..yi..yi ye..he..ena' ai'yi..ye..he.. ena' aiyi..ye..he..ena' eni..ya..he' ya'..he..na ya'hena akulawa' ni'yashi kulape'hu i'tati'niye 'si'ita pi'änni'hle 'si'ita nichihlhkai 'si'ita tanilth ki'ishi shi'shi ye'la 'si'ita tanilth ki'ishi ai'i..yi..yi ye..he..ena' ai'i..ye..he..ena' eniya hoi.

II

Hea' le'ya ena' hea' hea' ena' hea' ena' hea' ena' hea' ena' ya ena' hee'.

Ni'ye kachĕ' ku'na' niye' ku'lawa ine' aye kachĕ' pi'änni'hle seya'taspa alth'su na'si yaye' hena' tuhu' yi'ta eniya' Ya eniya' he eniya' ku'lawa.

---

[a] Ke from kĕm'me buckskin; pachu, one who wears the hair brushed back. The Zuñi name for Navaho is A'pachu, singular pa'chin, these Indians wearing their hair back from the face.

[b] See List of clans.

[c] The writer was not aware until a short time before her departure from Zuñi, in 1902, that the Great Fire fraternity songs were not in Zuñi but in the "Ke'pachu" tongue, since it is almost impossible to distinguish words amid the din of rattle and drum.

MAP SHOWING ROUTE FOLLOWED BY ꞋHLEꞋWEKWE (WOOD FRATERNITY)
IN QUEST OF THE MIDDLE PLACE

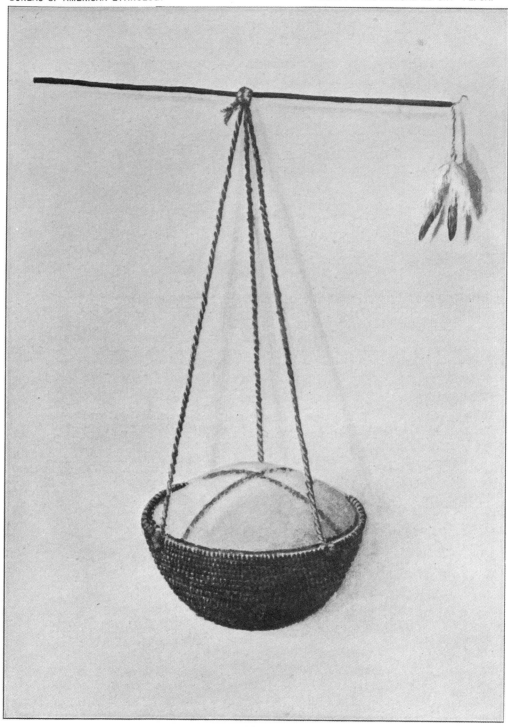

BASKET WITH MEAL CROSSED AND ENCIRCLED WITH CORN POLLEN, SYMBOLIC
OF THE FOUR REGIONS AND THE WHOLE WORLD

ORDER OF KOK'KO 'HLAN'NA

While this order is known as Kok'ko 'hlan'na (Great God), there are three anthropic gods associated with it, Kok'ko 'hlan'na, Shits'ukĭa, and Kwe'lele, who are supposed to live in the east near Shi'papolima,[a] home of Po'shaiyänki, the Zuñi culture hero.

The order of Kok'ko 'hlan'na can be joined only when these gods are summoned to the village by an illness which produces swelling of any part of the body. They possess great power over such maladies, but must not be called upon until all other efforts have failed to effect a cure.

The following story is implicitly believed by the Zuñis:

In the olden time the god Shumai'koli[a] traveled from the west to the east, and the Kok'ko 'hlan'na was passing a little to the west, and they met. Kok'ko 'hlan'na was the first to speak. He inquired of the stranger: "Who are you, and what is your business?" Shumai'koli replied: "Who are you, and what is your business?" "Well," said Kok'ko 'hlan'na, " I have medicine here that will quickly kill a man if I put it on him." Then Shumai'koli told him to try it on him if he wanted to. "All right," said the Kok'ko 'hlan'na, " I will." He then rubbed his medicine over the body of the Shumai'koli, who soon began to swell all over; even his fingers were four times their normal size. After being in this condition four or five days, Shumai'koli cried: " I am almost dead. You must take off your medicine; it will kill me." The Kok'ko 'hlan'na then removed his medicine, and said, " Now, let me see you try your medicine," and the Shumai'koli covered the Kok'ko 'hlan'na with his medicine, and almost immediately his legs and arms and every part of the body twisted like ropes; and he called to the Shumai'koli to remove his medicine at once or he would die, that he was nearly dead then; and the Shumai'koli removed the medicine. Then the Kok'ko 'hlan'na shook hands with the Shumai'koli and said: "Your medicine is better than mine. I could live but a short time with your medicine, while you could live a long time with mine. You are my elder brother, and you will come to my house." These gods have since this time lived near one another.

When a member of the Kok'ko 'hlan'na wishes another to join his order he makes known to him his wish. If the one invited accepts, he carries meal wrapped in a corn husk to the member, who becomes the fraternity father of the novice; but should the novice already be a member of another order of the fraternity, the meal gift is not necessary.

CEREMONY FOR THE CURE OF SORE THROAT

A ceremonial to cure a sore and badly swollen throat, observed by the writer in 1891, is here described:

Kok'ko 'hlan'na, Shits'ukĭa, and Kwe'lele (see plates XXVI, XXVII, and CXV) arrive near sunset and ascend to the roof of the house of the invalid, who is a young man. This is the signal for the patient to be placed on a pallet in the middle of the floor. The half-reclining body, facing east, is supported by the chosen fraternity father, who must, of course, be a member of the order of Kok'ko 'hlan'na. Only the patient and members of this order may be present. The

_____

a See p. 407.

invalid is nude, except the breechcloth. When the patient is a female she wears the usual clothes minus the pi'toni (a piece tied in front and falling over the back). The male members of the order group at the south wall and midway, facing the choir. The female members sit on the opposite side of the room. Blankets are arranged so as to form a dressing room for the personators of the gods at the east end of the room. The gods stamp and dance on the roof until it is time to descend through the hatchway into the chamber below, the custom being to enter the house about dusk. Shits'ukĭa (warrior or aid to Kok'ko 'hlan'na) carries giant yucca in the left hand and a rhombus in the right. Kwe'lele carries the yucca in the right hand and in the left sticks for producing fire by friction and an unlighted cedar brand. Shits'ukĭa precedes Kok'ko 'hlan'na, who carries giant yucca in each hand, down the ladder, as he always leads this god, who has tiny eyes.[a]

A female member of the order, holding her mi'li (insignia of the Mystery medicine order) and sacred meal basket, sprinkles meal as she leads the gods from the roof to the room; passing from left to right, they encircle the patient four times, the choir singing to the accompaniment of rattle and pottery drum. Upon halting, Shits'ukĭa, taking meal from his belt, runs a line with his four fingers across the body to the waist, beginning at the left shoulder of the patient; and Kok'ko 'hlan'na, standing before the patient, places his hands to the middle of his own forehead, as he clasps the yucca in both hands and then runs it over the meal lines indicated by Shits'ukĭa. Kwe'lele simply passes around the patient; but should Kwe'lele be chosen by the patient instead of the Kok'ko 'hlan'na, the places of these two gods would be reversed. The gods again pass around the invalid, and Shits'ukĭa draws the meal lines from the right shoulder across to the waist, and Kok'ko 'hlan'na repeats the strokes with the yucca. Again they encircle the patient, and the lines are drawn from left to right across the knees, which are close together, and the Kok'ko 'hlan'na repeats the motion with the yucca. After another round, Shits'ukĭa draws lines of meal from right to left over the knees, and Kok'ko 'hlan'na brings the yucca over, and again the meal lines are made across the back. Instead of beginning at the shoulders in crossing the back, he begins at the waist, running the lines upward to the shoulder. The yucca always follows the meal lines. After the back is crossed the arms of the patient are extended forward and kept close together while they are crossed with the meal and yucca. The palms of the hands are turned upward and crossed together in the same way. Kok'ko 'hlan'na now stands at the side of the patient, and removing his mask hands it to the patient's fraternity father, who places it over the invalid's

---

[a] A pregnant woman avoids looking upon the mask of Kok'ko 'hlan'na, that her child may not have small eyes, since the Zuñis regard large eyes as a mark of beauty.

head;[a] and after he expectorates through the small mouth hole in the mask, the fraternity father removes it and hands it to the wearer, who returns it to his head.

The three gods now retire behind the curtain. After removing their masks they return to the room, taking seats of their choice, and all the members of the division, except the three personating the gods, the woman who leads them, the fraternity father, and the invalid,[b] who remains on his bed, go to their homes for the evening meal. Those remaining, including the invalid, are served in the chamber of the invalid by his female relatives.

Members of the order return to the room of the invalid about 9 o'clock and resume their former seats. Kok′ko ′hlan′na, Shits′ukĭa, and Kwe′lele are personated during the night by different male members, who retire behind the curtains to don the dress. Female members wear the dress of other gods over their own, but not the masks. They receive their regalia behind the curtain and ascend with it to the roof, male members accompanying them to assist in dressing. When fully attired they descend into the room and dance. The night is consumed in dancing, the men and women wearing the costumes of gods according to the will of the director of the division. The women remove the regalia in the room, but not behind the curtain. At dawn three members of the order, who may be of any clan, make fire with the fire sticks of the Kwe′lele. They sit in the center of the room where the invalid reclined in the early evening. Kok′ko ′hlan′na, Shits′ukĭa, and Kwe′lele are now personated by those who performed over the invalid, the two former stamping about while the fire is being made. At the same time the director of the division bathes the Kwe′lele under each knee with medicine from a medicine bowl, and the bowl is afterward placed near the fire-makers. The man who produces the fire moves the crushed cedar fiber back and forth, and another lights the cedar brand from it and dips the brand in the medicine water. The director now carries the medicine bowl to the invalid, who reclines against his fraternity father seated against the north wall and west of the choir, and gives him several drinks directly from the bowl. The remainder of the medicine is afterward drunk by the invalid.

The three gods led by the woman who preceded them to the chamber now go some distance east of the village, and when they return the fraternity father places the invalid in his old position in the middle of the floor and leaves him. The gods encircle him four times, and two of them ascend to the roof, led by the woman as before. Kwe′-lele, who remains, stands with a foot on each side of the sick man's head, holding the fire stick in his left hand and the drill in his right. He also holds in his left hand four cakes of bread strung on a yucca

---

[a] When Kwe′lele is chosen his mask is placed over the patient's head instead of that of Kok′ko ′hlan′na.

[b] If the patient is able he may take a seat in the room wherever he chooses, but he must not leave it.

ribbon, three of which are in ring form while the fourth is a perforated disk. Holding his hands close together Kwe'lele, bending forward, moves them over the patient from the head down the center of the body to the feet. He now stands at each side of the shoulders and runs his hands down the body to the feet, and standing each side of the upper arms he runs his hands down to the feet, and repeats the same, standing over the forearms, which are extended down the body. Again standing each side of the lower legs, which are close together, he extends his hands toward the head, drawing them downward; passing around to the left side of the patient, and again standing each side of the head, he runs the hands down to the heart, laying the string of bread over it. With female patients the bread is laid upon the dress and not next to the nude body. He then leaves the house to join the other gods on the roof. The gods now depart, Shits'ukĭa leading, followed by Kok'ko 'hlan'na and Kwe'lele in file; they all encircle the village and pass on over the eastern road to their home near Shi'papolima.[a] After the gods leave the chamber the fraternity father hands the string of bread to the invalid, who eats three pieces and throws the fourth to a dog which has been brought into the room by his mother-in-law for the express purpose of receiving the bread.[b] The dog's eating the bread that has been laid upon the heart of the invalid is supposed to absorb the disease from the invalid. After the bread has been thrown to the dog the wife of the fraternity father places a bowl of yucca suds near him, and the fraternity father presents the invalid with four ears of corn, two prayer plumes, one to the Sun Father and the other to the Moon Mother, and a calico shirt or some such gift. Each member present dips a handful of suds and deposits them on the head of the invalid, after which the head is thoroughly washed by the wife of the fraternity father. The invalid becomes a member of the order of Kok'ko 'hlan'na through the treatment described, without further ceremony. A feast follows, furnished by the wife and immediate relatives of the invalid, who also send gifts of flour and meal to the house of the fraternity father.

INITIATION INTO THE ORDER OF O'NAYA'NAKĬA [c]

The ceremonial described was observed by the writer in 1891. The fraternity convenes on the 11th of November.[d]

The first day is consumed in decorating the tablet altar, preparing

---

[a] In reality they go a short distance from the village and exchange their regalia for their ordinary clothing, which is secreted under the blankets of several attendants, who follow the gods at a respectful distance. These same attendants bring back the masks and other paraphernalia of the gods, which is also hidden under their blankets.

[b] When the invalid is able to do so he goes to the door and throws the bread outside to the dog, but when this is impossible the dog is brought in by a female relative of the patient, or by a relative of his wife, should he be married. These women are not present during the ceremonial.

[c] Referred to by the fraternity as i'wenash'nawe (knowledge of sucking).

[d] One may belong to the three orders and every division of the Fire order or to only one or a portion of these. Though a member of the fraternity may be present at the meetings of other than his own orders, he participates only in the proceedings of the order or orders to which he belongs, except for taking part in the dancing.

the cups to serve as the base for the mi′wachi [a] to be given to the initiates, and making a dry or sand painting.   Four artists decorate the altar while others grind the paints.   The grinding is done on stone slabs 12 by 18 inches, slightly hollowed.   The blue-green paint is made from copper ore, the red from red ocher, the yellow from yellow ocher, and the black from a black clay combined with a conserve of fruit of yucca baccata.   All the members of Mystery medicine prepare prayer plumes. By sunset the altar is erected and the animal and other fetishes are placed before it, and the sand painting is completed.   The painting is made as follows: Four lines of white powder form a square, and segments of a circle are drawn with black on the inner side of the lines: the square, excepting the segments, which symbolize black rainclouds, is covered with white pigment, and cones of white are formed over the square.   Plate CXVI shows the altar previous to placing all the objects belonging with it and to the making of the sand painting.

A meal is now served to those present, but before the members indulge, a quantity of the food is collected and deposited before the altar.   After eating, the members leave the ceremonial chamber, and later in the evening, about 8 o'clock, they return one after another until the room is well filled.   The male members of the Mystery medicine order bring rolls of sheepskin on their backs, to serve as beds during their hours of sleep the next three nights.   The women, except the novices, return to their homes to sleep.

First night.   Each member of the order of Mystery medicine brings his mi′li, which is handed to the deputy director, who places it by the altar.   As the men of the order gather, they group on the south side of the room and toward the west end, where they chat and smoke. The female members and the women invited to dance take seats on the north ledge, until it is quite full; then they sit on the floor in front of those on the ledge.

The women to be healed sit on the floor at the east end of the room. They wear ordinary dress, with limbs and feet bare; many have their infants with them.   The male invalids, who are nude except a cotton breechcloth, gather on the south side of the room and near the east end.   Both sexes remove their moccasins on entering the ceremonial chamber.   By 9 o'clock both men and women of the order are busy with their personal adornment.   The feet and lower portions of the legs, and the hands and arms to the elbow, are painted white.   The men wear black-wool breechcloths; the women wear ordinary dress, with neck and limbs bare.   The novices—a woman, a girl of 10 years, and a girl of not more than 4 years, each with a fraternity parent by her side—sit on the north ledge near the altar, the woman being at the west end of the line, and the youngest girl at the east end.   The flutist sits immediately behind the altar and to the north side.   Three officers of the fraternity sit behind the altar and south of it.   The a′kwamosi

---

[a] See p. 416.

sits on his folded blanket in front of the altar and to the north side,
while a warrior of the fraternity has his seat in front of it to the south
side.

When all are assembled, the fraternity parents—two being men, the
other the A'wan 'sita[a] (Great Mother) of the fraternity (see plate
CXVII)—distribute meal from corn husks to each person present, the
meal being received in the palm of the left hand. The male members,
and afterward the women, sprinkle the meal over the altar and fetishes.
The a'kwamosi forms a cross of meal, symbolic of the four regions,
upon the stone floor near the altar, and places the medicine bowl in the
center and his prey-god fetishes at the points of the cross, and those
for the Zenith and Nadir by the side of the one at the eastern tip. The
song opens to the accompaniment of the rattle, and immediately a
woman deposits a vase of water by the a'kwamosi; at the same time
he raises the medicine bowl upward six times, and prays to the Beast
Gods of the six regions, while the warrior beats time with his eagle-
wing plumes. As soon as the medicine bowl is returned to the cross,
the drum is struck and the a'kwamosi dips a gourdful of water from
the vase; at the same moment the warrior stands before the altar and
whirls the rhombus, calling the clouds to gather quickly. This deafening noise continues throughout the consecrating of the water. Water
is dipped six times from the vase, and each time the gourdful of water
is held over the medicine bowl, while the a'kwamosi offers a prayer to
the appropriate Beast God. The six fetishes are dropped separately
into the bowl, a prayer being repeated each time invoking the presence
of these gods. Meal sprinkled into the water completes the consecration. The a'kwamosi now dips his eagle plumes into the water and
sprinkles the altar, while at the same time the other warrior of the
fraternity and another officer of the order wrap their blankets about
them and collect the food from before the altar in two basket trays,
which they rest on the blankets over the left arm, and leave the chamber to deposit the food in the river to the Beast Gods. The Great
Mother now hastens to the fireplace, and, lifting ashes in her right
hand, deposits them in a heap before the dry painting. Two men now
leave the choir, each having an eagle plume in each hand, and dip the
ashes with the plumes. The head is turned over the left shoulder, the
right arm is drawn back as far as possible, and with a sort of sweep it
is brought forward and the eagle plume held in the right hand strikes
the under side of the plume held in the left, the two men, side by
side, striking their plumes simultaneously. The ashes are thrown first
to the East, then to the North, West, South, Zenith, and Nadir, for
physical purification of those present. After repeating the throwing
of ashes to the six regions by striking the plumes, they dip them in

[a] Though white-haired and aged, she is considered the most efficient female theurgist in Zuñi.

the medicine bowl and sprinkle all present.   The two who carry out
the food from before the altar return, and the three novices begin to
dance, keeping in line before their seats, facing first the east, and then
the west.   They dance until the close of the practicing of the medicine, which consumes an hour.   The child of 4 years is one of the most
energetic and the best dancer in the line.   As soon as the three dancers
are on the floor, two other men leave the choir and, skipping and hopping about, gesticulate beast-like before the altar, and very soon their
bodies become the abiding places of the Beast Gods and they begin
practicing upon the patients.   A woman deposits a large bowl south
of the center of the room beside an aged woman who sits on the floor.

During the healing the theurgists throw themselves almost prostrate
on the floor and suck at the exposed parts of the bodies of the invalids,
and then ejecting into their hands the material supposed to have been
removed, throw the hands up, or wave them, and profess to deposit
the material in the large bowl presided over by the old woman.   As
each theurgist completes the drawing out of the disease, he gives a
kind of strangling cough and takes a gourdful of water which is
handed to him by the woman, and gargles his throat, expectorating
into the bowl.   Several of the infants are supposed to be ill, but from
the way their bright eyes glisten as their mothers dance them on their
laps, keeping time with the choir, one can hardly believe in their
suffering.   The babies sleep little during these hours, and seem to
delight in all they see.   As soon as the theurgists cease practicing, the
song changes, and all the women along the north ledge rise, and at the
same time the Great Mother gives a pinch of ashes to each officer and
member of the choir, and she and the two fraternity fathers, each holding two eagle-wing plumes in the right hand and ashes in the left, form
in line, facing north, and approach the novices.   When near them they
turn, facing south, each fraternity parent being immediately before
his child, and at the same time they hold the eagle plumes over their
shoulders, each novice catching the tip ends of the plumes of her fraternity parent.   The youngest novice has to be raised in order to
touch the plumes, the mother of the child securing her to the fraternity father's back by means of a piece of cotton cloth.   The wife or
sister of the fraternity father stands back of the novice, with a hand on
each shoulder of the latter.   In this way all advance toward the south
side of the chamber, in three files, the Great Mother's file being to the
west; then they turn, wheel fashion, and face the east, and the women
attendants take seats on the north ledge, while the fraternity parents
seat their children on the floor a short distance before the altar,
facing east and take their seats behind them.   Each fraternity parent
extends the feet on each side of the child and draws her head back
until it rests on the bosom, the eyes of the novice being covered by

the hands of the fraternity parent. A warrior, wearing his war pouch, and on his head his plume wand, now dances before the novices, bending and wildly gesticulating; passing around by the north side of the altar, he stands his two eagle-wing plumes upward in his bow wristlet and slips a bear's foot skin on his left hand. He takes one of the diminutive mounds from the sand painting, and returning by the south side of the altar, he throws himself, with one knee bent and the other leg extended backward, before the couple at the south end of the line, and places the material from the dry painting to the heart of the fraternity child of the Great Mother. Clawing over the novice, he indulges in extravaganza, throwing his arms outward and upward; he then returns to the altar, dances a moment or two before it, takes a second mound from the painting, and applies it to the heart of the novice midway the line. After the third novice has passed through the rite, the warrior returns to the first novice, growling and gesticulating, and throws himself forward and sucks at the spot where the material from the dry painting has been placed. Waving the supposed extracted material about his head, he approaches the altar, and, dancing wildly, passes by the south side and appears to deposit the extracted material in a bowl. In this particular ceremony the sucking is done at the heart only, and is for the purification of the heart. He no sooner sucks at the heart of the second novice than a female theurgist repeats the same rite with the girl at the south end of the line, and continues with the other two novices; one after another from the choir repeat the form, until every theurgist of the fraternity has drawn evil from the heart of the novice, each one aiming to outdo the other in extravaganza. No one omits to pass around the altar from the north side in going to the bowl to deposit the material supposed to be drawn from the hearts of the novices.

The women are as enthusiastic as the men, but are awkward, while the men are wonderfully graceful. At the conclusion of this ceremony each novice is assisted to her feet by the fraternity parent, who leads her to the altar, where they both pray, and afterward she is led to her place on the ledge on the north side of the room. When the novices have taken their seats the warrior carries out the bowl of supposed extracted material. Two men leave the choir and appear before the altar just as the Great Mother deposits ashes before it, and the former ceremony of sprinkling ashes for purification is repeated. Those present, still holding in their left hands the meal previously distributed, wave their hands four times around their heads, from left to right, whenever the dancers strike the ashes from their plumes.

After the sprinkling of ashes to the six regions is repeated, all but the really ill people stand and pray aloud. The prayer closes shortly before 2 in the morning, and the male members gather about the altar, and afterward the female members, to sprinkle meal and receive a draft of medicine water from the a'kwamosi. The women return to their homes two hours after midnight, but the men remain and sleep in the ceremonial chamber. The second morning finds the men occupied making prayer plumes and mi'wachi for the novices.

Second night. Most of the men have their bodies zigzagged in white, symbolic of lightning, and each man wears a wreath of yucca ribbon. The female theurgists wear their conventional dress and red-colored, fluffy eagle plumes attached to the forelock; their feet and legs halfway to the knee, and hands and arms midway to the elbow, are painted white. The altar and the floor before it are white with meal, sprinkled by the members of the fraternity, and a line of meal crossed four times extends from the altar to the ladder. The Beast Gods pass over this line to be present, for the time being, in the bodies of the theurgists. The animal fetishes by the altar influence the spiritual presence of the Beast Gods.

The ceremonial opens with the consecration of water, according to the ritual previously described. At 10 o'clock a warrior dances before the altar, not moving from the spot upon which he first stands. He holds an eagle-wing plume in each hand, which he extends alternately toward the altar. After a time he dips the plumes in the medicine water and sprinkles the altar, afterward sprinkling to the six regions. Two theurgists now leave the choir and dance wildly before the altar, afterward dashing madly about, growling like the beasts they represent. They are soon joined by two female theurgists. The warrior whirls the cloud cluster surmounted by Ä'chiyälä'topa (being with wings and tail of knives), which is suspended above the altar, by touching it with his eagle plumes held in the right hand, that the clouds of the world may gather over Zuñi. He also sprinkles the altar and choir at intervals, and sprinkles the women twice by dipping his plumes into the medicine water. After the theurgists who are now on the floor form in two files, three in each, and face first north and then south, the warrior gradually becomes wilder in his gesticulations before the altar, bending until he almost kneels before it, which he leaves every now and then to join the dancers or to heal the sick. A guest from the pueblo of Sia, who belongs to the Fire fraternity of that pueblo, goes to the fireplace and stamps in the fire and literally bathes himself in the live coals. He then takes a large coal in his right hand, and after rubbing his throat and breast with it he places it in his mouth. Others of the Fire fraternity also play with the coals, rubbing them over one another's backs. As the night wanes, the cries of the theurgists become louder and wilder, and the time of the dance grows faster. The women are as wild as the men. Mothers move their infants' tiny fists in time with the rattle, drum, and song. The men keep their upper arms rather close to their sides as they raise their hands up and down. The lines of dancers often break into a promiscuous mass. Now and then a man drags a woman to the floor, compelling her to dance. Again the dancers run about healing the sick. Two or more theurgists sometimes grab at the same patient simultaneously. The patient often rubs his hands up the back of the theurgist during the healing.

The a'kwamosi stands by the altar keeping time with his plumes, held in each hand and moved simultaneously up and down. An aged man, much crippled with rheumatism, who comes late in the evening, receives treatment from many of the theurgists, who seem especially interested in his case. The largest number of women observed on the floor at any one time is seven, and these, with the number of men crowding the floor, form a curious living kaleidoscope. The dance closes shortly before midnight. The a'kwemosi dips his plumes into the medicine water and places the quill ends to the lips of the Sia guests. First the men and then the women group about the altar, each receiving a draft of medicine water from the a'kwamosi, and sprinkle the altar with meal. Then the women leave for their homes with their wideawake babies on their backs. The men remain in the ceremonial room.

Third night. The ceremony is somewhat delayed by the making of flash-light pictures, much effort being necessary to succeed, as the fraternity at large make strong objection. The officers of the fraternity finally prevent any interference.

The members of the order are devoid of paint or other decoration, except the yucca wreath and fluffy eagle plume. At half past 10 o'clock the room is well filled, the choir having previously grouped in the designated place. The a'kwamosi is seated as usual by the medicine bowl at the altar, and the medicine water is prepared. A warrior of the fraternity now comes before the altar and moves his eagle-wing plumes up and down. In a moment or two the director dances before the altar and then proceeds to heal the sick. After sucking his first patient, who is a woman, he throws the supposed extracted material into the fire. His next subject is the a'kwamosi, from whose side he "draws" an object and throws it into the fire. He afterward deposits the material supposed to come from his patients in the bowl presided over by the aged woman. For some time he practices healing alone, when his exquisitely graceful movements can be clearly observed. When the director retires, the warrior moves from his position before the altar, and a second theurgist comes to the floor. Dipping his plumes in the medicine water, he sprinkles the choir and dances wildly before the altar, twisting and bending his body, and proceeds to practice on the patients. In a few moments he is joined by two female theurgists, who perform curious antics before the altar, bending first one knee and then the other. Gradually the number of theurgists on the floor increases, leaving, however, a sufficient body to continue the song. One of the practicing theurgists is a Sia guest invited to take part in the healing. He falls on one knee before the altar, his back to it, then rises and proceeds to practice. Touching one of the women with the tips of his two eagle-wing plumes, he extends his hand and receives the stone, which he professes to draw from the body by the touch of the plumes, and holds it up to view. The trick is beautifully and gracefully performed.[a] The Sia theurgist stamps in the fire with his bare feet, and runs about with a large live coal in his hand, finally rubbing it over his nude body. The scene is dramatic when the floor becomes crowded and the theurgists, jumping about in groups in squatting positions, manipulate their eagle-wing plumes as they approach the invalids. As one touches an invalid the others of the group draw near, waving their plumes, which are usually held in the left hand during the dance or sucking, and pointing them toward the sick one. Occasionally two theurgists practice upon an invalid at the same time, the others manipulating their plumes about him.

For a time no woman is on the floor; then one appears, doing her share in the healing. A warrior stands back and to the south of the altar, keeping time with a plume held in each land. A second warrior also beats time with his plumes while he remains seated at the south side of the altar. The a′kwamosi retains his standing position, keeping time.

At 11 o'clock the director of the fraternity and a woman leave the chamber, each carrying a pinch of meal, which they sprinkle outside, and a Sia Indian steps to the door and throws out a pinch of meal, afterward gargling his throat to cleanse it, and returns to the choir. All the dancers but one now leave the floor. He performs extravaganza before the altar for a time, and resumes dancing, when he is joined by a female theurgist, who gives the most peculiar screeches as she awkwardly jumps about the floor. After a time a man joins the couple and the three dance sidewise, one behind the other, up and down the room. In moving toward the altar they face south, and as they dance from it they face north.

Shortly after 11 the first of these dancers goes outside the house and gargles his throat, the second man returns to the choir, and the female theurgist is left alone on the floor. After dancing violently for a time she is joined by another woman, who holds her eagle plumes in her right hand. The two dance until twenty minutes after midnight. The position of the arms of the women in dancing seldom varies, the upper arms being kept close to the body, and the lower extended outward. When they take their seats all draw in a sacred breath from their eagle plumes, and the officers of the Mystery medicine order repeat a prayer. The warrior now carries out the bowl containing the extracted matter and buries the contents. The a′kwamosi administers

---

[a] The Sia are more expert than the Zuñis in the theurgistic performances and in playing with fire.

a draft of medicine water to each person present. The men, and afterward the women, gather about the altar and pray, and the women return to their homes, the men remaining in the ceremonial chamber.

Fourth night. The four walls of the ceremonial chamber are ornamented with paintings of the cougar in yellow, bear in black, badger white spotted in black, wolf in gray, and a second bear in dark gray followed by a cub. A black thread outlines each figure except the cub. The hearts are shown in red, with a line extending from the heart to the mouth in the same color. A red-colored fluffy eagle plume, insignia of Mystery medicine, is attached to the outline near the head of each animal. The altar is elaborate with its fetishes and other accessories.

Although the opening of the ceremonial is not until 11 o'clock, the personal adornment commences at 9, the men, as usual, painting first their own limbs and then the bodies of one another in red hematite and then in micaceous hematite. Both of the paints are scraped and mixed in water. The women decorate in white their own feet and legs halfway to the knee and their hands and arms midway to the elbow. Some time is consumed in this decoration, and the process is evidently enjoyed. Finally all is completed and the men group in the southwest end of the room.

Members of the A'pi"läshiwanni are privileged to be present at the meetings of all the fraternities, but they are not alone the privileged ones. Others may not only be present by invitation of the director of a fraternity, but they may be active in the healing. It is quite common for the director of a fraternity to invite members of another organization to join him in his ceremonies. On the present occasion two men and a woman of the Shu'maakwe fraternity and other guests from the Little Fire fraternity, one being a woman, arrive and are greeted with marked cordiality, though pronounced formality, and shown seats on the ledge at the west end of the room near the choir. The two theurgists from Sia, who have been present each night, are also cordially received and shown seats on the south ledge.

At the outset sacred meal is given from corn husks into the palm of the left hand and afterward medicine is distributed from corn husks. The meal is sprinkled on the altar and the medicine is taken into the mouth of the one who receives it and expectorated on the body and afterward rubbed over the body with the right hand. A warrior and another male member carry out food from before the altar, each providing himself with a pinch of meal from a basket before it, and the a'kwamosi, who sits as usual to the north side of the altar, after making a cross of meal upon which the medicine bowl is to stand, signals the choir to begin by raising the bowl. The ritual attending the making of the medicine water does not vary from that previously described.

The two who left the chamber to offer food to the Beast Gods return before the completion of the consecration of the water, and the warrior whirling the rhombus, steps back to give them room by the altar to sprinkle meal and to pray. At the close of the preparation of the medicine water the a'kwamosi stands and sprinkles it on the altar with his plumes, after which a female theurgist collects ashes from the fireplace with her plumes and deposits them in a heap before the altar. Immediately the drum is heard in addition to the rattle, and two men leave the choir for the floor and lift the ashes just deposited, with their plumes. One skips down the north side of the room, the other the south side; crossing at the far end, they return on opposite sides, proceeding in an ellipse. As they pass down the room they sprinkle the people with the ashes, and on their return they gracefully manipulate their plumes, still held in each hand. Meeting near the altar, they stand for a moment side by side, facing north, and then turn and face the west. Extending the right arm backward and the left arm forward, they simultaneously strike the plume held in the left hand with the one held in the right, by a long under sweep of the right hand, exclaiming at the moment, Hu......hu......hu...... hu......uh. The process of sprinkling the people and striking the plumes is then repeated. Again they lift ashes and sprinkle them to the East, North, West, South, Zenith, and Nadir, lifting ashes each time for each region. The sprinkling to the six regions is repeated and the two return to the choir, when two others leave it. At this time four women form a line, extending east and west, and dance. After extravaganza before the altar, the two men dash about, healing the sick. Other theurgists appear on the floor, and the number of dancers increases. Owing to the presence of invited guests, the novices adjourn to another place at midnight, to be decorated. Each fraternity parent is preceded by his fraternity child. The Great Mother, who is before the other fraternity parents, carries a kettle of kaolin mixed with water, to be used on the novices. As soon as they depart the floor is cleared, and though the choir remains in position, there is no music during the hour's absence of the novices, this being the only rest for the singers from the opening of the ceremony in the evening to the following morning at 7 o'clock or later.

After an absence of an hour the novices and their fraternity parents return, the wee one being carried on her fraternity father's back; the feet and legs halfway to the knees and the hands and arms halfway to the elbows are painted white. They wear the ordinary dress and red belt, and the hair is done up in the usual way. A circle of white paint with hawk down attached, symbolic of the clouds of the world, crowns the head. The chin and upper lip are also painted in kaolin and covered with the down. An owl and a raven feather are crossed on the wrist and held in place by yucca ribbons, the owl feather pointing outward, the other pointing inward. The novices are led to seats on the north ledge near the altar by their fraternity parents, the younger girl sitting on her mother's lap.

The return of the novices is the occasion for reopening the song, and in a few minutes the dancing begins, the director of the fraternity being the first to appear on the floor. He dances before the altar, bending and twisting his body and growling animal-like, every little while dashing up to an invalid and "drawing disease" from the body. During the fifteen minutes that he practices a warrior stands to the south side of the altar, holding his eagle plumes in each hand, constantly extending first one hand and then the other. When the director retires behind the altar the novices form in line and dance (the young child being held on the back of a woman by means of cotton cloth). Theurgists from time to time cease their healing to join in the dance. The noise of the choir increases in volume until the close of the medicine practice previous to the closing ceremony of initiation, except for five minutes allowed to all for rest. Occasionally the woman holding the child is relieved and sits for a while, but this is not often.

Five male and two female theurgists are soon at work upon the patients. Gradually others come to the floor until about twenty are dashing about madly among the sick. Sometimes four theurgists are sucking at one man. As the night wanes and the floor becomes more crowded the scene grows more and more wild and weird and the excitement is intense. The women appear even more excited than the men, though they are far from graceful, and their attempts at legerdemain are very poor. The Great Mother, however, is one of the experts.

Among the vast number suffering from real or imaginary ills a few are seriously afflicted. Though several theurgists pretend to extract from the writer's forehead (she is suffering from headache) material "shot" in by witches, it is impossible for her to discover the clever tricks. Large pebbles and yards of yarn seem to be drawn from her forehead. A Sia guest apparently extracts a large stone. Occasionally some one is caught nodding, and is at once wakened by a neighbor in no very kind tone. Sleeping at such times is regarded as most disrespectful to the Beast Gods, only young infants being accorded the privilege. At times the theurgists dance in groups; then again the men and women form into several parallel lines, facing first the south and then the north, as they dance back and forth from west to east. Usually there are more men than women on the floor. A theurgist from the Little Fire fraternity, followed by three of his fellows, who appear to be charmed by their leader, enters the chamber in semicrawling position, and after holding a crystal for a moment to the breast of an invalid—the crystal showing the seat of the disease—he touches the spot with his two eagle plumes with a trembling motion, and while one of the party sucks the spot he continues

b   *a*   *b*

a, ANCIENT 'HLA'WE; *b*, 'HLU'SIPOWE, FETISHES OF 'HLE'WEKWE, THE
SWORD SWALLOWERS

SHRINE OF THE GODS OF WAR, SHOWING TEHL'NAWE (STAVES) USED IN
CEREMONIAL OF ᵗHLE'WEKWE, THE SWORD SWALLOWERS

the motion with the plumes over the body. The theurgist who extracts the cause of the disease distorts his face and body in his efforts to be rid of the foreign material. Finally he draws many yards of yarn from his mouth. Again the leader with his followers approaches an invalid and rubs his plumes over the body with a peculiar trembling motion; and placing the crystal, which he holds in the left hand, against the body, he touches the plumes held in the right hand to the spot indicated by the crystal, and with the tip ends of the plumes draws disease near the surface and sucks the spot, and after great distortions he gradually succeeds in "drawing" several yards of string.

Most of the extracting of disease is done by sucking, but in some instances the plumes only are used to draw disease to the surface, when the material is caught with the hand. The best manipulating is near the writer. Stones varying in size from minute to that of a pigeon's egg, bits of old cloth, and strings of various kinds are exhibited by the theurgists. The men always show what they are supposed to have extracted, the hand being first waved toward the invalid, and with the exclamation, "Hu_____hu_____hu_____hu_____uh." Usually each theurgist waves the hand containing the extracted material before the altar previous to depositing it in the large bowl provided for the purpose, but the women, except the Great Mother, keep their hands closed while waving them, and no sound is heard when the hand is opened over the bowl. Though generally the theurgist casts the supposed extracted material into the bowl, the first time he usually throws it into the fire; then he takes a pinch of meal from the basket before the altar and leaves the chamber to sprinkle it outside with a prayer. Sometimes a theurgist wears the skin of a bear's foot on his left hand; again one is worn on each hand. When a dozen or more theurgists are on the floor, their bodies thrown forward until they appear like the animals they personate, growling and wrangling with one another, the scene is weird and impressive.

At half past 3 o'clock the healing performances close for a time. The dance ceases and the novices form in line behind their fraternity parents, who, facing south, extend an eagle plume over each shoulder, the ends of which are caught by the novice, while the wife or sister of the fraternity parent is behind and rests a hand on each shoulder of the novice. In this way they advance several steps toward the south and stand for a moment, when the Great Mother, who is at the west end of the line, turns toward the east, and they all swing wheel fashion. The shoulders of the novices are moved in time with the choir, and the novices make a similar motion with the plumes. Again they wheel around by the north and face west, when they receive consecrated water from the a'kwamosi, who administers it from a shell.

After this ceremony with the novices the dancing is resumed and the theurgists continue their practicing upon the sick. Three young and charmingly graceful boys, wearing white cotton breechcloths, their bodies painted white, now appear for the first time among the dancers, a number of whom are women. The adult novice is led upon the floor to receive her first lesson in healing. She is very awkward as she is dragged about by her fraternity father, who, after touching his plume to some portion of the body of an invalid, has the pupil suck the spot. She afterward pretends to deposit something from her mouth into her fraternity father's right hand, and he dashes, with her arm through his, to the bowl and, holding his hand close to it, appears to drop in some object. When novices receive their first instruction no objects are seen or sounds heard in making the deposit in the bowl. The wee one is carried on the back of her fraternity father, who throws himself almost prostrate upon the floor, jumps about in a squatting position, and performs curious feats when he is not extracting disease. The child takes no part in the healing, as one must have reached the age of discretion before attaining to the degree of practicing medicine. After some fifteen minutes the fraternity children are returned to their places, and they at once join in the dance, the younger one dancing with all the enthusiasm of her elders. One of the theurgists carries on his back a boy about eight years of age, who has been previously initiated into the order of Mystery medicine, but is not yet old enough to be active in his order. This man's actions are so violent that it is remarkable the child retains his position.

The Great Mother collects ashes from the fireplace and heaps them before the altar, and the ash-sprinklers who appeared early in the evening come again from the choir. They repeat the sprinkling of the ashes, and they dance in front of the altar longer and more violently than before. After the ashes are sprinkled, the a′kwamosi administers medicine water from the bowl with a shell to the men and women, and all sprinkle the altar with meal.

The novices now take seats on boxes in line facing east. A bowl of yucca suds is brought and the fraternity parent lifts suds with his two eagle-wing plumes and anoints the head of the novice. Afterward each member of the order dips suds with his eagle-wing plumes and deposits them on the head of each novice, and then the head is washed by the wife or sister of the fraternity parent, who gives prayer plumes and four ears of corn to the novice, and then draws his mi′li by the novice's lips, head, and shoulders. Each member of the order does likewise with his mi′li, and the ceremony of initiation into the order of O′naya′nakĭa is closed. Variations of a minor character occurred in the Mystery medicine order in 1884.

Soon after the order assembles, one of the theurgists, who is also a member of the Fire division, stands before the altar and dips the quill ends of his eagle plumes into the medicine water and presses the quills to his nude breast to receive the charm of the medicine, when he becomes extravagant in his beast-like performances and dancing. He raises first one foot then the other as high as possible, each time stamping firmly upon the floor; leaps about in the wildest manner; throws himself upon the floor, maintaining the most graceful attitudes; then suddenly rising, dances before the altar. After some minutes he runs into the back of his belt the two eagle-wing plumes he carries, and dashing forward to the fireplace takes a large coal and, dancing about with it first in one hand and then in the other a moment or two, puts it into his mouth, where it remains thirty seconds, during which time he indulges in extravaganza. He is soon joined by other men and by women, whose dusky forms, moving beast-like in light or shadow, according to the uncertain light of the embers in the fireplace, their eyes almost as bright as the coals in their mouths, which scintillate with every breath, carry one in imagination to the regions of Pluto. The longest time a coal is held in the mouth is one minute; the shortest, thirty seconds. There is considerable rivalry at such times, each one aiming to outdo the other, yet all are filled with the spirit of good nature. When the coal is removed from the mouth it is tossed into the fireplace with a peculiar quick and graceful motion. After a time the theurgist who came first to the floor dips the feather ends of his eagle plumes into the medicine water and places them to his mouth, then resumes his seat in the choir. Again the theurgists come forward two or three at a time and pelt the members of the choir with live coals, and then lighting large bunches of corn husks, shower the choir with the sparks, and each one runs the burning mass into his mouth.

When these men return to the choir the women begin dancing, but they are not long on the floor when a young man of the Pi'änni'hle (Sword) order appears wearing a war pouch; a wand is attached to the back of his head and a fluffy eagle plume tied to the forelock. He advances to the altar, and dipping the feather ends of his eagle-wing plumes into the medicine water, places them to his lips and rubs them over his nude body. After dancing wildly about the room for a short time, he secures a sword of his order from behind the altar, and, dancing before the altar and facing it, he gracefully throws his body forward, twisting and turning in beast-like motions. After a time he turns and faces the east, and dropping on one knee swallows the sword. When this rite has been repeated three times he places the sword by the altar. His movements are the perfection of grace, and the picture presented is most pleasing. The flutist, who sits behind the altar, puffs smoke each side of it at intervals. The healing of the sick begins soon after the sword swallowing, and the sword swallower and two girls conclude the dance at midnight. The remainder of the ceremonial corresponds with the one previously described.

FIRE ORDER OF THE MA'ᵗKE ᶜHLAN'NAKWE SWORD DIVISION

First night. The tablet altar is erected as usual the first day in the ceremonial chamber, and members are busy preparing prayer plumes, the floor being quite covered with medicine boxes and plumes. When the fraternity convenes for the night ceremonial, the novice's father calls for him (there being but one novice on the occasion described) and conducts him to a seat on the north side of the ceremonial chamber. Eight officers of the different orders of the Fire division, each supplied with a bundle of juniper (species not yet determined) splinters as long as from the heel to the bent knee, measured on the outer side of the leg, sit behind the altar. After the choir[a] sings one song to the accompaniment of rattle and drum, each officer takes bits of the root and blossom of yarrow (Achillea lanulosa) into his mouth and expectorates upon the splinters six times alternately, and deposits the bundle behind the altar. The novice now hands a husk of meal to some member of the order and returns to his seat; while the man receiving the husk hands it to the chosen fraternity father, saying: "The child wishes to join the order." The chosen one receives the meal, saying, " I wish for the good heart and health of my son," and he distributes the meal to each person present, depositing it in the palm of the left hand while the receiver remains seated.

The ᶜHlĕm'mosona of the Sword order now spreads a blanket some distance from the altar and removes the sword blades,[b] which are wrapped in an old buckskin, from a box and deposits them in the center of the blanket. Each member has his sword so marked that he readily selects it from the large number; he then attaches the feathered handle to it, these handles, when not in use, being kept suspended on the wall of an inner room of the ceremonial house. After all the swords are arranged with their handles, each member of the order sprinkles the altar with the meal which was given him by the novice, the novice alone taking meal from the meal basket to sprinkle the altar. They pass in file by the south side and around the altar and down the north side of the room to the east end, led by a female member of the fraternity carrying her mi'li and meal basket. The ᶜHlĕm'mosona follows the woman, and after him the other officers, and then the order at large. The novice follows his fraternity father around the altar, but afterward takes his seat on the ledge. When the ᶜHlĕm'mosona while returning to the altar reaches the ladder leading through the hatchway into the chamber, the director of the dance, who is midway in the file, begins the song. The sword is

---

[a] While all the members of the Great Fire fraternity may be present, only those of the Fire division are privileged to form the choir.

[b] These blades, which are of juniper, are as long as from the tip of the middle finger to the tip of the thumb, the fingers extended, and the thumb and four fingers crosswise, three-fourths of an inch wide, slightly curved and rounded at the end. They are rubbed with Congar grease and red hematite.

carried in the left hand and the rattle in the right. After one song
is sung, the ᶜHlĕm′mosona addresses his people, saying: " My grandfathers, my uncles, my sons, my elder brothers, my younger brothers,
to-night I commence my dance. Are any of my people sorry? I
want everybody to be happy to-night." The dance now begins, all
passing around the altar from the south side.

A woman of the order takes the novice by the left arm and leads him
through the line of dancers to the middle of the room, facing him east,
and stands behind him with her hands on his shoulders, moving one
and then the other forward, while the hands of the novice hang by his
side. After the dancers pass around the altar a second time, the woman
who leads them approaches the novice, the other woman at once retiring, and places her mi′li to his right shoulder, head, left shoulder, and
mouth, that he may draw in the sacred life breath of A′wónawil′ona,[a]
and returns to her place as leader of the file. Then the ᶜHlĕm′mosona
stands before the novice, and after swallowing his sword draws it
before the right shoulder, head, left shoulder, and lips of the novice,
as was done with the mi′li, and returns to his place. Each member
repeats the ceremony with his sword over the novice, the dancers in
the meantime continuing around the altar.

The fraternity father now stands before the novice, and after swallowing his sword[b] hands it to the novice, who makes an effort to pass
the sword down his throat. The sword is supposed to be swallowed
four times by the novice, and each time he returns it to the fraternity
father, who breathes four times upon it.[c]

On the present occasion, the novice failing each time to pass the
sword down his throat, his fraternity father swallows it instead.
After the sword swallowing, the novice, following his fraternity father,
joins the dancers, who remain but a short time longer on the floor.
After each one prays before the altar he hands his sword to the ᶜHlĕm′-
mosona, who deposits it on the buckskin which has been placed close
to the altar, the tips of the swords pointing to the west. The buckskin is folded over the blades, leaving the handles exposed. After
arranging the swords, the ᶜHlĕm′mosona takes his position near the
ladder, and, beginning with the ᶜhle′pekwĭn (deputy) to the ᶜHlĕm′-
mosona, deposits blossoms and bits of root of yarrow in the palm of
the left hand of each member of the Sword order who stands in line

---

[a] See p. 22.

[b] These Indians are so clever at legerdemain that when first observed the sword swallowing was
thought to be one of their tricks. To convince herself, the writer induced a member of this order,
after long persuasion, to visit her camp and swallow the sword. Great secrecy was observed while
the head-kerchief and leather pouch were removed and the sword swallowed, and the Indian to this
day feels that he was guilty of a great wrong in swallowing the sword without the ceremony which
should attend it.

[c] Unlike the ᶜHle′wekwe fraternity, it is exceptional, so a prominent member of the Great Fire fraternity states, for a novice to succeed the first night in swallowing the sword. He adds: "I failed
in every effort to swallow the sword the night of my initiation. I tried four times, but could not
succeed."

and to the novice. Some put the medicine into their mouths at once, while others wait until they are about ready to eat the fire. This medicine is chewed to protect the mouth when the fire is eaten. After the medicine is distributed, the 'Hlĕm'mosona places near the fireplace a bundle of the juniper splinters previously referred to, and the novice is again conducted by the woman to the middle of the floor. She turns him to face the east, and moves his shoulders as has been described, while the dancers pass twice around the altar. Again the female leader of the file of dancers goes to the novice as before, and the first woman returns to her seat; then the 'Hlĕm'mosona lights the bundle of splinters and puts them into the novice's mouth. When the fire is out he draws them over the novice's shoulders, head, and mouth, as previously described; this ceremony is repeated four times by each member of the order, a fresh bundle of splinters being used each time. After this ceremony the splinters are laid by the fireplace. The novice now passes with his fraternity father once around the altar and returns to his seat, and all sprinkle the altar with meal, and pray; then the warrior of the Fire division carries the partially burned splinters east of the town and deposits them at Ku'shilowa (red earth).

Second day. After six songs are sung to the six regions for snow, two members of the Fire order go in single file, the second man whirling the rhombus, to collect two young trees. They are preceded by another man, who carries a meal basket and sprinkles meal for a short distance north of the village. The trees which are selected are about 3 feet high, one being piñon, the other another species of pine. Three marks are made near the base and on the east side of each tree, denoting eyes and mouth. The trees are cut with a stone knife and are carried in the left arm to the ceremonial chamber, where the man who accompanied the tree collectors beyond the village, receives them and waves them to the six regions. The 'Hlĕm'mosona afterward puffs smoke from native tobacco in a reed over them and attaches a la'showannĕ of a single white fluffy eagle plume to each tree. The collectors of the trees are careful to bring young buds of spruce and piñon trees in separate husks, some of which are put into the medicine water; the remainder are afterward distributed to the fraternity at large. The women especially are anxious for the "bud medicine," as they call it, which is eaten when a woman is pregnant. If a boy is desired, she eats the buds of the pine; if a girl, she takes those of the piñon. The wish is always realized unless the woman's heart is bad. Upon the writer's asking for the buds from a pine branch brought to the village with a load of wood, a member of the Great Fire fraternity exclaimed: "Oh, they are no good; the bough was not cut from the tree while the old songs of the Ma'ʻke ʻHlan'nakwe were sung."

The man who receives the trees lays them north of the swords, which are still near the altar, with the marks indicating eyes and mouth upward, the upper portion of the tree pointing to the east. At midnight the trees are carried to the roof, and the piñon is placed to the west and the other to the east of the crossbar of the hatchway, the face symbols being to the east, where they remain until the close of the ceremonial on the fifth day. After the trees are placed in position the eight officers of the fraternity stand around them; the flutist plays, the warrior whirls the rhombus, while the 'Hlĕm'mosona prays and sprinkles meal upon the trees.ᵃ There is continuous dancing and sword swallowing on the second and third days until midnight, and an elaborate display of playing with fire on the third night. The visits of the Sword order to other houses are noted in the 'Hle'wekwe ceremonials.

A dry painting about 2½ feet square is made on the floor and near the altar on the fourth afternoon. The foundation of the painting is the ordinary yellow sand found near the village. Its groundwork is about half an inch in depth. The measurements are made with the right hand, from the tip of the thumb to the tip of the second finger and from the tip of the thumb to the tip of the index finger. The four sides of the square are measured in this way. The north line of the square is symbolic of the Hopi country; the west line, of the Navaho country; the south line, of the Mexican country; the east line, of the Rio Grande country; and the yellow line running through the center, which is of corn pollen, is symbolic of the Zuñi country, the heart and center of all. The black coloring is charred corncob mixed with other powdered pigment. The two human figures in the painting represent Na'ke'e, the original director of the Great Fire fraternity, and his fellow or younger brother. Zigzag lines extend out from each side of the figures, denoting lightning. The war pouch is indicated by a diagonal line across the body. A circular spot of corn pollen on the body represents the heart. Eagle-wing feathers are held in the hands. The black lines extending outward below the knees represent garters of blue yarn. Crosses over the surface of the painting, with a single grain of corn on each, indicate stars. When the painting is completed it is protected by placing a stone at each corner, upon which pieces of wood are crossed and a white embroidered blanket laid over the wood.

The painting is uncovered at night by the 'Hlĕm'mosona after the swords are distributed to their owners, who are grouped before the altar. If a blemish is found on raising the blanket from the painting the 'Hlĕm'mosona says, should it be near the pollen line: " I fear many of my people will die." If the defect is near another line, then the people of the country indicated by the line will die.

After passing once around the altar the Sword order forms in line.

ᵃ The trees are not referred to as such, but as tĕsh'kwi (not to be touched, sacred).

The two small trees are brought from the hatchway and as the 'Hlĕm'-mosona passes down the line, he draws the trees before the face of each dancer with a prayer, the dancer drawing a sacred breath from them. When all have drawn the sacred breath, or all that is best, from the trees they are placed beside the altar, and the Sword division visit the chamber where the Mu'waiye[a] rehearse, and dance and swallow the swords. On their return to their ceremonial chamber the novice is served with food, and then all present partake of it.

After the repast is finished dancing is resumed and continues throughout the night. At midnight the 'Hlĕm'mosona deposits prayer plumes and sprinkles meal in an excavation the depth of a man's arm in the Si'aa' te'wita at the base of the ladder east of the one which leads to the He'iwa ki'wi'sinĕ with prayers to Na'ke'e, the original director of the fraternity. After the deposition of the prayer plumes the 'Hlĕm'mosona covers the cavity with a stone and earth so cleverly that no one would dream of its existence. This spot in the plaza is most sacred to the Great Fire fraternity, as Na'ke'e is supposed to have disappeared into the earth as this point, and no one must sit on the ladder that runs up by this excavation or on the roof immediately above it when the Great Fire fraternity is present in the plaza, for an ĕt'tonĕ[b] of a shi'wanni (rain priest), who is also a member of the Great Fire fraternity, is kept in the old house to which the upper ladder leads.

Fifth day. At daylight on the fifth day the 'Hlĕm'mosona runs his hand over the pollen line of the painting in the ceremonial chamber and places the pollen he collects in a corn husk; and men and women hasten forward to take a pinch from the heart (which is considered good medicine for fecundity) of each figure, each one having a corn husk in which to place what is collected. The grains of corn are also eagerly sought. One, two, three, or four grains collected are planted apart from other corn the coming year, and the corn raised from this is not eaten, but kept till the next year and planted in the field with the other corn. After all the mi'wachi are removed from the altar, the 'Hlĕm'mosona brushes the meal on the floor about the altar to the dry painting with his eagle plumes and lifts the sand with his two hands and deposits it in a bowl, which a woman places near him, and carries it to the river where he deposits the contents. After the 'Hlĕm'mosona leaves the chamber a box is placed in the middle of the floor, with a blanket spread over it, upon which the novice takes his seat. The fraternity father, standing behind the novice, places over his shoulders a blanket (a gift) which has the sun emblem, painted on a piece of cotton cloth, sewed to the center of it, and steps before him, while his wife stands behind the novice with a hand on each shoulder.

---

[a] See p. 458.   [b] See p. 163.

The ceremony which follows is the same as described on page 502 at the close of the initiatory ceremonies of the order of O'naya'nakĭa.

Later in the morning the chins of the male members of the order are painted black and streaked with white, symbolic of rain clouds with falling rain. The neck is painted yellow, the remainder of the body black; the upper portion of the arms black, and the forearms and hands yellow; each scapula, the outside of both arms near the shoulders, the breasts, and the outer side of the legs at the kneejoint are crossed in double lines of white; the upper portion of the legs are white, a band of black encircles the legs about the knee, and the remainder of the legs and the feet are yellow. Sometimes these decorations vary, the lower leg being entirely yellow. Dance moccasins are worn. White and black beads, the latter made from a dried berry, pass over the right shoulder and under the left arm; the long hair is tied tightly at the nape of the neck with red yarn or a red garter, a yucca wreath knotted at both sides encircles the head, six eagle-tail feathers arranged like a spread tail, with a few yellow parrot feathers pendent at the base, ornament the left side of the head. A fluffy eagle plume colored red is tied to the forelock of such dancers as belong to the Mystery medicine order. A bow wristlet is attached to the left arm, and profusions of ko'hakwa, coral, and turquoise beads are worn as necklaces. Rattles are carried in the right hands, swords in the left. The ʰHlĕm'mosona carries a crooked prayer plume instead of the rattle, and his deputy has instead of the feathered handle to his sword a tablet carved in cloud designs and colored in blue-green, red, yellow, black, and white, and further embellished with the sun and a star. Two white fluffy eagle feathers tip the cloud design at the top of the tablet. The ʰHlĕm'mosona, the Ko'mosona (director-general of the ki'wiʰsiwe),[a] and the pa'mosona (scalp custodian), who are members of this fraternity, have each a serpentiform sword denoting lightning.[b]

The female members wear their ordinary dress, including moccasins, with a folded mi'ha passing under the right arm and fastened on the left shoulder; the arms and neck are bare, and they wear turquoise earrings and elaborate necklaces; the hair is done up in the usual manner, with a fluffy eagle plume attached to the forelock, and each carries a sword in her left hand and two eagle-wing plumes in her right.

A woman carrying a meal basket leads the dancers through the southeastern covered way in single file to the plaza. Passing to the north by the east side and around by the excavation in which the prayer plumes were deposited the previous night to Na'ke'e, they join

---

a See Ki'wiʰsiwe and their functions.

b The present warrior, who has been a member of the fraternity four years, was anxious to possess such a lightning sword, but the ʰHlĕm'mosona objected on the ground that he had not been a member of the organization long enough for the goodness of his heart to be tested.

the line of the 'Hle'wekwe fraternity, who have completed their dance and are retiring from the plaza.[a]

The members of the Great Fire fraternity pass once around the boxes of the 'Hle'wekwe before dancing, but the musicians on the notched sticks sit with bowed heads and do not play. Each dance is begun with a barbaric shout; then the dancers settle down into monotonous song. There is little or no variety in the step; first one foot, then another, is raised as they continue to encircle the boxes. The 'Hlĕm'mosona is the first to step from the moving circle. At this moment all cease to dance, and simultaneously, like well-drilled soldiers, commence dancing again, and reverse the swords, holding the blades upward, while the 'Hlĕm'mosona waves his serpentiform sword over the boxes and prays. At the close of the prayer the swords are reversed with the same precision, and the 'Hlĕm'mosona steps before the boxes and swallows his sword. Again they move on for a moment or two, when all turn and face the center; then the others in turn leave the circles in groups and swallow the swords.

As soon as one group returns to the circle others step out, some swallowing two swords at once, one man swallowing three. The first group faces north, the second faces west, another south, another east, and two other groups face east for the zenith and the nadir. The Great Mother of the fraternity swallows two swords at once. It is noticed that many of this fraternity run the sword through the mouth to moisten it before swallowing it, but this is not done by the 'Hle'wekwe fraternity. They dance five times around the boxes, swallowing swords each time, and as the boxes are encircled the fifth time the 'Hlĕm'mosona swallows his sword facing north, two men swallow theirs facing east, two men and one woman swallow theirs facing south (see plate CXVIII), the warrior with his lightning sword and another man and the Great Mother swallow two swords facing east.

Again three men face north, three men east, two men south, two men and two women south, one man and two younger boys east, the man swallowing three swords at once; and the 'Hlĕm'mosona again swallows his sword facing west. Passing around the circle he receives the swords from each person, resting the feathered handles over his right arm. When all the swords are collected he has all he can manage; he stands in the center of the circle, facing the east, and prays. After the prayer he motions the swords to the six regions and again passes to the dancers, that each may take his sword. When all have received their swords again those east of the ladder draw as near as they may to the others on the opposite side[b] and proceed with the dance, and at its close they make their exit from the plaza by the

---

[a] See p. 469. The 'Hle'wekwe fraternity and Sword order of the Great Fire fraternity hold synchronal meetings in January and February, and alternate in their dancing in the plaza.

[b] No one must stand directly over the excavation sacred to Na'ke'e or before the ladder.

eastern covered way. Ere the last of the dancers has disappeared from the plaza the music of the notched sticks is begun and the men and women form for the circle dance described in the ʹHleʹwekwe ceremonial. The circle gradually increases in numbers, through the untiring energy of the aʹmosi and the aʹmosonoʹʹkĭa. Much persuasion is often necessary in order to secure the dancers.

On retiring to the ceremonial chamber after the last dance the swords are handed over to the ʹHlĕmʹmosona and all pray before the altar. A feast brings the sword festival to a close.

ORIGIN OF THE SHOʹTIKĬANNA, ARROW DIVISION

One day a white arrow point, as long as from the tip of the middle finger to the second joint measured on the under side of the finger, dropped to the floor through the hatchway of the ceremonial chamber. The director of the Great Fire fraternity exclaimed: "What is this?" He lifted the arrow and, upon examining it, expressed thanks for the gift. He declared that Äʹchiyäläʹtopa (being with wings and tail of knives) must have dropped the arrow, wishing him to institute an arrow order. The director attached the arrow to a reed shaft, and after making three efforts he succeeded the fourth time in running the arrow down his throat to his heart. He afterward initiated others into the arrow swallowing, and so instituted the order of the Arrow. Only men belong to this order. The ceremonial occurs every fourth year in February, in connection either with the poʹsikishi (spruce tree) ceremony or with the paʹĕtʹtowe (Navaho dance). The arrow swallowing is always combined with sword swallowing and is synchronous with the sword or tree ceremonial of the ʹHleʹwekwe in February.

On the fourth day of the festival of the winter solstice the warrior of the Great Fire fraternity cuts a reed square across the ends, the length from the carpus to the tip of the middle finger. He places a bit of raw cotton in one end, and after filling the reed with corn pollen he stops the other end with cotton, then colors the reed red, leaving the cotton white, and attaches to the center of the reed a laʹshowannĕ (one or more plumes attached to cotton cord) composed of a fluffy under-wing eagle feather, banded turkey feather, and a tail feather from each of the birds of the six regions. A bead, which may be koʹhakwa or turquoise, is strung on the string attached to the laʹshowannĕ. The reed is wrapped in a corn husk and the warrior hands it to the ʹHlĕmʹmosona, who sits near the altar, the fraternity being convened in the afternoon. Holding the reed with both hands, the ʹHlĕmʹmosona prays: "Give me rains, give me corn, horses, all animal food, and other food and all clothing." Then he gives it to another officer of the fraternity, who repeats the prayer. The reed in this way is passed to the eight officers and to all males present, who repeat the same prayers. The warrior of the fraternity afterward places it in a basket.

The following morning, the order having spent the night in the fraternity chamber, the warrior, after taking his morning meal, carries the reed to his home; but soon afterward he visits O'pompia mountain, and after reaching a shrine dedicated to the younger God of War, he selects a tall tree near by. Climbing it, he attaches the reed to the topmost limb, with prayers to the spirit of the tree to intercede with the u'wannami (rain-makers) for cold rains and snows. On his return to the village he goes to the house of every man of the fraternity and notifies him to come to the ceremonial chamber at night, at which time all assemble and sit and smoke, and he announces that they will have the arrow dance in February.

The ceremony described was in connection with the Navaho dance[a] and was observed by the writer in February, 1891. Each member of the Arrow order makes three prayer plumes to Na'ke'e. Two are retained and one is given to the director appointed to collect the young piñon and spruce trees for the ceremonial. The indoor ceremony of the Arrow order is substantially the same as the Sword, the main difference occurring on the fifth morning. At sunrise on the fifth morning the men make suds and wash their heads. The one novice also washes his own head. The hair, which the men must attend to for one another, since no woman can come in or touch them, is parted over the head and done up in the usual knot, with a wreath of yucca around the head; a fluffy eagle plume dyed red is attached to the forelock and an elaborate wand is attached pendent to the back of the hair near the crown. Their feet and legs halfway to the knees, and hands and arms nearly to the elbow, are painted white. A serpentine line for lightning runs up the outside of the legs and upper arms and up each side of the chest and each side of the back. There are a few variations, one man having blue-green curves spotted in red and white over each scapula; another, blue-green up his right arm and yellow up his left, while all the curves on a third are of blue-green spotted in colors. A ribbon of yucca encircles the right wrist and a bow wristlet is worn on the left. The face is colored black to the line of the lips and painted white below; hawk down is applied over the white, and a small quantity of the down is stuck to the end of the nose. A line of micaceous hematite extends across the face below the eyes. A black breechcloth with blue embroidered ends is worn. Rattles are carried in the right hand.

Each one receives in his left hand from the 'Hlem'mosona the

---

[a] The participants in the Navaho dance dress similar to the Navahos.

arrow[a] he is to swallow and sprinkles the altar with meal from his
right hand; then he passes around the altar by the south side and takes
his position on the north side of the room and to the west end.

After the arrows are distributed the 'Hlĕm'mosona takes his stand
at the end of the line near the east wall. The novice, who has kept
his seat until now, passes to the middle of the floor and stands facing
east. The drummer, who uses a wooden drum on this occasion, stands
near the south wall and west of the fireplace. All dance in an ellipse
once around the altar and return to their places. A new song is
begun, when the 'Hlĕm'mosona advances to the novice and, facing
east, swallows the arrow. After the arrow swallowing is repeated by
all, the fraternity father draws his arrow before the shoulders, mouth,
and over the head of the novice. The novice makes four unsuccessful
efforts to swallow the arrow. The party now start for the Si'aa'
te'wita, preceded by the drummer, who takes his place on the east
side of the plaza. The leader wears a white cotton shirt, white
embroidered kilt, blue knit leggings, and dance moccasins. The
upper legs are exposed, but are not painted. He carries a pottery
meal basket and a po'nepoyannĕ[b] in his left hand, and uses his right
to sprinkle meal. Each dancer carries a bow and arrows in his left
hand, and in his right hand the arrow he is to swallow and also his
rattle (plate CXIX shows the Arrow order in the plaza). The boxes of
the 'Hle'wekwe are encircled four times, then all stand for a moment,
shouting, "Ha—ha—ha;" the arrow director steps before the boxes
and, facing them, waves his arrow gracefully from right to left over
them, then waving it in a circle, he turns from right to left and
swallows the arrow, facing east. Both the swords and the arrows
are held horizontally and placed to the mouth while the head is erect,
then the head is moved gradually backward as the instrument is
pushed down the throat. Great care is observed in the feat, only
three men venturing to dance while swallowing the arrow. One man
gives three quite violent pressures to the shaft after the arrow is
down the throat. Each one in turn steps before the boxes, faces east,
and swallows his arrow. One man, failing to swallow his arrow,
waves it over the boxes around which they dance, and is then successful.
Groups of two face the cardinal points as they swallow the arrows.
The arrow dance is repeated three times in the plaza, the order retiring after each dance to the ceremonial chamber, where after the

a These arrows are not individual property, but belong to the order. Some are covered with a
glossy brownish substance, while others have it half over them, and others only one-third of the way·
The arrows vary in size and form, many being slightly oval at the end, some are pointed, and all
are rounded or oval where they are attached to the shaft, which is slightly curved at this end.

b The Great Fire fraternity has a po'nepoyannĕ similar to the one of the 'Hle'wekwe (see p. 417,
note a).

third dance the ʻHlĕm'mosona, standing near the altar, receives the arrows and the dancers are provided with their swords for the closing dances. When the swords are carried for the first time, the ʻHlĕm'-mosona, on reaching the south end of the boxes, steps before them and, facing west, prays; then he and two others swallow their swords, and all by groups follow in succession in swallowing the swords, as heretofore described. The dance is suspended for a time, and the ʻHlĕm'mosona, stepping before the boxes, prays and swallows his serpentiform sword.

Immediately following the dance just described, the order of the Arrow, joined by the women of the Sword order, begins another dance, and soon the ʻHlĕm'mosona and a warrior of the ʻHle'wekwe appear from the western way, and stepping within the circle of dancers stand before the boxes and pray. The dancers, as usual, pass four times around the boxes before swallowing the sword, the leader of the dance shouts and hoots, and the ʻHlĕm'mosona steps before the boxes and the sword swallowing begins.

The following table gives the order in which the members of the Arrow order and the women swallow their swords during the last dance in the plaza:

Two men and one woman, facing north.	Three men and one woman, facing north.
Two men, facing east.	Two men, facing south.
Two men and one woman, facing south.	Two men and one woman, facing east.
Two men and one woman, facing south.	Two men and one woman, facing south.
Two men, one woman, and a girl, facing south.	Two men, facing east.
	Two men, facing east.
Three men and one woman, facing west.	ʻHlĕm'mosona, facing east.

At the close of the sword swallowing the ʻHlĕm'mosona, retaining prayer plumes in his right hand, collects the swords, resting them over his left arm, the feather handles pointing to his right. Each dancer lays his sword on the arm of the ʻHlĕm'mosona, who, holding the swords with both hands, stands before the boxes and prays that Ä'chiyälä'topa and the Beast Gods will intercede with the rain-makers for cold rains and snows. All the members stand with folded arms during the prayer, which lasts three minutes. The ʻHlĕm'mosona now passes around the ellipse, that each one may receive his one or more swords.

All but two now clasp hands and form into a broken circle, and the musicians at the boxes of the ʻHle'wekwe play on the notched sticks and sing, joined by the drummer, who stands to the north of the plaza. The dancers shake their rattles and sing as they jump back and forth toward the center of the circle, holding their swords in the left hand, the feathered handles pointing inward. This movement, so like one of the children's games of civilization, creates much glee among the dancers and many of the spectators, though some of

'HLE'WEKWE, THE SWORD SWALLOWERS, IN PLAZA

A'WAN 'SI'TA (GREAT MOTHER) OF MA''KE 'HLAN'NAKWE (GREAT FIRE FRATERNITY)

the latter express indignation at the burlesquing of the sacred circle dance. After a time the clasped hands are extended outward while they dance. When the Arrow order leaves the plaza the musicians change their song to melodious strains, and the circle dance is performed previous to the appearance of the 'Hle'wekwe. This fraternity, the Great Fire, and the circle dancers alternate in dancing in the plaza throughout the day. With each repetition of the latter the numbers are increased. When the Great Fire fraternity return to the ceremonial chamber for the last time the swords are handed over to the 'Hlĕm'mosona, who places them for the time being by the altar. The fraternity father gives the novice four prayer plumes, four ears of corn, and enough calico for a shirt. The head and hands of the novice are bathed by the wife of his fraternity father at the wife's house, and he enjoys a meal with him and others of the family, after which the wife of the fraternity father accompanies the novice to his house, carrying a bowl of food and the bowl his head was washed in as gifts from his fraternity father.

PO''SIKISHI—DIVISION OF THE SPRUCE TREE

At the present time this order has but two female members, and the trees handled by them are smaller than the others. While the celebration of the tree swallowing occurs only at initiation in the 'Hle'wekwe fraternity, it is not dependent upon this rite with the Great Fire fraternity. This festival is synchronous with the two fraternities.

The day the order convenes the member and novices each make three prayer plumes to Na'ke'e. The officers make, in addition to these, one to each of the Beast Gods of the six regions. Each man reserves two of his prayer plumes and gives one to the deputy director, who gathers all into a kĭa'ĕtchĭnĕ (a group of prayer plumes wrapped together at the base), which he places in a basket. The other prayer plumes are also placed in baskets, each man tying together the two he retains. The eight a'mosi (directors of the different orders) sit in the middle of the room around the baskets of plumes, while the others of the order, including the women, sit together and sing to Na'ke'e to the accompaniment of the wooden drum, no rattles being used. They begin thus: "We are to swallow the tree; we ask that our throats may not be made ill." The baskets of plumes are now placed on the ledge in the west end of the room, and they adjourn to their homes for the remainder of the night. The following morning about 9 o'clock they return to the chamber and sing six songs, one to the Beast God of each of the six regions, to intercede with the rain-makers for cold rains and snows. After these songs the deputy 'Hlĕm'mosona followed by a warrior whirling the rhombus, leaves with the kĭa'ĕtchinĕ he made the previous day, and as he passes out of the room the female members stand in line and sprinkle meal on the group of plumes. The two are led for a short distance north of the village by a man carrying a meal basket and sprinkling meal. He returns, and the others continue on their journey to collect two small trees, one pine and the other piñon, which are brought and deposited in the manner described in the January ceremonial of the Sword order, except that the la'showannĕ for each tree is an undertail banded turkey feather instead of the fluffy eagle plumes. A flint arrow attached to a shaft is placed between the trees when they are planted on the roof by the hatchway, to remain through the ceremonial. The directors hold a ceremony over the trees on the roof similar to the one described in January, and the trees are sprinkled with meal each morning by the members of the order. After the ceremony over the trees, there is no more singing during the night unless some one should cough. During the ceremonies in the fraternity chamber the feet must be kept close together, whether the person be sitting or lying down, and the arms must not be extended outward or upward except when using the sword or sprinkling the meal. Should this rule not be observed the corn would be stunted in its growth.

The flutist and a warrior to the fraternity sit on their sheepskins in the middle of the floor for awhile, the latter speaking in whispers to his rhombus, the other to his flute.[a]

After the early meal on the third morning in the ceremonial chamber the ᵗHlĕm'mosona selects a man as director and five others and sends them for pine trees, which are collected south of the village. Each tree is marked, before it is hewn, with three dots to denote the eyes and the mouth. All take their turn in cutting the trees, which are brought on the backs of the men, held in place by ropes; they arrive about sunset. The trees are slid down the ladder through the hatchway into the ceremonial room, where they are received by six men. As the trees descend the ladder, animal-like yells are given. All the trees remain in the middle of the room while the choir sings and the director puffs smoke from a reed cigarette through the boughs. The trees are afterward suspended by ropes from the ceiling at the east end of the room, the eyes and mouth sides upward. A feast is now served; but previous to eating, a quantity of the food is taken from all the bowls and placed before the altar by a warrior, and it is afterward divided by him into five heaps before the altar. Six

---

[a] The use of the rhombus and flute at this time is to bring snows and rains quickly. These instruments are placed by the heads of the flutist and the warrior when they lie down, and should one cough, the flutist plays and the warrior whirls his rhombus, and every one must immediately rise and stand until the music ceases, when all present draw a breath and the director and all sprinkle the altar with meal and ascend the ladder and sprinkle meal on the trees; then there is no more sleep during the night. Should a member be caught nodding, he is awakened by another member with lighted husks or sticks, and they must sing and dance until sunrise, when the altar and afterward the trees are again sprinkled with meal.

officers take seats behind the altar, and the a'kwamosi sits north
and the warrior south of it.   The 'Hlĕm'mosona now says: "I hope all
will be happy, no one will be sad or ill."   Then addressing the flutist
and warrior: "You remain here and make rains and snows for me."
Five men appointed to carry out the five heaps of food, offer it in
the river to the deceased members of the fraternity.   The warrior
whirls the rhombus and the flutist plays on his flute until the return
of the men, when all sprinkle the altar with meal.

The 'Hlĕm'mosona now gives young buds of spruce and piñon, which
are in separate husks, to the a'kwamosi, who gathers them into one
husk and proceeds to prepare the medicine water to protect the throat
from being injured by the sword.   He first deposits in the water
six pinches of the buds and then six stone fetishes, consecrating the
water with the ceremonies heretofore described.   After the consecration of the medicine water the order dances for a short time, and then
all retire for the night; but if anyone coughs, there is a repetition
of the flute playing and whirling of the rhombus and dancing the
remainder of the night.

The swords are made on the fourth morning.   The novice, who is
instructed by his fraternity father, makes his own sword.   When a
woman is initiated her sword is made by her fraternity father.   The
swords are fashioned like those of the Sword order, at the butt of the
tree, the trunk being slender (there are no serpentiform swords fashioned by the order of the Kĭä'lä'selo).   The swords are afterward
rubbed with cougar grease and red hematite.   This same hematite is
used by the Indians on their faces to protect them from sunburn, and
to color the plumes worn by the order of Mystery medicine and objects
sacred to the Bow priesthood.

The 'Hlĕm'mosona brings out six stone knives, each one a color of
one of the six regions, which are used to polish the swords.   When
the sword is completed the maker attaches a la'showannĕ of a turkey
feather to the top of the tree from which his sword is fashioned, and
the tree is deposited in the east end of the room, with the sword pointing
east.

If there is to be no initiation the dry painting described in the January ceremonial is omitted.   The 'Hlĕm'mosona, who sits at the south
end of the line of officers, now gathered near the east end of the chamber, rises and leads them to the altar, which they all sprinkle with
meal.   The altar is afterward sprinkled by the members at large, who,
after sprinkling the meal, pass by the south side around the altar and
return to their positions at the east end of the room.

The 'Hlĕm'mosona, with the sword end of his tree resting over his
left arm and the tree extending on the floor, now approaches the novice,

who has taken his position near the center of the room, facing east,[a] and gives him a sprig, which he holds in his left hand, of the same medicine that was distributed in the initiation into the Sword order. After giving the medicine, the ʻHlĕm′mosona turns and faces east, and running the top of the tree through the hatchway in the roof, swallows the sword at the end of the tree, while the order sings to the accompaniment of the drum. After withdrawing the sword he passes it before the lips and each shoulder of the novice, and places his tree across ropes near the ceiling at the east end of the room, and takes his place behind the altar. The deputy ʻHlĕm′mosona repeats the ceremony with his tree, and after placing it by the other near the ceiling, takes his seat by the ʻHlĕm′mosona. The other six officers of the fraternity repeat the ceremony with their trees each one when through taking his place behind the altar; and then each member of the order repeats the same ceremony, the order at large gathering near the drummer. The fraternity father of the novice now goes through the performance also and then runs the novice's tree through the hatchway and hands it to him, and the latter attempts to run the sword down his throat. When the novice fails, the fraternity father takes the tree and runs the sword four times before the lips of the former, who draws a breath each time. The fraternity father now returns the tree to the novice, who again fails to swallow the sword. Two other efforts are unsuccessful, and the fraternity father repeats the passing of the sword before the lips of the novice, and depositing it with the others, he returns to his place by the drummer. The afternoon ceremony closes with the singing of one song, after which a feast is enjoyed in the ceremonial chamber.

A few hours later preparations begin for the night ceremonial, which is a repetition of that described, the personal decorations being much the same as when they appear in the ceremony of the Sword division. After one dance in the ceremonial chamber, where each member of the order swallows the sword portion of the tree, they then take their swords with feathered handles instead of the trees and visit the house where the Mu′waiye of the ʻHle′wekwe fraternity[b] are rehearsing and dance and swallow the sword; returning to their chamber, young buds of spruce and piñon are administered by the deputy to the fraternity at large, and all retire for the night but the eight officers who visit Si′aa′ te′wita to deposit prayer plumes to Na′keʹe. The flutist plays, the warrior whirls the rhombus, and four keep watch to see that no intruder appears while the other two deposit prayer plumes. After the return of the officers from the plume planting, the fraternity are privileged to sleep in any part of the ceremonial chamber, and no amount of coughing necessitates their rising to dance.

---

[a] If there is more than one novice, the ʻHlĕm′mosona begins with the one at the north end.
[b] See p. 458.

The morning ceremony begins about 7 o'clock, when the 'Hlĕm'-mosona, holding six couples of eagle-wing plumes, representative of the six regions, takes his seat on a stool near the center of the room and not far from the fireplace. The a'kwamosi sits on his wadded blanket to the left, and the deputy sits on the right of the 'Hlĕm'mosona. When the deputy takes his seat he deposits a medicine bowl before the a'kwamosi, and immediately a female member of the fraternity places a vase of water and a gourd near him. The a'kwamosi combines, as before, young buds of spruce and piñon in one husk. The flutist sits facing the 'Hlĕm'mosona and the warrior stands before the a'kwamosi. The members of the order at large are grouped about the drummer on the southwest side of the chamber. The deputy first dips six gourd-fuls of water from the vase and empties them into the medicine bowl, each time motioning to the six regions; the a'kwamosi then takes a pinch of the spruce and piñon buds from the husk he holds in his left hand and deposits them in the left palm of the deputy, who takes them with his right hand and, motioning to the six regions, drops them into the medicine bowl. This is repeated six times, each time the a'kwamosi putting the pinch of buds into the deputy's left hand. Six stone fetishes are afterward dropped separately into the bowl, and the deputy takes his two eagle plumes in his right hand and draws them in the water from each of the four regions to the center, and moves them from the zenith to the center of the bowl and stirs the water for the nadir. The flute is played, the rhombus whirled, and the choir sings to the accompaniment of rattle and drum during the consecration of the water. When this is done the 'Hlĕm'mosona hands the deputy the six pairs of eagle plumes separately, which he lays over the bowl, the tips toward the altar. Then the 'Hlĕm'mosona rises and, carrying a meal basket, advances to the altar, preceded by the flutist playing and the warrior whirling the rhombus, and followed by the deputy, with the a'kwamosi and another officer on each side. The other members of the order, the drummer excepted, follow the officers. After taking a few steps all halt while one song is sung. Again they advance, with the beginning of a new song, and stand until it is finished. Again advancing, they halt while a third song is sung; then they proceed to the altar, and the fourth song is sung. The flutist does not halt after reaching the altar, but proceeds at once to his place behind it and continues playing on the flute. The warrior stands in front and south of the altar and whirls the rhombus. The song is enlivened with animal-like calls upon the Beast Gods to intercede with the Council of the Gods for rain. When the singing ceases, the deputy deposits the medicine bowl near the altar, and all sprinkle the altar with meal and then depart, carrying their bedding to their homes. But they soon return to the ceremonial chamber, where the men have their heads washed by the female members of the fraternity, each of whom afterward washes her own head.   After the morning meal in the ceremonial chamber, preparations are begun for the outdoor festival.

While black paint is being applied to the lower portion of the face they sing to Na'ke'e, accompanied by the drum and rattle: "Your people are now preparing for the dance; they are happy; they wish the cold rains and snows to come."   When all is ready they ascend the ladder, each with his tree, led by a woman[a] carrying her mi'li and meal basket, from which she sprinkles meal as she advances.

The ceremonies in the plaza are identical with those described in the Sword order.[b]   There are three dances with the trees in the plaza. At the close of each dance the party returns to the ceremonial chamber, the leader places her meal basket near the two trees by the hatchway, and all sprinkle the trees with meal before descending into the chamber.   Each one pulls his tree after him and lays it in the middle of the floor, with the knife pointing toward the east, the "eyes" of each tree looking upward.   This is the convenient way for placing the tree so as to carry it out.   After resting a while the dancers sprinkle meal over the altar and return to the plaza to dance and swallow the tree sword.   After the third dance the trees are returned to their former elevated position near the ceiling, and the swords with feathered handles are used instead of the trees in the closing dance.   On their return the last time to the ceremonial chamber the members of the order take meal from the basket before the altar in their left hands and stand around the room close to the wall, the drummer standing west of the fireplace.   The 'Hlĕm'mosona, beginning with the officer at the south end of the line, the officers being assembled in the east end of the room, administers the medicine water.   He passes around, first by the north wall, giving each one a draft, while all sing to the accompaniment of the rattle and drum.   Again beginning with the officer at the south end of the line, he takes a shellful of water into his mouth, refilling the mouth when necessary, and each one of the order throws his head back while the 'Hlĕm'mosona sprays the throat with the medicine water from his mouth, that the larynx may not suffer from the sword swallowing. He then sets the bowl before the altar and takes a corn husk filled with diminutive and slightly sweet black seeds and places one in each person's mouth; then he returns the husk to the altar.   Ascending the ladder, he brings in from the hatchway the two small trees and arrow, and standing in the middle of the chamber and facing east he moves the trees and arrow up and down in time with the song, and passes to each one, beginning with the officers, who sprinkle the trees with the

---

[a] It is the custom for a woman of an order to ask the director for this position, for should he select one, the others might feel aggrieved.

[b] The danger incurred in swallowing the sword carved from the trees renders the sight anything but pleasing to the stranger, but the Indian spectators become so enthusiastic at this ceremony that they are without thought of accident to the dear ones, for "only those of wicked heart can be injured."

meal held in the left hand, for his physical purification. The trees are passed four times to be sprinkled in the same manner, and again four times, when each person, catching the la'showannĕ of each tree in his left hand, draws a breath as quickly as possible; but he must not let go the la'showawe until his neighbor has caught them with his left hand. The 'Hlĕm'mosona returns to the middle of the floor, and after prayers he again passes the trees four times before the order, when each one catches the la'showawe and passes the feathers through his mouth, in order that any of the medicine left in the mouth from the swords may adhere to the plumes.[a] The 'Hlĕm'mosona again returns to the middle of the floor for a moment and again passes the trees rapidly before all, each one having time only to pick off a bud or two. Every effort is made to get the buds of the spruce or piñon, according to the wish of the individual, for a male or female child. Returning to the middle of the floor, the 'Hlĕm'mosona holds the trees until the song ceases. Still holding the trees, he addresses his people, saying: "We will have no more of this until another year [four years hence.] I hope my people will be happy and keep well. I hope our dance and songs will bring cold rains and snows, and that all may have bountiful crops. Now, throw up your arms." And all obey at once.

The two small trees are now placed with the larger ones, and the 'Hlĕm'mosona unwraps the arrow point from the shaft, while each member of the Sword order takes his sword with the feathered handle in the left hand and, expectorating four times upon it, waves it around the head four times, from left to right, for physical purification. The sword is then separated from the handle and the 'Hlĕm'mosona places the swords in the skin, which is wrapped carefully over the contents and laid in the box.

The following morning the novice's head is washed by the wife or daughter of the fraternity father, who gives four prayer plumes, four ears of corn, and some yards of calico to the novice. The trees, including the two small ones, are carried, by a different set of men from those who gathered them, some 4 miles north of the village to the top of a mesa and dropped into a deep fissure, the sword ends pointing to the east.

U'HUHUKWE (EAGLE DOWN FRATERNITY)

This fraternity takes its name from u'kĭa, down; reference to the down of eagles and other birds and of native cotton. The U'huhukwe embraces four orders: O'naya'nakĭa (Mystery medicine), Ma'᾽ke (Fire), Hä'lo (Ant), and It'sĕpcho (Jugglery). The last-named order has no female members. The women, however, are most active during the

---

[a] "If all of the medicine should not be removed from the mouth, it would pass down and make the throat sick."

exhibitions with fire and are quite as enthusiastic as the men in the chase with the flaming brand. The ceremonies of the Ant order are similar to those practiced by the Ant fraternity.

CEREMONIAL OF INITIATION INTO O'NAYA'NAKĬA

Members of the fraternity prepare te'likinawe (prayer plumes) in the ceremonial chamber the first morning, and before sunset the tablet altar (see plate LVIII), which is one of the most attractive to be found in Zuñi, is erected and the fetishes placed about it.

The U'huhukwe have some good animal fetishes of stone, one a well-cut image of the bison, the horns being well defined, which is the only representation of this animal observed by the writer among the Zuñis, who claim to have but little knowledge of the bison, as they say it belongs to the east. It is, certainly, an unimportant factor in Zuñi at the present time. The bear fetish is 10 inches long; the other animal forms are somewhat smaller. The human figure (female) is about 18 inches high. Figures in human form are very rare in Zuñi, while they are common in Sia.

The ceremonials are so like those of the other orders of O'naya'nakĭa (Mystery medicine) that the writer will describe only the ceremonies of the fourth night, when the novices appear for the first time.

The members are busy by 8 p. m., preparing for the ceremonies. The feet and legs to the knees and the hands and arms nearly to the elbows, of both men and women, are painted white. The rest of the bodies of the men are striped or starred in white. A line of micaceous hematite runs across the face under the eyes, and a circular spot of the same is on the chin and each cheek. A fluffy eagle plume, colored red with dry pigment, is tied to the forelock, and a wreath of yucca ribbon adorns the head. A bow guard is worn on the left wrist. The women wear the ordinary woven dress, and elaborate necklaces adorn the necks of both the men and the women. When the toilets are complete the women take their seats on the north ledge, near the east end of the room, and the men group on the south side near the west end. When the men indicate their intention of beginning the song, the women gather on the south ledge and to the east of the men, but they do not use the rattle. Each fraternity father leads his one or more fraternity children to the ceremonial chamber, each fraternity child bearing the large buckskin which is the payment to the fraternity father for initiation into the order of O'naya'nakĭa. After the novices have assembled each one is decorated by his fraternity father as described on page 499. Yucca ribbons are knotted around the wrists and forehead of each novice, and a fluffy eagle plume is tied to the left side of the head, not to be removed until four days after the ceremonial, during which time no animal food or grease can be eaten.   When the decoration of the novices is completed they take their seats in line on the north ledge, near the west end, the wife of the fraternity father sitting on the left of the fraternity child or children and the elder sister of the fraternity father sitting on the right.   The a'kwamosi has his assigned seat on the north side of the altar and the deputy director sits on the south side.   The warrior, protector of the altar and fetish medicine, sits in front of the altar, just beyond a mound of food deposited to the gods.   The flutist sits back of the altar.

There are two rolls of corn husks containing native tobacco, each roll having a prayer plume on each side.   One roll is in a niche in the north wall near the altar, and one is in a niche in the south wall immediately opposite the other.   The ceremony begins with the handing of the rolled husks to the a'kwamosi, who opens them, and with the native tobacco and corn husks makes cigarettes.   The a'kwamosi, the deputy, and the flutist all retain their seats while each smokes one of the cigarettes, blowing the smoke over the altar and mi'wachi,[a] the a'kwamosi and deputy from the front and the flute player from the back.   The mound of food placed near the altar at the evening feast is now divided by the warrior into two heaps, with a space of 8 or 10 inches between.   A vase of water is brought by a woman and placed before the a'kwamosi, who raises and lowers the empty medicine bowl six times.   As soon as he touches the bowl he begins a prayer song in low, impressive tones, which continues until the completion of the medicine water.   Dipping a gourd of water from the water vase, he holds it over the medicine bowl while he repeats a prayer to the Cougar of the North to be present in spirit, and then empties it into the bowl.   The second gourdful is held while he repeats a prayer to the Bear of the West.   With the third gourdful he offers a prayer to the Badger of the South, with the fourth a prayer to the White Wolf of the East, and with the fifth he prays to Ä'chiyälä'topa (a being with wings and tail of knives) of the Zenith.   The sixth gourdful, as soon as it is dipped from the vase, is emptied into the bowl with prayers to the Shrew of the Nadir.   Six fetishes are now taken from a leather pouch, and each one is raised six times in the right hand, while the two eagle plumes taken from the medicine bowl are held in the left hand.   Each fetish is deposited at its appropriate point of the compass, those of the Zenith and Nadir being laid by the fetish of the East.   After all the fetishes are placed the a'kwamosi takes the one of the North and holds it over the bowl, and after raising and lowering it six times he drops it into the bowl.   The remaining five fetishes are passed separately through the same ceremony.   Six pinches of meal are afterward sprinkled into the bowl, each pinch being raised and lowered six times

---

[a] Mi'wachi is plural for mi'li (see p. 416).

before it is cast upon the water. The two eagle plumes which the a'kwamosi has in his left hand are now transferred to the right, and the quill ends are dipped six times into the water, the plumes being held in a perpendicular position. Each time the a'kwamosi stirs the water with the plumes, at the same time giving a most beast-like growl, he invokes the prey animals of the six regions to give their spirits to the bodies of his people that they may have the power to penetrate the flesh and see disease.

After the consecration of the water the a'kwamosi dips the feather ends of the plumes into it, and taking a plume in each hand sprinkles the altar, striking the underside of the plume held in the left hand with the one held in the right, keeping both plumes in a horizontal position. The sprinkling of the altar is repeated four times, and then the a'kwamosi throws meal six times over the altar. Though the music of the choir and the whirling of the rhombus are continuous throughout the consecration of the water, the impressive tones of the a'kwamosi and the sweet music of the flute are distinctly heard. Two members of the choir now collect the food in front of the altar and throw it into the river, to be borne to the Beast Gods, and the dance begins with both men and women, the warrior being a conspicuous dancer.

The room gradually becomes crowded with those suffering from some real or imaginary malady. While such persons are often relatives of the members of the fraternity, others who wish to be cured may be present. The dancing and healing of the sick being similar in all orders of Mystery medicine, the writer will mention only certain features in this ceremonial.

Those men who have not already removed their shirts and trousers bare their bodies as soon as the first dancers take the floor. At the beginning of the dance two members of the choir, their bodies painted white, join in the dance. Suddenly they spring before the altar, and bending their bodies low dip the eagle plumes[a] which they carry into the medicine water and sprinkle the altar, each striking the left plume on the underside with the right one. Again dipping the plumes into the medicine bowl, the water is sprinkled to the North, West, South, and East. Each time the feather is struck the dancer cries, "Uh......hu." After the sprinkling to the four regions has been repeated four times the two return to the choir and two others come to the floor. Dipping their plumes into the medicine bowl, they repeat the sprinkling to the four regions, calling upon the Beast Gods to come. No women dance while the water is being sprinkled, but immediately after the sprinkling three women, dressed in white cotton gowns and red sashes, and holding an eagle-wing plume in each hand,

---

[a] The eagle plumes carried by both men and women are referred to as klä'kläli a'siwe (eagle hands), and when once taken in the hands must not be laid down until the close of the ceremony.

take the floor, and thereupon a member of the choir rushes in the wildest manner to the center of the room, dancing with the women for a while, then performing the most curious and weird antics before the altar, while he invokes the Beast Gods. After a time he fairly pulls the a'kwamosi from his seat, barely giving him time to remove his cotton clothing, and leads him around in the most curious manner. The old a'kwamosi has not the grace and symmetry of the younger man, and he appears very awkward. The leader presently throws himself before the altar and, slipping his left hand into one of the bear's feet without removing the two eagle plumes it holds, dashes about wildly. He circulates among the choir, growling and drawing the bear's claws over the naked backs of the men, and frightening the dancing women by threatening to do the same with them. The women dance about forty-five minutes and leave the floor, but the man continues his violent movements for an hour. In the meantime a juggler appears before the altar. He moves his eagle plumes over the human image with queer incantations until it is supposed to catch the tips of a plume with each hand, when the juggler elevates it, apparently by having the image hold the tips of the plumes. The illusion is perfect. A woman now takes a pinch of ashes from the fireplace, and after sprinkling the altar she deposits some in the palm of the right hand of all present. When the ashes have been distributed, the assemblage groups before the altar, the men first and afterward the women. Each person passes the ashes from right to left three times around the head and throws them upon the altar. After all return to their seats two young men representing the Chapparral cock skip about gracefully for a moment or two and, throwing their bodies almost prostrate upon the floor, take ashes from the fireplace with their plumes and dance gracefully, one to the right and one to the left of the altar, throwing the ashes upon it by striking the left plume with the right, as heretofore described. Again they lift ashes from the fireplace and sprinkle all present with it. Returning to the fireplace for more ashes, they throw them to the six regions, beginning at the North. The sprinkling to the regions is repeated four times. Every time the ashes are thrown they cry, "Uh_____hu." The two return to the choir, and the a'kwamosi administers the medicine water, dipping it from the bowl with a shell, to all present, after which he repeats a long litany. At the end of each supplication the people join in the prayer. At the close of the litany the a'kwamosi is joined by all in a long prayer to the Beast Gods. The pe'kwĭn sits throughout the ceremonial with bowed head, except when the a'kwamosi lights a cigarette and, taking one whiff, passes it to his deputy to finish. The dance closes at daylight and the novices receive their gifts in the manner heretofore described.

After the ceremony with the novices, and as the first rays of sunlight

come through the eastern window, the men assemble before the altar
and pray. The women go outside of the house to offer their prayers
to the Sun Father, but return to sprinkle meal upon the altar and pray.
The Kĭa'kwemosi, rain priest of the North, who is a member of the
U'huhukwe, removes the animal fetishes from before the altar and,
blowing the meal from them, gathers them into his arms. The owners
of the mi'wachi collect them, carefully blowing off the meal, and in a
few moments the altar is bared of its adornments. A little later the
altar itself is taken apart and stored away until required for future use.

The February ceremonial, in which initiation into the Mystery medicine order occurred, was very much the same as the one described, with
the addition of playing with fire, and there was a greater display of
jugglery. The features not given in the December meeting are here
described.

There is an elaborate display of fire on the third and fourth days of
the meeting of the fraternity, the members appearing in the street
before the ceremonial house and on the house tops with blazing brands
of cedar fiber. Three He'hea and six Na'wisho (anthropic gods) appear
for the occasion, though only the He'hea go to the ceremonial house
of the U'huhukwe. The He'hea gods have their nude bodies covered
with white kaolin and lined by drawing the finger nail through the
paint. A yellow crescent is painted on the back of each (see plate
CXX). As soon as they enter the ceremonial chamber they are pelted
with fire from cedar brands, and they escape to the street, where they
create great amusement by their pantomimical conversations. Being
in the street does not save them, for they are followed by men and
women with flaming brands. who chase the gods up the ladder to the
roofs, where they get more pelting with fire by members of the fraternity, especially the women (see plate CXXI). The gods at times climb
a pole, perform gymnastics on the ladders and a pole suspended horizontally before the ceremonial house. The men and women of the
fraternity also pelt one another with fire, not even sparing the face.
A very pretty sight is a run of about a thousand yards, in a kind of
meander, by two of the men of the fraternity, both carrying flaming
masses of cedar fiber, the foremost one flying like the wind and the
other apparently no less fast, but he does not catch the foremost.
The men are nude except for the black woven breechcloth. The
women wear their ordinary dress and knitted leggings, and their feet
are bare. The women especially seem to enjoy the fun. Two tricks
worthy of mention are performed at night in the ceremonial chamber.
A yucca rope apparently passes through the body of another, the rope
being held by a man at each end. The illusion is perfect. Another
trick is the changing of a basket tray of balls of blue mush. The
writer, taking one, finds it to be as pliable as firm mush. The tray,
with the balls of mush, is afterward raised high and waved to the six

regions with prayers for snow, when it is again passed and the balls are found to be as hard as stones. A third time the basket is passed, after prayers have been offered, and the balls are in the same condition as when first examined. The U'huhukwe and Hä'lo'kwe (Ant) are considered the most expert jugglers in Zuñi.

On the closing evening an aged member with white hair appears with a flaming brand at the house of one of the women of the fraternity who is tardy, and entering without ceremony starts her out before his flaming brand. Though this woman is hourly expecting to become a mother, she is allowed no freedom of action; she must not omit her duty to the fraternity.

CEREMONIAL OVER A SICK MAN

In connection with this fraternity the writer witnessed a ceremonial over a sick man at his house. The patient was suffering from smallpox. Many theurgists had been called in, but none had effected a cure; accordingly the Kĭa'kwemosi, who is also a theurgist of the U'huhuhwe, was appealed to. He was surprised at the beginning of the ceremony by the presence of Mr Stevenson and the writer, who had taken the guard at the door unawares while he was sleeping at his post. One of the officiating theurgists even declared that the presence of the visitors would be fatal to the invalid, but Mr Stevenson and the writer nevertheless remained.

The room was dimly lighted by an old Zuñi lamp resting on the chimney place. The Kĭa'kwemosi sat upon a low stool in the center of the large room, facing east. He was clothed in a suit of pure white cotton and his black wavy locks were flowing. The head-kerchief so constantly worn had been removed. A bowl of medicine water, two eagle plumes, and a vessel of sacred meal were on the stone floor before him. He looked haggard and seemed to have aged since the afternoon. The patient, a young man, partially reclined upon a blanket spread upon the floor on the north side of the room. His body was supported by his mother. Two theurgists acted under the direction of the Kĭa'kwemosi, one standing in front of the sick man, holding an eagle-wing plume in each hand, the other holding two eagle-wing plumes in his right hand and a bowl of medicine water in his left, from which he filled his mouth and sprinkled the man's nude body, waving the plumes in the right hand over him. The mouth being emptied of the water, he joined the other theurgist in incantations over the sick. During the sprinkling of the medicine water and the passing of the eagle plumes over the body, which was done with a graceful waving gesture, the Kĭa'kwemosi, with the sacred meal basket in hand, rose and stood before the patient and placed pinches of sacred meal in spots over the body, calling upon the Beast Gods to give him power to call the disease to one of the meal spots, that it might be drawn from the patient. "If the prayer is not answered and the disease does not show itself, the heart of the patient is not good."

The Kĭa'kwemosi, in company with his associates, visited the patient four nights, one of the Beast Gods being appealed to each night to be present and send pure winds from the four quarters of the earth to heal the sick. The first night the Cougar of the North was appealed to to send the pĭsh'lankwĭn pi'naiye (north wind); the second night the Bear of the West was invoked to send sun'hakwĭn pi'naiye (west wind); the third night prayers were addressed to the Badger of the South to send ta'wiakĭa pi'naiye (south wind); the fourth night the Wolf of the East was besought to send te'wana pi'naiye (east wind).

Only the mother and the doorkeeper, besides those officiating, were present. The prayers of the Kĭa'kwemosi, which were repeated aloud, must not be heard by any other person, else he would not be granted the desired power. It must be borne in mind, however, that the Kĭa'kwemosi officiated not in his capacity as rain priest, but as a member of the order of Mystery medicine of an esoteric fraternity. His high priestly position gives him additional power, as the A'shiwanni (rain priests, of whom the Kĭa'kwemosi is the head) must be absolutely pure of heart.

'CHI'KĬÄLIKWE (RATTLESNAKE FRATERNITY)

The 'Chi'kĭälikwe fraternity is a division of the U'huhukwe and was created in this way: A member accidentally stepped on one of the bowls of medicine before the altar, breaking the bowl and spilling the medicine and also turning over a carving of the rattlesnake which stood before the tablet altar. Some of the fraternity were very angry with the man and violent words followed, until it was declared by the offender's friends that a division of the fraternity must occur. The division was called the Rattlesnake, for the reasons that the carved snake had fallen over and been bathed in the medicine-water spilled from the bowl, and that the fraternity quarreled like angry snakes.

The functions of the two fraternities are the same.

HÄ'LO'KWE (ANT FRATERNITY)

This fraternity has four orders—O'naya'nakĭa (Mystery medicine); Hä'lo (Ant), sometimes called Pe'pe (Broom), because broom straws are used in brushing from the body of the invalid the pebbles "shot" into it by the ants after they have been brought to the surface by the theurgists; It'sĕpcho (Jugglery), and Ä'chiya (Stone knife). The fraternity is sometimes referred to as the Ä'chiya ti'kĭannĕ.[a]

The male membership of this fraternity is large, but in 1896 there were only four female members. Only men belong to the Ä'chiya order.

_____

[a] Ti'kĭannĕ is another name for ti'kili (fraternity).

SWORD SWALLOWERS OF MA'KE 'HLAN'NAKWE (GREAT FIRE FRATERNITY)

DANCE OF ARROW ORDER OF MA''KE 'HLAN'NAKWE (GREAT FIRE FRATERNITY)

Initiation into the Hä'lo'kwe order sometimes occurs on the first night of the meeting of the fraternity for initiation into Mystery medicine, which initiation takes place on the last night. The fraternity father, having prepared te'likinawe (prayer plumes) to the ants of the six regions, goes at sunset to the home of the novice, who accompanies him over the southern road to an ant-hill. On reaching the spot they stand facing east while the fraternity father offers a prayer. After the prayer the fraternity father gives the novice a portion of the prayer plumes which he carries, depositing the others separately on the ant-hill, then the novice plants his there one by one. The prayers offered during the planting of the plumes are for rains to fructify the earth and that the ant gods will give them power to cure disease.

The order of Hä'lo'kwe are the agents of the ant gods, and as such heal disease caused by these gods, who "shoot" the pebbles from the ant-hills into those who micturate or step upon them. The pebbles produce all sorts of cutaneous troubles and sore throat, and relief is obtained by the theurgists' bringing the pebbles to the surface, through their prayers and incantations, and brushing them from the body with bunches of broom straws.

When the patient is treated in the ceremonial chamber he sits upon a low stool in the center of a mi'ha (white, embroidered blanket) laid on the floor. A line of meal is sprinkled from the edge of the blanket to meet the line of meal which extends a short distance before the tablet altar (see plate CXXII); the line is then continued over the blanket and along the floor to the ladder; and then, beginning in the center of the blanket, a line is extended to the north ledge; and, again, a line of meal is carried from the center of the blanket to the south ledge, that the ants, their spirits, may come over the meal road and be present. The patient is present four nights, and the process of healing is most curious and interesting. A number of the theurgists surround the patient. Each has his two eagle-wing plumes and a bunch of broom straws in his left hand and a gourd rattle in his right, and with the most weird incantations they invoke the ant gods to be present and give them power to "see the disease." The Yellow Ant of the North is the one specially appealed to the first night; the second night the Blue Ant of the West has the special prayers; on the third night the Red Ant of the South is the special object of prayer, and the White Ant of the East is appealed to the fourth night. Occasionally there is a wild animal-like cry when one of the Beast Gods is invoked to influence the ant gods to give the theurgist power to see disease. After a time pebbles are brushed off in showers from the patient's nude body. The Zuñis and the Sia observe the same method in curing disease caused by angry ants.

On the fourth morning the novice goes with his fraternity father to a deserted ant-hill, and stepping firmly on the ground he extends his right foot over the hill. Standing on his toes he takes the tips of the fraternity father's eagle-wing plumes in each hand and then stoops over the ant-hill while the fraternity father repeats a prayer. The novice does not relinquish the plumes until after he rises.

The prayer plumes made for novices of the Ä'chiya order are in length from the inner side of the bend of the elbow to the tip of the middle finger, the sticks are painted yellow, and eagle plumes and feathers of the birds of the six regions are attached. These offerings are to Ä'chiyälä'topa (the being of the Zenith with wings and tail of knives), who gave the knife to the Hä'lo'kwe.

Shu'maakwe

The Shu'maakwe is named from shu'minnĕ, a spiral shell, because this fraternity treats the disease known as ku'sukĭayakĭa, which is a terrible twisting of the body, convulsions. If the pain strikes the back of the neck, the head twists and the afflicted one falls. The remedy is to sprinkle urine on a heated stone over which crushed medicine is sprinkled. The invalid, if he is an adult, is carried in a blanket by four men to the fraternity chamber, where the principal men of the fraternity are assembled; the altar is erected and a meal painting is made before it. The director of the fraternity makes a square of four central stalks of yucca, symbolic of the four winds, by crossing them at the corners and tying them; he then lays the square upon the painting. When the patient arrives, he is rubbed with the medicine from the hot stone, and then the director, while four songs are sung, manipulates the square over the head of the invalid, down the back, arms, breast, legs, and over the feet. He then rolls the square between his flattened hands, and after a short time the yucca drops from his hands in the four original pieces. Should the director fail to undo the four knots during the rubbing of the yucca, the patient would surely die.

The Shu'maakwe has for its patron gods the Shumai'koli of the six regions and their attendant Sai'apa warriors. These gods are supposed to live in Chi'pia, which is in the east and near Shi'papolima, the home of Po'shaiyänki (Zuñi culture hero). The fraternity comprises two orders—Shumai'koli and Fire. It is stated in the chapter on "Origin and functions of esoteric fraternities" that the Shu'maakwe was organized by the Shumai'koli when they visited Häl'ona on the special invitation of the pe'kwĭn (sun priest). The origin of the Shu'maakwe fraternity is explained in the following legend:

When the Shumai'koli came to this world through Ji'mi'kĭanapkĭatea in the northwest, the Sun Father commanded them to go to his house in the east. The distance was great, and all the Shumai'koli and all who accompanied them—men, women, and children—became foot-sore from long travel. The Sun Father gave them medicine—one kind to drink, the other to use externally—which cured the feet at once. After a time the Shumai'koli and their people moved from the Sun Father's house, going by his command to live at Chi'pia, not far distant. After the Shumai'koli visited Häl'ona when they initiated a man of the Chaparral cock clan into the secrets of the medicine, and the songs which the Sun Father gave to them,[a] they went to the west and descended into a body of water. The waters flowed neither to the north, the west, the south, nor the east. Since that time the Shumai'koli have lived in these two places, the waters and Chi'pia, and at each place they have their representatives of the six regions.

The Shumai'koli masks are to be found in the Hopi and Sia villages, and no doubt the other Rio Grande Indians personate these gods. A man must remain four days in his home previous to wearing a Shumai'-koli mask. "Should he not do this the mask would stick to his face and break the skin, and he would become crazy and die in four days. Men have been known to become crazy, and consequently many of the fraternity fear to wear the mask." The question arises, To which tribe may be accredited the origin of these gods? The Zuñis not only have their own masks of Shumai'koli, but now possess those of the Sia Indians, through the friendship existing between the mo'sona (director) of the Shu'maakwe of Zuñi and the Sia people. The people of this pueblo number, all told, little over 100, and have had no one privileged to personate the Shumai'koli for some years. During a visit of the director of the Shu'maakwe to Sia it was decided that the Shumai'koli masks of the Sia should be given to the Shu'maakwe fraternity of the Zuñis. The director of the fraternity, wishing to make some return for the high trust reposed in him, said to the Sia: "You no longer have with you those privileged to personate the Ko'yemshi;[b] all those who understood the preparation of prayer plumes for the Ko'yemshi have died. Bring one of your young men to Zuñi and we will initiate him into the Ko'tikili (mythologic fraternity) and teach him the prayers to be made to the Ko'yemshi, and he can in turn teach others, and you will again be able to personate these gods."[c] Accordingly, a delegation of Sia priests, who were also theurgists, came to Zuñi with a young man in the winter of 1891. The youth was initiated into the fraternity of Ko'tikili at the annual ceremonial of voluntary initiation, when several Zuñi boys were received, the director of the Shu'maakwe acting as his fraternity father.[d] Having prepared prayer plumes for the novice, the fraternity father told him how and when these offerings were to be made to the A'wan Kok'ko (Council of the Gods). The youth, after being properly initiated, was able, on his return to Sia, to impersonate the Ko'yemshi. This interchange of rites and masks exists to a considerable extent among the Pueblo tribes.

---

[a] See p. 411.

[b] See p. 33. The Ko'yemshi are to be found among the Hopi and Rio Grande Indians.

[c] Gods may be personated only by those who understand the prayers to be addressed to them and have the knowledge of making the prayer plumes for the special gods to be personated.

[d] See "Voluntary initiation into the Ko'tikili."

The director of the Shu'maakwe fraternity must be of Po'yi'kwe (Chaparral cock) clan and his pe'kwĭn must be a child of that clan.[a] Other officers must be of 'Ko''loktakwe (Sand-hill crane), Pi'chikwe (Dogwood) and Tä'kĭakwe (Frog) clans, or children of these clans. The officers have the septum of the nose pierced, this ceremony occurring in the early morning, when the members at large hasten to lap the blood as it flows from the wound. The piercing is done with a splinter of archaic wood, a bundle of it being in the keeping of the director of the fraternity. The aperture is plugged with a bit of wood so perfectly fitted that it is scarcely perceptible. The plug is removed for ceremonials, and the quill end of an eagle plume is thrust through the opening.[b] Sometimes two plumes are worn on opposite sides. A man having the septum pierced must observe continence for one year. At the expiration of this time he captures a wood rat (neotoma), and roasting it eats it, that his blood may not be made impure by terminating his period of continence.[c]

The director of the Shu'maakwe is also a shi'wanni (rain priest), his clan being Po'yi'kwe, and he therefore has an ĕt'tonĕ. His deputy and the warrior of his fraternity are present at the ceremonies over his ĕt'tonĕ.

The Shu'maakwe possess in addition to their remedies for convulsions infallible medicine for rheumatic affections and cramps of the limbs. This medicine is something more than fetishistic, and can be classed as bona fide materia medica. The medicines of this fraternity comprise a variety of plants, several of which, after being ground, are compounded into small cakes and sun dried, and then used as medicine internally and externally. The writer can testify to its efficacy in external use for rheumatism, since it relieved her and also a member of her party after other medicines failed. These cakes have a pungent odor. A number were secured and deposited in the National Museum.

The Shu'maakwe, like other fraternities, invite women who are not members to participate in the dance and in the grinding of medicines. The director visits the houses of such women as he desires and invites them to be present, giving each a small quantity of meal wrapped in a corn husk.

CEREMONIAL OF INITIATION INTO THE SHU'MAAKWE

First day. The early part of the day is consumed in repainting and erecting the tablet altar, working upon masks, and preparing prayer plumes, in some instances the women painting their own plume sticks. At 3 p. m. the a'kwamosi (maker of medicine water) draws a cloud

---

[a] See List of clans.

[b] The wearing of the plumes through the septum is not confined to Shu'maakwe ceremonials. One is priviliged to wear the plume in the ceremonies of any other fraternity in which he holds membership, and it is usually displayed.

[c] It was observed that in a Hopi fraternity ceremonial bits of a charred mole were taken into the mouths of the members during the night. The mole, it is understood, was used in ceremonials by the early Japanese.

symbol with meal at the base of the altar, and all the members who are in Zuñi, minus one woman, gather in the ceremonial chamber. Such members as possess a mi'li of the fraternity on entering the chamber hand them to an officer, who deposits them for the time being in a basket tray. These fetishes, each having a zigzag stick symbolic of lightning standing in the heart of the plumes, are afterward placed in line before the altar. The younger brother Bow priest, who is a warrior to the fraternity, leaves the chamber after the completion of the meal painting, but soon returns, when he is greeted and returns greetings as though he has not before been present. An aged woman of the fraternity places two boxes and two home-manufactured stools in line north and south before the altar. The warrior takes his seat south of the altar, facing east, and is soon joined by three other officers. As soon as the warrior is seated all present remove their moccasins. One woman having suffered an injury to her left foot is allowed to retain the moccasin. The a'kwamosi consecrates the medicine, as previously described, dropping in concretion fetishes sacred to the field instead of those in animal form, and while the choir sings to the accompaniment of rattle and pottery drum the a'kwamosi sprinkles the altar. The director sits on the north ledge and near the altar, and a female member who sits beside him deposits a basket of prayer plumes in the northwest corner of the room—the only office she is observed to perform, though she retains the seat throughout the ceremonial. The four novices, who are all males, sit on the ledge not far from the director. The male members are gathered on the south ledge, near the west end of the room, and the female members sit on the same ledge, but more to the east. There are present twenty-five men, three young boys, five girls from 6 to 11 years of age, and six women. Three of the women are old, and one, known as the A'wan ᵗsi'ta (Great Mother) is too aged to participate, but exhibits unlimited interest in all her dim eyes are able to see; the next oldest woman acts in her place. In a short time the novices take their seats on the boxes and stools and the first four officers sit on their wadded blankets before them. Each officer places a corn-husk package of meal in the right hand of the novice opposite him, and clasping the hand with both of his repeats a long prayer. At its close he holds the hand containing the husk to the novice's mouth, that he may draw a breath from the meal, the novice praying at the same time. This ceremony continues but a few moments, when the four officers return to their former positions. Then the a'kwamosi sits before them and repeats a litany, to which all respond; at its close the sacred breath is drawn. The four novices now pass to everyone present, giving to each a pinch of meal from the husk referred to. The meal received is wrapped in a bit of corn husk and tied, and each member starts for

Ku'shiloa (red earth), a short distance east of the village, to plant prayer plumes and sprinkle meal.

When the writer returns to the ceremonial chamber at half past 7 in the evening she finds a number of members already gathered about the south ledge chatting by the light of a low fire. As the women come in they take seats on the north ledge. After about twenty men have arrived, the deputy a'kwamosi and another officer leave the chamber with corn husks containing offerings, which they take from behind the altar, and a warrior at once removes the food which was deposited near the altar before the evening repast and carries it out to offer it in the river to the gods. The two return in an hour with the empty husks, which they deposit in their former place by the altar. A youth now removes a bunch of gourd rattles from the wall and distributes them to the members of the choir. The a'kwamosi and a warrior sit on the north ledge, near the altar, and the novices also sit on this ledge. The deputy a'kwamosi and a second warrior sit on the south ledge apart from the choir. Three women join the choir, which now begins the song to the accompaniment of the rattle and pottery drum. At the sound of the music a young man clad only in a breechcloth, with his hair done up in the usual way and carrying a rattle in his right hand, who is to personate one of the Sai'apa gods, leaves his seat at the east end of the room and goes to the center of the floor. One foot, which has been severely injured, is bandaged, and he walks with a limp, which, however, he soon forgets in his interest in the dance. Poised on one foot, he stamps several times with the other; then drawing up the foot as high as possible, with a sudden spring he spins around like a top, usually revolving three times, but on several occasions he turns five times when balancing on the left foot. Though he endeavors to do the same when poised on his right foot, he fails to turn more than three times. His figure is most symmetrical and his motions graceful. Now and then he stands before the altar and inhales the sacred breath of the fetishes. For fifty-eight minutes he dances without the slightest evidence of fatigue. At the close of this dance the women gather before the altar to sprinkle meal and inhale the sacred breath, and then return to their seats. The men also sprinkle the altar and pray, and then the fraternity is adjourned for the remainder of the night.

On the second day some of the masks and other paraphernalia are completed. Many objects are then added to the altar. Three masks are deposited before it, the others are placed on the ledge behind the altar and covered with a mi'ha (white embroidered blanket).

Second night. By 8 o'clock most of the company have assembled. The director, his deputy, and a warrior sit on the north ledge near the altar. Other officers sit on the south side of the altar. The four novices sit on the north ledge near the three officers. Five women and five girls sit on the north ledge, nearer the eastern side of the room, the Great Mother of the fraternity sitting to the east end of the line. The choir, which is grouped in its usual place, begins the song in low tones. After the first stanza two men leave the choir and carry away to offer to the gods the food which was placed before the altar when the evening meal was served.

A woman of the fraternity, who has been absent from the village, now appears for the first time. She takes her seat with the others of her sex and at once removes the moccasins, and each of the four novices gives her a pinch of meal from his husk, which she receives in the palm of her left hand. She wraps it in a bit of husk, forming a rectangular package, as the others did on the first afternoon of the ceremonial. Her fraternity father hands her a prayer plume, and then she leaves the chamber, accompanied by the fraternity father, and proceeds to Ku'shilowa, where she plants her plumes and sprinkles the meal. Though the night is cold and the wind piercing, she is not deterred from complying with the demands of her cult. After the first song the choir enjoys a social smoke and chat for fifteen minutes. When the second song begins two young men start the dance by pulling several of the girls to the floor, and these are joined by three of the choir. Other women (one who is soon to become a mother has her belt so arranged by the acting Great Mother as to hide the form as much as possible) are induced to join the ring, until all the women excepting the Great Mother are dancing. Others from the choir step in until a circle of twenty is formed. They dance around from left to right, all but two holding hands. There is always a break in the circle, symbolic of the road or passageway of life. Two young men who are to personate Sai'apa gods are in the center of the circle. They take their positions, wearing their cotton trousers and shirts, but almost immediately each of the two removes his clothing and fastens around his waist a fringe of buckskin 6 inches deep and tipped with bits of conical tin. The two men dance back and forth in the circle, which is constantly moving, with a monotonous side step. This dance continues thirty minutes, when all the dancers pass to the altar and inhale the sacred breath of life. Coffee is now served to the men, and after a ten-minute chat the song is resumed, the personator of the Sai'apa of the previous evening being joined by a companion. The balancing on one foot is varied by jumping and hopping about the room, crying out in wild, weird tones. The two men are cheered by the others, who cry in a similar way. After dancing thirty minutes the dancer of the previous evening leaves the floor and his place is filled by a warrior of the fraternity, who is far from graceful in the springing motion. An aged woman and two girls now begin dancing. They aim to follow the men in the springing figure, but their feet are raised only a few inches above the floor. The women, as well as the men, stop frequently before the altar to inhale the sacred breath. The woman and girls dance thirty minutes, the former vehement in her motions and in her efforts to have the girls, who appear to be novices in the dance, display more enthusiasm. When these female dancers leave the floor one of the first male dancers, who has been on the floor an hour, goes out into the bitter night wind, his body glistening with streaming perspiration. Three other women and two men then take the floor and dance thirty minutes, when their places are filled by others. As each dancer leaves the floor he prays before the altar and sprinkles meal. All the members sleep in the ceremonial chamber.

Third day. The members of the fraternity are occupied in decorating masks and preparing other paraphernalia. The ceremony of the third night is similar to that of the second night.

Fourth day. The fourth day is a busy one in completing the paraphernalia for the closing scenes and in preparing prayer plumes, which they plant during the afternoon. At sunset the town is in commotion over the arrival of a Shumai'koli god from Chi'pia, attended by two Sai'apa. They are accompanied by a number of the fraternity, most of them grouped, forming the choir, and the whole party is led by a female member of the fraternity carrying a pottery basket of sacred meal.

The Shumai'koli is in gorgeous array. The mask, which covers the face only, is flat and colored yellow, in personation of the Shumai'koli of the North, and the eyes protrude. The mask is crowned with a bunch of long, banded turkey-tail plumes, some of which are tipped with fluffy white eagle plumes. At the base is a band of short, black turkey feathers, somewhat fluffy. Two fluffy white eagle plumes are each side of and at the base of the standing feathers. A white wool embroidered sash passes around the mask outside the feather band, and is attached at the back so as to have the two streamers, which are securely fastened together, fall straight down the back, thus covering the entire back of the mask. Plate CXXIII shows mask of Shumai'koli of the Zenith.

The Shumai'koli wears a white cotton shirt with full sleeves, a mi'ha fastened on each shoulder and falling below the calves of the legs, and a white cotton fringed sash around the waist fastened at the back. A mass of buckskin fringe tipped with conical bits of tin hangs from the waist in front. A gray skin having a white streak down the back, which is not over 12 inches long, is attached to the blanket dress about midway on the front. Tight-fitting trousers fringed on the outer sides extend to the feet. These trousers are removed for the indoor ceremonies and the legs are painted white. Dance moccasins are worn, with anklets blocked in black and white porcupine quills. Hanks of native blue yarn with sleigh bells attached are tied around the legs below the knees and fall in tassels on the sides. A strip of reddish buckskin, somewhat longer than the arm and 5 inches wide,

with six eagle-wing plumes attached, is tied to each arm near the
shoulder and allowed to hang free. A silver-mounted bow guard is
worn on the left wrist and a fox skin hangs from the right. A black
staff, slightly longer than an ordinary walking cane, ornamented at the
top and midway with small eagle plumes, is carried in the right hand,
a mi'li and a prayer plume being carried in the left. A diminutive
blue crook, symbolic of longevity, the color symbolizing A'wonawil'-
ona, the supreme life-giving power, and the Sun Father, is attached
to the prayer plume.

The Sai'apa masks cover the head. The face of one is colored blue,
the other yellow, symbolic of the sun and of the moon. The backs
of both are white decorated with a tadpole in the center. Each has a
narrow strip of light-colored fur running up the center of the face.
Five cylinders about 5 inches in length, circled in yellow, blue, and
black, run back from the forehead on the top of the mask. Feathers
are so placed in the front of the tubes as to project forward in line with
them. From each side of the mask fall long, slender, padded horns,
each one of which, where attached, is so turned as to form a ring.
Two fox skins encircle the base of each mask. The heads of the
animals are crossed in front, the tails hanging at the back. The body
of each Sai'apa is painted white. The person of one is covered with
a bunch of yucca held on by a yucca ribbon passed around the waist.
The other wears a war pouch in the same way. Anklets of spruce twigs
complete their dress. They carry a burning cedar brand in the right
hand and a bunch of giant yucca in the left. The Sai'apa speak and
act the reverse of what they mean. They ask for food when they are
not hungry; when they wish to smoke they declare they have no
desire for tobacco.

Upon reaching the village, the Shumai'koli, the two Sai'apa, and
others go at once to the ceremonial house, the Sai'apa moving their
burning torches as they proceed. On reaching the house they dance
about for a time in the street and then, since a tall cedar tree bars
the lower doorway, ascend the outer ladder to the roof. The choir
descends into the chamber, but the Shumai'koli and the Sai'apa remain
for some minutes on the roof, the former running about in a peculiar
manner, while the latter brandish the burning brands. It is dusk
before the three gods descend into the chamber. Previous to the
descent the Sai'apa extinguish their brands by striking them against
the hatchway.

Fourth night. The night ceremonial begins at 10 o'clock. Two
blankets have been hung near the northeast end of the room so as to
form a dressing room. About 9 o'clock the personal decoration of the
members of the fraternity begins. Some of the men have their bodies
and limbs colored in solid white, with streaks of white down the feet
and hands; others have serpentine lines of white over their bodies
and limbs, while others are spotted in white to represent the heavens.

They give one another much assistance, marking the scapula and back with the greatest care. On such occasions the paint is always applied with the fingers. The female members paint in white their lower arms, hands, lower legs, and feet. Those who are to personate the Sai'apa, consisting of two men and a boy, are painted in white from neck to toe. They should appear perfectly nude at the indoor ceremonials, dispensing even with the yucca and war pouch. "The Sai'apa lived in this world before any kind of raiment was known, and therefore never had any; and it is by the strict injunction of these gods that all apparel be dispensed with by their personators." [a]

The women wear black-wool dresses embroidered in blue, with red belts. The hair is done up as usual; the necks are bare and adorned with many necklaces. When the personal adornment is completed each one receives a bit of root in the mouth from the a'kwamosi. This they chew, and then ejecting it into their hands, rub first their own bodies, then those of the others, that they may not become fatigued in the dance.

The pottery drum has been made ready with its covering of hide. A member removes the bunch of rattles from the wall, and at 10 o'clock the choir is heard, accompanied by the rattle and drum. The first song consumes an hour. At its close a woman places a vase of water near the deputy a'kwamosi, who sits by the south side of the altar. The cloud bowl containing the bits of root, which has stood to the north side of the altar, is now placed south of the medicine bowl. The a'kwamosi deposits six pebble fetishes for fructification to the four sides of the medicine bowl and two others for the Zenith and Nadir to the east of it. Each fetish is held in the right hand while he offers a prayer. At the moment the first fetish is deposited a warrior rises and, standing before the altar, whirls the rhombus, the flutist, who sits behind the altar, plays, and the choir begins the second song, accompanied by the rattle and drum. After the a'kwamosi arranges the fetishes, his deputy, taking a gourd of water from the vase, waves it to the six regions with prayers for rain; then he waives it in a circle, symbolic of the whole world, and empties a portion of the water into the medicine bowl and the remainder into the cloud bowl. Six gourdfuls are passed through the same form and deposited into the bowls. Afterward two gourdfuls are emptied into the bowls without ceremony, and the a'kwamosi begins the consecration of the water in the medicine bowl, dipping in the pebble fetishes, etc., as described on page 492. At the same time the deputy a'kwamosi deposits bits of root in the cloud bowl and whips the water rapidly with a reed held at an angle of about 45°. [b]

---

[a] After a discussion, continuing over an hour during the afternoon, it was decided that the Sai'apa should wear breechcloths at the request of the writer.

[b] The Sia hold the reed perpendicularly and are greater experts in their manner of producing the suds, which rise high above the bowl, but do not fall over.

When the a'kwamosi has consecrated the water a cigarette of native tobacco wrapped in corn husk is handed to him, and leaving his stool he bends forward on his knees and draws smoke from the cigarette six times, each time blowing the smoke into the bowl of water, bringing his mouth close to the bowl. After the sixth time he waves the cigarette toward the altar, then to the six regions and in a circle, and thrusts the lighted end into his mouth for a moment. Then he hands the cigarette to the cloud-maker, who repeats the same rite over the cloud bowl and continues his work. All music and the rhombus cease, and the a'kwamosi dips his eagle plumes into the consecrated water and sprinkles the altar while he chants a prayer; at the same time the warrior carries off the food from before the altar. Men and women now form into a circle and dance from left to right, the three Sai'apa dancing back and forth within the circle. The cloud-maker continues the preparation of the clouds, a ceremony requiring three-quarters of an hour. The suds frequently fall over the bowl to the floor. When this occurs he lifts them with his reed and returns them to the mass. When he completes his task he rises, and standing before the altar throws suds over it, lifting them with his reed, while he chants a prayer in very low tones. After the dance has progressed for a time the master of ceremonies removes the yellow-faced mask from its place behind the altar and carries it, concealed with a piece of new cotton cloth, to the east end of the room for the man who is being dressed behind the blankets to personate the Shumai'koli of the North. The dress of this god is the same as described, with the exception of the leggings. He emerges from the dressing room and, stepping within the circle, begins to dance. The dance closes at 1 a. m., when all except the master of ceremonies, the Great Mother, the four novices, two Sia guests, and the writer leave the chamber to visit the He'iwa, Chu'pawa, and Mu'he'wa ki'wi'siwe,[a] where members of these ki'wi'siwe and girls chosen by young men appointed for the purpose spend the night in dancing. Not a word is spoken by those who remain in the ceremonial chamber. Once the master of ceremonies lights a cigarette and hands it to one of the novices. The two Sia guests smoke constantly.

The Shumai'koli and Sai'apa are absent an hour, the others returning in three-quarters of an hour. Upon his return the a'kwamosi chants a prayer before the altar, while the four novices rise and stand in line, five women alternating with the men, who clasp the hands of women beside them. The fingers are entwined, the novices' hands being above. In this position the chain of hands is kept in motion from right to left, the women slightly bending their knees. Three women and a little girl stand on the ledge behind the men, each one placing a hand on each shoulder of the man before her. At the con-

---

a See Kı'wi'siwe and their functions.

clusion of his prayer the a'kwamosi takes his mi'li from the altar and passes it with a prayer before the mouth of each novice, who draws the sacred breath. The motion of the novices' hands ceases but twice, and then only for a moment each time, except when the corn is placed to their lips, until 6 o'clock in the morning. The women relieve one another in attending the novices.

Thirty minutes after the ceremony with the mi'li the dance begins, and the Shumai'koli of the North backs out of the dressing room to the middle of the floor, and suddenly begins turning around like a top in a manner similar to the Sai'apa. The Shumai'koli dances two minutes, when he is joined by an officer of the fraternity from the seat formerly occupied by the a'kwamosi, the latter being now seated at the west end of the room. The Shumai'koli, with his associate to his right, the latter carrying the bowl of medicine water in his left arm and an ear of corn in his right hand, approaches the novice at the west end of the line, and the man dips the ear of corn into the medicine water, and with the Shumai'koli's hand upon the corn he puts it to the mouth of the novice. Each novice has the corn put to his mouth, after it has been dipped each time into the medicine water. As the lips are touched each novice ceases to move his hands. The Shumai'koli touches the corn only for the first novice, but he stands by while the corn is put to the lips of the second, and then returns to the floor to dance. After the corn is passed to the four novices, the medicine bowl and corn are deposited near the altar, and the officiating officer resumes his seat on the north ledge, by the altar; but in a few minutes he joins the Shumai'koli, and they stand before the two novices whom the Shumai'koli omitted, while the officer prays. Again the Shumai'koli returns to the floor, and after dancing a few minutes he retires to the greenroom, having been in the chamber just thirty minutes.

A charm fashioned of wood and similar to one of the bars of the suspended form above the altar is carried by a young man whenever the Shumai'koli appears, the bearer manipulating the bar before the god, which appears to have mystic control over the Shumai'koli. The writer has observed the same thing among the Hopi Indians. The bearer of the charm also carries a cedar-fiber brand, which, however, is not lighted until later.

The three Sai'apa now come to the floor and dance most gracefully, the younger of the three, a lad, remaining on the floor an hour and three-quarters, dancing violently all the time. He succeeds in turning but three times while poised on the left foot, though he makes numerous efforts to do better. He can turn but twice while balanced on the right foot. The leg is always drawn up as high as possible. The Sai'apa are soon joined by dancers of both sexes, each one dancing until fatigue compels retiring. Many dance thirty minutes, while others keep on the floor an hour, and a few dance two hours."

To prevent fatigue the dancers lift a quantity of suds from the cloud bowl and rub them on their legs. Before each dancer leaves the floor, the eagle-wing plumes that are carried are passed four times over the lips of each novice, beginning with the one at the west end of the line. The plumes are held diagonally to the mouth and drawn downward. Afterward each dancer passes the right hand across his or her forehead and then across some part of the body of the novice, generally the breast or legs first. Again rubbing the hand across the face it is passed over some portion of the body of the novice. This is repeated four times with each novice. As each male member finishes this ceremony he returns to the choir, so that the choir is at no time deplete of its members. The five remaining Shumai'koli appear separately in regular order and dance. After the god of the North comes the one of the West, with blue face mask, then red for the South, white for the East, all-color for the Zenith, and black for the Nadir. The cloud decorations on the faces of the masks differ. The ceremony of dipping the corn into the medicine water and placing it to the lips of the novice is repeated with the appearance of each Shumai'koli. The same ceremony is repeated by the Shumai'koli of the Zenith and Nadir over two Sia guests, which is a mark of very delicate courtesy. The novices remain standing as long as a Shumai'koli is present, but as soon as the god retires, the novices and the women sit down until another appears, but the clasped hands continue in motion.

As the hour for the rising of the morning star approaches, the participants exhibit much anxiety to know the instant the star appears above the horizon; there is, therefore, continual ascending of the ladder. The straw mat which covers the hatchway is raised as each one goes forth to look for the star. About this time an old woman deposits a great heap of corn husks and a cedar-fiber brand near the fireplace and makes a large fire. Finally the appearance of the star is announced by the withdrawal of the mat from the hatchway. The bar charm is laid aside by its bearer, who immediately lights a heap of corn husks and runs with the blazing mass to the choir, pelts the singers, and afterward dances violently, still holding the husks; and again pelts the choir and again dances. A number of dancers now congregate on the floor. Rushing to the fire, the young man gathers more husks and lighting them pelts the male and female dancers. Another and another light great bunches of the husks until the room is ablaze, women and children vying with one another, one of the

---

a This fraternity seems more devoid of decency in the ceremonial chamber than the others. both sexes using the same urinal, which stands in a convenient place in the room, members of other fraternities leave the chamber for such purposes.

enthusiastic participants being a girl less than 6 years of age. Cedar brands succeed the husks and a grand mêlée ensues. A warrior runs up the ladder and descending with an armful of husks ignites them and runs about among the people with them blazing in his arms. The excitement grows greater and greater as the male and female members run around pell-mell, showering one another with sparks. Clubs are thrown upward, and much dodging is necessary to avoid being struck. Another and another join in the excitement until only the drummer and two companions remain in the choir; but the cries and yells of the dancers drown all other sounds. The women do not seem to mind in the least the sparks showering over their bare necks and arms. They are too crazed with excitement to be conscious of physical pain. The aged woman, whose usefulness as a member of the fraternity has long since passed away, is aroused by the fire display and her old wrinkled face brightens with a lively interest as she touches the writer, when she is near, and exclaims: "Kokshi! kokshi!" (good! good!) It must have been many a day since this creature played an active part in these weird scenes, which a pen picture can scarcely describe, especially the fighting with the great firebrands.

The Shumai'koli of the Nadir leaves the floor soon after the beginning of the fire display, but the Sai'apa remain on the floor to the last. Just previous to the close of this barbaric scene the tree which was removed from the lower entrance and carried up the ladder and then down into the chamber early in the evening is taken from the room through the lower door and stood outside, the door being left open. After the fire fight, prayers are offered before the altar, and the tree, which has a la'showanně composed of a banded turkey feather, a fluffy white eagle plume, and feathers of the ᵗsi'liliko (Falco sparverius deserticolus, desert sparrow), hawk, and ᵗhlai'aluko (Sialia arctica, mountain bluebird), attached to the topmost branch, is planted in the center of Si'aa' te'wita, and the fraternity dance around it for two hours and then return to the ceremonial chamber to enjoy a feast. Later in the morning the fraternity reappear in the plaza, and after dancing around the tree all return to the chamber to remain, except the charm-bearers and those who personate the gods.

As is the custom with other fraternities, youths and maidens are appointed by this fraternity to procure dancers from the town at large, the youths choosing the women and the girls the men. The youths, who are designated as a'mosi (directors), wear black shirts of native weave, trimmed in bright red and green ribbons, or velveteen shirts, when this material can be secured, velveteen knee breeches, deerskin moccasins and leggings colored a reddish brown, and red garters. The breeches and leggings have lines of silver buttons on the outer sides. Lines of micaceous hematite under the eyes denote

HE'HEA GODS ON THEIR WAY TO CEREMONIAL CHAMBER OF U'HUHUKWE (EAGLE-DOWN FRATERNITY)

U'HUHUKWE (EAGLE-DOWN FRATERNITY) CHASING HE'HEA GODS WITH THEIR FIRE BRANDS

officership. The girls wear the conventional dress, with a white blanket wrap bordered in red and blue, and white moccasins with highly polished black soles. Both sexes wear turquoise earrings and profusions of ko'hakwa, turquoise, and coral beads, and the girls wear their silver necklaces in addition to these. Each youth carries a ball of yarn and a large needle to be used in securing the blanket wraps of those who dance. The dancers usually form two concentric circles. The drummer sits east of the tree and uses a wood drum covered with hide. As the dancers become fatigued, or when for other reasons they do not wish to remain on the ground, they drop out at the close of a dance; but their places are soon filled.

The six Shumai'koli appear both separately and in couples in the plaza and dance. Two Sai'apa are in attendance (see plate CXXIV). Each Shumai'koli is accompanied by a charm-bearer;[a] whenever he waves the charm the Shumai'koli backs off a distance and then starts forward while the charm-bearer vigorously manipulates the charm to draw the god to him. The two Sai'apa perform a variety of antics; they climb the tree and run up the ladders to the houses above, begging for melons and bread, which they deposit beside the tree. The Sai'apa return at intervals to the ceremonial chamber. At times none of the gods are to be seen in the plaza, but the dance is continuous. At sunset two of the Shumai'koli gods and the Sai'apa, one of the latter whirling the rhombus, depart over the eastern road with those who accompanied them to the village.

Preparation of medicine. The day preceding the ceremony is consumed in collecting medicinal plants. A plant closely resembling water cress (not yet classified), but having a much more pungent odor, is gathered at the base of the mesa north of Kwïl'li yäl'lännĕ (Twin mountain), several miles north of Zuñi.

When the writer enters the ceremonial chamber about 10 o'clock the room appears in general confusion, though the tablet altar has been erected. Six mi'wachi are placed in line on the cloud symbol of white meal. The mi'li of one of the officers of the fraternity stands on the meal line, which extends outward from the cloud symbol. A sacred meal basket is on the line before the mi'li, another meal basket is to the north, and two medicine bowls with serrated rims stand on the north and south sides of the altar. The other bowls and a basket tray are for the use of the medicine cakes (see plate CXXV). A large quantity of some variety of plant is heaped near the southwest corner of the room, with a quantity of squash blossoms scattered over it. Near by, and also on the south side of the room, is another mass of plants which appear to be the same as the former, only younger, the latter having white blossoms, the whole plant measuring less than 12

---

[a] The charm-bearer does not appear in the picture, being absent when the photograph was taken.

inches in height. Near this heap is a quantity of root about 3 inches
in diameter. On the north side of the room, and more to the east,
is a quantity of wild sage and a bowl containing the flower tips of
the plant. Groups of men are near each collection of plants and at
once begin work. The plants in the southwest end are broken into
bits and deposited in large bowls together with the squash blossoms.
The younger plants are also separated and put into bowls, the roots
are prepared and cut into small pieces and deposited in bowls, and the
leaves are removed from the stems of the sage and also placed in
bowls. One plant is separated into small clusters and placed in bowls
with a small quantity of water that it may remain fresh. The work is
industriously pushed forward, and by 2 o'clock all the medicine is
arranged and the floor is in order. Six very old grinding stones or
mills, much worn from use, are placed on the floor on the north side
not far from the altar, upon skins and cloths, with just space enough
between the mills and the ledge for the grinders to kneel. The grinding begins. The medicine of all the fraternities is ground principally
by invited guests, who also take part in the dancing, the girls and
women relieving one another.

As the grinders and dancers arrive they take seats on the north
ledge, near the east end of the room. Other women also sit in this
locality, and several sit near the choir. When all are present the
a'kwamosi, who carries a meal basket in his left hand, gives a pinch
of meal to each female, and prays about a minute over each. The
meal is received in the left hand, but it is changed to the right when
the women go to the altar to pray and sprinkle the meal. Six grinders are now dressed by the warrior and another member of the fraternity. Only the pi'toni and the moccasins are removed. The usual
woven dress is covered with a mi'ha fastened on the right shoulder
and passing under the left arm, and a white cotton fringed sash is worn
tied at the back. The hair is hanging and tied loosely with a red
garter at the nape of the neck; a white fluffy eagle plume is attached
to the fore part of the head. The neck and arms are bare, and silver
beads, bangles, and rings are worn, besides the elaborate necklaces of
ko'hakwa, turquoise, and coral. Each girl is led separately to the mill
by the a'kwamosi, who carries an eagle-wing plume in each hand, the
girl holding the tips of the plumes. She passes behind the mills, while
the a'kwamosi walks before them. They now face one another, the
girl still holding the plumes. The first girl is led to the most western
mill, the others follow in succession. After each girl is in position
the a'kwamosi places a hand on each shoulder and motions her to the
six regions, carrying the head forward and back for the Zenith and
the Nadir. An aged woman and a man take seats before the mills.
Each has a large bowl of the mixed plants to the right; there are also
two small bowls containing bits of turquoise and ko'hakwa (white shell

beads). These two perform the double duty of supplying the mills with the medicine and rearranging the elaborate ornaments of the grinders when necessary, each having three mills and three grinders in care. The song is now begun to the accompaniment of the rattle. One woman remains near the choir but she does not sing. The song is low and in minor key. The aged man and woman who sit by the mills deposit on each mill bits of turquoise and ko'hakwa, which the girls crush to powder; to this several pieces of the root medicine are added. The various plants are lifted from the bowl dripping wet and squeezed before placing on the mills; sometimes a little water is added. Each additional plant is ground as it is placed on the mill. The grinding appears to be hard work, and the girls' heads bob up and down as they proceed with the grinding. At times the a'kwamosi wipes the dripping faces of the girls by slipping a cloth under the long bangs without pushing the hair aside. When the medicine is thoroughly crushed, fully an hour being required to reach the desired result, the grinder works it into cakes and hands it to the attendant, who deposits it in one of the large bowls used for this purpose which stands north of the altar. The a'kwamosi assists the grinders from the mills in the same manner as they are led to them. Their dress and adornments are removed and placed on others who are to take their places at the mills. The garters are also removed from the hair.

As soon as the second party takes its turn at the mills the character of music changes, the drum is used in addition to the rattles and the songs appear to be martial in character, the time being more rapid than before. A youth in the choir is an attentive listener, wishing to learn the songs.[a]

At this time the a'kwamosi stands before the altar keeping time with his feet and two eagle plumes held in each hand. He dips the tips of his plumes into the medicine water and touches them to the four serrated points of the bowl and motions them up and down for the Zenith and Nadir; he afterward sprinkles the altar and fetishes and the crossbar above the altar with the medicine water and starts the latter whirling. Afterward he dances in the middle of the floor for a time and returns to the altar to repeat the sprinkling and whirling of the crossbar, which must be kept in motion. Five men and ten women begin the dance in groups of three, a man between two women. The a'kwamosi leads the dancers. He holds a corn husk horizontally, catching it at each end and his two partners hold each an eagle-wing

---

[a] During this ceremonial the writer discovered that the Shu'maakwe songs were not in the Zuñi tongue, but in Pima. The officers of the fraternity were much annoyed because of her discovery. There is still much to be learned concerning this fraternity, the most interesting features being its origin and its association with the Pimas. Friar Marcos de Niza mentions in the account of his travels in the present New Mexico that he met an old Cibolan Indian among the Pimas. If it be true that Cibola and Zuñi land are one and the same, then the old man Niza referred to was a Zuñian.

plume in the same manner. The four men who follow catch the ends
of the plumes held by their partners. The acting Great Mother follows alone, with her eagle plume. They all pass around the room in
an ellipse from west to east, starting from the south side with a forward step with the right foot, then the left, each time, especially the
men, raising the foot high; the women are not very successful in their
efforts to raise their feet high from the floor. The arms are extended
outward in unison with the music. The song is spirited and the drum
and rattles resound through the room. The dancing, which is most
pleasing, continues until sunset, when the a'kwamosi dips ashes from
the altar, which he has previously placed there from the fireplace,
and sprinkles the dancers. The sprinkling of the dancers is repeated
four times and then ashes are lifted and thrown out of the door,
when all inhale a sacred breath. The sprinkling of the ashes is for
physical purification. Each male dancer passes his hands over his
face, the entire body dripping with perspiration, and rubs them over
the faces of his partners, then passing his hands over his breast and
arms rubs their arms, but he does not touch their breasts. After
repeating the rubbing over his legs, he rubs his hands over the lower
legs of his partners, and the backs are rubbed in the same manner.

At sunset the two sets of grinders stand in line north and south in
the east end of the room and face east. Each grinder has a female
vis-a-vis who is supplied with a bowl of yucca suds, and each grinder
has her forelock and then her hands washed with the suds by the
woman immediately before her. They are bathed in turn, the woman
at the south end of the line beginning with the grinder before her.
The a'kwamosi stands behind each grinder, with a hand on each
shoulder.

The grinding, with the full ceremonies, is repeated on the following
day, and the day after the ceremonial chamber is deserted, the male
members of the fraternity being at work in the fields of the director
of the fraternity. On their return after sunset they are entertained
at a sumptuous feast by the wife and family of the director at their
house, the female members of the fraternity first assisting in waiting
upon the men and afterward enjoying a feast themselves with the women
of the household. Grinding, with the ceremonies described, is repeated
on the next day, and the following day more plants are gathered, and
on the seventh day the grinding and dancing are repeated. The dancing
continues until sunset, then, after a rest of a couple of hours, is resumed
and continues until midnight. After the dance closes at sunset a corn-
husk package about 9 inches in length and several inches across, containing sun-dried cakes of the freshly prepared medicine, is given
to each grinder and dancer who has participated by invitation. The
dancing at night is the same as previously described, many taking their
turn on the floor. During the intervals between the dances the men rub

their partners' arms and also their legs as far as the knees with medicine, carefully manipulating the limbs to relieve them of fatigue and
give them strength to continue in the dance. At the close of the dancing at midnight medicine water is administered to all. The following
morning a tree is planted in the center of Si'aa' te'wita and the dancing
and appearance of the gods in the plaza occur as previously described.
Much persuasion is often required to induce the women to take part,
though they are evidently expecting, from their appearance, to participate. Sometimes the men force them into the dance. Both men and
women are attired in their best clothing. As the afternoon advances
the number of dancers grows larger until three concentric circles are
formed, embracing in all 150 dancers. The dancers go round from
right to left, holding one another's hands, the men singing to the accompaniment of the drum. The two Sai'apa are busy throughout the day
ascending ladders to compel the spectators on the house tops to come
down and take part in the dance, and collecting loaves of bread, which
they place in the tree around which the men and women dance. Several times a Sai'apa climbs the tree to place the bread in the uppermost
forks. As dancers become fatigued they drop out of the circle and
others take their places. At sunset the circles remain stationary while
all inhale the sacred breath of A'wonawil'ona,[a] and then all the dancers
leave the plaza; but another circle is at once formed by others, and
the dance continues until dusk, when the ceremonial is concluded.

The Shumai'koli precede the Sai'apa over the eastern road and are
supposed to lie down and sleep at Shu'mĭnkĭa, on the road to Chi'pia,
and when the Sai'apa follow, each brandishing a flaming cedar brand,
and find the Shumaikoli sleeping they waken them, and catching them
by the waist carry them off to Chi'pia, whence they came.

Certain features appear in some of the ceremonies of the Shu'maakwe
that the writer has not observed, as they never happened to be brought
out when she was in Zuñi, though she has seen them in the Shumai'koli
performances among the Hopi Indians, these Indians and the Zuñis
having the same name, Ya'ya, for the male characters introduced.
The minute description given by the pe'kwĭn and other Zuñis accords
perfectly with the scenes observed in the Hopi villages. The Ya'ya
create general amusement among the spectators when at sunset the
Shumai'koli of the West appears in the plaza and separates the circle
of dancers by grabbing the men's wrists. The women at once go to
their homes, and do not see the Ya'ya put in blankets and dropped
through the hatchway into the ceremonial chamber.

In 1902 the director of the Shu'maakwe fraternity with an associate
visited Laguna for the purpose of receiving the six Shumai'koli masks
of the pueblo, since all those privileged to use these masks had died.
They were consigned to the keeping of the director of the Zuñi fra-

---

[a] See p. 22.

ternity. The masks, carefully wrapped, were brought to Zuñi on the backs of burros. The writer was present at the ceremonial held by the Shu'maakwe fraternity on the return of the director from Laguna and she notes here the variations from the ceremony previously described.

The occasion of this ceremonial is twofold. A woman and a young girl are to be initiated into the fraternity, and the Laguna masks of the Shumai'koli are to be brought out for the first time in Zuñi. The men who are to personate the gods go to Ku'shilowa about half an hour before sunset. As they leave the ceremonial chamber the writer enters and finds six Shumai'koli and three Sai'apa masks on a large blanket spread on the north side of the chamber and a short distance before the altar. The masks are receiving the finishing touches, and other regalia are being arranged. Men not employed on this work are grouped on the south side of the room, singing to the accompaniment of the rattle. A woman of the fraternity who is to lead the gods to Zuñi sits on a stool facing east. In a short time the woman, followed by the charm-bearer, proceeds to Ku'shilowa, to return with the gods who appear after sunset. Two Shu'maikoli and two Sai'apa masks are conveyed under cover of blankets to Ku'shilowa. It will be remembered that these gods live in the east.

In a short time all Zuñi is out on the house tops and in the streets to view the coming of the gods. As soon as they are observed in the distance a fraternity father, followed by a novice, comes to the ceremonial house, but does not enter. The two stand just west of the entrance, the novice being west of the fraternity father. The man looks to the east, but the woman holds her head down and appears to be deeply impressed with the solemnity of the occasion. In five minutes the other novice follows her fraternity father and they stand west of the first couple; this man also looks to the east and the girl looks downward.

When the gods enter the village the children are wild with excitement. Animal-like cries are heard in the ceremonial chamber, and the voices of the choir are more vigorous in the song. The female leader of the gods carries her mi'li and meal basket in the left hand and throws out meal with her right as she advances. The man who follows carries the charm referred to, which he manipulates that the gods may follow. The two Shumai'koli, of the North and of the West, come next and are followed by two Sai'apa. The foremost Sai'apa has the back of the mask colored yellow for the North, being the attendant to the Shumai'koli of that region; the other has his mask blue, for he is attendant to the Shumai'koli of the West. On reaching the ceremonial house, the female leader takes her position east of the fraternity fathers and novices, and faces east. The charm-bearer stands south of her, facing east, and holds his charm above his face

with his left hand and shakes a small gourd rattle with his right,
while he sings a low chant, reminding one of the intoning of a Catholic priest. The two Sai'apa strike the top, left, base, and right
of the door frame with their burning brands and join the Shumai'koli
in the dance. The gods dance for a time with a slow step, raising
first one foot and then the other to the music of the choir within. The
time is changed and they dance more rapidly. After thirty minutes
the female leader and the charm-bearer retire to the chamber. The
gods prolong the dance for a few minutes, and the man who has charge
of the tree, which now stands east of the entrance, places his hand on
the back of the Shumai'koli of the North and directs him to the entrance
of the ceremonial chamber, when he stoops and goes in. The other
Shumai'koli follows, also directed by the man. In the meantime the
two Sai'apa continue to dance, but they soon join the others in the
chamber. The tree attendant now carries in the tree. The dancing
of the gods in the chamber is violent and continuous for some time,
then the masks are removed and all indulge in a feast. The all-night
ceremonial is the same as previously described.

Ma'^tke 'San'nakwe (Little Fire Fraternity)

The Ma'^tke 'San'nakwe fraternity comprises four orders: O'naya'-
nakïa (Mystery medicine), It'sĕpcho (Jugglery), Ma'^tke (Fire), and
Pa'yatämu (God of music, flowers, and butterflies).

This organization has a large membership, many of the members
being among the wealthiest of the pueblo. Its theurgists are equal
to any in Zuñi, Nai'uchi,[a] the warrior of the fraternity, standing at
the head of the Zuñi medicine men. There is no physician anywhere
who is kept busier with patients than this remarkable old man, to
whom the writer is indebted for much of the material comprised in
this monograph. The rules for the convening of this fraternity are
the same as those followed by others where the mysteries of medicine
are practiced. Though the members of the Little Fire fraternity play
with fire at other gatherings, their most elaborate fire display occurs
but once in four years, this being the time of the celebration of the
lighting of the first fire by the Sun Father, according to Hopi belief.
In fact, the members of this fraternity participate in the great fire
dance only once in eight years, for the reason that a division occurred
in the fraternity many years ago, but within the recollection of some
of the older men. According to the statement of an aged theurgist,
who was about ten or twelve years of age when the trouble arose and
at the time a member of the Little Fire fraternity, but who joined the
opposing party, a man and a woman were the cause of the break in
the fraternity, their conduct being a subject for the severest censure,

---

[a] Since deceased.

especially as all must observe continence at such times. Certain members of the fraternity wished to expel the woman from the fraternity and retain the man, while others desired to expel the man and retain the woman. The latter faction finally declared itself a separate organization. The man remained with the parent fraternity while the woman went with the new one. The new body, on selecting a chamber for their meetings, found it to be infested with cimex, and so the branch fraternity was named Pe'shä'silo'kwe (Cimex). Plate CXXVI shows the altar of the Cimex fraternity before all the fetishes have been placed. A medicine bowl is on each side of the meal line, a prayer-meal basket south of the line, and a large shell on the line of meal. The dry painting in the foreground shows the bears of the four regions; that of the West is followed by her cub. The color symbol is not adhered to, the Bear of the North being in gray instead of yellow; the Bear of the West in black instead of blue-green; the Bear of the South also in black instead of red, and the Bear of the East in yellow instead of white, upon a ground of green, which represents the vegetation of the world. The blue-green color is bordered in black and white blocks, denoting the cloud houses of the four regions, and the blocked circle denotes the cloud houses of the world. The decoration of the bar extending above the altar shows the sun blue-green, moon yellow, stars white, Cougar of the North yellow, Cougar of the West blue-green, Bear of the East white, spotted in black. The rituals of the two organizations are the same, though there are variations in their altars and dry paintings. The Little Fire and Cimex fraternities alternate in the quadrennial ceremonial referred to.

CEREMONIAL OF INITIATION INTO O'NAYA'NAKĬA

The four days' ceremonial here described is one of the most elaborate of the Little Fire fraternity, and embraces about all to be found in the various ceremonies, except the quadrennial.

First day. The wall of the ceremonial chamber has been freshly decorated with a blue frieze, edged with cloud symbols in black. The north wall has a painting of a cougar in blue-green. The color symbol is not adhered to in this instance also, as yellow is the color for the North and blue-green for the West. The morning is consumed in decorating and arranging the altar and in preparing prayer plumes to the Beast Gods and deceased members of the fraternity. A tiny, closely covered vase said to contain blossoms and the root of the te'nas'säli, combined with the hearts of butterflies and dragon-flies, belonging to Nai'uchi, is deposited before the altar on the south side, with the animal fetishes, etc.

Night ceremony. Each member of the fraternity on entering the chamber is greeted by those present, and after removing his moccasins the newcomer advances to the altar and sprinkles meal. Each member of Mystery medicine hands his or her mi′li[a] to an officer of the fraternity, who places it by the altar.

Plate CXXVII shows altar fully embellished. The tablets forming the altar are carved and painted in cloud symbols. Faces of the Sun Father and Moon Mother cap the rear slats. Ä′chiyälä′topa (being with tail and wings of knives) stands upon the topmost clouds. Ku′pïshtaya, the lightning-makers, are represented on the middle slats with the dragon fly, an important rain symbol, below. The morning and evening stars cap the front slats upon which the cougar of the North (yellow) and of the West (blue-green) are painted. A carved rattlesnake is before the left front slat. This fraternity having a large membership in Mystery medicine, there are a number of mi′wachi (plural for mi′li), to be seen, composed of brilliant plumes, two of which stand on the meal line. The following enumeration shows the position of the principal objects: 1, ear of corn; 2, giant yucca; 3, dry painting—an eagle is figured on the bed of the painting with pieces of banded gypsum, the head is designed in black, mounds of colored grains of corn dot the disk (further description on page 560); 4, medicine bowls; 5, prayer-meal baskets; 6, bowls for ground medicine; 7, food offerings; 8, arrow points; 9, three crystals; 10, basket of plume offerings; 11, pouch of warrior of fraternity; 12, bear's-foot skin; 13, animal fetish, 14, cut-stone fetish. Flutes of the order of Pa′yatämu of the Little Fire fraternity hang on the wall above the altar.[b]

One is impressed with the quiet which prevails, for the whispering of the women can not be heard at the other end of the room, while the men talk almost as low, only one speaking at a time, the others remaining most attentive listeners. They tell of their feats in war; of the killing of some of the hated Navahos; how their parents were brutally murdered by the enemy, or how they surprised the enemy and gained advantage over him. While reciting the most thrilling adventures they do not fail to indulge in the keenest ridicule of the enemy, the listeners at such points joining in a low but hearty laugh. While the orator speaks he scarcely raises his voice as high as the moderate tones of civilized man, and at times lowers it to a whisper. The delicate modulations of his voice are remarkable, and his gesticulations the poetry of motion. Smoking of cigarettes made of commercial tobacco is continuous at this time. The native tobacco is used only for ceremonial smoking. Pipes are not used by the Zuñis.

After 9 o'clock the room becomes crowded. The choir groups on the south side toward the west end of the room, some sitting on the ledge, while others roll their blankets into wads for seats. There are

---

[a] See p. 416.
[b] The dry painting described is not made until the fourth afternoon.

five novices—one young woman, two young men, a small boy, and an old man. The young girl sits by the side of one of the young men upon the ledge at the west end of the room and to the north of the altar; the other young man and the boy sit upon the same ledge at the south side of the altar, and the old man, who is a cripple from rheumatism, sits upon the floor with the other members of the fraternity.[a] The leader of the choir beats on a te'pehan (a vase-shaped pottery drum), and the other members of the choir use the gourd rattles. The ceremonial opens with the making of the medicine water, when there is no longer any semblance of quiet. At the first stroke of the drum the choir simultaneously commences the song, to the accompaniment of the rattle, and the noise is deafening.

Preparation of medicine water. A large vase of water is brought in by a woman and placed opposite the medicine bowl, which stands before the altar and by the side of the a'kwamosi (maker of medicine water), who sits to the north of the altar. He at once begins the preparation of the medicine water,[b] but his prayers, offered in low tones, invoking the Beast Gods to be present, can not be heard because of the music of the choir; at the same time notes can be heard from the flute, which is played by a young man who sits behind the altar. The chief warrior stands before the altar and whirls the rhombus. He also keeps the cloud symbol suspended above the altar in rotary motion, calling upon the rain-makers to gather quickly and send rain. The a'kwamosi prays for power to see disease, and that it shall be carried off by the four winds.

Invocation of the Little Fire fraternity

> Lion of the North, give me power to see disease.
> Bear of the West, give me power to see disease.
> Badger of the South, give me power to see disease.
> White Wolf of the East, give me power to see disease.
> Eagle of the Zenith, give me power to see disease.
> Shrew of the Earth, give me power to see disease.
> Thou, my Sun Father, give me power to see disease.
> Thou, my Moon Mother, give me power to see disease.
> All ye ancient ones, give me power.

Three medicines of the Beast Gods: (1) The medicine of the Cougar and Bear, which is white and said by the Indians to be a mineral deposit from dripping water; (2) a grayish root medicine of the Badger and Wolf; and (3) a blackish root medicine of the Eagle and Shrew, are found only on two mountains—Yällän Ko'han, (White mountain), in the west, and Ka'pachu mountain, near Acoma. When these medicines are required by a fraternity some twelve members, including the director, his deputy, and the warrior, are each provided with six prayer plumes. The stick of one is colored yellow for the Cougar of the North, another blue for the Bear of the West, another red for the Badger of the South, another white for the Wolf of the East, another all-color for the Eagle of the Zenith, and another

---

[a] It is usual for the novice not to appear until the fourth night of the ceremonies.
[b] See p 492   There is but little variation in the consecration of the water by the fraternities.

black for the Shrew of the Nadir. The plume offerings are made to these animals, which use the medicines as their food. The offering of the plumes propitiates the Beast Gods, so that they good-naturedly walk away. After the deposition of the plume wands with prayers and the sprinkling of meal, the medicine is hastily collected. These three medicines are given separately at ceremonials to the members of the fraternity, and when one is ill a small portion of each of the three is sprinkled in water and drunk.

The a'kwamosi dips water from the vase six times. Each gourd of water he holds above the medicine bowl while repeating a prayer, after which he empties the water into the bowl. He drops six animal fetishes, one for each of the six regions, which have been placed in position, north, south, east, and west of the medicine bowl—those for the Zenith and the Nadir being laid to the east into the bowl separately. He next sprinkles sacred meal into the water six times, for the six regions, and then dips the quill ends of his eagle plumes into the medicine water, and holding them perpendicularly raises and lowers them six times. At the close of the consecration of the medicine water the flute and rhombus cease. The flute is returned to its place before the altar and the rhombus is replaced in the niche in the wall. The a'kwamosi now stands, and dipping the feather end of his eagle-wing plumes into the water sprinkles the altar. The plume in the left hand is held in a horizontal position and struck on the underside at right angles with the plume held in the right hand. The song, rattle, and drum continue, with an occasional intermission of a few seconds, until midnight, when a corn husk is made funnel-shaped and filled with tobacco. This cigarette is passed to all present, including the women, and each one, holding the small end to the mouth, takes a whiff. All the women (except the novice) now return to their homes, escorted by members of the fraternity, who are specially detailed to perform this office, for women must not walk the streets at night alone. When sleeping, the female novice, covered with a blanket, lies upon a single sheepskin on the floor immediately in front of where she sat. The other novices take the same position in relation to their seats, while the remainder of the men, who must not sleep out of the fraternity chamber during the ceremonial, scatter around the sides of the room. Food is brought to them by the women of the fraternity and also of their clans. Though the men take no food at their homes, they are free to pass in and out of the ceremonial house as they choose, often going out for a few hours to look after their crops and herds.

Second day. The morning is consumed in preparing prayer plumes and in chatting and smoking. In the afternoon the grinding of medicine is begun, when the large room is filled with the members of the fraternity, many of the women having their infants with them. A girl, attired in ordinary dress, sits at the east end of the room behind a stone slab laid upon several sheepskins, the wool side down, pounding with a stone hatchet a mineral, the medicine of the cougar and bear, which she afterward grinds and deposits in an ordinary eating bowl. Sheepskins are laid in line on the floor on the north side of the room and west of the center, and two blankets are placed on them. Buckskins are laid on the blankets, a piece of canvas is spread over these, a piece of new cotton cloth covers the canvas, and on this is placed a cotton cloth which has evidently been used many times for the same purpose, as it is thoroughly dyed with the medicine. Three stone mills, such as are used for grinding grain for daily consumption, are placed at an angle of forty-five degrees on this cushion, leaving just space enough between them and the wall for the grinders to kneel. Two of the grinders are dressed, each by a young man of the fraternity. A mi′ha (white embroidered blanket) is worn as a dress over the ordinary black wool gown. Earrings, bangles, rings, and most elaborate necklaces of ko′hakwa, turquoise, coral, and silver beads, are worn. The hair, which has been plaited to make it wavy, is tied with a red garter at the nape of the neck, and a fluffy eagle plume is tied to the forelock. Each grinder is led to her place by a warrior of the fraternity by holding the tips of his eagle-wing plumes. The girl, still holding the tips of the plumes, on reaching the mills goes to her place behind them, while the warrior, who passes before them, extends his arms over the mills. When the girl kneels behind a mill, her guide takes his seat before her and the mill, and holding her clasped hands between his own waves them to the six regions with a prayer. Then a male attendant to each grinder takes a seated before each mill. The one before the mill to the east places the bowl of the ground medicine before the mill over which he presides. The man presiding over the center mill places a bowl of the ground grayish root medicine of the Badger and Wolf by his side; and the one who attends the third mill deposits by his side a bowl of crushed sunflowers.[a]

A few bits of archaic shell beads and a minute quantity of the root of the te′nas‵säli are crushed in each mill, and then a quantity of the root medicine of the Cougar of the North is added, the grinders bending their bodies and bobbing their heads in harmony with the song of twenty men, accompanied by rattle and drum. The Bear, Badger, and Wolf medicines are afterward ground in turn. The choir wear only their trousers rolled above their knees and a profusion of necklaces.

Dancing begins late in the afternoon, after the grinding ceases. A man of the choir dances his infant on his knee to the time of the music, and the little one looks before it with the most unconcerned expression. One man, three women, and two little girls, each about six years old open the dance. In a short time these dancers are joined

---

[a] The director of the fraternity asserts that there are six different plant medicines besides the above, each plant the property of a beast god of one of the six regions, and that they are found in the crater of a mountain north of the pueblo of Laguna.

by four more women. A man desiring a certain woman to dance pulls off her knit leggings, for she must not appear on the floor as a dancer with her leggings on. All the officers of the fraternity, except the warriors, when not on the floor sit back and to the north side of the altar. The choir is jovial, and the younger brother Bow priest causes great merriment by frequently approaching it and giving instruction how to sing. After a time two young men join the dancers. The director hands a lighted cigarette to a man in the choir, who puffs it and returns it, when the director takes a whiff and hands it back to the man, who smokes it a moment, then passes it around. The representatives of the beast gods frequently break out in animal-like cries. The a'kwamosi dips his eagle plumes four times in the medicine water, sprinkling the altar each time. The choir closes by the drawing in of the sacred breath of A'wonawil'ona[a] and all repeat a prayer, after which there is an intermission until night. At night the novices occupy their same positions. The choir assembles as on the previous evening, the leader beating on a pottery drum, the others using the gourd rattle. The choir opens with a low chant, but their tones grow louder and the noise is deafening during the making of the medicine water. The music and dancing continue until midnight, when the fraternity adjourns until morning.

Third day. The mi'wachi for the novices are prepared by their fraternity fathers during the morning. In the afternoon five slabs are placed, as the three were on the previous day, for grinding medicine. The women are dressed and led to the mills, as before described, except that the plume worn by one of them is colored red with dry pigment. Bits of archaic shell and te'nas'säli root are deposited on the mills before the grinding begins. During the grinding of the first medicine (that of the Cougar of the North) the attendant at the center mill deposits two pieces of corn husk on the mill, and the girl takes them in each hand and rubs the metate for a while, then lays them aside, and continues grinding. When reduced to a powder the medicine is bluish gray. It is placed in the bowl by the attendants, who lift it with an eagle plume held in each hand. Any medicine adhering to the mills is scraped off with stone knives. The medicine plant of the Bear of the West is next placed on the mills, bits of archaic shell and an atom of the te'nas'säli having been first crushed. Upon the completion of the grinding of this medicine, it is collected in the same manner and placed in a bowl. Then the medicine of the Badger of the South is ground with bits of shell and te'nas'säli, and it is deposited in the first bowl containing the medicine of the Cougar of the North. Upon completion of the medicine of the White Wolf of the East, bits of shell and te'nas'säli having been ground with it, it is

ᵃ See p. 22.

placed in the bowl containing the medicine of the Bear of the West. If any of the medicine falls from the slab during the grinding, one of the warriors hastens to replace it with an ancient stone knife. Occasionally during the grinding the attendants run stone knives over the mills crosswise, to loosen the material from the stone. Each set of grinders, who work about thirty minutes, is assisted to rise by the two warriors, who stand before the mills and extend two eagle-wing plumes. The women, touching the tips of the plumes held by the warriors with each hand, pass from behind the mills at the east end. When the grinding is completed for the day the warriors place the bowls of medicine and stone knives by the altar. The grinders gather a short distance east of the mills and are relieved by young men of some of their adornments, including the finger rings. The elaborate necklaces and earrings are not removed. The red garters are taken from the hair, allowing it to fall loosely over the shoulders, but the plumes are allowed to remain. The women step aside and change the white embroidered robe for the ordinary Zuñi dress and take seats upon the ledge on the south side of the room. The mills are removed while the dress is being changed.

The last five grinders advance to the middle of the room and form into two lines, extending east and west, lengthwise of the room, two women in the south line, three in the north, and a man forming a center line between the two. Each woman holds two eagle-wing plumes horizontally in the right hand.[a] One of the plumes has a fluffy eagle feather attached to its tip. The woman wearing the feather colored red has one of the same color attached to her eagle plume, feathers of this color being worn by members of the order of Mystery medicine. The upper arms are extended horizontally and the forearms perpendicularly. The lines begin dancing from east to west, all facing south; at the west end of the room they simultaneously turn, facing north, and dance sidewise to the east. These variations are continued throughout the dance. The two grinders in the south line are soon joined by a third woman, and the man in the middle by the elder brother Bow priest. The two men wear the black breechcloth, supported by a silver belt, the ends of which are embroidered in dark blue, and fall so as to form a kind of short skirt. The young man has a band of yucca around his hair, which is parted in the middle and done up in the usual knot in the back; the elder brother Bow priest has a fluffy eagle plume colored red tied to his forelock. He also wears his war pouch. Both men are adorned with many necklaces.

Every little while the elder brother Bow priest leaves his position in the dance, and approaching the choir and the group of women throws his body forward, growling and gesticulating like a bear; again he

---

[a] In the night ceremony the plumes were held in the left hand.

SHUMAI'KOLI AND SAI'APA GODS IN PLAZA; CIRCLE DANCE

WILLOW DANCE OF 'KO'SHI'KWE (CACTUS FRATERNITY), DIRECTOR IN FOREGROUND BEARING PO'NEPOYANNĚ, SACRED FETISH OF THE FRATERNITY

rejoins the dancers, continuing the growling. After dancing about thirty minutes he orders the old woman guarding the fire to stir up the embers, and at the same time he removes his war pouch and beads, and places them beside the altar. He lays the plume from his head and his two eagle-wing plumes in front of the altar. When the coals are well alive he dances forward and runs his right arm to the elbow into the coals, and, taking a large bunch of corn husks in each hand and lighting them from the coals, he rushes wildly to the choir, scattering the sparks over the nude bodies of the men. Relighting the husks, he goes to all the women, fairly showering them with the sparks. The babies look up in mild wonderment when a spark falls upon them, but no sound comes from the little ones. The men and women are struck over their faces as well as their bodies with the burning husks. Several times during the performance the elder brother Bow priest calls upon his assistant warrior and others to whip him with the burning husks, he at the same time running them over his nude body. An old woman who refuses the elder brother Bow priest's request to whip him with the firebrands, preferring to receive rather than to inflict the punishment, has her face and head pelted by him. This weird scene closes with the elder brother Bow priest's putting the burning husks into his mouth and chewing them. He now procures a rod about 3 feet in length and 1½ inches in diameter and calls upon one of the men to strike him with it, the rod having been first wet with medicine water. Those who anticipate strokes have the entire body bathed with the water. The man on refusing to strike the elder brother Bow priest receives from him a blow across the back, when the man who is struck procures a similar rod and strikes the elder brother Bow priest, who stands erect, extending both arms, and requests the man to strike him across the chest. The rod is used with such force that it breaks into three pieces.

A large bunch of yucca baccata is now brought out by the second warrior, who deals several of the men severe blows, the elder brother Bow priest receiving the stroke of the yucca across his extended right arm, which does not bend from the stroke, although the yucca is held in both hands and much force is used in striking; then across the left arm with the same result, and across the chest. After each blow is given the man holding the yucca places his hand over his mouth and gives an animal-like call. After the yucca is laid away the elder brother Bow priest takes a bear's foot skin from the altar, and drawing it over his right hand he rushes toward his brother warrior and, holding him closely, runs the claws up and down his body; then, returning it to the altar, he resumes his place in the dance, which continues two hours, the dancers stopping every thirty minutes for a rest of a moment or two. After the elder brother Bow priest and his associate warrior cease dancing they don their cotton shirts, trousers, and head-ker-chiefs. The dance continues, however, and the former dancers, minus the warriors, are joined by two young men, two women, and a little girl not over 8 years of age. The young men wear the breechcloth and wreaths of yucca ribbon tied in fanciful knots at the side and passing around the forehead at the edge of the hair, which is parted in the middle. At the same time the male and female novices leave the chamber, guided by an officer, to offer prayers to the Sun Father as he disappears for the night. The men wear pure white cotton clothing; the girl, the ordinary Zuñi dress. The girls who ground the medicine are seated on the north side of the room near the east end. As each woman or girl retires from the dance she puts on her pi'toni.[a]

Two women, one an albino, each bearing a large bowl of water, enter the chamber at sunset and deposit the bowls on the floor near the east end of the room, the bearers of the bowls standing between them and the east wall and facing west. A third woman takes her position between the two water-carriers, and the water is consecrated by the two warriors, who repeat a long prayer, when the medicine grinders, who approach in twos, are baptized, the elder brother Bow priest receiving one, and another warrior the other. Each warrior extends his left arm across the girl's back, placing his left hand upon her left shoulder and his right hand upon the right shoulder. The head is bent while the woman opposite bathes the forelock; the hands and wrists are afterward washed thoroughly. Throughout this cere-mony, which is repeated with all the medicine grinders, the warriors and women repeat scarcely audible prayers. After the baptizing the grinders resume their seats upon the ledge, the two warriors take seats on low stools in front and facing them, and the elder brother Bow priest repeats a litany, which is responded to by the second warrior with "Eh!" (Yes). During the prayer, which seems to be of little interest except to the grinders, women are bringing in vessels of bread, meat stews, sliced melons, and dried peaches. At the conclusion of the litany the elder brother Bow priest offers a grace over the food, when bits of food are gathered from each vessel and placed in a heap before the altar. After all have enjoyed the feast the assembly separates.

Third night. Sixteen members of the Ko'tikili (Mythologic frater-nity) are gathered in a chamber of a dwelling. The walls are intensely white, and a line of cord extends across the room near the west end. Freshly painted masks of the 'Cha'kwena (certain anthropic gods) to be worn in a dance which is to occur in four days are suspended from a line. The masks are covered with a strip of calico, but the long beards appear below the cloth. As usual, this group is interested in

[a] A piece of cotton cloth tied in front and falling over the back. The Zuñi women would as soon appear in public without the pi'toni as a civilized woman would without a dress; but this article must not be worn during certain ceremonies.

the recitation of a story of some great exploit of the Gods of War. At the conclusion of the story the song opens, to the accompaniment of the hide drum, with a low chant, swelling louder and louder as the song continues. Mr Stevenson and the writer linger but a short time here and proceed to the house of the Little Fire fraternity, where a group of men are telling stories and smoking, previous to the convening of the fraternity. One of the men possesses remarkable powers as an orator. His voice is at all times perfectly clear and distinct, though he never raises it above a low tone, and many times drops it to a whisper. The women sit dozing in their end of the room. At 10 o'clock the group scatters, leaving the main body of the room clear. The floor is sprinkled by a man filling his mouth with water and ejecting it, Chinese fashion, over the floor.

Then the sixteen members of the Ko'tikili enter in single file and advance toward the altar; turning, they face south and dance from west to east, then from east to west, and so on, indulging in curious hoots. Twelve dancers carry gourd rattles in the right hand, while the others carry in the same hand food wrapped in corn husks, to be offered to the Kok'ko awa (all the anthropic gods). They all carry large bunches of yucca in their left hands, narrow ribbons of yucca encircle their heads, the hair being parted in the middle, with the usual knot at the back. Dressed deerskins are worn; the limbs are bare, but the feet are covered with moccasins. Each has a tortoise-shell rattle attached to the calf of the right leg immediately below the knee. They dance and sing to the accompaniment of the rattles and drum of skin. One of the chief features of this dance is a graceful movement of the gourd rattles, the dancers waving them around their heads from the right in a circle, at the same time delicately and gracefully shaking and manipulating them. During the dance the members of the Little Fire fraternity remain quiet spectators.

At the close of the dance, at midnight, the dancers take seats on the north side of the room, the ledge having been previously covered with skins and blankets. Each one is supplied with a cigarette, which has been lighted by a member of the Little Fire fraternity, who takes a whiff before handing it to a dancer. The latter smokes once and returns it to the donor, who takes one whiff and returns it to the dancer, who continues to smoke it. When the cigarettes are consumed the dancers approach the altar, each taking a pinch of meal from the basket in front of it, sprinkle the altar and pray, and then return to their seats. The a'kwamosi, carrying a bowl of medicine water, passes to the dancers and gives each a drink of the holy water from a shell. He afterward gives a draft to the members of the Little Fire fraternity, including the women and children. When the visiting dancers leave the houses, the men of the fraternity gather before the altar and repeat

a prayer, at the same time sprinkling the sacred meal.   After the men
are through, the women advance in a body and pray and sprinkle meal
upon the altar.   One mother, holding a naked infant, guides the little
hand to take the meal from the pottery basket before the altar and
sprinkle it.

The women now return to their homes, while the men and the novices sleep, as before, in the ceremonial room.   The meal sprinkled
about the altar is carefully swept away and the mi'wachi are taken out
and the meal blown off the feathers, when they are again placed in
position.

Fourth day.   During the afternoon several men are busy in the
ceremonial room preparing the dry painting, shown in plate CXXVII,
which is some 5 feet in front and south of the altar.   The disk, which
is about 3 feet in diameter, is surrounded by an elevation of 4 or 5
inches, forming a basin.   The wall, which symbolizes the galaxy, is of
ordinary sand, and when it is perfectly smooth, the red, white, and
black varieties are sprinkled over the ground color.   The red and
white sands are ground from the red and white sandstone; the black
is charcoal.

Previous to the evening ceremony the scene is weird.   The candles
have not yet been lighted, and the tawny faces of the Indians are first
in light, then in shadow, according to the freak of the fire that burns
in the quaint fireplace.   A circle of men, with two in the center, sit
in the middle of the floor.   The north and south ledges are filled with
men.   A few women in half-reclining positions are in their end of the
room apparently tired out.   The novices occupy their former positions.   Another young girl, who has not appeared on the previous
occasions, sits sleeping to the right of the juvenile novice.   The flute
player is in position behind the altar.   The elder brother Bow priest
enters and takes his seat in the center of the circle, and all of this
group, except five, smoke cigarettes.   Though constant smoking is
indulged in, there is but little conversation, which is carried on in a
very low tone.   The men in the circle are busy splitting yucca and
preparing wreaths, wristlets, armlets, and garters.   While this work
is in progress, the elder brother Bow priest leaves his position, takes
a bowl of the medicine prepared the previous afternoon, and passing through the crowd gives each person a portion, each one being
provided with bits of corn husk in which to place the medicine.
Having some of the medicine left after all are helped, he again passes
around and deals out the remainder, each one receiving it in a pouch
of dressed deerskin.[a]   The sunflower powder, which is now distributed
by the elder brother Bow priest to male members only, is used for a

---

[a] This medicine is taken for a variety of maladies.   It is placed in the mouth and ejected, generally
on the palm of the hand, and the hand is then rubbed over the afflicted part of the body.   It is
sometimes mixed with a little water and drunk.

number of purposes. It is sprinkled upon personators of the gods, that they may aid the one using the medicine to have a brave heart; and when a man has a distance to go he takes a bit of the flower medicine into his mouth and spits it out, that he may follow the right road, meet no enemies, be well received by all peoples whom he may visit, and be preserved from all accident and ill health during his journey.

On the completion of the yucca adornments they are carried by the men who prepare them and placed on the novices where they sit. After the two young men novices are adorned with the yucca, they join the group in the center of the room and have their nude bodies washed in a deep red paint. The boy and the old man are painted in the same manner. The young girl has her face, hands, and arms, and her feet and legs to the knees, washed with the red paint, after which the men have the scalp knot painted with thick white paint on each breast, scapula, and knee in as heavy a line as the forefinger can carry. The girl has two bands of white around each arm, several inches apart, and the scalp knot is painted between the lines on the top of the arm. The five novices now have their chins, upper lips, and eyebrows painted white and covered with down from the breast of the hawk. A circle of white paint is also made on the top of the head, to which the down is attached. The down decoration is symbolic of clouds. Although the tickling of the feathers must be torture, the novices never touch the face after the feathers are put on. The novices now return to their seats and the male members of the fraternity proceed to prepare for the ceremony, each man decorating himself after first donning a black woven breechcloth. They adopt various designs in white paint, representing the eagle, the chaparral cock, the bear, the cougar, the badger, the white wolf, and the coyote. The white wolf is represented by the elder brother Bow priest and the second warrior, whose entire bodies are covered with white paint. Two little boys represent the heavens. The Zuñi coil or seal is painted in red on the palms of the hands of the two boys, as here represented, ▣'. After the men complete their decorations the women come forward and paint in white their hands and arms to the elbow and their feet and legs to the knee. The choir on this occasion, which sits as usual on the south side of the room, is composed of both sexes, the women holding two eagle wing plumes in the left hand and gourd rattles in the right; the men also have rattles.

The a'kwamosi and pe'kwin sit each side of the altar upon low stools, while the warriors resume their positions as protectors of the altar. The flute player occupies his assigned position behind the altar. The preparation of the medicine water is begun, and when completed each member of the choir takes a drink from a shell dipped into the bowl.

During the early part of the ceremony the room gradually becomes filled. All those belonging to the fraternity who have any ailment whatever avail themselves of this opportunity to be cured. After the medicine water is passed around, two characters representing the chaparral cock, each holding an eagle-wing feather in each hand, leave the choir and hop and skip birdlike to the altar; facing it, they extend their hands outward and then draw them back, keeping the hands and plumes in line, their movements being very graceful. In a few moments they skip to the fireplace, and each lifts ashes with his plumes, and returning to the altar they sprinkle it with the ashes. Again lifting the ashes, they skip to the outer door, which is on the south side of the room, and throw the ashes out. Gathering more ashes, they throw them to the north of the room, and continue the same operation for the west, south, and east. Returning to the altar, they dance for a while, and then repeat the gathering and sprinkling of ashes toward the four regions; and returning to the outer entrance they repeat the sprinkling. Once more gathering ashes, they place them in a little heap in front of the altar by the food which was deposited previous to the afternoon meal. Each time the ashes are thrown (which is for physical purification) the men exclaim, "Sh....,..u...._u'."

These men return to their positions in the choir, and the fraternity fathers of two of the novices, the spirits of the Cougar and Bear being present in their bodies, appear on all fours and jump around the altar, growling in the most savage manner. In a short time they are joined by two others bearing the spirits of the Badger and the White Wolf, and after indulging in extravaganza before the altar, invoking the continued presence of the Beast Gods, each one takes a novice in charge. The little boy's fraternity father carries him upon his back, the child's feet dangling. The other novices are led by their instructors, who dash wildly about among the people. When first leading the novices the theurgists maintain an upright position, but they growl and make hideous noises; afterward they throw themselves and the novices almost bodily on the floor, and in this way they approach an invalid and suck at some spot upon the body. The theurgists are given the power through the Beast Gods to see into the body and detect disease and bring it forth, that they may see with the physical eye what they have already seen with the mind's eye. It is but the work of an instant. Suddenly the doctor raises himself and with the palm of his right hand receives from his mouth what he is supposed to have sucked from the body of the invalid. The legerdemain is perfect. Amid a wild noise, and between a shout and a growl, the hand is thrown around the head and the supposed extracted material is deposited in a bowl which is guarded by an aged woman, who has a vase of water and a gourd by her side, so that she can give water to those who need it. The people seem to believe implicitly in this humbuggery.

After the novices are fairly instructed they, the small boy excepted,[a] make awkward attempts at healing the sick.

As all those forming the choir are members of the order of Mystery medicine, they take turns in leaving their places to practice on the sick. The women, though far less graceful than the men, appear wilder; they cry out louder and gesticulate more vehemently. One very old woman with perfectly white hair, known as the Great Mother of the fraternity, seems wilder than any of the men.

After a time a theurgist, whose body is inhabited by the spirit of the Cougar, advances on all fours to the altar and taking his mi'li from the altar raises and lowers it and then moves it sidewise, invoking the Beast Gods to give him power as their agent; then he backs down the long room, never taking his eyes off the mi'li, which he holds upward before his face, moving it to and fro. He is followed by men in whose bodies the Bear, Badger, and Wolf are spiritually present, the former carrying the little novice on his back, as before. They leave the house to visit the ceremonial chamber of the U'huhukwe (Eagle down fraternity), which is also holding a meeting.

After each member of the choir has had a turn in healing Nai'uchi, the elder brother Bow priest comes to the floor as the White Wolf, and he is by far the most graceful man who appears. He wears his warrior plume wand attached to the crown of his head and extending backward, and the inevitable fluffy eagle feather, colored red, attached to his forelock. The war pouch worn earlier in the evening has been removed. He moves about in a beautiful, graceful way, sucking at the shoulders, limbs, or feet of the invalids. Several others perform after the elder brother Bow priest takes his seat by the altar.

After the party returns from visiting the U'huhukwe the elder brother Bow priest removes the large bowl from the side of the old woman, brings it to the altar, and waves it in a circle; then he carries it from the house and empties the contents in an excavation in the earth which has been made for the purpose near by and carefully fills the excavation. After the removal of the bowl, a girl of 12, one of 6 years, and a little boy whose body is painted to represent the heavens, form in file and dance. The eldest girl is on the north end, the younger girl on the south, and the boy between. They dance up and down sidewise, first facing south, then north, turning at each end of the room. At the same time the elder brother Bow priest dances before the altar, dipping his eagle plumes into the medicine water and sprinkling the altar by striking the plumes in the manner before described. Going to the cardinal points, he sprinkles in the same way north, west, south, and east; he is then joined by a man representing the Bear, when the

---

[a] Members of Mystery medicine must have arrived at years of discretion before they are instructed in healing.

two repeat the sprinkling of the altar and the four regions. Returning to the altar, they dance before it for a long time, throwing their
eagle plumes out and then drawing them in by a movement of the
shoulder. At times each runs an arm through the other's, making
the right hand of one appear to be the left hand of the other. This
causes great amusement among the people, particularly when each
one, showing evidence of weariness, desires that the other should act
as his support. This is the only exhibition of mirth throughout the
entire ceremonial. The dance closes at dawn with the two repeating
the sprinkling of the four regions with the medicine water, after
which the elder brother Bow priest, as protector of the altar, resumes
his seat by it and the other returns to the choir. The women go
outside the house to sprinkle meal to the rising sun. The candles
are now extinguished so that the first light of day may be seen
through the eastern window, and first the men and afterward the
women assemble before the altar to offer their prayers to the approaching Sun Father; and as the first light comes into the room the
novices step within the circle of the sand painting. Their feet and
limbs are bathed with the sands, and this most attractive painting is
destroyed. A long prayer is repeated by all as the novices stand
within the circle. They remain standing while medicine water is
administered, first to those immediately before the altar and afterward
to the invalids scattered throughout the room. The group in front
of the altar now disperses, each person taking his mi'li from it.
The medicine stones forming the wings and tail of the bird in the dry
painting are gathered from the sand by their owners, and the novices
are seated and receive their mi'wachi and prayer plumes with the
same ceremony as described in Great Fire fraternity. Later in the
day the novices, in company with their fraternity fathers, go a distance from the village and plant the prayer plumes given them by the
fraternity.

SUN DANCE OF THE PE'SHÄᵀSILO'KWE (CIMEX FRATERNITY)

The Zuñis are filled with the wildest superstitions concerning this
ceremonial, which is celebrated once in four years by the Little Fire
and the Cimex fraternities alternately in the month of March. It is
believed that the original fire was the gift of the Sun Father, the
wood being stacked high over an excavation by the Hopi Indians, just
as is done at the present time, and lighted by the sun's rays. The
writer has observed several sun dances of the Little Fire and Cimex
fraternities. The one described occurred in March, 1904.

The fraternity convenes on the 2d of March and holds a four nights'
ceremonial similar to the one described in the preceding pages relating to the Little Fire fraternity. On the third day of the meeting
ten men bring on their backs from the woods south of Zuñi each

a load of ai'iko (juniper, species not yet identified), and deposit it in the ceremonial chamber, where it remains until the rising of the morning star, at which time it is carried to the Si'aa' te'wita. A circular excavation about 2½ feet in diameter is made, and a smaller one is dug in the center of this, in which prayer plumes and medicine are deposited. These are covered with earth, and the wood is piled in and over the excavation until it reaches the roof of the He'iwa (North) ki'wi᷾sinĕ, which stands on the north side of the plaza. The pile is lighted and allowed to burn until only coals remain, when two members of the Cimex fraternity rake the coals out of the bed, scatter them over a considerable surface, and beat them with long poles about 4 inches in diameter until they are broken into small pieces. The coals which have lost the red color are gathered in a mound over the excavation with wooden shovels; the finer coals are next brushed to the mound with a bunch of juniper twigs, and finally the shovels are used to pack the mound into a symmetrical form. The plaza is then swept to make ready for the arrival of the fraternity, and it is not long before the dancers appear, led by a woman wearing an ordinary black dress with a mi'ha (sacred embroidered blanket) fastened close about her neck. She also wears a number of necklaces and a pair of fine white deerskin moccasins with black soles, and she carries in her right hand a mi'li and in her left a meal basket. She is followed by a man whom the writer terms the sprinkler. He wears a white cotton shirt and an embroidered kilt ornamented with a band of blue-green, at each end of which a game of sho'liwe [a] is painted. The band symbolizes the vegetation of the world. The kilt is held on with an embroidered sash and a woman's red belt fastened at the right side. He also wears blue knit leggings, tied below the knee with blue yarn, which hangs in tassels and is ornamented with sleigh bells, and dance moccasins. In addition to the many necklaces he wears a hank of blue yarn. A bunch of yellow and green parrot plumes is attached to the forelock, and a wand, composed of long parrot-tail feathers and two fluffy eagle plumes with an aigret of yellow parrot plumes at the base, the whole finished off with long streamers of red and green ribbons, is attached upright to the back of the head. The hair hangs loosely down the back. The other male dancers wear white embroidered kilts with white fringed sashes and women's red belts fastened at the right side and fox skins pendent at the back. The feet and legs are bare. A hank of black or blue yarn is tied around the right wrist and a bow wristlet is on the left. Yarn is also tied around the throat in addition to the beads, and an eagle-tail plume is suspended to the yarn at the back of the neck. They wear wreaths of yucca ribbon tied in fanciful bows or knots at each side of the head. There is a daub of yellow paint on each scapula,

---

[a] See Games.

each arm below the shoulder, and each breast. Each one carries a large, unpainted gourd rattle in the right hand and two eagle-wing plumes and a corn-husk package of meal in the left. The two novices carry each a blanket, one red and one black, gifts from their fraternity fathers, rolled into as small a package as possible, and quantities of prayer plumes. The women wear the ordinary black dress, with a white blanket bordered in red and blue fastened over the shoulders. Their feet and limbs are also bare. Each has a fluffy eagle plume, colored red, tied to the forelock. They wear turquoise earrings and many necklaces, and they also carry two eagle-wing feathers and a corn-husk package of meal in the left hand; they have nothing in the right.

The dancers go direct from the ceremonial chamber to the plaza in single file, the female leader being immediately before the sprinkler. The men sing and shake their rattles. They dance in a circle around the coal bed. Then the sprinkler approaches the coals and sprinkles them with the medicine water from the bowl. A feather wand is used for the sprinkling.[a] Returning to the line of dancers he sprinkles the one next to him, and the man leaves the line and dances about the fire, performing animal-like antics, and sprinkling the meal from his corn-husk package over the coals, he jumps into them and dances a moment or two. He returns to the line and the sprinkler repeats the ceremony over the coals and then sprinkles the next dancer, who repeats the ceremony of the former. None seem more enthusiastic or more ready to jump into the coals than the two young novices. There is no special time for remaining in the burning bed. Some are able to endure it much longer than others. The women do not remain in the fire so long as the men. After all the dancers have passed through the fire they retire from the plaza to the ceremonial chamber.

To those who had not before observed this ceremony it would still appear as remarkable, but the writer finds it quite different from those previously observed. There is a waning of enthusiasm and the fire is not so great. On previous occasions the men ran their arms into the glowing coals in addition to dancing in them. Altogether the scene in former years was more weird and exciting.

Eight bowls containing medicine prepared from yarrow (Achillea millefolium) stand in line before the altar in the ceremonial chamber. The dancers are bathed in the medicine before they go to the plaza. The first four in the line of dancers use the medicine from the four bowls on the north side and the next four from those on the south, the line of dancers alternating in this way before going to the plaza. The bathing is repeated previous to each visit to the plaza to prevent burning.

The Zuñi declare that elaborate exhibitions of jugglery occurred within the memory of some of the aged men. Men were apparently butchered limb by limb, the members being cast into the fire. Sometimes the throat only was cut. The butchered man was gathered in a mi'ha and carried to He'iwa ki'wiᵗsinĕ and the mi'ha dropped through the hatchway, when the man rose in perfect condition. "One who passes through this ordeal never dies, but lives to old age to sleep to awake in Ko'thluwala'wa" (abiding place of the Council of the Gods). An aged salt-gatherer from Hopi, who passed through Zuñi, described to the writer some of the scenes with the fire in his own village, declaring that he himself had been cut to pieces and cast into the fire.

There are five men of this fraternity who have, in addition to the medicine practices observed by the fraternity, a form known only to themselves that came from the Snake fraternity of the Hopi Indians, which originally comprised four orders—Mystery medicine, Snake, Jugglery, and the Dead. The director of the first order, becoming ill some years since, determined that after his death this medicine should not remain in the Hopi land, where disputes were constantly arising between the Navahos and Hopis as to who possessed the most valuable medicine. The director declared that his medicine was too valuable and dear to him to be the subject of dispute, and he sent his younger nephew to Zuñi to bring to him at once his elder nephew, who had gone thither many years before, at the time of a famine in the Hopi country, and, marrying a Zuñi woman, had remained at that pueblo. On appearing before his uncle the elder nephew was instructed in the secrets of the medicine, and the medicine bags, fetishes, etc., were given to him, with instructions from the uncle to carry all to Zuñi and to form a small fraternity, or an order in a fraternity. The nephew remained with the Hopis four days after his uncle's death and then returned to Zuñi. He waited two years before saying anything of the secrets told him, and then, being a member of the Mystery medicine of the Little Fire fraternity of Zuñi, he invited four of his fellows to meet at his home, where he organized the order. The four were fully initiated, and he became the director of this special body of medicine men.

This order extracts disease inflicted by witchcraft, but the mode followed is in some respects different from that observed by the orders of Mystery medicine of the Zuñis. While the latter draw out disease by sucking, first bringing the cause of the disease to the surface by penetrating the flesh with the eye or by placing pinches of meal over the body praying that the trouble will be located by a meal spot, the Hopi order locates the cause of disease by the sense of touch after placing meal spots over the body, and the doctor has within himself the power of healing—he is therefore a shaman and not a theurgist. He uses his hands altogether in drawing material from the body. There is a great desire on the part of other members of the Little

Fire fraternity to join the Hopi order, but the director refuses all increase of membership, declaring it to have been the wish of his uncle to keep his secrets confined to a few. The paraphernalia belonging to this order remained for a long time in the home of the director, but during a visit of the writer to Zuñi it was removed to the home of his fraternity child of the Little Fire fraternity, who is a woman and the wife of a Mexican captured (when a child) by the Zuñis and afterward adopted into the tribe.[a] When an invalid desires the presence of a shaman of the Hopi order, he wraps meal in a corn husk and a member of the family is dispatched with it, with a request for the doctor to visit the invalid. The shaman, like the theurgist, is usually paid after each visit with calico, cotton, or food, according to the wealth of the family, since it is always understood that these doctors expect proper compensation for their services.

Some time ago reports came to Zuñi that a man of the Snake fraternity at Mŭrshŏng'nuvi intended creating an order such as the one described, or, rather, reestablishing it, and the Zuñi director hastened to Mŭrshŏng'nuvi, but the old man declared that he had had no such intention. He said: " I know well that the deceased director did not intend that anyone should continue the order among the Hopi, and we should be afraid to do so."

Considerable jealousy is felt by the Zuñis over the feats performed by the Hopi. A theurgist of the Little Fire fraternity, referring to the Hopi jugglers, declared them to be great. He said:

Once, when a friend and I were visiting Walpi, a member of the order of Jugglery of the Snake fraternity called to us to give him a head-kerchief. My friend handed his to the man, who first held it at diagonal corners; then he pulled it, first through one hand and then through the other, beginning each time midway of the head-kerchief, on the bias. He then pressed it to his breast and presently threw down two snakes, which at once moved about. The head-kerchief was nowhere to be seen. He secured the snakes, and, pressing them to his breast, the head-kerchief soon reappeared.

ORDER OF PA'YATÄMU OF THE LITTLE FIRE FRATERNITY

Though the present Zuñis, as a class, believe the Little Fire fraternity to have originated with the Hopis and to have been introduced by them into the A'shiwi ritual, they do not credit the order of Pa'yatämu of this fraternity as coming from the Hopi Indians; yet the two peoples' ideas of the god of music are so similar that it is more than probable that he has been borrowed by one or the other. The Zuñi legend regarding the origin of the order of Pa'yatämu is as follows:

The gods of war while strolling about the country some 3 miles east of Zuñi, were attracted by very sweet music and they proceeded to learn its source. On approaching the mesa Shun'te'kĭaya they discovered that the music issued from a spring (bearing the same name as the mesa; and also A'mitolan te'poula, rainbow covering

[a] This Mexican is not allowed to observe the masked dances, but they occur in his house (when he must absent himself), since he has left the home of the mother-in-law for a residence of his own.

entrance) at the base of the mountain. Here they found Pa'yatämu^a playing on his flute, while eight beautiful maidens ground corn and sang.

On their return to the village the Gods of War told of their visit to Pa'yatämu and of his beautiful music, and when the Little Fire fraternity was preparing for a ceremonial the director dispatched a member of the fraternity for Pa'yatämu requesting that he come and play his flute while their maidens ground medicine. The god complied with the request, and remained four days and nights, accompanying on his flute the maidens in their songs as they ground. On the fifth morning he passed his flute to the lips of those present that the sacred breath might be drawn from the flute, and then he departed for his home at Shun'te'kĭaya.

Again, when the Corn maidens were to dance, a warrior and another member of the Little Fire fraternity were sent to ask Pa'yatämu to be present for the occasion. He arrived the night previous to the dance and went at once to the ceremonial chamber of the fraternity, where he remained until morning. At sunrise he accompanied a warrior of the fraternity to Si'aa' te'wita and took his seat on the north side of the häm'pone (pavilion) erected for the dancers and just outside of it to the east, a position similar to the one occupied by him when he observed the Corn maidens dance the first time in I'tiwanna.^b Pa'yatämu played for a portion of the dances, which were called sho'kowe (name of Pa'yatämu's flute), to distinguish them from those dances when Pa'yatämu did not play. Before leaving I'tiwanna, he presented his flute to a member of the fraternity, and initiated him into the secret of playing upon it. The god of music never again appeared to the fraternity. This man in turn initiated nine other members, forming an order which he named Pa'yatämu, after the god, and himself became the director of the order. A flute was fashioned after the one presented by Pa'yatämu for each member of the new order.

The novice receives from his fraternity father a flute and the te'na^tsäli, mixture of the order. The order plays at the time of the ^tHla'hewe ceremonial (see page 180). Many of the prayer plumes offered to Pa'yatämu are much longer than those commonly offered to the gods, and are very attractive (see plate CXXVIII).

^tKo'shi'kwe (Cactus Fraternity)

Membership in the ^tKo'shi'kwe is confined to males. A man who kills an enemy but does not take the scalp, and one cured of a wound

---

^a Pa'yatämu causes flowers, especially the te'na^tsäli, to bloom with the music of his flute, and with it he calls together the butterflies of the world. The te'na^tsäli, a plant supposed to bear blossoms of the colors of the six regions, is collected once in four years by those specially designated for the purpose. Two prayer plumes to the sun and moon, two to Pa'yatämu, and two to te'na^tsäli are made by each collector and deposited just previous to collecting the plant. The A'shiwanni and the esoteric fraternities, except the Bow priesthood and Cactus, have both the root and flowers of the te'na^tsäli. It is claimed by the directors of the order of Pa'yatämu of the Little Fire and Cimex fraternities that they combine with the flowers of the te'na^tsäli the hearts of butterflies and dragon flies. This is known as the sun medicine. The te'na^tsäli is ground in the fraternity chamber amid great ceremony. All the flutes belonging to the order are played, while the musicians stand before the altar. The te'na^tsäli is deposited in a large shell, which stands on the cloud symbol of meal at the altar, and crushed with a smaller shell by the director of the order of Pa'yatämu.

The te'na^tsäli is always used by the Hunters fraternity in connection with their ceremonial hunt, but they do not possess the hearts of the butterflies and dragon flies. The powdered flowers and root of the te'na^tsäli are administered in small quantities to the male members of the fraternities. No woman must have this powder, as, if she were married, she would be unfaithful to her husband; if unmarried, she would be filled with amorous desires.

The same powder is taken into the mouth and spit out upon the body for psychic purification, and it is also spit out when one is traveling to insure following the right course.

^b See p. 48.

from arrow, bullet, or dog bite, is eligible for membership in the
ꞌKoꞌshiꞌkwe. If a man is struck by a flying bit of cactus during an
outdoor ceremony and is caught as he runs off, he joins the fraternity.
A member of the Cactus fraternity can not join the Aꞌpiꞌꞌläshiwanni
(Bow priesthood) until he has taken four scalps.

A shrine of the Cactus fraternity is in an arched cave in the
western wall of Toꞌwa yälꞌlännĕ (Corn mountain). Great numbers
of teꞌlikịnawe (prayer plumes) are deposited here by the fraternity;
and some distance below this shrine is a shelf containing a large bed
of cactus (Opuntia arborescens). This entire bed is the property
of the Cactus fraternity, and it is never touched except by order of
the director of the fraternity. A single plant about 2½ feet high,
which is isolated from the others and very symmetrical, is a most
important object to the fraternity. Offerings are deposited at the
base of this plant and upon it when cactus is to be collected by the
fraternity.

When a boy has been restored to health by a member of this fraternity his father goes to the man who cured him, carrying sacred meal in
his right hand, which he places in the left hand of the other. If a man
is cured, he goes himself, saying: "I wish to join the ꞌKoꞌshiꞌkwe."
The fourth day after the request has been made the man appealed to
prepares four prayer plumes of feathers of the birds of the six regions
and the eagle and turkey plumes as offerings to the deceased members
of the fraternity. The same night he visits the house of the novice and
presents the prayer plumes, saying: "My child, deposit these to the
north, west, south, and east, to the deceased ꞌKoꞌshiꞌkwe." The fraternity convenes the fifth day after the prayer plumes are given to
the novice. Continence is observed from the time the plumes are
given until the fifth day following the closing ceremonies. Should
continence be broken, the flesh would become filled with cactus needles
and the offender would die.

The ceremonial of initiation here described occurred in October,
1896. The fraternity meet in the morning, and the members proceed
to prepare prayer plumes to be offered to the Gods of War and the
Kuꞌpĭshtaya (lightning-makers), that they will intercede with the uꞌwan-
nami (rain-makers) to send rains upon Zuñi. The moꞌsona (director)
prepares, in addition to these plumes, four others and a laꞌshowannĕ
with a long string of cotton cord, to which a bit of turquoise is strung.
The deputy carries the plumes to the cactus bed at Corn mountain
and winds the string attached to the laꞌshowannĕ about the large
cactus plant which stands alone; the string is so delicately woven
over the plant that it appears like a web. He plants at the base of
the cactus the plumes which he carries, and also deposits food near
the plant to the deceased officers of the fraternity. He then cuts

SCALP HOUSE

SCALP POLE IN CENTER OF PLAZA

a small cactus, brings it home in his left hand, and gives it to the director, who places it at the hatchway on the roof of the ceremonial chamber. The tablet altar is erected in the afternoon. The fraternity tell stories, chat, and smoke (they do not sing or dance) until midnight, when they retire. No woman must be touched, spoken to, or even looked upon during the ceremonial. When a woman carries food to the chamber she stamps upon the roof and disappears before anyone ascends to receive the food. There is a little singing and dancing on the second day, both in the morning and the afternoon, and the story-telling and smoking is repeated until midnight, when all retire. They are all up at sunrise, and one of the members is at once dispatched on horseback to a small canyon northeast of Zuñi to collect long willow switches for the ceremonial. Before the willows are cut prayers are offered and meal sprinkled over them. The director prepares a laʹshowannĕ and then cuts yucca glauca leaves into bits about the size of a match and divides all of the pieces except two between five men. A sixth man, who is designated as the director of the other five, receives the laʹshowannĕ and the two extra pieces of yucca, which indicates that he is to collect a cactus plant to be used by the officers of the fraternity and a piece of cactus for the novice. They start at once for Corn mountain, where the director of the party attaches the laʹshowannĕ to the large cactus plant and all sprinkle the plant with meal and pray for rain. The cactus to be used in the ceremonial is now collected. The director cuts but two pieces—the plant which is to be used by the officers and a small piece for the novice. The others count their bits of yucca, each one cutting as many pieces of cactus as the yucca indicates. Each man covers his pile of cactus with cedar branches, wraps it with rope, and carries it home on his back. At a point east of Zuñi, where the Shumaiʹkoli gods and their warriors are supposed to have rested on their return from their visit to Zuñi (see p. 411), the willow and cactus-bearers are met by the director, his deputy, warrior, the novice, and his fraternity father, who stop within 50 yards of the willow and cactus-bearers, who stand abreast and begin their song as soon as the others are near; the others are also in line, and all but the novice sing. The two parties sing different songs. Both sides advance very slowly, and when they meet in a small "wash" all sit down and the director of the cactus party pulls out the piece of cactus for the novice and ejects medicine from his mouth over it; all then rise and come out of the "wash." The novice places his left foot on a deserted anthill and his right foot before him on the ground, while the warrior stands in front of him and the others group a little distance behind. His head is turned to the south and his left shoulder, which has been bared of the shirt sleeve, is raised as high as possible; the arms hang.

The elder brother Bow priest, who is one of the warriors of the fraternity, takes the cactus in his right hand and passes in a circle around the novice; returning to the north side of him, he stops, faces north, and calls upon the Ku'pïshtaya of the North to be present and make the boy's heart good and brave and to give long life. Again he encircles the novice, passing from left to right, and facing the west repeats the same call upon Ku'pïshtaya. Passing around the novice once more, he halts at the south and makes the prayer; passing around him again, he halts at the east and prays. Another circle is made and he halts at the west and gives the call upon the Ku'pïshtaya of the Zenith. Again passing around, he halts at the south and calls upon the Ku'pïshtaya of the Nadir. The novice does not change his position during this time. The warrior now strikes the novice across the left shoulder and throws on the ground to his left such of the cactus as remains, and then joins the group. The fraternity father helps the novice on with his shirt sleeve, and all proceed in file to the village. The director of the fraternity leads, followed by his deputy, warrior, fraternity father, novice, director of cactus collectors, and others. On reaching the village the director of cactus collectors secures six archaic stone knives belonging to the Shi'wanni of the West and places them in couples before the altar of the 'Ko'shi'kwe. When the others reach the ceremonial chamber the fraternity father takes from a basket tray before the altar and hands to the novice a prayer plume made by himself, which is in length equal to the distance from the inner side of the elbow to the tip of the thumb. This is an offering to the Gods of War. The cactus-bearers lay each piece of cactus separately on a bench placed for the purpose in the northeast end of the chamber. The two extra pieces of cactus and the long willows are placed north of the altar, and all but the novice exchange their clothing for the black woven breechcloth. The novice sits on the north side of the room, with his fraternity father to his right. The choir group at the south side with rattles and a drum made of wood covered with hide; the 'Ko'shi'kwe do not possess a pottery drum. The pe'kwïn takes his seat on the south side of the altar and before it and proceeds to consecrate medicine water, a member of the fraternity having placed a vase of water and gourd by him. As soon as the pe'kwïn lifts a gourd of water to empty it into the medicine bowl, the choir begins singing to the accompaniment of the rattle and drum, and the warrior standing before the altar whirls the rhombus. The songs are addressed to the Ku'pïshtaya and his pe'kwïn, 'Si'kïahaya, and the deceased A'pi''läshiwanni (Bow priesthood), that the fraternity may be able to use the cactus without injury. Six small stones are then dropped separately into the water.

At the conclusion of the consecration of the water the warrior ceases to whirl the rhombus, but the music continues. The deputy rises and takes a bunch of willows (the willows are 10 or 12 feet long) in his left hand and a piece of the cactus which was placed beside them in his right. The director also takes a bunch of the willows in his left hand and the other piece of cactus in his right. The elder brother Bow priest and another warrior take willows in both hands and the four then dance. The novice now removes his clothes, puts on a black woven breechcloth, and stands before his fraternity father, who with a hand on each shoulder moves first one and then the other slightly forward, while the novice is continually moving his prayer plume up and down. After dancing a while the four officers stand before the boy and pray for rain, for a good heart, and for the health of the novice. The director then places the switches and cactus before the novice's mouth, shoulders, head, and heart, with a prayer that his heart may be pure. The prayer and placing of the willows are repeated by the other officers; then all the members take either cactus or switches, or both, and repeat this ceremony with the novice. Some one then takes the place of the fraternity father in holding the novice's shoulders while the former repeats the ceremony with the cactus and willows. The director now takes the two pieces of cactus[a] in each hand and gives them to the novice, who dances around with the cactus, running it under his arms and about his body. There is no need for medicine on the body now, as the medicine was put on his cactus at the time it was collected. The novice dances all alone for about half an hour and then resumes his seat on the left of the fraternity father. The fraternity now enjoys a repast and a smoke, and the ceremonies are thus ended for the day.

At early dawn all but the leader of the song and his alternate and the fraternity father and the novice go to the well, where they make a small fire and heat water, and after washing their heads in yucca suds bathe their entire bodies. The novice accompanies his fraternity father to his house, where water is heated and the fraternity father washes his own and the novice's head in yucca suds and bathes his own and the novice's body. The wife may heat the water, but the man and wife do not speak to each other, and the man does not look at his wife. The leader of the song and his alternate remain in the ceremonial chamber to prepare medicine. They afterward heat water in the fireplace and bathe without leaving the chamber. On the return of the fraternity to the ceremonial chamber they chew native squash seeds, the blossoms of which have been dried in dark rooms, and seeds of a burr (not yet classified), and eject the mixture into the palms of the hands and rub their bodies to prevent injury from the cactus. All, including the fraternity father and novice, now prepare for the dance. They wear the native black woven breechcloth, a yucca wreath arranged around the head, and a fluffy eagle plume tied to the forelock;

---

a The cactus is always soaked in water for a short time before using.

their feet are bare. Bunches of willows are carried in each hand by all except the director, who carries a po'nepoyannĕ[a] belonging to the A'pi''läshiwanni and leads the others to Si'aa' te'wita. They proceed in file, waving the long willows gracefully as they move with slow, measured steps, chanting in low tones their prayers to the new day, while the drummer beats lightly upon the drum. The scene is most impressive. They reach the plaza just as the sun rises above the horizon; after forming an ellipse and dancing twice around, the director turns his face inward, which is the signal for all to do likewise. They cease moving and the director steps within the circle, and holding his po'nepoyannĕ upward asks that his people may have good health, that their hearts may be pure, and that they may so please the gods that all good may come to them and to all peoples. They then leave the plaza as they came.

After breakfasting in the ceremonial chamber they prepare for a second visit to the plaza. The bodies are painted white with kaolin, which contains the mixture of the chewed squash blossoms and seeds and the burr seeds, this medicine is the property of the Gods of War. The elder brother Bow priest has the upper portion of his face colored black, the portion below the upper lip painted white and dotted over with hawk down, symbolizing clouds; a bit of the down is stuck on the end of the nose. The others have their faces painted a brownish red, with a line of micaceous hematite across the face, under the eyes, and a spot of the same on each cheek. All wear the breechcloth and a belt, from which falls a deep fringe of goat's wool, with here and there an eagle plume attached, and a fox skin. Pendent at the back leather armlets, elaborate necklaces, hanks of blue yarn, with sleigh bells attached, tied around the leg below the knee, and moccasins. The hair is flowing and tied at the nape of the neck with red ribbons or garters. A yucca wreath is worn and a fluffy eagle plume colored red is attached to the forelock. The two warriors wear their war pouches. While the others are completing their dress, the leader of the dances, whose place is always midway of the line, and his fellow sit by the bench of cactus and eject the mixture of squash blossoms and seeds over each piece, and rub the cactus one way repeatedly with long fluffy eagle plumes, afterward sprinkling bits of hawk down over it. When the cactus is all prepared the pe'kwĭn of the fraternity goes to the bench, and the leader of the dances takes a piece of cactus in each hand and places them in the hands of the pe'kwĭn. He gives two pieces of cactus to another officer and his alternate gives two pieces to each warrior, the officers also carrying willows. Each of the other members carries a bunch of willows, while the director, who precedes the fraternity, bears the po'nepoyannĕ (see plate CXXIX), they all go to the plaza through the eastern

---

[a] See p. 598, note a.

covered way in the manner heretofore described. They pass around by the east side to the north, and after they dance around twice they stand in an ellipse and dance for a time. Then while they step very slowly a warrior runs to the West. The other warrior (elder brother Bow priest), following him, strikes him over the left shoulder. The director runs to the South and the deputy follows him, hitting him over the left shoulder. Then the elder brother Bow priest runs to the East, the other warrior following and striking him over the left shoulder. The deputy then runs in a circle indicating the Zenith and the director strikes him on the left shoulder, and the warrior runs in a circle indicating the Nadir and the elder brother Bow priest strikes him on the left shoulder. They then join the dancers.

There are four dances in the plaza after the sunrise dance; at the close of each dance the fraternity retire to their ceremonial chamber. Cactus is carried in the first three dances by the four officers only, but the willows are dispensed with for the fourth dance, and all carry large pieces of cactus in each hand. The mixture of squash blossoms and seeds is taken into the mouth of each member before he leaves the ceremonial chamber. At times the dancers leave the circle and use the cactus right and left, and all so unfortunate as to be near enough to be struck have no doubt as to its effect.[a] It is observed that when members strike one another they usually run the cactus one way, and it is always run through the mouth in the same manner. There are some exciting scenes, especially when the two warriors leave the plaza and return with huge pieces of the plant and enter into bouts with it, each one vying with the other in his exhibition of indifference to the pain inflicted by the other. The dancing and fighting with cactus in the plaza continues until after sunset, when the fraternity return to their chamber, where they enjoy a repast. After smoking and chatting for a time, they dance again and fight with cactus in the ceremonial chamber until sunrise. At this time the fraternity father hands a corn husk to the novice and leads him to a painting which was made on the floor in front of the altar before sunset the previous day.[b] The novice steps upon the painting, with his face to the altar, but in a moment he faces the east, and then as quickly as possible turns around on the painting four times, and stepping outside the painting stoops and hunts out the grains of corn, depositing them in the corn husk. Then the deputy administers medicine water, the director at

---

[a] When the cactus breaks off in the outdoor dance the members note the circumstance, and if it strikes a man or boy, the member catches him, if possible, and he is led to the ceremonial chamber, where he is painted and dressed like the others and comes out in the next dance. He carries switches in the dance, accompanies the party when the cactus and willows are buried, and plants the prayer plumes given him by the man who caught him and who becomes his fraternity father, but he may not use cactus until he is fully initiated.

[b] The painting is a ground color of powdered kaolin on ordinary sand laid about an inch thick on the floor. Figures of the Ku′pĭshtaya of the six regions form a circle on the disk. A diagonal line, symbolic of the galaxy, crosses the disk and different-colored grains of corn represent stars. Cloud symbols extend from the periphery of the disk toward the altar.

the same time collecting the sands of the painting with eagle-wing feathers and the hand and deposits them in a piece of cloth which is at once carried, with the cactus and switches, to the place beyond the village where the novice was first struck with cactus. The director and pekwĭn lead, each carrying willows held with the right hand and resting over the left arm. A portion of the cactus, which is now much broken from use, is carried on the willows. A warrior follows with the cloth containing the sands. The fraternity father comes next, carrying the yucca wreaths that were worn, and the novice carries the long plumes given him by his fraternity father. An excavation is made, and the willows and cactus are first deposited, then the yucca wreaths, and then the sands from the painting are spread over the whole. All plant prayer plumes, and the excavation is then covered with earth.

The party returns to the ceremonial chamber, where the other members await them. The novice takes his old seat and the warrior stands before him. The fraternity father, who sits to his right, says: "Now you are a cactus man. Should any Kok'ko [anthropic god] hit you once, do nothing; if he hits you twice, do nothing; if he hits you three times, do nothing; if he hits you four times, then take his yucca from him and whip him; break the beak and the feathers on his mask. Don't be afraid; no one can hurt you."[a] The novice replies: "It is well. I am glad to hear this." This closes the ceremony, and all return to their homes and sleep alone on sheepskins with the wool side down, for the cactus needles continue to work out of the flesh. The squash seeds are chewed and rubbed constantly over the wounds. Though there is considerable annoyance from the needles embedded in the flesh, a complaint is never heard.

The cougar medicine of the 'Ko'shi'kwe, which is a root, comes principally from the high valleys about the Jemez mountains in New Mexico and is traded to the Zuñis by the Cochiti Indians, who understand the value of the cougar medicine for some diseases. Only the 'Ko'shi'kwe of Zuñi (according to the statements of the members of this fraternity) recognize its value for wounds. This root is used in conjunction with the burr seeds previously referred to, the root and seeds being chewed and then applied to the wound.

A'PI'ᵀLÄSHIWANNI (BOW PRIESTHOOD)

It has been stated that the Bow priesthood was organized by U'yuyewi and Ma'sai'lema (Gods of War) after the A'shiwi (Zuñis) reached I'tiwanna (site of the present Zuñi), and these gods are supposed to have been represented in direct succession since that time by the elder and younger brother Bow priests, who are at the head of the organization and who carry the sacred traditions of their divine predecessors.

---

[a] The personators of the Kok'ko are afraid to use their switches on members of the 'Ko'shi'kwe, as after one stroke a member of this fraternity tells the god to strike again, and it is regarded as cowardice to refuse, and the consequence is the mask of the personator of the Kok'ko is soon dilapidated. No one must interfere in the affray.

Although the Bow priesthood is embraced in the esoteric fraternities of the Zuñis, it is in a way quite distinct from the others and is always referred to as a priesthood. The Bow priesthood, having to do more especially with the lightning-makers, communicating usually directly with them, and not through other gods, is differentiated from the other fraternities.

Though the Kĭa′kwemosi (rain priest of the North) consults with the first body of A′shiwanni (rain priests), it is his prerogative to choose the elder brother Bow priest. This high office, however, usually falls, when vacant, to the younger brother Bow priest, unless some other member of the organization has become more famous in war when his scalp trophies win for him the highest honors conferred on any member of this body. Though the offices of elder and younger Bow priests are for life, the incumbents may be impeached for sufficient cause.[a]

INSTALLATION OF THE ELDER BROTHER BOW PRIEST

A meal painting is made (see figure 33), by the pe′kwĭn (sun priest) at sunrise on the floor of a room in the dwelling of the Shi′wano′‘kĭa, the

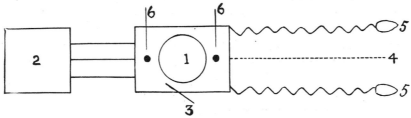

Fig. 33.—Meal painting made for the ceremony of the installation of the elder brother Bow priest. 1, circle of meal about 8 inches in diameter, symbolic of the waters of the world—a disk is afterward formed by filling in the circle with meal; 2, square of meal, symbolic of a mesa with rain, indicated by the three lines, falling upon it; 3, parallelogram, symbolizing the boundary of the Zuñi territory; 4, straight road of truth; 5-5, lightning; 6-6, position of the men when standing on the meal painting.

Priestess of fecundity, when the first body of A′shiwanni and officers of the esoteric fraternities (the Ko′tikili, mythologic fraternity, excepted) gather in the same order as described in the initiation of associate shi′wanni.[b] Upon completion of the painting, the Kĭa′kwemosi takes position west of the disk and faces east, and the novice stands facing the Kĭa′kwemosi, who, placing his hands over the novice's shoulders, speaks to him of his duties and obligations, and adds: "You must have a good heart and your thoughts must be pure, that the rains may fall upon our land, that we may have all food." He then clasps the novice's hands, holding them so that his thumbs are on the top of the hands, and prays. At the close of the prayer he draws the clasped

---

[a] In 1903 Nai′uchi′ and Me′she, elder and younger brother Bow priests, upon being reduced to the ranks ceased to attend the meetings of the fraternity.

[b] See A′shiwanni (Rain priesthood).

hands to his mouth and breathes upon them, and extends them to the novice's mouth, who draws all that is good from the Kĭa′kwemosi.

Each shi′wanni—and afterward the officers of the fraternities, in order—stands in the place of the Kĭa′kwemosi and repeats his commands, the novice remaining in position with folded arms. The novice afterward offers a prayer to the Sun Father to give him a good heart that his prayers for the welfare of his people may be heard, and he prays to the Gods of War to intercede with the Sun Father and Kok′ko A′wan (Council of the Gods) to send rains. The newly ordained elder brother now chooses from among the Bow priesthood his fellow, who comes forward and stands before him while he repeats what the Kĭa′-kwemosi has said, after which he takes his seat to the right of the Kĭa′kwemosi, who now rises and standing before the newly chosen one repeats the ceremony similar to that held over the elder brother, after which each shi′wanni and the officers of the fraternities follow in turn. The younger brother Bow priest now takes his seat to the right of the elder brother Bow priest, and the pe′kwĭn offers a prayer to the Sun Father for the well-being and good heart of his people, which is followed by prayers by the elder brother Bow priest, who again invokes the Gods of War. Nothing is said in the entire ceremonial in connection with the enemy. When the writer inquired of the elder brother Bow priest why there was no reference to war he was shocked, and replied: " Only prayers for good and rains are offered, no thought being given at such times to the enemy."

CEREMONIAL OF INITIATION INTO THE BOW PRIESTHOOD

Although this organization is much occupied with its various duties and obligations, it celebrates but two festivals—the scalp ceremonial, or initiation of the victor into the A′pi‘‘läshiwanni, which occurs every three or four years and after the return of a victor; and the o′wina-hai′ye (harvest dance) annually, in October, which is a thanksgiving for the crops.

The mere killing of an enemy does not entitle the victor to become a member of the A′pi‘‘läshiwanni; he must bear as trophies the scalp and at least a portion of the buckskin apparel as actual proof of his prowess. Thus the Zuñis, like other primitive peoples, make trophy-bearing a requisite of distinction as warriors. Though the scalp is necessary for initiation into the A′pi‘‘läshiwanni, one who does not take the scalp is not debarred from honorable recognition—he joins the fraternity of the ′Ko′shi‘kwe (Cactus). At least such was the case until the cessation of intertribal wars; and now that scalping has virtually ceased, the scalp ceremonial is still held every three or four years, by command of the elder brother Bow priest, for two reasons—to please the Gods of War, that they will intercede with the Sun Father and Council of the Gods for rain, and that the organization may not become extinct.

The Zuñis having been driven to step aside from legitimate procedure, the elder brother Bow priest selects some desirable man and initiates him into the A'pi‘ᵗläshiwanni. In 1896 there were only fifteen members of the fraternity, a number of these being aged men. The scalps used at these times are taken from the scalp vase, in which such trophies have rested since the establishment of the present Zuñi, or perhaps earlier, and the ceremonial is identical with that which occurred when the victor returned with the fresh scalp.

The elder brother Bow priest having decided upon a time for the ceremonial, notifies the scalp custodian, who in turn requests the elder brother Bow priest to designate the man to serve as elder brother to the victor, each victor having a member of the A'pi‘ᵗläshiwanni to accompany him throughout the ceremonial as elder brother. The acceptance of such appointment is optional, and occasionally the priest finds difficulty in securing a man. When he has secured one, the elder brother Bow priest chooses two warriors and two men of the Coyote clan to personate warriors, preceding the victor on returning from battle. These men are known as the pa'sewikĭa. Then the ᵗsi'hakoshona'kwe (scalp-washers) and their fellows are appointed. The number of scalp-washers and scalp-kickers depends on the number of scalps taken. If but one scalp is taken, there are two scalp-washers, and the scalp is divided with an archaic stone knife; if two are taken, there is no division of the scalp, but so complete is the dual system that whenever an odd number occurs the scalp must be divided. One scalp-washer and his alternate must be paternal uncles of the victor; if the father has no brothers, then the nearest male relatives, grandfather excepted, on the paternal side. The same relations are held with the elder brother and the other scalp-washer and his fellow. The i'tätononakwe (scalp-kickers) must be paternal aunts of the victor and elder brother; if there are no aunts, then the nearest paternal female relatives, grandmother excepted.

It was the writer's privilege to witness the ceremony described, which in this instance began in October, 1891. The evening of the day on which the actors are selected the pa'sewikĭa, equipped with rifles, leave the pueblo on horseback and spend the night a distance north of the village. They start on their return at sunrise, and upon the discovery of the first ant-hill they dismount.

The two warriors, each having eight olive shells (Olivella biblicata), stand a short distance away, while the other two, who have each a string of shell beads that will encircle the thumb, given them by the elder brother Bow priest, stoop by the ant-hill. The two warriors hold the shells in the right hand close to the mouth, while the others hold theirs in the left hand, also over the mouth. One of the stooping men maintains silence, while the other whispers the following prayer:

Our great Sun Father rises and comes forth from his night house.
My fathers, the beast gods of the six regions, arise, come forth.

Addressing the ants they continue their prayers:

To you of the six regions whose homes cover the earth I give shells.

The two warriors now deposit their olive shells and the other two the strings of shells at the apex of the ant-hill.

Yellow ant, blue ant, red ant, white ant, all color ant, black ant U......hu...... we......u......hu......we......u......hu......we......u......hu......we.

To you whose homes are covered with the mountain tops [a] I give shells—A′hayuta yellow, A′hayuta blue, A′hayuta red, A′hayuta white, A′hayuta all color, A′hayuta black. [b]

Rain-makers Bow priests, ꞌSi′kĭahaya, ꞌKĭä┤lawanni, Ku′pĭshtaya. [c]

When we meet the enemy a little arrow storm wind will rise. [d]

When we meet him on the road near by he will never more inhale the sacred breath of day.

I inhale the sacred breath of day.

All come quickly, the enemy comes from ambush. A Navaho is killed, we inhale the sacred breath of day.

They now discharge their rifles and, mounting, ride a few steps and halt, when the spokesman at the ant-hill repeats Uh......., then each man fires one shot. Proceeding a few steps farther, they halt, and the same man repeats Uh......hawanawe′, when each one fires a shot. Again they proceed a short distance and halt, when the same man repeats Uh......iwolokĭa′, when they again fire one shot and, advancing a few steps, they halt and the man repeats Uh......Pa′wi ash′kĭa, and again each fires a shot, and then they proceed direct to the north side of the pueblo.

The victor and elder brother are side by side, each flanked by a fellow. A great crowd has congregated to receive the party, whose approach has been observed by the pa′mosona (scalp custodian), who, facing the pa′sewikĭa, speaks:

You have met the enemy. He will nevermore inhale the sacred breath of day.

The war hoop (a′wakikapna) is now repeated four times by all. The pa′mosona continues, addressing the populace:

The enemy is destroyed. Who will be our great father Bow priest? [e]

Who now is to become a Bow priest? [f]

Well! who will kick the scalp? His younger mother (elder aunt), his elder sister (younger aunt).

Who will wash the scalp? His younger father (elder uncle), his elder brother (younger uncle).

Well! (said by pa′mosona). Good! (said by all).

---

[a] The unexpressed idea is that the homes of the Gods of War are roofed with mountain tops. The permanent home of these gods is supposed to be in the crater of an extinct volcano.

[b] Reference to the Gods of War presiding over the six regions—yellow for the North, blue for the West, red for the South, white for the East, all-color for the Zenith, and black for the Nadir.

[c] ꞌSi′kĭahaya travels in the rain by day; ꞌKĭä┤lawanni travels at night; he has long hair (comet or meteor); Ku′pĭshtaya travels in the midst of fog. These celestial beings are mighty warriors.

[d] The unexpressed idea is that there will be a little wind of arrows, or, in other words, the air will be filled with arrows.

[e] Referring to what member of the Bow priesthood will act as elder brother to the victor.

[f] Referring to one who has taken a scalp.

The war whoop is now given and they cry "teya" (more). After the second and third war whoops they again cry "teya." After the fourth they cry "alth'nate" (a little more). The pa'mosona now expectorates upon a bit of cedar bark, waves it to the six regions, and throws it upon the ground, and then the pa'sewikïa retire to their homes.

The victor and the warrior, who acts as elder brother, give each a tiny vase filled with rain water and a diminutive gourd dipper, which were given them by the Kïa'kwemosi, to the pa'mosona, and about 3 o'clock the same afternoon the pa'mosona takes a piece of scalp, every vestige of hair having long since disappeared, from the great pottery vase (colored black) which remains permanently in the scalp house (see plate cxxx).[a] "This vase was captured from the Navahos so long ago that no one's grandfather knows when." Dividing the piece of scalp in two, the pa'mosona proceeds on foot about 2 miles north of the village to a sequestered spot surrounded by hillocks and ravines. Here the two pieces of scalp are deposited, one of the vases of rain water and a gourd being placed by the side of each. The pa'mosona makes a small fire between them, and sprinkles an extensive circle of meal, embracing the surrounding ridges symbolizing the enemy sitting around the camp fire. Immediately upon the return of the pa'mosona to the village, the victor and elder brother, with their bows and arrows, hasten (on foot) to the place to make a reconnaissance. Discovering the camp fire, one exclaims, "I think there is an enemy." Each cuts a juniper twig, some 3 inches in length, from the top of the tree with an archaic stone knife belonging to the elder brother Bow priest. Four equilateral triangular cuts are made at the twig and it is then snapped off. One now passes to the right around the circle of meal, the other to the left, and when on opposite sides they draw their bows. The twig is held in the left hand while the arrow is shot. Each shoots his arrow into one of the bits of the scalp. The arrow is not removed, and the bit of scalp is placed in the toga, the shaft passing over the region of the heart, the feathered ends touching the chin. The juniper twig is also carried in the toga. The tiny vase of water and the gourd are transported in the blanket, which is carefully secured about the waist.

During the absence of the victor and the elder brother the pe'kwĭn makes an excavation, about 8 inches square and 20 inches deep, on the plain about 400 yards north of the village and directly south of where the scalps are to be hoisted for the first time. A mound of loose earth 10 inches in diameter is now raised on each side of the excavation and

---

[a] The scalp house is a conical structure covered with earth, standing out on the plain several hundred yards north of Zuñi. It has been moved since the writer became acquainted with these people to make room for the extension of the pueblo, corrals, etc. The mound opens at the apex and is covered with a stone slab and several flat baskets, one upon the other.

is covered with white meal. A line of meal extends eastward[a] from the excavation a distance of 9 feet. The line is crossed four times at equal distances with meal. The pe'kwĭn now places two bits of yucca in X form on each cross line, and on each of these X's is set a round flat stone, the stones being used to hold the yucca in place. The crossed yucca indicates tracks of the chaparral cock to the house of the ant (figure 34). "This bird is valuable because he can convey messages, and the enemy can not tell from his footprints whence he comes, for the feet point both ways." The mounds are symbolic of the homes of the Gods of War and the square of the home of the ants at Shi'papolima.[b] "Ants destroy the footprints of the Zuñis from the eye of the enemy." After the pe'kwĭn completes his work he returns to the village. The victor and the elder brother soon approach over the plain, bearing

Fig. 34.—Excavation and meal mounds symbolic of Shi'papolima and homes of the Gods of War.

the divided scalp in their togas. When they come within 500 yards of the village they remove the pieces of scalp from the arrows and attach them to a slender pole 5 feet high, which the pa'mosona has planted in the ground for the purpose, and the two take seats on the ground about 6 feet north of the pole and facing the village, the victor to the right of the elder brother. They busy themselves trimming the juniper twigs which they have brought with them. These twigs are twice the length from the tip of the middle finger to the tip of the thumb, the fingers extended. Here they sit for an hour. In the meantime the warriors and members of the Ant fraternity gather in a circle near by.

Each warrior having prepared two prayer plumes to the Gods of War and wrapped them together at the base, plants them on an ant-hill

[a] According to a prominent priest of Zuñi, this meal line used to extend westward, so that the people passed up toward the east, as Shi'papolima is in the east.
[b] See p. 407.

near by, before he joins the group. The victor takes a bit of red pigment from a small buckskin medicine bag and deposits it on a scrap of paper and, removing the divided scalp from the pole, he and the elder brother each bore a hole through the portion of scalp he holds and draws a buckskin thong through it; then breaking off a bit of the scalp each runs a thong through it and attaches it to the larger piece. The two pieces of scalp are now tied to a juniper twig, a fluffy eagle plume having been previously attached to each twig. The bark is picked off the lower end of the twig the length of the four fingers crosswise, and the red pigment is rubbed over the bared place. The pa′mosona and his vice now appear and each one twirls juniper bark in the faces of the victor and the elder brother, and going a distance to the north they throw away the bark.

During this time the warriors and the members of the Ant fraternity enjoy a social smoke. The arrival of the pe′kwĭn (sun priest), the Shi′wanni of the West, and the elder brother Bow priest brings the social gathering to a close. The latter presents to the victor and elder brother each a reed cigarette colored red and so surrounded with feathers of the eagle, turkey, and birds of the six regions that the reeds can not be seen. The cigarettes and plumes are afterward offered by the victor and elder brother to the Gods of War. The pe′kwĭn and the Shi′wanni of the West now stoop side by side, facing north; the elder brother Bow priest faces them. The Shi′wanni of the West removes from a corn husk a strip of cotton cloth less than 2 inches wide and a reed, colored black and filled with native tobacco. He rolls the strip of cotton and then lights it by striking flint (this being a common way of furnishing light for cigarettes outdoors) and hands the roll and reed to the pe′kwĭn, who lights the cigarette from the burning cotton. A second cigarette is now lighted and the two are smoked by the group. The remaining bits of the cigarettes are placed in corn husks by the pe′kwĭn, who carries them later in the evening to his home, and the following morning he takes them to the ceremonial chamber of the Kĭa′kwemosi and there deposits them in a large basket tray, where they remain eight days. These are afterward attached to the images of U′yuyewi and Ma‛sai′lema.[a]

About 200 mounted men, wrapped in blankets and armed with rifles and revolvers, and crowds of pedestrians gather around the meal-covered mounds. The A′pi‛tläshiwanni and the Ant fraternity, preceded by the victor, his elder brother, and the elder brother Bow priest, advance slowly and with measured steps to the meal mounds, singing the following refrain, which is low and musical:

Ha′‛ma, ha′‛ma Shi′waiyu, shi′waiyu, wai′yu, wai′yu
Ha′‛ma,   ha′‛ma   rain priests,   rain priests,   wai′yu,   wai′yu
Wai′yuma hai′‛na yu′liwa yu′liwa hi‐‐‐‐hi‐‐‐‐hi‐‐‐‐hi‐‐‐‐hi‐‐‐‐
Wai′yuma   hai′‛na   coming,   coming.

---

[a] See p. 597.

The above is repeated four times as the warriors and Ant fraternity proceed. The idea is that the scalp is symbolic of the A'shiwanni because it brings rains. As heretofore stated, it is the special duty of the A'shiwanni to fast and pray for rains.

The Kĭa'kwemosi stands west of the excavation. The priest of the po'nepoyannĕ or pa'ĕttonĕ (the sacred fetish of the fraternity), clasping two pa'ĕttowe (plural for pa'ĕttonĕ) to his breast, stands to the right of the Kĭa'kwemosi, whose first associate is to his right. The remainder of the first body of A'shiwanni stand by in line. The i'tatononakwe (scalp-kickers) arrive, and passing behind the warriors and around by the north of the line of A'shiwanni to the west they take their positions a short distance from the A'shiwanni. They wear their ordinary dress, with white blankets bordered in red and blue over their shoulders. The quill ends of two feathers of the chaparral cock—one an upper tail feather and the other an under tail feather—have been crossed and placed in line by their brothers in consanguinity between the second and middle toes of the left foot, the tips of the plumes pointing toward the foot, and the moccasins carefully drawn over. "The feathers give courage, for knowledge and courage come from this bird, who is the keeper of courage." After the girls reach the scene, the same brothers tie similar but somewhat larger feathers to the left side of the head with a strand of the hair and a cotton string already attached to the plumes. The plumes must not be removed for four days.

Each i'tatonona holds in the right hand two prayer plumes and meal wrapped in corn husks. The vice pa'mosono'ʻkĭaᵃ (female aid to the scalp custodian) stands north of the meal line in a soiled cotton garment with a conventional black blanket about her shoulders.ᵇ The four women mentioned are the only Zuñi women present at this feature of the ceremony.

The elder brother Bow priest now directs two youths to stand north and south of the mounds and clasp each other's left hand with arms raised over the excavation. The youth who stands on the north side of the mound is of the Deer clan, the other of the Bear clan. Each youth is led up the meal line to his place by the elder brother Bow priest. The victor and the elder brother, stepping on the crossed yucca, pass up the line of meal and under the clasped hands, each carrying the cedar twig with the pieces of scalp and fluffy eagle plume attached. As soon as they pass under the hands, the twigs are received by the pa'mosona and the aid, who afterward lay them on the ground a short distance southwest of the mounds, and the priest of the pa'ĕttowĕ clasps the victor to his breast while the Kĭa'kwemosi

---

ᵃ There was no pa'mosono'ʻkĭa at this time, the former having been accused of witchcraft and dismissed.

ᵇ Women holding this office may be of any clan, but must have passed the child-bearing period, for should a pa'mosono'ʻkĭa have an infant the deceased enemy would cause its death. Though the appointment is for life, the pa'mosono'ʻkĭa is subject to impeachment.

MAIDENS RETURNING FROM THE HOUSE OF VICTOR WITH GIFTS FOR THEIR SERVICES IN GRINDING

PU'PANAKWE, CHOIR OF A'PI'ꞮLÄSHIWANNI (BOW PRIESTHOOD)

embraces the elder brother.   The arms are placed around one another. The two then reverse places and are embraced.   Each time long prayers are repeated by the two priests, and the victor and the elder brother pray and are afterward embraced by the remaining A'shiwanni.   The two i'tatononakwe place their left arms through the right of the victor and the elder brother.   The victor and an i'tatonona visit one ant-hill, the other couple another ant-hill, both hills being near the meal mounds, and plant their prayer plumes at the apexes of the hills.   The sticks of the women are colored black and are offered to the rain-makers, while those of the men are red and are offered to the Gods of War for the destruction of the enemy.   Each woman divides the prayer meal she carries with her companion and the two sprinkle it over the plumes and ant-hills.   The women do not speak, as a woman not past the child-bearing age must not speak at the house of the ants on this occasion.   The men pray aloud and deposit the prayer plumes.   The elder brother Bow priest is the third to proceed up the meal line, and by his request the writer follows him.   When all the warriors have passed over the meal line and under the hands, the populace follow, the equestrians dismounting for the purpose.   "They step over the sacred road of meal to the home of the ants, that they may keep their lives when passing about the country or contending with the enemy."   The first body of A'shiwanni and priest of the pa'ĕttowe are exempt from this feature of the ceremonial, as their place is at home and not amid the dangers of travel and war.   When all have passed over the meal line, the pa'mosona deposits he'we (wafer bread) as a food offering to the ants in the excavation, and destroys the mounds by running his left foot over them and drawing the earth into the opening.

After the deposition of the plume offerings on the ant-hills the party returns to the group and all pass on to the village.   The i'tatononakwe, who must not look to the right or the left, start the scalps with the left foot and so keep them before them, never using the right foot for this purpose.   The victor and the elder brother follow after the i'tatononakwe, and the elder brother Bow priest precedes the Ant fraternity and the A'pi ᶜᵀläshiwanni, who follow a short distance in the rear. The scalp custodian, his aid, and the vice pa'mosono''kĭa come next, and after them the populace, some on foot and others mounted, making the air ring with rifle and pistol shots and the war whoop.   Each person, except the scalp-kickers, carries a bit of cedar bark in the left hand.

The worst element in their barbaric nature seems to be aroused.   If the mere dramatization produces such frenzy, what must have been the scenes when the victor in reality returned from battle with scalps of the hated Navaho!

The village is encircled four times from right to left, coil fashion,[a] until they find themselves within the te'wita 'hlan'na (large plaza), where they are joined by women and children, and all form into four concentric circles.

The scalp-kickers lift from the ground with the left hand the twigs to which the scalps are attached and wave them before handing them to the pa'mosona, who stands facing west. As soon as the pa'mosona receives the twigs, the elder brother Bow priest approaches, and the pa'mosona picks off a bit of scalp and attaches it to the arrow of the elder brother Bow priest, who afterward passes around the inner circle four times from left to right. The first time around he runs his arrow over the ankles of the men and women as he passes; the second time, he draws it above their knees; the third time, it is drawn by the waist; the fourth time, over the head, that their hearts may be pure and know no fear. Each time as he reaches the starting point all present expectorate upon the cedar bark and carry it around the head four times from left to right for physical purification, the elder brother Bow priest waving his arrow held in the right hand at the same time. After the fourth movement all males give the war whoop and the elder brother Bow priest shoots the arrow containing the bit of scalp to the north, the home of the hated Navaho. At this hour the plaza and Indians are bathed in moonlight, and the scene, though barbaric, is most picturesque.

After the shooting of the arrow, symbolic of the destruction of the enemy, the pa'mosona and his aid attach the bits of scalp to a pole about 20 feet long, which has rested against the crumbling wall of the old Catholic Church; it is then planted in an excavation previously made for it in the center of the plaza by the pa'mosona, his vice, the victor, and the elder brother (see plate CXXXI). This pole must not be touched after it is hoisted. The victor and the elder brother, who must not be touched by another after the hoisting of the pole, alternate in keeping guard over it until the crowd disperses for refreshment.

The first body of A'shiwanni and others return to their homes. The members of the Bow priesthood, with the victor and scalp-kickers, after again passing four times around the village coil fashion, adjourn to their ceremonial chamber, where a feast is served. Later the populace gather around the scalp pole and dance throughout the night. The scalp dance is repeated twelve nights, and is under the very shadow of the old church erected by the Spanish invaders two hundred years ago with the hope of bringing these people to the Christian faith. None are too aged and few too young to participate

---

[a] The coil, often conventionalized into the square by the Zuñis, the significance of which they carefully conceal, is their seal, and "wherever found it surely indicates that the A'shiwi have passed that way and were at one time the owners of the land."

STEVENSON]   A'PI⁽ᵀLÄSHIWANNI   587

in this dance and song of rejoicing for the destruction of the enemy.
Young children are led to the dance by their mothers, who offer
prayers to the Gods of War to give the lives of the enemy to the Zuñis.
Occasionally a wish is expressed that the Navahos, who are celebrated
among the Indians of that section for their fine peach orchards, may
eat peaches enough to kill them.

The victor must not touch animal food, grease, or salt for ten days,
and his food must be cold, for should hot food be taken at this time
he would become corpulent—something the Zuñis aim to avoid; yet
the women, at least many of them, become so with age. For the
same period he must observe continence, by command of the Gods of
War. His elder brother and the scalp-kickers must observe this fast
four days. The victor and scalp-kickers remain as far as possible
from the fireplace, though only embers rest on the hearth.ᵃ They
do not remove any part of their clothing during the four nights, not
even the moccasins. The victor and his elder brother must not smoke
for four days, and they, with the scalp-kickers, must not be touched
by another or receive anything directly from the hands of another for
the same period, the superstition being that death would result from
disobedience of this edict.

The first four nights are spent by the victor, the elder brother, and
the two scalp-kickers in the ceremonial chamber, when the men must
remain apart from the women and not speak to them. Each night the
warriors assemble and sing and brandish the war club, the victor
joining in the songs. Some say the original clubs were thrown from
the heavens by Mo'yächun ⁽hlan'na (Great star), warrior of the heavens.

The victor and members of the Bow priesthood each prepare eight
prayer plumes as offerings to the Gods of War, the second morning,
the victor and elder brother making theirs in the ceremonial house of
the Bow priesthood, while the other warriors prepare theirs in their
dwellings. The prayer plumes are joined in couples, and the following
morning deposited on ant-hills at the four cardinal points. Similar
ones are made on the fifth day and planted on ant-hills, and on the
eleventh day they are duplicated and likewise deposited.

On the fifth day the elder brother of the victor stands by the scalp
pole six consecutive hours, and when he desires to depart the crowd
endeavors to prevent him. He finally gets away by promising to
bring something good to the plaza, and when he returns with meat
and melons there is great scrambling. The kïep'yätonanně (war pouch)
of buckskin, originally from apparel of the enemy, is made by the elder
brother of the victor on the fifth day. One braid of three strips of buckskin and three braids of two strips each are made and sewed in parallel
lines close together upon a strip of cotton cloth. The ends of the

---

ᵃThese men have a superstitious dread of being near the fire at this time.

strips are attached to a roll or stuffed piece of buckskin about 9 inches long and 2½ inches in diameter in the center, the ends tapering, and an arrow point is attached where they are fastened to the strap on each side. (When a second enemy is scalped the same number of braids of buckskin, with the same number of strips in each, are added, the cotton strip being broadened sufficiently. For the scalping of the third enemy two arrow points are attached to the band, each about 4½ inches from either end of the strap. On the scalping of a fourth enemy two more arrow points are added on opposite ends, about the same distance as the two former are from the end of the strap. After scalping a fifth enemy, two more arrow points are added, the same distance apart on opposite ends of the strap, when the arrows nearly meet midway of the strap. No more are added after the placing of the eight arrow points, the warrior having received the highest honors.) The band passes over the shoulder, the pouch hanging at the waist. A twisted wristlet is formed of two buckskin thongs, also originally from apparel of the enemy with olive shells strung on them. The kĕm'poyannĕ, a skullcap of perforated buckskin with a full tuft of hawk plumes, is another badge of office.

The fifth morning the scalp-kicker and his aid bathe the entire body of the victor, when his blood-stained hands are washed for the first time since the scalping. The water used must be cold, and he must remain away from the fire during the bathing. At noon on the fifth day the pu'panakwe—a body of eight singers, who may be of any clan, chosen for life by the elder brother Bow priest to serve the fraternity at this ceremonial—form into two choirs, four men in each group, at each end of the long ceremonial chamber of the Bow, the choir for U'yuyewi (elder God of War) sitting at the east end and that for Maᵗsai'lema (younger God of War) sitting at the west. Each choir is provided with an archaic pottery drum, vase-shaped, cream-colored, and decorated, and a hooped drumstick. One of these sticks has a zigzag line denoting lightning running up the handle. These particular drumsticks are in the keeping of the pa'mosona, and are supposed to be the original ones used at Hän'ᵗlipĭnkĭa. A man of each choir acts as director, his hand serving the purpose of a baton, and another as drummer. The pa'mosona presides over the choir of U'yuyewi and his vice over that of Maᵗsai'lema. These epic songs are ancient and no innovations must be introduced. The pa'mosona and his vice are kept busy for a time gathering together ha'shiya (shakers; from ha'shi to shake).

A sufficient number of girls having arrived, the dance begins. Four girls, having removed the pi'toni (cotton piece which hangs over the shoulders), stand before the choirs, two at one end of the room and two before the choir at the other end. These girls may be married or single. They wear the usual black woven dress, with their necks and limbs bare; also a red belt, a string of silver beads around the neck, and silver bangles. The hair is done up in the usual manner. The dancers at the east end stand upon a rectangular wooden slab, 8 feet in length and 15 inches wide, laid in the floor, facing the choir, with their feet close together, their arms hanging and their hands clasped. Those at the west end have similar positions.

While the choirs pray, the drummer at the east end of the room gives one loud stroke upon his drum, which is returned by a stroke from the other drummer, in obedience to the command given at Hän'-ᵗlïpïnkïa,[a] that the beings who appeared from below the earth at that time shall hear and be present. The drummer at the east end now begins an accompaniment to the song, which is low and slow during the first stanza, the girls keeping time by motions with the knees and arms. After a minute there is another single stroke at the east end, which is returned by the drummer at the west, and the song and dance begin in earnest. The girls at once turn and face the room. The two at the west end extend their right upper arms outward and the right lower arms upward, their left arms are extended slightly forward, and hang. The arms of the girls at the east end are reversed, their right arms pointing downward, their upper left arms upward, as they begin. The positions of the arms are constantly reversed during the dance.

The pa'mosona, who stands north of the line of dancers in the east end of the room, wears cotton trousers and shirt, with a red blanket around him. The vice pa'mosona, who is attired in much the same fashion, and the vice pa'mosono'⁽kïa, wearing her usual dress, including moccasins, with black blanket, stand north of the line of dancers at the west end of the room. Each of the three and each member of the choir holds a bit of cedar bark in the left hand.

The girls dance from south to north and back, sidewise, in unison with the choir. At certain portions of the song, where the Gods of War are appealed to to destroy the enemy, the cedar bark is spit upon and carried around the head four times from left to right, when all expectorate. When the dancers retire, no set remaining longer than ten minutes on the floor, they return to their seats on the north or south side of the chamber, when they immediately put on the pi'toni and moccasins, and other girls fill their places. The choirs pray each time the change is made and after the dancers take their positions. This dance closes at half past 1 o'clock in the afternoon, and the pa'mosona and his vice place the drums side by side in the center of the chamber. Removing the hide, they take from the inside of each drum two chaparral cock feathers, diagonally crossed, and two pieces of yucca leaf crossed in the same fashion, indicating the footprints of the bird, and hold them in their left hands with the cedar bark while

---

[a] See p. 36.

they pray, when they are returned to the drums, where they remain throughout the ceremonial. The hide covers are laid loosely upon the drums, which are placed in the northeast corner of the room, behind the line of mills on which the family grain is ground. This chamber, as well as all other ceremonial chambers, is used by the family of the house when not set apart for ceremonial purposes.

The ᵗsi'hakoshona'kwe receive the scalps about 3 o'clock in the afternoon of the fifth day from the pa'mosona, who, assisted by his vice, removes them from the pole. The scalps remain attached to the cedar twigs, with the fluffy eagle feathers in place. The pole, which is not scaled but uprooted for the purpose of removing the scalps, is stood against the wall of the church until the scalps shall be again attached. The scalp-washers and their fellows are elaborately attired. The leg of one pair of trousers is red, the other yellow, a broad tuck extending down the side, each tuck being ornamented with three large medallions of gilt paper. Another pair has one yellow leg, the other a large plaid of yellow, black, and brown, with similar tucks and medallions. The other two wear velveteen trousers. The four wear black native woven shirts trimmed in red and green ribbons. The two ᵗsi'hakoshona'kwe wear women's white blankets, bordered in red and blue, folded, and tied over the shoulder. The hair is done up in the common knot in the back, parted over the head, and looped and tied with red and green ribbons at the sides. All wear the kĕm'poyannĕ and each has a streak of micaceous hematite across the right eyelid and under the eye, indicating officership.

The ᵗsi'hakoshona'kwe, each with his fellow (one, with his fellow, must be of the clan of the victor's father, the other, with his fellow, of the clan of the father of the warrior who assists as the victor's elder brother), proceed abreast to a secluded spot on the river bank a mile or so west of the village, where they bathe the scalps in yucca suds, a cavity being made in the earth to serve as a basin. The scalps are afterward rubbed with kaolin, for rain, and a bit of the scalp is taken into the mouth, that the Zuñis may have brave hearts and that the Gods of War will empower them to destroy the enemy. "Should the victor possess a good heart, the killing of the enemy brings much rain."

The ᵗsi'hakoshona'kwe return to the ceremonial chamber at the close of the dancing of the ha'shiya. Before they enter, the cedar twigs with the scalps are placed over the door between the adobe wall and the lintel. They approach the A'piᵗl〱shiwanni, who stand in a group to receive them. After the reception they all smoke commercial tobacco, and after the smoke one of the ᵗsi'hakoshona'kwe beats upon one of the drums, while the others sing. In a short time the newly appointed pa'mosono'ᵗkĭa, wearing ordinary dress, arrives, followed by two o'tai-lasho'nakwe (dancing girls) in the conventional black gown; but they are afterward elaborately attired, one by the victor and the other by the elder brother to the victor, each with a white embroidered kilt tied across the shoulders, necklaces of precious beads, and hanks of native blue yarn around the wrists hanging in tassels. The vice pa′mosono′ʽkïa and the two ᵗsi′hakoshona′kwe take seats on the north ledge and near the west end of the room. A number of ha′shiya now return, having added to their dress a white blanket bordered in blue and red.

When all is ready the ᵗsi′hakoshona′kwe with their fellows leave the chamber abreast, and removing the cedar twigs from over the doorway carry them with their bows and arrows in their left hands; each has a single arrow in the right hand. They proceed a few steps and wait for the remainder of the party, which is not long in appearing. The elder brother Bow priest follows after the scalp-washers, the victor and his elder brother comé next, and then the other warriors in couples, followed by the vice pa′mosona (the pa′mosona having preceded the party to the te′wita ʽhlan′na (large plaza), and two o′tailasho′-nakwe and the ha′shiya. Each couple on emerging from the chamber separates, and two lines are thus formed. The ha′shiya join in the lines, while the two o′tailasho′nakwe dance back and forth between the lines to the music of the song and drum. The drum is of wood, the ends covered with hide.

As the procession advances to the plaza it is joined by several girls from 6 to 10 years of age, placed there by their mothers, who are quite as enthusiastic as the men. The enthusiasm, however, does not reach its height until the plaza is entered and the pole with the scalp attached has been raised by the pa′mosona and his vice. While the scalp is being tied to the pole, the elder brother Bow priest cries to the crowds on the house tops and in the plaza to join in the dance. After the placing of the pole the pa′mosona and his aid stand close by it and pray. The party from the ceremonial chamber dance around the pole for an hour in two concentric circles, facing each other, while the o′tailasho′nakwe dance between them, and the drummer stands near the pole. When this party leaves the plaza a small circle is formed around the pole, the drummer now standing within the circle, which must never be entirely closed, but is gradually increased as the populace of both sexes and all ages join in the dance, which continues throughout the night, until the plaza seems one mass of motion. There are no other dances in the plaza on the fifth day, and the only dancing on the sixth day is by the populace around the scalp pole, but the A′piʽläshiwanni sing in the ceremonial chamber until midnight.

On the seventh day the ha′shiya dancing begins in the ceremonial house at 2 o′clock and closes at 3. Afterward all pass from the ceremonial chamber to the plaza, led by the elder brother Bow priest. The pu′panakwe carry their pottery drums and group on the east and west sides of the te′wita ʽhlan′na, one party representing U′yuyewi and the other Ma'sai'lema. Two ha'shiya dance before each choir. Those who are to represent the side of the younger God of War are attired by young men designated for the purpose in a house on the west side of the plaza, and those for the other side in the ceremonial house of the priest of 'su''hlan'na (great shell), on the north side of the plaza. The pu'mokĭakĭanawe (hatchet-bearers) also dance in the plaza.[a] The ha'shiya repeat their dancing on the eighth day in the ceremonial chamber and in the plaza. On the same day members of the Eagle clan assemble in a large room of one of the clan to prepare corn meal and flour.

The corn and wheat to be consumed by the A'pi'''läshiwanni during this ceremonial is the gift of the father of the victor, who belongs to the Eagle clan, the victor himself being a member of the Turkey clan. The girls and younger women of the clan do the grinding and remove the corn from the cob, while the crones toast the corn after it has passed through the coarser mill. The grinding is done to the accompaniment of a drum and a choir of five young male singers. An elaborate feast is served to the party of workers after midday. At sunset the corn meal and flour are carried to the house of the victor, where each grinder is presented by the hostess with a large bowl of hot stew or basket of bread, which she carries to her home. (Plate CXXXII shows the girls returning home with bowls of food.) The same afternoon the o'tailasho'nakwe dance, first before the house of the elder brother Bow priest, then around the village, and finally in the te'wita 'hlan'na, the dancers being in single file and proceeding like a great serpent. It is designated by the writer the meander dance. This dance is for the destruction of the enemy.

On the ninth day the elder brother Bow priest grinds bits of shell and turquoise beads to be offered to the Gods of War. Afterward he joins the A'pi'''läshiwanni in the ceremonial chamber, when the ha'shiya again dance from 2 until 3 o'clock. After the dance the pa'mosona and vice pray over the drums, as before described, but only one drum is now opened, and it is afterward placed in the northeast corner of the room. The other drum is carried to the plaza, to which place the pa'mosona and vice and the vice pa'mosono''kĭa hasten. Seven pu'panakwe are seated on a ledge in front of the house, on the west of the te'wita 'hlan'na, and one takes his seat on a chair and the drum is placed beside him (see plate CXXXIII). They all smoke while they await the hour for the dance.

Eight girls, four for each side, to take part in the pu'mokĭakĭanawe dance, gather in the house on the west side of the plaza and in the house of the priest of 'su''hlan'na, where many necklaces, etc., are added to their already elaborate apparel. The girls wear, in addition to the pi'toni, white blankets bordered in red and blue, and over these

---

[a] A description of this dance will be given hereafter.

bright-colored shawls of foreign manufacture. The four girls in the house of the priest of ᵗsu′ᵗhlan′na are led to the entrance of the plaza at the northeast street by the pa′mosona, and the four girls in the other house are led to the southwest covered way by the vice pa′mosona, two men of the pu′mokĭakĭanawe awaiting each set of girls. The party at the northeast corner represents U′yuyewi, and that at the southwest corner Maᵗsai′lema. As has been stated, "the Sun Father relegated all land north of the road of day to U′yuyewi, and all south to Maᵗsai′lema."

The pa′mosona and his aid and the vice pa′mosono′‵kĭa have seats on the ledge at the south end of the line of pu′panakwe; the warrior of the Ant fraternity, the victor, and the elder brother sit on raised seats around the drum. The most aged member of the Bow stands by a ladder north of the group, holding his war club. The pa′mosona rises and sprinkles meal over the top of the drum and hooped drumstick which lies upon it, and offers a lengthy prayer for rain. He afterward lights a cigarette of corn husk filled with native tobacco, and drawing the smoke he puffs it into the meal on the drum, holding his mouth very close, and again prays for rain. The choir and those about it, the vice pa′mosono′‵kĭa excepted, smoke similar cigarettes. The warrior of the Ant fraternity repeats the puffing of the smoke over the meal and prays. The others wave their cigarettes in the direction of the drum, and the music begins.

The warriors of the Ant fraternity, the victor, and the elder brother join in the song, keeping time with their war clubs. The dancers start with the beginning of the music, each side having been joined by two warriors wearing ordinary cotton clothing, moccasins, and the war pouch. Two of the warriors have the kĕm′poyannĕ; the others wear red silk bandas around their heads. Each carries a war club in his left hand. The two male pu′mokĭakĭanawe on the side of the warriors wearing the kĕm′poyannĕ have white embroidered kilts fastened at the right side, a white cotton fringed sash passing around the waist and looped at the right side, and a fox skin pendent at the back. Strings of black stone archaic beads and shell beads pass over the right shoulder and under the left arm; hanks of native blue yarn are worn around the neck and wrists, hanging in tassels; silk bandas adorn the head, in addition to two eagle tail feathers standing from a heavy aigret of hawk feathers at the back. The hair is done up in the conventional knot. The white cotton trousers are tucked in the leather leggings, and moccasins are worn. The hands are colored pink, and the chin is painted in vertical lines in the same color. The two pu′mokĭakĭanawe on the other side are dressed in similar fashion, one, however, wearing an elaborate buckskin shirt trimmed with fringes and triple rows of silver buttons; he wears no banda. Each carries a wooden hatchet in his left hand, with a lock of horsehair hanging from the end of the handle symbolic of a scalp.

The pu'mokĭakĭanawe start simultaneously from the diagonal corners of the plaza in couples, the women alternating with the pu'mokĭakĭanawe and the warriors. The women extend their left hands to the backs of the men, indicating that the Navahos have fled. In this way the two parties reach the center of the plaza west of the scalp pole. On meeting, the couples from the southwest corner separate, allowing the others to pass between the lines. The moment they separate the men transfer their war clubs and hatchets to the right hand, and the women use their right hands instead of their left, indicating, "Go, Navahos; the Zuñis have no fear." The two parties cross to the opposite sides, and after going just outside the plaza, the leaders separate; turning outward, and pass around toward the plaza, and return to it. When midway, those belonging to the northeastern entrance separate into two files, allowing the other couples to pass between them. This figure is repeated four times. The last time an innovation occurs which causes general merriment among the mass of spectators. Two men appear just behind the dancers from the southwest covered way, as United States troops after the Zuñis, one wearing high boots, light-blue army overcoat, and black felt hat; the other, blue army trousers, fatigue army coat, and gray felt hat. The first carries a gun, and the second a pick and a stick of wood. The two remain with the dancers until the close of the dance.

The warriors lead in the next figure. They start out in couples from opposite sides of the plaza as described, but soon separate, those from the southwest corner passing up the west and east sides of the plaza, and those from the other side separating and passing immediately inside the lines of the other party. On reaching the middle of the plaza the left hand is changed, as before, for the right; on reaching the corners the separated couples come together, each couple passing down between the lines exactly as the figure is danced in the Virginia reel, and they cross to the other side of the plaza. This figure is repeated four times. The step in each is a sort of quick pace. As soon as the song ceases the choirs join in prayer, which grows louder and louder, but the voices are never raised above moderate tones.

The pu'mokĭakĭanawe are scarcely out of the plaza when one of the governor's aids cries out to the people to dance around the scalp pole, calling for some one to bring a drum. The pottery drum is never used for this dance. Twelve young men are soon gathered around the pole, the drummer standing outside the small circle, which rapidly increases to large proportions. The step is slow and regular as they pass from left to right. By 9 o'clock at night concentric circles fill the plaza, the air resounds with songs and war whoops, and the excitement is great. On the tenth day the o'tailasho'nakwe dance.

On the eleventh day the ha'shiya dance in the chamber on the west side of the plaza, and afterwards in the plaza itself, when they wear for the first time the elaborate dress and the spread-eagle tail upon their heads.

The o'tulasho'nakwe is repeated on the eleventh day. The men are dressed elaborately. The leader of the dance carries a spear having a handle about 6 feet long, with an aigret of raven plumes and a single eagle tail feather attached where the spear joins the handle. All who can by any means secure a gun or pistol carry it, while others less fortunate carry hatchets and hammers. The girls wear black gowns, white blankets bordered in red and blue, white buckskin moccasins, and leggings, the hair being done up in the usual manner. Both men and women have bead necklaces in profusion. This dance begins before 5 o'clock in the afternoon, in the house of the elder brother Bow priest, and the dancers afterward form a square before his house; then they begin the meander figure, advancing almost imperceptibly with a hop step, raising the foot but slightly from the ground. Only the men sing; the women extend their arms out and bent slightly upward from the elbow, and move them with a kind of shake which seems to be caused by the motion of the body. The men now and then, at the proper time in the song, gracefully extend the right arm as they sing for the enemy to be destroyed. There is one variation in this dance. All turn simultaneously to the left, and as they do so they bend the left side, and keeping the feet close together move three steps sidewise to the right, emphasizing each step with the voice. This is varied by bending to the right and taking three steps to the left. These figures are repeated as they proceed through the village.

The drummer is west of the sixty-one dancers, who present a most brilliant picture. As they enter the narrow street they straighten out in single file, passing through the eastern covered way to the Si'aa' te'wita, the sacred dance court, and thence on to the northwest corner of the village, dancing for a time before the house of the Shi'wanni of the East, who lives on the west side of the village, where they repeat the meander figure; they then pass in single file to the plaza beyond, where they dance. Again they straighten out in single file and enter the narrow street leading to the western covered way; thence to the large plaza, where great crowds of spectators have gathered, including about fifty equestrians.

The o'tailasho'nakwe disperse at dusk, and the pu'mokĭakĭanawe come by the northeast and southwest entrances to the plaza. The party from the northeast is halfway across the plaza when those from the opposite side appear. They advance facing each other in two lines, fifty in each line, afterward dancing sidewise across the plaza. This party is hilarious, and the song is quite different from that of the previous dance. Men, women, and children of both sexes and all ages form the motley crowd. All the men carry either bows and arrows, guns, or pistols, and there is an incessant firing, which seems to delight even the youngest dancers, who never flinch at the report of the firearms. After crossing the plaza they pass around the scalp pole, forming two broken opposing circles (the drummer keeping within the inner circle), and dance around the pole. The firearms and clubs are brandished, and the drumming and singing never cease during the dance. A number of dancers leave the plaza by the western covered way for the west side of the village, where one of their number fires a gun and all run up the street they have just passed down, fleeing, as they say, from the fire of the Navaho; and they are derided by the spectators for being cowards. When this dance is over a crier calls to the populace to come close around the pole and dance, and there is a scramble for places, the young children being as eager as their elders to be first at the pole. The circle soon grows to be very large, and the dance continues until dawn.

The first body of A'shiwanni prepare prayer plumes on the eleventh day in the ceremonial chamber of the Kĭa'kwemosi, each making four. The Shi'wanni of the Nadir, as elder brother Bow priest, makes four additional offerings to the Gods of War, and the younger brother Bow priest also makes four to these gods. The sticks of all these prayer plumes are the length from the metacarpus to the tip of the second finger and taper at the upper end. The first feather is attached about 2 inches from the top. When the plumes are to project abruptly from the side of the plume stick, the quill ends are softened by placing them in the mouth. The cotton cord which binds the plumes to the sticks is fastened in a buttonhole loop. The black paint used to color the sticks offered to the Gods of War is taken from an archaic cup hollowed out of a piece of wood. After the prayer plumes to be offered by the elder and younger brother Bow priests to the Gods of War are completed, the younger brother Bow priest rubs the lower portion of the feathers on a red paint stone, the dry color adhering to the plumes. The la'showawe (plumes attached to cotton cord) are also rubbed with the dry color, after which the elder brother Bow priest removes an olive shell from his war bracelet and hands it to the younger brother, who strings it on his la'showannĕ; the elder brother, removing a second shell, attaches it to the cord of his own la'showannĕ, and each ties his la'showannĕ to the topmost plume (an eagle tail feather) of a prayer plume. All the plumes used are from male birds.

Upon completion of the prayer plumes, each shi'wanni wraps his own in a corn husk, tying it with a thread of yucca. The pe'kwĭn (sun priest) uses a greater variety of feathers than the others, for he adds the plumes of the birds of the six regions that are specially associated with his office.   After the Kĭa'kwemosi completes his prayer plumes, he adds fresh plumes to two long-necked gourds, each gourd being provided with a sprinkler (a reed about 12 inches long and ¼ inch in diameter).   Four white fluffy eagle plumes are attached equidistant around the upper edge of a white cotton cord netting, which covers a portion of the bulb of the gourd, and a la'showannĕ of the same plumes is tied near the upper end of each sprinkler.   These jugs are afterward placed on the meal painting in the chamber of the A'pi'ᵗläshiwanni and are carried in a later ceremony by the ᵗkĭa'punakwe (water-bearers or sprinklers).

The wood idols of the Gods of War are completed on the eleventh day.   U'yuyewi is made by the aged member of the Deer clan (see plate XIX), and his batons and games are made at the same time and place by two other members of this clan.   Maᵗsai'lema and his appointments are made by three members of the Bear clan in the house of the man who carves the image.ᵃ   During the afternoon, after the completion of the images, the warriors, independently of one another, go to the two houses and deposit two prayer plumes in upright position in the yucca belt around each image.

At sunset the maker of the image of the younger God of War, accompanied by two members of his clan bearing the staffs and games of Maᵗsai'lema, carries the image, hidden under his blanket, to the house of the maker of U'yuyewi, and stands it on the floor near the north end of the room, some 3 feet south of the other image, both effigies facing east.   Other prayer plumes are added, and finally the idols are almost wholly obscured by the plumes.   The images are guarded until midnight by men of the two clans, appointed, respectively, by the elder and the younger brother Bow priest, when they with their belongings are taken to the ceremonial chamber of the warriors by those who fashioned them and the men designated to carry the paraphernalia.   They are received separately by the pe'kwĭn (sun priest) with great ceremony, and stood beside the meal painting, previously made by him on the floor in the west end of the room.

The idol of the elder God of War is stood on the northwest corner of the painting, that of the younger on the southwest corner, the paraphernalia of each idol being placed by its side and just behind it.   Six plume wands in clay holders extend in line before each image.   The two nearest the image of U'yuyewi have their sticks colored red, and are offerings to the Gods of War to destroy the enemies of the world;

ᵃ These images are made only at the time of initiation and at the winter solstice.   It is stated in the winter solstice ceremonies that wood of a pine tree struck by lightning is selected for the former occasion, and cottonwood is used on the latter, to bring rain.

the other four are colored black, and are offered to the deceased warriors for rains. Those before Ma⁺sai′lema have their sticks colored for the six regions, the one nearest the image being yellow, the following blue, then red, white, all color, and black, for the destruction of the enemies of the six regions.

Three po′nepoyannĕ,[a] two belonging to the A′pi⁺ᵗläshiwanni and one to the priest of ᵗsu′ᵗhlan′na,[b] are bound together at the base with red flannel and stood on the meal line, extending from the cloud symbol, and the ᵗsu′ᵗhlan′na is placed near it on the line. The ĕt′tonĕ of the Kĭa′kwemosi, covered in its blanket of native cotton and wrapped with strings of precious beads, is deposited on the meal painting, with the two gourd jugs of the ᵗkĭa′punakwe each side of it, and a line of mi′wachi along the back of the cloud symbol.

An all-night ceremonial is held in the chamber, when the epic songs of the Gods of War are sung, and at sunrise the pa′mosona removes the divided scalp from its elevated position in the plaza and attaches it to a pole about 8 feet high, planting it in the northwest corner of the plaza. A meal painting similar to the one in the ceremonial chamber is supposed to be made on the north side of the plaza at sunrise, but on the occasion observed the pe′kwĭn did not complete it until half past 8 o′clock. The painting in the ceremonial chamber is in the west end of the room.

By 9 o′clock the first body of A′shiwanni, except the pe′kwĭn, and elder and younger brother Bow priests are assembled in the ceremonial chamber, the A′shiwanni sitting on a ledge in line behind the meal painting, between the two ᵗkĭa′punakwe, who are supposed to be virgins. The A′shiwanni are dressed in pure white, but the ᵗkĭa′punakwe are elaborately attired, each wearing an embroidered kilt fastened at the right side with an embroidered sash which is also tied at the right side. One wears a native blue knit shirt over that of white cotton, and both are adorned with corals, ko′hakwa (white shell), and turquoise beads in profusion. The hair is done up in the conventional knot, with a red silk banda round the head; a white fluffy eagle plume is attached to the scalp lock, and dance moccasins are worn. A line of micaceous hematite three-quarters of an inch in width crosses the nose and extends under each eye. The victor and his elder brother wear

---

[a] The po′nepoyannĕ of the Bow priesthood consists of an ear of corn surrounded by reeds, six are colored, each for a region and are filled with grains of corn of the six colors and other seeds. The remainder of the reeds contain native tobacco. The reeds are obscured by a pyramid of eagle plumes (which must have been dropped by the eagle in his flight, not plucked) and the base is covered with cotton cloth wrapped with cotton cord to which shells and precious beads are strung. The keeper of the two po′nepoyannĕ belonging to the A′pi⁺ᵗläshiwanni is designated the priest of the pa′ĕttowe (pa from A′pachu, Navaho). One of these fetishes is carried to battle; the other remains at home.

[b] The ᵗsu′ᵗhlan′na is a large shell most precious to the Zuñis. Not only its keeper, who bears the title of priest of the ᵗsu′ᵗhlan′na, but his vice, must be of the Badger clan, because this shell was originally the property of a member of this clan. The occasion must always be eminently worthy of the presence of the great shell. The songs of the ᵗsu′ᵗhlan′na are very old, and known only to four men of the Badger clan.

MEAL PAINTING AND FETISHES OF A'PI˙ʟ̈ÄSHIWANNI (BOW PRIESTHOOD) IN PLAZA

M. Wright Gill.

PA'MOSONO''KÏA, FEMALE ASSOCIATE TO SCALP CUSTODIAN, AND TWO HÁ'SHIYA DANCERS IN PLAZA

velvet trousers, a white cotton shirt with a native blue woven shirt over it, red-brown moccasins; the hair is done up as usual. Their toilets are made at their homes, and after coming to the ceremonial chamber each has a large white buckskin doubled and tied at the throat, hanging over the shoulders and caught at the waist by an embroidered sash looped at the right side. They wear turquoise earrings and elaborate necklaces. When they are thus attired, the elder brother Bow priest empties a handful of meal into the belts of the victor and his elder brother, which they carry to the makers of the two idols, the victor giving his meal to the man of the Bear clan and the elder brother giving his to the man of the Deer clan. They return at once to the ceremonial chamber, when the elder brother Bow priest anoints their faces with a paste made of the fat of the prey animals of the six regions and the rattlesnake.ᵃ The ‛kǐa′punakwe rub a red pigment on the faces of the warriors and afterward apply micaceous hematite over the nose and upper portion of the cheeks and stipple it on the eyelids. Each warrior smokes until his turn comes to be decorated, all appearing to be in the happiest mood.

The pe′kwǐn returns to the chamber of the Bow priesthood at this time and stands with his red blanket wrapped around him (he is dressed in white like the other A′shiwanni). The victor takes his seat facing east, on a chair placed by the elder brother Bow priest about 5 feet before the cloud symbol. Leaning back in his chair he extends his feet with an air as though he intends to make himself as comfortable as possible for the ordeal. The elder brother Bow priest now places a cloth around him, barber fashion, and stands behind the chair, pressing both hands on the victor's forehead, while the pe′kwǐn, who is provided with a small black and highly polished archaic pottery vase and an old medicine bag (the vase is supposed to contain a black paint brought from the undermost world; the bag contains corn pollen), prepares to paint the face. He dips a stick of yucca needle into the paint pot and proceeds to color the lower portion of the face, the dividing line passing under the nose and across the cheeks. He afterward applies corn pollen to the upper portion by stippling with a mop of raw cotton. A corn husk is laid over the black portion during this process to protect it from the pollen. When the coloring of the victor's face is completed, he rises and his elder brother takes his seat for the same operation, during which time the victor stands north of the chair and slightly before it, wearing the gravest expression possible. When the pe′kwǐn has finished with the elder brother, the victor again takes the seat and the warrior of the Ant fraternity covers the chin, upper lip, end of nose, and forehead with eagle down, and a wreath of the same,

---

ᵃThe Bow priesthood are the only Zuñis who kill the rattlesnake. The rattle is an amulet worn as a protection from the enemy, and the fat or oil of the snake is rubbed on the face, that the enemy may fear the one using this grease as he fears the snake.

held in place by a paste of kaolin, is fashioned around the crown of the head. The whole decoration symbolizes "the heart must be pure that the prayers breathed into the plume offerings may be wafted to the deceased A'shiwanni that they may send much rain." The black on the chin denotes heavy rain clouds; the pollen, all vegetation, and the down, lighter clouds. The circle of down on the head symbolizes the clouds of the world. After the eagle-down decoration the pe'kwĭn places in the mouth of each an arrow point, which may not be removed until sunset. A deerskin hood (see plate LX), with the plume wand of the A'pi"läshiwanni attached to the crown, is worn. The victor and his elder brother are now in full attire, including the war pouch placed over the shoulder and the bow wristlet. The war club and the quiver with bow and arrows complete the toilet. The elder brother Bow priest is careful to examine each quiver to see that it contains the full number of arrows, one for each of the six regions. The victor and his elder brother take their prayer plumes from the meal painting, and afterward all of the prayer plumes are removed by their owners, each warrior having deposited two.

By this time the makers of the idols of U'yuyewi and Ma^ʿsai'lema arrive, and the chatting and laughing of the warriors at once cease and not a word is spoken after the two men enter the chamber. The warriors take position, standing on the north side of the room, the Ah'shiwanni remain at the west end, and the elder brother Bow priest stands south of the painting and before it, whirling the rhombus and calling for rains. When the whirling of the rhombus ceases the pe'kwĭn returns the mi'wachi,[a] which have embellished the painting, to their individual owners. The ĕt'tonĕ of the Kĭa'kwemosi and the large shell are placed in two baskets lined with raw cotton, and the other fetishes are divided among certain warriors. The pe'kwĭn removes all the objects from the north side of the painting systematically, handing the image of U'yuyewi to the elder brother and the paraphernalia to the appropriate parties. The objects are now removed from the south side, the image of Ma^ʿsai'lema being handed to the victor and the paraphernalia to others. All leave the chamber and proceed to te'wita ʿhlan'na in couples. The elder brother Bow priest leads, whirling the rhombus, with the pe'kwĭn by his side; the other A'shiwanni follow, and after them a man of the Deer clan; the elder brother to the victor, with a warrior to his left, comes next; two couples follow, and then the victor, with a warrior to his left, and preceded by a man of the Bear clan. The bearers of the paraphernalia of the Gods are near the end of the procession.

Upon reaching the plaza all but the A'shiwanni form into single file and dance, after which the objects are placed on the meal painting in the plaza. The image of U'yuyewi is stood on the east side and that

---

a See p. 416.

of Maᵗsai′lema on the west, just as they were on the cloud symbol in the chamber. The elder brother Bow priest and the elder brother of the victor stand east of the cloud symbol, while the victor and the younger brother Bow priest stand west of it, and the warriors sit in line on each side of the painting. The objects are guarded by two warriors standing with long spears at the south of the painting, the A′pi‛ᵀläshiwanni, except the elder and younger brother Bow priests, the victor, and his elder brother, taking turns at the post (see plate CXXXIV).

The pu′panakwe are grouped on each side of the plaza to furnish music for the ha′shiya, who are dressed as on the previous day, a number of girls being in the two chambers to take their turns in the dance. The pa′mosono′‛kĭa leads the ha′shĭya from the ceremonial house of the priest of the ᵗsu′ᵗhlan′na to the east side of the plaza and stands north of them while they dance (see plate CXXXV), and the vice pa′mosono′‛kĭa leads the ha′shiya from the chamber on the west side of the plaza and these girls dance on this side of the plaza. The pa′mosono′‛kĭa and vice each carry a fanciful bunch of grass (colored red with dry pigment and arranged by the warriors (see plate CXXXVI[a]), which is waved around the head four times, from left to right. The grasses are afterward deposited at Shop′ᵗhlua yäl′läkwi (a shrine to the Gods of War a short distance north of the village).

After the first dance of the ha′shiya the pu′mokĭakĭanawe, equipped with rifles, pistols, clubs, and bows and arrows, coming by the northeast entrance, cover the greater part of the te′wita ᵗhlan′na. The dancers, led by two warriors, appear in opposing lines, preceded by a drummer, who keeps a little off to one side. Two women dance between the lines. While this party is still dancing, a similar set approaches the plaza by the southwest covered way. Males of all ages are in this dance. Those not so fortunate as to have firearms carry clubs, sticks, etc. The party from the northeast entrance closes its dance first and crowds around the meal painting to pray; the other party also prays before the painting at the close of the dance and retires from the plaza.

Those who are to personate the Sha′läko, giant couriers to the rain-makers, the coming year now make their appearance, accompanied by two warriors designated to lead them to the plaza. Each one who is to personate a Sha′läko carries a spruce bough. After the dance, which is for great rains, that the earth may be bountiful with food for man and game, they group before the painting and pray, and then leave the plaza. The pu′mokĭakĭanawe now return. They dance repeatedly throughout the day, their number increasing each time until the opposing lines are quadrupled and the air is dense with arrows and rings of the war whoop. After each dance the dancers gather

---

[a] The writer is indebted to the pa′mosona for securing these specimens, which are now in the National Museum.

before the meal painting to sprinkle meal and pray. The ha'shiya dance on, apparently oblivious to all that is going on around them, and there is no attempt at harmony between the drums and the songs of the pu'panakwe and those accompanying the other dancers.

During the latter part of the afternoon the plaza is free for a time from dancers, except the ha'shiya. At this time the priest of the ᵗsu'ᵗhlan'na stoops immediately before the meal painting and four buckskins are thrown over him, and thus secluded from view he blows the great shell for rains and good hearts of the people. At the same time the elder brother Bow priest stands east of the painting and the younger brother Bow priest west of it, each whirling a rhombus for the clouds to gather. After the ceremony with the shell the drummers of the pu'mokĭakĭanawe and dancers reappear in the plaza; those coming from the northeastern entrance are accompanied by the elder brother to the victor, and those from the southwestern by the victor. The victor and elder brother each carry on their heads a basket tray of red he'we (wafer bread), such as is offered to the deceased enemy. As they run in and out of the line of dancers, each followed by two women, they cry: "We are anxious to meet the Navaho who comes." When the baskets of bread fall to the ground it is indicative of the killing of the foe, and they exclaim: "We have destroyed the Navaho." The pa'mosona and vice hasten to gather up the bread into the baskets, every scrap being picked from the ground, and as the dancers pass they catch at the bread with their mouths. The baskets of bread are afterward placed by the scalp pole, which is now near the northwest corner of the plaza and not over 8 feet high. After dropping the trays of bread, the victor and his elder brother return to their positions by the cloud symbol. Though the noise of the four drums, with the singing and the war whoop, is distracting to one not accustomed to it, the members of the Bow do not grow weary of the noise or of beating time to the drums with their war clubs and arrows.

The nightly dancing around the scalp pole arouses these people, but the dances on the closing day of the ceremonial fire them to the extreme. Infants observe these ceremonies without the slightest fear, while the mothers' interest is intense. The ha'shiya continue to dance. At intervals a warrior steps before the cloud symbol, and waving one or more arrows four times from right to left over the painting, throws them toward the pu'panakwe grouped on the west side, when a member of the choir from one side or the other comes forward, and lifting the arrows waves them four times from left to right over the cloud symbol and carries them to his seat. Gifts of calico and other things are now thrown by the warriors, their relatives, and friends. Some of these gifts are rather costly, one being an imported shawl worth several dollars. The love of display and the desire to exceed one's neighbors are not confined to enlightened people. As each gift is

caught it is waved over the meal painting from left to right. The
gifts are divided among the ha'shiya, after they cease dancing, by the
men who receive them, amid cheers from the populace. A warrior
having left the plaza to add to the warmth of his clothing, presents an
incongruous spectacle on his return, clad in a well-worn Prince Albert
coat and black cloth trousers, with a war pouch over his shoulder, a
buckskin skullcap on his head, and carrying his war club.

Some time before sunset two files of women, sixteen in each file,
each carrying a bowl or basket of food upon her head, come to the
plaza. They wear black dresses with blue embroidery, black blankets,
white buckskin moccasins with black soles, and the silver beads and
bangles, which are never omitted in ceremonies. Great pride is felt
by the women in their appearance when they carry food for ceremonial purposes, no matter what the ceremony may be. One file, led by
the elder brother to the victor, approaches by the northeast entrance;
the other file, led by the victor, reaches the plaza by the southwest
way. The former deposit their bowls and baskets on the ground
about the pu'panakwe on the east side of the plaza; the others deposit
theirs about the pu'panakwe on the west side. The drummer of
pu'panakwe on the east side prays with the elder brother, and the one
on the west side prays with the victor. Afterward the drummer clasps
the hands of each woman of his side and prays. At the close of the
prayer, he moves his hands (still holding hers) three or four times
before her lips, that she may draw from him the sacred breath, or all
that is good of him. The women depart as they come, followed by
the elder brother and the victor.

Many of the bowls of food from each side are placed near the meal
painting by the pa'mosona and his vice, for the A'shiwanni and warriors. The food in the remaining vessels is consumed by the pu'panakwe, the pa'mosona and pa'mosono''kïa eating with those on the east
side, while the vice pa'mosona and vice pa'mosono''kïa eat with the
pu'panakwe on the west side of the plaza. Before any food is taken
by the pu'panakwe the drummer puffs smoke from his cigarette over
the hooped drumstick, which lies on the top of the drum, and prays;
and the pa'mosona deposits food from the collation in the basket
containing the red he'we to the north side of the scalp pole, and the
vice pa'mosona places food in the basket to the south side. Food is
also gathered from the bowls and baskets on the east side of the meal
painting and placed in the basket to the north, and from those on the
west side and placed in that to the south of the scalp pole.

After the return of the victor and the elder brother to the plaza, they
stand west of the meal painting, facing east, and the pe'kwïn removes
the arrows from their mouths; and the elder brother to the victor,
passing before the cloud symbol, returns to his place on the east side
behind the painting. These two, who have not eaten or drunk during

the day, now do full justice to the feast. After the A'shiwanni and warriors have satisfied their appetites, the populace is allowed to partake of the remaining food, and the pu'panakwe also distribute what is left of their feast. After the repast the ha'shiya resume dancing, and the pu'mokĭakĭanawe soon appear through the northeast entrance, the men wearing every variety of costume. Many of the women carry an arrow. As they pass by the food left in the bowls they grab it and eat it as they proceed.

There is no evidence that the participators in this extended ceremonial are weary, their energy and interest appearing as keen as on the first day. As sunset approaches, the pe'kwĭn, accompanied by the elder brother Bow priest whirling the rhombus, and the two ᵗkĭa'punakwe visit He'patina (see plate XL), departing through the southwest covered way, to deposit the jugs of water and the prayer plumes, which they take from the cloud symbol. The party returns within thirty minutes. The ha'shiya continue to dance, and as each set begin they bend the knees to the slow, soft music of the choir, but after a minute or two the song becomes louder and more rapid, and the dancing begins in earnest. The pa'mosono'ᵗkĭa and her vice each wears a mi'ha instead of their blanket wraps, and a white fluffy eagle plume is tied to the forelock. They receive bits of cedar bark from the pa'mosona and his vice. At this time the first body of A'shiwanni sprinkle the meal painting and objects about it with meal. The elder brother Bow priest stoops behind the image of U'yuyewi and the younger brother Bow priest stoops behind that of Maᵗsai'lema, each placing his hands on the idol before him. A warrior holds the po'nepoyannĕ, and the other fetishes are held by the pe'kwĭn and others. The idols and fetishes are not lifted from the ground, but gently rocked upon it from right to left. The two guardsmen at their posts move their spears in the same manner until sunset. The dancing on each side of the te'wita ceases at sunset, and the pa'mosono'ᵗkĭa, her vice, and others expectorate on cedar bark and wave it with their left hands around their heads for physical purification.

The idols and their paraphernalia are now removed from the painting by the pe'kwĭn and returned to the parties who brought them to the plaza. The elder brother Bow priest and four other warriors form a group in the center of the plaza by an ancient pottery drum which contains a cream-colored decorated archaic vase filled with water and seeds. A circle, comprising the victor and his elder brother, who carry the effigies, the other A'piᵗläshiwanni, the first body of A'shiwanni, and women, is formed around the group. The hands are not held, but the women catch hold of the men's blankets.

It is asserted that at the original ceremonial at Hän'ᵗlipĭnkĭa a son of the drummer, who was at the head of the Coyote clan, held the scalps, and that upon his father's death he took his place as drummer, the father having taught him the songs, and another man of the Coyote clan held the scalps; and since that time the holder of the scalps in this dramatization is either of the Coyote clan or a child of the clan,[a] the scalp holder continuing to take the place of the deceased drummer.

The songs accompanying this dance are supposed to be the same as those sung at the time the seven beings appeared from the earth at Hän′‛lipĭnkĭa by the commands of the Gods of War.[b]

The following persons compose the circle, each man's aunt on the paternal side, or the next nearest female relative on that side, being to his left. The aunt is referred to as elder sister.

Shi′wanni of the North, Dogwood clan; paternal clan, Coyote. Elder sister, Coyote clan.

Shi′wanni of the West, Dogwood clan; paternal clan, Corn. Elder sister, Corn clan.

Shi′wanni of the South, Badger clan; paternal clan, Turkey. Elder sister, Turkey clan.

Shi′wanni of the East, Eagle clan; paternal clan, Sun. Elder sister, Sun clan.

Pe′kwĭn, Shi′wanni of the Zenith, Dogwood clan; paternal clan, Bear. Elder sister, Bear clan.[c]

Priest of the ‛su′‛hlan′na, Badger clan; paternal clan, Dogwood. Elder sister, Dogwood clan.

Associate priest of ‛su′‛hlan′na, Dogwood clan; paternal clan, Badger. Elder sister, Badger clan.

Priest of pa′ĕt′tonĕ, Badger clan; paternal clan, Sand-hill crane. Elder sister, Sand-hill crane clan.

Vice priest of pa′ĕt′tonĕ, Badger clan; paternal clan, Sand-hill crane. Elder sister, Sand-hill crane clan.

Warrior, Sand-hill crane clan; paternal clan, Badger. Elder sister, Badger clan.

Warrior personating elder brother to victor (holding the effigy of U′yuyewi), Dogwood clan; paternal clan, Sand-hill crane. Elder sister, Sand-hill crane.

Warrior, Turkey clan; paternal clan, Dogwood (carries paraphernalia of U′yuyewi). Elder sister, Dogwood clan.

Victor (holding the effigy of Ma‛sai′lema), Turkey clan; paternal clan, Eagle. Elder sister, Eagle clan.

Warrior, Dogwood clan; paternal clan, Eagle (carries paraphernalia of Ma‛sai′lema). Elder sister, Eagle clan.

Warrior, Sand-hill crane clan; paternal clan, Corn. Elder sister, Corn clan.

Warrior, Tobacco clan; paternal clan, Badger. Elder sister, Badger clan.

Warrior, Eagle clan; paternal clan, Dogwood. Elder sister, Dogwood clan.

Warrior, Bear clan; paternal clan, Badger. Elder sister, Badger clan.

Warrior, Corn clan; paternal clan, Dogwood. Elder sister, Dogwood clan.

Warrior, Badger clan; paternal clan, Sun. Elder sister, Sun clan.

The circle dance continues far into the gloaming, until all the songs given by the Divine Ones at Hän′‛lipĭnkĭa, which are among the most melodious the writer has heard, are sung. The step is slow, from left to right, in perfect unison with the song, and the change from the hilarious songs and dances of the day to this quiet, peaceful, dignified ceremony is most impressive. When the dance ceases all disperse in perfect quiet; not a word is spoken.

---

[a] See List of Clans.

[b] See p. 36.

[c] The present Shi′wanni of the Nadir is also elder brother Bow priest and is present in the latter capacity forming one of the group within the circle.

The idols are carried to the ceremonial chamber, where the warriors spend the night singing, the first body of A'shiwanni being present. The scalp is removed from the pole for the last time by the pa'mosona, and at midnight he and his assistant, accompanied by the elder brother Bow priest and four other warriors, fully equipped, place the scalps in the pottery vase in the scalp house. Cigarettes colored red and red bread are also deposited at the scalp house as offerings to the deceased Navahos. The bread is made by the i'tatononakwe out of meal and water, and is colored with a red mineral. The batter is made with the left hand and put upon a baking stone with the same hand. To do so, they say, is awkward, but the hand which is used to prepare their own food must not be used for making this bread. The stone upon which it is baked is at once destroyed. Partly smoked cigarettes and plume offerings are deposited at Shop'ᵗhlua yäl'läkwi.

At daylight the victor and his elder brother, each accompanied by a warrior who assists in carrying the paraphernalia, proceed to deposit the idols at their respective shrines. That of U'yuyewi is deposited at Te'wan ko'han o'nan pä'nina; that of Maᵗsai'lema at Shi'äkĭa yäl'lannĕ. "In the olden time, the Sun Father designated the country north of the road of day to U'yuyewi and that south of it to Maᵗsai'lema," and images of these gods are accordingly placed at the shrines after the scalp ceremonial. The shrines at which the idols are placed are as follows:

ROAD OF DAY

North	South
Te'wan ko'han o'nan pä'nina.	To'wa yäl'lännĕ.
Day white road descending.	Corn mountain.
ᵗHlä' kĭaᵗhlona o'nan pä'nina.	Shi'äkĭa yäl'lännĕ.
Name of a tree road descending.	Stone sharpener mountain.
ᵗHla'wulᵗhlia yäl'lännĕ.	O'pompia[a] yäl'lännĕ.
Eagle's nest mountain.	Sack of meal hanging mountain.
Kwĭl'li yäl'lännĕ.	Ke'ya yäl'lännĕ.
Twin mountain.	Whitewash mountain.
	No'ponia[b] yäl'lännĕ.
	Face mountain.
	U'hana[c] yäl'lännĕ.
	Wool mountain.

After a scalp ceremonial, these shrines, beginning with Te'wan ko'han o'nan pä'nina and Shi'äkĭa, are taken in rotation, the idol of

---

[a] O from owe, flour (wheat or corn); pom'pia, hanging. "Two girls from Shun'teᵗkĭaya were gathering grasses to make baskets to hold prayer plumes, when they met the elder God of War. He invited them to his house on the mountain top. Here they saw a diminutive sack of flour hanging from a tree, and great was their surprise when they observed the grandmother of the gods make bread from the flour in the sack. Although the woman took but the smallest quantity of the flour, she made a great basket of bread from it."

[b] So named because "the face and head of Ko'loowisi (Plumed Serpent) were seen above the waters at this point by the A'shiwi, who were on To'wa yäl'lännĕ to escape the great flood."

[c] "The Gods of War killed many mountain sheep on this mountain, and the grandmother, in sweeping the wool of the sheep from the house, swept it down the mountain side until it was quite covered with wool."

the elder God of War being placed north of the road of day, and that of the younger God of War south of it. The image is set up and the prayer plumes are planted in a row on each side at right angles with the image, and the paraphernalia are arranged much as they were in the plaza. Meal is sprinkled from the idol outward between the lines of prayer plumes. Both gods bear the name of A′hayuta at the winter solstice and at other times when only rain and all things good are thought of and hearts are peaceful. Although the road of the sun divides the shrines of these gods, neither one must be thought of in connection with the north side at the winter solstice when rain is desired, and therefore at this season the elder god is always deposited on U′hana yäl′länně, and the younger on To′wa yäl′länně. Should an idol of U′yuyewi be placed north of the road of the sun at this time, "the rains and winds would be very angry and there would be too much cold."

Plate cxxxvii shows five images of U′yuyewi and paraphernalia removed from the shrine on Kwĭl′li yäl′länně and placed by a monument erected by a topographical party of the United States Geological Survey. Of the nine carvings, beginning with the one at the left, the first three are idols of U′yuyewi; the five lines on each side of the idols and near the base represent the hands of the gods; figure 4, the war club; figure 5, the earthly arrow; figure 6, a tablet surmounted with a serrated design symbolizing cumulus clouds. The crescent is immediately below the cloud symbol. The full moon is symbolized by the circular opening, and the star by the cross. Figure 7 represents the lightning arrow; figures 8 and 9, idols of U′yuyewi. Three of the images still retain the serrated projections which symbolize the umbilicus.

Plate cxxxviii shows the shrine on Kwĭl′li yäl′länně, with the latest idols in place and the displaced images with their paraphernalia heaped about.

Plate cxxxix shows idols of the God of War, removed from an ancient cave shrine in the west wall of To′wa yäl′länně and stood outside to be photographed.

Although the A′piʻläshiwanni have many shrines dedicated to the Gods of War, the most sacred spot, perhaps, is the crater in the volcanic cone at the Zuñi Salt lake (see plate lxxxix), which is supposed to be the present home of these gods.[a]

The philosophy of the Indian, as of man wherever found and at whatever stage of culture he may have arrived, is the result of his desire and his efforts to understand the mysteries of nature. With the exception of the Lightning fraternity, which originated virtually

---

[a] All of the shrines of the Gods of War and a number of other illustrations in this paper were secured by Mr Stevenson in 1881.

under her own eye, the author has not attempted in the foregoing pages to give any explanation of the origin of the religious organizations other than that entertained by the Zuñi mind. These children of the human family are highly imaginative. The soul of the Zuñi expands with adoration toward the supreme mysterious power that controls all things, without form yet embracing form, the breath of life—even life itself; and toward the gods, whose forms are visible in the heavens above, in the earth beneath, and in the waters under the earth, who are only less mighty than the supreme power, and who bless the good and punish the wicked.

While it remains to be learned definitely by what people or peoples the elaborate rituals of the Zuñi were instituted it is assumed that they originated with the Zuñi themselves. What part clanship played in the dawn of the ritualistic life of the Zuñi is also yet to be determined. It is certain that for a long time past membership at large in the fundamental religious bodies of the Zuñi has not been dependent on ties of clanship, though in certain cases succession to office in fraternities does depend on clanship.

Before any exposition of the origin of the fundamental religious organizations and of the rituals can be offered, a comparative study of the Pueblos must be made. For this work the passing hours are golden, for not only are the villages losing their old-time landmarks, but the people themselves are changing, are adapting themselves to suddenly and profoundly altered environment; and the Zuñi at least, whose religion teaches them to speak with one tongue, to be gentle to all, and to subdue the passions, thereby winning the favor of their gods, are, under the influences of modern conditions, losing the restraining power of this religion, and, as a result, are changing for the worse.

GRASS WAND CARRIED BY PA'MOSONO''KĬA, FEMALE ASSOCIATE TO
SCALP CUSTODIAN

IDOLS OF ELDER GOD OF WAR FROM SHRINE ON KWĬL'LI YÄL'LĂNNĔ (TWIN MOUNTAINS)

SHRINE ON KWĬL'LI YÄL'LÄNNĔ (TWIN MOUNTAINS), SHOWING LATEST IDOLS OF ELDER GOD OF WAR IN PLACE, AND DISPLACED IDOLS

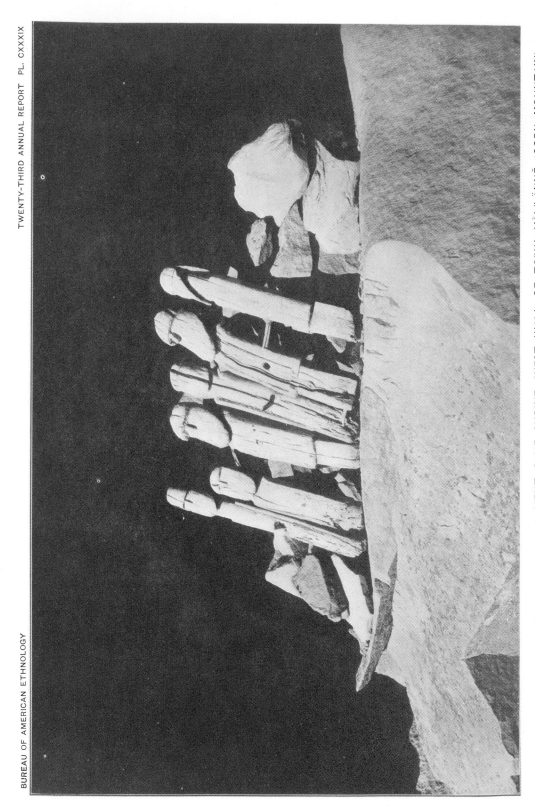

IDOLS OF ELDER GOD OF WAR FROM ANCIENT CAVE SHRINE, WEST WALL OF TO'WA YÄL'LÄNNĚ (CORN MOUNTAIN)

INDEX

618   INDEX

O